TRADE UNIONS OF THE WORLD 1992–93

TRADE UNIONS OF THE WORLD 1992–93

3rd Edition

This edition revised and updated by

MARTIN UPHAM

with a contribution on the United Kingdom by Tom Wilson

TRADE UNIONS OF THE WORLD 1992–93

1st Edition 1987
2nd Edition (revised and updated) 1989
3rd Edition (revised and updated) 1991

Published by Longman Group UK Limited, Westgate House,
The High, Harlow, Essex, CM20 1YR, United Kingdom

Distributed exclusively in the United States and Canada
by Gale Research Inc., 835 Penobscot Building, Detroit,
Michigan 48226, USA

ISBN 0-582-08194-7

Printed in Great Britain by BPCC Wheatons Ltd, Exeter

A catalogue record for this publication is available from the British Library

Contents

Introduction

In the four years since its first appearance *Trade Unions of the World* has established an unrivalled reputation as an indispensable guide to labour movements. This third edition builds on the strengths of earlier editions and adds to them. From its predecessors it inherits its country by country format and the provision of political and economic background. It has proved possible on this occasion to achieve a greater consistency of information relevant to the structure and behaviour of trade unionism. Thus country entries normally contain an indication of the nation's economic structure including (where available) the breakdown of the workforce between agriculture, industry and services. It is hoped that the comparative value of the book has been enhanced thereby.

But where earlier editions drew all matters of direct bearing upon trade unionism under a common title, the third edition presents this information under two distinct headings. Under the heading *Industrial relations* will be found detail concerning the legal and behavioural background and the involvement of government. Under the heading *Trade unionism* is information about the structure and behaviour of a country's unions.

At the end of the book international organizations of trade unionism are to be found in a separate alphabetical sequence, to which a list of acronyms refers. It is particularly gratifying to be able to give a full entry in this edition to the World Confederation of Labour. The (English language) titles and acronyms of national trade union centres are given in one consolidated index.

It has also been possible to achieve greater consistency of content. Thus trade union density—a vital indicator of strength—is given in almost every case, while certain countries with brief entries now receive more equal treatment. Any current inequities in this respect owe more to the relatively undeveloped nature of a country's industrial relations than to any elusiveness of information.

The third edition does resemble its predecessors in being built around national trade union centres. Having provided general information under the headings *Industrial relations* and *Trade unionism* its next aim is to profile each country's peak association. In many metropolitan countries this is a relatively simple matter, but outside the most industrialized regions there often exists a pluralism not only of unions but also of union centres. The book's aim is to reflect this pluralism fully. Where there are no centres at all leading trade unions are profiled.

Since the compilation of the second edition enormous changes have swept the trade union world. In the industrialized countries trade unions still seek to minimize the impact of structural economic change which depresses the significance of manufacturing and elevates that of services. Their differential success in staunching declining density often depends on the policy-making structure of the country in question, with the trade union movements of Germany and Sweden for example more successful than those of the United Kingdom or the United States. But there is no necessary connection of this type as the evolution of a single trade union centre in Japan seems to indicate.

Beyond the most industrialized countries the most dramatic developments have been those consequent on the political revolutions of 1989 in Eastern Europe. At first sight these seem to have had the effect of building a greater plurality of trade union representation in the place of the single centre model invariably to be found in communist countries. On closer inspection the picture appears more complex. Each Eastern European union centre sought to renew itself during the period in which virtually all of society's institutions fell under popular questioning. Their success varied. In Germany the union structure of the West extended itself to absorb trade unionists in the East, leaving little trace of the FDGB; Germany's unions thus responded to unification in parallel fashion to the Federal German state.

In Hungary—where economic changes predated 1989—several union centres now exist with none being able to claim the allegiance of a clear majority. Poland anticipated pluralism by a decade when Solidarity erupted onto the scene in 1980. But here the position is complicated by Solidarity's political role which has allowed the former official union centre (now the OPZZ) to build a new identity for itself in opposition to government. In Czechoslovakia CS-KOS commands the support of the vast majority of the country's trade unionists. In Romania and Bulgaria the ability of the relaunched official unions to continue in a dominant position while faced with smaller but ambitious rivals is as yet unclear.

In all cases however new and old centres do have to survive in a competitive environment. Along this path of structural change the USSR has travelled least far. The main unions there have revised their statutes and their name but claim the same level of support as their official predecessors. The extent to which their membership competes with or overlaps the membership of rival unions is as yet unclear.

Other communist countries such as Cuba or Vietnam have retained a single trade union system. The official structure was briefly challenged in China by the Workers' Autonomous Federations but consolidated its position after June 1989. However the trend undermining official structures is apparent in several countries of the developing world where a shift towards plural trade union representation marches in step with the decay of the one-party state. Even more striking is the extent to which official union centres in several African countries have established themselves as independent organizations and centres of opposition.

The co-existence of independent unions and rival centres is not just a mirror image of an increasingly privatized economy. In a number of these countries state ownership of the means of production persists so that the decline of the single trade union system may more plausibly be attributed to a crisis of representation which afflicts all institutions founded in the communist era. Yet such problems are not confined to the former Eastern Bloc; they are evident in France and Italy in the different form of declining union density. Moreover pluralism may have different roots as submerged national identities seek to express themselves after decades underground.

The changing institutional framework has consequences for international trade unionism. There are still three world centres, but the ICFTU has gained the adherence of some key former WFTU affiliates. Other peak national associations redefining their role in a pluralistic political environment are reluctant to align themselves with a world centre. In other respects the most striking feature is how little international trade union bodies have evolved in a period when multinational business organizations have grown stronger.

The publishers and the editor are grateful to the many organizations world-wide who responded to our questionnaire and other enquiries. Their assistance and that of key members of their staff has been invaluable in bringing many important union organizations out of the shadows. Other important sources have been the publications of the ILO, the ICFTU and the WFTU and the US Department of Labor's *Foreign Labour Trends*. Every effort has been made to achieve accuracy. Any errors of fact or later developments should be reported to the Editor of *Trade Unions of the World 1992–93* Longman Group UK Ltd, Westgate House, The High, Harlow, Essex, CM20 1YR, United Kingdom. Suggestions for further improvements will also be welcome.

Martin Upham

TRADE UNION ORGANIZATIONS
BY COUNTRY

Afghanistan

Capital: Kabul

Population: 14,825,013
(1989)

Political system. The Afghan monarchy was overthrown in 1973, and a republic was declared. The new régime was however overthrown in April 1978 when the (communist) People's Democratic Party of Afghanistan (PDPA) took power and became the sole political party allowed to operate. After a series of personnel changes and internal party conflicts, and in the light of mounting opposition from a range of mainly Islamic guerrilla groups, the Soviet Union intervened militarily in December 1979, although Soviet forces subsequently were withdrawn by February 1989.

Under a new Constitution introduced in November 1987 political parties were allowed to be formed, but all candidates in elections to the National Assembly held in April 1988 belonged to the National Front of Afghanistan (an umbrella organization for all organized political activity); the PDPA was understood to be in a minority in the Assembly. The Constitution provides state protection for all forms of property, including co-operative, mixed, private and state-owned.

Economy. Agriculture, based mainly on livestock rearing and herding and on the growing of cotton and fruits, is the dominant activity of the Afghan economy, accounting for some two-thirds of the working population (including nomads), for about two-thirds of net material product (NMP) and for about half of all exports. Industry, which accounts for about 13–14 per cent of NMP and is largely state-controlled, includes the mining of precious and semi-precious stones and of copper ore, gas production (partly for export to the Soviet Union) and the manufacture of cotton textiles, chemical fertilizers and leather products. A considerable semi-legal "black" economy in foreign goods exists in Kabul.

System of industrial relations. Afghanistan has ratified neither ILO Convention No. 87 (Freedom of Association and Protection of the Right to Organize, 1948) nor Convention No. 98 (Right to Organize and Collective Bargaining, 1949).

Trade unionism. As a consequence of government repression combined with the lack of any significant industrial base, trade unionism scarcely existed in Afghanistan prior to the late 1970s other than in the form of co-operative benefit societies established in a small number of plants and institutions. Following the 1978 revolution, the new régime established the Central Council of Afghan Trade Unions (CCATU) which began to organize a trade union structure. The work accelerated considerably after the pro-Soviet *coup* of 1979, but trade union members are still only a small fraction of the working population. There are no trade unions outside the CCATU. The councils of representatives of the "trade union primary organizations", the basic unit of the structure, are empowered to conclude enterprise collective bargaining agreements.

Central Council of Afghan Trade Unions (CCATU)

Address. P.O. Box 756, Kabul
Phone. (93) 23040/23057
Cables. CCATU KABUL
Telex. 372 AF

3

Leadership. Abdul Satar Purdeli (president); Ahmadullah Poya (vice-president); Tela Baz Habibzai (secretary, international relations)

Membership. The CCATU represents local, rather than national, trade union groups. By September 1988 there were approximately 300,000 members organized in 35 provincial, subprovincial and city councils and in 2,810 "trade union primary organizations".

History and character. The CCATU was set up by the left-wing military government which came to power in 1978, but—according to the present CCATU leadership—"unsuitable figures" were placed in the union organization and it "became isolated" from the workforce. The Soviet intervention of December 1979 was followed by a restructuring of the CCATU and, according to official figures, a rapid and continuing growth in membership from the level of about 28,350 individual members in 59 organizations in early 1980. The first congress of the CCATU took place in 1981. Although formally a non-party organization, the CCATU is closely identified with the ruling PDPA, and its role is substantially to implement party policies. Union representatives are commonly elected to serve in *jirgas* (assemblies).

Structure. The supreme organ of the CCATU is the congress, which elects a central council. The central council plenum, held at least twice a year, decides policy between congresses. Fifteen members of the council form the presidium, seven members of which (the president, vice-president and five secretaries) form the secretariat, which is responsible for the day-to-day running of the movement.

Policies. The CCATU defines its main policies as (i) providing leadership for the nation's trade union movement; (ii) improving the working and living conditions of wage-earners; (iii) strengthening the state sector and the national economy; and (iv) "defending the gains made by the *Sowr* (i.e. 1978) Revolution". The CCATU has consistently promoted the government's policy of "national reconciliation" since its introduction in early 1986. Among its current activities are (i) participation in decision-making at national, district and plant levels on production and broader industrial matters; (ii) literacy campaigns and other educational, cultural and sporting activities; (iii) organization of "self-defence groups" to safeguard enterprises against subversion (32,000 workers were mobilized in such groups in early 1988); (iv) organization of "work emulation drives" to boost productivity; and (v) participation, in its own right and in forums, in solidarity with workers' organizations in other countries. A current major objective is to provide assistance in attaining the objectives of the national First Five-Year Plan (for 1986–90).

Publications. *Kar* (weekly newspaper, circulation 26,000); *Information Bulletin* (quarterly English-language; circulation about 200).

International affiliation. WFTU.

Albania

Capital: Tirana   **Population: 3,300,000**

Political system. Since the end of World War II Albania has been a one-party state under the Albanian Party of Labour (APL), as the Communist Party was renamed in 1948. Under the 1976 Constitution the People's Socialist Republic is based on the dictatorship of the proletariat, with the APL as the sole directing political power and with Marxism-Leninism as the ruling ideology. There is a unicameral People's Assembly to which elections are held on a single list presented by the APL-led Albanian Democratic Front.

In the late 1940s and 1950s Albania was a member of both the Council for Mutual Economic Assistance (CMEA or Comecon) and of the Warsaw Treaty Organization, but as the rift between it and the Soviet Union developed it relinquished its membership of these two bodies in 1962 and 1968 respectively. Although Albania is ideologically largely isolated, some *rapprochement* has developed latterly with neighbouring Greece, with other non-communist European countries, and with some East European states. However, the Constitution laid down that Albania may not grant concessions to "capitalist, bourgeois and revisionist monopolies and states", nor create foreign or joint economic or financial institutions with them nor accept credits from them.

Albania was the last of Europe's centrally planned economies to show signs of internal unrest. In December 1989, Enver Hoxha's successor President Alia was reported to have "firmly and categorically denied that events taking place in Eastern Europe could ever happen in Albania". However political disturbances grew during 1990 and alternative political parties emerged. In March 1991 the first free elections in 60 years were held, though against the wishes of the new parties, which would have preferred a delay. The easy winners were the Albanian Party of Labour, the country's communist party, which gained most of the rural vote, while the new parties fared well only in urban areas. The Party of Labour won 68 per cent of the vote and 162 seats in the 250-member single chamber parliament, to 25 per cent and 65 seats for the Democratic Party, the largest of the opposition groups.

However, the results—which led to a Party of Labour government—were not accepted by the Opposition. The Democratic Party campaigned for new elections and industrial agitation culminated in a general strike. In June 1991 the Party of Labour government was forced to resign; a new non-party government of "national salvation" was agreed to by communists, the Democratic Party and the unions to run the country until fresh elections could be held in 1992.

Economy. The principal mainstays of the Albanian economy are agriculture and mining. Agriculture is organized on a collectivized and largely co-operative basis, and accounts for about 30 per cent of total social product; tobacco and cotton are grown as well as food crops. There are major mineral deposits, and Albania is the world's second largest exporter of chromite (chromium ore). Industry includes the processing of agriculture and mineral raw materials, chemicals and fertilizers. Locally extracted petroleum is refined and there are considerable hydroelectric resources. Albania is the poorest and least-developed country in Europe but the 1986–90 economic plan aimed to secure major progress in the transformation into an industrial-agricultural country.

System of industrial relations. The traditional Albanian pattern is one where the government fixes wages and hours and conditions of work, and in mid-1987 wage differentials were introduced for the first time among certain groups of skilled workers as a means of providing incentives. Disputes are resolved by conciliation without recourse to strike action. The trade unions administer social insurance regulations and have responsibilities in the enforcement of health and safety rules. Albania ratified both ILO Convention No. 87 (Freedom of Association and Protection of the Right to Organize, 1948) and No. 98 (Right to Organize and Collective Bargaining, 1949) in 1957, but withdrew from the ILO in 1967.

While 1990, which ended with steps in the direction of political liberalization, brought relatively little industrial unrest, 1991 saw a series of strikes which continued after the March general elections. Coal miners struck in January in support of opposition calls to postpone the elections, and in May organized an underground hunger strike for better social conditions. A four-day general strike was launched towards the end of the month which paralyzed the whole country. It was directed towards demands for pay rises of up to 100 per cent following a government offer of 30 per cent increases, but demands were also raised for an inquiry into the deaths of four people in Shkoder following clashes with the security forces just after the elections. The State Radio reported that one tenth of the population was taking part in the strikes.

5

Trade unionism. The Albanian trade union movement took shape after 1945, and its framework was established by the 1950 Constitution and the 1956 Labour Code. There are union branches in each workplace, which elect workplace trade union committees, and there are also ward committees and district councils. Unions are organized by industry on a regional basis, with a general congress meeting every five years (last in 1987) to elect the membership of the Central Council of Albanian Trade Unions (TUA).

As recently as its Seventh (1989) Plenary Session the Central Council of Albanian Trade Unions emphasized its orientation towards fulfilling its commitments under the country's economic plan. With 600,000 members, its position in society seemed impregnable.

By February 1991 however the TUA President Sotir Kocollari reported that "there are tendencies . . . to create so-called free trade unions . . . (which) . . . are not in the interests of society"; in March the TUA in fact launched its own federation, which it claimed was independent, to rival an independent force in the mines. A democratization process for the whole Council was announced shortly after.

The independent unions in Albania made their presence felt from the beginning of the year. They started in the mines, where strikes had already taken place, recruiting (according to *Free Labour World*) 7,000 miners in 200 enterprises. The formation of an "initiating commission for the creation of independent trade unions" was announced soon after. On April 4 this Commission called for a general strike to protest against the post-election violence. In May a general strike was launched and during its course the independent unions pressed demands, in parallel with the opposition Democratic Party, for fresh elections, and mounted demonstrations in Tirana, Shkoder and other cities. In June 1991 the pressure finally broke the government which resigned to make way for an administration of "national salvation".

Këshilli Qëndror i Bashkimeve Profesionale të Shqiperisë
Central Council of Albanian Trade Unions (TUA)

Address. Bulevardi Dshmort e Kombit, Tirana
Leadership. Sotir Korollari (president)
Membership. 600,000.
Affiliated unions. Agriculture Trade Union; Construction, Communications and Communal Economy Trade Union; Education, Culture, Trade and Health Trade Union; Industry, Mines and Energy Trade Union.
International affiliation. Recorded as a WFTU affiliate, but does not participate in its work.

Independent unions

No details are available of the independent unions.

Algeria

Capital: Algiers   **Population: 21,050,000**
                                        (estimated mid-1984)

Political system. Algeria achieved independence from France in 1962 following a lengthy armed struggle spearheaded by the Front de Libération Nationale (FLN), and a republican

Constitution was adopted in 1963. The FLN is the sole permitted political party, and under the 1976 Constitution is the guide to the revolution and the leading force in society; it constitutes the vanguard, leadership and organization of the people with the aim of building socialism, and its leadership holds the decisive responsibilities in the state. The unicameral National Assembly is largely dominated by officials of the FLN and government officials. The 1976 National Charter set out the aim of building a socialist society and achieving socialism, and specified the principle of non-alignment in foreign policy. Modifications to the National Charter were approved in a referendum in January 1986 making provision for greater emphasis on the private sector of the economy, alongside a "pragmatic socialism", and on the principles of Islam.

The new Algerian constitution of February 1989 opened the way to a market economy and a more liberal and pluralist society.

Economy. Following independence in 1962 the Algerian economy suffered an initial setback with the departure of most of the French settlers who had provided much of the country's management and skills. The main agricultural estates, together with most manufacturing and banking, were brought under state ownership and control in the 1960s. Rather under half of arable land is either state-owned or held by co-operatives, the main crops being cereals, grapes and citrus fruits.

Nearly all of Algeria's export revenue derives from oil and gas, this sector having been either nationalized or brought under majority state control in 1971, but dependence on oil revenues makes the economy extremely vulnerable to fluctuations in the international price of petroleum, particularly as many development projects were based on the high prices obtained in the late 1970s.

The 1985–89 economic development plan continued the strategy of the previous plan in aiming to decentralize away from the northern coastal area, to improve agricultural output, and to split many of the large state corporations into smaller units with greater management freedom and financial self-responsibility, while at the same time seeking to encourage small-scale private agricultural and industrial enterprises.

By early 1990 however unemployment was running at 22 per cent, and reducing it was the prime objective of the National Employment Promotion Commission established in 1989 under the Finance Law of that year. Following its recommendations the government in January 1990 inaugurated a package of small business and training support.

System of industrial relations. Widespread consultations on industrial relations with national and international participation occurred in 1989 following the inauguration of the new Constitution. This endorsed freedom of association in line with ILO conventions, collective bargaining and participation at company level, and amended the legal provisions governing dispute settlement procedures. The participants included the main union centre UGTA and the farmworkers' union (UNPA).

In February 1990 three laws laid down a new framework for industrial relations activity. The right to strike exists following the exhaustion of procedure and after a positive ballot result but striking workers may not be replaced by the management. Minimum service must be maintained in essential services. There must be regular employer–employee consultations on work matters and there are provisions for conciliation, mediation and arbitration. In the event of a dispute there will be conciliation by a new Conciliation Board of two representatives each from employers and employees; where conciliation fails there is appeal to the new Labour Tribunal on Social Affairs, another bipartite body with a magistrate in the chair. The matter may be referred after mediation to the new National Arbitration Commission, a bipartite body chaired by a Supreme Court judge.

Trade unionism. Prior to independence the French trade union centres maintained regional organizations in Algeria and there were also independent federations. Following independence, however, the Union Générale des Travailleurs Algériens (UGTA), which was linked with the FLN, became the sole centre and it remains the sole legal (non-peasant) labour organization.

Under the constitutional changes of 1989, trade unions have been re-conceived as independent bodies rather than channels of management. This presents a particular challenge to the UGTA which has to adapt to new circumstances in which its central representative role is not guaranteed. An early challenge to its status was made by the Algerian Journalists' Movement which is composed of journalists who had left their UGTA-affiliated union. It held its first conference in October 1989.

Union Générale des Travailleurs Algériens (UGTA)
General Union of Algerian Workers

Address. Maison du Peuple, Place du 1er mai, Algiers

Leadership. Tayeb Benlakhdar (secretary general)

History and character. The UGTA was created in 1956 as part of the FLN, and after independence replaced all existing union federations. Legislation adopted in 1971 named the UGTA as the sole recognized labour organization and provided that it should set up a trade union section in any work unit with more than nine workers. A 1975 ordinance made UGTA the sole bargaining agent, and a provision of the 1976 Constitution placed all mass organizations under the protection and control of the party. This provision was rescinded by the 1989 Constitution.

International affiliations. OATUU, ICATU. The UGTA disaffiliated from the ICFTU in 1963.

Andorra

Capital: Andorra la Vella   **Population: 49,000**

Political system. Andorra is a co-principality, with each of the two co-princes (the President of France and the Bishop of Urgel in Spain) being represented by a Viguier and a permanent delegation. There is a 28-member General Council, which is organized not on party political lines but through loose political or interest groupings; since the beginning of 1982 there has been a Head of Government and an Executive Council.

Economy. Since the early 1950s traditional agriculture and forestry have been replaced by tourism and increasingly commerce as the principal economic activities of Andorra, while mineral resources are also exploited.

System of industrial relations. Andorra is a conservative state which traditionally has resisted any attempts to establish a formal system of industrial relations.

Trade unionism. Until recently there were no trade unions in Andorra. However, in 1990 the Andorran Workers' Union was formed claiming several hundred members.

Angola

Capital: Luanda   **Population: 9,694,000**

Political system. The former Portuguese province of Angola became independent in November 1975. Immediately preceding independence there was a mass exodus of the white and mixed-race population, and hostilities resumed between the three main liberation movements which had nominally formed a joint transitional government in January 1975. The Popular Movement for the Liberation of Angola (MPLA), with large-scale Cuban military support, established itself as the effective, and generally internationally recognized, government; however, parts of the country continued to be controlled by the National Union for the Total Independence of Angola (UNITA) which received South African support across the border from Namibia.

Lengthy negotiations resulted in a December 1988 agreement to a phased withdrawal from Angola of all Cuban forces. However six months later the ceasefire agreement collapsed and civil war was renewed with the United States continuing to finance UNITA and Cuban troops still involved in the fighting. Talks between UNITA and the MPLA with third party participation were resumed in April 1990 and lasted throughout the year. In December 1990 the MPLA decided at its Congress to replace Marxism–Leninism with "democratic socialism" as its ideology. The last Cuban troops returned to Cuba in the third week of May 1991, and on May 31st the final peace agreement between the MPLA and UNITA was signed. It provides for integration of the two armies under international supervision and elections late in 1992.

Economy. Following independence and the consolidation of control by the MPLA, many enterprises were taken into the public sector, notably those hitherto owned and managed by Europeans. The Constitution lays down that the state should promote and develop the public sector and also foster the establishment of co-operatives; certain areas of the economy such as banking, insurance, petroleum and various public utilities and services are reserved exclusively for the public sector, which overall covers about 80 per cent of all industry and commerce. A new economic and financial programme launched in 1988 sought to improve productivity through the restructuring of state-owned enterprises, to ensure that such enterprises were accountable in terms of profit, and to allow for the development of small-scale private enterprises.

The Angolan economy was traditionally based largely on agriculture and diamond mining. However, the departure of European experts, the continuing internal fighting and adverse climatic conditions, combined with depressed price and demand conditions in the international markets, have resulted in low export revenue from the staple commodities of coffee and sugar, while the market for diamonds has also been depressed. On the other hand the level of oil production has risen (particularly in the north of the country) and oil accounted for some 90 per cent of export revenues.

By 1990 external debt was US$6,000 million and the impact of the civil war (which had caused 70 per cent of revenue to be diverted to military spending) was compounded by drought. However in 1989 Angola joined the IMF and the World Bank and in 1990 it began to implement a series of economic policy changes which would cut public spending, alleviate taxes and deregulate prices. If the peace agreement survives Angola may be able to exploit its vast natural wealth which makes it potentially one of the richest countries in Africa. In 1985–87, 79 per cent of the labour force was employed in agriculture, 9.5 per cent in industry and 16.7 per cent in services.

System of industrial relations. Angola ratified ILO Convention No. 98 (Right to Organize and Collective Bargaining, 1949) in 1976 but has not ratified Convention No. 87

9

(Freedom of Association and Protection of the Right to Organize, 1948). Angola also ratified Conventions 29 and 105 on forced labour in 1976, but the ILO has noted that sanctions involving compulsory labour can be imposed for breaches of labour discipline and participation in strikes.

Trade unionism. Under Portuguese rule to 1975 there existed occupational "syndicates"; these organizations functioned mainly to provide welfare services, and free collective bargaining and strikes were banned. Members of these syndicates were predominantly Europeans and *assimalados*, and independent African trade unionism was illegal. However, several underground or exiled unions gave their support to the independence struggle, these becoming identified with the rival factions among the independence forces. Following the winning of power by the MPLA, the União Nacional de Trabalhadores Angolanos (UNTA) became and remained the sole union centre.

União Nacional dos Trabalhadores Angolanos (UNTA)
National Union of Angolan Workers

Address. Avda Brazil 235-1, CP 28, Luanda
Phone. 32441/3
Telex. 3387 An Unta
Leadership. Pascual Luvualu (secretary general)
Membership. 600,000.
History. The UNTA was formed in the late 1950s, and through the 1960s worked both in exile abroad and underground at home, organizing co-operative production in areas held by MPLA forces. Other trade union centres, linked to the rival liberation movements, also existed in the 1960s and early 1970s, but following independence in 1975 and the assumption of control of most of the country by the MPLA, these ceased to function.
International affiliations. OATUU; WFTU.

Antigua and Barbuda

Capital: St John's

Population: 84,000
(1988)

Political system. Antigua and Barbuda, formerly a West Indian Associated State, became independent in 1981 as a full member of the Commonwealth and has a bicameral parliament (comprising an appointed Senate and an elected House of Representatives). The Antigua Labour Party (ALP), and previously the Antigua Trades and Labour Union with which it is affiliated, have been the dominant political force since the 1940s with the exception of 1971–76 when the administration was formed by the Progressive Labour Movement. In the 1984 elections to the House of Representatives the ALP won all the seats except that of the island of Barbuda. The most recent parliamentary elections were held in March 1989.

Economy. The economy is heavily dependent on tourism, although this is subject to severe fluctuations in line with world economic factors and in particular the strength of the economy of the United States which is the main source of tourists; two US bases on

Antigua also provide foreign exchange revenue. Agriculture is based mainly on locally consumed crops; there is little manufacturing industry apart from the production of rum and some garment-making. Legislation was approved in 1982 which was designed to encourage the establishment of an offshore banking sector.

Unemployment in Antigua and Barbuda was above 10 per cent at the end of the 1980s. The best-paid jobs are found in the tourism sector.

System of Industrial Relations. Provision for the registration of trade unions was first made in the Trade Union Ordinance No. 16 of 1939, and the Antigua Trades and Labour Union (ATLU) dates from that year. The Trade Union Ordinance was superseded by the Angitua Labour Code Act No. 14 of 1975. As an independent country Antigua and Barbuda ratified both ILO Convention No. 87 (Freedom of Association and Protection of the Right to Organize, 1948) and No. 98 (Right to Organize and Collective Bargaining, 1949) in 1983.

Trade unionism. Trade union density in Antigua and Barbuda was estimated to be as high as 28 per cent in 1987. There are two rival centres, each of which was strongly involved in the March 1989 elections. The ATLU—which gained a new leader in 1989—is closely associated with the ALP, the country's dominant party. The AWU is linked to the Progressive Labour Movement and gained some ground in the later 1980s. There is also an Antigua and Barbuda Public Servants Association (ABPSA) which gained formal recognition from the government in 1988 following an intervention by the Caribbean Public Services Association.

Antigua Trades and Labour Union (ATLU)

Address. 46 North Street, St John's
Phone. 20090
Leadership. William Robinson (president); Noel Thomas (general secretary)
Membership. 10,000
History and character. The ATLU was founded in 1939 and functioned for many years as both a trade union and a political party. It remains closely tied to the Antigua Labour Party, its political offshoot, which has held power since 1976.

The ATLC's relationship with the ALP is of considerable assistance to it: in 1988 it negotiated a favourable agreement on behalf of casual workers in the public service, while in 1989 it founded a new government-funded regional education centre in conjunction with the CWC.

Publications. Workers' Voice.
International affiliations. CLAT.

Antigua Workers' Union (AWU)

Address. Freedom Hall, Newgate Street, St John's
Phone. 20441/2; 22005
Cables. AWUNION
Leadership. Malcolm Daniel (president); Keithlyn Smith (general secretary)
Membership. 5,000 (1981).
History and character. Originated from a split in the ATLU in 1967, and is linked to the Progressive Labour Movement (founded in 1970 as the political arm of the AWU), the principal opposition party.

The AWU defeated the ATLU in a poll for recognition at the Royal Antiguan Hotel in 1989.

Publication: Trumpet.
International affiliations: ICFTU; ITF.

Argentina

Capital: Buenos Aires

Population: 31,506,000
(1988)

Political system. Seven years of military rule ended in 1983 — in the wake of the Falklands (Malvinas) armed conflict with the United Kingdom in 1982, and in the face of a situation of economic crisis and popular unrest — with the election of a President and of a bicameral parliament. The Chamber of Deputies is directly elected and the Senate is nominated by the provincial legislative bodies; the President is chosen by a directly elected electoral college. As of 1988 the Chamber of Deputies was fairly evenly balanced between the governing Radical Civic Union and the (Peronist) Justicialists.

In July 1989 the Peronist victor of the presidential elections Carlos Menem entered office succeeding President Raúl Alfonsín. His free-market policies have brought deep splits to both the Peronist movement and the trade union movement.

Economy. Agriculture accounts for about 15 per cent of gross domestic product and manufacturing for about 25 per cent. Argentina is a major exporter of grain and beef and agricultural produce and processed products represent two-thirds of total exports.

The manufacturing industry has been severely hit by the effects of inflation, deteriorating competitiveness in world markets, caused in part by the rapidly depreciating foreign exchange rate, and the worldwide recession of the early 1980s which resulted in increased unemployment and depressed real wages.

Argentina has been affected over a long period of years by a very high rate of inflation, which has had serious consequences for the internal economy and the external position (the foreign debt standing in mid-1988 at US$56,000 million), and has also been reflected in sharp conflicts with the politically developed trade unions. Within two years of the restoration of civilian government the annual inflation rate had risen to over 1,000 per cent, and in June 1985 a severe austerity programme (the Austral Plan) was introduced including a wage and price freeze and a sharp reduction in government spending.

Since 1987 Argentina has received large-scale assistance from the IMF and also from the World Bank in the context of an overall rescheduling of public-sector and private-sector debt, and this programme has in addition included debt-equity swaps. As part of the complementary structural adjustment Argentina has been implementing further austerity measures, seeking the modernization of production and privatizing certain unprofitable state undertakings and other activities.

Annual inflation in July 1989 — the month of President Menem's accession — was 196.6 per cent. Real wages had fallen sharply in the first half of the year and unemployment had risen by 1 per cent over the previous 12 months. The President, and his economic advisor Nestor Rapanelli embarked on a programme of economic liberalization — "major surgery without anaesthetic" according to Menem — which included maximum prices for basic commodities and devaluation of the austral. A long list of public sector candidates for privatization was drawn up and negotiations opened up with the IMF, despite the fact that Argentina had, hitherto, been excluded from the Plans of US Treasury Secretary Brady for debt reduction.

By the end of 1989 however there had been a steep drop in purchasing power and the Menem government faced mounting social and union opposition to its economic policies. In January 1990 the President announced that a further package of measures would be put into effect and declared his intention to seek a social pact with both sides of industry. Measures to suppress the growth of public sector wages were imposed however and the government's aim at the end of 1990 was to eliminate its spending deficit by March 1991.

System of industrial relations. Argentina ratified ILO Convention No. 87 (Freedom of Association and Protection of the Right to Organize, 1948) in 1960 and No. 98 (Right to Organize and Collective Bargaining, 1949) in 1956.

The right to belong to a trade union was formally restored in September 1982, and the right to strike in 1983 (although the government retained powers to ban individual strikes). At the same time the trade unions were brought into tripartite discussions with government and business on questions relating to the transition to democracy and the economic crisis. Government proposals for major trade union reform were severely weakened in 1984 (*see below*). Undeterred, the government pressed on and succeeded in passing two pieces of legislation, in December 1987 and March 1988, which are being seen as significant steps in Labour Reform. The December Act broadened collective agreements on wages and conditions in both the public and private sectors with "sector" level and company level bargaining allowed. However, only trade unions (and employers) clearly representative of a particular trade or industry were permitted to be the bargaining parties. The government's provisos were that all such agreements are binding on both sides and only valid when ratified by the Ministry of Labour which could refuse to endorse any agreement it felt might threaten public order or which were not felt to be in the public interest, a decision not subject to legal appeal. However, collective bargaining would no longer be suspended on grounds of economic emergency. The government retained for itself the right to set pay guidelines in certain circumstances to suit its anti-inflation policy. But it opted for codes of conduct to be agreed on by both unions and employers to resolve disputes, rather than using legislation to curb strikes (in December 1987, the government ratified ILO Convention No. 150—Collective Bargaining, 1981). The reform process was extended, after a great deal of opposition from employers and sections of the Radical party, by an Act of March 23, 1988, which recognized the right of workers to form or be (or not to be) members of a union of their choice. Equally, trade unions might become members of their preferred federations, confederations and affiliates to international union organizations. However, unions could only represent workers and participate in negotiations, be it in the public or private sectors, if the Ministry of Labour had been assured of their representative status. Where workers were deemed to be members of a *bona fide* union, it was the employers who were empowered to act as the collectors of union dues. Trade unions were allowed to set up mutual benefit societies and co-operatives and were still allowed to retain their controversial role of administering social welfare (a vast system of health provision, education, tourism, sports facilities; a monopoly bitterly opposed by government and employers alike).

According to a 1990 report, two thirds of the disputes in Argentina between 1986 and 1989 occurred in the public sector. These were unlikely to fall when real wages of public sector employees had dropped 53 per cent in the first three months of 1990. In October 1990 after the failure of Congress to pass such a measure during the previous six months, President Menem signed a decree curbing the rights of workers in "essential industries" to strike. The decree applied to public health, transport, water supply, gas, oil, phones, education and the judiciary. In all these sectors wage increases were made the subject of strict procedures including compulsory arbitration before action might be taken; while for its duration unions must guarantee to maintain essential services. In January and February 1991 the decree received its first serious test in a major rail strike.

Trade unionism. Trade unionism took root early in Argentina, the first trade union in Latin America—the printers' union—being formed in 1857, and from the beginning of the twentieth century onwards various attempts were made to form national trade union centres. These efforts were unsuccessful, however, until the formation of the Confederación General del Trabajo (CGT) in 1930. The CGT, through periods of contrasting fortunes, has remained since the 1940s a major force in Argentine politics and the bastion of Peronism (*see below*), and although trade unionism was suppressed by the military junta from 1976 it resurfaced strongly in 1982–83 in demonstrations and general strikes in a transitional phase from rigid authoritarianism preceding the restoration of full civilian rule at the end of 1983.

President Menem's free market policies provoked a crisis in Peronism and in the CGT. The CGT had by November 1989 split into two factions for and against Sr Rampanelli's programme with opposition led by the Confederation's redoubtable General Secretary Saúl Ubaldini. The Ubaldini faction fiercely resisted the call for a voluntary two-year strike ban and was displaced by a "Menemista" group at the head of the official CGT apparatus.

Confederación General del Trabajo (CGT)
General Conferation of Labour

Address. Brasil 1482, Buenos Aires
Phone. (98-54-1) 27-75-50
Leadership. Saúl Ubaldini (secretary general)
Membership. 2,500,000. Represents 90 per cent of the country's unions.

History and character. The CGT was founded in 1930, but in its early years its status was challenged by competing syndicalist, anarchist and socialist federations, and railway unions still provided 50 per cent of the membership in 1942. After becoming Minister of Labour and Social Welfare following a military coup in 1943, Col. Juan Domingo Perón began to build a relationship with the CGT as part of his politics of charismatic, authoritarian populism (which has been characterized as a form of proletarian fascism, with no exact parallel elsewhere). Perón was dismissed in October 1945, but a strike called by the CGT won his release from detention and paved the way for his election as President in 1946. From then, until Perón's fall and exile in 1955, the CGT leadership consolidated its influence through its relationship with the Peronist movement. The overthrow of Perón in Sept. 1955 was met with widespread resistance by the trade unions, and several hundred workers and others were killed in an abortive Peronist uprising in June 1956. Government-appointed officials took over the running of unions, and the CGT was formally disbanded, though retaining an underground identity. The CGT then entered a long period of internal conflict over the question of its relationship to successive civilian and military governments and with the exiled Perón. In 1961 the CGT was returned to union control and in 1963 it held its first open congress since Perón's fall. Under its secretary general, Augusto Vandor, who advocated "Peronism without Perón", the CGT reached an accommodation with the military régime which took power in 1966, but following bitterly disputed union elections in 1968, it broke into rival pro- and anti-government factions, the dissidents forming the "CGT of the Argentines". In elections in March 1973 the Peronist candidate Héctor Cámpora became President of Argentina, preparing the way for the election of Perón himself as President in Sept. 1973. On his death in July 1974, Perón was succeeded by his widow María Estela (Isabelita); Isabelita Perón retained considerable support from the CGT, but relations were strained by worsening economic conditions and the operation of a wage restraint policy which bitterly divided the unions. In June-July 1975 the implementation of that policy provoked the first CGT-led strikes against a Peronist government and the resignation and flight from the country of the Minister of Social Welfare. Following the military *coup* which deposed Isabelita Perón in March 1976, government-appointed officials took control of the CGT, and it was officially dissolved in 1979. Different factions of the underground but increasingly open CGT were already leading protests and strikes in 1982–83, however, before the restoration of the right to strike in mid-1983 and the return to civilian rule later that year.

A trade union reform bill introduced by the incoming civilian government of President Alfonsín at the end of 1983 met with vigorous opposition from the CGT; the CGT objected in particular to clauses binding unions to hold elections within 180 days under the supervision of the judiciary and using a system of proportional representation. Alfonsín had made union reform a principal plank in his election manifesto in 1983 and had repeatedly criticized the close links between the CGT leadership and hard-line members of the previous military government, as well as suggesting that union funds had been misapplied by corrupt CGT leaders, and in a statement attached to the bill the government declared that "the republic has democratized itself in the political sphere but not in the union one". The bill was approved in the Chamber of Deputies, where Alfonsín's Radical Civic Union party held the majority, but in March 1984 it was defeated in the Senate, where the Peronist Justicialist National Movement dominated. A much watered-down package, which had been negotiated with the CGT, was approved by both Houses in mid-1984; the measure set out new rules for the conduct of trade union elections, making union leaders responsible for updating voting lists and suspended a decree invoked under military rule whereby union leaders were denied access to "social work" funds (such funds had been seen as a source of corruption). The CGT's legal status had been withheld by the government due to the enormous financial debt it had incurred under the military government, estimated at tens of millions of US dollars. However, following the mediation of the ILO in September 1986, the CGT's legal status was restored on Nov. 7, 1986, coinciding with the Confederation's first congress for nearly 11 years, attended by 1,300 delegates for 155 organizations. Saúl Ubaldini, the secretary general, was returned for a two-year term.

The CGT called one-day general strikes on Jan. 24, March 25, June 13, and Oct. 9, 1986, to protest against government austerity measures under the Austral Plan, especially wage controls, and to demand a moratorium on repayments of the foreign debt. The last of these strikes, the seventh since Alfonsín came to power, produced an absenteeism rate in Buenos Aires, the main manufacturing centre, estimated by the government at 60 per cent and by the CGT at 80–90 per cent, with an accompanying protest demonstration by 100,000. Critics of Saúl Ubaldini argued that his concealed intention was to destabilize the government and Ubaldini — a hard-line Peronist — was widely regarded as the effective leader of opposition to Alfonsín. In 1987, the CGT called three one-day general strikes in protest at the government's austerity measures, with Saúl Ubaldini, on the occasion of the Nov. 4 stoppage, demanding the resignation of the ministers in charge of economic affairs and that the government cease paying interest on the foreign debt (then standing at US$54,000 million). Despite such activity work stoppages in the private sector showed a marked decline druing the year, militancy being mainly confined to the public sector. The CGT called further general strikes on April 14 and Sept. 12, 1988, making a total of 12 since President Alfonsín came to power. The latter strike was widely supported, again by public sector workers, whose low incomes have been further eroded by current economic policies (schools had been closed for the previous six weeks as teachers maintained a strike for a minimum monthly wage of approximately 110 dollars).

Although previously hostile to any restrictions on pay bargaining, the CGT initially welcomed the March 23, 1988 labour legislation (*see above*), believing that it genuinely respected principles of trade unions' autonomy and freedom of association, especially through conferring legal status on shop stewards for the first time. Its one reservation was that the law did not provide for workers' participation in the management of companies and denied the unions access to a company's financial and economic information.

In the last year of the Alfonsín administration however the CGT again turned to militant opposition to the government and a new strike wave hit Argentina early in 1989. Its honeymoon period with the new Peronist President Menem was brief, and by the autumn it was again split into factions, this time over whether or not to support the government's free-market measures and voluntarily to renounce the right to strike.

Splits in the CGT. The peculiarly powerful status of the CGT has contributed to its almost perpetual factional divisions.

In December 1984 the then four-way split of the CGT (*CGyT*, led by Jorge Triaca; *Independientes*, led by Ramón Baldassini; *Ex 25*, led by Osvaldo Borda; and *Verticalistas*, led by Saúl Ubaldini) was healed, with Ubaldini becoming secretary general of the unified CGT. As of late 1986 Ubaldini remained in control of the greater part of the CGT — being re-elected as secretary general at a "normalizing congress" held in early Nov. 1986 — but a significant minority bloc, seen as less hostile to the government's efforts to stabilize the national economy, was led by Lorenzo Miguel, the leader of the metalworkers' union (Unión Obrera Metalúrgica — UOM). Three powerful unions which negotiated wage deals with the government in July 1986 without reference to Ubaldini — the UOM and the unions of state workers (ATE) and construction workers (UOCRA) — were reportedly seeking to restrain Ubaldini.

The CGT's latest split occurred in the autumn of 1989 when Saúl Ubaldini and his supporters who opposed President Menem's economic policies were deposed by a "Menemista" faction.

International affiliations. ICFTU; ORIT.

Other co-ordinating organizations

Consejo Co-ordinador Argentino Sindical (CCAS)
Argentinian Trade Union Co-ordinating Council

Address. Venezuela 3342, 1211 Beunos Aires
Leadership. Miguel Gazzera (secretary general)
International affiliations. WCL; CLAT.

Co-ordinadora Nacional de Agrupaciones "Augustin Tosco" (CONAT)

Address. Jujuy 771, Beunos Aires
Leadership. Luis Canay
International affiliation. WFTU.

Australia

Capital: Canberra   **Population: 16,804,000**
(1989)

Political system. The Commonwealth of Australia came into being in 1901 and is a fully independent member of the Commonwealth. Final and full legal independence from the United Kingdom was constitutionally achieved in March 1986. There is a bicameral Parliament with a directly elected Senate (with 12 members for each of the six states and two for each of the two territories) and a directly elected House of Representatives (with currently 148 members representing broadly equal electorates). From 1949 to 1972 and again from 1975 to 1983 the federal government was formed by the Liberal/National (Country) Party coalition and from 1972 to 1975 and since 1983 by the Labor Party.

The Australian Labor Party, led by Bob Hawke a former ACTU Secretary, came to power in 1983 and in the 1990 elections won a historic fourth consecutive term of office. Labour won five of Australia's six states in the 1991 state elections.

Economy. The Australian economy has traditionally been based on cereals and livestock (meat and wool), but more recently the export of coal and coal products, of iron and other ores, and of manufactured goods has become increasingly important.

Australia has huge deposits of coal, nickel, iron ore, uranium and bauxite and is one of the world's principal sources of diamonds. Nearly three-quarters of Australia's petroleum requirements are met from domestic production. The mining sector overall accounts for nearly 40 per cent of all exports, although providing only a small level of employment.

Rather over 40 per cent of exports are still of agricultural produce or products, especially meat, dairy products, cereals, sugar and wool. Manufacturing industry, which accounts for about 20 per cent of gross domestic product, is centred principally around the metallurgical and engineering sectors.

The economy has since the early 1980s been affected by falls in the world market prices of many of Australia's commodity exports.

Civilian employment in Australia was 7,400,000 in 1988, of which 1,940,000 was in industry, 410,000 in agriculture, and 5,380,000 in services. Unemployment fell back

1 per cent during the year to 7.2 per cent but climbed thereafter to reach almost 10 per cent by the spring of 1991. Economic growth rose past 4 per cent in 1989 but fell to less than half of that rate in 1990.

System of industrial relations. Australia ratified both ILO Convention No. 87 (Freedom of Association and Protection of the Right to Organize, 1948) and No. 98 (Right to Organize and Collective Bargaining, 1949) in 1973.

As of 1989 Australia had ratified 46 of the ILO's 166 Conventions and was in the process of ratifying Convention 1561, (Workers with Family Responsibilities).

Trade union role in prices and income policy. A pattern of centralized wage negotiation with quasi-judicial arbitration and settlement, as opposed to company-by-company collective bargaining, has generally prevailed since the establishment of the Commonwealth Conciliation and Arbitration Commission (CAC) in 1904.

The authority of the CAC to enforce its judgements was substantially eroded after 1969, but its status was restored following the return of the Labor government in March 1983. The new government concluded a tripartite Prices and Incomes Accord with the Confederation of Australian Industry (CAI) and the ACTU at the country's first national economic summit held on April 11–14, 1983. Under this Accord the government undertook to reflate the economy, while business accepted price surveillance, dividend restraint and a resumption of centralized wage-fixing, and the unions agreed not to press wage demands beyond the level of inflation. Under the agreement the CAC was to set half-yearly pay awards on the basis of movements in the consumer price index.

On Sept. 4, 1985, the government and the ACTU negotiated a two-year extension of the Accord whereby, in return for a reduced wage claim and agreement by the ACTU to the modification of a 4 per cent productivity claim to a phased-in 3 per cent increase in occupational pensions (superannuation), the government would support the ACTU claim for a 3.8 per cent pay claim before the CAC, and would also reduce personal income taxes by an amount equal to the after-tax equivalent of a 2 per cent wage increase. The superannuation funds would be controlled by the unions. In Nov. 1985 the CAC awarded the fully-indexed 3.8 per cent ACTU national pay claim in full, provoking threats by the CAI to walk out of the Accord. By this time, however, there was mounting concern at the general economic situation, and in March 1986, 64 employers' groups, representing 250,000 businesses, resolved to withdraw from the Accord, on the ground that the ACTU was "in effective control" of the CAC and the government.

On June 11, 1986, following evidence of worsening trade deficits, the Prime Minister warned that it would be necessary to accept cuts in real wages and the postponement of tax cuts if the nation's economic difficulties were to be overcome; the government would not interfere with the current ACTU pay claim of 2.5 per cent, but would seek to avoid any further increases in 1986 and to spread the 3 per cent superannuation increase over three years. In response, Simon Crean, the president of the ACTU, stated that further wage discounting (i.e. keeping wages below inflation) was unacceptable. On June 26 the CAC agreed only to a 2.3 per cent pay increase and to reject the 3 per cent superannuation productivity package, triggering strikes in the oil, dock and other sectors. The federal budget announced on Aug. 19 proposed wage restraint, with increases in 1987 kept to the level of 2 per cent, and postponement of tax reductions from Sept. 1 to Dec. 1. Simon Crean subsequently said the ACTU would be prepared to negotiate a new agreement under the prices and income accord.

It was reported in early October 1986 that the leadership of the ACTU had abandoned its commitment to full wage indexation, but wanted the government to give greater incentives for investment in industry. An ACTU conference on Nov. 6 endorsed a proposed two-tier system, to be advanced in wage negotiations in 1987, with full wage indexation for lower paid workers and bargaining on an individual company or industry basis for the higher paid. The Labor government was said to support the idea provided it did not lead to wage increases beyond the 6 per cent envisaged in the August budget (compared with projected price inflation of 8 per cent).

Protagonists of the Accord noted that under it by 1986 there had been three years of growth at an annual rate of 5 per cent, with effective wage restraint and relatively low unemployment of 8 per cent. Critics pointed to the 9 per cent inflation rate, the severe balance of payments deficit, and a foreign debt which had reached US$52,000 million, arguing that the boom had been financed by borrowing and that the Accord represented a throw-back to discredited wage-restraint policies of the sort which had been prevalent in the major Western economies in the late 1960s and much of the 1970s. The Australian economy had been built on the surpluses generated by commodity exports, allowing the growth of tariff-protected industries and a high-wage economy; however, the prices of many of those commodities had fallen. These critics maintained that Australians still looked to government rather than to the workings of the free market for economic success.

Establishment of "two tiered" wage system. The Australian Conciliation and Arbitration Commission on March 10, 1987, announced its abandonment of wage indexation and the introduction in its place of a "two tiered" system intended to allow for greater wage flexibility by providing for two separate categories of wage increases. Under the so-called "National Wage Case Decision" (which was formally approved by the ACTU at a special conference held in early April), a "first tier" 10 dollar flat rate increase (2.5 per cent of average weekly earnings) was granted in March 1987 and an additional 6 dollars was given in February 1988. (In mid-December 1987 the ACAC had deferred any decision on a national wage increase in order to allow additional time for an assessment of the impact on the economy of the global share price fall in October 1987). The adjustments were not tied to the cost of living. Additional "second tier" wage rises, up to a maximum of 4 per cent, were linked to productivity performance. These were largely to result from agreements on, *inter alia*, changes to work and management practices, reduced demarcation barriers and increased multi-skilling, preferably negotiated at the plant and enterprise level. According to a report by the Organization for Economic Co-operation and Development (OECD) published in August 1988, the flow-through from the "second tier" awards was slower than anticipated.

For the first six years of the Labour Government wages rose at a slower rate than inflation. The 1989 Government – ACTU Accord agreed to tax cuts for the middle income bracket, pay increases of A$20–30 over two years, and an additional phased pay increase for the low paid. The IRC more or less endorsed these provisions, though it tied them to productivity, and pay was thought (after tax cuts) to outstrip inflation in the year. The IRC is examining the structure of Australia's pay award system with a view to eliminating "leap-frogging", a practice ACTU itself opposes.

The number of days lost in industrial disputes continued to fall from 1983 up to 1989, and in the last year dropped back by 30 per cent. However that year saw a major strike by the Australian Federation of Airline Pilots (AFAP) for a 30 per cent rise in defiance of any centralized setting of wages at the country's domestic airlines. The union faced stiff opposition from the government and was gradually worn down. In a landmark case the employers successfully brought a common law action against it, winning damages of A$6,600,000, a verdict which raises doubts as to whether or not there is a legal right to strike under a system so centralized as that of Australia.

Trade unionists' rights and immunities. Entrenched union power has helped to secure for labour a wide range of benefits and extra payments, with widespread restrictive practices which employers are increasingly seeking to challenge. At the institutional level, unions are shielded from actions by parties injured by industrial action, and legislation passed by the previous government giving the right to sue to third parties affected by "secondary boycotts" has found little application. The platform of the opposition Liberal-National parties coalition argues that mandates of the federal and state arbitration commissions should be made more flexible, to take account of the ability of individual industries to pay, and that steps should be taken towards introducing a system of collective bargaining, starting with voluntary negotiation of legally enforceable contracts in companies employing 50 or fewer people. Many employers also favour a phased introduction of US-style collective bargaining as a means to link wage increases more closely to productivity. The system of setting wages and conditions at present is based on the federal conciliation and arbitration commission and similar statutory bodies in each of the states. A statement issued on Sept. 24, 1986, and signed by leading employer groups, the ACTU and the government, indicated a willingness to re-examine issues relating to restrictive practices and productivity. An agreement reached in April 1988 between the Confederation of Australian Industry (CAI) and the ACTU on employee participation appeared to provide a framework for a more constructive approach to industrial relations. The areas identified in the statement issued by the two sides for the encouragement of participative practices were consultation and the sharing of information, the introduction of new technology and management practices, changes in work organization, the improvement of training and skills development opportunities and the introduction of schemes for employees to participate financially in the enterprise.

"Australia Reconstructed" report. The ACTU and the government's Trade Development Council (TDC) issued jointly in late July 1987 a report titled "Australia Reconstructed", containing the findings of senior union officials on employer-union relations in five European countries and their relevance to Australia. The report put forward a comprehensive series of recommendations on the restructuring of the Australian economy and the enhanced participation of the unions in that process. It called for "a central national economic and social objective, negotiated, set and given substantial support by all major parties e.g. government, unions, business and community groups". The recommendations included policies for trade and industry (including the establishment of a National Development Fund), a national skills and training plan, a cohesive industrial and social wage programme, and "strategic unionism" i.e. extending union activities beyond the traditional fields of wages and working conditions. The report was endorsed by the ACTU at its annual congress in September 1987, but received a mixed reception from employer groups. For instance, the Confederation of Australian Industry (CAI) claimed that implementation of the report would lead to an increase in bureaucratic procedures, which was "a prescription totally at odds with Australia's current needs".

The Industrial Relations Act 1988 was a major statute modifying the legal framework of Australia's industrial relations. While maintaining the (constitutionally prescribed) involvement of the state at each level it strengthened the role of the Industrial Relations Commission (IRC). To its power to resolve industrial disputes, demarcation disputes at the national level, and to register unions, the Commission now adds the power (under Section 115) to certify agreements which are unique and thus inconsistent with broader awards. This is a very important consideration in Australia, where the pay of some 85 per cent of employees is regulated by state or federal awards. Though these tend to be company rather than industrial based there is power at State level to make a "common award" which will generalize the terms of an agreement.

Section 115 (which allows companies and unions to negotiate local agreements subject to the approval of the IRC) may prove important in opening up the path for enterprise agreements. Section 118 facilitates the right of unions to cover a wide range of workers at a single plant. Another section effectively requires all unions to have membership of at least 1,000 by 1991, affecting a very large number of Australian unions (*see below*).

Trade unionism. Trade unionism developed strongly among the nineteenth-century

British settlers, and there were some 200 unions operating by 1890. The pattern has traditionally been one of craft unionism and, despite a trend in more recent years towards large
industry-wide unions there were still 308 unions in 1988. Of these the 18 largest ("large"
being defined as those with more than 50,000 members), accounted for 52.2 per cent of the
unionized workforce. By contrast 226 unions with less than 5,000 members accounted for
only 7.9 per cent of union membership. Nearly half the unions in that year (with only 1.7
per cent of the membership) had fewer than 1,000 members. The attractiveness of amalga-
mating has now increased with provisions in the new Industrial Relations Act which
extended the defences of legal standing only to unions with a membership above a
minimum of 1,000. The once-powerful, rural-based Australian Workers' Union has tended
to decline, and blue-collar unions have lost much of their earlier pre-eminence in the face
of the rise of white-collar and public sector unionism. The public sector, which employs
one-third of the workforce, is progressively becoming the most unionized area of the
economy. Enterprise unionism, although not unknown, has generally been strongly
opposed by the majority of unions, which have supported the practice of negotiating
industry-wide agreements regardless of the varying circumstances of individual
employers. There is one dominant and politically important central organization, the
Australian Council of Trade Unions (ACTU).

The Biennial ACTU Congress was held in Sydney in September 1989. It was dominated
by strategic issues facing the unions. Both the then leaders insisted that ACTU was
doomed unless it made itself more relevant: estimates had shown that only 100,000 of the
new 1,600,000 jobs created since 1983 were unionized. Density which had fallen to
42 per cent might fall to 20 per cent by 2010 unless drastic changes were made, in the view
of Secretary Bill Kelty, who called on unions to rationalize in order to cut their number to
two or three per enterprise and their overall strength to 20. Congress called for a wage
strategy to raise living standards in 1990–92, for a sweeping social welfare programme,
and for improvements in occupational health and safety.

Political ties of organized labour. There is a close relationship between the Australian
Labor Party and the mainstream of the organized labour movement, with trade union
delegates attending party conferences and unions sponsoring MPs; however, the direct
influence over the party has weakened since the 1960s. The Communist Party of Australia
(which has never won a seat in Parliament) has some influence in various trade unions,
including the metal workers', shipwrights', railway workers', transport workers',
dockers', miners' and teachers' unions. The small influence on the unions of the minor
Socialist Party of Australia (a pro-Soviet breakaway from the Communist Party of
Australia) was reduced with the expulsion from the party in 1982 of its then president,
Patrick Clancy, the federal secretary of the Building Workers' Industrial Union, and other
trade unionists who resisted the party's attempt to dictate policy to their unions.

The Victoria state equal opportunity board ruled in February 1987 that an employee
could not be dismissed for refusing to join a union if the union in question had substantial
political affiliations. The case at issue involved an engineering worker who had refused to
join the Amalgamated Metal Workers' Union (AMWU), an affiliate of the Victoria state
Australian Labour Party. In its decision the board claimed that the ties between the
AMWU and the Labour Party were "clearly of a political nature"; it further accused the
AMWU of initiating industrial action for purely political ends. Commentators stated that
national ramifications were expected from the ruling, because South Australia and New
South Wales had equal opportunity laws similar to those in Victoria.

The largest union in Australia is probably still the Shop, Distributive & Allied
Employees' Association with a membership in excess of 200,000 closely followed by the
Amalgamated Metal Workers' Union. At the end of the 1980s there was an acceleration of
the merger process among Australian unions. In August 1989 the Administrative and

Clerical Officers' Association (ACOA) amalgamated with the Australian Public Sector and Broadcasting Union, Australian Government Employment to form the Public Sector Union (PSU) with around 90,000 members. In the same year the Miners' Federation merged with two smaller unions to form the United Mineworkers' Federation of Australia, and the Metalworkers' Union merged with the Supervisors' and Draughtmen's Union. However an attempt to merge the Building Workers with the Engine Drivers was thrown out in a ballot by the latter, and the Ironworkers' Union failed to merge with the Australian Workers' Union.

The Municipal Officers' Association ballotted in April 1991 on amalgamation with the Australian Transport Officers' Federation of Australia and the Technical Service Guild of Australia to form the Australian Services Union. The new union will be prodominantly in the public sector and have 70,000 members. In the spring of 1991 the Australian Insurance Employees' Union ballotted its members on a proposal to amalgamate with four others, the Australian Bank Employees' Union, the AMP Society Staffs' Association, the Trustee Companies Officers' Association and the Wool Brokers Staffs' Association, to form the Finance Sector Union of Australia. A December 1989 ruling of the Industrial Relations Commission granted jurisdiction over all workers at a new aluminium company in Tasmania, to the Federated Ironworkers, a development which could only accelerate rationalization.

Australian Council of Trade Unions (ACTU)

Address. 393 Swanston Street, Melbourne, Victoria 3000
Phone. (03) 663 5266
Telex. AA 33943
Fax. (03) 663 4051
Leadership. Martin Ferguson (president; formerly the federal secretary of the Federated Miscellaneous Workers Union of Australia; William Kelty (secretary)
Membership. 2,600,000 (more than three-quarters of the country's trade union membership) in 146 affiliated unions. Since 1988, the number of unions has been reduced as a result of the amalgamation of unions objective of the ACTU.
History and character. The ACTU was founded in 1927. It has no political affiliation, although it has traditionally enjoyed a close and at one time dominating relationship with the Labor Party. Bob Hawke, the present Labor Prime Minister, is a former ACTU president. Several leading federations of white-collar unions affiliated to the ACTU in the 1979–81 period, hastening the change in its former blue-collar image.
Structure. The supreme policy-making body of the ACTU is the biennial congress. The executive body is the 38-member executive. There are ACTU state branches (known as trades and labour councils) for each of the six states of Australia. The state branches each elect one member of the executive, and have wide discretion in dealing with intrastate industrial and political issues.
Policies. The ACTU is committed to a programme of socialization. The ACTU assists in arbitrating industrial disputes, including those involving strike action by affiliated unions, and enjoys considerable authority and influence.

ACTU's policy is to encourage amalgamation of existing member unions, in part to reduce disruptive demarcation disputes and in part to assist in the development of powerful, professionally managed and institutionally sophisticated unions able to deal with modern companies on a more equivalent footing. Industry-wide unions are also seen as better fitted to cope with the problems posed for narrowly recruited skill-based craft unions by new technology.

Affiliated unions. There are 146 unions affiliated to the ACTU including:

1. **Public Sector Union**, 5th Floor, 191–199 Thomas St, Haymarket, Sydney, NSW, 2000.
   Phone: (02) 281 5899. Fax: (02) 281 9245.
   Leadership: P. Robson and J. Palmer (secretaries); P. Prince, R. Omdale (joint presidents).
   Membership: 90,284.

2. **The Amalgamated Footwear and Textile Workers' Union of Australia**, Ground Floor, 132–138 Leicester Street, Carlton, Victoria, 3053.
   Phone: (03) 347 2956; 347 2766. Fax: (03) 347 4049.
   Leadership: W. A. C. Hughes (secretary); J. Roughley (president).

3. **Amalgamated Metal Workers Union**, 136 Chalmers Street, Surry Hills, NSW, 2010.
   Phone: (02) 690 1411. Fax: (02) 698 7516.
   Leadership: George Campbell (secretary); R. T. Scott (president).
   Membership: 195,000.

4. **Association of Foremen and Supervisors**, P.O. Box 390, Mona Vale, NSW, 2103.
   Phone: (02) 997 4704.
   Leadership: J. Grant (secretary); Alf Pace (president).

5. **The Australasian Meat Industry Employees' Union**, Labor Council Building, Suite 5, 5th Floor, 377–383 Sussex Street, Sydney, NSW, 2000.
   Phone: (02) 264 2041; 264 2279.
   Leadership: T. Hannon (secretary); L. Day (president)

6. **Australian Bank Employees' Union**, 18 Drummond Street, Carlton South, Victoria, 3053.
   Phone: (03) 662 3577; Telex: Public Telex Service ME044.
   Leadership: M. L. Hingley (secretary); K. M. Westgarth (president).
   Membership: 78,070.

7. **Australian Federated Union of Locomotive Enginemen**, P.O. Box 250, North Melbourne, Victoria, 3051.
   Phone: (03) 328 3550; 328 4735. Fax: (03) 328 2719.
   Leadership: K. Matthews (secretary); R. D. Bradford (president).
   Membership: 9,000.

8. **The Australian Insurance Employees' Union**, 310 Queen Street, Melbourne, Victoria, 3000.
   Phone: (03) 670 8301. Fax: (03) 670 8188.
   Leadership: K. W. Davern (secretary); H. R. Purvis (president).

9. **Australian Postal and Telecommunications Union**, P.O. Box 436, Carlton South, Victoria, 3053.
   Phone: (03) 347 8922. Telex: 33044. Fax: (03) 348 1285.
   Leadership: Paul Watson (secretary); M. Anthony (president).

10. **Australian Public Service Federation**, P.O. Box 387, Carlton South, Victoria, 3053.
    Phone: (03) 347 2488. Fax: (03) 347 0462.
    Leadership: L. N. Riches (secretary); B Dittmer (president).

11. **Australian Railways Union**, 6th Floor, Labor Council Building, 377 Sussex Street, Sydney, NSW, 2000.
    Phone: (02) 267 6116; 264 3735. Fax: (02) 264 2896.
    Leadership: R. Jowett (secretary); P. E. Dunne (president).
    Membership: 34,200.

12. **Australian Teachers' Union**, P.O. Box 415, Carlton South, Victoria, 3053.
    Phone: (03) 348 1700; Facsimile: (03) 347 6330.
    Leadership: D. Robson (secretary); D. Foggo (president).
    Membership: 180,000.

13. **Australian Telecommunications Employees' Association/Australian Telephone and Phonogram Officers' Association**, 139 Queensberry Street, Carlton, Victoria 3053.
    Phone: (03) 348 1022; 348 1059. Telex: AA33677. Fax: (03) 347 3448.
    Leadership: I. M. Musumeci (secretary); I. McLean (president).

14. **The Australian Workers' Union**, P.O. Box 384, Redfern, NSW 2016.
    Phone: (02) 690 1022. Fax: (02) 690 1020.
    Leadership: E. R. Hodder (secretary); W. Ludwig (president).

15. **The Building Workers' Industrial Union of Australia**, P.O. Box C337, Sydney, NSW, 2001.
    Phone: (02) 267 3929; 264 5993. Telex: 25836; Fax: (02) 262 1465.
    Leadership: Tom McDonald (secretary); B. W. Ethell (president).
    Membership: 100,000.

16. **The Clothing and Allied Trades Union of Australia**, 64 Kippax Street, Surry Hills, NSW, 2010.
    Phone: (02) 281 9177. Fax: (02) 281 9129.
    Leadership: Anna Booth (secretary); K. Boyd (president).
    Membership: 25,000.

17. **Commonwealth Bank Officers' Association**, P.O. Box 3719, Sydney, NSW, 2001.
    Phone: (02) 281 6211. Fax: (02) 281 6240.
    Leadership: K. Scott (secretary); A. G. Redford (president).
    Membership: 34,000.

18. **Electrical Trades Union of Australia**, 52 Bay Street, Rockdale, NSW, 2216.
    Phone: 597 4499. Fax: (02) 597 6354.
    Leadership: Terry Johnson (secretary); R. C. Cuckman (president).

19. **Federated Clerks' Union of Australia**, 2nd Floor, 53 Queen Street, Melbourne, Victoria, 3000.
    Phone: (03) 629 3801. Fax: (03) 614 3250.
    Leadership: T. W. Sullivan (secretary); J. P. Maynes (president).

20. **The Federated Engine Drivers' and Firemen's Association of Australasia**, P.O. Box C337, Clarence Street, Sydney, NSW, 2000.
    Phone: (02) 267 3929; Telex: AA25836; Fax: (02) 262 1465.
    Leadership: J. Cambourne (secretary); M. McDonald (president).

21. **Federated Ironworkers' Association of Australia**, 51–65 Bathurst Street, Sydney, NSW, 2000.
    Phone: (02) 264 2877. Telex: 176770 (IRONWK). Fax: (02) 261 1701.
    Leadership: S. Harrison (secretary); R. Redmond (president).

22. **The Federated Miscellaneous Workers' Union of Australia**, 1st Floor, 365–375 Sussex Street, Sydney, NSW, 2000.
    Phone: (02) 267 9681. Telex: AA75879. Fax: (02) 267 3778.
    Leadership: J. Lawrence (secretary); Chris Raper (president).
    Membership: 137,000.

23. **Federated Municipal and Shire Council Employees' Union of Australia**, 1–3 O'Connell Street, North Melbourne, Victoria, 3051.
    Phone: (03) 326 6001. Fax: (03) 326 5313.
    Leadership: Paul Slape (secretary); J. Foyle (president).

24. **Federated Ship Painters and Dockers' Union of Australia**, 36 Mort Street, Balmain, NSW, 2041.
    Phone: (02) 810 3617.
    Leadership: R. Galleghan (secretary); A. Milne (president).

25. **National Union of Store Workers, Packers, Rubber and Allied Workers**, 132–138 Leicester Street, Carlton, Victoria, 3053.
    Phone: (03) 347 7455. Fax: (03) 347 6630.
    Leadership: Greg Sword (secretary); L. Jamieson (president).
    Membership: 93,600.

26. **Hospital Employees' Federation of Australia**, P.O. Box 655, Carlton South, Victoria, 3053.
    Phone: (03) 663 8224. Fax: (03) 663 8225.
    Leadership: R. Colley (secretary); K. Williams (president).

27. **Municipal Officers' Association of Australia**, 116–124 Queensberry Street, Carlton, Victoria, 3053.
    Phone: (03) 348 1788. Fax: (03) 347 5050.
    Leadership: Steve Gibbs (secretary); Tony Tuohey (president).

28. **Printing and Kindred Industries Union**, 594–596 Crown Street, Surry Hills, Sydney, NSW 2010.
    Phone: (02) 690 1000. Telex: 71708. Fax: (02) 699 1061.
    Leadership: John Cahill (secretary).
    Membership: 46,640.

29. **Australian Nursing Federation**, 373 St George's Road, North Fitzroy, Victoria, 3068.
    Phone: (03) 482 2722. Fax: (03) 482 2330.
    Leadership: Marilyn Beaumont (secretary).
    Membership: 80,000.

30. **Seamen's Union of Australia**, 289 Sussex Street, Sydney, NSW, 2000.
    Phone: (02) 267 3801. Fax: (02) 261 5897.
    Leadership: Patrick Geraghty (secretary); J. Steele (presiding officer).

31. **Shop, Distributive and Allied Employees' Association**, 9th Floor, 53 Queen Street, Melbourne, Victoria, 3000.
    Phone: (03) 282 0400. Fax: (03) 614 6264.
    Leadership: J. De Bruyn (secretary); James Maher (president).
    Membership: 201,787.

32. **Transport Workers' Union of Australia**, P.O. Box 211, Carlton South, Victoria, 3053.
    Phone: (03) 347 0099. Fax: (03) 347 2502.
    Leadership: Ivan Hodgson (secretary); K. Cys (president).
    Membership: 98,000.

33. **Vehicle Builders' Employees' Federation of Australia**, 3–11 Howard Street, West Melbourne, Victoria, 3003.
    Phone: (03) 326 8011. Telex: 30705. Fax: (03) 326 8097.
    Leadership: Wayne Blair (secretary); W. Taylor (president).
    Membership: 30,000.

34. **Waterside Workers' Federation of Australia**, P.O. Box 344, Haymarket, NSW, 2000.
    Phone: (02) 267 9134. Fax: (02) 261 3481.
    Leadership: T.I. Bull (secretary); J. Beggo (president).
    Membership: 8,113.

Publication. ACTU Bulletin.
International affiliations. ICFTU; ICFTU-APRO; CTUC; TUAC.

The Building Workers' Industrial Union remains, exceptionally and in common with the Seamen's Union of Australia, an ACTU affiliate which is also affiliated to the WFTU. The Miners' Federation is affiliated to the IMO.

CHRISTMAS ISLAND

Population: 3,214

Political system. Christmas Island has been an Australian territory since 1958.

Economy. The sole economic activity of significance is the mining of phosphates; until 1981 this was conducted by the British Phosphate Commission as managing agent for the Australian and New Zealand governments, and subsequently by the Phosphate Mining Corporation of Christmas Island Ltd (PMCI), which is owned by the Australian government. The PMCI workforce was reduced from 1,628 in mid-1981 to 619 by mid-1986; the phosphate reserves are close to exhaustion and the Australian government is seeking to establish alternative employment on the island.

Trade unionism. There is one union, the Union of Christmas Island Workers.

Union of Christmas Island Workers (UCIW)

Address. P.O. Box 185, Christmas Island, Indian Ocean 6798
Phone. 644 UCIW, Christmas Island, Indian Ocean (radio telephone through Perth)
Leadership. Gordon M. Bennett (secretary); Cheng Hang (president)
History and character. The UCIW was formed in the late 1970s with the assistance of the Australian Council of Trade Unions (ACTU), of which it is an affiliate. Under the leadership of Gordon Bennett the workforce in 1979 won parity in pay and conditions with Australian workers, although this only hastened the shedding of labour as the phosphates industry contracted (*see above*). The UCIW is now the most significant political force on the island, and has recently been in dispute with the Australian government over arrangements for the winding down of the phosphate industry, compensation for displaced workers, and the provision of alternative employment. Most UCIW members are of Chinese origin (the majority population on the island), whereas most employees in the services industry are Malays, and most mine managers and civil servants are white Australians.

Austria

Capital: Vienna

Population: 7,563,000
(1988)

Political system. Austria's republican Constitution was restored in 1945 immediately following the defeat of the German forces, although the country remained under allied occupation until 1955. From 1945 to 1966 there was a coalition between the Socialists and the (conservative) Austrian People's Party (until 1947 with the participation of the Communist Party). Thereafter the People's Party alone provided the government until 1970; the Socialists from 1970 to 1983 (initially in a minority position); and from 1983 the Socialists in coalition with the small (liberal) Freedom Party which had not hitherto been represented in government. A Socialist-People's Party coalition government took office in November 1986. There is a bicameral parliament, with the *Nationalrat* being elected directly under a system of proportional representation and the *Bundesrat* being elected by legislative assemblies of the nine provinces. Austria has been a member of EFTA since that organization's establishment in 1960.

Economy. The Austrian economy is predominantly industrial, with manufacturing accounting for nearly 30 per cent of gross domestic product; agriculture accounts for only about 4 per cent, although the country is largely self-sufficient in food. Fifty five per cent of the workforce is employed in services. The period of allied occupation saw the establishment of state corporations in large parts of the mining, metallurgical, engineering, chemical and petroleum industries (now grouped within the ÖIAG holding company), and the state sector accounts for nearly a quarter of industrial production; however, some parts of the state sector (notably Voest-Alpine) were experiencing financial difficulties in the early 1980s, and in 1987 legislation was approved providing for the ÖIAG to reduce its holdings in most of the nationalized undertakings to a bare majority. In 1990 the state-owned industries were restructured into 150 smaller firms and a rationalization programme was inaugurated. An increasing proportion of manufacturing has become concentrated in fields such as electronics and chemicals and away from the more traditional heavy industries, and the government has encouraged the development of the technological sector. Tourism is a major component of the economy, accounting for a large surplus within the country's current external balance. Austria imports a considerable proportion of its energy requirements, due in part to continued ecological and environmental objections to both hydroelectric and nuclear power facilities.

Economic growth in 1989 was 3.8 per cent, a slight decline over the figure for the previous year, and assisted in the reduction of the annual deficit. Unemployment fell to 5 per cent while inflation rose slightly to 2.5 per cent. Some 6.5 per cent of the workforce are legal foreign workers, and in June 1990 the Parliament voted to allow this proportion to rise to 10 per cent.

System of industrial relations. The setting of Austrian industrial relations is the Social Partnership, an informal mechanism joining employers and unions, agriculture and government. Elaborate consultative arrangements draw vested interests into the decision-making process before legislative proposals are presented to Parliament; the state sustains unified employer and employee organizations. The 1980s saw mounting criticism of the Social Partnership from the Freedom Party and the Greens but it continues to command majority support.

The Social Partnership shapes the behaviour of the partners. The last really serious strike wave was in 1965. There were no strikes at all in 1989, though a stoppage at the Daimler truck plant in February 1990 was the longest in Austria for 30 years. It lasted five days.

Austria ratified ILO Convention No. 87 (Freedom of Association and Protection of the Right to Organize, 1948) in 1950 and No. 98 (Right to Organize and Collective Bargaining, 1949) in 1951.

Trade unionism. Organized trade union activity in Austria developed in the second half of the nineteenth century, with legal protection for the formation of trade unions being extended in 1870. The first federation of trade unions (the Provisional Committee of the Austrian Trade Unions) was established in 1893. Apart from "free unions", which were closely associated with the Social Democratic Party, the Christian Social Party from around 1900 also contributed to the development of Christian trade unions. After the civil war of February 1934, the Social Democratic Party and its allied trade unions were dissolved and a United Trade Union was founded, controlled by the Christian groups. This organization was itself dissolved following the *Anschluss* (German annexation) in 1938, and workers and employers were brought into the German Labour Front. Only three weeks after the liberation of Vienna by Soviet troops on April 13, 1945, the Österreichischer Gewerkschaftsbund (ÖGB—the Austrian Federation of Trade Unions—*see below*) was formed, uniting former members of Christian, Socialist and Communist unions. The pattern of trade unionism established after 1945 was one of industrial unionism, whereby all manual workers in a plant belong to one union regardless of job demarcation lines. There are 15 national trade unions, all of which are affiliated to the ÖGB. The reputation of Austrian trade unions since 1945 has been one of a moderate and disciplined reformism, with the ÖGB co-operating with government in the pursuit of policies of balanced growth. Collective bargaining agreements are signed by the ÖGB and are governed by law. Union density in 1989 was stable at 60.1 per cent.

There also exist Chambers of Labour, which are established by law and funded by contributions from the wages and salaries of employees. There is a Chamber of Labour in each of the nine Austrian provinces and they are united in a body called the Austrian Chambers of Labour (OAKT). The Chambers of Labour are involved in practically every aspect of Austrian daily life, and their main role is to serve the interests of employees at both provincial and federal level. They carry out a wide range of functions including advice on employment, legislation, housing, urban policies, education, transport, health, and the provision of training, cultural activities, statistical and technical information, health and safety etc. All proposals for legislation at local, provincial and federal level must be submitted to the Chambers of Labour for expert appraisal before being considered by the appropriate legislature. In addition, the Chambers of Labour play an important role in nominating representatives on to a wide range of public bodies. In essence, they are there to represent the interests of the working population in Austria and they work very closely with the trade unions. There are parallel employers' chambers.

Österreichischer Gewerkschaftsbund (ÖGB)
Austrian Federation of Trade Unions

Address. Postfach 155, 1011 Vienna, Hohenstaufengasse 10–12

Phone. (0222) 534 44

Telex. GEWEBUND-WIEN

Fax. (0222) 533 52 93

Leadership. Friedrich Verzetnitsch (president); Alfred Dallinger, Josef Hesoun, Rudolf Nürnburger, Rudolf Poder, Hilde Seiler, Rudolf Sommer (Vice-Presidents); Karl Drochter, Mag. Herbert Tumpel (Executive Secretaries).

Membership. 1,644,408 (1989) of which 68.9 per cent is male.

History. The ÖGB was formed in Vienna in 1945 as a federation of 16 occupational unions, eight regional organizations and three fractions (Socialist, Communist and Popular Party, the last becoming the Christian fraction in 1951, *see below*). It played an active role in the post-war emergence of Austria as a democratic, neutral nation. It has emphasized policies of co-operation with government to achieve orderly growth, a joint commission of employers and unions (set up in 1957) meeting under the aegis of the federal chancellor, to review and to some degree control prices and wages. The ÖGB is non-party in character but there are groups of Christian, Socialist and Communist trade unionists within its structure, which are represented on the National Board (*Bundesvorstand*), as are members of other minority groups.

In allowing this participation the ÖGB resembles the Confederation of Venezuelan Workers and the *Histradut* in Israel. The four major parties draw up lists for elections to the executive and, while the Social Democrats always predominate, there is a minority voice which helps to stop absolute identification between party and union. Social Democratic influence in the ÖGB is great, but is certainly surpassed by the influence of the ÖGB in the Party: many senior union leaders have been or are in Parliament or Ministers.

In November 1989 the ÖGB at last broke with its long-standing policy of dealing only with official unions in Eastern Europe, and since that time has energetically supported the new independent unions there.

Structure. The highest forum is the quadrennial national congress, the delegates to which are elected by the members of the 15 national unions affiliated to the federation in accordance with their membership strength. Between congresses, the highest policy-making body is the *Bundesvorstand*, comprising the presidium, delegates of the 15 unions and representatives of minority groups. Day-to-day work is done by the presidium, which comprises the president, three vice-presidents and two executive secretaries. There is also an audit commission elected by the national congress to monitor the financial activities of the ÖGB and adherence to congress resolutions. There are provincial and district offices throughout the country. The ÖGB is a voluntary occupational association independent of any political party, and it is financed primarily by its membership. It concludes collective bargaining agreements (its affiliated unions being empowered only to negotiate such agreements), represents the interests of its membership in the legislative sphere, and offers welfare and social insurance programmes, and occupational training.

In 1989 the Commercial, Clerical and Technical Employees remained the largest ÖGB affiliate with 20.7 per cent of Federation membership. The Metalworkers, with 14.6 per cent are the second largest. Eight of ÖGB's 15 unions registered membership increases in 1989.

Affiliated unions (membership figures relate to 1989).

1. **Gewerkschaft der Bau- und Holzarbeiter** (Building and Woodworkers), Postfach 76, 1010 Vienna, Ebendorferstrasse 7.
   Phone: (0222) 42-36-41. Telex: 114833. Fax: (0222) 42-36-41-258.
   President: Josef Hesoun.
   Membership: 184,689.
   Publication: Bau Holz.

2. **Gewerkschaft der Chemiearbeiter** (Chemical Workers), 1062 Vienna VI, Stumpergasse 60.
   Phone: (0222) 597 15 01-03. Fax: (0222) 597 2101/23.
   President: Gerhard Linner.
   Membership: 58,523.
   Publication: Chemiearbeiter.

3. **Gewerkschaft Druck und Papier** (Printing and Paper Trade Workers), Postfach 91, 1072 Vienna, Seidengasse 15–17.
   Phone: (0222) 93-82-31/32.
   President: Herbert Bruna.
   Membership: 23,301.

4. **Gewerkschaft der Eisenbahner** (Railway Workers), 1051 Vienna V, Margaretenstrasse 166.
   Phone: (0222) 55-46-41/45.
   President: Franz Hums.
   Membership: 114,251.

5. **Gewerkschaft der Gemeindebediensteten** (Municipal Employees), 1090 Vienna IX, Maria-Theresien Strasse 11.
   Phone: (0222) 34-36-00. Telex: 114316. Fax: 275 34 3600.
   President: Rudolf Pöder.
   Membership: 169, 657.
   Publication: *Der Gemeindebedienstete* (monthly).

6. **Gewerkschaft Land-Forst-Garten** (Agricultural and Forestry Workers), 1010 Vienna I, Wipplingerstrasse 35/37.
   Phone: (0222) 534 44.
   President: Josef Wegerer (acting).
   Membership: 18,549.

7. **Gewerkschaft Handel, Transport, Verkehr** (Workers in Commerce and Transport), 1010 Vienna, Teinfalstrasse 7.
   Phone: (0222) 534 54. Fax: (0222) 53 454/325.
   President: Peter Schneider.
   Membership: 37,846.

8. **Gewerkschaft Hotel, Gastgewerbe, Persönlicher Dienst** (Hotel and Restaurant Workers), 1013 Vienna, Hohenstaufengasse 10.
   Phone: (0222) 534 44. Telex: 11 43 16. Fax: (0222) 53 35 293.
   President: Franz Erwin Niemitz.
   Membership: 52,812.
   Publications: Zeitung der Gewerkschaft Hotel, Gastgewerbe, Persönlicher Dienst.

9. **Gewerkschaft Kunst, Medien, Freie Berufe** (Artists and Media Workers), 1090 Vienna IX, Maria-Theresien-Strasse 11.
   Phone: (0222) 34-36-00.
   President: Stefan Müller.
   Membership: 16,310.

10. **Gewerkschaft der Lebens-und Genussmittelarbeiter** (Food, Beverage and Tobacco Workers), 1080 Vienna, Albertgasse 35.
    Phone: (0222) 42-15-45. Fax: (0222) 42 15 45/20.
    President: Dr Leopold Simperl.
    Membership: 40,113.
    Publications: Der Lebensmittelarbeiter.

11. **Gewerkschaft Metall-Bergbau-Energie** (Metal Workers, Miners and Power Supply Workers), 1041 Vienna IV, Plosslgasse 15.
    Phone: (0222) 501 46-0. Fax: (0222) 65 65 51.
    President: Rudolf Nürnberger.
    Membership: 240, 221.

12. **Gewerkschaft Öffentlicher Dienst** (Public Employees), 1010 Vienna I, Teinfalstrasse 7.
    Phone: (0222) 53454.
    President: Siegfried Dohr.
    Membership: 229, 851.

13. **Gewerkschaft der Post- und Fernmeldebediensteten** (Postal and Telegraph Workers), 1010 Vienna I, Biberstrasse 5.
    Phone: (0222) 512-55-11. Telex: 112042. Fax: (0222) 512 55-11-52.
    President: Norbert Tmej.
    Membership: 79,357.

14. **Gewerkschaft der Privatangestellten** (Commercial, Clerical and Technical Employees), 1013 Vienna, Deutschmeisterplatz 2.
    Phone: (0222) 34-35-20. Telex: 114114. Fax: (0222) 34 35 20 1388.
    President: Lore Hostach.
    Membership: 340,348.
    Publication: *Augestellten*.

15. **Gewerkschaft Textil, Bekleidung, Leder** (Textile, Garment and Leather Workers), 1013 Vienna, Hohenstaufengasse 10.
    Phone: (0222) 534 44.
    President: Ing. Harald Ettl.
    Membership: 38,580.

Publications. *Solidarität* (monthly newspaper, circulation 1,300,000); *Arbeit und Wirtschaft* (monthly journal, circ. 30,000); *Hallo* (monthly youth journal, circ. 90,000); *Gew Nachrichtendienst* (weekly information bulletin, circ. 14,000); *Rednerdienst* (circ. 14,000).
International affiliations. ICFTU, ETUC, TUAC.

Fraktion Christlicher Gewerkschafter im Österreichischen Gewerkschaftsbund
Austrian Trade Union Federation—Christian fraction

The address, phone and telex numbers are as for the ÖGB as a whole.
Leadership. Rudolf Sommer (president); Alkuin Pecher, Herbert Selner, Franz Stocker, Gertraud Wawersich (vice-presidents).
Membership. 230,000.
History. The Christian fraction of the ÖGB was formed in 1951, replacing the Popular Party fraction which had been formed in 1945. It describes itself as "non confessional, non political".
It continued to maintain links with independent unions in Eastern Europe while official ÖGB contacts lapsed.
Affiliated unions. The Christian trade unionists' sections of the 15 national Austrian occupational unions (listed under the ÖGB main heading).

Publications. FCG-Magazin; Standpunkt.
International affiliations. WCL; ETUC.

Fraktion des Gewerkschaftlichen Linksblocks im ÖGB

Address. Höchstädtplatz 3, 1206 Vienna
Phone. (0222) 33-56-01
Telex. vstwn 114162
Leadership. Anton Hofer
Character. Left-wing faction of the ÖGB.
Publication. Die Arbeit.
International affiliation. WFTU.

Bahamas

Capital: Nassau

Population: 247,000
(1988)

Political system. The Bahamas became independent in 1973 as a full member of the Commonwealth and has a bicameral parliament. Since 1967 the government has been led by Sir Lynden Pindling's Progressive Liberal Party (PLP), which derives its main support from the islands' black community; in 1986 the PLP won 31 seats in the House of Assembly, the Free National Movement 16 and independents two.

Economy. The main economic sectors are tourism (accounting overall for two-thirds of employment, with 25 per cent of the workforce being in the hotels and catering field) and offshore banking and finance. Industry and agriculture are relatively undeveloped. Despite continued high unemployment, the general standard of living is one of the highest in the Caribbean.

System of industrial relations. The Bahamas ratified ILO Convention No. 98 (Right to Organize and Collective Bargaining, 1949) in 1976, but has not ratified Convention No. 87 (Freedom of Association and Protection of the Right to Organize, 1948).

Trade unionism. Trade unions developed after World War II. The first union centre was the Bahamas Federation of Labour, founded in 1942, but this ceased to function as a federation in 1969. The trade union centre is now known as the Commonwealth of the Bahamas Trade Union Congress.

The Commonwealth of the Bahamas Trade Union Congress (CBTUC)

Address. P.O. Box C.B. 10992, 104 Bethel Ave, Stapledon Gardens, Nassau
Phone. 1-809-323-7124
Leadership. Arlington L. Miller (president); A. Leonard Archer (secretary general)
Membership. 11,000. There are 10 affiliated unions.
History and character. The Commonwealth of the Bahamas Trade Union Congress was established in its present form in 1971. The CBTUC's main activities, at present, revolve around the organization of unorganized workers and the agitation for modern labour laws which would offer employment protection for workers, as well as the legalizing of severance and redundancy payments.
International affiliations. ICFTU/ORIT; CCL.

Bahrain

Capital: Manama

Population: 489,000

Political system. Bahrain (comprising the island of Bahrain itself and a number of smaller islands) became fully independent in 1971 having previously been a British protected state. The Amir rules through an appointed cabinet under a Constitution ratified in 1973;

the National Assembly was dissolved in 1975. The ruling family is Sunni Moslem, whereas the majority of the population is Shia.

Economy. The economy is largely dependent upon petroleum (although reserves of oil are expected to be exhausted during the 1990s). Approximately a fifth of gross domestic product is derived from petroleum and mining, a quarter from trade and finance and another quarter from manufacturing, while over 80 per cent of export revenue is derived from the petroleum industry. Oil exploration, production and marketing are centralized in the government-owned Bahrain National Oil Company; the government also has a major holding in petroleum refining, gas exploitation, aluminium smelting, extrusion and rolling, petrochemicals, ammonia and methanol production, and iron ore pelletizing. The Arab Shipbuilding and Repair Yard Company is jointly owned by the seven members of OAPEC.

Bahrain's banking business comprises developed domestic and offshore sectors, and there are few limitations on the movement of capital or other funds.

Nearly 60 per cent of Bahrain's workforce comprises foreigners (mainly manual labourers from the Indian sub-continent), but foreigners as a whole represent only a third of the total population. However, it was announced in May 1986 that all expatriate workers would have to leave the country upon the expiry of their contracts unless they were about to be retired.

The Gulf Crisis led to a decline in business confidence in Bahrain, reflected in a fall in share prices on the new Stock Exchange, and led to the government postponing plans to reduce its share in state-owned enterprises.

System of industrial relations. The first organized strike in Bahrain occurred in 1938, with demands including the replacement of the British "political agent", the expulsion of foreign workers from the Bahrain Petroleum company (BAPCO), and the right to organize trade unions. Bahrain has ratified neither ILO Convention No. 87 (Freedom of Association and Protection of the Right to Organize, 1948) nor Convention No. 98 (Right to Organize and Collective Bargaining, 1949).

Underground trade unionism, partly communist-inspired, existed in the 1950s, and a strike of BABPCO workers in 1965 developed into a general strike. Following independence in August 1971 the government maintained the ban on trade unionism, although strikes occurred in 1972 and again in 1974. In 1983 the government for the first time recognized an organization for the representation of industrial workers, the **General Committee for Bahrain Workers**. This is a joint committee of management and workers and exists in only eight major designated companies. There is also an (unrecognized) pro-WFTU **Union of Workers of Bahrain**, chaired by Husayn Abdullah and apparently linked to the tiny and illegal Bahrain National Liberation Front; the support for this group is unclear. The WFTU and ICATU have complained of continuing arrests and violations of trade union rights in Bahrain, including allegations of the torture of activists.

Bangladesh

Capital: Dhaka
(1989)

Population: 114,718,395

Political system. Bangladesh (formerly East Pakistan) effectively secured its separate independence in 1971 and became a member of the Commonwealth in 1972 with republican status. After a decade of disturbed political conditions, power was assumed in April 1982 by Gen. Hossain Mohammad Ershad, the Army Chief of Staff. Parliamentary elections which were held in May 1986 but which were boycotted by one of the main opposition groupings resulted in an overall majority in the unicameral parliament for the pro-government Jatiya Party. Following further industrial and political unrest a state of emergency was declared in November 1986, while subsequent controversial parliamentary elections in March 1988—boycotted by the principal opposition parties—again produced an overwhelming Jatiya Party majority.

It was only late in 1990 that the Jatiya Party lost power to an opposition coalition led by the widow of Sheikh Mujib Rahman, the founder of Bangladesh.

Economy. Bangladesh is essentially an agricultural country, with a high density of population and a very low per capita gross national product. Some two-thirds of the workforce are engaged in agriculture and less than 5 per cent in manufacturing, with the jute industry as the largest single industrial source of employment. There is a very high incidence of unemployment and under-employment, although this is difficult to quantify accurately. Raw jute and jute goods account for some 60 per cent of export, but both output and market conditions are subject to wide fluctuations.

Many industrial concerns were nationalized in 1971 upon the establishment of the new state of Bangladesh (mainly companies previously owned by citizens from West Pakistan). However, President Ziaur Rahman adopted a policy in the late 1970s of a return of substantial parts of the nationalized sector to private ownership, while Gen. Ershad, in June 1982, announced a major programme of denationalization, notably of the jute and textile industries.

Bangladesh initiated a sequence of five-year development plans in 1973–74, the latest being for the period 1985–89. However, these have been liable to severe modification as a result not only of major policy changes but also of the effects on the economy of devastating flooding and other natural disasters to which the country is prone.

The latest of these occurred in April 1991 when a massive cyclone caused the deaths of an estimated 150,000 in the Bay of Bengal. There is a civilian labour force of perhaps 34,500,000, of whom 18,000,000 work in the countryside. Its size is set to continually expand: in 1988 alone a further 3,000,000 were added to the population. Unsurprisingly emigration is maintained at a high rate—some 750,000 Bangladeshis have left their country to work abroad since 1976.

System of industrial relations. Pakistan ratified ILO Convention No. 87 (Freedom of Association and Protection of the Right to Organize, 1948) in 1951, and Convention No. 98 (Right to Organize and Collective Bargaining, 1949) in 1952; Bangladesh in turn ratified both Conventions in June 1972. However, the rights assured by these Conventions have been almost continuously threatened or weakened by the operation of contradictory national legislation, at times under conditions of martial law. In practice a high degree of union activity appears to have persisted throughout the last 40 years regardless of the edicts of military and other governments, often serving as a vehicle for political dissent. In recent years, the imposition of martial law did not suffice to stifle union activities; restrictions imposed on trade unions in 1982 were repealed in April 1983, and a further ban on union activities on March 1, 1985, was lifted as of Jan. 1, 1986. However, according to the World Confederation of Labour in February 1986, the authorities "adopt an authoritarian and repressive attitude to the majority of autonomous and independent organizations, whilst on the other hand they remain tolerant with regard to the forces which identify themselves with the government".

The ILO *Report of the Committee of Experts on the Application of Conventions and Recommendations* (1985) noted that under the Industrial Relations Ordinance of 1969, as amended in 1980, supervisory staffs are barred from union membership, although

Article 9 of ILO Convention No. 87 states that only police and armed forces may be excluded from its scope, and that there are also restrictions on the right of workers to belong to unions of their own choosing, especially for public servants, whose associations may not participate in any political activity. The *Report* noted in respect of public servants that only employees of the railways and the post and telecommunications may form trade unions. The 1969 Ordinance also allows the registrar to cancel the registration of a trade union if the number of members is below 30 per cent of the workers of the establishment or group of establishments for which the union was formed, in contravention of the Convention. The *Report* also noted that under the Essential Services (Maintenance) Act of 1952 (supplemented by similar legislation of 1958), it is an offence punishable by up to one year in prison for any person employed by the central government to terminate his employment without the employer's consent, and that this provision was apparently used with some frequency to inhibit employees from leaving their employment.

Many of these observations reappeared in the ILO's *Report of the Committee of Experts on the Application of Conventions and Recommendations* (1988). The Committee noted that its recommendations for the repeal of the Essential Services (Maintenance) Act, 1952 have yet to be implemented in full. It draws the attention of the government of Bangladesh to its obligations under ILO Convention No. 29, which it ratified in 1972, and points out that "even regarding employment in essential services whose interruption would endanger the existence or the well-being of the whole or part of the population, there is no basis in the Convention for depriving workers of the right to terminate their employment by giving notice of reasonable length".

As concerns Bangladesh's obligations under ILO Convention No. 87, the Report notes that the practice of supervising trade union records, including its finances, by governmental authorities "is incompatible with the right of workers to organize their internal administration". The Committee has recommended to the government that it limit these powers "in order to bring them into conformity with the Convention". In addition, the Committee has also asked the government to review its existing powers to restrict the right of association of persons carrying out functions of management and administration; to limit the right to join a trade union to persons actually employed in the establishment or group of establishments concerned; to prohibit civil servants from forming or joining an association of their own choosing, and to dissolve a trade union whose members are less than 30 per cent of the total proportion of workers in the establishment or group of establishments in which the trade union has been set up.

In November 1989 the 1969 Ordinance was amended by the Industrial Relations (Amendment) Ordinance 1989 which prohibited dismissed employees from holding union office, permitted officers of any union—except the general secretary or president—to be transferred without their consent from one place to another, and reduced the number of unions by amending the definition of an establishment. In its last years in office the administration became no friendlier to unions: employment laws simply did not apply in the Export Processing Zones and workers in essential services (a very widely drawn category) remained forbidden to strike.

Although the 1989 Ordinance was met by the unions with a protest day, there was little other action on the industrial scene in 1989. Twelve strikes were recorded, often in transport, with the most significant in any sector being a three-day stoppage at the Adamjee Jute Mills.

Trade unionism. Trade union activity in Bangladesh has a long and at times bloody history, dating back to a revolt by tea plantation workers in 1920 (when the country was part of British-ruled India) and the formation in that year of the All India Trade Union Congress. The East Pakistan Trade Union Federation was formed following the creation of

Pakistan in 1947, and split into five factions shortly before the achievement of independence by Bangladesh in 1971.

Union density in Bangladesh is low. In March 1989 there were 3,905 unions in the country with a total membership of 1,175,878. This membership set against such a large civilian workforce puts unionization at the low rate of around 3 per cent, not helped by the strong powers held by the outgoing government which in 1988–89 cancelled the registration of no less than 80 unions for violations of the Industrial Relations Ordinance.

There is a high degree of politicization among the unions of the country: 17 of the 18 federations are associated with political parties, and it is normal for a party to have a union wing. Political relationships can advance or retard a federation's cause. Thus President Ershad's Jatiyo Sramik (National Labour) Party became in the four years from its foundation the largest federation in the country with 339 affiliated unions and nearly 300,000 members.

Opposed to Jatiyo Sramik is the Sramik Karmochary Oikya Parishad — SKOP (Workers' and Employees' United Front) which was launched in 1984. SKOP loosely coordinated the activity of federations independent of the President. In the year of its foundation SKOP achieved an agreement for public sector workers, but in 1986 and the years following its position was undermined. SKOP unions attempted to unite in opposition to the Ershad government's privatization proposals from 1987 onwards but with only partial success. After the return of the government parties in the 1988 elections SKOP worked with the Opposition and played a part in ousting the Ershad régime. There is no accepted national trade union centre, and there is considerable fluidity and confusion in respect of the status of trade union confederations. The ICFTU-APRO Committee on Affiliation Questions found in April 1987 that there were 17 or more trade union centres, and also 10 "labour fronts" linked to political parties, and that "trade union leaders often seemed to shift their loyalties for various considerations". The ICFTU itself, however, in December 1987 accepted into affiliation three new Bangladesh affiliates, the Jatiya Sramik Party (JSP), the Bangladesh Free Trade Union Congress (BFTUC), and the Bangladesh Jatiyatabadi Sramik Dal (BJSD), with a claimed total membership of 723,000 (compared with the 550,000 membership of the ICFTU's other affiliate, the Bangladesh Jatio Sramik League, BJSL).

The WFTU officially claims six affiliates: the Bangladesh Trade Union Kendra (BTUK); the Jatio Sramik Jote; the Jatio Sramik League; the Bangladesh Ganotantrik Sramik Federation; the Jatio Sramik Federation; and the Jatio Sramik League of Bangladesh. It is not clear that all of these have any current existence.

Bangladesh Jatio Sramik League (BJSL)

Address. 68/2, Purana Paltan (G.P.O.Box 3625), Dhaka-2
Phone. 282063
Leadership. S.M. Rumi (president); Majibur Rahman Bhuiyan (general secretary)
Membership. 550,000.
History. The Bangladesh Jatio Sramik League (BJSL also known as the Jatio Sramik League, JSL) was founded in 1969, its first conference being opened by Banghbandhu Sheikh Mujibur Rahman (the leader of Bangladesh, as Prime Minister and then as President, from its formation until his assassination in Aug. 1975). The BJSL played an active role in the war for independence in 1971, training 40,000 Sramik League fighters. In Dec. 1974 the government declared a state of emergency, banning strikes and restricting trade union activities. In 1975 the rival centres—Bangladesh Trade Union Kendra (BTUK) and the Bangladesh Sanjukta Sramik Federation (BSSF)—were dissolved by the government of Sheikh Mujibur and the BJSL became the only recognized trade union centre in the country (and the Bangladesh Krishak Sramik Awami League became the only legal political party); many thousands of trade unionists belonging to anti-government groups were imprisoned. In

Aug. 1975 a new government dissolved all national trade union centres, although grass-roots trade unionism continued. After 1978, a breakaway group from the BJSL formed an organization affiliated to the WFTU. The BJSL now states that it believes in a "free and democratic trade union movement".

Affiliated unions. Bangladesh Building and Wood Workers' Federation; Bangladesh Chemical Workers' League; Bangladesh Food and Allied Workers' League; Bangladesh Forest Workers' Federation; Bangladesh Garment Workers' Federation; Bangladesh Ghat Sramik Union; Bangladesh Jute Bailing and Press Workers' Federation; Bangladesh Jute Workers' Federation; Bangladesh Metal Workers' League; Bangladesh Press and Packaging Sramik Karmachari Federations; Bangladesh Textile Workers' Federations; and others.

Publication. Nayabarta.

International affiliation. ICFTU/APRO.

Bangladesh Sanjukta Sramik Federation (BSSF)

Address. 23/2 Topkhana Road, Dhaka

Cables. SIDNUR DACCA

Leadership. Mukhlesur Rahman (president); Siddiqur Rahman (treasurer)

History and character. The BSSF leaders, Mukhlesur Rahman and Siddiqur Rahman were arrested on Nov. 6, 1985 and each given sentences of one month in prison for their part in leading a strike at the Adamjee Jute Mills, the largest jute factory in Asia, and where the BSSF is the strongest union among the 30,000 workers.

International affiliation. WCL.

Jatio Sramik Jote

Address. 20/4 Joykali Mandir Road, Dhaka 1203

Phone. 281933

Telex. POST BOX. G.P.O. 2410 DHAKA

Leadership. 75,630.

History and character. The Jatio Sramik Jote (JSJ) claims descent from the (Bangladesh) Jatio Sramik League founded in 1969 (*see separate entry*). The JSJ states it is concerned with the protection of workers' rights; improvement in living conditions; the political education of industrial workers; the promotion of workers' unity; the integration of the trade union movement with democratic movements, and creating greater awareness of global issues, particularly international peace. The highest body of the JSJ is its Central Committee consisting of 41 members who are elected bi-annually by a general council of 530 elected members. It has several zonal committees which co-ordinate the work of their respective zones. The JSJ regularly conducts workers' education programmes.

Publications. Trade Union Review (quarterly, in English); *Press Release*; and *Jote.*

International affiliation. WFTU.

Barbados

Capital: Bridgetown   **Population: 255,000**
(1988)

Political system. Barbados became a fully independent member of the Commonwealth in 1966, and has a bicameral parliament. After the 15 years in which the government was formed by the Democratic Labour Party (DLP), the 1976 and 1981 general elections to the House of Assembly were won by the Barbados Labour Party which is affiliated to the Socialist International; however, the DLP—which describes itself as a "democratic socialist party"—again came to office in a landslide victory in general elections to the (lower) House of Assembly in May 1986.

Though the DLP suffered defections resulting in the formation of the New Democratic Party, it continued in government under Erskine Sandiford.

Economy. The economically active population was estimated at 119,300 in mid-1987, but the unemployment rate rose in the 1980s to level out at about 18 per cent. Some 63 per cent of employed persons were employed in the government and services sector and just over 12 per cent in manufacturing.

The Barbados dollar is pegged to that of the USA, and this link makes the competitiveness of Barbados's exports dependent to a large extent on the strength or weakness of the US dollar; moreover, export revenue is highly vulnerable to fluctuations in the domestic US economy. Tourism accounted in the mid-1980s for rather over half of all earnings from exports of goods and services, while as a result of problems in both regional and international markets the share of manufactured goods fell from around 30 to only about 18 per cent. Prior to the 1970s sugar, molasses and rum were the largest single source of foreign earnings, but this share fell during the 1980s to only about 5 per cent due to lower production and the generally depressed international sugar market.

In 1988 the Government achieved a budgetary surplus, allowing it to fund acceptable public sector wage increases in 1989. However, although employment in 1988 rose to nearly 100,000 this was not enough to prevent an increase in unemployment which was running at a rate of 18 per cent at the end of the year. The government's Development Plan aims to reduce the rate to 15 per cent by 1993.

System of industrial relations. Following riots in 1937, the British government in 1939 passed legislation, the Trades Disputes (Arbitration and Equity) Act, legalizing the formation of trade unions. Barbados ratified ILO Convention No. 87 (Freedom of Association and Protection of the Right to Organize, 1948) and Convention No. 98 (Right to Organize and Collective Bargaining, 1949) in 1967.

Trade unionism. Union density in Barbados for 1987 was assessed at 28.8 per cent. The main union centre is the Barbados Workers' Union (BWU) which has in membership 25,000 of the country's 34,000 trade unionists. It stayed loyal to the DLP after the split which led to the formation of the NDP. Significant unions outside the BWU are the National Union of Public Workers (NUPW)—the largest public service union—, the Barbados Union of Teachers (BUT), the Barbados Secondary Teachers' Union (BSTU) and the National Democratic Workers' Union (NUDW) formed in 1988. They negotiated side by side in the 1989 public sector wage talks though they settled separately. The dissatisfaction of BUT members with their 1989 settlement led to the resignation of their President and General Secretary.

Barbados Workers' Union (BWU)

Address. "Solidarity House", Harmony Hall, P.O.Box 172, St Michael, Bridgetown

Phone. (809) 426 3492 (general office); (809) 436-6079 (general secretary); (809) 435-5505 (labour college)

Telex. 0392-2527 WB

Cables. BARUNION

Fax. (809) 436-6496

Leadership. David Giles (president); Sir Frank L. Walcott (general secretary)

Membership. 20,000.

History and character. The BWU, a general workers' union, was registered in Oct. 1941, and was a direct descendant of the Barbados Progressive League formed after the 1937 disturbances. In its early years it recruited mainly from among ships' carpenters, foundry and port workers and sugar factory employees, but it absorbed a clerks' union in the 1950s and thereafter developed a significant white-collar element. Frank L. Walcott became general secretary in 1948. The BWU from the first participated actively in politics, its first president being Grantley Adams, the founder of the Barbados Labour Party (in 1938) and Prime Minister of Barbados from 1954–58 and of the short-lived West Indies Federation from 1958–62, while the first BWU general secretary was Sir Hugh Springer, the former Governor General of Barbados. A split developed in the early 1960s when the union leadership transferred support to the somewhat more left-wing Democratic Labour Party, led by Errol Barrow (which took power in 1961 and held it continuously until 1976), breaking with the Barbados Labour Party. Grantley Adams led a breakaway group called the Barbados Progressive Union of Workers in 1963 (although this soon folded). The BWU was recognized as the bargaining agent for a wide range of occupations in 1966. The BWU runs a labour college, providing training in industrial relations and union affairs, which receives a government subsidy, and there is also an associated BWU Co-operative Credit Union.

Affiliated unions. There are no affiliated unions. The BWU recruits members in all occupational fields, and negotiates directly with companies on behalf of the different sectors of its membership.

Publication. The Unionist (a newspaper).

International affiliations. ICFTU/ORIT; CCL; CTUC.

National Union of Public Workers (NUPW)

Address. P.O. Box 174, Bridgetown, Barbados

Phone. (809) 427-7774 (general secretary); (809) 426-4971; (809) 426-1764; (809) 426-0422

Cables. BACSA

Leadership. Keith Yearwood (president); Joseph Goddard (general secretary) since 1973

Membership. 8,000. The NUPW recruits predominantly in the public sector.

History and character. Founded in January 1944 and registered as a Trade Union in 1964; name changed in 1971 from Barbados Civil Service Association (BACSA) to National Union of Public Workers.

In July 1985, the NUPW established a public workers' academy, the first of its kind in the English-speaking Caribbean. The political orientation is broadly social democratic, but there is no current party orientation. The NUPW emphasizes worker education, the maintenance of collective bargaining in the public sector, as opposed to unilateral decision-making by government.

Publication. The publication of *The Public Worker* has been suspended in favour of a monthly radio broadcast.

Regional affiliations. Caribbean Public Services Association (CPSA), founder member 1970; Caribbean Congress of Labour (CCL).

International affiliations. PSI, PTTI, FIET, ICFTU.

Belgium

Capital: Brussels   **Population: 9,880,000**

Political system. Belgium is a constitutional monarchy with a bicameral parliament. A major division exists between the Flemish-(Dutch)-speaking north and the French-speaking south, with Brussels forming a bilingual (though predominantly francophone) unit in the centre of the country and with a small German-speaking community in the east.

Flanders and Wallonia each have their own elected regional assembly, while Brussels is still administered through the Ministry for the Brussels Region.

In 1981 a centre-right coalition was formed by the two Christian democratic and the two liberal parties, but in 1988 this was replaced by a five-party coalition of the two Christian democratic parties, the two socialist parties and the (Flemish nationalist) People's Union under Wilfred Martens.

Economy. Belgian's civilian labour force is divided between industry (37 per cent), agriculture (5 per cent) and services (58 per cent). During the 1980s, the heavy industry of the country (concentrated in the south) suffered a severe decline; growth has tended to favour the north, exacerbating regional tensions. The return of the Socialists to coalition with the Christian Democrats (displacing the Liberals) did not alter the main thrust of economic policy.

In May 1988 Mr Martens' ninth government embarked on a new programme which continued economic austerity, introduced tax reforms and increased federalization. Belgium abolished its two-tier exchange rate system, cut withholding tax from 25 to 10 per cent, and began the reorganization and deregulation of financial markets. The result was growth of 4.4 per cent, inflation at a five-year average of 2.6 per cent, high investment, a sound balance of payments surplus, and containment of the ever-spiralling public debt, an objective of governments since the early 1980s. Nevertheless at around BF 7,000,000 million it still represented some 125 per cent of GDP and remained the country's major economic challenge—annual interest rates absorb the equivalent of 10 per cent of GDP.

In May 1990, Belgium announced its intention to peg the franc more closely to the Deutschmark, effectively creating a Deutschmark zone covering Belgium, the Netherlands, Luxembourg and Germany. It has direct experience of monetary union following the establishment of a common currency zone with Luxembourg (controlled by the National Bank of Belgium) as long ago as 1921 and it was (like all its neighbours) a founder member of the Community, adhering to the EMS from an early date.

Under the constitutional reform implemented in 1989, the three regions have autonomy in matters of industrial and employment policy, public works and communications, provided they respect the free movement of persons and capital within the country as a whole. The national government remains responsible for monetary and incomes policy.

System of industrial relations. The foundations of the present structure of collective bargaining in Belgium were laid during the period of social reconstruction after World War II, although the first government attempts to regulate industrial conflict had been made towards the end of the nineteenth century. Workers' organizations which are recognized as "representative" are empowered to negotiate collective agreements with similarly recognized representative employers' organizations within the framework provided by the National Labour Council (established in 1952); such agreements are binding on all employees in the industry concerned, whether or not union members. The ILO *Report of the Committee of Experts on the Application of Conventions and Recommendations* (1985) noted that the rights of individual unions under this system could be impaired by: (i) the obligation placed on a trade union to be affiliated to an organization represented on the National Labour Council in order to be considered representative in the private sector and to be able to sit on a joint committee (1968 legislation); (ii) the similar obligation placed on public sector unions if they are to take part in the work of the general bargaining committees (1974 legislation); and (iii) the fact that provisions of a collective agreement concluded outside a joint body are deemed null and void if they are contrary to agreements concluded within the National Labour Council or its committees. The Committee observed that the workers members of the National Labour Council consist entirely of representatives of workers' organizations chosen by the King from among the candidates put forward by the interoccupational organizations that are federated at the national level, and it has pointed out on many occasions that these provisions may prevent a union that is the most representative in a given branch of activity from participating in collective bargaining in its own sector. (It cannot be doubted, however, that the present system in use in Belgium has proved satisfactory to the great majority of Belgian trade unions.) Belgium ratified ILO Convention No. 87 (Freedom of Association and Protection of the Right to Organize, 1948) in 1951 and Convention No. 98 (Right to Organize and Collective Bargaining, 1949) in 1953.

The agreement of November 1988 provided a framework for negotiations during the next two years, covering around 70 per cent of the workforce. It allowed for wage increases of between two and four per cent, a renewed commitment to the country's training objectives, the extension of early retirement agreements, and progress on shorter working hours. The CSC and FGTB registered their discontent at the lack of progress in lowering the enterprise threshold for health and safety committees. In March 1990 both sides of industry used the Council to promulgate an agreement providing for negotiations prior to the introduction of nightwork, thus avoiding the need for legislation on the matter.

In the public sector, where the government is the employer, pay was regulated less amicably. Strikes occurred in many sectors as different groups of employees sought to catch up with the private sector after the restrictions of 1981–88, and the last disputes were not resolved until May 1989.

Trade unionism. Collective bargaining in Belgium tends to be carried out at the sectoral level though employers have stated their preference for undertaking it at the level of the plant. At the national level there are two major union confederations in the shape of the confessional (though increasingly secular) Confederation of Christian Trade Unions (CSC/ACV) and the smaller social democratic (FGTB/ABVV). For many years the two trade union centres (which account for about 90 per cent of union members) kept apart, a habit reinforced by their political links (the CSC/ACV with the Christian Democrats, the FGTB with the Socialists) and poor personal relations between leaders. However each undertook a restructuring to accommodate the Belgian nationalities in its ranks during the 1980s, and—with new leaders at the helm—they jointly welcomed the constitutional proposals of Prime Minister Martens for his eighth government in 1988. There are two other union centres: the General Federation of Trade Unions in Belgium (CGSLB) has 220,000 members and the National Union of the Public Service (UNSP/NUOD) has 100,000: each is independent of the two main confederations. Between them the unions have achieved high density—around 70 per cent of the workforce.

The Belgian state has traditionally supported comprehensive industrial relations arrangements and structures. A Law of 1968 which accords national collective bargaining status to "representative organizations", applies to employers' organizations as well as to trade unions: an individual employer may conclude an agreement only in respect of his own enterprise. The central employer and employee organizations participate in Belgium's tripartite Central Economic Council (Counseil Central de l'Economie—CCE, established in 1952) which reports twice yearly to the Government on the country's economic status. It is also responsible for maintaining wage indexation, the occasion of the schism which separated the Christian Democrats and Socialists in government in 1981. Some idea of the value of the CCE to employers and employees may be glimpsed from their use in January 1989 of a dissenting memorandum to express reservations about government proposals to intervene in collective bargaining.

Another institution, the National Labour Council, is bipartite, comprising representatives of labour nominated by the king from the central union confederations as well as representatives of the employers. The country's pay rates progress within the terms of a central agreement signed by the FEB, the FGTB and the CSC with the involvement of the

Ministry of Labour. Under the auspices of the National Labour Council agreements between "representative" organizations bind all parties.

Confédération des Syndicats Chrétiens (CSC)
Confederation of Christian Trade Unions

Address. 121 rue de la Loi, 1040 Brussels
Phone. (02) 233-34-11
Telex. 61770 CSCACV
Leadership. Willy Peirens (president); Robert D'Hondt (secretary general)
Membership. 1,336,000

History and character. From its earliest stages the Belgian labour movement was troubled by the division between socialists and Christians. In 1886 the Christian Weavers of Ghent established the Ligue Antisocialiste des Ouvriers du Coton, the germ from which CSC grew, in opposition to the first International developed from 1864 by Karl Marx. Thereafter Christian trade unions grew in a somewhat haphazard way, often in connection with the development of co-operatives, mutual savings banks and workers' improvement and self-help bodies. In Flanders, the model for Christian syndicalism was taken from the Medieval craft guilds. By 1901 there were 62 Christian associations with 11,000 members.

In 1904 the Secrétariat Général des Unions Professionelles Chrétiens de Belgique was formed, and between 1904 and 1908 "professional federations", with nearly 40,000 members, were created covering a wide range of trades and industries. In 1909 the Confédération Nationale des Syndicats Chrétiens et Libres was formed, with separate organizations for Dutch-speaking Flanders and French-speaking Wallonia, as part of the Ligue Démocratique Belge; in 1912 the organizations for Flanders and Wallonia were fused, and the confederation held its first convention autonomously from the Ligue Démocratique Belge. Membership, standing at 129,000 in 1914, slumped during World War II. In 1923 the federation received its present name. In the inter-war years, the authority of local unions declined and that of the national professional federations increased. All normal trade union activity ended after the German occupation of Belgium in 1940, but the CSC office resumed its work on the day Brussels was liberated (Sept. 4, 1944).

In 1960 the CSC and the FGTB, the socialist centre, began the process of formulating common positions on various issues; the willingness to work together was reflected in the conclusion in the 1960s of a wide range of agreements with employers for the 40-hour week and other benefits.

During the 1970s a greater regional devolution of powers was carried out by the CSC, in parallel with the broader political process whereby increasing regional autonomy was granted to the three regions of Brussels, Flanders and Wallonia. The CSC established regional executives in 1974, and in 1978 special committees for the three regions were established at national headquarters.

During the recession of the early 1980s the CSC called for work-sharing programmes to be adopted, but the employers proved unwilling to follow this lead in any significant way. The unions also faced challenges to the right to strike and exercise union powers, and to social security benefits. In the late 1980s, under the leadership of Willy Peirens, the CSC developed a much closer relationship with the FGTB.

Structure. A general congress, to set policies and elect officials, is held at least every four years, and an annual ordinary congress may be held in other years. The general council, which meets at least twice a year, sets policy between congresses, and is composed of about 560 representatives of the *centrales professionelles* and regional federations. The 55-member national committee, which meets monthly, deals with current policy developments, and the 35-member national bureau, normally meeting twice a month, is charged with giving effect to the decisions of the superior bodies. The secretariat-general attends to affairs on a day-to-day basis. The division of Belgium on language grounds is reflected in the existence of three regional committees.

Political relationships. The CSC has no organizational ties to any political party, and since 1945 CSC officials have not taken political office, other than at the minor local level. Officially, the Christian Workers' Movements—Mouvement Ouvrier Chrétien (MOC) and Algemeen Christelijk Werkersverbond (ACW), which are themselves mutually independent coalitions of autonomous organizations—give political expression to CSC policies; however, the MOC (in Wallonia and Brussels) has since 1972 been a pluralistic movement (with elected candidates belonging to different

41

political parties) and in March 1985 members of the MOC and the CSC Regional Committee for Wallonia founded a political party called Solidarité et Participation (SeP). On the Flemish side, the ACW looks to the Christelijke Volkspartij (CVP) for the implementation of its policies. The CVP, and its French-speaking counterpart the Parti Social Chrétien, has been in power since 1981, and Dr Wilfried Martens, the Prime Minister, is a member of the CVP.

Affiliated unions. The following are the *centrales professionelles* of the CSC:

1. **Centrale Chrétienne de l'Alimentation et des Services** (Food and Services), rue de l'Association 27, 1000 Brussels.
   Phone: (02) 218-21-71
   President: W. Vijverman; secretary: E. Delecluyse.

2. **Centrale Chrétienne de l'Energie, de la Chimie et du Cuir** (Energy, Chemicals and Leather), Avenue d'Auderghem 26, 1040 Brussels.
   Phone: (02) 231-00-90
   President: Alfons Vangenechten; secretary general: Marcel Sommereyns.
   Membership: 75,000.

3. **Centrale Chrétienne des Industries Graphiques et du Papier** (Graphic and Paper Trades), Avenue d'Auderghem 26–32, 1040 Brussels.
   Phone: (02) 231-00-90.
   Secretary general: Marcel Neirynck.

4. **Centrale Chrétienne des Metallurgistes de Belgique** (Metalworkers), rue de Heembeeck 127, 1120 Brussels.
   Phone: (02) 215-88-40. Fax: (02) 241-48-27.
   President: Tony Janssen, secretaries: Frans Bellon. François Cammarata, Marc de Wilde.
   Membership: 240,000.
   Publications: *Métal Info-Agenda.*

5. **Centrale Chrétienne des Ouvriers du Transport et des Ouvriers Diamantaires** (Transport and Diamond Workers), Entrepotplaats 12–14, 2000 Antwerp.
   Phone:(03) 231-47-85. Fax: (03) 231-47-81.
   President: John Janssens.
   Membership: 35,000.

6. **Centrale Chrétienne du Personnel de l'Enseignement Technique** (Technical Education), Avenue d'Auderghem 26–32, 1040 Brussels.
   Phone: (02) 230-3229. Fax: (065) 360733
   President: Jean Luc Masux; secretary general: J.P.Leclerq.
   Membership: 8,000.
   Publication: *Action CCPET*

7. **Centrale Chrétienne des Professeurs de l'Enseignement Moyen et Normal Libre** (Teachers in Secondary Education and Teacher Training), Avenue d'Auderghem 26, 1040 Brussels.
   Phone: (02) 231-00-90.
   President: J. Vlaminck; secretary general: G.Trommelmans.

8. **Centrale Chrétienne des Services Publics** (Public Services), d'Auderghem 26, 1040 Brussels.
   Phone: (02) 238-72-11. Fax: (02) 230-45-62
   President: Filip Wieërs; secretary-general: Guy Rasneur.
   Membership: 120,000.
   Publication: *Ere Nouvelle.*

9. **Centrale Chrétienne des Travailleurs du Bois et du Batiment** (Wood and Building Workers), rue de Trèves 31, 1040 Brussels.
   Phone: (02) 230-85-70. Fax: (02) 230-74-43.
   President: A.Desloovere; secretary-general: R.Jongen.
   Membership: 181,000.
   Publication: *CHB-TCB.*

10. **Centrale Chrétienne des Travailleurs de la Pierre, du Ciment, de la Céramique et du Verre** (Stone, Cement, Ceramic and Glass Workers), Avenue d'Auderghem 26–32, 1040 Brussels.
President: August De Decker; secretaries: Leo Dusoleil, Raymond Groetembril.

11. **Centrale Chrétienne des Travailleurs du Textile et du Vêtement de Belgique** (Textile and Clothing Workers), Koning Albertlaan 27, 9000 Ghent.
Phone: (091) 22-57-01. Fax: (091) 20-45-59.
President: André Duquet; secretary-general: Ludwig Meulman.
Membership: 115,000.

12. **Centrale des Francs Mineurs** (Miners), Avenue d'Auderghem 26–32, 1040 Brussels.
Phone: (02) 231-00-90.
President: André Daeman; secretary: Frans Vanderlinden.

13. **Centrale Nationale des Employés (Région Nord)/Landelijke Bediendencentrale**, Beggaarden-straat 1, 2000 Antwerp.
Phone: (03) 234-15-00.
Secretary general: L. Stragier.
Regional organization for Flanders and (with Région Sud) Brussels.

14. **Centrale Nationale des Employés (Région Sud)**
President: Georges Sels; general secretary: José Roisin.
Regional organization for Wallonia and (with Région Nord) for Brussels.

15. **Federation des Instituteurs Chrétiens de Belgique** (Christian Teachers) Koningsstraat 203, 1210 Brussels.
Phone: (02) 217-40-50. Fax:(02) 219 4761.
General president: Guy Bourdeaud'hui; secretaries: Régis Dohogne, Louis Van Beneden.
Membership: 48,000.
Publications: *Christene School/Pedagogische Periodiek; Wisselwerking/Actua; Educateur Belge/Directoire Pedagogique.*

16. **Service Syndical Sports** (Sport), Poel 7, 9000 Ghent.
Phone: (091) 24-00-42.
President: E. Laenen; secretary: M. Lippens.

17. **Syndicat Chrétien des Communications et de la Culture** (Posts, Telecommunications, Railways, Shipping, Radio and TV etc.), Avenue d'Auderghem 26, 1040 Brussels.
Phone: (02) 238-7211.
General president: Micheal Bovy.
Membership: 54,800.
Publications: *De Rechte Lijn; Le Bon Combat.*

18. **Union Chrétienne des Membres du Personnel de l'Enseignement Officiel**, Avenue d'Auderghem 26, 1040 Brussels.
Phone: (02) 231-00-90.
President: A Pollet; secretaries: E. Bodson, J. Luyten.

Publications. Volksnacht (1,000,000 copies weekly); *Info CSC* (120,000 copies weekly); *Syndicaliste CSC* (22,500 copies fortnightly); *ACV Vakbeweging* (56,000 copies fortnightly).
International affiliations. WCL; ETUC; TUAC.

Fédération Générale du Travail de Belgique (FGTB)/Algemeen Belgisch Vakverbond
Belgian General Federation of Labour

Address. Rue Haute 42, 1000 Brussels
Phone. (02) 506-82-11
Telex. Trabel 24-620

Fax. (02) 513-47-21
Leadership. François Janssens (president); Mia de Vits (secretary-general)
Membership. 1,014,065 (1989).
Affiliated unions and structure. Following an Extraordinary Congress of May 1978, the FGTB statutes provided for three inter-regional organizations covering Flanders, Brussels and Wallonia which correspond to the country's regional authorities. These are: Vlaamse Intergewestelijke ABVV, grouping 24 Flemish branches, Interregionale Wallonne FGTB, grouping 10 Flemish branches and the Brussels Interregional Organization.

Affiliated unions.

1. **The "Cadets"** (students and pupils), Rue Haute 42 – B1000 Brussels.
   Phone: 02/506.82.11.
   Membership: 9,900.

2. **Centrale Générale F.G.T.B. – Algemene Centrale ABVV** (General Union of Manual Workers from the building, timber, glass, paper, chemicals, oil industries), Rue Haute 26/28 – B1000 Brussels.
   Phone: (02) 513-06-25. Fax: (02) 514-16-91
   President: Juan Fernandez.
   Membership: 262, 025.

3. **Centrale Générale des Services Publics CGSP/Algemene Centrale der Openbare Diensten ACOD** (Public Services General Trade Union), Place Fontainas 9/11, B1000 Brussels.
   Phone: (02) 508-58-11. Fax: (02) 508-59-02.
   President: Roger Pitton.
   Membership: 208,873.
   Publication: *Tribune.*
   International affiliations: CISL, CES, ISP.

4. **Centrale de I'Industrie du Livre et du Papier/Centrale der Boek-en Papiernijverheid** (Book and Paper Industry Trade Union—manual workers), Galerie du Centre, Bloc 2, Rue des Frippiers 17, B1000 Brussels.
   Phone: (02) 511-09-66. Fax: (02) 511-30-20.
   National secretaries: Robert Leloup, Roger Sagon.
   Membership: 14,084.

5. **Centrale des Métallurgistes de Belgique (CMB)/Centrale der metaalbewerkers van België (CMB)** (Belgian Metalworkers Union — manual workers), Rue J. Jordaens 17, B1000 Brussels.
   Phone: (02) 647-83-14 Fax: (02) 647-83-92.
   Secretary General: Michel Cossaer.
   Membership: 178,310.

6. **Centrale des Ouvriers Textiles de Belgique (COTB)** The Belgian Textile Workers Union—manual workers), Opvoedingsstraat 143, B9000 Ghent.
   Phone: (091) 21-75-11. Fax: (091) 21-08-93.
   President: Donald Wittevrongel; national secretary: Luc Vanneste.
   Membership: 33,885.
   Publication: *Militant.*
   International affiliation: ITGLWF.

7. **Centrale Syndicale des Travailleurs des Mines de Belgique/Belgische Mijnwerkerscentrale** (Belgian Mine Workers Trade Union), Boulevard d'Avroy 7C B.8/33, B4000 Liege.
   Phone: (041) 23-78-52.
   President: Lucien Charlier.
   Membership: 13,568.

8. **Centrale des Travailleurs de l'Alimentation et de I' Hotellerie/Centrale der Voeding en Hotelarbeiders** (The Food and Hotel Workers Trade Union — manual workers), Rue des Alexiens 18, B1000 Brussels.

Phone: (02) 512-97-00. Fax: (02) 512-53-68.
President: Arthur Ladrille.
Membership: 57,095.

9. **Centrale du Vêtement et parties similaires de Belgique/Centrale der Kleding en aanverwante vakken van België** (The Belgian Clothing and Related Professions Union—manual workers), Ommeganckstraat 32, B2018 Antwerp.
Phone: (03) 233-56-72. Fax: (03) 226-40-09.
President: Jef Hoymans; general secretary: René Stabel.
Membership: 28,228.
Publication: *Info*.
International affiliation: ITGLWF.

10. **Syndicat des Employés, Techniciens et Cadres de Belgique (S.E.T.Ca)/Bond der Bedienden, Technici en Kaders van België (B.B.T.K.)** (Trade Union of Belgian Employees, Technicians and Executives—private sector), Rue Haute 42, B1000 Brussels.
Phone: (02) 512-52-50. Fax: (02) 511-05-08.
President: Karel Boeykens.
Membership: 181,022.

11. **Le Syndicat des Ouvriers Diamantaires/Belgische Diamantbewerkersbond** (The Diamond Workers' Trade Union), Lange Kivietstraat 57 B. 1, B2018 Antwerp.
President: Constant Denisse.
Membership: 3,131.

12. **Union Belge des Ouvriers du Transport (UBOT)/Belgische Transportarbeidersbond (BTB)** (Belgian Union of Transport Workers), Paardenmarkt 66 B2000 Antwerp.
Phone: (03) 224-4-11. Fax: (03) 234-01-49. Telex: 73070.
President: Remi van Cant.
Membership: 23,944.
Publications: *De Haven*; *De Zee*; *De Binnenvaant*; *BTB-Wegwijs/UBOT en Route*.
International affiliations: ITF.

History and character: The FGTB traces itself to a Trade Union Committee established by the Belgian Workers' Party (POB) in 1898. It became the Belgian Trade Union Confederation in 1937. In 1945 the FGTB was founded uniting a number of trade union federations on the basis of a statement of principle declaring its political independence. In 1978 it was restructured to reflect Belgium's nationalities and in 1988 welcomed Prime Minister's Martens' constitutional proposals.

The FGTB is still governed by its 1945 *Statement of Principles*, and is formally committed to social and economic democracy, the socialization of major industrial and financial institutions, regulation of multinationals and management of nationalized industries by workers and consumers. Despite this, the new leadership of Janssens and De Vit, which took over in 1989, marked an important change which installed a graduate leadership at the head of the FGTB for the first time.

Publications. Syndicats; *Die Nieiwe Werker*.
International affiliations. ICFTU; ETUC; TUAC.

Other inter-occupational federations

Centrale Générale des Syndicats Libéraux de Belgique (CGSLB)
General Confederation of Liberal Trade Unions of Belgium

Address: (social office) Boulevard Baudoin 11, 1210 Brussels; (administrative office) Konig Albertlaan 95, 9000 Ghent.
Phone: (social office) (02) 218-57-44; (administrative office) (091) 22-57-51
Fax: (social office) (02) 218-62-91; (administrative office) (091) 21-04-74
Leadership. Willy Waldack (national president)
Membership. 220,000.
Publications: *Le Syndicaliste Libéral*.

International affiliations. TUAC.

History and Character. The CGSLB was founded in 1891 and has links with the Belgian Liberal Parties. Unlike the two main union centres, it declined to separate into regional organizations during the prolonged constitutional crisis of the 1980s.

Union Nationale des Services Publics (UNSP)/Nationale Unie der Openbare Diensten (NUOD)
National Union of the Public Services

Address. Rue du Pavillon 54, 1210 Brussels.
Phone. (02) 215 66 70
Leadership. G. Van Acker (president); F. Malfrooid (general secretary).
Membership. 100,000
History and character. The UNSP/NUOD is the successor organization to the Cartel des Syndicats Indépendants de Belgique, dissolved in 1985.

Belize

Capital: Belmopan   **Population: 182,000**
                                                (1988)

Political system. Belize (known until 1973 as British Honduras) became independent in 1981 as a full member of the Commonwealth, and has a bicameral parliament. Due to a longstanding claim to all or part of Belize's territory, Guatemala has refused to recognize that country's independence, and Britain has continued to maintain an armed presence there.

The centre-left People's United Party was in office for 30 years from 1954 (between 1964 and 1981 under a system of internal self-government), but it was defeated in December 1984 in general elections by the centre-right United Democratic Party which won 21 out of 28 seats in the House of Representatives.

Economy. Belize's main economic activities are agriculture, fisheries and forestry, with sugar, citrus products, fisheries products and bananas being major sources of export revenue; however, agricultural output is liable to severe disruption through disease, drought, flooding and hurricanes. Belize has in the 1980s been adversely affected by low world prices for sugar (which accounted in 1987 for rather over 35 per cent of the value of exports). Clothing (mainly for export) is also an expanding industry, whereas timber (formerly the country's main export) is now of relatively small importance although there are considerable forest reserves. Marijuana also represents an important (though unofficial) element in Belize's economy and export revenue.

System of industrial relations. Belize ratified ILO Conventions No. 87 (Freedom of Association and Protection of the Right to Organize, 1948) and No. 98 (Right to Organize and Collective Bargaining, 1949) in 1983.

Trade unionism. Following labour unrest in the 1930s the British authorities legalized trade unionism in 1941, the first registered union being the British Honduras Trade Union (1943). This was subsequently known as the General Workers' Union and from 1960 (following the merger with a British Honduras Development Union) as the General

Workers' Development Union (GWDU). The GWDU is now known as the United General Workers' Union while the WCL/CLAT affiliate is the Christian Workers' Union. The National Trades Union Congress of Belize has all but one trade union in its membership.

Christian Workers' Union

Address. 23 George Street, Belize City
Phone. (02) 2150
Leadership. Desmond Vaughn (president)
Membership. 673
History and character. This organization was founded on July 14, 1963. It is a general workers' union, including municipal workers, domestic servants, road construction workers, port employees, oil company employees, etc.
International affiliations. WCL/CLAT.

National Trades Union Congress of Belize

Address. Racecourse Street, Belize City
Phone. (02) 2857
Leadership. Cyril Davis (president)
Membership. 2,650.
International affiliation. CCL.

United General Workers' Union

Address. 1259 Lakeland City, Dangriga
Leadership. Antonio González (president); Pablo Lambey (general secretary)
History. Founded 1979 by amalgamation of the Belize General Workers' Development Union and the Southern Christian Union.

Benin

Capital: Porto Novo   **Population: 4,450,000**

Political system. Benin (named Dahomey until 1975) became a self-governing republic within the French Community in 1958 and gained full independence in 1960; thereafter the country experienced four military *coups* between 1963 and 1969. Mathieu Kérékou came to power in a further military *coup* in 1972, and in 1974 he declared that a socialist society would be established with Marxism-Leninism as "the revolutionary philosophy—the basis and the guideline of our revolutionary movement". The Benin People's Revolutionary Party (PRPB) was formally established as the sole legal party in 1975, and in the 1977 Constitution this was defined as the vanguard detachment and leading nucleus of the people and of the revolution of Benin. In elections to the unicameral National Revolutionary Assembly in 1979 and 1984 the PRPB presented the sole list of candidates. Following a series of social conflicts in which students and civil servants were prominent, the Party renounced Marxism-Leninism in December 1989.

Economy. Agriculture (largely subsistence) represents the dominant factor in Benin's economy, accounting for nearly half of gross domestic product and engaging about half of the total working population. The main cash crops are palm oil and cotton, but both of these have been severely affected by drought and disease. At the end of 1974 it was announced that a number of financial institutions and a telecommunications firm had been nationalized, and that the assets of foreign oil companies operating in the country had become national property; however, the majority of domestic trade is still within the private sector, and it was officially stated in early 1987 that in the context of a structural adjustment plan under way particular attention would be paid to private investors. A development plan for 1980–90 provided for an increase from about 11 to about 15 per cent by 1985 in the share of gross domestic product represented by the industrial sector (largely small-scale processing of primary output).

Fewer than 100,000 of the population are categorized as employed (nearly half of these being engaged in the community, social and personal services). In total, the public sector employs 43 per cent of the workforce. Benin ratified ILO Convention No. 87 (Freedom of Association and Protection of the Right to Organize, 1948) in 1960 and Convention No. 98 (Right to Organize and Collective Bargaining, 1949) in 1968. Conventions Nos. 29 and 105 on forced labour were ratified in 1960 and 1961.

Trade unionism. Several trade union centres, with different international affiliations, were active in the 1960s and early 1970s, but in 1974 the government of President Kerekou established a single trade union centre, the UNSTB.

Union Nationale des Syndicats des Travailleurs du Bénin (UNSTB)

Address. B.P. 69, Cotonou
Phone. 315613
Telex. 5200 MINAFFET
Leadership. Romain Vilon Guezo (secretary general; also a member of the Benin People's Revolutionary Party politburo and Vice-President of the Permanent Committee of the National Assembly) was dismissed in February 1990. Gregoire Agbahe (first deputy secretary general)
Membership. 300,000 in 16 sectoral federations.
History and structure. All pre-existing unions and federations were absorbed into this organization in 1974. The UNSTB a designated mass organization of the PRPB, and there were no trade unions outside its structure. However, several federations threatened to secede in 1989 following its failure to back industrial action, notably by civil servants. In January 1990 UNSTB declared its intention to become independent of the Party. A special assembly the following month dismissed Romain Vilon Guezo, the general secretary of UNSTB since its inception.
International affiliations. OATUU. The UNSTB resolved to leave the WFTU in February 1990.

Bhutan

Capital: Thimphu

Population: 1,534,122
(1989)

Political system. Bhutan became a member of the United Nations in 1971 and of the non-aligned movement in 1973. A partly elected National Assembly was established in 1953, a

Royal Advisory Council in 1965 and a Council of Ministers in 1968. However, power is in practice exercised by the hereditary king (assisted by the Royal Advisory Council), together with the Council of Ministers, the National Assembly and also the head of the country's Buddhist lamas.

Economy. Bhutan's economy is almost entirely dependent upon agriculture and forestry, which account for over 90 per cent of the active workforce. To complement the traditional handicrafts and carpet weaving, a number of industrial estates have been established to encourage small-scale enterprises, mainly for the manufacture of certain basic consumer goods. However, manufacturing employs only about 2 per cent of the economically active population. In 1982–83 the government transferred all of its workshops, the telephone company and the tourist agency to private management. Much non-agricultural work is carried out by foreign nationals, especially from Nepal and India.

System of industrial relations. Bhutan has ratified neither ILO Convention No. 87 (Freedom of Association and Protection of the Right to Organize, 1948) nor ILO Convention No. 98 (Right to Organize and Collective Bargaining, 1949).

There is no Ministry of Labour in Bhutan. Wages, terms and conditions outside those of the Royal Civil Service are fixed by the Government, which requires workers and employers to have a contractual agreement in writing. The structure of wages is monitored.

Trade unionism. Trade unionism is not permitted and does not appear to exist.

Bolivia

Capital: La Paz   **Population: 6,900,000**
                                                    (1988)

Political system. From 1964 (when a military *coup* ended 12 years of civilian administration) until 1982, Bolivia was governed almost continuously by a series of military régimes. In 1982 Hernán Siles Zuazo of the (democratic socialist) National Revolutionary Movement of the Left (MNRI) was sworn in at the head of a coalition of the MNRI, the (Marxist) Movement of the Revolutionary Left (MIR), the Communist Party, and the Christian Democratic Party. In 1984–85 successive widespread strike actions were orchestrated by the Bolivian Workers' Central (COB) against the government's economic and social policy, and fresh elections in July 1985 resulted in a narrow relative majority in the bicameral Congress for the centrist Historic Nationalist Revolutionary Movement (MNRH); the presidential election was inconclusive, but the MNRH's candidate, Víctor Paz Estenssoro, was eventually selected by Congress and was sworn in in August of that year. He was succeeded in August 1989 by a new President Jaime Paz Zamora whose liberal economic policies broadly resembled those of his predecessor.

Economy. The mainstay of the Bolivian economy is tin, the principal mines having been nationalized by an earlier Paz Estenssoro government in 1952 and grouped together in Comibolo, on whose board the mineworkers' federation (the FSTMB) secured majority representation in 1983. The collapse of the price of tin in the international markets in late 1985 led to the imposition by the new government of severe austerity measures—including tight demand management, structural reform and a massive reduction in Comibolos' work force—which were again met by serious industrial unrest over the next three years.

Agriculture accounts for only about 16 per cent of gross domestic product, although for about half of the workforce. While few agriculture exports enter the official statistics, there is large-scale illicit trade in coca (the base for cocaine and estimated to be worth US$600 million in 1986), which has contributed to tension with the US authorities.

By mid-1985 annual inflation had risen to about 20,000 per cent and the external debt to nearly US$5,000 million, while the official rate of exchange had fallen by the end of 1986 to around 2,000,000 pesos to the dollar.

In 1987 the government introduced a currency reform and an economic reactivation plan to promote industrial and infrastructural investment, and to boost exports. In the same year a number of innovative arrangements were reached in effect to reduce or refinance Bolivia's external debt. Meanwhile the country's hyper-inflation had broadly been brought under control.

In 1989 Bolivia had a workforce of 1,830,000, of which 870,000 were engaged in agriculture, 670,000 in services, and 290,000 in industry and construction. The workforce experienced a series of pay freezes under an IMF/World Bank programme intended to cut Bolivia's enormous national debt. By 1991 exports had fallen sharply while imports had risen; a number of major companies had closed down and unemployment reached 25 per cent of the workforce. Inflation in 1990 ran at 18 per cent, causing a fall in purchasing power and major protests (*see below*).

System of industrial relations. Bolivia ratified ILO Convention No. 87 (Freedom of Association and Protection of the Right to Organize, 1948) in 1965 and Convention No. 98 (Right to Organize and Collective Bargaining, 1949) in 1973. The ILO *Report of the Committee of Experts on the Application of Conventions and Recommendations* (1985) noted appreciable recent progress in Bolivia towards free trade unionism. However, the *Report* also drew attention to the denial of the right to organize to home, domestic and casual workers; the impossibility of setting up more than one union in an enterprise; the wide powers of supervision of the labour inspectorate over trade unions; the possibility that trade unions may be dissolved by administrative authority; and the power of the executive to prohibit strikes by imposing compulsory arbitration.

The *Committee of Experts' Report* for 1988 noted with concern the current high levels of unemployment, estimated at 18.9 per cent and underemployment, estimated at 64 per cent, and drew attention to Convention No. 122 (Employment Policy 1964), ratified in 1977, which calls on governments implementing adjustment policies to ensure that they promote employment and the satisfaction of basic needs. Further, the committee hoped the government would make provision for consultations with representatives of both employers and workers in the implementation of employment policy.

In January 1988, the ICFTU's Inter-American Regional Organization wrote to the government demanding an inquiry into the arrest, on Jan. 11, of Filomen Escolar, a leading Bolivian trade-unionist, a council member of the COB and a former leader of the FSTMB. He was arrested while attending a union meeting in Cochabamba.

Bolivia's Labour Code (under which employers and not unions fund union representation) dates from the 1930s but its revision is under discussion. The Ministry of Labour is required to recognize legally elected union representatives. In 1989 unions and employers reached an agreement on the ratio of union representation but this was ruled unlawful by the Supreme Court.

Like its predecessor, the Zamora government, used tough methods in response to trade union unrest. A 90-day state of siege was ordained in November 1989 when it felt a teachers' hunger strike for more pay was threatening counter-inflationary policy. The Interior Ministry claimed that 500 unionists were detained at this time, but the national union centre COB put the figure at 3,000. The COB staged general strikes in January 1989 and April 1990. From December 1990, union unrest built up again around a nine-point programme put to government by the COB, and in March 1991 the COB mounted another general strike against Zamora's socio-economic orientation.

Trade unionism. The first significant labour organization in Bolivia began in the first decade of the twentieth century. The La Paz Federation of Labour (Federación Obrera de La Paz), organized from 1908–10, was built on pre-existing guild structures, and was strongly influenced by Liberal politics. The first congress of Bolivian workers assembled in 1921, and the 1920s and 1930s were marked by violent conflicts between anarchist and Marxist factions. The history of trade unionism in modern Bolivia, however, is essentially that of the Bolivian Workers' Central (Central Obrera Boliviana—COB), and its most powerful industrial affiliate, the mineworkers' union Federación de Sindicatos de Trabajadores Mineros de Bolivia (FSTMB). The FSTMB was founded in 1944, and in the April 1952 revolution of the National Revolutionary Movement (MNR) led by Víctor Paz Estenssoro which overthrew military rule, the tin miners served as an armed militia. Following the revolution the FSTMB led in creating the COB, with Juan Lechín Oquendo (the FSTMB executive secretary until June 1986) assuming the position of COB executive secretary. Lechín was appointed Minister of Mines in the MNR government of Víctor Paz Estenssoro, presiding over the nationalization of the tin mining industry as Comibol. For some years thereafter the FSTMB and the COB played a major part in sustaining MNR rule and in 1960 Lechín was elected Vice-President of Bolivia.

In January 1964, however, Lechín was expelled from the MNR for his opposition to government plans to rationalize Comibolo, which was making heavy losses, by removing the FSTMB veto over management decisions, cutting the workforce, and expelling Communists from leadership positions in the union. The disaffection of the miners and the resultant unrest contributed to a split in the MNR, the destabilization of the civilian government, and a military *coup* in November 1964 led by Gen. René Barrientos. Juan Lechín was deported (to Paraguay) in May 1965, precipitating a general strike and several days of heavy fighting between miners and industrial workers and the armed forces in which there were numerous casualties. Further serious disorders occurred in mining areas later the same year, with at least 30 deaths officially reported. In June 1967 tin miners in Oruro, Huanini and Siglo Veinte, in sympathy with guerrillas led by Ernesto (Che) Guevara (who was captured and subsequently killed in Bolivia in October 1967), proclaimed the region a "free territory" and 21 miners were killed during the suppression of the insurrection. Following the death of Barrientos in April 1969 successive civilian and military governments of varying political complexions failed to achieve political stability in the country, and militant and at times insurrectionist tactics remained a feature of the activities of the COB and the FSTMB, despite the extended periods of exile imposed upon Lechín and other union leaders. All trade union activity was officially banned from November 1974 to January 1978, although this ban was only partly effective, and the COB was likewise officially suspended from 1971 to 1978. In November 1979 a military *coup* was followed by a general strike by the COB in which more than 200 people were killed. Widespread but futile resistance in La Paz and the mining areas was reported following a *coup* in July 1980, the new régime again banning the COB and all trade union activity. Lechín and Simon Reyes, another leader of the FSTMB, were arrested in July 1980 but freed into exile shortly afterwards; an abortive attempt at a military *coup* was supported by a general strike call by the (banned) COB.

The ban on the COB was lifted in May 1982 and a civilian government under President Hernán Siles Zuazo was installed in October 1982, with the COB rejecting a request by Siles to participate in the government. The COB vigorously opposed the attempts of the Siles government to implement austerity measures to combat hyper-inflation. In August

1983 the COB presented a programme which included: (i) a rejection of any negotiations with the International Monetary Fund (IMF), and a moratorium on payments of the external debt; (ii) the establishment of worker-control in private sector enterprises; (iii) the establishment of joint management by workers and government in the public sector; (iv) the control of private banking by a government agency; (v) control of the government's emergency agrarian programme by the peasants' federation (the CSUTCB); and (vi) majority worker participation in all state decision-making organizations.

In September 1983 the government conceded majority representation on the board of Comibol to the FSTMB, but rejected the main themes of the COB programme. Austerity measures introduced in November 1983 led to a general strike called by the COB, and in the period until the installation of the Paz Estenssoro government in August 1985 a pattern became established whereby the increasingly enfeebled government announced various austerity measures and then withdrew or sharply modified them in the face of strikes called by the COB.

On Aug. 29, 1985, the new government announced austerity measures approved by the IMF which have set the tone of government policy up to the present. These included the devaluation of the peso, wage freezes, sharp reductions in government subsidies, the repayment of foreign debts and price freedom. Such a policy critically revolved around the restructuring of both the private and state-owned mines, with an estimated 27,000 miners losing their jobs between 1985 and 1988. In protest the COB organized a series of general strikes with particular effect in the mining sector throughout 1985 and 1986, to which the government responded with declarations of states of siege (Sept. 19, 1985 and Aug. 28, 1986) and the temporary detention or internal exiling of union leaders. On July 25, 1986, the COB staged a national "referendum" in which 98 per cent of the 1,500,000 who participated were claimed to have voted against the repayment of foreign debts and the government's economic measures. Between Aug. 22–27, 1986, up to 5,000 miners marched on La Paz, but the government confirmed its intention to close seven of the 24-state-owned mines and sell nine to miners' co-operatives. The government claimed that the march, broken up by the army 60 km. from the capital, had been intended to lead to the overthrow of the government. A mass hunger-strike organized by the COB in April 1988 was estimated to have involved 4,000 workers, especially redundant miners, in opposition to government social and economic policies. On April 29 and 30, students and teachers sympathetic to the hunger strikers clashed with police in Potosi. President Paz Estenssoro in response agreed to provide alternative stop-gap employment for unemployed miners.

In September 1989, the COB convention was held at which the Communist General Secretary Simon Reyes was replaced by Victor López, an associate of Reyes' predecessor Juan Lechín. Most of the other leadership positions remained in the hands of the Left. In December leaders of the Movement of the Revolutionary Left (MIR) were expelled from the COB. Under Left leadership the COB has returned to its former willingness to use general strikes as a negotiating weapon. In December 1990 the COB met government with a nine point plan for social amelioration, which included a 30 per cent basic wage rise and the honouring of agreements between the government and rural workers: frustration led to another general strike in March 1991. In the mines, the influential COB affiliate FSTMB continued to oppose privatization or the introduction of joint ventures.

Union density in Bolivia is estimated at 29 per cent.

Central Obrera Boliviana (COB)
Bolivian Workers' Central (Confederation)

Address. CP6552, Calle Sucre 916, La Paz
Leadership. Victor López (general secretary).

Membership. The COB is the Bolivian trade union centre, and all the national unions except the transport workers are affiliated to it. Its membership of 200,000 includes some members of popular organizations such as housewives' and tenants' associations.

History and character. See above: Trade unionism.

International affiliations. Affiliation to the WFTU was confirmed by the WFTU General Council in October 1988.

Federación de Sindicatos de Trabajadores Mineros de Bolivia (FSTMB)
Trade Union Federation of Bolivian Mine Workers

Address. Plaza Venezuela 1470, La Paz

Phone. (02) 340574

Leadership. Juan Lechín Oquendo resigned as executive secretary on June 14, 1986, and was subsequently replaced by Victor López Arias.

Membership. 27,000.

History. The FSTMB originated in 1944, when Juan Lechín was elected its leader at the founding convention. It rapidly established itself as the most powerful and militant Bolivian union (for subsequent history, *see Trade unionism* above).

Botswana

Capital: Gaborone   **Population: 1,256,000**
                                                                            (1989)

Political system. Botswana (until 1963 the British High Commission territory of Bechuanaland) became a fully independent member of the Commonwealth with republican status in 1966, and has a largely elected National Assembly together with a House of Chiefs. Since the pre-independence elections of 1965 all general elections have been won overwhelmingly by the Botswana Democratic Party (most recently in 1989).

Economy. Although diamond and other mining (particularly copper-nickel) and meat processing produce a large proportion of Botswana's export revenue, they represent only a relatively small source of employment; the government holds a share in most of the mining activities and in the main meat processing plant. Export revenue and the strength of the main industries are liable to severe fluctuations, in the case of meat products because of the incidence of drought and of cattle disease, and in the case of mining because of the volatility of the world markets for diamonds and copper.

In the 1980s as a whole Botswana maintained an average growth rate of 10 per cent, though this impressive performance was not enough—with many Botswanans returning home after working abroad and high population growth—to prevent unemployment remaining high. In the 1985–87 period 43.2 per cent of Botswana's labour force worked in agriculture, 4.9 per cent in industry and 51.9 per cent in services. This represents a major shift since the mid-1960s when agriculture, which in Botswana is composed mainly of subsistence or pastoral activity, accounted for 89 per cent of employment. The country now has a fast-growing urban working class and its GNP per capita is now the largest in Southern Africa after South Africa. The Seventh (1991–97) Development Plan forsees an expanded role for the private sector and reduced dependence on mineral exports.

System of industrial relations. Botswana has not ratified ILO Convention No. 87

53

(Freedom of Association and Protection of the Right to Organize, 1948) or Convention No. 98 (Right to Organize and Collective Bargaining, 1949) although unions are legal and have been active since before independence.

Trade unionism. The principal organization is the Botswana Federation of Trade Unions, formed in 1977. It was reported early in 1988 that unions are not allowed to employ full-time officials.

Botswana Federation of Trade Unions

Address. P.O. Box 440, Gaborone
Phone. 52534
Leadership. B.C. Ntune (chairman); Ronald Baipidi (secretary general)
Membership. 6,870 (1983).
International affiliations. OATUU; ICFTU. Botswana has been host to the Southern African Trade Union Co-ordination Council since it was launched in December 1984 (*see* separate entry).

Brazil

Capital: Brasilia   **Population: 135,560,000**

Political system. Brazil came under military rule in 1964, although under the 1967 Constitution there was a limited degree of popular representation in a bicameral parliament. The first truly multiparty elections for 20 years were held in 1982, when the progovernment Social Democratic Party (PDS) won the largest number of seats, followed closely by the Christian Democratic Party of the Brazilian Democratic Movement (PMDB). The members of the Federal Senate and Chamber of Deputies, together with representatives of the ruling parties in the 23 states, formed an electoral college for the indirect election of a president in 1985. This was decisively won by the candidate of the Democratic Alliance which included principally the PMDB and the Liberal Front (dissident PDS members), although the military initially supported the official PDS candidate, and a civilian government was sworn in, made up of members of the PMDB and defectors from the PDS. Congress in May 1985 approved a constitutional amendment providing for direct presidential elections in the future. Elections in 1986 resulted in a PMDB majority in the bicameral Congress, whose members formed a Constituent Assembly. A new Constitution drawn up by it was promulgated in October 1988, providing among other things for enhanced workplace rights and the freedom for all workers (including public servants) to form autonomous labour unions and to strike.

In January 1990 President Sarney handed over office to President Collor de Mello of the National Reconstruction Party, the first Brazilian president to be elected by universal suffrage for 29 years. President Collor had won the 1989 Presidential elections only by a surprisingly narrow margin against the candidate of the Workers' Party (PT), Louis Inacio de Silva commonly known as "Lula". Lula is a former Metalworkers' Union leader who was imprisoned for leading the first strikes in the early 1970s.

Economy. Brazil is one of the leading newly industrialized countries of the world, but after a period of rapid expansion in 1964–74 its economy was severely affected by the oil price explosions of the 1970s. Heavy external borrowing and IMF assistance became necessary, and by the mid-1980s the external debt amounted to about US$100,000 million, with annual repayment obligations of around US$10,000 million. A recovery was evident in 1983, when the visible trade surplus rose sharply, but the inflation rate also increased, to around 200 per cent in each of the three years 1983–85, and subsequently on occasion rose to an annualized rate of as much as 16,000 per cent.

The economic productive base is founded firstly on broadly based manufacturing and secondly on agriculture, with mining as an important third component. However, various of the commercial crops are subject to sharp price and demand fluctuations on the international markets, while coffee and cocoa in particular are also liable to be severely affected by disease and local climatic conditions. The state sector has accounted for about half of industrial output, but although an important part of the new civilian government's economic recovery programme and reduction of public expenditure has been to privatize a number of these concerns and to close others, little actual progress has been achieved in this direction.

Brazil made efforts during the mid- and later 1980s to reschedule its massive external debt; as the negotiations faltered Brazil in 1987 suspended certain interest payments and principal repayments, but in the course of 1988 agreements were reached on rescheduling of both commercial and official indebtedness.

Successive governments have inaugurated plans to resolve Brazil's economic difficulties: the Cruzado Plan (February 1986), the New Cruzado Plan (June 1987) and the Summer Plan (introduced by President Sarney in January 1989). Each of these entailed greater or lesser measures of monetary control with the special aim of reining in an inflation rate which was near to 1,000 per cent in 1988 and over 300 per cent the following year; each of them provoked trade union and general unrest in opposition to the perceived impact on living standards; each of them failed to achieve major objectives. Unable to command assent to his proposals, President Sarney ceded office early to his successor, and in March 1990 President Collor's Brazil Novo Plan which if anything was tougher than its predecessors, was inaugurated.

The Brazil Novo Plan aimed to curb inflation, reduce the public sector, cut public spending and liberalize trade. It placed an embargo on bank withdrawals, strictly regulated the price of goods and services and inaugurated quarterly adjustments to the minimum wage to prevent erosion of the real earnings of the poor. However the savagely deflationary impact of the measures became clear in April and May as a wave of redundancies began in the private sector and culminated in a programme of public spending cuts which included making one quarter of Brazil's civil servants redundant.

One year after it entered office the Collor administration was no nearer achieving its economic objectives than its predecessors had been. Inflation in early 1991 was 905 per cent, the minimum wage had fallen, and the President's election promises to create a welfare state has not materialized. Autolatina, the carmaker, announced 8,000 redundancies—a 16 per cent cut and one of the biggest ever in the private sector—in February of that year.

System of industrial relations. Brazil ratified ILO Convention No. 98 (Right to Organize and Collective Bargaining, 1949) in 1952, but has not ratified Convention No. 87 (Freedom of Association and Protection of the Right to Organize, 1948). The ILO *Report of the Committee of Experts on the Application of Conventions and Recommendations* (1988) notes with concern the application of Convention No. 9 (Forced Labour, 1930) ratified in 1951. It was responding to a report from the National Confederation of Industrial Workers (CNTI) that forced labour and debt bondage still persist in certain regions of Brazil despite government explanations of the difficulty of detecting such violations and enforcing labour laws in remote regions. However, the Committee responded favourably to an agreement of July 9, 1986, signed by the Ministry of Labour, the Ministry of Reform and Agricultural Development, the National Confederation of Agriculture and the National Confederation of Agriculture Workers (CONTAG) to deal with all kinds of slave labour ("trabalho escravo").

Unrest under military rule, 1978–85. Industrial unrest became marked from 1978 onwards, notably among the metalworkers, among whom Luis Inacio da Silva, "Lula" (the president of the São Bernardo Metalworkers' Union until his enforced removal in 1980, and unofficial leader thereafter) was prominent. Factory commissions, organized independently of officially sanctioned union structures and negotiating directly with management (especially in large foreign-owned plants) were a factor in this activity. Leaders of the unrest were known as *autênticos* or *combatives*, and were critical of the prevailing machine-unionism. The government responded by a series of "interventions" — i.e. assuming control of union offices and assets and appointing their own officials—and trials of labour leaders in military courts. The *combative* approach was reflected in the formation of the Partido dos Trabalhadores in 1980 and the holding of two conferences in 1981, under the banner of the *Oposiçao Sindical* (itself formed after the 1964 *coup*, but which had had little impact), which brought together *autênticos*, and non-trade union groups, aimed at strengthening grass-roots support. A *Unidade Sindical*, formed in 1979, in contrast comprised mainly conservative and communist machine-unionists concerned that radical trade unionism would reverse the régime's trend to greater liberalization (the *abertura*, begun in the late 1970s).

A weakening in the severity of repressive control became apparent in the latter stages of military rule, allowing increasingly open activity: all leading factors in the union movement attended a National Workers' Congress (CONCLAT) in Aug. 1981 and began preparations to form a national inter-trade federation in defiance of the law (*see below*). The first attempt at a general strike (although with mainly local impact in the São Paulo area) since the introduction of military rule was on July 21, 1983, the government responding by placing five unions under "intervention" and suspending 69 union officials. In the following months part of the labour movement formed a national inter-trade federation, the Central Unica dos Trabalhadores (CUT). Similarly, military tribunals in February–March 1984, in a series of trials, dismissed charges brought under the national security laws against prominent figures including Jair Meneguelli (leader of the newly formed CUT), Luis Inacio da Silva, and José Francisca da Silva (president of the CONTAG—*see below*).

Trade unionism under civilian rule. Government control was greatly relaxed following the introduction of civilian government in March 1985 so as to: (i) permit the formation of national and regional confederations representing workers from more than one industrial sector; (ii) allow unions from March 1986 to determine their own electoral rules (rather than as previously the Labour Ministry); and (iii) end orders banning many prominent activist leaders from taking part in union affairs. However, such relaxations were dwarfed by changes in the labour regulations voted for by the Constituent Assembly in May 1988. Hailed as the most fundamental reform for 40 years, it allowed the unrestricted right to strike for all workers, including public sector workers in "essential" areas, a reduction in the working week from 48 to 40 hours, a six-hour shift limit, maternity leave of 120 days for female workers and a five-day paternity leave for males, indemnity for workers dismissed without justification, the right of workers (including public servants) to form unions, and that unions would no longer be subject to control by the Ministry of Labour.

Right to strike and collective bargaining. Numerous strikes during 1985–86 divided the government over the extent to which existing authoritarian labour legislation should be applied. Automatic wage increases were built into the government's Tropical (or Cruzado) Plan, initiated on Feb. 28, 1986, which guaranteed that wages would rise by a minimum of 60 per cent of the inflation rate. When economic performance proved sluggish during

1986, the government embarked on "Phase Two" of the Cruzado Plan. This, together with rationalization in the state sector (involving the immediate closure or merger of 15 state-sector companies, with a further 32 to follow) provoked widespread protest. On Nov. 27, 1986, the CUT called a stoppage in Brasília and Rio de Janeiro, followed on Dec. 12 by a 24-hour general strike staged jointly by the CUT and the CGT. Throughout 1987 and 1988 consistently rising inflation triggered the indexation mechanism, thereby ensuring regular wage increases for the public sector. When the cost of buying off labour unrest in institutions of Higher Education (a 49.86 per cent pay increase) was taken into account, the total public sector salary bill had, by government estimate, already devoured 92 per cent of all federal government revenue by early 1988. The government claimed that public sector wages now outstripped those of the private sector and, if left unchecked, would account for 4.2 per cent of GNP in 1988 (as compared to 2.4 per cent in 1987). The government, on April 7, 1988, instigated a wage freeze for the public sector and suspended the indexation wage mechanism, the *unidade de referencia de precos* (URP) for two months. In response, the CUT and CGT called a series of disruptive strikes involving public sector employees, and President Sarney dismissed the chief of staff of the Armed Forces, Air Force Brig. Paulo Roberto Camarinha, when the latter complained that public sector employees (which included members of the armed forces) were the victims of discrimination, since the freeze involved neither the private sector (where collective agreements on wages, productivity deals and overtime rates predominate) nor the legislative and judicial branches of the government. In September 1988 Rio de Janeiro's mayor declared the city bankrupt and some 100,000 municipal employees were denied their salaries for the month. In response to the crisis, tripartite talks were held in early November 1988 towards the formulation of an "anti-inflationary social pact", and this led to an agreement on a 60-day period of voluntary pay and price restraint (especially on essential foodstuffs) in an attempt to reverse the upward trend of inflation, recorded at 27.75 per cent for October. However, this attempt at conciliation was severely compromised as the government moved to end the 12-day strike by 25,000 workers at the Volta Redonda steel mill, 100 miles south of Rio de Janeiro, the largest in Latin America. On the evening of Nov. 9, 1,000 troops with armoured cars clashed with an estimated 2,000 workers occupying the mill. Three workers were killed and a reported 34 others wounded. The incident sparked off an immediate national strike of 40,000 refinery workers of the state-owned Petrobras Company. Jair Meneguelli, president of the CUT, accused the government of ordering the army's "brutal invasion" and urged other union leaders to break off all social pact talks as well as summoning a national meeting of delegates from unions, popular organizations and political parties to decide on how to respond.

Altogether the union confederations called three general strikes between 1985 and 1989. By 1991 however, enthusiasm for national protest action was waning as it became increasingly apparent that the unions' mobilizing ability was being hampered by disunity between them.

In rural areas union leaders campaigning for land reform have been the victims of a murderous and unpunished campaign by gunmen. In the region of Rio Maria in the Eastern Amazon, 173 people were killed in land conflicts between 1980 and 1991. They included two presidents of local branches of the National Rural Workers' Movement, Joao Canuta who was killed in 1985, and his successor Expedito Ribiero de Souza, shot in 1991. The most celebrated victim of the gunmen was the leader of the CUT-affiliated Rubbertappers' Union and ecologist Chico Mendes. Chico Mendes had received a United Nations prize for "making an outstanding contribution to the life of our planet" for his work to protect the Amazonian forests from landowner depredation. He was shot dead in December 1988.

The Church Land Commission records that there have been only 24 trials following the 1,630 land reform murders committed in Brazil since 1964. The CUT in 1990 questioned the destination of internationally raised funds intended for land reform claiming that money raised as long ago as 1988 had not yet reached the countryside.

Trade unionism. Labour organization in Brazil began in the first decade of the twentieth century. Two general confederations, the Confederación Nacional de Trabajo (CNT) and the communist-led Confederación General del Trabajo (CGT), were formed in the 1920s, but under the government of Getúlio Vargas (1930–45) unions were restructured on corporatist lines, with Mussolini's example in Italy as a model; strikes were prohibited, union structures absorbed into the state, and agricultural workers forbidden to organize. After 1946 greater freedom was allowed and the CGT reorganized, but attempts to create a unified national trade union centre were unsuccessful. Tight government control resumed after the 1964 military *coup*, with union affairs dominated by pro-government officials exercising authoritarian control. During the 1970s, although nominal rights to free collective bargaining and to strike existed, they were in practice largely negated by active government intervention in union affairs, and most strikes were declared illegal under the national security laws. Brazilian trade unionism has never developed the militant character associated with certain other Latin American countries. In the early 1980s there were 5,000 unions financed by the union tax on all workers (*see below*), and an elaborate system of labour courts.

Union tax. The financing of the Brazilian labour organizations has been based on the union tax (*imposto sindical*), a compulsory levy equivalent to a day's pay for each worker, which is divided between local, provincial and national unions and the Labour Ministry; the 20 per cent allocated to the Labour Ministry was in theory to provide for unemployment benefits, although in practice these were rarely available. Right-wing machine-unionists and the Moscow-line Communist Party (PCB) alike propose that the tax should be retained; the *combatives* have argued for its abolition on the ground that the tax entrenches monolithic structures.

Development of national confederations since 1981. Movement towards the reorganization of the Brazilian labour movement on a national basis began with the holding in August 1981 of the first National Workers' Congress (CONCLAT). This brought together urban and rural workers and all ideological tendencies and agreed on the need for a unified national labour federation. However, a 54-member organizing commission established to prepare for such a body was politically fractured and plans for a second CONCLAT to be held in 1982 were abandoned. On Aug. 26–28, 1983, a CONCLAT attended by 5,000 delegates set up the first national trade union centre, the CUT. Conservative- and communist-led unions, including the main occupational federations, boycotted the formation of the CUT, after protracted negotiations failed to secure their attendance. They objected to the arrangement whereby workers could organize themselves and elect delegates if their own unions refused to participate, and claimed that the CONCLAT would over-represent the liberal professions. The *combatives*, however, the main force behind the formation of the CUT, argued that they had made sufficient concessions in acceding to participation by unrepresentative existing occupational federations and confederations. The non-participants at the August congress staged their own congress on Nov. 5–7, 1983, there creating a rival semi-permanent organization which took the name of the National Co-ordination of the Working Classes (Coordenacão Nacional des Classes Trabalhadores, also known as CONCLAT). This body was officially not described as a trade union centre, but as a deliberative and executive body to prepare the way for the formation of such a centre. In the view of the CUT, this CONCLAT was dominated by accommodationist conservatives (*pelegos*) and communist machine bosses. Technically both the CUT and the CONCLAT were illegal, Brazilian labour law not permitting the formation of collective organizations of unions representing workers in different occupations, but the government conceded tacit acceptance. Following the return of civilian government in March 1985, prohibitions on national and regional inter-trade organizations were lifted. On Nov. 5–6, 1985, the CUT and the CONCLAT co-operated for the first time in leading a general strike for wage and hours demands in the São Paulo area. In late 1985, a third, conservative-led organization, the União Sindical Nacional was formed, and in March 1986 the CONCLAT was reformed as a permanent organization to be called the Central Geral dos Trabalhadores (CGT). A number of independent unions continued to remain outside the CUT and CGT.

Central Geral dos Trabalhadores (CGT)
Central General de Trabajadores
Workers' General Confederation

Address. Rua da Glória 152, 01510 São Paulo, SP

Phone. (011) 35-88-27

Leadership. Joaquim dos Santos Andrade (president); Valder Vincente de Barros (secretary general). Joaquim dos Santos Andrade, a leading *pelego*, was appointed president of the São Paulo Metalworkers' Union (said to be the largest union in Latin America, with 70,000 members) after the 1964 *coup*. He defeated the challenge of a CUT candidate to win re-election to that post in 1984.

Membership. The inaugural congress in March 1986 was attended by representatives of 1,341 unions claiming to represent 30,000,000 workers. The unions were classified by sector as 606 industrial, 347 rural, 222 service, 93 white-collar, and 73 public service.

History and character. The CGT was founded on March 23, 1986, at the second national congress of the Clase de Trabajadora de Brasil (CTB), convened by the CONCLAT. The CGT was created to give permanent form to the work of the CONCLAT, and was described as the successor to the previous CGT banned by the military government in 1964. In establishing the new organization, the congress rejected ILO Convention No. 87—adopted by President Dutra in 1948 but never ratified by the Brazilian Senate—which provides for full freedom and autonomy for trade unions, on the ground that this "divides the Brazilian trade union movement", a decision reflecting the basis of the new CGT in machine unionism of both the "yellow" and communist type.

Publication. CGT (magazine).

International affiliation. It was resolved at the founding congress that the CGT would be independent and maintain fraternal relations with all three international organizations (i.e. ICFTU, WFTU and WCL).

Central Unica dos Trabalhadores (CUT)
Workers' Central Union (Brazilian Workers' Centre)

Address. Rua Ouvidor Peleja 112, 04128 São Paulo, SP

Phone. (011) 577-48-33

Telex. (011) 542 82

Leadership. Jair Meneguelli (president); Avelino Ganzer (vice-president). Luis Inacio da Silva ("Lula") is often referred to as an unofficial leader of the CUT and is also president of the Partido dos Trabalhadores (PT), founded in 1980 as a political expression of the *combative* wing of the labour movement and which won six of 479 seats in the Chamber of Deputies in the general election of Nov. 15, 1982.

Membership. 1,1014 unions with 12,500,000 members were represented at the second CUT congress held Aug. 1–3, 1986. The main active industrial strength of the CUT in the early stages was largely confined to a few areas, notably the São Paulo "ABC" industrial region, where there is strong local organization. The 3rd congress was held in September 1988.

History and character. The CUT was created at a national workers' congress (CONCLAT) held in the industrial town of São Bernardo do Campo on Aug. 26–28, 1983, and attended by 5,000 delegates representing 912 trade unions, associations and federations. The congress was boycotted by major conservative and communist-led unions, which subsequently formed their own organization (under the name of CONCLAT—later CGT—*see above*). The founding congress elected a co-ordinating committee of seven and a national council of 83; Jair Meneguelli, the president of the São

Bernardo Metalworkers' Union, was elected chairman of the co-ordinating committee and Paulo Renato Paim, general secretary. Policies agreed at the founding convention included the non-payment of the national foreign debt, refusal to comply with IMF demands, the introduction of unemployment pay, a cut in the 48-hour work week, automatic three-monthly wage adjustments, the repeal of the national security laws and an end to government "interventions" in union affairs. The first CUT congress was held Aug. 24–26, 1984, although the CUT was still considered organization-ally weak and with only patchy effective support. The second congress was held in August 1986, and adopted a manifesto calling for agrarian reform, an unlimited right to strike and full trade union autonomy, non-payment of the foreign debt, a guarantee of popular participation in setting up the Constituent Assembly, a "New Economic Order", and a "struggle for peace and disarmament". This second congress was attended by delegates from 39 countries.

Publication. CUT Boletim Nacional.

International Affiliations. None.

Other major union confederations

Confederação Nacional das Profissões Liberais (CNPL)
National Confederation of the Liberal Professions

Address. SCS, Edifício Gilberto Salomão, 13° andar Salas 1.306/1.312, 70305 Brasília, DF

Phone. (061) 223-1683

Telex. (061) 3883

Leadership. Zoilo de Souza Assis (president); Carlo Alberto Schmitt de Azevedo (secretary general).

Membership. 2,500,000 in 17 federations. Members are business administrators, lawyers, librarians, accountants, engineers, nurses, pharmacists, doctors, architects, chemists, biologists, journalists, dentists and other white-collar and professional workers.

History. Was organized in February 1953 to represent the scattered and disparate members of the white-collar and professional sectors. In May 1985 the CNPL achieved its goal of securing legislation according to unions of liberal professions the same status as other trade unions.

International affiliations. Confederação Latino-Americana de Associações de Profissionais Universitários (CLAPU); FIET.

Confederação Nacional dos Trabalhadores na Agricultura (CONTAG)
National Confederation of Agricultural Workers

Address. Edifício CONTAG, Av. W3 Norte, Q 509, 70,750 Brasília, DF

Phone. (061) 274-4500

Leadership. José Francisco Da Silva (president)

Membership. 9,000,000 organized in 2,600 unions and 22 federations.

History. Rural workers were first granted the right to organize in 1944, but bitter landowner opposition ensured that little was done until 1962 when the government of João Goulart passed measures favourable to the development of rural unionism. Against this background the CONTAG was formed on Dec. 20, 1963. Following the 1964 military *coup*, CONTAG officers were replaced by government appointees. After 1979, however, encouraged by the rise of urban unionism and the relative liberalization of government policy, and assisted in many areas by Roman Catholic priests, rural unionism began to emerge again. This has, however, been met by considerable landowner-sponsored violence: in 1980-81 alone according to the CONTAG, seven union leaders, two union lawyers and 18 ordinary workers were killed for their participation in organizing work, and the police were often seen as being controlled by powerful local landowners. The CONTAG was reportedly the only national industrial federation which actively opposed the military government. The civilian government of President Sarney in May 1985 announced a programme of agrarian reform, intended to redistribute plots of land to 1,500,000 peasant families, but the implementation of this programme has triggered further violence and has been relatively unsuccessful.

Publication. O Trabalhador (monthly newspaper).

Confederação Nacional dos Trabalhadores no Comércio (CNTC)
National Confederation of Workers in Commerce

Address. W-5 Sul Quadra 902, Lote 705, 70,390 Brasília, DF
International affiliation. ORIT.

Confederação Nacional dos Trabalhadores em Communicações e Publicidade (CONTCOP)
National Confederation of Workers in Communications and Advertising

Address. SCS-Quadra 11, Edifício Serra Dourada 7° andar, Grupo 705/709, Brasília, DF, CEP 70,315
Phone. (061) 224-7926
Telex. (038) 611792
Leadership. Ankonio Maria Thaumatuigo Cortizo (president)
Membership. 300,000.
History. Founded 1964.
International affiliations. ICFTU; ORIT.

Confederação Nacional dos Trabalhadores nas Empresas de Crédito (CONTEC)

Address. Av. W4, SEP-SUL EQ 707/907 Lote E, 70, 351 Brasília, DF
Phone. (061) 244-5833
Telex. (061) 2745
Leadership. Lourenço Ferreira do Prado (president)
Membership. 200,000.
History. Founded 1958.
International affiliation. FIET.

Confederação Nacional dos Trabalhadores em Educaçao do Brasil (CNTE)
National Confederation of Education Workers of Brazil

Address. Edifício Venãncio III s. 10/2, Setor de Diversões Sul, 70,3000 Brasília, DF
Phone. (061) 225-1003
Leadership. Niso Prego (president)
Membership. 600,000 in 31 associations.
History. Founded 1952 and changed its name from the Brazilian Teachers' Confederation (CPB) at its 1988 congress.
Publication. CPB Notícias (monthly).

Confederação Nacional dos Trabalhadores em Estabelecimentos de Educação e Cultura (CNTEEC)
National Confederation of Workers in Education and Culture

Address. SAS, Quadra 4, Bloco B, 70,070 Brasília, DF
Phone. (061) 226-2988
Leadership. Miguel Abrahão Neto (president)
Membership. 11 federations and 140 unions.
History. Founded 1965.

Confederação Nacional dos Trabalhadores na Indústria (CNTI)
National Confederation of Industrial Workers

Address. Av. W/3 Norte, Quadra 505, Lote 01, Brasília, DF, CEP 70,300
Phone. (061) 274-4150
Telex. (061) 4230

Leadership. José Calixto Ramos (president)

Membership. 9,000,000 in four national and multistate federations, 59 other federations, and more than 1,000 local unions. Members are in a wide range of industrial occupations.

History. The CNTI was founded on July 19, 1946. Co-ordinates and provides legal assistance to member organizations.

Publications. Tribuna Sindical (bi-monthly official publication); *Tribuna Jurídica* (supplement to *Tribuna Sindical*).

International affiliations. Affiliation to ORIT has been discontinued.

Confederação Nacional dos Trabalhadores em Transportes Marítimos, Fluvais e Aéreos (CNTTMFA)
National Confederation of Sea, River and Aviation Workers

Address. Av. Pres. Vargas 446-22°, 20,071 Rio de Janeiro, RJ

Phone. (021) 223-8329

Leadership. Aloysio Ribeiro (president)

Membership. 400,000 in eight federations and 180 unions.

History. Founded 1957.

Confederação Nacional dos Trabalhadores em Transportes Terrestres
National Confederation of Land Transport Workers

Address. SBS, Edifício Seguradoras, 11° andar, 70,072 Brasília, DF

Phone. (061) 224-5011;

Telex. (061) 1593 CTTT

Fax. (061) 225-5235

Leadership. Orlando Coutinho (president); Nilo Tochetto (secretary-general); José Dias Trigo (finance secretary)

Membership. About 385,310 in 154 unions and nine federations.

History and character. Was formed in 1952 at the instigation of the existing unions of transport workers. Orientation is pluralist. Is subdivided into five regional federations.

Publication. Folha do Transporte (monthly).

International affiliation. ITF.

Brunei

Capital: Bandar Seri Begawan   **Population: 243,000**
                                                          (1988)

Political system. Brunei Darussalam (Brunei) became a fully independent member of the Commonwealth in 1984, having hitherto been a British protected state from 1888 to 1971. It had been largely self-governing since 1959 under a treaty which was amended in 1971 so as to transfer responsibility from Britain for internal public order. Since 1962, following an unsuccessful internal rebellion, a state of emergency has been in force under which the Sultan has ruled by decree. Major responsibilities within the Cabinet are held by the Sultan (as Prime Minister) and by other members of the royal family.

Economy. The Brunei economy is largely dependent on the production of petroleum and gas, and on oil refining and gas liquefaction. Together, these account for almost all of Brunei's exports and some three-quarters of gross domestic product; the state has participation in most oil and gas activities. Brunei has only a small agricultural sector and imports a high proportion of its foodstuffs, while little rubber is now produced. In view of the probable exhaustion of oil and gas reserves around the end of the 1990s, efforts are being made to increase agricultural production, to establish processing and manufacturing sectors and to develop an international financial services sector. Per capita income is among the highest in the world, and there is a well-developed system of welfare services and other social benefits. About a third of the workforce comprises foreigners, principally from the Philippines and Malaysia. The government's policy is to favour *bumiputra* (Malay and indigenous) participation in economic activity, as long as the relevant skills exist.

The country's fifth national development plan, covering the period 1986-90, succeeded at reducing dependence on revenues derived from petroleum and natural gas reserves and helping with the creation of new private sector industries.

Trade unionism. Unions have legal status, although they are little developed. Reported unions are:

1. **Brunei Government Junior Officers' Union**, P.O. Box 2290, Bandar Seri Begawan.

2. **Brunei Government Medical and Health Workers' Union**, P.O. Box 459, Bandar Seri Begawan.

3. **Brunei Oilfield Workers' Union**, P.O. Box 175, Seria.

4. **Royal Brunei Custom Department Staff Union**, Custom Dept., Kuala Belait.

Bulgaria

Capital: Sofia   **Population: 8,933,000**
                                                          (1990)

Political system. Bulgaria was declared a people's republic in 1946 after the left-wing Fatherland Front had seized power in 1944; in the first post-war elections in 1947 the Bulgarian Communist Party emerged with an overall majority. A new Constitution was adopted in 1971 (replacing that of 1947), which defined the republic as a socialist state of the working people, headed by the working class and with the Bulgarian Communist Party (BCP) as the leading force (in close co-operation with the Bulgarian Agrarian People's Union). In (unopposed) elections to the unicameral National Assembly in 1986 there was a sole list of 400 candidates nominated by the Fatherland Front (including 276 from the BCP).

At a conference in early 1988 the BCP agreed a general policy of "restructuring", representing "the transition of power in the name of the people to power through the people"—in particular through the establishment of a system of "socialist self-government". Meanwhile regulations adopted in late 1987 had provided for a mandatory choice of candidates in all parliamentary and local elections and the inclusion of candidates other than those nominated by official organizations (although all would require endorsement by the Fatherland Front).

In November 1989 popular uprisings led to the ousting of the longstanding head of state

Todor Zhivkov who was replaced by a Communist reformer Peter Mladenov as Party chief. After an internal party struggle accompanied by further popular unrest, Peter Mladenov assumed the Presidency and led a rapid renewal of the BCP (now renamed the Bulgarian Socialist Party) which positioned it well to win Bulgaria's first free elections in June 1990. Disturbances continued in the second half of 1990 and led to the resignation of the BSP government in December.

Economy. Under the former Constitution, the socialist economic system was defined as being based on the public ownership of the means of production, developing in a planned manner towards a communist economy as part of the world socialist economic system. Ownership constituted state ownership (by the whole state), co-operative ownership, ownership by public corporations or personal ownership. State ownership applied in particular to plants and factories, banks, natural resources, transport and communications. Foreign trade was the exclusive right of the state.

Under the "new economic mechanism", introduced from 1982, more use was made of prices, wages and profits as factors in economic flexibility, with greater decentralization of decision-making to the labour collectives and use of incentives. Since 1978 the "brigade" had been the principal enterprise unit, and it was announced in 1984 that wage ceilings for brigades had been removed, to allow workers to benefit from their increased productivity.

The process of "restructuring" agreed in early 1988 included "the transference of socialist property to the work teams for management and administration" and the introduction of "socialist competition".

Before 1989, Bulgaria operated a system of five-year plans, the ninth, for the period 1986–90, laying special stress on technical re-equipment and automation. It also participated in the comprehensive programme of the Council for Mutual Economic Assistance (CMEA or Comecon), in which context particular emphasis was placed on Bulgaria's developed electronics industry. Legislation approved in 1980 permitted the establishment of joint economic ventures involving Bulgarian companies and enterprises from non-communist countries.

System of industrial relations. Before 1989 only minor changes had been made in Bulgaria's industrial relations.

The ILO *Report of the Committee of Experts on the Application of Conventions and Recommendations* (1985) noted, with reference to the application of ILO Convention No. 87 (Freedom of Association and Protection of the Right to Organize, 1948), which Bulgaria had ratified in 1959, that under Section 7 of that country's Labour Code "the acquisition of legal personality by any occupational organization was conditional on the approval of the central management of the occupational organization that already existed". Bulgaria also ratified Convention No. 98 (Right to Organize and Collective Bargaining, 1949) in 1959.

Role of trade unions in "restructuring". A major reappraisal of the role of trade unions took place following the adoption by the BCP leadership of the policy of *preustroistvo* ("restructuring"), which in the economic sphere was based on "the transference of social property to the work teams for management and administration" and the decentralization of decision making at all levels. New labour legislation strengthening the role of the work teams came into effect at the beginning of 1987, and decrees reorganizing enterprises along "self-management" lines were approved by the BCP and the government in July of that year.

According to a BCP resolution in January 1988 *preustroistvo* also envisaged reorienting the economy towards better technological development and the phasing out of "non-competitive enterprises with a large unskilled labour force". Enterprises and their workforces were required to be more responsive to market forces, with wage policy more closely linked to productivity and salaries realigned according to a new assessment of "the creative imput of professional work to social progress". Wage levelling tendencies were to be eliminated by the introduction of performance-related incentives and the removal of wage ceilings, while the minimum wage was to be replaced by a "guaranteed social subsistence income" for low earners. Enterprise social programmes, such as housing, pre-school groups, cultural and leisure facilities, now had to be financed from profits, rather than from centralized national funds, as previously.

Workplace organization. Within a "self-managing" enterprise workers were organized into teams, lead by team councils, which sent delegates to a General Assembly of Workers' Delegates and an Economic Council, responsible for negotiations with the enterprise management. Corresponding to the work teams and the General Assembly in an enterprise, trade unions were represented at the level of "basic organizations" and "enterprise organizations"; the CCTU estimated that there were around 74,000 basic organizations and around 8,000 enterprise organizations. The supreme body of each enterprise organization was the Delegates Assembly, comprising the chairmen of each basic organization in an enterprise, which in turn elected an executive committee. The Delegates Assembly decided to which trade union the workers in an enterprise affiliated and chose candidates for elections to local councils and more senior trade union bodies.

Disputes. The CCTU stated that "under socialism there is no objective basis for such differences between the trade union and the state bodies which could eventually culminate in a strike", and that problems were resolved by a "joint discussion" influenced by the "leading role of the Communist Party". The basis of all these arrangements was fatally undermined by the popular uprising of October-November 1989.

A major strike wave was the centrepiece of the downfall of the Zhivkov régime. Beginning with small partial stoppages it grew during November and December 1989 to major proportions. At one point The CITUB President Kristo Petkov estimated that 250 of the country's biggest enterprises were hit by industrial action. In 1990 there were estimated to have been 300 strikes during the first three months alone. These were largely spontaneous: the independent union Podkrepa claimed to be in the leadership of only 30 of them. The June 1990 elections (won by the BSP) brought only a brief hiatus. Renewed strike activity and continuing discontent culminated in a general strike called by the independent union Podkepa which led to the fall of the BSP government in December.

Trade unionism. Bulgarian trade unions first appeared in the 1880s, and the General Workers' Trade Union Association was formed in 1904. Trade unionism assumed a revolutionary character, with labour playing a part in the revolution of 1944. Unions were incorporated into the structure of the state thereafter.

According to an official Bulgarian trade union publication published in 1984, the Bulgarian trade unions united "98 per cent of all working people" and constituted a "non-state, self-initiated organization of voluntary participation". "The relations between the Party (i.e. the Bulgarian Communist Party, BCP) and the trade unions", it was maintained, "stem from their common class basis and objectives. The party exerts an ideological and political influence over the trade unions and gives scientific guidelines to their activity. Yet the party's policy towards trade-union internal organizational activities is one of non-interference".

A significant proportion of trade union members are working peasants, represented in the Fatherland Front government by the Bulgarian Agrarian People's Union; in 1985 about 27 per cent of total agricultural output came from peasants' private plots. The Trade Union of Agricultural and Food Industry Workers, with 1,154,000 members was the largest affiliate of the Central Council of Trade Unions (CCTU).

A CCTU secretary, Kosta Andreev, wrote in mid-1988 that "given that in a society of self-management workers collectives themselves may solve economic problems through their self-management bodies (and that therefore there is no longer any need for intermediaries), unions will no longer have any reason to take a direct part in enterprise manage-ment". Instead, the unions would act as "social guarantors" by making sure that self-management functioned correctly, and Andreev cited cases where the unions had successfully overturned bureaucratic decisions which had harmed individual "self-managing" collectives, and also where the unions had prevented profiteering or abrogation of contracts by collectives. Andreev added that the aim of the unions "to create the best possible conditions for ensuring the complete success of the new management methods, and to prevent decisions taken by administrative (or other) bodies above them from being imposed on the collectives" meant rejecting the unions' previous role in transmitting downwards decisions taken by state and party planning bodies. He acknowledged that this role had reduced the unions to the status of "an auxiliary body in the economic apparatus" and that the excessive centralism and bureaucracy which had developed as a consequence had led to "a weakening of the workers' confidence in the unions". Andreev asserted that a complete reorganization of trade union structures to make the leading bodies more respon-sive to the grassroots was almost complete. His argument was upheld when the CCTU structure dissolved almost immediately under the impact of political change.

In December 1989, faced with trade union pluralism the CCTU opted for an approach similar to that of the Bulgarian Communist Party, the leadership resigning and the Council changing its name to the Confederation of Independent Trade Unions of Bulgaria (CITUB). In February 1990 the old CCTU statutes were completely overhauled, and later in the year the CITUB withdrew from the WFTU. While Podkrepa campaigned for the opposition in the June elections, the CITUB stayed neutral. It still has the following of a much larger membership than Podkrepa and has inherited all the assets of the CCTU. However the comparative membership strength of the two began to be clarified due to Podkrepa's policy of insisting that new members leave CITUB before they join it.

There was a trade union aspect to the movement which overthrew the Zhivkov régime from its inception. The first independent union Podkrepka (Support) was formed by intel-lectuals in February 1989. Its first President Konstantin Trentchev was imprisoned with several other activists in June, but Podkrepka's Statutes and Programme were published in September, and by December it claimed 100,000 members. Podkrepa led a number of strikes in 1990, and in the June 1990 elections sponsored candidates standing as part of the (opposition) Union of Democratic Forces. Its paper membership is substantially smaller than that of CITUB though reliable comparative figures are difficult to obtain. Like CITUB however it faced difficult choices between political and industrial action during 1990, but reasserted itself in December to launch the general strike which brought down the government.

Confederation of Independent Trade Unions of Bulgaria (CITUB)

Address. pl. D. Blagoev 1, Sofia
Phone. 86-61
Telex. 22446
Leadership. Krysto Petkov (president, appointed December 1990)
Membership. 3,600,000.
History and character. The CITUB is the restructured Central Council of Trade Unions (CCTU), which was established following the 1944 revolution. The Central Council participated in central-ized price and wage fixing by government; member trade unions were responsible for seeing that labour standards were adhered to (with powers to give orders to managers), and had the formal right to make legislative proposals in this sphere. Under the "self-management" policy the CCTU and its affiliates were assuming an increasingly consultative role. Trade unions had responsibility for administering social security and welfare programmes, and provided a wide range of cultural, educa-tional, health and welfare facilities.

International affiliations. Withdrew from the WFTU in 1990.

As early as 1987 the CCTU was reorganized in parallel with the slow move towards decentralization taking place in the country as a whole. Ten new federations were established in addition to the 16 already in existence. But the collapse of the communist régime meant that the CCTU was faced with increasing competition from independent unions. At its Fifth Extended Plenum on Nov. 25, 1989, the independence of Bulgarian Trade Unions was proclaimed by 150 elected representatives, the "conciliatory and yielding" posture of the official unions was repudiated and there was a widespread view that the confidence of working people could be regained only if the unions became uncompromising defenders of their interests. In a founding resolution the Bulgarian Trade Unions were proclaimed independent of political organizations. The CCTU now moved swiftly to reorganize and rebuild its image. At the Sixth Extended Plenum (Dec. 26) the entire collective leadership headed by Petur Dyulgerov was removed and replaced with a new team led by Krysto Petkov, a formidable critic of Solidarnosc.

During January 1990, a consultative ballot (plebiscite) was held among union members which revealed substantial support for diversity of forms of property, opposition to the participation of political parties, and agreement with the newly independent unions entering the forthcoming elections on their own platform. Contacts were established with the ILO in January and a discussion initiated in all workplaces in advance of an Extraordinary Congress. The number of federations was now raised to 50 and open elections held for delegates to the Congress. It was reported that the haemorrhage of members suffered since November had been staunched by these measures.

Petkov's position was legitimized at the Eleventh Extraordinary Congress of Feb. 17–18, 1990 which elected him unopposed as Chairman and changed the Statutes to launch the Confederation of Independent Trade Unions of Bulgaria (CITUB). The Extraordinary Congress then became the Constituent Congress of CITUB and inaugurated a two-month period when it invited federations and unions to affiliate or leave it in freedom. Contacts were opened with the ETUC, and the CITUB discontinued CCTU's affiliation to the WFTU. CITUB criticized the BSP and stayed officially neutral during the June 1990 elections in Bulgaria. It also opened up negotiations with the government for a new general agreement in the course of which the National Union of Business Managers of Bulgaria took part for the first time. This was CITUB's first venture into tripartitism.

Podkrepa
Support

Address. Kniaz Donkunov 39, Sofia
Phone. (2) 390052
Leadership. Konstantin Trentchev (general secretary); Mr Choulev (vice-president).
Membership. 400,000.
History and character. Founded by six intellectuals in February 1989 and immediately applied for official registration. It declared its aims to be the defence of members' interests and opposition to arbitrariness and encroachments by unscrupulous firms and state enterprises. Despite the imprisonment of several leaders, Podkrepa published its Statutes and Programme in September. It grew from 60 members at the time of Zhivkov to more than 70,000 by the time of its first Congress in March 1990.

Podkrepa was a founder member of the opposition Union of Democratic Forces (UDF) and is one of the most powerful voices within it for free market policies. It sponsored several candidates of the UDF in the June elections, but indicated in advance that it intended to remain a union federation, not a political party, and would not have organizational ties with any members who became government ministers. On the eve of the elections it was the strongest force of the UDF and could claim a membership of 400,000.

In the event the BSP won the elections and Podkrepa continued its industrial activities unhampered by the presence of a number of its candidates in the National Assembly. The public perception of it is influenced by the controversial views of Mr Trentchev who strongly advocates the rights of the Turkish minority, who met ex-King Simeon in the Spring of 1990, and who advocated the sale of all big Bulgarian industry to multinationals and the export of unemployed labour. These are not necessarily official Podkrepa views however, and although Trentchev was easily elected General Secretary at the March Congress he was surrounded by a five-strong executive which was meant to develop into a collective leadership. The views of other members of the leadership may be gauged by the comments of Vice President Choulev, who in the autumn of 1990 described the BSP's economic programme as "shock without the therapy". Its demands include a call for all economic and social reform to be discussed with the unions, for a minimum wage, and for pay to be indexed in line with the cost of living. In the autumn of 1990 Podkrepa and other independent union forces again became the focus for discontent: it launched a general strike in December against the slow pace of reform, and it was sufficiently well supported to bring down the government. Late in 1990 Podkrepa was denounced by CITUB for "giving priority to political goals".

International affiliations. Has established contacts with the ICFTU, and its miners' section has applied to join the Miners' International Federation.

Edinstvo

History and character. Founded in 1990 as an independent centre of labour but did not at that point have a developed platform. CITUB thought it discerned in its early statements "some ideas of left-wing socialist trade unionism (with a touch of trotskyism and co-operativism)".

Burkina Faso

Capital: Ouagadougou   **Population: 8,776,000**

Political system. Burkina Faso (named Upper Volta until August 1984) became a self-governing republic within the French Community in 1958 and gained full independence in 1960. Following a military *coup* in 1966 there were 12 years of alternating periods of military and mainly civilian rule. An elected government was overthrown by another *coup* in 1980, with further *coups* taking place in 1982 and 1983. As a result of this last, a left-wing National Revolutionary Council was established by Thomas Sankara, together with a largely civilian Cabinet; however, many of the ministers belonging to the Marxist Patriotic League for Development (Lipad) were replaced in 1984. However, in October 1987 the NRC was in its turn overthrown by the "Patriotic Front" which, while not acting as a political party as such, described itself as "a grouping of political, anti-imperialist and democratic mass organizations".

In March 1990 the Patriotic Front began the process of formulating a new constitution, and a draft was approved by the Assembly in December. The draft provides for a multiparty system and presidential elections—the first since 1978—during 1991.

Economy. Some 9 per cent of the Burkina population lives in the towns. In 1985–87, the labour force was divided between agriculture (86.6 per cent), industry (4.3 per cent) and services (9.1 per cent). Much of the agriculture is subsistence farming or nomadic herding. The West African area within which Burkina Faso lies has been subject to long periods of drought, and this, together with widespread disease, has sharply reduced agricultural output. Moreover, poor infrastructure facilities make the transportation of produce difficult. These are limited mineral resources, while manufacturing (mainly textiles and the processing of tobacco and food products) accounts for only about 10 per cent of total gross domestic product and about 8 per cent of the workforce. Most factories and similar enterprises are privately owned, but almost all of these are of very small scale.

Burkina Faso has a large trade deficit and is heavily dependent on multilateral and bilateral sources of finance.

The government's overall development efforts are hampered by the existence of a significant black market or parallel economy.

System of industrial relations. Burkina Faso (as Upper Volta) ratified ILO Convention No. 87 (Freedom of Association and Protection of the Right to Organize, 1948) in 1960 and Convention No. 98 (Right to Organize and Collective Bargaining, 1949) in 1962.

Trade unionism. Trade union activities began in Burkina Faso (then Upper Volta) at least as early as 1947, when the Union Syndicale des Travailleurs Voltaïques (USTV) was established, and by 1978 six trade union centres were in existence. Although relatively small in scale—with a total membership put at only 12,500 in the late 1970s—the unions have been significantly involved in the unsettled political history of the country. In January 1966 the régime of President Maurice Yameogo was brought down by army intervention following a general strike. President Aboubakar Sangoule Lamizana was likewise deposed in a *coup* in November 1980 following several weeks of strikes and protests led by teachers and supported by the four main trade union federations. The successor military régime led by Col. Saye Zerbo banned the right to strike in November 1981, describing it as a "luxury which our economy cannot allow in the difficult world situation". The ban on strikes was partly lifted in February 1982, although severe restrictions remained in force. Following a further *coup* led by junior army officers in November 1982, which installed a People's Salvation Council (CSP) government, restrictions on trade unions were greatly eased and trade unionists dismissed under Zerbo were permitted to apply for their former jobs. In August 1983 a leftist faction of the CSP led by Capt. Thomas Sankara took power in a military *coup*. Relations between the new régime and the trade unions deteriorated following the arrest and detention in February 1985 of some 20 union leaders who had signed a declaration protesting against the introduction of economic austerity measures. Discontent among the unions—particularly among the teachers—formed part of the background to the *coup* of October 1987 in which Sankara was overthrown and killed in another internal *coup* led by his one-time friend and colleague Captain Blaise Compaoré. Relations with the unions have since improved; pay and conditions have been reviewed and more than 1,000 dismissed teachers reinstated.

As of September 1988 there were four union centrals all affiliated to the OATUU (although the extent to which they were all functioning was unclear), and a number of autonomous unions. A new confederation, the General Confederation of Labour of Burkina Faso (CGTB) was established in October 1988, which grouped some half dozen autonomous unions. The new CGTB was said to have no political or religious affiliation.

Confédération Nationale des Travailleurs Burkinabés (CNTB)
National Confederation of Workers
(formerly Confédération Nationale des Travailleurs Voltaïques—CNTV)

Address. B.P. 445, Ouagadougou
International affiliation. OATUU.
Leadership. Emanuel Oudrago

Confédération Syndicale Burkinabè (CSB)
Trade Union Confederation of Burkina
(formerly Confédération des Syndicats Voltaïques—CSV)

Address. B.P. 299, Ouagadougou
Leadership. Yacinthe Onedrago (secretary general)
History and character. The CSB, apparently the most active of Burkina Faso's union organizations, was founded as the CSV by 20 independent unions in 1974. It was dissolved by decree by the

government of Col. Saye Zerbo on Nov. 24, 1981, and its secretary general, Soumane Touré, was arrested. The new CSP government released Touré, and abrogated the dissolution decree on Dec. 24, 1982. Touré was again arrested in May 1983 for his part in stirring student unrest to demand the release of Capt. Thomas Sankara, the leader of a faction within the CSP (*see above*). He was released after Sankara took power in August, but was subsequently arrested again in January 1985 for having stated that members of the ruling National Revolutionary Council were guilty of embezzlement. The CSB was affiliated to the Marxist Patriotic League for Development (Lipad), whose role in the government had been sharply reduced in the previous few months. The organization has come closer to the government since the overthrow of Thomas Sankara. The CSB held its fifth congress in May 1988 at which it demanded greater freedom and democracy, pay increases, and improvements in health care and education. Together with the representatives of the other centrals, the CSB presented a list of these and other grievances to the government after the congress.

International affiliation. OATUU.

Organisation Nationale des Syndicats Libres (ONSL)
National Organization of Free Trade Unions
(*formerly Organisation Voltaïque des Syndicats Libres—OVSL*)

Address. B.P. 99, Ouagadougou
International affiliations. ICFTU; OATUU.
Leadership. Boniface Kabore (secretary-general)
History and character. The ONSL was founded in 1960 and by 1983 its membership had risen to 6,000.

Union Syndicale des Travailleurs Burkinabés (USTB)
Trade Union Federation of the Working People of Burkina Faso
(*formerly Union Syndicale des Travailleurs Voltaïques—USTV*)

Address. B.P. 831, Ouagadougou
History and character. The USTB was founded (as the USTV) in 1947 as a branch of the French Confédération Générale du Travail (CGT), reorganized into the USTB in 1985 and claims to have 35,000 members in 45 affiliated organizations.

International affiliations. WFTU; OATUU.
Leadership. Boniface Samdah

Burundi

Capital: Bujumbura

Population: 5,450,000
(1989)

Political system. Burundi (formerly part of the Belgian-administered Ruanda-Urundi UN-trust territory) achieved full independence in 1962 as a kingdom, but following two successive *coups* in 1966 was declared a republic. Tribal antagonism between the Tutsi and the majority Hutu led to serious internal unrest between 1969 and 1972 and the confirmation of the Tutsi as the dominant influence in the country. Violence again flared in late 1988. The Party of the Union for National Progress (UPRONA, originally created in 1958) was formally recognized as the sole political party in a Constitution promulgated in 1974. President Jean-Baptiste Bagaza, who had led the country since 1976, was deposed on Sept. 3, 1987, in a military *coup*, and a Military Committee of National Salvation (MCNS) took power; UPRONA remaining the sole party.

In the early part of 1990 President Buyoya rejected a multi-party system for democracy within a single party. However an end to military rule was promised for the end of the year, and in December an extraordinary UPRONA Congress elected him as Chairman of a Party to replace the ruling Military Council for National Salvation.

Economy. The Burundi economy is centred almost exclusively on agriculture (largely subsistence) and is also conditioned by the country's landlocked position, its high density of population and its low per capita income. The principal cash crop is coffee (which accounts for some 90 per cent of export revenue but whose international markets and prices are subject to wide fluctuations), although tea is also being developed as a second export crop. Manufacturing, which accounts for only about 10 per cent of gross domestic product, is based mainly on the processing of agricultural products, and is principally small-scale, although there are some larger productive units in existence or under construction for the coffee, cotton/textiles and sugar industries.

Burundi's GNP per head is one of the lowest in Southern Africa. Only 7 per cent of the population lives in towns. Of the labour force, 92.9 per cent worked in agriculture in 1985–87—a proportion almost unchanged in 20 years, 1.6 per cent in industry, and 5.5 per cent in services.

System of industrial relations. Burundi has ratified neither ILO Convention No. 87 (Freedom of Association and Protection of the Right to Organize, 1948) nor No. 98 (Right to Organize and Collective Bargaining, 1949). Conventions 29 and 105 on forced labour were ratified in 1963, but the ILO has questioned the imposition of compulsory cultivation, porterage, public works, and penal labour.

Trade unionism. All previously existing unions were absorbed into the Union des Travailleurs du Burundi (UTB) in 1967, this being closely linked to the ruling party (UPRONA). A former organization, the Fédération des Syndicats Chrétiens Ouvriers et Paysans du Burundi (FSCOPB), founded in 1958 and associated with the Belgian Confédération des Syndicats Chrétiens (CSC), had been closely linked with the Hutu tribe, and many of its members had been killed in conflicts with the Tutsi (the ethnic basis of the UPRONA).

Union des Travailleurs du Burundi (UTB)
Union of Burundi Workers

Address. B.P. 1350, Bujumbura

Phone. 3850

Leadership. Marius Rurahenye (secretary general)

History and character. Since its inception in 1967, the UTB has been closely identified with the ruling régime. When President Bagaza was overthrown in September 1987, the union quickly affirmed its support for the new Military Committee for National Redemption. There are 18 affiliated sectoral organizations.

International affiliation. OATUU.

71

Cambodia

Capital: Phnom Penh

Population: 6,838,033
(1989)

Political system. The People's Republic of Kampuchea (PRK) was proclaimed in January 1979 following a military intervention by Vietnamese troops in support of Kampuchean resistance forces opposed to the ruling *Khmer Rouge* (Democratic Kampuchea) régime. Under its 1981 Constitution, the PRK is an independent sovereign state "moving step by step toward socialism". There is only one legal political party, the Kampuchean People's Revolutionary Party (KPRP). Despite controlling most of Kampuchea, the PRK government is not recognized by a majority of the member states of the United Nations, which instead recognizes the opposition Coalition Government of Democratic Kampuchea (CGDK) or Cambodia, formed in June 1982.

Fighting continued throughout the 1980s, with Russia and Vietnam backing the PRK government and China arming the *Khmer Rouge*. In 1989 the Vietnamese withdrew their troops. In 1990 the United Nations drew up a peace plan for Cambodia which it hoped would be acceptable to all the parties which had fought over the country's territory since 1982: the Vietnam-backed government of Hun Sen, and the three factions of the National Government of Cambodia—the *Khmer Rouge*, the supporters of Prince Sihanouk (former head of state), and the Khmer People's National Liberation Front (KPNLF). However these peace talks collapsed in June 1991.

Economy. The country's infrastructure, industrial sector and financial institutions were completely disrupted by war between 1970–75 and the subsequent programme of complete nationalization adopted by the *Khmer Rouge* government. Under its 1981 Constitution the PRK government directs the economy which is comprised of three sectors; state, co-operative and family (private). The country's first five-year plan was introduced at the fifth KPRP congress held in October 1985, with "export and thrift" as the primary economic guidelines. Cambodia was heavily, dependent on aid from the Soviet Union and Vietnam in the 1980s.

However, in 1991 the government reported that Soviet aid to Cambodia had been cut by 80 per cent compounding the difficulties caused by the poor rice harvest the previous year. It was reported to be looking for foreign companies to join in joint ventures in an attempt to reduce the chronic budget deficit.

System of industrial relations. Cambodia became a member of the International Labour Organization in 1969 but has ratified neither Convention No. 87 (Freedom of Association and Protection of the Right to Organize, 1948) nor No. 98 (Right to Organize and Collective Bargaining, 1949).

Trade unionism. A single-trade-union system is in place under government control.

Kampuchean Federation of Trade Unions (KFTU)

Address. Phnom-Penh
Leadership. Mat Ly (chairman, also a member of the politburo of the ruling KPRP); Chhim Nguon and Duong Savang (vice-chairmen)
History and character. The KFTU was founded following the establishment of the present régime in 1979. A political report delivered at the fifth congress of the ruling KPRP in October 1985

called for the building up of the KFTU as the "training school of the working class for economic and administrative management . . . (it) must take part in state management and in the management and defence of production bases". The KFTU held its second congress on Oct. 1–3, 1988, with the participation of 350 delegates representing trade union organizations throughout the country. The congress elected a new 49-member executive committee, and an 11-member permanent committee.

International affiliation. WFTU.

Cameroon

Capital: Yaoundé

Population: 9,540,000
(estimated mid-1984)

Political system. The United Republic of Cameroon was formally established in 1972 in succession to the Federal Republic of Cameroon; this in turn had been created in 1961 from the former trusteeship of French Cameroon (independent since 1960) and the British trusteeship of Southern Cameroons. The name of the country was changed in 1984 to the Republic of Cameroon. The sole legal party (which holds all the seats in the unicameral National Assembly) is the Rassemblement Démocratique du Peuple Camérounais (RDPC) which was established in 1985 to replace the Union Nationale Camérounaise; however, since 1987 rival lists of RDPC-approved candidates have been permitted. One of the principles of this former UNC was "to establish the union of all Cameroonians in peace, justice and solidarity" on the basis of "planned liberalism", the balanced development of the nation, self-sufficiency and "private initiative within the framework of the conditions of the national development plan".

Economy. Agriculture still represents the major sector of the economy, accounting for about a third of gross domestic product, but the industrial sector accounts for a further quarter. The principal agricultural exports, cocoa and coffee, are both subject to severe international market fluctuations. Industry is based principally on aluminium smelting, on the processing of raw agricultural materials and increasingly on oil production and refining. The sixth five-year programme (1986–91) aims to increase food self-sufficiency through agricultural modernization (with the goal of an eventual food surplus) and to encourage small and medium-sized industries and crafts.

In fact after 1986 Cameroon was unable to maintain its steady economic growth. Unemployment rose to an estimated 12 per cent and Cameroon became dependent on external loans. The situation will not be helped by a fast expanding workforce, and in April 1990 President Biya inaugurated a National Employment Fund to promote job creation. The fund is thought likely to aim at increased flexibility in the labour market.

System of industrial relations. Cameroon ratified ILO Convention No. 87 (Freedom of Association and Protection of the Right to Organize, 1948) in 1960 and Convention No. 98 (Right to Organize and Collective Bargaining, 1949) in 1962. Strikes are illegal where conciliation and arbitration procedures have not been exhausted and workers are restricted to joining unions affiliated to the sole trade union centre. Cameroon also ratified Conventions 29 and 105 on forced labour in 1960 and 1962, but the ILO has noted that compulsory communal work could be extracted under the country's Labour Code, and that legal provisions setting up the National Civic Service sanction the imposition of compulsory labour.

The Board of the Fund is tripartite in composition, and includes three employers' and two employees' representatives, selected from nominations by the most representative workers' organizations.

Trade unionism. Unions developed on the French model, with divisions along political lines, and at the beginning of the 1960s there were about 100 unions and several competing centres, including centres affiliated to the WFTU and the International Federation of Christian Trade Unions (IFCTU), the predecessor of the WCL. The number of unions fell rapidly during the 1960s and in 1971 the surviving four unions dissolved themselves to form the sole trade union centre (Syndicat Central Unique), subsequently known as the National Union of Cameroon Workers (Union Nationale des Travailleurs du Caméroun, UNTC), and now called the Organisation des Syndicats des Travailleurs Camérounais *(see below)*.

Organisation des Syndicats des Travailleurs Camerounais (OSTC)
Organization of Cameroon Workers' Unions

Address. B.P. 1610, Yaoundé

Leadership. Dominique Fouda Imah (president)

History and character. The UNTC held an extraordinary congress in December 1985 at which it was dissolved and the OSTC created in its place. The congress followed the appointment of the previous UNTC president, Jérôme-Emilien Abondo, as Minister of Defence. The centre is closely linked to the ruling party, the RCPD.

International affiliation. OATUU.

Canada

Capital: Ottawa **Population: 29,094,000**
(1989)

Political system. Canada was established as a British dominion in 1867 and is now a fully independent member of the Commonwealth. Under legislation enacted in 1981–82 the Canadian Constitution was "patriated" with the effect that Canada was enabled to amend its own Constitution in all respects. Canada has a bicameral parliament comprising an appointed Senate and an elected House of Commons. The Federal government was formed by the Liberal Party almost continuously from 1963 to 1984, when the Progressive Conservatives were returned to office with a large majority (being re-elected in 1988).

Economy. The Canadian economy is closely linked with that of the United States, and about 70 per cent of Canada's trade is with the USA. In the 1970s and early 1980s the then Liberal governments pursued a policy of economic nationalism, and a Foreign Investment Review Agency was established with a major aim of ensuring that any direct foreign investment in Canada was of significant benefit. Moreover, under the National Energy Programme it was intended to reduce from 70 to 50 per cent the foreign-owned share of the Canadian oil and gas industry. The Progressive Conservative government which came to office in 1984 abolished the FIRA and required only that new foreign investments should be of "net benefit". A US–Canadian free trade agreement began to operate in 1989, designed to eliminate over a 10-year period most cross-border tariffs on mutual trade in goods and services.

In 1989 Canada had a labour force of 13,503,000 of whom 12,486,000 were in civilian employment. Around 6,000,000 of the labour force were women.

System of industrial relations. The Canadian system of industrial relations is marked by decentralization and industrial militancy, though this does not generally take a political form. Some 90 per cent of all agreements are concluded between a single employer and a single union. Despite the lack of federal, provincial or even sectoral bargaining systems, more employees (possibly as many as 50 per cent) are covered by agreements than are members of unions. The legal framework is complicated by the existence of separate industrial jurisdictions for each of the country's 10 provinces, and in recent years unions have found sharp divergences in their standing under the law in different parts of the country.

While Canada ratified ILO Convention No 87 (Freedom of Association and Protection of the Right to Organize, 1948) in 1972 it has not ratified Convention No 98 (Right to Organize and Collective Bargaining, 1949). The ILO's first ever information and study mission visited Canada in September 1985, in response to a CLC complaint about the labour policies of Ontario, Alberta and Newfoundland. It subsequently found that all three provinces and British Columbia had restricted collective bargaining and the right to strike to a point unacceptable by ILO standards.

In 1989 the ILO brought two further criticisms to the Canadian government for violating the freedom of association convention in its use of the Back to Work legislation, once in June during a railway dispute and once in November concerning postal workers.

Labour legislation exists both at the federal and provincial levels. Ontario (with one third of the country's organized workers) introduced a 1988 Pay Equity Act which allowed comparability of jobs done predominantly by women with jobs done predominantly by men. By late 1989 dissatisfaction with its limited application had led the Pay Equity Commission to propose amendments to provide additional mechanisms of evaluation. The Province also passed a radical law compensating the disabled for lost working time and considered new health and safety legislation in 1989.

However in British Columbia, a 1987 law ("Bill 19") severely restricted the right to strike and created an Industrial Relations Commission with wide powers to intervene in disputes and impose arbitration. After a general strike and an attempt by the BC Attorney General to obtain an injunction to prevent a repetition of it, industrial relations calmed as unemployment fell and the Provincial Federation of Labour retreated from its militant stance.

In October 1989 the Supreme Court ruled in a dispute between Pacar of Canada and its unions that employers may unilaterally change working conditions when collective bargaining contracts expire. The Court had ruled in 1987 that the right to freedom of association did not include the right to strike. In a further blow to organized labour the Federal Court ruled in March 1990 that the reference to "life, liberty and security of the person" in the Canadian Charter of Rights does not imply the right to strike. There was however some consolation for the unions in that the Federal Court also found the heavy penalties imposed upon longshoremen under the government's "back to work" legislation to be unconstitutional.

Until 1988 Canada's unions mounted trenchant opposition to the Conservative government. Most unions continue to oppose the Canada – United States Free Trade Agreement (FTA) which came into force on Jan. 1, 1989 and in 10 years will remove all tariffs on 50 per cent of US or Canadian goods. Opposition to the FTA was a principal theme of the CLC's opposition to the Mulroney Conservatives in the 1988 election and the Congress publishes a monthly monitor of its effects, claiming the resultant loss of thousands of jobs, and mounting risk to Canada's social programmes.

The CLC also spearheaded an attack on the Goods and Services Tax and held a referendum on it in April 1990. However there was some mellowing of union opposition following the Conservatives' return to power: a meeting of Mr Mulroney and the CLC President was held in March 1989 (though not repeated) and the CLC rescinded its boycott of participation in state-sponsored organizations.

Trade unionism. In 1989, 36.2 per cent of the Canadian non-agricultural workforce was unionized (29.7 per cent of the civilian workforce), continuing the gradual fall from the 1983 peak of 40 per cent. In absolute terms however, union membership increased to 3,944,000 with a rise of 381,000 (10.7 per cent) over the same period. Union density is higher in the public than in the private sector, a development which occurred very rapidly between the mid-1960s and 1980 and which laid the basis for the later clashes of the unions with the Mulroney government and several provincial administrations. There are significant differences between the provinces with Quebec having the highest density at 41 per cent, and most industrial workers to be found there or in Ontario.

The three biggest unions, CUPE, the NUPGE and the PSA are all CLC affiliates in the public sector. The CAW reached fifth position by absorbing two unions active in the fishing industry. Another union to grow was the CLC-affiliated Canadian Union of Postal Workers which almost doubled its membership in 1989 following a ruling of the Canadian Labour Relations Board to the effect that workplace-based postal workers and letter carriers should be consolidated into one union. However the merger was opposed by a large number of members of the Letter Carriers Union of Canada which formerly organized them.

Quebec unions — which have a centre of their own — have expressed particular concern about the dominance of English in industrial relations at a time when 80 per cent of the province's workforce is French-speaking. They wish to see tighter monitoring of companies' observation of the "French promotion programme" prescribed by legislation.

The major Canadian national centre is the Canadian Labour Congress (CLC), formed in 1956 with a membership of 2,200,000, some 58 per cent of organized workers. It supports the New Democratic Party whose "social democratic principles go to the heart of our being" according to its president Shirley Carr. Other centres are the Quebec-based Centrale des Syndicats Nationaux (CSN), with 235,000 members from which the Confédération des Syndicats Démocratiques (CSD with 45,000 members) broke away; the non-partisan Canadian Federation of Labour (225,000 members) and the Confederation of Canadian Unions (CCU) with 35,000 members. The US-based Teamsters union had a 100,000-strong Canadian branch in 1989. There are also important unions in teaching and the health service without affiliation either to a Canadian or American centre, such as the Quebec Teaching Congress which had affiliated 102,314 members in 1989.

In 1989 Canada had 917 unions in all divided between national (i.e. Canada-based) organizations (228), International (i.e. United States-based) organizations (63), and 626 organizations which were either indirectly chartered or independent locals.

Links to USA. Initially the Canadian labour movement was most closely linked to that of Britain but subsequently the relationship with the United States became more dominant. With many Canadian plants owned by firms based in the United States, it is not surprising that cross-border union links have been strong, but the trend is for Canadian unions to split away. The CAW left the United Auto Workers in 1985, after 50 years' affiliation following years of disagreement over the Canadians' demand for full national control of wage bargaining, strike authorization and staff appointments. The schism followed breakaways from the United Paperworkers' International Union in 1974, and the Oil, Chemical and

Atomic Workers' Union in 1980 as well as rupturing of international links among woodworkers and food workers.

Membership of international unions (many affiliated to the AFL – CIO) fell from over half of all unionists in the early 1970s to its lowest ever level of 6.9 per cent in 1989, when there were thought to be 63 of them. Compared with 1980 the numbers represented by international unions were down by 294,000 to 1,300,000.

Canadian Labour Congress (CLC)
Congrès du Travail du Canada

Address. 2841 Riverside Drive, Ottawa KIV 8X7
Phone. (613) 521-3400
Telex. 053-4750
Fax. (613) 521 4605
Leadership. Shirley Carr (president); Richard Mercier (secretary-treasurer)
Membership. 2,200,000
History and character. The CLC was formed in 1956 by the merger of the former Trades and Labour Congress (TLC) with the Canadian Congress of Labour (CCL). The TLC represented mainly craft unions and the CCL mainly industrial unions, in both cases with their affiliates having international headquarters predominantly in the United States. But by 1983 the three largest affiliates were all public sector unions, the PSA, CUPE and NUPGE, with the United Steelworkers of America fourth largest.

The CLC supports the New Democratic Party and its policies tend to correspond to the social democratic outlook of that organization. Unlike other Canadian national centres the CLC has affiliates whose members pay a proportion of their membership dues to the party. It is the largest Canadian centre, with 57.8 per cent of unionized workers in 1989 affiliated to its member unions. Following the 1988 election there was a clash between CLC affiliates over relations with the NDP, but no change resulted.

The CLC Convention met in Montreal in May 1990 attended by 2,000 delegates. It adopted two major documents to guide CLC resistance to what the Congress calls the Big Business Conservative Agenda: *A Plan of Political Action* was passed unanimously while *A New Decade: Our Future* was adopted in principle as the basis of a discussion until the 1992 Congress, scheduled to be held in Vancouver.

Structure. Some 90 unions are affiliated in all and convene biennially to discuss federal matters and make policy. Much of the time of the CLC office is spent lobbying at the federal level for legislation based on these policies. There is a provincial federation of labour in each province and there are local labour councils organized on similar principles. The CLC is predominantly English-speaking, but the francophone minority in Canada is recognized by the simultaneous publication of all documents in both languages. A Women's Bureau was established in 1972 reflecting the increasing size and importance of female membership. The CLC is committed to affirmative action and voted overwhelmingly for the freedom of choice for women over abortion at its 1988 convention.

Affiliated unions. There are about 90 affiliates including those constituted as Canadian branches of United States international unions. Details of the major affiliates follow. Unions affiliated to the AFL – CIO are marked with an asterisk.

1. **Amalgamated Clothing and Textile Workers' Union**, 601–615 Gervais Drive, Don Mills, Ontario M3C 1Y8
   Phone: (1) 416 441 1806; (1) 800 268 4064.
   Fax: (1) 416 441 9680.
   Leadership: Jack Sheinkman (president); John Alleruzzo (Canadian director).
   Membership: 25,000 (Canada).
   Publications: *Labour Unity*; *Action*.

2. **Canadian Brotherhood of Railway, Transport and General Workers**, 2300 Carling Avenue, Ottawa K2B 7G1.

Phone: (613) 829 8764.
Fax: (613) 829 6815.
Leadership: J.D. Hunter (president).

3. **Canadian Paperworkers' Union**, 255 St Jacques St. West, Montreal, Quebec H2Y 1M6.
Phone: (514) 842-8931.
Fax: (514) 843 5712.
Leadership: Donald Holder (president).
Membership: 65,000.
Publication: *CPU Journal*.

4. **Canadian Union of Public Employees**, 21 Florence Street, Ottawa, Ontario, K2P OW6.
Phone: (613) 237-1590.
Fax: (613) 237-5508.
Leadership: Jeff Rose (national president).
Membership: 356,000 (1989).
History and structure: CUPE is Canada's largest union, formed in 1963 by a merger of the National Union of Public Service Employees and the National Union of Public Employees. It has some 2,200 locals covering all the country's 10 provinces.

5. **Communications and Electrical Workers' Union of Canada**, 141 Laurier Avenue West, Suite 906, Ottawa K1P 5J3.
Phone: (613) 236-6083.
Leadership: Fred Pomeroy (president).

6. **Energy and Chemical Workers Union (ECWU)**, 9940–106 Street, Suite 202, Edmonton, Alberta T5K 2N2.
Phone: (403) 422 7932.
Fax: (403) 424 2505.
Leadership: R.C. Basken (president).
Membership: 35,000.
History and character: The ECWU was formed in 1980 by a merger of the Canadian Chemical Workers Union and the US-based Oil, Chemical and Atomic Workers' International Union.
Publication: *The Journal*.

7. **International Association of Machinists and Aerospace Workers**, 331 Cooper Street, Suite 600, Ottawa K2P OG5.
Leadership: Valerie Bourgeois (vice-president).

8. **International Woodworkers of America**, 2088 Weston Road, Weston, Ontario M9N 1X4.
Leadership: J.J. Munro (president).

9. **National Automobile, Aerospace and Agricultural Implement Workers Union of Canada (Canadian Auto Workers, CAW)**, 205 Placer Court, North York, Ontario, M2H 3H9.
Phone: (416) 497-4110.
Fax: (495) 6559.
Leadership: Robert White (president).
Membership: The CAW was boosted in 1989 by the adherence of two fishermens' unions, making it the fifth largest in Canada and bringing it to 160,000.
History and structure: The CAW was founded in September 1985 after splitting from the United Auto Workers based in Detroit.

10. **National Union of Provincial Government Employees**, 2841 Riverside Drive, Suite 204, Ottawa, Ontario, KIV 8N4.
Phone: (613) 526-1663.
Fax: (613) 526-0477.
Leadership: James Clancy (national president).
Membership: 297,200 (1989).
History and structure: NUPGE is Canada's second largest union. It has 13 components, including unions representing provincial government employees in nine of the country's

provinces. In Quebec its presence is via associate membership of the Syndicat des Professionelles et Professionels du Gouvernement du Québec (SPGQ).

11. **Public Service Alliance of Canada**, 233 Gilmour Street, Ottawa, Ontario K2P OP1.
    Phone: (613) 560 4200.
    Fax: (613) 567 0385.
    Leadership: Daryl Bean (president).
    Membership: 171,900 (1989).

12. **Service Employees' International Union**, 1 Credit Union Drive, Toronto, Ontario M4A 2S6.
    Phone: (416) 752-4770.
    Leadership: S E Roscoe (vice-president).

13. **United Food and Commercial Workers' International Union***, 61 International Boulevard, Rexdale, Ontario M9W 6K4.
    Phone: (416) 675 1104.
    Fax: (416) 675-6919.
    Leadership: Clifford Evans (Canadian director).
    Membership: 160,000 (Canada).

14. **United Steelworkers of America***, 234 Eglinton Avenue East, 7th floor, Toronto, Ontario M4P 1K7.
    Phone: (416) 487-1571.
    Fax: (416) 482 5548.
    Leadership: Gérard Docquier (national director for Canada).
    Membership: 160,000.
    Publication: *CLC Today/CTC Aujourd' hui* (a news magazine published 10 times a year, circulation 20,000).
    International affiliations: ICFTU; ORIT (some affiliates are also directly affiliated to international trade secretariats of the ICFTU); TUAC.

Canadian Federation of Labour (CFL)

Address. 107 Sparks Street, Suite 300, Ottawa, Ontario KIP 5B5
Phone. (613) 234-4141
Fax. (613) 234-5188
Leadership. James A. McCambly (president); Austin Thorne (secretary-treasurer)
Membership. 225,000
History and structure. Founded in 1982, the CFL is a national centre whose 14 affiliates have members in all parts of Canada and most industrial sectors. Its aim is to promote the interests of Canadian workers through direct, regular, non-partisan involvement in national affairs. To this end it sponsors "Working Ventures Canadian Fund Inc.", a venture capital fund designed to help employees take a more pro-active role in economic activities through investment in growth-oriented enterprises, new job creation and shares in the rewards of ownership. This Fund is the first national labour-sponsored venture capital found in Canada. The CFL president, James McCambly, was before 1982 the executive secretary of the executive board for the country's 14 building trades unions.

The executive council comprises the president and secretary-treasurer plus one vice-president for each affiliated union and provincial council of labour of which there are 10. The provincial councils represent affiliates and their members in all provincial matters, especially legislation.

Affiliated unions. The 14 affiliates of the CFL are as follows: International Association of Heat and Frost Insulators and Asbestos Workers; International Brotherhood of Boilermakers, Iron Ship Builders, Blacksmiths, Forgers and Helpers; International Union of Bricklayers and Allied Craftsmen; International Brotherhood of Electrical Workers; International Union of Elevator Constructors; International Union of Operating Engineers; International Brotherhood of Painters and Allied Trades; Operative Plasterers' and Cement Masons' International Association; Sheet Metal Workers' International Association; United Association of Journeymen and Apprentices of the Plumbing and Pipe Fitting Industry of the United States and Canada; Canadian Association of

Professional Radio Operators; Manitoba Association of Health Care Professionals; Canadian Health Care Guild (formerly the Alberta Association of Registered Nursing Assistants); Canadian Office Employees Union.

Centrale des Syndicats Démocratiques (CSD)
Centre of Democratic Trade Unions

Address. 801, 4c rue, Québec City, Québec G1J 2T7

Phone. (418) 529-2956

Leadership. Claude Gingras (president); Robert Legare (secretary); Jeannot Picaird (treasurer).

Membership. There are 43,700 paid-up members, 80 per cent of whom are male, in 425 local unions.

History and character. The CSD was founded in 1972 following a rift in the Confédération des Syndicats Nationaux (*see below*) over organizational and ideological issues. CSD is non-partisan and practises direct democracy.

Structure. The 307 non-federated affiliates are organized into seven sectoral sub-groups. There are, in addition, three non-affiliated federations. There is an executive committee (president, vice-president and secretary-treasurer), a steering committee, plenary assembly and a congress.

Publication. La Base.

Confederation of Canadian Unions (CCU)

Address. 13311/2, St Clair Avenue West, Toronto, Ontario M6E 1C3

Leadership. Garry Worth (president); John B. Lang (secretary-treasurer)

Membership. 15 affiliated unions with 35,000 members in all.

History and character. Founded in 1969 as a rank and file controlled confederation.

Confédération des Syndicats Nationaux (CSN)
Confederation of National Trade Unions

Address. 1601 Ave de Lorimier, Montréal, Québec H2K 4M5

Phone. (514) 598-2121

Telex. 055-60905

Fax. (514) 598 2052

Leadership. Gérald Larose (president); Pierre Paquette (secretary general)

Membership. 250,000 (50 per cent women). Although the CSN has a Canada-wide charter, the vast majority of its membership is in the (mainly French-speaking) province of Québec, which has a labour force of about 3,000,000.

History and character. The CSN originated in Sept. 1921 as the Confédération des Travailleurs Catholiques du Canada (CTCC, Confederation of Catholic Workers of Canada). The two main influences in the subsequent development of the CTCC were the efforts of the Catholic clergy to create confessional unions, and the nationalist resistance within the union movement to the attempt of the American Federation of Labour to control Canadian trade unionism. Membership in the organization—which was at that time concentrated mostly in the textile, clothing, pulp and paper, and metalworking industries, and the retail trades—had reached 94,000 by 1960, when the CTCC became officially secular and changed its name to the CSN.

The CSN's membership more than doubled form 1960 to 1970 with the unionization of the public sector in Québec. There was a split in 1972, with more conservative unions opposing the confrontation between the CSN and the Québec government, and breaking away to form the CSD (see above). Membership fell to 160,000 in 1976, but has grown steadily since then, with expansion in the public and private sectors. By 1990 it had reached 250,000.

Structure. As of January 1991 there were 2,047 affiliated local unions (*syndicats*). These unions each have a regional affiliation to one of 22 regional councils (*conseils centraux*) and a sectoral or professional affiliation to one of nine member industrial federations: Federation for Social Affairs; Federation for Commerce; CSN — Construction; National Communications Federation; Metalworkers Federation; Paper and Forest Workers Federation; Professionals and Managers

Federation of Quebec; Public Service Workers Federation; National Federation of Teachers in Quebec.

Policies. The CSN favours democratic socialism. Current major issues are: (i) the creation of jobs through reductions in working hours, negotiated introduction of new technology, and policies favouring growth in the processing of raw materials and a more dynamic role for state-owned corporations; (ii) positive discrimination programmes to favour the employment of women, young people and other minorities; (iii) the protection and expansion of state welfare schemes; and (iv) the use of sectoral bargaining to extend the benefits of unionization to non-unionized areas. At its 1990 Congress, the CSN was given a mandate to support and promote the political independence of Quebec.

The CSN is currently opposing the plans of the federal government to liberalize trade with the USA; these plans would expose Québec's industrial base to competition from frequently more efficient US manufacturers, while potentially benefiting western provinces of Canada producing raw materials.

The CSN's constitution prohibits it from being affiliated to, aligned with or giving support to any political party.

Representation on government bodies. The CSN sits on several consultative bodies at both federal and provincial level, including the Canadian Employment and Immigration Commission and the Commission de la Santé et de la Sécurité au Travail du Québec. It is also part of the Canadian delegation to the ILO.

Publication. Nouvelles-CSN (fortnightly bulletin, circulation 35,000).

International affiliation. TUAC. The CSN was affiliated to the WCL from 1946 to 1986 (serving as the WCL's representative in North America), but ended its affiliation as of June 1986.

Cape Verde

Capital: Cidade de Praia   **Population: 369,000**

Political system. Cape Verde became formally independent of Portugal in 1975, it being initially intended that the islands should become fully integrated with Guinea-Bissau (whose independence had been recognized by Portugal in 1974). After the independence of both territories the African Party for the Independence of Guinea and Cape Verde (PAIGC) continued to operate in both countries; however, following the adoption of a separate Cape Verdian Constitution in 1980 and the overthrow of the existing government in Guinea-Bissau two months later, a separate African Party for the Independence of Cape Verde (PAICV) was formed in early 1981 and the Constitution was amended to exclude all references to the issue of union with Guinea-Bissau.

Until 1991 Cape Verde had a unicameral Parliament nominated on a single list drawn up by the PAICV. However in September 1990 the ruling PAICV agreed to constitutional reform which separated party and state. In January 1991 elections were held for the 79-member Assembly which resulted in victory for the newly formed Movement for Democracy (MPD); in February 1991 the Presidential elections were won by Antonio Monteiro and he took office in March.

Economy. Cape Verde has few natural resources. Some three-quarters of the population are dependent upon subsistence agriculture, but prolonged periods of drought have necessitated the import of over 90 per cent of food requirements, a large proportion of it under aid programmes. Much of the rural workforce is under-employed. Together with foreign aid, a major contribution to the economy is made from remittances from nationals working or residing abroad (who are estimated to number nearly 1,000,000), although the flow of such remittances has recently been rather stagnant. Fish processing and canning provide a limited amount of employment.

Carlos Veiga, Prime Minister of the new democratic government promised his government would struggle against "sub-human living conditions" by concentrating on promoting fishing, tourism, services production and industry.

System of Industrial Relations. Cape Verde has not ratified ILO Convention No. 87 (Freedom of Association and Protection of the Right to Organize, 1984) but ratified Convention No. 98 (Right to Organize and Collective Bargaining, 1949) in 1979.

Trade unionism. There appears to have been no organized trade union activity before independence from Portugal.

The monopolistic position of he UNTC-CS may be at risk following the defeat of the PAICV in the January 1991 Assembly elections.

União Nacional dos Trabalhadores de Cabo Verde—Central Sindical (UNTC-CS) Trade Unions of Cape Verde Unity Centre

Address. BP 123, Praia, São Taigo
Leadership. Julio Ascensao Silva (general secretary)
History. On May Day 1976 the Organizing Commission of Cape Verde Unions was formed as a complement to the Guinea-Bissau National Union of Workers (UNTG). Two years later the UNTC-CS was established; it is the only union centre and is closely associated with the ruling (and sole legal) party, the PAICV.
International affiliation. OATUU.

Central African Republic

Capital: Bangui   **Population: 2,951,000**

Political system. The French territory of Ubangui-Shari became a self-governing republic within the French Community in 1958 as the Central African Republic and gained full independence in 1960. Jean-Bedel Bokassa assumed power in 1966, and from 1976 ruled as Emperor of the Central African Empire. In 1979 he was deposed by David Dacko who was himself overthrown in a bloodless military *coup* in 1981 by André Kolingba. The Military Committee of National Recovery formed in 1981 was dissolved in 1985 when a predominantly civilian Cabinet was appointed. A fresh Constitution introduced in 1986 provided for the establishment of the Reassemblement Démocratique Centrafricaine as a sole legal party, which accordingly in 1987 won all the seats in a newly created National Assembly.

During 1990 it came under some pressure to permit a multi-party system but, following a special party congress in October, rejected it. However, the appointment in March 1991 of Edouard Flank as Prime Minister was presented by President Kolingba as evidence of the Republic's "determination to pursue the democratic process".

Economy. The economy stagnated in 1980–83, particularly in 1983, due to drought, and although in 1984 output in both agricultural and non-agricultural areas increased, subsequent low world commodity prices and currency fluctuations had serious consequences for the external balance. A government programme was launched in 1986 to stimulate investment and output in the productive sectors of the economy, coupled with continued action to restrain public consumption. In 1985–87, 83.7 per cent of the labour force was engaged in agriculture (mainly subsistence), 2.8 per cent in industry, and 13.5 per cent in services.

System of industrial relations. Several labour federations were in existence at the time of independence in 1960, and the Central African Republic ratified ILO Convention No. 87 (Freedom of Association and Protection of the Right to Organize, 1948) in 1960 and Convention No. 98 (Right to Organize and Collective Bargaining, 1949) in 1964.

The Central African Republic ratified Conventions 29 and 105 on forced labour in 1960 and 1964, but the ILO has noted that legal provisions in respect of the suppression of idleness remain for the imposition of compulsory labour and farming, and that forced labour may be imposed as a punishment for political dissidence. The ILO has expressed serious concern at the continuing breaches of its conventions on freedom of organization ratified by the government but not honoured.

Trade unionism. Under Bokassa, the General Union of Workers of Central Africa (Union Générale des Travailleurs du Centrafrique, UGTC), with its affiliated occupational federations, was the sole permitted organization. In 1973 and again in 1977 general secretaries of the UGTC were dismissed as a result of their participation in anti-government activities. As of 1979 the UGTC, which was an ICFTU affiliate, had 15,000 members. In response to internal unrest President Dacko suspended the right to strike in early 1980; in May 1981 he dissolved the UGTC after it attempted to break the ban on strikes, and announced the formation of a new body, the National Confederation of Central African Workers (CNTC). However, all trade union activities were suspended after the military *coup* in September 1981. Since then the CNTC appears to have resumed functioning, but it has had a precarious existence. The confederation's secretary general was reported to have been seriously harassed by vigilantes of the ruling party in February 1988.

Confédération Nationale des Travailleurs du Centrafrique (CNTC)
National Confederation of Central African Workers

Address. BP 2141, Bangui
Leadership. Jean-Richard Sandos Oualanga (secretary-general)

Chad

Capital: N'Djaména   **Population: 5,273,000**
                                                                    (1987)

Political system. Chad became a self-governing republic within the French Community in 1958 and achieved full independence in 1960. Following an army *coup* in 1975 (when the National Assembly was dissolved) there ensued a prolonged intensification of internal dissension and secessionist movements, and various agreements on national unity all proved short-lived. Fighting again broke out in 1983 in the north between governmental and Libyan-backed forces. An agreement reached in 1984 on a withdrawal of Libyan troops remained largely unimplemented. President Habré's forces gradually consolidated their hold over major parts of the centre and south, although factional conflict continued in these areas. A ceasefire was agree in late 1987, but this too was largely unobserved.

Economy. Since the 1970s the Chadian economy has been almost continuously disrupted by civil conflict, and the situation has been severely aggravated by drought conditions, interrupted on occasion by torrential rains which have broken communications links. Some 90 per cent of the population is occupied in agriculture (largely subsistence, together with livestock rearing and nomadic herding) and fishing in the richly stocked Lake Chad. Industry, based mainly on agricultural products, accounts for only about 4 per cent of gross domestic product. Chad is among the countries with the lowest gross national product per head, and is heavily dependent on external financial assistance for economic survival.

The second phase of an IMF/World Bank structural adjustment programme was inaugurated in May 1991 and was expected to include wide-scale privatization and slimming down of the public sector. There is no welfare state and many public services are thought to be earmarked for privatization.

System of industrial relations. Chad ratified ILO Convention No. 87 (Freedom of Association and Protection of the Right to Organize, 1948) in 1960 and Convention No. 98 (Right to Organize and Collective Bargaining, 1949) in 1961. The ILO has welcomed government undertakings to reform the Labour Code so as to halt official intervention into collective bargaining. It has also requested the repeal of the measures prohibiting trade unions from political activity, suspending strike action nationwide, and prohibiting unionization among public employees. Chad ratified Conventions 29 and 105 on forced labour in 1960 and 1961, but the ILO has noted that legal provisions persist for the exaction of forced labour for penal purposes, including punishment for participation in strike action.

Trade unionism. French unions maintained branches in Chad before independence in 1960. Strikes have been illegal since 1975 and public employees have been barred from trade union membership since 1976. Trade unions are also prohibited from engaging in political activity, and while collective bargaining is permitted, collective agreements require government approval.

Before 1988 there were two trade union centres, the Trade Union Confederation of Chad (CST) and the National Union of Workers of Chad (UNATRAT) which reflected tribal and geographical cleavages. A great deal of their energy was absorbed by rivalry and eventually a decision was taken to establish a national negotiating team to achieve unity. In November 1988 the National Union of Chadian Trade Unions (UNST) was launched under a new general secretary.

Union Nationale des Syndicats de Tchad (UNST)
National Union of Chadian Trade Unions

Leadership. Laoujoura Sa-N'Doudijnang (general secretary)

Membership. Estimated at 40,000, of whom 16,000 are in the private sector.

History and character. The UNST was formed by a merger of the tribally and geographically divided CST and UNATRAT in November 1988. Its chief objectives include the building of a trade union culture in Chad and the extension of membership into a large part of the public sector. To this end it launched the Federation of Planning Ministry Workers in 1990 and proposes to open a new federation for employees of the agricultural ministry. In 1990 and 1991 UNST ran a series of union training courses, with assistance from the Public Services International, intended to develop collective bargaining skills. Some 1,000 public sector workers had been trained by January 1991.

Chile

Capital: Santiago   **Population: 12,900,000**

Political system. As a result of elections in 1970 the Christian Democratic government of Eduardo Frei was succeded by a left-wing coalition headed by Salvador Allende. This latter, however, was overthrown in 1973 in a military *coup*, following which Congress was dissolved and the country was administered by a military junta. The junta's leader, Gen. Augusto Pinochet, was in 1981 inaugurated as President for an eight-year term under a new Constitution which also among other things formally prohibited Marxist and totalitarian groups and removed the rights of employees of the state and in essential public services to strike. During the 1980s there were increasing signs of opposition, manifested in demonstrations, strikes, acts of violence and calls by anti-government groupings for an early transition to full democracy, and for periods the country was under states of emergency or siege. Political parties were in 1984 allowed to function under certain circumstances and in 1987 formally to register. A referendum in 1988 failed to endorse an eight-year extension of President Pinochet's term of office, and presidential and legislative elections were held in December 1989. These resulted in the election of the Christian Democrat Patricio Aylwin at the head of a coalition of centre-left parties.

Economy. Following the military takeover in 1973 the junta embarked on a reversal of the policies of the Allende administration, including the return to private ownership of many of the enterprises nationalized during the previous three years, the encouragement of foreign investment, the dismantling of many import barriers and the adoption of a fully free-market economic system.

The later 1980s were marked by rapid economic growth in Chile, averaging more than six per cent in the six years to 1989. In 1989 the actual figure was 10 per cent, sharply reducing the unemployment rate to five per cent at one point, with mining, industry and transport showing the biggest take up of jobs. In 1989 real wages rose by 3.1 per cent though that year's inflation was 2.14 per cent. Of 4,430,000 civilian employees, 1,000,000 are employed in industry, 1,340,000 in services, and 2,040,000 in agriculture.

System of industrial relations. Chile has never ratified either ILO Convention No. 87 (Freedom of Association and Protection of the Right to Organize, 1948) or No. 98 (Right to Organize and Collective Bargaining, 1949).

At the end of October 1978 the government ordered elections for unions in the private sector, the first such elections since 1973. Announcing the elections (for which four days' notice was given), the government stated that to ensure the "depoliticization of the unions", no current office holder could stand for re-election; no one who had been active in party politics or a member of a political party in the past 10 years would be allowed to stand; there would be no formal presentation of candidates; and that the Labour Ministry had the power to annul any election result if the chosen candidate was found to be a "militant". According to official figures, 450,000 workers took part in the elections.

Government decrees in July 1979 restored a limited right to strike for the first time since 1973. These decrees: (i) revoked a special statue protecting the job security of copper miners; (ii) made trade union affiliation and the payment of union dues voluntary; (iii) allowed collective bargaining but restricted the bargaining arena to the individual workplace (thereby undermining the peasant unions, which had been organized on the basis of contracts covering farm workers by provincial district); (iv) stipulated that a strike could be called only if approved by a secret ballot and after compulsory arbitration; and (v) limited strikes to a maximum period of 60 days, the employer having the right to declare a lock-out and hire other labour after 30 days. Strikes were prohibited in any sector connected with national security, public services, the "normal supply of the market" or the "public interest". The essential elements of the decrees were subsequently entrenched in a new constitution which took effect in 1981 after approval in a referendum the previous year. The first legal strike under the new regulations was held in the El Teniente copper mine in April 1981.

In July 1987 Chile codified 12 employment laws but in such a way that unions continued to complain that their activities were fragmented under legislative pressure. President Pinochet did not respond to these complaints, but the Aylwin régime was committed to labour law reform. It introduced draft legislation into Congress from May 1990 onwards to legitimize the formation, of central union organizations and regulate their finances, permit industry-wide collective bargaining, and eliminate unjustified dismissals.

Even under the unreformed Code there were more than 2,300 collective agreements in 1989, many of them of two years' duration. Strikes were brief and relatively few and there was no compulsory arbitration in the 25 strategic industries in which strikes are not permitted. In May 1990 the CUT met the employers' organization CPC and the government to make a three-way agreement governing labour/management relations which: recognized the need for economic growth and the primacy of private enterprises; acknowledged that both sides of industry had the right to protect their own interest; and emphasized discussion and negotiation as the preferred means of resolving disputes.

Trade unionism. Trade unionism took strong roots in Chile and the first centre, the Federation of Chilean Workers (Federación Obrera de Chile, FOCH), was formed in 1909. Legalized trade unionism and collective bargaining developed in the 1930s under the Popular Front government, and in 1936 the Confederación de Trabajadores de Chile (CTCH) was created; this, however, broke into socialist and communist factions during the 1940s. A reunified centre, the Central Única de Trabajadores de Chile (Central Union of Workers, CUT), was created in 1953, its membership including Christian Democrats, socialists and communists.

In 1970 the CUT strongly backed the accession to power of Allende, and several CUT leaders became ministers in the Allende government. Industrial unrest in the copper mines and strikes by lorry owners and other small businessmen destabilized the Allende government, paving the way for the 1973 *coup*, following which the CUT was banned. Strikes were declared illegal, collective bargaining suspended and some unions disbanded. Numerous trade unionists were executed, imprisoned or exiled, and the government intervened actively in the surviving unions by controlling their assets or appointing their officers.

Opposition to the Pinochet government has been marked since 1981, in part reflecting an economic crisis which followed several years of successful economic performance. In February 1982 Tuscapel Jiménez, the leader of the union of public employees, was found murdered shortly after announcing plans to establish a broad-based trade union front to oppose the government's economic policies. In May 1983 the copper workers' union, the CTC, led a day of national protest, which led to widespread arrests of trade unionists and others. Following this 60 labour leaders including those of the CTC formed a coalition of labour groups opposed to the régime known as the National Workers' Command (CNT) to campaign for "the re-establishment of democracy and the free exercise of labour rights", and immediately initiated a long series of days of protest, which frequently triggered violence and mass arrests. Its co-founders included the National Trade Union Co-Ordinating Body (CNS), the ICFTU-backed Democratic Workers' Centre (Central Democrática de Trabajadores, CDT), the Confederation of Private Sector Workers (CEPCH) and the United Workers' Front (Frente Unitario de Trabajadores, FUT). The CNT embraced both left-wing and Christian Democratic elements, and although officially illegal established itself as the effective major trade union centre in the country.

Following disturbances associated with two days of protest called by the CNT in September 1985 the leaders were arrested and charged with violations of the national security law; Rodolfo Seguel (the copper workers' leader) and CNT general secretary Arturo Marínez were released on Nov. 27, 1985, after further protests called by the CNT on Nov. 5–6 in which four people died, and their own participation in a hunger strike, but Manuel Bustos Huerta of the CNS was kept in detention until January 1986.

An attempt by the CNT to hold its first national convention in April 1986 was prevented by the government. Thereafter in an effort to improve the effectiveness of trade union opposition, the CNT worked towards the creation of a pluralistic single trade union confederation, and its efforts bore some fruit with the formation of the CUT in 1988.

Despite being technically illegal under pre-1990 legislation, there were by 1990 three national union centres in Chile, the Unified Workers' Centre (CUT), the Democratic Workers' Centre (CDT) and the Chilean Workers Central (CTCh). With union density assessed at 11 per cent, some 50 per cent of all unionists are affiliated to the CUT, which inherited its acronym from the centre of pre-Pinochet years, and which survived an early challenge from the Pinochet régime when its leadership was sent into internal exile. The CDT was in 1990 divided between factions favouring closer political involvement (and greater distance from the Communists) and preferring a closer relationship with the CUT. The CTCh was led by figures closely associated with Pinochet and is strongly attached to private enterpise. The most significant individual union remains the Confederation of Copper Workers (CTC).

Central Unitaria de Trabajadores (CUT)
Unified Workers' Centre

Address. Santa Monica 2015, Santiago

Leadership. Manuel Bustos (president)

History and character. The CUT was formed by a conference of trade unionists from the National Workers' Command (CNC), the National Campesino Confederation, and the (previously unaffiliated) Teachers' Union in Santiago in August 1988. Its first President was Manuel Bustos of the CNS and its first Vice-President Arturo Matínez of the CNT. These leaders were sent into internal exile in September 1988 for calling a strike the previous year and not released until the autumn of 1989. The CUT backed the candidature of President Aylwin in 1989 and organizes more than half of Chile's trade unionists and has held discussions with a faction of the CDT with a view to merger.

International affiliation. The CUT has an ICFTU co-ordination committee but no affiliation. It received a WFTU delegation in May 1989 and some individual unions are affiliated to the WFTU.

Central Democratica de Trabajadores (CDT)
Democratic Workers' Centre

History and character. Like the CUT and CDT was in opposition to the Pinochet régime during its last years, and lost the affiliation of the National Campesino Confederation to the larger body in 1988. In January 1990 it split into two factions when an attempt was made to expel its President Eduardo Ríos for his criticisms of the Aylwin election platform. Ríos survived this attempt and also remained leader of the dockers' union. The leader of the rival faction Hernol Flores announced in April 1990 that it would open merger talks with the CUT.

International affiliation: ICFTU.

Central de Trabajadores Chilena (CTCh)
Chilean Workers Central

History and character. The CTCh was formed in March 1989 by a number of unions which had been members of the Economic and Social Council which President Pinochet established in 1984. They oppose partisan domination of unions and links with the Communist Party.

Confederación de Trabajadores del Cobre (CTC)
Confederation of Copper Workers

Address. Mac-Iver 283, Quinto Piso, Santiago
Phone. 392776-380835-331449
Membership. 20,000 (1983) in nine unions
Publication. Revista De Los Trabajadores Del Cobre.
History and character. A day of national protest called by the CTC in May 1983 led to the deaths of two demonstrators and the arrest of 10 leading members of the CTC, including the president, Rodolfo Seguel. Following strikes in the copper mines, Seguel was released but stripped by the government of his post as president of the union, although his dismissal was not acknowledged by the union. Seguel was re-arrested in Sept. 1983 but released later the same month, and spent a further two months in detention from Sept. 1985.

In early 1986 Seguel and other CTC leaders were re-elected by the union's congress despite court orders barring them from taking part in trade union activities, but Seguel stepped down in Nov. 1986.

In April 1989 the CTC convention elected a new Christian Democratic leadership in preference to the Left Alliance. After the failure of negotiations between these factions, the Christian Democrats filled all official posts.

China

Capital: Beijing   **Population: 1,112,298,677**

Political system. The People's Republic of China was formally established in 1949 with the final defeat on the mainland of the Nationalist forces of Generalissimo Chiang Kai-shek by the Communist forces led by Mao Tse-tung (Mao Zedong). Under the 1982 Constitution the People's Republic is defined as "a socialist state under the people's democratic dictatorship led by the working class and based on the alliance of the workers and peasants". Although in the preamble the Communist Party is described as leading a broad patriotic front composed of democratic parties and people's organizations and embracing all socialist working people, it is not given any special status in the main articles of the Constitution. Nevertheless, effective overall control is exercised by the Communist Party. The National People's Congress elected indirectly in 1988 was composed as to nearly 70 per cent of members of the Communist Party; it is the highest organ of state power, with the Standing Committee acting as its permanent body.

A period of increasing political liberalization ended in June 1989 with the crushing of pro-reform demonstrations in Tiananmen Square and the replacement of the conciliatory Party Leader Zhao Ziyang with a new premier, Li Peng.

Economy. The 1982 Constitution lays down socialist public ownership of the means of production as the basis of the socialist economic system. The state economy is the sector of socialist economy under ownership by the whole people, while rural people's communes, agricultural producers' co-operatives and other forms of co-operative economy belong to the sector of socialist economy under collective ownership by the working people. The individual economy of urban and rural working people, operated within the limits prescribed by law, is a complement to the socialist public economy, and the Constitution specifies that the state protects the right of citizens to lawfully own earned income, savings, houses and other lawful property and the right of citizens to inherit private property. The state "practises economic planning on the basis of socialist public owner-ship".

In 1988 Chinese civilian employment was estimated at 543,300,000 of whom 96,600,000 were employed in industry, 323,000,000 in agriculture, and 123,600,000 in other sectors. The 1980s indeed were a decade of relaxation for China's command economy. The commune system was ended, free markets for farm products were devel-oped. State businesses began to pay orthodox taxes instead of transferring their entire profits to the government. Central product allocation was reduced and (within limits) private businesses permitted. Certain coastal regions were allowed economic autonomy and to develop cautious trading relations with neighbouring capitalist states. Finally in the summer of 1988 trade in privately owned land was made legal. From the autumn of 1988 however these market-oriented reforms were in trouble: panic buying had set in and there were runs on the banks; inflation was soaring towards 20 per cent.

Following the events in Tiananmen Square and the crushing of the political reform movement there was a significant restoration of central control. Credit was restricted and confined to the state sector, price controls were reimposed and the decentralization of foreign trade was reversed. These measures met with some success, in economic terms. China's current account deficits of 1988 and 1989 were turned into a surplus in 1990 and in early 1991 and output rose fast. Real GNP on one estimate rose by more than 8 per cent in the 12 years to 1990. Despite the post-1989 roll-back state-owned businesses are still responsible for little more than half of output, with collective and individual businesses catching up fast.

System of industrial relations. China has ratified neither ILO Convention No. 87 (Freedom of Association and Protection of the Right to Organize, 1948) nor Convention No. 98 (Right to Organize and Collective Bargaining, 1949). Under the 1982 Constitution a previous nominal right to strike provided by the 1975 Constitution was withdrawn, and grievances are settled through mediation and arbitration.

Labour contract system. The Chinese economy has been adversely affected by the prevailing pattern of employment whereby workers in state enterprises normally hold their jobs for life (even in some cases enjoying informal hereditary rights). This has led to under-employment in some workplaces, with very low productivity, combined with labour shortages in others. Since 1980 China has experimented with a labour-contract system, which allows for workers to be laid-off or dismissed, and by mid-1986, 3,500,000, or 4 per cent of all employees of state-owned units, were contract employees. As from October 1986, the labour contract system was extended to all new workers in state enter-prises, with an unemployment benefits scheme established as a safety net.

A sharp increase in unemployment in 1990 resulted from the imposition of austerity measures; in the early part of 1991 this was countered by relaxation of the money supply.

During most of the 1980s party cadres were removed from the factories as autonomy was increasingly permitted. A law of March 1988 put enterprises under the control of professional managers who received performance-related bonuses. Since 1989 there has been a return to party control and an increasing presence of officials in the factories.

Trade unionism. Trade unions developed in the first quarter of the twentieth century in harness with the nationalist and revolutionary politics of the Kuomintang (KMT), and by 1927 an All-China General Labour Federation (founded 1925) claimed 3,000,000 members. Following the establishment in 1927 of KMT rule under Chiang Kai-shek in Shanghai, however, many trade unionists were executed, and thenceforth the unions were restricted, with national and general federations prohibited, and government-sponsored "yellow" unions installed. The Red Army under Mao Zedong which took power in 1949 was peasant-based, but in 1948 the Communist Party (CPC) had organized the All-China Federation of Trade Unions (ACFTU). This functioned as the sole trade union centre until

1966 when it was abolished (as were all trade unions) during the Cultural Revolution. The ACFTU was restored in 1978 as part of the process whereby the excesses of the Cultural Revolution were denounced as the product of a conspiracy by the so-called "gang of four".

The ACFTU stands at the apex of a pyramid comprising 15 national industrial councils, 29 provincial councils and 536,000 trade union primary organizations. Some 80 per cent of (non-peasant) workers are in trade unions, those outside being predominantly new workers awaiting the formal processes of admission. However, many of the factories operating in rural areas are not unionized, and disregard labour and welfare regulations. Each factory is required to elect a workers' congress, with various powers over management in the labour standards and welfare areas (and sometimes powers to appoint managers), and the branch unions act as secretariats for these congresses. Unions are financed by a payroll tax on workers and factories; 60 per cent of the funds are allocated to the workplace union, 35 per cent to the provincial union, and 5 per cent to the ACFTU. The funds support 50,000 workers' schools, "halls of culture", etc.

A continuing programme initiated in June 1984 seeks to transform the 460,000 grass-roots trade union organizations into "workers' homes", raising the level of services (such as dormitories, canteens, etc.) provided in workplaces and involving the workers more closely in production and productivity matters. The criteria for a workers' home are that: (i) "there is a revolutionary-thinking leading group with relatively young members . . . "; (ii) that it is "successful in mobilizing (workers) in promoting technical and technological progress and in organizing socialist labour emulation drives"; (iii) that it succeeds in promoting study and a developed political consciousness; (iv) that it is "successful in promoting democratic management of the enterprise . . . and in performing its functions as the working body of workers' congresses"; (v) that it does "a good job in guaranteeing the welfare of workers and staff members"; and (vi) that it works well to strengthen trade union organization at the supra-enterprise level. By the end of 1985, 200,000 of the grass-roots trade union organizations were considered to be qualified as "workers' homes". The development of the "workers' homes" concept is officially accredited with having encouraged more workers to apply for membership of the grass-roots organizations.

Trade unions and the new enterprises. Economic liberalization in China during the 1980s has encouraged the promotion of economic enterprises outside of the traditional state and collective sphere. There are now several kinds of Sino-foreign joint ventures, owned by individuals, shareholders or partners, and a number of wholly foreign-owned enterprises. A large proportion of the foreign-invested enterprises are located in the Shenzhen Special Economic Zone, located just across the border from Hong Kong. During 1987, a relatively high number of strikes were staged in Shenzhen, most of which appeared to have been spontaneous actions deriving from employer violation of workers' rights. A high proportion of the disputes involved temporary workers lacking legal protection in the absence of comprehensive labour laws (legislation introduced in late 1986 had, however, confirmed the right of foreign investors to hire and fire workers). The ACFTU reported in mid-1987 that trade union organizations had been established in 32 per cent of Sino-foreign joint ventures, co-operative enterprises and wholly foreign owned enterprises. As for trade unions in the emerging private sector, the *China Daily* newspaper reported on April 29, 1988, that the first ever trade union in a private firm had been established in Shenyang (Xinhua province). The new union was automatically affiliated to the ACFTU.

Independent trade unionism featured strongly in the reform movement which flowered briefly in 1989. The Workers Autonomous Federations (WAF) were founded on May 19, and claim to have suffered the loss of 30 members killed in the shootings on June 4. On May 25 the Beijing WAF claimed that "in the entire people's patriotic movement, led by the students since April, the majority of the Chinese workers have demonstrated a strong wish to take part in politics. At the same time they also realize that there is not yet any organization which can truly represent the wishes expressed by the working masses". The WAF went on to call for "an entirely independent, autonomous organization, built up by the workers on a voluntary basis, through democratic processes . . . not controlled by other organizations". The WAFs seem to have had particular success in Shanghai; there and elsewhere they focused on income discrepancies, poor working conditions, the lack of democracy at the workplace, the lack of involvement in policy-making, and the deterioration of living standards.

On June 2, the ACFTU called for the crushing of the independent unions and repeated its view at a meeting of the ILO shortly afterwards. However the First Secretary and Vice President of the ACFTU, Zhu Hou Ze favoured the reform movement and this led to his dismissal in December 1989; he was replaced by Yu Hon-Gen, former President of the National Coal Corporation. The leader of the Beijing Federation, Gou Hai Feng, expressed similar views and was arrested in August, charged with having set fire to a bus.

On June 14, the Public Security Bureau declared the WAFs illegal. A number of their members were posted on wanted lists and some were certainly sentenced to death. On June 16 delegates to the UN Special session on Prevention of Discrimination and Protection of Minorities heard of 13 workers executed for "counter-revolutionary crimes" and 67 arrested for their involvement in WAFs. Nonetheless, in July there were reports of the founding of "solidarity" unions intended to emulate Poland's Solidarnosc.

Around the time of the first anniversary of the Tiananmen Square events the authorities released several hundred prisoners incarcerated since June 1989. It was thought however that none of the WAF leaders was among them and also that the official position that only 45 of these were still held might be an underestimate.

As repression intensified the Workers' Autonomous Federations organized underground. They were reported to be prepared either to supplant the official unions or to compete with them, acknowledging that the dismissal of Zou Hou Ze indicated sympathy with reform at the highest levels of the official union movement.

All-China Federation of Trade Unions (ACFTU)

Address. 10 Fuxingmenwai Street, Beijing

Phone. 367849

Cables. 1930

Leadership. Ni Zhifu (chairman); Wang Houde, Chen Bingquan, Zhang Ruiying, Zheng Wantong, Li Rongguang and Li Peiyao (vice-chairmen); Yu Hon-Gen (first secretary).

Membership. The Workers' Daily reported on Oct. 14, 1988, that China's trade unions (all of which are ACFTU-affiliates) now had a membership of over 100,000,000, accounting for 89.7 per cent of the country's total (non peasant) workforce.

History and character. The first All-China Labour Congress was held in 1922, and the All China General Labour Federation was founded at the second such conference held in 1925. In 1948 this was reformed in areas controlled by the CPC under its present name, and was extended to other areas of the country after the CPC took power throughout the country (except Taiwan) in 1949.

The ACFTU was organized on the Soviet model on the principle of democratic centralism, and until 1966 it and its associated unions were active at workplace level, principally in the areas of education, labour safety, welfare and propaganda. During the Cultural Revolution, however, trade unions were replaced by workplace "revolutionary committees" and the ACFTU was itself dissolved in December 1966. Trade unions were denounced as "counter-revolutionary" in purpose and methods. Following the death of Mao in 1976, however, the "gang of four" were arrested and many of the policies adopted in the late 1960s reversed.

The ACFTU held its first congress since 1957 in Oct. 1978 and its newspaper, *The Workers' Daily*, which had been suppressed in 1966, resumed publication in the same month. In a statement to the congress, Ni Zhifu, the chairman of the federation and a member of the Communist Party Political Bureau, recorded that:

"In December 1966 the office building (of the ACFTU) was occupied by force and *The Workers' Daily* was closed and sealed, at the personal instigation of Jiang Qing (Mao's widow and one of the "gang of four")...Many trade unions at the provincial, municipal and autonomous regional levels, as well as basic-level trade unions, were battered and crushed. Their office buildings were occupied by force, properties divided and files lost...In 1975 the party Central Committee decided to prepare for the convocation of the ninth national congress of trade unions. The sinister cohorts of the gang of four usurped the leadership of the preparatory group for this congress, turning the preparatory group into a secret liaison centre carrying out their conspiracies, did many evil things and tried to change the trade unions into their tools for usurping party and state leadership."

The first union to resume its activities, after 12 years' suspension, was the All-China Federation of Railway Workers' Unions, which began its national congress at the end of Oct. 1978.

Today, according to the ACFTU, the "Chinese trade unions, under the leadership of the Chinese Communist Party, work independently and on their own...with the four modernizations as the central task...to bring into full play the role of the Chinese working class as the main force in developing socialist material and spiritual civilization".

Deputies represent the trade unions at all levels in the people's congresses, and the unions participate in the formulation and implementation of policies and laws regarding labour.

The ACFTU held its 11th congress between Oct. 22–28, 1988. In a speech delivered at the opening session of the congress, the general secretary of the Chinese Communist Party (CCP), Zhao Ziyang admitted that the party had, in the past, neglected the trade unions' function of protecting workers' rights and interests. He also recommended that trade union leaders be elected, as opposed to the current practice whereby leaders are appointed or dismissed by party committees or company directors. In his opening speech to the congress, Ni Zhifu, who was re-elected ACFTU chairman, said that unions must be given the right to supervise, criticize, report and charge any state administrative departments guilty of encroaching on workers' interests. Ni also called for social welfare reforms and the establishment of arbitration courts to hear labour disputes.

Since 1983 the ACFTU Constitution has required that the establishment or dissolution of a union be undertaken only with its national permission. Once founded a union must affiliate. This became a highly significant matter in 1989 with the emergence of the WAFs which declined to work within the official structures. Nevertheless a willingness to rethink the Federation's role was apparent even before 1988. The organizational counterpart to Zhao Ziyang's speech was the appointment in 1988 as ACFTU First Secretary and Vice-President of Zhu Houze, former Deputy Director of the Rural Development Research Centre. Zhu had been fired as head of the Party propaganda department in February 1987 because he was associated with the policies of the then Party Leader Hu Yaobang who had failed to stop student demonstrations.

As ACFTU First Secretary Zhu probably encouraged moves to invigorate Worker Congresses and to make unions more responsive to welfare concerns of workers. He also appears not to have prevented members from participating in the reform and democracy movements of 1989, and in December of that year he was replaced by Yu Hon-Gen, former President of the National Coal Corporation.

Structure. Supreme authority is vested in a national congress to be held every five years (last in 1988). Between congresses authority resides with the executive committee (currently comprising 229 members elected by the congress), which elects the chairman, vice-chairmen and members of the presidium. When the executive committee is not in session, the presidium (which has 19 members) exercises the functions and powers of the executive committee. A 12-member secretariat attends to day-to-day affairs. There are 29 trade union councils for the provinces, autonomous regions and municipalities, and 15 national industrial unions: Railway Workers' Trade Union; Civil Aviation Workers' Trade Union; Seamen's Trade Union; Road Transport Workers' Trade Union; Postal and Telecommunications Workers' Trade Union; Machinery and Metallurgical Workers' Trade Union; Petroleum and Chemical Workers' Trade Union; Coal Miners' and Geological Workers' Trade Union; Water Conservancy and Electrical Workers' Trade Union; Textile Workers' Trade Union; Light Industry Workers' Trade Union; Building Workers' Trade Union; Agricultural and Forestry Workers' Trade Union; Financial and Commercial Workers' Trade Union; and

Educational Workers' Trade Union. The industrial unions have their own national executives, elected by their respective congresses.

Publications. The *Workers' Daily* (daily, in Chinese, circulation 2,700,000); *Chinese Trade Unions* (quarterly, in English); *Chinese Trade Union Bulletin* (bimonthly, in English, French, Spanish and Japanese).

International affiliations. Recorded as an affiliate by the WFTU, but does not participate in its work and does not appear in WFTU membership totals.

Workers' Autonomous Federations (WAF)

Membership. At their peak the WAFs claimed to represent over 100,000 workers in more that 40 industries and sectors of Beijing.

History and character. WAFs were founded by around 100 workers who joined the student protests in Beijing's Tiananmen square in May 1989. They established a makeshift office in the Square and published leaflets criticizing the government and the official trade unions. Prominent among the membership were steelworkers (from the Capital Iron and Steel Plant), railway workers, aviation workers, restaurant cooks and lawyers. During the period immediately before the suppression of the students' demonstrations, stoppages were organized in a large number of Beijing enterprises. Leaders of the WAFs were detained even before the army shut off the Square on June 4. Other WAFs were founded in China's main cities. The WAFs now function only in clandestinity.

Among their guidelines for action were:

"The organization should be an entirely independent, autonomous organization, built up by the workers on a voluntary basis, through democratic processes, and should not be controlled by other organizations.

"The fundamental principle of the organization should be to address political and economic demands, based on the wishes of the majority of the workers, and should not just remain a welfare organization.

"The organization should possess the function of monitoring the party of the proletariat – the Chinese Communist Party.

"The organization should have the power, through every legal and effective means, to monitor the legal representatives of all state and collective enterprises, guaranteeing that the workers become the real masters of the enterprise. In other enterprises, through negotiation with the owners and other legal means, the organization should be able to safeguard the rights of the workers.

"Within the bounds of the constitution and the law, the organization should be able to safeguard all legal rights of its members.

"Membership of the organization should come from individuals on a voluntary basis, and also group or collective membership in branches of various enterprises."

(Published on May 28, 1989 in Tiananmen Square).

Colombia

Capital: Bogotá   **Population: 33,000,000**

Political system. Following the overthrow in 1957 of the dictatorship of Gen. Gustavo Rojas Pinilla, the presidency of Colombia has broadly alternated between the Liberal and Conservative parties, with the Cabinet being effectively bipartisan; however, upon winning the 1986 election Virgilio Barco Vargas formed a wholly Liberal administration. In elections to the bicameral Congress the Liberals have consistently been the largest single group although not always with an overall majority. Colombia has been subjected to considerable internal unrest since the mid-1970s, but negotiations with representatives of various of the left-wing guerrilla movements have led to partial truces with certain groups. Drug trafficking, principally in marijuana and cocaine, has played an important role in respect of both the political and the economic life of the country.

Public life was scarred by an increasing series of assassinations of political and trade union figures during President Barco's last three years in office. He was succeeded in August 1990 by President César Gaviria on a platform of economic and social reform.

Economy. Agriculture accounts for about a quarter of Colombia's gross domestic product and manufacturing (principally food-processing and textiles, and also motor vehicles) for over 20 per cent. Coffee represents nearly half of all exports, but price and demand are subject to considerable fluctuations in the international markets.

The Barco government in 1986 set out as its economic priorities a reduction in unemployment, the implementation of agrarian reform, the elimination of the budget deficit and an improvement in the external situation through the stimulation of exports. Colombia's current external debt amount to some US$15,000 million.

The rough division of employment in the country is 2,000,000 in industry, 4,000,000 in agriculture and 6,000,000 in services. Unemployment in Colombia, which reached an all-time high of 17 per cent in 1985, had fallen by 1990 to below 10 per cent partly through the agency of the state training service SENA. Growth in the later 1980s averaged four per cent and external indebtedness was far lower than that of other Latin American countries. However inflation was still running at between 20 and 30 per cent and there were dramatic extremes in the distribution of income and wealth. Colombia has a minimum wage, which was raised by 26 per cent at the end of 1989, but real wages fell in every year but one in the years 1984–89.

System of industrial relations. Following Colombia's ratification in 1976 of ILO conventions No. 87 (Freedom of Association and Protection of the Right to Organize, 1948) and No. 98 (Right to Organize and Collective Bargaining, 1949), in November 1977 Colombia enacted laws under which the trade unions became independent legal bodies, formally ending their direct political ties.

The ILO *Report of the Committee of Experts on the Application of Conventions and Recommendations* (1985) noted that Colombia could be considered in breach of the Conventions in respect of: (i) the prohibition placed on trade unions from taking part in politics; (ii) the prohibition on federations and confederations from calling strikes; (iii) the prohibition on strike action in a "very wide range of services that are not necessarily essential"; (iv) the powers of the government to impose compulsory arbitration in labour disputes after 40 days and to terminate strikes affecting the interest of the national economy; (v) the temporary suspension of the right to strike under emergency powers; (vi) the automatic dismissal of trade unionists who have taken part in illegal strikes; and (vii) the interference by government in the internal affairs of unions, including their constitutional arrangements and the election of officers. The government of Colombia argued that many of these restrictions should be seen in the context of a country struggling to overcome the problems of economic underdevelopment. In contrast to some other Latin American countries the trade unions have not themselves been major vehicles for political unrest; nevertheless, the high level of politically motivated violence which has long prevailed in Colombia has been reflected in a number of deaths of trade unionists. The influence of the trade union centres has been reflected in their participation over many years in governmental and quasi-governmental bodies operating in the social and economic fields, such as the National Council of Labour.

In February 1987, the Supreme Court of Justice set guidelines for the dismissal of workers in unlawful strikes. According to the ruling, the Ministry of Labour must ensure that a worker has been an active participant, thereby meriting dismissal under Article 450 of the Labour Code. However, it would be considered unjust to sack a worker for playing a "passive" role in a strike. It was for the Ministry of Labour to decide the degree of an individual's participation and it could specifically authorize dismissal.

Apart from ILO Conventions, Colombia's employment standards are laid down in the Constitution and the country's Labour Code, which regulates the right of association, organization of unions, federations and confederations, collective bargaining agreements, the right to strike and other union rights. The government has the right to withdraw legal recognition from trade unions. For all its protective nature, the significance of the Code is attenuated by the existence of a large informal and unregulated Colombian economy.

Collective bargaining revolves around two-year agreements; where disputes occur, the Code provides for a series of steps to be taken before a strike call may be issued. In the public sector arbitration is compulsory in the event of a dispute; in the private sector both sides usually strive to avoid it. A CUT attempt to mount a general strike against the economic policies of the Barco administration in October 1988 did not command widespread support. Where industrial strikes occur, the government may respond with severity, as in the case of a miners' strike of April 1990 at the giant El Cerrejón mine, where tanks and troops were used.

Large numbers of trade unionists fell victim to gun squads from 1988 onwards, and the rate of murders increased in the months preceding the 1990 presidential elections, despite undertakings from President Barco that they would be given special protection. In May the vice-president of the CTC was killed and by the end of the year the toll approached 1,000 for the three-year period. While some of the killings were linked to drug barons and landowners, unions accused the security forces of complicity in some instances.

Trade unionism. Labour organization began to appear from the first decade of the twentieth century, and a strike against the US-owned United Fruit company in 1928 resulted in the "massacre of the banana workers" when several hundred were killed when the army fired on demonstrators. Trade union organizations were legalized following the accession to power of a Liberal government in 1930. The Trade Union Confederation of Colombia (Confederación Sindical de Colombia, CSC) was formed in 1935; this soon split but reformed as the Confederation of Workers of Colombia (Confederación de Trabajadores de Colombia, CTC). The CTC, which was closely linked with the Liberal Party, was severely weakened for some years by its unsuccessful attempt in 1946 by a general strike to prevent an incoming Conservative government from coming to power, and the Union of Workers of Colombia (Unión de Trabajadores de Colombia, UTC) was formed in 1946 with the sponsorship of the Conservative Party. After the overthrow of Gen. Rojas Pinilla, the CTC and UTC in 1958 entered a social pact with the government. The communist Trade Union Confederation of Colombian Workers (Confederación Sindical de Trabajadores de Colombia, CSTC) was founded in 1964, and the WCL-affiliated General Confederation of Labour (Confederación General del Trabajo, CGT) was founded in 1971.

All four trade union confederations took part in a general strike in September 1977 in which about 18 people were killed in clashes between strikers and the security forces; the CTC and the UTC participated in the general strike despite their close links with the (ruling coalition) Liberal and Conservative parties, respectively.

In October 1981 the armed forces placed Bogotá under military control to avert a supposed plan to stage an insurrection in connection with a general strike called by the

CSTC. Following this the government suspended the legal status of the CSTC. A state of siege imposed in May 1984 was partially lifted in October 1984 when President Betancur annulled decrees forbidding meetings relating to political or trade union activities. (A previous state of siege had been in force for 30 years to June 1982.) The communist CSTC had called a general strike on June 20 to protest against the state of siege and the government's economic policies; the strike was declared illegal but paralyzed public transport.

Due to the increased pace of "disappearances" together with assassinations of opposition party and trade union leaders and their supporters and members by paramilitary groups (estimated at over 1,000 disappeared and 1,200 dead for 1986–1987), the CUT called "The Day of the Right to Life, Trade Union Freedoms and Against the Repayment of the External Debt" on Aug. 19, 1987, and protests throughout the country demanded government measures to stem the level of violence and "military terrorism". Following the assassination of Jaime Pardo Leal, President of the Patriotic Union (UP), the country's leading opposition party, the CUT called a general strike on Oct. 13, 1987.

On March 4, 1988, 21 members of SINTRAGO, the agricultural workers union, were reported murdered by paramilitary death squads. In response, the CUT called a national day of action on March 9, but to little effect because a further massacre of 28 agricultural workers was reported on April 3. Opposition forces accused the military of being responsible for this growing political violence, suspecting them of directly supporting the paramilitary groups. (Between April 21 and May 2, 1988, six trade union leaders were killed, including the president of SINTRAGO, Hernán Usaga. According to Amnesty International, Sr Usaga was the twelfth trade union leader of the banana plantation workers of the Urabá region to be murdered since February 1988). On July 27, the CUT called another general strike and along with the CGT sent an open letter to Colombia's President Virgilio Barco Vargas outlining plans to end the crisis. The unions advocated immediate general wage increases to offset the huge increases in basic commodity prices, the reduction of the working week to 40 hours, the introduction of unemployment benefit, the application of the ILO Conventions Nos. 87 and 98 and the dissolution of the paramilitary groups. While the CUT and the CGT prepared for a national referendum (due to be held from Sept. 14–20) to reinforce its campaign for fundamental political change, it was reported that a further 22 workers, including 18 miners in the province of Antioquia, had been murdered by death squads between July 14–22, 1988.

Trade union density in Colombia is estimated at 11–12 per cent for 1988, representing some 1,400,000 organized workers, of whom more than 300,000 are in the public sector. While trade unions tend to be concentrated in industrial areas, there are agricultural labourers' unions—notably among sugar and banana workers—which have borne a large number of the gunmen's attacks referred to above. Colombia's 2,210 unions and 93 federations were, until 1988 mostly organized into four national centres. The dominant centre is the Central Union of Workers (CUT) which holds the affiliation of about 55 per cent of the Colombian labour movement. The Confederation of Democratic Workers of Colombia (CTDC) holds about 25 per cent, the CGT 6 per cent and the CTC 4 per cent. Some 10 per cent of trade unionists are members of independent unions and federations.

The most significant trade union event in 1988 was the founding in August of the CTDC which was launched at its founding Congress as an avowedly anti-CUT body. The Conservative Party supporting Union of Workers of Colombia (UTC) was dissolved to make way for it, as was the Trade Union Confederation of Colombian workers (CSTC). It also gained the adherence of a faction of the CTC, whose ICFTU affiliation for 1988 slumped in consequence to 60,000. Nevertheless the trend during 1988 was for the Left-leaning CUT to defy this realignment and grow at a faster rate than the CTDC.

Central Unitaria de Trabajadores (CUT)
Central Union of Workers

Leadership: Jorge Carrillo Rojas (president); Angelino Garzon (secretary general)

History and character: The CUT is the dominant union centre in Colombia. It was formed on a Marxist platform in 1986 out of a fusion of former affiliates of the CTC and the now defunct UTC. It has been willing to use the general strike as a weapon to press economic demands, but received a setback in October 1988 when a strike call received inadequate support and the President Carrillo Rojas resigned for a temporary period.

In April 1988 the CUT gained the adherence of the Cartagena Portworkers' Union from the CTC, but in August it suffered the defection of the large FETRABOC federation. This was followed in April 1989 by a further defection, this time of the UTRACUN federation. While having friendly links with the CTDC both federations maintain their independence.

International affiliations. The CUT is not affiliated to the ICFTU, but one part of it (led by its President Jorge Carrillo) set up the United Front of Democratic Workers (FUTC-CUT) in December 1988 which affiliated to the ICFTU with over 400,000 members. Communist members of the former CSTC (a faction of which was a founding organization of the CUT) maintain links with the WFTU though these stop short of formal affiliation.

Confederación General del Trabajo (CGT)
General Confederation of Labour

Address. Av. 19 No. 13A-12, Piso 7°, Bogotá

Phone. 2835817; 2835818; 2835896

Leadership. Julio Roberto Gomez Esquera (president); José Corredor Nuñez (first vice-president); Julio Roberto Gomez Esguerra (secretary general)

History and character. The CGT was founded on May 1, 1971 as the successor to the Acción Sindical Colombiana (ASICOL), a breakaway from the UTC. The CGT, which affiliated to the WCL, saw itself as opposed to the subservience of the CGT and the UTC to the political parties to which they were linked, and to their bureaucracy and corruption. The CGT received legal recognition in 1975. It describes its orientation as being to humanist-socialism, fundamentally Christian but not clerical. It emphasizes trade union pluralism and freedom, and independence from all political parties, government, employers and the Church, and seeks to work not just as a trade union centre but through other popular organizations such as co-operatives, peasants' leagues, mutual societies, etc., to the end of rebuilding society.

On Aug. 13, 1988, the Congress of the CGT decided to postpone moves to establish a single union confederation, due to the confused social situation at the time. However, it confirmed its commitment to joint action with the other confederations. In March 1989, Laureano Rodríguez, a CGT vice-president, disaffiliated from the Confederation to help establish the independent federation UTRACUN (formerly part of the CUT).

Publication. *Organo Informativo* (newspaper).

International affilations. WCL; CLAT.

Confederación de Trabajadores de Colombia (CTC)
Confederation of Workers of Colombia

Address. Calle 39, No. 26A-23, Barrio de la Soledad, Bogotá

Phone. 2682084

Fax. 2688576

Leadership. Apecides Alviz Fernández (president); Ramón Márquez Iguarán (secretary general)

History and character. The CTC developed in the 1930s (see above) and has traditionally been linked with the moderate free-enterprise Liberal Party (PL), one of the two principal Colombian parties. A former president, José Raquel Mercado, was assassinated by the revolutionary leftist M-19 movement in 1976.

The size of the CTC was considerably reduced in 1988 when the Cartagena Port Workers Union switched affiliation to the CUT, while the FETRABOC federation of Bogota became independent.

Publications. *Liberación Obrera* (monthly).
International affiliations. ICFTU; ORIT.

Confederación de Trabajadores Democráticos de Colombia (CTDC)
Confederation of Democratic Workers of Colombia

Leadership: Mario Valderrama (president); Alfonso Vargas (secretary general).

History and character: The CTDC was established in August 1988 by the dissolution of the former Trade Union Confederation of Colombian Workers (CSTC) and the Union of Workers of Colombia (UTC) together with a faction of the CTC. It is intended to rival the larger CUT which it has not yet surpassed, though it grew steadily in 1988. The CTDC Secretary-General is Alfonso Vargas who held the same position in the UTC.

International affiliations. The CTDC has no international affiliation though it applied to the ICFTU for recognition in 1989.

Comoros

Capital: Moroni   **Population: 459,000**

Political system. The Comoros, formerly a French overseas territory accorded internal self-government in 1961, declared itself independent in 1975. (Mayotte, one of the four islands in the archipelago, voted in 1976 to remain within the French Republic and has the status of an overseas territorial collectivity, but the Comoros government regards the island as an integral part of its national territory). Following a *coup* in 1978 a Federal Assembly was set up, and a one-party system was introduced in 1979 with the Union for Comoran Progress established as the sole legal party.

Economy. Agriculture occupies over 80 per cent of the workforce, although there is high unemployment and rural under-employment. Most of this activity is on a subsistence basis with production seriously affected by erosion and drought, and markets for the few agricultural and agriculture-based exports are liable to wide fluctuations. The Comoros' economy has been severely disrupted by domestic upheavals and natural disasters and the country depends heavily on assistance from France and from Arab states in the Gulf area, and on agreements with the European Communities.

System of industrial relations. The Comoros ratified ILO Conventions No. 87 (Freedom of Association and Protection of the Right to Organize, 1948) and No. 98 (Right to Organize and Collective Bargaining, 1949) in 1978.

Trade unionism. The existence of one central organization, the Union des Travailleurs des Comores (Union of Workers of the Comoros, B.P. 405, Moroni), has been reported, with affiliation to the OATUU.

Congo

Capital: Brazzaville

Population: 2,100,000
(1988)

Political system. The Congo became a self-governing republic within the French Community in 1958 and achieved full independence in 1960. After some years of disturbed political conditions, a military *coup* took place in 1968, and in the following year a nominally Marxist regime was established under the Parti Congolais du Travail (PCT) as the sole political party. Under the Constitution the chairman of the central committee of the PCT is also president of the republic and head of state. There is a unicameral People's National Assembly whose members are elected from a sole list presented by the PCT. A 20-year treaty of friendship and co-operation with the Soviet Union was signed in 1981, but the Congo also has close links with France.

Economy. From the late 1960s the main sectors of the economy have under successive regimes been nationalized or otherwise become state-controlled. Agriculture occupies about a third of the workforce, mainly on a subsistence basis but with plantation cash crops including coffee and cocoa (both subject to wide demand and price fluctuations in the international markets), sugar and palmoil. Petroleum production began in 1960 and expanded rapidly in the late 1970s and early 1980s, eventually accounting for some 90 per cent of export revenue—resulting in part in the Congo having one of the highest gross national products per head in sub-Saharan Africa. Depressed oil prices, however, led to the adoption of a structural readjustment programme in mid-1985, involving the shelving of certain planned investment projects, a re-scheduling of the external debt, and in 1987, to the opening of various state-owned enterprises to private-sector investment.

System of industrial relations. Congo ratified ILO Convention No. 87 (Freedom of Association and Protection of the Right to Organize, 1948) in 1960, but has not ratified Convention No. 98 (Right to Organize and Collective Bargaining, 1949). The ILO *Report of the Committee of Experts on the Application of Conventions and Recommendations* (1985) observed that the CSC is designated by name in a decree as the sole trade union and that it benefits from compulsory check-off from the pay of all workers which was introduced in 1973. Under the 1975 labour code primary-level unions are obliged to conform to rules laid down by the CSC.

Trade unionism. Trade unionism developed under French rule but is now coordinated under one recognized body, the Confédération Syndicale Congolaise (CSC).

The CSC is no longer simply a regulator of trade union affairs. Although its general secretary remains a member of the political bureau of the ruling party, it has shown an increasing desire for independence, in support of which it called a general strike in September 1990.

Confédération Syndicale Congolaise (CSC)
Congolese Trade Union Confederation

Address. B.P. 2311, Brazzaville
Phone. 811923
Telex. 5304
Leadership. Jean-Michel Bokamba-Yangouma (secretary-general, re-elected June 1986).
Membership. 130,000.
History, structure, policy and character. The CSC was formed in 1964 as a result of the amalgamation of three main trade union centres previously linked to French union organizations, together with other labour organizations. The CSC comprises three levels of organization. At the base are

union sections, union and district committees, and enterprise-based organizations. At an intermediate level are committees of the regions and of Brazzaville commune, together with 13 professional federations. The Confederal Congress is the CSC sovereign body, meeting every four years. A 271-member Confederal Council runs the CSC in between congresses; it comprises an executive commission and a verification and control commission responsible for organization and finance. The CSC describes its policy as strongly socialist and for the liberation of the economy from foreign capital. It is strongly integrated into the ruling party.

The CSC General Secretary Jean-Michel Bokamba-Yangouma is a member of the political bureau of the PCT. However, within the Confederation a strong independence movement has gathered, leading to threats of secession on the part of some federations. In response to this pressure the CSC called a general strike for its independence form the PCT on Sept. 16, 1990.

Affiliated unions. The CSC includes 13 professional federations, covering workers in: Agriculture and Forestry; Science, Sport, Education, Information and Culture; Post and Telecommunications; Financial Institutions; Sea, Railway and River Transport; Health and Social Affairs; Public Works and Buildings; Banks and Insurance; General and Municipal Administration; Commerce; Industry and Metallurgy; Mines and Oil; and Road and Air Transport, Hotels and Tourism.

Publication. *Voix de la Classe Ouvrière (VOCO).*

International affiliations. The CSC claims to be affiliated to all three world labour organizations, the ICFTU, WFTU and WCL, together with the OATUU. Its affiliation is claimed by the WFTU.

Costa Rica

Capital: San José   **Population: 2,950,000**

Political system. Since a brief but bitter civil war in 1948 Costa Rica has generally had presidents alternately from conservative groupings and from the National Liberation Party (PLN). In its earlier periods of office the PLN undertook a major programme to reform, including the dissolution of the army, a programme of nationalization (especially of the banks) and the establishment of a developed system of social security. In elections in 1986 the PLN (which is affiliated to the Socialist International) both retained the presidency and remained the largest party in the unicameral Legislative Assembly (although in each case with a reduced overall majority).

In early Summer 1990, the Arias administration was replaced by another under the Christian Democrat President Calderon, which immediately announced measures to cut external debt by raising taxes, prices and import tariffs.

Economy. In the early 1980s the internal and external strength of the Costa Rican economy began to deteriorate sharply, due largely to an adverse change in the terms of trade, and substantial arrears of payment accumulated on external debt. Upon its election to office in 1982, the PLN administration instituted an emergency programme involving austerity measures which included the removal of food subsidies and increases in prices in the public services. Over the succeeding years the government disposed of major parts of the state-owned economic sector and sought to implement structural and fiscal reforms at the instigation of the IMF, but encountered difficulties in its efforts to secure rescheduling of the country's external debt.

Costa Rica's main export crops are coffee and bananas, but the prices and levels of demand of each of these are liable to severe fluctuations in the international markets. Moreover, requirements for labour on the coffee estates vary seasonally so that there is frequent widespread rural under-employment, while in 1984 the major US-owned banana producer (United Brands) announced that it was withdrawing from its Costa Rican operations following a protracted strike on its plantations. Manufacturing (principally concerned with food processing) has latterly been operating well below capacity.

Costa Rican GDP grew at approximately 5 per cent in 1989, a year in which inflation dropped to 12 per cent, half the previous year's figure. Wages are increased at the start of each year by 75 per cent of the anticipated rate of price rises for that year with adjustments in mid-year if inflation outstrips expectations. The level of unemployment is the subject of controversy between government departments, which put it variously at 5.5 per cent or 3.8 per cent at the end of 1989. 27.3 per cent of the workforce is engaged in agriculture, 25.2 per cent in personal services, 19.2 per cent in commerce, 17.2 per cent in manufacturing and mining. The Ministry of Labour estimates that 85 per cent of employment is in the private sector.

System of Industrial Relations. The Constitution guarantees basic workers' rights, including a minimum wage and limitations on hours of work; the rights to lock out and to strike (except in public services) are guaranteed. There is an office of conciliation in the Department of Labour which handles collective disputes, with a labour court beyond this.

Costa Rica ratified ILO Conventions No. 87 (Freedom of Association and Protection of the Right to Organize, 1948) and No. 98 (Right to Organize and Collective Bargaining, 1949) in 1960. The ILO *Report of the Committee of Experts on the Application of Conventions and Recommendations* (1985) criticized the government of Costa Rica for failing to ensure the access of trade union officials to plantations, and also for prohibiting strikes in "a very wide range of services declared to be public that are not essential services in the strict sense of the term".

In May 1989 President Arias's Minister of Labour announced the agreement with the unions of a new draft regulation which would promote union development by giving protection against firings of activists but its introduction into law was blocked by fierce opposition from employers and *Solidarismo* (*see below*). In 1989 the ICFTU submitted a complaint to the ILO about the activities of the Costa Rican government in promoting *Solidarismo*, which it saw as a barrier to an independent trade union movement.

Though not legal, strikes do take place in the public as well as in the private sectors. In the late 1980s they were generally of short duration and those involved sometimes achieved local success. A five-day local general strike in Limón in August 1989 was less successful. Under President Arias there was some willingness to accommodate the unions in order to preserve labour peace.

Trade unionism. The first artisans' union was recorded in 1905, and the growth of trade unionism (including the appearance of the first trade union centres) was fostered by favourable labour legislation introduced by the government of President Rafael Calderon Guardia from 1940 to 1943.

At least 15 per cent of the employed labour force is in unions, with the bulk being in the public sector where protection is greater. The unions in Costa Rica face a powerful rival in the Catholic-inspired *Solidarismo* movement which is presented as an alternative to their activities. *Solidarismo* was created in Costa Rica in 1947 but was intensively active in the 1980s, and the new President Calderón has promised legislation to favour its further development. In 1989 *Solidarismo* claimed 140,000 members in 1,213 associations. If accurate these figures give it a following of similar size to that of the unions, but some estimates place its membership at a lower level.

The associations tend to be affiliated either to the Solidarista Union (SURSUM) or to the Pope John XXIII School (whose affiliates tend to be active in agriculture). Their guiding principle is harmonious relations between employers and employees: members gain practical benefits such as credit unions in return for which they renounce the right to strike. In January 1990 the associations established their own bank, financed by the American agency USAID.

Under Article 273 of the Labour Code, only five people are needed to form a *Solidarismo* association whereas the figure for unions is 20. This discrepancy was the subject of the ICFTU complaint to the ILO in 1989, together with evidence that employers were pressurizing their workforce to join such associations. The 'Solidarist' Act of 1984 granted the associations special legal status. The six national union centres are vehemently opposed to *Solidarismo*, arguing that employer preference for it is eliminating independent unionism. In the banana plantations this is already the case. Nevertheless, in January 1989 *Solidarismo* employees at Tres Rios Textiles did hold a brief and successful strike to gain greater control over their association, and there have been other manifestations of discontent.

According to official figures, Costa Rica had 436 independent unions in September 1988. The six centres do not cover them all, notably the National Teachers' Association (ANDE). The two left-led centres (CUT and CTCR) seem to have suffered more from loss of members to *Solidarismo*, though they are not identical in orientation and only CUT is a WFTU affiliate. Though figures are unreliable, it seems likely that the ICFTU affiliate CATD is the largest of the six centres.

Central de Trabajadores Costarricenses (CTC)
Costa Rican Workers' Union

Address. Apartado Postal No. 4137-1000, Calle 20, Av. 3–5, Casa No. 321, Continguo a la Iglesia "La Medalla Milagrosa", San José

Leadership. Alsimiro Herrera Torres (secretary general)

Membership. 13,522 (1988).

History and character. The CTC was created by the regional organization of Christian unions, CLASC, as the Federation of Christian Workers and Peasants of Costa Rica (FOCC) in 1964, and took its present name in 1972.

International affiliations. WCL; CLAT.

Confederación Auténtica de Trabajadores Democráticos (CATD)
Democratic Workers' Union

Address. Apartado Postal No. 7–1100, San Juan de Tibas, San José

Leadership. Prof. Carlos Vargas (secretary general)

Membership. 23,572 (1988).

History. Founded 1978; politically independent.

International affiliation. ICFTU.

Confederación Costarricense de Trabajadores Democráticos (Rerum Novarum)
CCTD
Costa Rican Confederation of Democratic Workers

Address. Apartado Postal No. 2167–1000, San José

Phone. 22-19-81

Leadership. Miguel Calderón Sandi (secretary general)

Membership. 17,687 (1988).

History and character. The CCTD originated in 1943, with the sponsorship of the Roman Catholic Church, as the Central Costarricense de Sindicatos "Rerum Novarum", and adopted its present name in 1966.

International affiliations. ICFTU; ORIT.

Confederación de Trabajadores de Costa Rica (CTCR)
Confederation of Workers of Costa Rica

Address. Casa Sindical Carlos Luis Falla, 50 metros norte, Iglesia St. Teresita, 952 San José

History. This group appears to have been formed as a breakaway from the leftist Confederación Unitaria de Trabajadores (CUT) in 1985, taking the original name from the early 1940s of an organization which was subsequently reorganized as the General Confederation of Workers (CGT) and then as the present CUT. The CTCR is allied with the Costa Rican People's Party (PPC)

Confederación Nacional de Trabajadores (CNT)
National Confederation of Workers

Address. Apartado Postal No. 440-1000, San José

Phone. 33-05-44

Leadership. Oscar Vega Hernández (president); Gilbert Brown Young (secretary general)

Membership. 14,013 (1988). There are 14 affiliated federations, unions and associations.

History and character. The CNT was founded in Oct. 1983.

Publications. Several booklets on debt crisis, democratic alternatives to problems of central America.

International affiliation. ICFTU.

Confederación Unitaria de Trabajadores (CUT)
United Confederation of Workers

Address. Apartado Postal No. 186-1009, San José

Phone. 21-47-09

Leadership. Mario Devundas Brenes (president); Juan Rafael Morales (vice-president); Rodrigo Ureña Quiros (secretary general)

Membership. CUT claimed 48,000 members in 1987 but is likely to have lost members to *Solidarismo.*

History and character. Was founded in Nov. 1980 by the merger of the Federación Nacional de Trabajadores Públicos (National Federation of Public Workers) and the Confederación General de Trabajadores (CGT, General Confederation of Workers). The CUT is associated with the left-wing Coalición Pueblo Unido (PU), and considers itself the sole truly class-orientated union federation in Costa Rica. It claims to have signed the most collective bargaining agreements and brought about the most strikes of any federation, and to be the largest and most broadly based of the federations. Policies include opposition to the IMF and opposition to the use of Costa Rica as a base for counter-revolutionary activity. CUT is allied to the Popular Vanguard Party (PVP).

Structure. Biennial national congress; national steering committee meeting every three months; executive committee meeting every 15 days.

Affiliates. Federación Nacional Campesina (National Peasants' Federation), with 10 unions; Federación de Trabajadores de la Enseñanza Superior (Federation of Workers in Higher Education), with four unions; Federación Nacional de Trabajadores Industriales (National Federation of Industrial Workers), with eight unions; Federación Sindical de Trabajadores de Plantaciones (Federation of Plantation Workers), with eight unions.

Publication. Unidad Sindical.

International affiliations. WFTU; CPUSTAL.

Other organizations

The National Teachers' Association ANDE (30,000 members) is independent of the centres as are two other teachers' unions SEC (13,000) and APSE (8,000).

Côte d'Ivoire

Capital: Abidjan   **Population: 9,460,000**

Political system. Côte d'Ivoire became a self-governing republic within the French Community in 1958 and gained full independence in 1960. Since independence the country's government has been formed by the Parti Démocratique de la Côte d'Ivoire (PDCI) led by Félix Houphouét-Boigny, which is in practice the only political party and which holds all the seats in the unicameral National Assembly. The PDCI's aim has been to consolidate the country's independence on the basis of a free-enterprise economy, in co-operation with other West African states, and the maintenance of good relations with France.

Economy. Côte d'Ivoire is one of the world's major producers and exporters of coffee and cocoa (prices and demand for which, however, are subject to wide fluctuations in the international markets) but also has a relatively large manufacturing and industrial sector. Manufacturing (much of it owned and managed by foreigners) was initially centred on goods hitherto imported but has more recently moved towards export products.

Côte d'Ivoire experienced rapid economic expansion and development in the 1970s, but in the early 1980s encountered economic difficulties as export revenues declined; public expenditure cuts introduced to rectify this situation led to outbreaks of civil and industrial unrest. Major reschedulings took place in 1986–88 of portions of Côte d'Ivoire's external debt of over $8,000 million, while a suspension of debt service payments was announced in mid-1987 in view of a collapse in export earnings. During this period Côte d'Ivoire received assistance from both the International Monetary Fund and the World Bank, and continued to divest itself of a considerable part of the commercial enterprises in which it had a stake and to enhance the role of the private sector as part of a structural adjustment programme.

System of industrial relations. Côte d'Ivoire ratified ILO Convention No. 87 (Freedom of Association and Protection of the Right to Organize, 1948) in 1960 and Convention No. 98 (Right to Organize and Collective Bargaining, 1949) in 1961. The ILO has questioned the powers of the president to submit industrial relations disputes to compulsory arbitration when he considers public order is jeopardized, powers which apparently contradict Convention 87. However the government is reported to be considering reform of its Labour Code to bring it into conformity with the principles of freedom of association.

Industrial unrest was recorded in the period 1980–83 as a consequence of the economic recession, principally among professional and white-collar workers. Secondary school teachers were dismissed after striking in Jan. 1983, on the grounds that their action had been politically motivated. Shortly afterwards, unrest involving teachers, doctors, pharmacists, dentists and veterinary surgeons lasted for more than two weeks before being ended by a presidential decree threatening fines and imprisonment under 1963 legislation allowing for the conscription of workers for those who failed to return to work. There was further unrest in 1987, again involving teachers. Eleven officials and members of the teachers' union, the *Syndicat national des enseignants du second degré de la Côte d'Ivoire* (Synesci) were arrested in September-October 1987 and conscripted into the army. Synesci, like other teachers' unions, is outside the UGTCI and is one for the few autonomous organizations in Côte d'Ivoire; the protest was largely inspired by government moves to incorporate the union more closely into the ruling order. The detainees were released and reinstated between June and October 1988 in reconciliatory moves ·by the president.

Trade unionism. Trade unions developed under French rule and at independence in 1960 three national trade union centres were in existence. In 1962, however, a single trade union system organized through the Union Générale des Travailleurs de Côte d'Ivoire (UGTCI) was set up under the leadership of the ruling PDCI and this has remained in force.

In April 1990 the leadership of the UGTCI was reported as seeking to protect its organization's status by regaining control over "rebellious affiliates which had aligned themselves with the protesters and strikers". Outside the UGTCI the independent behaviour of the teachers' unions has been matched by that of the bankers' unions; each disowned leaders who refused to present their demands to President Houphouët-Boigny. A Federation of Free Trade Unions has also been reported which claims the adherence of 20,000 members. Twenty-nine of its leaders were detained to prevent them staging a protest march in April 1990.

Union Générale des Travailleurs de Côte d'Ivoire (UGTCI)
General Union of Workers of Côte d'Ivoire

Address. Bourse du Travail à Treichville 05, B.P. 1203, Abidjan 01

Phone. 32-26-65, 32-95-23

Leadership. Hyacinthe Adiko Niamkey (secretary general)

History and character. The UGTCI was formed in 1962 by merger of the four existing trade union centres; these previous centres had maintained affiliations to the rival international trade union centres, and these affiliations were ended. The UGTCI is closely tied to the PDCI ruling party, which has held power since independence in 1960, and describes itself as advocating "trade unionism of responsible participation".

Structure. Congress met in 1968, 1977 and 1984. The UGTCI has a 30-member executive committee and a 50-member steering committee. There are 55 affiliated basic trade unions, organized on an occupational basis, nine regional (departmental) unions and 31 local unions.

Publication. *La Voix du Travailleur* (circulation 20,000).

International affiliations. OATUU; has amicable relations with the ICFTU, the WFTU and AFL-CIO (USA).

Cuba

Capital: Havana   **Population: 10,500,000**
                                                                 (1988)

Political system. Revolutionary forces led by Fidel Castro overthrew the Batista regime at the beginning of 1959. A Marxist-Leninist programme was proclaimed in December 1961, and in 1965 the existing leading political organization was transformed into the Communist Party of Cuba. A new Constitution, which came into effect in 1976, defines the republic as a socialist state of work people and other manual and intellectual workers and as part of the world socialist community, with the Communist Party as the leading force. The state organizes and directs the economic life of the country in accordance with a central social and economic development plan; it also recognizes the right of small farmers to own their land and other means of production, and guarantees the right of citizens to own personal property. There is a unicameral National Assembly (elected indirectly by municipal assemblies from candidates approved by the Communist Party), and this in turn elects a Council of State as its permanent organ.

Economy. From 1960 under the Castro regime the economy has become increasingly socialized.

The economy continues to be heavily dependent upon sugar and tobacco, but both of these crops are not only subject to severe fluctuations of demand and price in the international markets, but are also liable to be seriously affected by disease and climatic conditions such as drought, hurricanes or torrential rains. Although Cuba has vast reserves of nickel, demand for this also has been adversely affected by international market conditions. Most manufacturing industry is related to the processing of agricultural products and the production of consumer goods. Over half of Cuba's external trade is conducted with the Soviet Union, which also provides large amounts of aid; Cuba's economic planning is co-ordinated with that of its partners in the Council for Mutual Economic Co-operation (CMEA or Comecon).

During the 1980s, Cuba experienced continuing economic difficulties associated principally with the fall in international prices for sugar, tobacco and nickel, and renegotiated part of its approximately $3,500 million debt with Western countries.

By the end of the 1980s tourism had begun to match the contribution of staple crops to the Cuban economy. In 1988 there were 3,740,600 civilian workers including 269,000 agricultural workers of various kinds, 66,000 in co-operatives, 155,100 in administration and 387,300 in commerce.

System of industrial relations. Cuba ratified ILO Conventions No. 87 (Freedom of Association and Protection of the Right to Organize, 1948) and No. 98 (Right to Organize and Collective Bargaining, 1949) in 1952. However, collective bargaining was ended in 1959 and a labour code adopted in 1961 abolished the right to strike. The UN Commission on Human Rights decided to send a mission in August 1988 to investigate charges by the ICFTU that Convention No. 87 is not being honoured and that only the CTC is allowed by law to represent Cuban workers.

Collective agreements are regulated by Decree 74 (Aug. 9 1983) and are also covered by the Labour Code of 1984 which established a dispute precedure. Article 44 of the Constitution prohibits the right to strike.

Trade unionism. Trade unions appeared in Cuba in the nineteenth century, and the first workers' congress was held in 1898. The Confederation of Workers of Cuba (Confederación de Trabajadores de Cuba, CTC) was formed in 1939 and was thereafter the only important trade union centre. The CTC (now the Central de Trabajadores de Cuba) has been the sole trade union centre since the assumption of power by Castro.

Central de Trabajadores de Cuba (CTC)
Workers' Central Union of Cuba

Address. Calle San Carolos y Peñalver, Municipio Centro-Habana, Prov. Ciudad Habana
Phone. 7-4901
Telex. 511263 CTC, CU
Leadership. Roberto Veiga Menendez (secretary general, also a member of the Communist Party politburo and a vice-president of the WFTU)
Membership. 17 national unions organized by industrial sector with 2,910,000 members.
History and character. The present CTC traces its origins back to the formation of the Confederación de Trabajadores de Cuba, founded in 1939. This organization established itself as the only trade union centre of consequence but its history was marked by violent internal feuds, with killings by rival factions. Important elements of the CTC sought accommodation with the regime of President Fulgencio Batista from 1954, and when Batista fled the country on Jan. 1, 1959, several

leaders of the confederation, including its secretary general Eusebio Mujal, followed suit. Following the assumption of power the CTC received its present name, and in November 1959 disaffiliated from the ICFTU, subsequently becoming the principal supporter of the WFTU in the Americas. In May 1960 the secretary general of the CTC, David Salvador, was removed from office and imprisoned, and at the next national congress only one list of candidates was presented. The congress held in 1966 adopted a platform which defined the role of the trade unions as being to supervise the increase in output and efficiency, expand social facilities, and apply wage scales and production quotas, and denied them any role in the formulation of policy. The sixteenth CTC congress was held in Havana on Jan. 24–28 1990. The main issues under discussion were errors and shortcomings in production, corruption in workers' collectives and union organizations, and the readiness of workers to clear away impediments to the construction of socialism. The 2,514 delegates heard a speech from President Castro which asserted the community of interests between the governors and the governed.

Publication. Trabajadores (circulation, 100,000)
International affiliations. WFTU; CPUSTAL.

Other organization in exile

Solidaridad de Trabajadores Cubanos (STC)
Cuban Workers' Solidarity

Address. Apartado 50, Zona Postal 1204, San Antonio de los Altos, Estado Miranda, Venezuela
Leadership. Pedro Perez Castro (secretary general)
International affiliation. CLAT.

Cyprus

Capital: Nicosia

Population: 686,000
(1988)

Political system. Cyprus became fully independent in 1960 and a member of the Commonwealth in 1961, with a republican Constitution designed to secure representation of both the Greek and the Turkish communities in the unicameral House of Representatives and in the various governmental organs. The Turkish community withdrew from the central government in 1963, and following intervention by Turkish forces in 1974, a separate Turkish-Cypriot administration was established in the northern part of the island in 1975. The "Turkish Republic of Northern Cyprus" (TRNC) declared by the Turkish-Cypriot parliament in 1983 (and recognized internationally only by Turkey) covers about a third of the entire island and contains about a quarter of the total population. Despite numerous efforts under UN auspices, no substantial progress has been achieved towards a settlement of the intercommunal dispute.

In the (southern) Republic of Cyprus the presidency was won in early 1988 by Georgios Vassiliou, an Independent supported by the pro-communist AKEL, the socialist EDEK and the recently formed Liberal Party. There is a centre-right majority in the unicameral House of Representatives, but the President is effectively not dependent on a majority in the legislature. In the TRNC the presidency is held by Rauf Denktash; since 1985 the government has been formed by the National Unity Party founded by him and the social democratic Communal Liberation Party (which together have a majority in the unicameral Assembly).

Economy. Most of the citrus groves, manufacturing industry and tourist facilities, and also the major port of Famagusta, lie in the area of the TRNC. The events of 1974 involved a massive exchange of population between the two parts of the island as Greek-Cypriots fled south and Turkish-Cypriots north. This necessitated a major restructuring of the economy of both parts with assistance from the Greek and Turkish governments as appropriate.

In the south, agricultural production has expanded, with a large export trade in fruit and vegetables; tourism has been developed; and an export trade in locally manufactured clothing and footwear has been established. In 1988 an agreement came into effect envisaging the achievement of a full customs union with the European Communities in two stages over 15 years.

In the north, which is relatively internationally isolated other than from Turkey, there has been a stagnation of the economy, with a low rate of growth combined with high rates of inflation and unemployment.

System of industrial relations. In independent Cyprus freedom of association was constitutionally guaranteed and Cyprus ratified ILO Conventions No. 87 (Freedom of Association and Protection of the Right to Organize, 1948) and No. 98 (Right to Organize and Collective Bargaining, 1949) in 1966.

Trade unionism. The British colonial authorities vigorously repressed the underground trade union movement in the 1930s, primarily because of its associations with nationalist and communist politics; however, unions not considered to be a security risk were permitted in 1937 and there was rapid growth thereafter.

Cyprus has been in effect partitioned since 1974 and different trade unions operate in the two parts of the island. However, a conference held in London in November 1984 and attended by representatives of the various Greek and Turkish trade union centres adopted a communiqué stating a belief that "the interests of Cypriot workers can only be met within an independent, sovereign, territorially integral, non-aligned federal republic, bi-communal in its constitutional and bizonal in its territorial aspects.... As trade unionists representing the vast majority of Cypriot workers, we recognize our special responsibility for initiating and supporting measures aimed at combating chauvinism and fostering rapprochement and understanding between the two communities". In general the various centres have in recent years concentrated on trade union "bread-and-butter" issues rather than wider political questions. The principal Greek centres are the Pancyprian Federation of Labour (PEO), affiliated to the WFTU, and the Cyprus Workers' Confederation (SEK), affiliated to the ICFTU, and the principal Turkish centre is the ICFTU-affiliated Cyprus Turkish Trade Unions Federation (Türk-Sen).

In 1985, SEK and TURK-SEN reached an agreement under ICFTU auspices providing for reciprocal visits and closer co-operation on union issues. For two years the agreement was not implemented but it was reactivated in 1987 following another ICFTU visit to the island. the unions claim that a number of benefits have accrued from the better relations between them. More than 500 TURK-SEN members, who worked all their lives in the Greek zone, have been able to claim their right to retirement thanks to the intervention of SEK. Several TURK-SEN delegations have been received at the SEK head office and the authorization of the President of the Turkish zone is no longer required for return visits by SEK. At the beginning of 1990 a joint co-ordinating committee was created by the two unions.

Greek organizations

Cyprus Civil Servants' Trade Union (PASYDY)

Address. 3 Dem. Severis St, Nicosia 136
Phone. (02) 442278, 442337, 441841
Leadership. A. Papanastassiou (president); G. Iacovou (general secretary)
Membership. 13,181.
Publication. *Dimosios Ypallilos* (fortnightly newspaper).

Demokratiki Ergatiki Omospondia Kyprou (DEOK)
Democratic Labour Federation of Cyprus

Address. 25 Const. Paleologos Avenue, P.O. Box 1625, Nicosia
Phone. (02) 456506
Leadership. Renos Prentzas (general secretary)
Membership. 3,482 in four affiliated unions.
History. Founded in 1962 after a split in the SEK (*see below*); virtually disappeared in the 1970s
but has recovered since 1982.
Publication. *Ergatikos Agonas.*
International affiliation. WCL.

Pankypria Ergatiki Omospondia (PEO)
Pancyprian Federation of Labour

Address. P.O. Box 1885, 31–35 Archermos St, Nicosia
Phone. (02) 4732192
Telex. 3073 OLVIA
Fax. 443382
Leadership. Andreas Ziartides (president); Avraam Antoniou (general secretary)
Membership. 75,000.
History. The PEO was founded in 1941 as the Pancyprian Trade Union Committee and
reorganized in 1946. There are 11 affiliated occupational unions, including the 10,000 members
of the Union of Cyprus Pensioners. The PEO engaged in discussions and joint actions with other
unions in 1986 in a successful effort to rebuff attempts by employers' organizations to reduce or
repeal cost of living allowance (COLA). Its 20th Congress in November 1987 focused on: (1) the
possible means of reconciliation between the two Cypriot communities through a reopened dialogue
under UN auspices with the aim of creating a non-aligned, demilitarized, federal state; and
(2) economic and social problems due to rising unemployment and the country's agreements with
the EEC.
Publication. *Engatiko Vrima.*
International affiliation. WFTU.

Pankyprios Omospondia Anexartition Syntechnion (POAS)
Pancyprian Federation of Independent Trade Unions

Address. 1 Menandrou Street, Nicosia 136
Phone. (02) 442233
Leadership. Costas Antoniades (president); Kyriacos Nathanail (general secretary)
Membership. Eight unions with 1,200 members.
History and character. The POAS was founded in 1956, and has recruited mainly among white-
collar staff. It has no political affiliations.
International affiliation. WCL.

Synomospondia Ergaton Kyprou (SEK)
Cyprus Workers' Confederation

Address. P.O. Box 5018, Nicosia
Phone. (02) 441142
Telex. 6180 SEKCY
Fax. (02) 476360
Leadership. Michael Ioannou (general secretary)
Membership. Seven federations, organized on occupational lines, with a combined membership of just under 53,016 two-thirds of whom are men.
History and character. Founded in Oct. 1944. In its early years the SEK met with bitter opposition from both the communist-controlled unions and, because of its support for self-determination for Greek Cypriots, from the colonial government. In 1949 SEK delegates took part in the founding conference of the ICFTU. Many of its leaders were arrested, imprisoned or killed during the struggle for independence in the late 1950s, seriously weakening the organization, but recovery took place in the 1960s. The SEK's political orientation is social democratic, but it supports no political party. Its policies include: (i) the introduction of a national health scheme; (ii) equal pay and rights for women; (iii) introduction of a low cost housing scheme for workers; (iv) industrial democracy; (v) maintenance of automatic cost-of-living adjustments in wages in line with increases in the retail price index. (The Greek Cypriot unions in March 1986 held a one-day strike to protest against employer demands for an end to the inflation-linking system.)
Structure. At the beginning of the 1960s, the SEK was composed of 232 free general unions, representing all kinds of workers, in as many towns and villages. In 1962, with ICFTU technical advice, the SEK was reorganized into "pancyprian federations", each of which was responsible for organizing workers on an occupational, island-wide, basis. The seven federations are: Industrial Employees' Federation Hotel Employees' Federation; Construction Workers, Miners and Allied Trades Federation; Government, Military and Public Services Federation; Transport, Petroleum and Agricultural Employees' Federation; Private Employees' Federation; and Semi-Government Employees' Federation.
Publication. *Ergatiki Phoni* (Workers' Voice) (weekly newspaper).
International affiliations. ICFTU; ETUC.

Turkish organizations

Devrimci İşçi Sendikalari Federasyonu (Dev-İş)
Revolutionary Trade Unions' Federation

Address. 8 Serabioglu Street, Nicosia
Phone. 90-520-72640
Leadership. Hasan Sarica (president) Bayram Çelik (general secretary)
Membership. Two unions with 3,200 members. These are the Revolutionary General Labour Union (DGIS, founded 1975) and the United Public Cooperative, Agricultural and Other Services and Craft Workers' Trade Union (EMEK-IŞ—also founded in 1975).
History and character. Founded in December 1976 by the merger of EMEK-IŞ and DGIS, themselves founded in 1975. The Federation describes itself as a progressive, class-based and politically-independent organization, and includes among its policies the search for a solution to the internal division of Cyprus on the basis of agreements reached between leaders of the two communities in 1977 and 1979.
Publications. *Dev İşin Sesí* (Voice of Dev/İş); *Genç İşli* (Young Worker); *Kuzey Kiblistaki Sendikalandan Habeller* (News from Trade Unions in Northern Cyprus).
International affiliation. WFTU.

Kibris Türk Isçi Sendikalari Federasyonu (Türk-Sen)
Cyprus Turkish Trade Unions Federation

Address. 7-7A Şehit Mehmet R. Hüseyin Str., P.O. Box 829, Lefkoşa, Mersin 10

Phone. (02) 472444
Telex. 2530 Turkoop
Cables. TURK-SEN, LEFKOSA-KIBRIS
Leadership. Hüseyin Curcioğlu (president); Lüfti Özter (general and financial secretary); Halil Bilener (organizing and educational secretary).
Membership. 15 unions with 12,000 members.
History and character. Founded 1954, registered 1955. The Türk-Sen constitution does not allow for any party political activity or link. Türk-Sen operates a chain of eight pharmacies in (Turkish-occupied) northern Cyprus, providing drug supplies to members on a low mark-up basis, and has established a "workers' development co-operative", which has set up building materials factories and constructed several hundred houses.
Structure. Triennial congress of 45 delegates from the affiliated unions; management committee; executive committee of nine members, including three full-time officials, namely the president and the two secretaries, which meets at least once per week.
Publication. İşçi Postasi (weekly newspaper, produced on its own printing press.)
International affiliations. ICFTU; ETUC; CTUC; Confederation of Turkish Trade Unions.

Czechoslovakia

Capital: Prague   **Population: 15,636,000**
                                                        (1989)

Political system. A people's republic was established in Czechoslavakia in 1948 following the resignation from government of the remaining non-communist members. Under the 1960 Constitution (as amended) the guiding force in society and in the state was the Communist Party, itself associated with other political parties and people's organizations within the National Front; this Front presented the sole list of candidates for election to the bicameral (federal) House of the People and to the Czech and Slovak national councils (in the two separate republics within the Czechoslovak Socialist Republic.) The Czech and Slovak republics have responsibility for all matters except principally foreign affairs, defence, foreign trade, transport and communications.

A brief period of reform in 1968 (the "Prague Spring") was abruptly terminated by a Russian invasion in August. From then on Czechosolvak society was deeply repressive, despite the publication of a human rights manifesto (Charter '77) by a number of dissident intellectuals. However, following the collapse of the Berlin Wall in 1989 discontent with the Czech regime resurfaced rapidly. The desire for reform was harnessed by the broadly-based Civic Forum which called a general strike in late November that shortly led to the collapse of the régime. In elections held in 1990, the Communist Party performed poorly; a government committed to political and economic liberalization took power and Vaclav Havel, a playwright and dissident often imprisoned for his views, became the country's first post-Communist President.

On March 4, 1991, all of Czechoslovakia's main political groups and institutions reached agreement on the framework for a new constitution. Its principles would be: (i) a federative state consisting of two equal and sovereign republics in the Czech lands and Slovakia; (ii) the republics to be linked by free will expressed in a declaration of coexistence; (iii) the federal constitution would be the fundamental document of the state; (iv) all powers not explicitly given to the federal state in the constitution would rest with the republics. Despite this agreement tensions between the nationalities were growing and there was a powerful separatist movement in Slovakia. On March 10 President Havel acknowledged the right of Slovakia to split away but disputed that such a desire was held by a majority of Slovaks.

Economy. Under the 1960 Constitution the country's economy is based on the socialist system and directed by plan. The means of production are socially owned; socialist owner-ship includes both national property (e.g. mineral wealth, the means of industrial produc-tion and banks) and co-operative property. Within agricultural co-operatives the land of members remains their personal property but is jointly farmed by the co-operative. Small private enterprises based on the labour of the owner himself are permitted.

Czechoslovakia's system of five-year planning is integrated and co-ordinated within the comprehensive programme of the Council for Mutual Economic Assistance (CMEA or Comecon). The country is among the most industrially developed of Comecon member states, with industry accounting for about 60 per cent of net material product (NMP) as against less than 10 per cent for agriculture and forestry; comparable figures for employ-ment are 40 and 14 per cent respectively.

"Restructuring" legislation was introduced in 1987 to provide for the devolution of responsibility away from central planning to individual enterprises in both the industrial and commercial and the agricultural sectors.

Since December 1989 successive governments have steered a progressively more definite course towards economic liberalization. However the consequences of this have been felt in industrial areas, and have fuelled discontent, especially in Slovakia where the national unions threatened a general strike to retain the prime minister of their choice.

System of industrial relations. Czechoslovakia ratified ILO Conventions No. 87 (Freedom of Association and Protection of the Right to Organize, 1948) and No. 98 (Right to Organize and Collective Bargaining, 1949) in 1964. The ILO *Report of the Committee of Experts on the Application of Conventions and Recommendations* (1985) noted that the government contended that the unity of the trade union movement (whereby 97 per cent of all workers were members of the Revolutionary Trade Union Movement, ROH) had come about by a free decision of the workers, and that legislation of 1973 in any case made provision for the possibility of workers freely constituting other trade unions. The Committee stated, however, that a de facto trade union monopoly did exist, and that the ROH was granted a preferential status in a range of legislation; thus, for example, the ROH was referred to by name in Article 5 of the 1960 Constitution and the Labour Code of 1965 provided for collective agreements to be concluded on behalf of the workers by the organs of the ROH. The Committee also noted that members of collective farms were not covered by the provisions of the labour code concerning trade union bodies, but the government stated that those members of co-operative farms who engaged in activity of an industrial character had already joined trade unions and the others were excluded by virtue of the nature of their activity and employment status; these persons were members of the Union of Co-operative Farmers.

New draft legislation was introduced in 1990 on trade union rights and social security. Under pressure from the new union centre CS KOS (*see below*) consultations were held with the unions on a proposed new Labour Code. The law on union recognition was amended by Parliament along lines drafted by CS KOS in July 1990, and as a result is now in line with ILO standards. However a large amount of industrial relations legislation from the pre-1989 era remains on the statute book.

Trade unionism. A highly developed but fragmented pattern of trade unionism existed in Czechoslovakia before World War II. Unions were dissolved during the war, but after liberation in 1944, competing Christian, social democratic and communist unions were re-established. Following the consolidation of the position of the Communist Party as the ruling force in 1948, however, the Central Council of Trade Unions (ÚRO) became the sole trade union centre, organizing the Revolutionary Trade Union Movement (ROH). Under the Dubcek government in 1968 the trade unions were radically reorganized, allowed to assert their own independent identity, and accorded an ultimate right to strike. Notwithstanding the Soviet-led occupation of the country in August 1968, the ÚRO congress held in March 1969 reaffirmed its support for the reforms; however, this residual defiance was effectively suppressed later that year following the replacement of Dubcek as First Secretary of the Communist Party.

Trade unions participated in the formulation of economic plans and had direct responsibilities in the provision of social and welfare services. Enterprise managers had to seek the support of the unions before any changes in the terms and conditions of workers could be made, and the unions ensured observance by employers of employment and work safety regulations. Disputes between workers and employers were generally settled by trade union branch arbitration commissions: in 1987 almost 5,000 commissions dealt with some 36,000 disputes.

The ÚRO was involved in drafting a new Labour Code, which Miroslav Zavadil, the ÚRO chairman, described as "a legal document guaranteeing the social certainties of the working people and contributing to the intensification of discipline and to the more flexible deployment of the labour force". At its 11th Congress in April 1987 the ROH gave its full support to the current policy of economic restructuring in Czechoslovakia, and in the keynote address Zavadil spoke of the need to restructure the work of the unions in order to simplify the organization of the ROH to eliminate the "formalism and bureaucracy" which persisted in several trade union bodies. This restructuring was the purpose of amendments to the ROH statutes which were approved at a special ROH national conference in September 1988.

By comparison with, for example, Bulgaria, the involvement of the unions in the revolution of autumn of 1989, was tardy. When it came, it took the form of "Strike Readiness Committees" which spread rapidly across the country. By December 1989 they were thought to have mobilized more than 5,000,000 workers and an Association of Committees (ASC) was formed. In the face of this competition the official centre crumbled despite an attempt at restructuring to come to terms with the new reality. Each enterprise in Czechoslovakia organized elections early in 1990 (many under ASC supervision) and sent delegates to a national congress at which the Confederation of Czechoslovakian Trade Unions (CS KOS) was founded.

CS KOS declined to affiliate to the WFTU and quickly demonstrated its independence with the threat of a general strike to force the government to consult it on new union rights and social security regulations. Like URO it has eight million members and has affiliated to the ICFTU on this figure. There are some small independent unions but in terms of size they do not compete with CS KOS.

Confederation of Czechoslovakian Trade Unions (CS KOS)

Address. nám. Antonía Zápotockého 2, 113 59 Prague 3
Phone. 2113
Telex. 121517
Leadership: Igor Pleskot (president)
Membership: Around 8,000,000
International affiliations: URO was affiliated to the WFTU (which has its headquarters in Prague), but in May 1990 CS KOS affiliated to the ICFTU.
History and character: CS KOS was founded in March 1990 at a national congress whose delegates were chosen at nation-wide enterprise elections. It inherited the assets of the former

Central Council of Trade Unions (URO) which had been the only union centre under the old régime. Like URO which in fact was composed of a Czech and a Slovak Council, CS KOS has a Confederation of Trade Unions for each nation. The Slovak Confederation threatened a general strike in May 1991 against the dismissal of the Slovak prime minister and his replacement by a Christian Democrat.

The origins of CS KOS lay in the strike committees which came into being in November and December 1989. Briefly URO sought to come to terms with them: its President Miroslav Zavadil resigned on 26th November and his successor Karel Henes offered negotiations. Henes announced that the URO had severed its connections with the Communist Party its plant-based party cells dissolved, and it was relaunched as the Action Committee on Dec. 11. In practice however the issue was resolved by defections from the Action Committee to the Association of Strike Committees [ASC]. Negotiations were broken off but the Action Committee was never in a position to re-establish itself. In practice the ASC approach appears to have been decisive in that its reform objectives ensured trade union unity despite the existence of some small independent centres.

Publication. Prace (Czech); *Praca* (Slovak).

Denmark

Capital: Copenhagen   **Population: 5,133,000**

Political system. Denmark is a constitutional monarchy with a unicameral parliament (*Folketing*). General elections are frequent but defeats in the *Folketing* do not necessarily lead to a government's fall from office. In 1982 the Social Democratic government gave way to a series of Centre-Right coalitions under Prime Minister Poul Schluter, leader of the Conservative Party. He pursued policies designed to curb public sector employment, but experienced greater difficulties with these after the recession of 1987. Severe austerity measures, including cuts in welfare benefits and incomes policies characterized his government's attempts to offset the cost of Denmark's imports. In December 1990 his attempt to gain support for tax reforms at a general election backfired, allowing the Social Democrats to register a large increase in seats from 55 to 69. The Coalition stayed in power with a slim majority.

Economy. Denmark became a member of the European Communities in 1973, having previously been a member of the European Free Trade Association since its formation in 1960.

Some 67.4 per cent of Danish employment is in services, 26.7 per cent in industry and 5.9 per cent in agriculture. The country experienced rapid growth of its economy and labour force up to 1987, followed by two years of recession. A recovery in 1989 was assisted by higher than usual export growth, but the problems of the 1980s—a structural deficit in the balance of payments (exacerbated by the need to import some three quarters of the country's energy requirements), and rising unemployment, persisted. At the start of 1991, unemployment had reached a rate of 9.7 per cent in stark contrast to the country's record on inflation, which remained steady at 2.5 per cent after falling during 1990. Denmark has an unusually large public sector, but the public monopoly of job placement activity was terminated in July 1990.

System of industrial relations. Denmark ratified ILO Convention No. 87 (Freedom of Association and Protection of the Right to Organize, 1948) in 1951 and Convention No. 98 (Right to Organize and Collective Bargaining, 1949) in 1955.

Wage controls. Collective agreements providing for wage indexation linked to price inflation were suspended by the new centre-right government in 1983 (retroactively as from Oct. 1982) for a period up to Jan. 1985, and the suspension was in May 1984 extended to Jan. 1987. Since 1899 it had been the established practice in Denmark that questions of wages, hours and working conditions were a matter for collective bargaining between the two sides of industry. In comment the ILO *Report of the Committee of Experts* (1985) stated that the "right to negotiate wages and conditions of employment freely with the employers and their organizations, is a fundamental aspect of freedom of association, and . . . any restriction on the free fixing of wage rates should be imposed as an exceptional measure . . . without exceeding a reasonable period"; a period of four years was, in the Committee's view, excessive and in contravention of Convention No. 87. The government in response argued that the restrictions were justified as an aspect of anti-inflation policy, and pointed out that restrictions had simultaneously been placed on profits and dividends. Since 1987 the two sides of industry have again been free to conclude wage indexation agreements.

The 1987 Central Wage Agreement between the main union and employer centres covered (unusually) the four years following, and under it there were moderate increases and some progress towards reducing working hours. There was provision for a mid-term review. The first two years' life of the agreement also saw days lost through industrial action fall from over 137,300 to less than 53,000. Consultations were undertaken by both sides of industry early in 1991 as to negotiating objectives for the next agreement. The government view was that increases should be kept to 3.5 per cent coupled with cuts in taxes. There were signs that the unions, concerned over high unemployment, were mainly interested in obtaining greater job security and improved pensions but the Metal union prioritized a shorter working week.

Trade unionism. Unions developed in the nineteenth century, and the Federation of Danish Trade Unions (Landsorganisationen i Danmark, LO) was founded in 1898. In 1899 unions and employers reached a basic agreement on the right to organize and industrial partnership which has formed the bedrock of subsequent trade union growth and policies. The unions also administer unemployment insurance schemes directly on behalf of the government.

Union density in Denmark is extremely high at 80 per cent. The main union centre the LO has not far short of 1,500,000 members, the great bulk of Denmark's trade unionists. In this it compares favourably to the Danish Employers' Confederation (DA) which has never been able to achieve such coverage and is restructuring to improve its representativeness. But organizational change is also under discussion at the LO which has reduced its number of affiliates to 30 and allocated them at its November 1989 Congress to five "cartels" which may eventually become bargaining units. This is the latest in a series of contested attempts by the LO centre to reorganize its structure along industrial lines. The process of rationalization has been assisted by the amalgamation of craft unions, the growth of the general workers union SiD (which holds one quarter of LO membership), and a legal requirement that a union's unemployment insurance fund must have at least 5,000 members in order to qualify for state assistance.

Financial support for political parties. The Specialarbejderforbundet i Danmark (Special Workers' Union or Federation of General Workers, SID), representing unskilled and semi-skilled workers, announced in April 1985 that it would spend DKr 180 m in a propaganda campaign aimed at bringing down the centre-right coalition government because of its incomes policy. (The largest political party, the Social Democrats, normally spent less than a tenth of this amount in a general election campaign.) Under current law, trade unionists cannot contract out of the use of part of their union dues for party political purposes, and in 1984–85 several major unofficial strikes were staged by workers objecting to other workers leaving the Special Workers' Union because of their refusal to make contributions to the Social Democrats.

The Social Democratic Party (SDP) appoints two members of the LO executive committee, and the LO reciprocally appoints two members of the SDP executive.

Other centres. While many clerical employees of government are members of LO-affiliated unions, the Federation of Civil Servants' and Salaried Employees' Organizations (FTF) also holds affiliations from unions they join. The strongest influence in the FTF is probably that of the teachers' and nurses' organizations, but it has important private sector affiliates too, notably in banking. There are separate representative centres for academics, supervisors and technicians.

Landsorganisationen i Danmark (LO)
Danish Confederation of Trade Unions

Phone. 31 35 35 41

116

Telex. 16 170 Io dk

Fax. 31 37 37 41

Leadership. Finn Thorgrimson (president); Hans Jensen (vice-president); Erik Hemmingsen (treasurer)

Membership. In 1990 the LO had 1,422,969 members organized in 30 affiliated unions, an increase since 1987 of 10,202. Some 48 per cent of affiliated members are female.

International affiliations. ICFTU; ETUC; TUAC; NFS. The LO maintains an International Solidarity Fund, established in 1980, and jointly [with the FTF] sponsors the Danish Trade Union Council for International Development Cooperation.

Publications. LO Bladet (weekly); *Danish Labour News.*

Affiliated unions and structure. The Commercial and Clerical Employees Union HK is now the LO's biggest affiliate, having increased its membership by 5,521 since 1987; the second largest union (formerly the largest) is the National Union of General Workers (SiD) which has 313,235 members, having grown by 6,918 members since 1987. National Affiliates of the LO are as follows, with membership figures as at January 1990.

1. **Blik- og Rørarbejderforbundet i Danmark** (The National Union of Plumbers), Alholmvej 55, DK-2500 Valby.
   Membership: 8,731.

2. **Dansk Beklædnings- og Textilarbejderforbund** (The National Union of Garment and Textile Workers), Nyropsgade 14, DK-1602 Copenhagen V
   Membership: 25,033.

3. **Dansk Bogbinder- og Kartonnagearbejderforbund** (National Union of Bookbinders and Allied Workers), Grafisk Forbundshus, Lygten 16, 2. DK-2400 Copenhagen NV.
   Membership: 8,740.

4. **Dansk El-forbund** (The National Union of Electricians), Vodroffsvej 26, DK-1900 Frederiksberg C.
   Membership: 26,396.

5. **Dansk Frisørforbund** (The National Union of Hairdressers), Lersø Park Allé 21, DK-2100 Copenhagen Ø.
   Membership: 5,065.

6. **Dansk Funktionærforbund** (The National Union of Workers in Service Trades), Upsalagade 20, DK-2100 Copenhagen Ø.
   Membership: 20,264.

7. **Dansk Jernbaneforbund** (The National Union of Railwaymen), Tjenestemændenes Hus, Bredgade 21,3, DK-1260 Copenhagen K.
   Membership: 10,624.

8. **Dansk Kommunalarbejderforbund** (The National Union of Municipal Workers), Nitivej 6, DK-2000 Frederiksberg C.
   Membership: 121,297.

9. **Dansk Litografisk Forbund** (The National Union of Lithographers), Grafisk Forbundshus, Lygten 16, DK-2400 Copenhagen NV.
   Membership: 5,294.

10. **Dansk Metalarbejderforbund** (The National Union of Metalworkers), Nyropsgade 38, DK-1602 Copenhagen V.
    Membership: 140,771.

11. **Dansk Postforbund** (The National Union of Postal Workers), Vodroffsvej 13A, DK-1900 Frederiksberg C.
    Membership: 15,102.

12. **Dansk Tele Forbund** (The National Union of Telecommunications Workers), Rolfsvej 37, 1, DK-2000 Frederiksberg C
    Membership: 9,782.

13. **Dansk Typografforbund** (The National Union of Typographers), Grafisk Forbundshus, Lygten 16, DK-2400 Copenhagen NV.
    Membership: 9,510.

14. **Fotografisk Landsforbund** (The National Union of Photographers), Grafisk Forbundshus, Lygten 16, DK-2400 Copenhagen NV.
    Membership: 1,870.

15. **Gastronomisk Landsforbund** (The National Union of Skilled Kitchen Staff), Apollovej 31B, DK-2720 Vanl¢se.
    Membership: 7,450.

16. **Hærens Konstabel- og Korporalforening (HKKF)** (The National Union of Enlisted Military Personnel in the Army), Trommesalen 3, DK-1614 Copenhagen V.
    Membership: 4,495.

17. **Handels- og Kontorfunktionærers Forbund i Danmark** (The National Union of Commercial and Clerical Employees — HK), Post Box 268, H.C. Andersens Boulevard 50, DK-1501 Copenhagen V.
    Membership: 322,990.

18. **Hotel- og Restaurantpersonalets Forbund i Danmark** (The National Union of Hotel and Restaurant Workers), Vendersgade 24 and 31, DK-1363 Copenhagen K.
    Membership: 8,677.

19. **Husligt Arbejderforbund** (The National Union of Cleaners and Domestic Workers), Rådhuspladsen 77, DK-1550 Copenhagen V.
    Membership: 79,591.

20. **Kvindeligt Arbejderforbund i Danmark (KAD)** (The National Union of Female Workers), Ewaldsgade 3, DK-2200 Copenhagen N.
    Membership: 96,653.

21. **Landsforeningen Danske Klubfolk** (The National Union of Employees in Recreation and Youth Centres), St. Kongensgade 79,4, DK-1264 Copenhagen K.
    Membership: 4,629.

22. **Malerforbundet i Danmark** (The National Union of Painters), Thomsgaardsvej 23C, DK-2400 Copenhagen NV
    Membership: 13,757.

23. **Murerforbundet i Danmark** (The National Union of Bricklayers), Mimersgade 47,3, DK-2200 Copenhagen N.
    Membership: 12,335.

24. **Nærings- og Nydelsesmiddelarbejder Forbundet (NNF)** (The National Union of Food and Allied Workers), Post Box 1479, C.F.Richsvej 103, DK-2000 Frederiksberg C.
    Membership: 42,290.

25. **Pædagogisk Medhjælperforbund (PMF)** (The National Union of Nursery and Childcare Assistants), St. Kongensgade 79, DK-1264 Copenhagen K.
    Membership: 24, 918.

26. **Socialpædagogernes Landsforbund** (The National Union of Social Pedagogues), Brolæggerstræde 9, DK-1211 Copenhagen K.
    Membership: 17,472.

27. **Snedker-og T¢mrerforbundet i Danmark** (The National Union of Joiners, Cabinetmakers and Carpenters), Mimersgade 47, DK-2200 Copenhagen N.
    Membership: 47,393.

28. **Specialarbejderforbundet i Danmark** (The National Union of General Workers—industrial,

building & construction, transport and agricultural sectors), Nyropsgade 30, DK-1602 Copenhagen V.
Membership: 313,235

29. **Tjenerforbundet i Danmark** (The National Union of Waiters), Vendersgade 31, DK-1363 Copenhagen K.
Membership: 5,209.

30. **Træindustriarbejderforbundet i Danmark** (The National Union of Woodworkers), Mimergade 47, 2, DK-2200 Copenhagen N.
Membership: 21,396.

The LO constitution guarantees the sovereignty of member unions, leaving the Confederation to coordinate. The Congress of the LO is its highest authority—convened every four years—which lays down objectives and policies (800 delegates). The 400-strong General Council is responsible for updating activities and objectives in the years between Congresses. An Executive Board, elected by Congress, is responsible for the daily management of the ILO. It has 24 members of which two are appointed by the Social Democratic Party. Departments within the LO include: Analysis, Press and Information, Working Environment, Cooperation, Labour Market, Equality, Research and Technology, Social Policy, Trades Councils, Shop Steward Training, International Affairs dept., Publications, Legal dept., Training and Education, Culture/Leisure, Youth, Public Sector, Economics.

History and character. The LO was founded in 1898 in an attempt to co-ordinate the nascent Danish labour organizations. From its inception it has participated in collective bargaining to improve wages and conditions, while working with the Social Democratic Party to promote social legislation.

The LO is Denmark's main trade union centre. Within traditional areas of employment it dominates, with density sometimes as high as 95 per cent. Approximately one third of its membership is in the public sector, one third is in companies affiliated to the DA, and one third is in other private companies. From time to time rationalization of the union structure along industrial lines has been discussed and special reports on the matter were considered at the 1987 and 1989 Congresses.

Other organization

Funktionærernes og Tjenestemændenes Fællesråd (FTF)
Federation of Civil Servants' and Salaried Employees' Organizations

Address. Niels Hemmingsensgade 12, Postbox 1169, 1010 Copenhagen K
Phone. (01) 15-30-22
Fax. (01) 91-30-22
Leadership. Martin Rømer (chairman)
Membership. 360,000 (60 per cent female), in 106 affiliated unions which represent teachers, civil servants, bank employees, local government employees, insurance employees, merchant seamen's officers, and other white-collar employees.
History and character. The FTF was founded in 1952 by 11 organizations of white-collar employees who were outside the broad labour movement. Among the concerns prompting its creation were the failure of salaries to keep pace with wage increases awarded to manual workers, and the desire for leadership which would be politically neutral (i.e. unlike that of the socialist-inclined LO). The LO and FTF had achieved a working relationship by 1973, after the LO had earlier regarded the new organization with some hostility. The FTF is independent of any political party, and is represented on 160 government committees, but its apolitical stance has tended to weaken over the years.
Publications. Fællesrådet (monthly); *FTF Information* (monthly).
International affiliations. ETUC; TUAC; ICFTU; NFS.

Djibouti

Capital: Djibouti

Population: 370,000
(1987)

Political system. Djibouti, formerly the French Territory of the Afars and Issas, became independent in 1977 following a referendum on the issue. There is a unicameral Chamber of Deputies for elections, to which, since 1981, only the Popular Rally for Progress (RPP, an affiliate of the Socialist Inter-African) is permitted to present candidates. Over half the population is nomadic, and there have in recent years been on occasion large influxes of refugees from Somalia and Ethiopia. Tension persists between the majority Issas (of Somali ethnic origin) and the Afars (of Ethiopian ethnic origin), with the latter maintaining that the dominant Issas exercise discrimination against them.

Economy. Djibouti has few natural resources, little arable land and hardly any industry. The country depends to a large extend on foreign aid, together with expenditure by the French armed forces stationed there by agreement and by (mainly French) expatriates. A free trade zone has been created to encourage the establishment of new industries. There is a considerable entrepôt trade based on the strategic position of the seaport, the airport and the railway link to the Ethiopian capital of Addis Ababa. Djibouti has a developed financial services sector, which benefits from the absence of exchange control and the free convertibility of the Djibouti franc.

System of industrial relations. Djibouti ratified ILO Conventions No. 87 (Freedom of Association and Protection of the Right to Organize, 1948), No. 98 (Right to Organize and Collective Bargaining, 1949) and Nos 29 and 105 on forced labour in 1978.

Trade unionism. Trade unions developed under French rule. One organization, the General Union of Djibouti Workers, has been identified.

Union Générale des Travailleurs de Djibouti (UGTD)
General Union of Djibouti Workers

Address. B.P. 489 Djibouti
Leadership. Ahmed Osman Moussa (secretary general)
International affiliation. OATUU. Observer status with ICATU.

Dominica

Capital: Roseau

Population: 81,000
(1988)

Political system. Dominica, formerly a West Indies Associated State, became a fully independent member of the Commonwealth in 1978 with republican status. There is a unicameral House of Assembly comprising 21 elected members and nine nominated senators. The Dominica Labour Party formed the administration from 1961 to 1979 but then, after a period of unrest and interim government, the "liberal, democratic and anti-communist" Dominica Freedom Party (DFP) came to office in 1980.

Economy. Dominica's principal economic activity is agriculture, and in particular the growing of bananas which accounts normally for about half of all exports. However, the banana industry has been periodically subject to heavy damage by severe hurricanes, torrential rains and disease, and is also prone to wide fluctuations. An Industrial Development Corporation was set up in 1974 to promote the establishment of new industries, and the DFP government has encouraged private-sector (including foreign) investment both directly and through joint ventures with the public sector. The government has also sought to improve infrastructural facilities.

Despite the vulnerability of Dominica's export trade, progress was made in the mid-1980s in reducing inflation, unemployment and also the trade deficit. An essential part of the DFP's economic strategy (with IMF support) has been the encouragement of private-sector investment and the concentration of the public sector on securing favourable conditions and the infrastructure necessary for the development of private-sector activities.

Unemployment fell in the late 1980s as banana production and construction provided new job opportunities for younger workers. Inflation in the early part of 1989 was above 9 per cent.

System of industrial relations. Dominica ratified ILO Conventions No. 87 (Freedom of Association and Protection of the Right to Organize, 1948) and No. 98 (Right to Organize and Collective Bargaining, 1949) in 1983; collective bargaining is freely practised and there is also recourse to mediation and arbitration by government.

Trade unionism. There is no trade union centre; the Dominica Trade Union fulfilled this role in the 1950s, but was subsequently weakened by the defection or its members to non-affiliated organizations. Relations between the various organizations were poor during the 1960s and early 1970s, but have since improved.

The CSA is the major public service union in Dominica though two other unions have bargaining rights with some of the Statutory Boards, public corporations and quasi-governmental institutions in the public sector. The country's four other unions are general organizations operating mainly in the private sector.

Civil Service Association (CSA)

Address: Valley Road/Windsor Lane, Roseau
Phone: (809) 44 82101/2
Leadership: Arthur R. Smith (president); Alvin A. Thomas (general secretary)
Membership: 1,500.
History and character. The Dominica Civil Service Association (DCSA) was founded in 1939 with Henry Letang (deceased) and John Bully as its first President and Secretary respectively; it was not until 1960 that steps were taken to change the status of what was in fact a Staff Association to that of a Trade Union. The Dominica CSA therefore became a registered Trade Union in 1961 under the Trade Union and Trade Disputes Ordinance Cap. 120 of the 1961 Revised Laws of Dominica with Ted Boyd (then Registrar General) as president, Arthur C. B. Watty as Secretary and Claude Bruney as Treasurer.

The CSA is the major public service union in the state. From 1967 and in keeping with the Dominica Constitution Order of 1967 (with similar provisions in the 1978 Independence Constitution Order), the Association has been recognized as the sole Bargaining Agent for all grades and categories of public officers in the State except police officers.

Publications. Newsletters; *Viewpoint*.
International affiliations. PSI, ICFTU.

Dominica Amalgamated Workers' Union (DAWU)

Address. 40 Kennedy Avenue, P.O. Box 137, Roseau
Phone. 83048

Cable. TECWUN

Membership. 3,500.

History and character. The DAWU was founded as the Dominica Banana Employees' Association in 1960, adopted the name Technical, Clerical and Commercial Workers' Union in 1961, and its present name in 1965.

Up until 1988 the Union had led several battles against foreign-owned companies, but it became less militant that year following a change of leadership.

Publication. Expression (occasional).

International affiliations. WCL; CLAT.

Dominica Trade Union (DTU)

Address. 70–71 Queen Mary Street, Roseau

Phone. 2903

Leadership. R. L. Kirton (president), Veronica Nicholas (general secretary)

Membership. 720

History and character. Founded in 1945, the DTU was at its peak in its earliest years, having over 8,000 members from a wide occupational spectrum in the 1945–50 period. Until the 1960s it remained the only union in Dominica, but the labour movement fragmented thereafter and the DTU declined. Its members today are mostly agricultural labourers, peasants, sharecroppers and maids. It has no current political affiliations, and its one-time political influence (when successive First Ministers were DTU members) has diminished.

Publications. Former publications have been abandoned because of lack of finance.

International affiliation. ICFTU.

Waterfront and Allied Workers' Union (WAWU)

Address. 43 Hillsborough Street, Roseau

Leadership. Louis Benoit (president); Curtis Augustus (general secretary)

Membership. 3,000.

History and character. Founded 1965. The Union successfully used boycotts of loading or unloading against two employers in 1988 to force concesssions in negotiations.

International affiliation. ICFTU.

Dominican Republic

Capital: Santo Domingo **Population: 6,859,000**
(1988)

Political system. More than 30 years of authoritarian rule by Generalissimo Rafael Trujillo ended with his assassination in 1961, and in the following year Juan Bosch of the Dominican Revolutionary Party (PRD, affiliated to the Socialist International) was elected President. This government, however, was overthrown in 1963, and in the course of an attempt in 1965 to reinstate him the USA intervened militarily to stop the ensuing civil war. Joaquín Balaguer of the anti-Marxist Social Christian Reform Party (PRSC), or Reformist Party, was elected President in 1966 and was re-elected in 1970 and 1974. The PRD successful in the 1978 and 1982 elections but Joaquín Balaguer was again elected President in 1986. There is a bicameral National Congress, in which since 1986 the PRSC has enjoyed an overall majority in the senate but only a relative majority in the Chamber of Deputies.

The presidential election of May 1990 was surrounded by controversy and accusations of fraud. After a recount, the Central Electoral Board announced that the incumbent President, Joaquín Balaguer, had won a narrow victory.

Economy. The economy of the Dominican Republic is dominated by the agricultural sector. Although sugar has traditionally been the principal crop, output is periodically adversely affected by hurricanes; the international market for sugar is liable to severe fluctuations (as are the markets for the alternative coffee, cocoa and tobacco); and in 1984 the major US plantation owner, Gulf and Western, announced its intention to withdraw from the country (selling its holdings to other US-based interests later that year). There are substantial deposits of bauxite, but the fall in the international price caused the cessation of production in 1984. The manufacturing industry is mainly centred around the processing of agricultural products, while tourism is a major and growing earner of foreign exchange.

Increasingly serious balance-of-payments problems and a rapidly growing foreign debt (about $4,000 million by 1987) have necessitated sharp austerity measures throughout the 1980s; these in turn have given rise to considerable industrial and social unrest as the government has sought to comply with conditions specified by the International Monetary Fund as necessary for the continuation of financial assistance.

The economy of the Dominican Republic grew by 2.9 per cent in 1989, a great improvement over the previous year. Out of 2,200,000 civilian employees that year, 7.2 per cent were in industry, 32.2 per cent were in agriculture, and 28.3 per cent were in services. However, the unemployment rate exceeded 28 per cent and inflation continued to be high at 41.2 per cent. The country still had debt equivalent to 70 per cent of GDP. Early in 1989 the Republic ceased making interest payments to commercial banks but it is honouring its debts to international financial institutions; the government declined to make an agreement with the IMF however for fear of instigating internal discontent.

System of industrial relations. Although the Dominican Republic ratified ILO Conventions No. 87 (Freedom of Association and Protection of the Right to Organize, 1948) in 1956, No. 98 (Right to Organize and Collective Bargaining, 1949) in 1953, and No. 105 (Abolition of Forced Labour, 1957) in 1958, the Committee of Experts on the Application of Conventions and Recommendations noted, in a report in December 1987, that the country's Labour Code still excludes agricultural, agro-industrial, stock raising and forestry concerns not employing more that ten workers continuously and permanently; that public employees are excluded from the Labour Code and thus effectively prevented from organizing (or even campaigning) for their own unions; that the Labour Code prohibits the right of "political" and "sympathy" strikes and imposes other major restrictions on the right to strike; and that counter to the government's claim that there was no forced labour in the country, there was ample evidence of the seasonal rounding up of Haitian citizens for the cane harvest, organized by clandestine labour groups (in Haiti and Dominican territory) with the collusion of the CEA (State Sugar Board). The majority of such Haitians worked in sub-human conditions (namely excessively long days "at times up to 16 hours under the supervision of armed guards") and received the lowest wages in Dominican agriculture. In response, the government assured the Committee that a bill to guarantee against the removal of trade unionists, and to protect trade union leaders in the negotiation of collective agreements or other trade-union activities, had been submitted to Congress. The government also stated that Haitian plantation workers were no longer being engaged. Clandestine workers crossing the border from Haiti were, however, said to be difficult to monitor and control.

Industrial unrest. The centre-left Dominican Revolutionary Party (PRD) government of President Salvador Jorge Blanco, elected in May 1982, faced serious unrest arising from its imposition of austerity measures in an attempt to meet its external debt difficulties. Disorders, leading to at least 100 deaths, broke out on April 23–25, 1984, in response to the announcement of price rises backed by the International Monetary Fund (IMF). To pre-empt a general strike called for May 1, the government used troops to occupy union offices and arrest union leaders, among them the leader of the General Central of Workers (CGT), Julio de Peña Valdéz. Four died in general strikes called in early 1985, but the government responded by reducing the prices of some essential goods, and went on to make further concessions following a 24-hour general strike in June 1985 which also won support from many non-union workers and small businesses. The success of strikes reflected the unprecedented unity of the various trade union federations (with the principal exception of the pro-PRD government Unión General de Trabajadores Dominicanos, UGTD), whose rival political affiliations had previously commonly precluded collective action, and the activities of neighbourhood strike committees. However, many trade upon activists were detained for short periods at different times during the year. For the first time in the country's history, workers took part in a national general strike on July 28, 1987. This followed the first national trade union forum, of Feb. 7, 1987, which sought to establish the basis for unity in action between the various trade unions.

In June 1989 a number of local unions and political parties began a series of actions to protest against the breakdown of essential services. The same month negotiations opened between the government and seven national centres over the level of the minimum wage. The talks were prolonged, and it was only under threat of a national general strike that the wage board in October conceded a significant rise together with undertakings that the President would freeze rents, cut the prices of basic goods and maintain permanent consultations with the unions. Throughout the year there was discontent in the health service, punctuated by strikes.

Trade unionism. Workers' organizations developed in the 1920s and a Dominican Confederation of Workers (Confederación Dominicana de Trabajadores, CDT) was formed in 1930. Trujillo's assumption of power later that year, however, led to the dissolution of the CDT; some unions nevertheless continued to exist, and Trujillo sponsored his own trade union centre, the CTD; this expired after his assassination in 1961 and was replaced by independent rival centres, including affiliates of the regional organizations of the three main world trade union organizations, i.e. the WFTU (CPUSTAL), the ICFTU (ORIT) and the WCL (CLAT). However, the Balaguer government from 1966–78 was generally unsympathetic to the trade unions and the Trujillo labour code remained in operation. About 13 per cent of the workforce is organized, and the various trade union centres tend to be unstable with frequent breakaways and ruptures. The fragmentary legacy of the Trujillo Labour Code still haunts Dominican unions.

There are currently nine trade union centres, including affiliates of the regional organizations of all three international trade union centres, i.e. CPUSTAL (WFTU), ORIT (ICFTU), and CLAT (WCL), and centres linked to each of the three main parties (i,.e. the Social Christian Reform Party—PSRC, the Dominican Liberation Party—PLD, and the Dominican Revolutionary Party—PRD). In September 1988, two of the centres, the National Confederation of Dominican Workers (CNTD) and the General Union of Dominican Workers (UGTD) announced a decision to merge though the rump of the UGTD remained in existence.

A new centre, the Independent Workers' Centre (CTI) was recognized in March 1990. It has links to the Democratic Workers' Party (PDT). Some unions are unaffiliated, notably the Union of the Workers of the Dominican Electrical Corporation (SITRA-CODE).

124

Central General de Trabajadores (CGT)
General Workers' Centre

Address. Juan Erazo 133, Santo Domingo, D.N.

Phone. 682-0600; 688-3932; 688-4584

Leadership. Francisco A. Santos (secretary-general)

Membership. Labour Secretariat unofficially reports 11 federations and 100 affiliated unions. However, these statistics do not reflect the recent split. Other sources indicate the current membership (combined total of both factions) is about 50,000.

History and character. The CGT was formed in 1972 from a previous United Workers' Front for Autonomous Trade Unions-Central of Trade Unions of Dominican Workers (FOUPSA-CESITRADO); this was the more left-wing faction (created in 1962 and identified with the Dominican Revolutionary Party — PRD — then led by Juan Bosch) of the previously united FOUPSA (itself created in 1961). The FOUPSA-CESITRADO opposed the US-led military intervention in 1965. The CGT is now split into the CGT and the CGT/Mayoritaria (Majority); the CGT faction is seen as communist-influenced by the Socialist Bloc (Bloque Socialista, BS) and Dominican Workers' Party (Partido de los Trabajadores Dominicanos, PTD).

International affiliations. Permanent Congress of Labour Unity of Latin American Workers (CPUSTAL); WFTU.

Central Obrera Dominicana (COD)
Dominican Workers' Centre

Address. Padre Castellanos 179 (altos), Santo Domingo, D.N

Phone. 685-8475

Leadership. Rafael Pimentel (secretary-general)

Membership. The country's Labour Secretariat unofficially reports eight federations with 37 affiliated unions. Some sources estimate membership at 3,000.

International affiliations. Part of international group attempting to form the Latin American Workers' Association (ATL) but otherwise has no international affiliations.

Central de Trabajadores Clasistas (CTC)
Classist Workers' Centre

Address. Tunti Cáceres No. 60 2da. Planta, Santo Domingo, D.N.

Phone. 685-1409

Leadership. Jacinto de los Santos (secretary-general)

Membership. Labour Secretariat unofficially reports three federations and 27 unions. (The CTC was founded in January 1985, with 4,766 members).

International affiliations. WFTU.

Central de Trabajadores Independientes (CTI)
Independent Workers' Centre

Address. Juan Erazo No. 139, Santo Domingo, D.N.

Phone. 688-3932; 687-3834

Leadership. Rafael Santos (secretary-general)

Membership. (This Confederation was officially recognized on March 23, 1990 and is determining its organization and affiliations.)

International affiliations. (*See Membership* above).

Central de Trabajadores Mayoritaria (CTM)
Majority Workers Centre

Address. Calle Seybo 98, Santo Domingo, D.N.

Phone. 689-9028; 565-0881

Leadership. Nelsida Altagracia Marmolejos (secretary-general)

Membership. Labour Secretariat unofficially reports five federations with 46 affiliated unions. CTM claims 10 federations and 125 unions with 175,000 members. Other sources place membership at about 50,000 or more.

History and character. This faction of the CGT formed in December 1983, is controlled by the left-wing pro-Cuban Dominican Liberation Party (PLD) led by former President Juan Bosch (who left the PRD in 1973 to form the PLD). It held its first Congress in October 1986 which approved its affiliation to the WFTU.

International affiliations. Permanent Congress of Labour Unity of Latin American Workers (CPUSTAL); WFTU.

Publication. Noticias Sindicales (monthly).

Central Unitaria de Trabajadores (CUT)
Unity Centre of Workers

Address. Calle Vicente Noble 14, Santo Domingo, D.N.

Phone. 685-8885; 685-2807

Leadership. Efraín Sanchez Soriano ("Pocholo") (secretary-general)

Membership. Labour Secretariat unofficially reports seven federations and 33 affiliated unions. Other sources point to 4,766 members.

History and character. Founded in 1978 by members of the pro-Soviet Dominican Communist Party (Partido Comunista Dominicano, PCD).

International affiliations. Permanent Congress of Labour Unity of Latin American Workers (CPUSTAL); WFTU.

Confederación Autónoma Sindical Clasista (CASC)
Autonomous Confederation of Classist Unions

Address. Juan Erazo 37, Apartado Correos 309, Santo Domingo, D.N.

Phone. 687-8533; 687-8537

Leadership. Gabriel Del Río Doné (secretary-general)

Membership. Labour Secretariat unofficially reports 24 federations and 141 affiliated unions. CASC claims 21 federations and 154 national unions with 164,000 members. Other sources estimate current total membership at 40,000.

History and character. Founded in 1962 by the Latin American Confederation of Christian Trade Unions (CLASC), and originally known as the Confederación Autónoma de Sindicatos Cristianos. The CASC has a significant role in the rural areas through its associated Instituto Nacional de Formación Agraria y Sindical (INFAS). It is politically independent but Social Christian in orientation and has supported the rightist Social Christian Reform Party (Partido Reformista Social Cristiano, PSRC) led by President Joaquín Balaguer (who took office again in August 1986). It was reported in May 1988, that the CASC had concluded a co-operation agreement with the Haiti *Central Autónoma de Tabajadores Haitianos*, a CLAT affiliate, with the double intention of solving the persisting problem of Haitian seasonal labour in the Dominican Republic and of encouraging new avenues of solidarity between both peoples.

International affiliations. CLAT; WCL.

Confederación Nacional de Trabajadores Dominicanos (CNTD)
National Confederation of Dominican Workers

Address. Avenida Duarte No. 270, Santo Domingo, D.N.

Phone. 682-5457 and 687-6937

Leadership. Mariano Negrón Tejada, (secretary-general)

Membership. Labour Secretariat unofficially reports 16 federations and 142 affiliated unions. CNTD and other sources indicate over 100,000 members. However, this figure includes members of CONACAD, an agrarian workers' group.

History and character. The CNTD (like the leftist CUT) originated in the United Workers' Front for Autonomous Trade Unions (FOUPSA) founded in 1961; when FOUPSA split the more right-wing faction in 1962 took the name National Confederation of Free Workers (CONATRAL). The CONATRAL adopted a "neutral" position at the time of the US-led intervention in 1965 and received the assistance of the US-backed American Institute for Free Labour Development (AIFLD). The CONATRAL in turn became the CNTD in 1971. In September 1988, the CNTD and the UGTD (see below) announced the merger of both bodies in order to fight jointly for the trade union demands. They called on the rest of the trade unions to unite in a single organization.

Publication. Libro del Militante.

International affiliations. ORIT; ICFTU.

Unión General de Trabajadores Dominicanos (UGTD)
General Union of Dominican Workers

Address. Ave. 27 de Febrero, No. 59, Santo Domingo, D.N.

Phone. 685-0807

Leadership. Juan Pablo Gómez, (secretary-general)

Membership. Labour Secretariat unofficially reports 12 federations and 86 unions. However, a large part of the UGTD left in 1987 (and joined the CNTD in 1988), seriously depleting membership. UGTD claimed 100,000 members prior to the 1987 split. Some sources feel that actual membership may be as low as 6,000.

International affiliations. None currently due to its current undetermined legal status.

Sindicato de Trabajadores de la Corporación Dominicana de Electricidad (SITRACODE)
Union of Workers of the Dominican Electric Corporation

Address. Calle Mauricio Baez No. 32, Santo Domingo, D.N.

Phone. 685-7279; 689-1394

Leadership. Eliaser Batista Matos, (secretary-general)

Membership. SITRACODE is a national union, unaffiliated to any of the principal Dominican labour confederations. Its membership comprises the workforce of the state-owned Dominican Electric Corporation (CDE).

Ecuador

Capital: Quito   **Population: 10,500,000**

Political system. After prolonged periods of political disturbance, there ensued more than 10 years of relative stability in 1948–60, followed by a decade of less settled conditions and then a period of military rule from 1972 to 1979. In 1988 the conservative President León Febres Cordero (who was not eligible for re-election) was succeeded by Rodrigo Borja Cevallos of the Democratic Left (affiliated to the Socialist International), who had the support of Popular Democracy to secure a legislative majority.

The union view of the government is that the restrictions it has imposed on union rights are more severe than those of its predecessor: the President has declared that 'the unionization of the public sector is the shortest road to the dissolution of the state' (*Free Labour World*, 31 May 1990).

Economy. Traditionally the economy had been based largely on agriculture, with plantation crops providing the country's main export. From 1972, however, petroleum has played an increasingly important role, particularly with the formation in that year of a state oil corporation, CEPE, which acquired foreign participations in existing foreign operations in the country, and with Ecuador's membership of OPEC in 1973. By the early 1980s petroleum was providing some three-quarters of export revenues, but the easing of the international oil market, combined with depressed markets for the traditional agricultural exports (accentuated by severe climatic conditions), resulted in increasing external imbalances and rising external debt. This in turn led to the adoption of stringent austerity measures and to conflict with Congress, with organized labour and with students, particularly in the context of attempts by the government to limit increases in the minimum wage.

By the beginning of 1987 Ecuador's external debt had grown to some $8,000 million, and an existing suspension of service payments was extended in the wake of a major earthquake in March of that year which disrupted oil supplies for export. A substantial rescheduling of debt was subsequently arranged with creditors, but in 1988 the new government imposed further stringent measures to conserve foreign exchange, increase economic growth, reduce inflation and cut the budget deficit.

The Rodrigo Borja government reduced inflation in 1989 to 54 per cent from its level of 86 per cent the previous year, but unrest was fuelled by a continuing deterioration in the value of the real wage. Nominal unemployment in 1989 was eight per cent but in reality underemployment may affect more than one third of the workforce. Such new jobs as were created during the year were in the large informal sector and insufficient to absorb new entrants to a workforce which grew by one quarter between 1982 and 1989. The most recent figures for employment by sector place 17 per cent in the industrial sector, 52 per cent in the agricultural sector and 24 per cent in services.

System of industrial relations. Ecuador ratified ILO Convention No. 87 (Freedom of Association and Protection of the Right to Organize, 1948) in 1967 and Convention No. 98 (Right to Organize and Collective Bargaining, 1949) in 1959. The 1978 labour code guarantees workers the right to join trade unions of their own choosing. However, under this and other enactments certain public servants are formally prohibited from setting up trade unions and from striking (although in practice associations of such employees do exist and are dealt with by the government for collective bargaining purposes); unions are not legally permitted to participate in the activities of political or religious parties; and the instigators of work stoppages may be liable to imprisonment. In addition the right to bargain collectively is reserved exclusively to works' councils, and may not be asserted by federations or confederations. The government in a report to the Committee of Experts on the Application of Conventions and Recommendations in 1987, indicated that it was prepared to revise sections of the labour code in respect to Convention No. 87 but was reflecting on the "timeliness" for such legislative reforms. The Committee of Experts has also sought repeal of a 1967 decree which formally makes collective action illegal for those organizing and participating in it and punishable by periods of imprisonment with forced labour (which also contravenes Convention No. 105 Abolition of Forced Labour, 1957, which Ecuador ratified in 1962).

A large number of sugar workers were shot or accidentally drowned in clashes with troops in October 1977, leading to a postponement of the return to civilian rule. The FUT has called a number of general strikes in recent years, with the support of its three member trade union centres, to protest against austerity measures and to demand increases in the minimum wage. On Aug. 30, 1988, the new government of President Rodrigo Borja announced a stringent economic emergency plan. The FUT denounced the plan as inspired by the IMF but postponed a decision to call a general strike. Instead, it presented a list of demands to the government which included requests for the dismantling of paramilitary groups, automatic six-month wage increases tied to inflation, a freeze on the prices of basic goods and utlities, the municipal control of public transport, a moratorium on debt repayments, and the elimination of peasant debts with the National Development Bank and the demarcation of indigenous territories.

The 1989 Report of the ILO Committee of Experts reiterated its view that several provisions of the Labour Code are incompatible with ILO Convention 87 including prohibitions on union membership in the public sector, insistence that members of works' committees be Ecuadorean, dissolution of these councils when union membership falls below 25 per cent, prohibition of union involvement in religious or political activity, and penalties of imprisonment for those who instigate work stoppages. Ecuadorean legislation was also still considered unsatisfactory in respect of its forced labour provisions. In 1989 the average number of disputes (of all kinds) in progress during any given month was 117.

Trade unionism. The right to join unions was recognized in the 1928 Constitution and associations developed from that decade though the first centre (CEDOC) was not established until 1938 with the assistance of the Catholic Church. CEDOC adopted its name to reflect greater secularization in 1972 but continued to follow Christian trade union practice by sustaining a large number of welfare activities. The CTE was founded in 1944 and CEOSL in 1962.

Today, union density in Ecuador is in the range 12–17 per cent and there are four union centres: the ICFTU affiliate CEOSL; the WFTU affiliate CTE; and the two halves of CEDOC, which split in 1976, the one affiliated to the WCL (CEDOC-CLAT), and the other (CEDOC-CUT) more radical. The centres have a loose co-ordinating organization, the United Workers' Front (FUT) which was founded in 1971 and in which CEDOC-CUT is active. The President of FUT is Jose Chavez of CEOSL and he led it in a general strike against austerity in 1988, though in 1989 the CTE declined to co-operate. A number of important unions do not affiliate to any of the centres.

Central Ecuatoriana de Organizaciones Classistas (CEDOC)
Ecuadorean Centre of Class Organizations

Address. Calle Río de Janeiro 407 y Juan Larrea, Casilla Postal 3207, Quito

Phone. 55 36 40

Leadership. Ramiro Rosales (president); Jorge Muñoz (secretary general)

Membership. 50,000.

History and character. The CEDOC was established in 1938, with the assistance of the Roman Catholic Church, as the Ecuadorean Confederation of Catholic Workers. It affiliated to the International Federation of Christian Trade Unions (IFCTU, the predecessor of the World Confederation of Labour, WCL) in 1952, and to the regional organization of the IFCTU, CLAT, on its formation in 1954. In 1972 the organization adopted its current name, reflecting the loosening of earlier ties with the Church (although the affiliation to the religious-influenced WLC, through CLAT, remains). The CEDOC assists members by providing or organizing a range of services, including legal aid, social and cultural clubs, neighbourhood committees, co-operatives, credit unions, and local workers' education institutes. Its orientation is humanistic, and it has no political affiliation. There are 16 provincial federations, 11 occupational federations and 1,089 affiliated unions.

Following government decrees of June 1988 aimed at extending control over private social institutes, which apply to training centres like that of the Ecuatorian Institute for Social Education (*Instituto Ecuatoriano de Formación Social*—INEFOS) which handles CEDOC's training projects, the latter reported the matter to the International Labour Conference in Geneva. CEDOC protested that if government interference was allowed in union training, this would be a step to wider interference in union affairs.

Publications. Unidad (30,000 copies); *Revista de los Trabajadores* (quarterly, 10,000 copies); various studies on labour and general social and economic issues.

International affiliations. WCL;CLAT.

Confederación Ecuatoriana de Organizaciones Sindicales Libres (CEOSL)
Ecuador Confederation of Free Trade Union Organizations

Address. Casilla Postal 1373, Quito

Phone. 522-511

Cables. CEOSL QUITO

Leadership. José Chávez (president); Julio Chang Crespo (secretary general)

Membership. 150-200,000

History and character. The CEOSL was founded in 1962. The ICFTU/ORIT protested to President León Febres Cordero in June 1988 about the arrest and mistreatment of ORIT vice-president and president of the CEOSL, José Chávez, following his arrest during a 24-hour general strike of June 1. The strike was organized by CEOSL and the United Workers Front (FUT). CEOSL is probably the largest of the four national centres.

International affiliations. ICFTU; ORIT.

Central de Trabajadores del Ecuador (CTE)
Ecuadorean Workers' Centre

Address. Olmedo y Benalcazar, Casilla Postal 4166, Quito

Phone. 219933

Leadership. Edgar Ponce (president)

Membership. 50–100,000.

History and character. The CTE was founded in 1944 and is leftist in orientation.

International affiliations. WFTU; CPUSTAL.

Ecuadorian Central of Class Organizations Marxist (CEDOC-CUT)

Address. 846 Flores, Quito

Phone. 593-2-51-40-13

Leadership. Fausto Dutan (president)

Membership. Approximately 10–20,000.

National Confederation of Mechanics and Artisans

Address. 1014 Ave. 18 De Septiembre, Quito
Phone. 593-2-56-90-61
Leadership. Nicanor Campana Quinteros (president)
Membership. Over 200,000.

National Confederation of Public Servants (CONASEP)

Address. 155 Yanez Pinzon, Quito
Phone. 593-2-23-19-01
Leadership. Lic. Alberto Gutierrez Gonzales (president); Jacinto Posligua (secretary general)
Membership. Approximately 200,000.

National Educators' Union (UNE)

Phone. 593-2-52-76-66
Leadership. Ernesto Alvarez (president)
Membership. Approximately 70,000.
Character. No formal affiliation, but key elements in leadership have ties to the Ecuadorian Popoular Democratic Movement (MPD).
International affiliation. The Chinese-Albanian Line Communist Party.

National Professional Drivers' Federation

Address. 841 Ave. Salinas, Quito
Phone. 593-2-54-77-89
Leadership. Nelson Leon Sarmiento (secretary general); Rodolfo Pogge Cedeno (secretary for finance)
Membership. Approximately 80,000.
International affiliation. International Transport Workers' Federation.

Egypt

Capital:Cairo   **Population: 53,300,000**

Political system. King Farouk was overthrown in 1952 by a group of nationalist officers, and Egypt was declared a republic in 1953. The conclusion of a peace treaty with Israel in 1979 led to the suspension of Egypt from most Arab organizations and of diplomatic relations with other Arab states, although this isolation gradually became less marked in the course of the 1980s. Political parties had been banned in 1953, but the Arab Socialist Union (ASU) was established in 1962 as the sole political organization permitted to present candidates for election to the National Assembly. In 1976 the ASU split into three groupings, of which two were eliminated from the unicameral parliament in 1979 and 1984 respectively. The third grouping, the Arab Socialist Party, merged in 1978 into the newly formed ruling National Democratic Party; this bases itself on the principles of democratic socialism and supports Islamic law as a principal source of legislation, and won overwhelming majorities in 1979, 1984 and 1987.

Economy. Major parts of the economy were nationalized in the 1950s and early 1960s, and the public sector still accounted in the early 1980s for about three-quarters of industrial production. However, following the 1973 Arab–Israeli war, an "open door" policy was increasingly adopted, while up to 50 per cent of investment in the five-year plan period starting in 1987 was to be accounted for by the private sector.

Out of a 1988 civilian workforce of 12,500,000 2,500,000 work in industry, 4,500,000 in agriculture, and 5,500,000 in services. Egyptian inflation is officially estimated at 26 per cent. Unemployment reached the rate of 14.7 per cent in 1989, exacerbated by rapid population growth and the return of expatriate workers from abroad. A likely result of the Gulf War is the return of large numbers of Egyptians who have traditionally found work in other Arab countries: more than 1,000,000 were employed in Iraq in 1989. In response the government has promulgated a Plan to create nearly 400,000 jobs in 1990–91, boosting the labour force to 13,600,000.

The public sector is imposing on increasing strain on the national budget; in 1990 the government felt compelled to raise wages there by 15 per cent because of the rate of inflation, yet its employees already accounted for one fifth of the national budget. Reduction of their numbers seems unlikely while unemployment is so high. Substantial reforms were introduced into its administration in 1988 and 1989, when the rate of return on capital reached 18 per cent, prompting the ETUF to express fears that the principle of workers' representation on boards might be put into jeopardy.

The ETUF has traditionally opposed the expansion of the private sector, where only a small minority of its members are to be found, but it is unlikely that the public sector can absorb the large numbers annually joining the workforce.

System of industrial relations. Egypt ratified ILO Convention No. 87 (Freedom of Association and Protection of the Right to Organize 1948) in 1957 and Convention No. 98 (Right to Organize and Collective Bargaining, 1949) in 1954. The ILO *Report of the Committee of Experts on the Application of Conventions and Recommendations* (1985) noted that under national law there is (in contravention of Convention No. 87), a legally prescribed single-trade-union system with the ETUF as the named central organization. The *Report* additionally noted that there is a system of compulsory arbitration and mediation; that the right to strike is not guaranteed; and that the Public Prosecutor may call for the removal from office of the executive committee of a trade union organization responsible for the abandonment of work or deliberate absenteeism in a public service or a service meeting a public need. The Egyption government maintained that the single-trade-union structure reflected the historical unity of the Egyptian trade union movement, was favoured by the workers' members of the People's Council, and was also in accordance with the obligations of the ETUF to the Organization of African Trade Union Unity (OATUU), which favours a single-trade-union system at the national level. The government also noted that the system of compulsory arbitration and mediation was one favoured by the workers themselves, and that in practice no action was taken against persons who participated in a number of strikes in 1983–84. In respect of the application of Convention No. 98, the *Report* observed that the labour code provides that any clause in a collective agreement jeopardizing the economic interests of the country shall be null and void. The Committee of Experts welcomed the decision of the Supreme State Security Court to acquit 37 railway workers arrested in July 1986 on charges of incitement, organization and participation in a strike.

The ETUF operates under labour legislation from the Nasser period when public sector workers were given virtual guarantees of permanent employment but did not have the right to strike. Collective bargaining occurs in the private sector which is widely expected to expand in the 1990s. When in dispute the ETUF prefers to resolve matters through the courts rather than by industrial action.

Trade unionism. The first trade union appeared in 1899 and thereafter unions tended to develop in association with contending political factions. Legal recognition was given to trade unions in 1942 and the Egyptian Trade Union Federation (ETUF) was established in 1957 as a centre for all existing unions.

Further legislation in 1952, 1959, 1964, 1976 and 1981 affirmed Egypt's pioneering status in the Arab trade union world. The ETUF is charged with respresenting the interests of all organized labour at government and international levels. Apart from negotiating successes on behalf of key groups such as the mines' and quarries' workes, unions have found it useful to work through the People's Assembly, where half the seats are reserved for them and for the farmers by constitutional right. Its recent successes include resolving a dispute over cuts in bonuses and food allowances at the Helwan Iron and Steel Works in August 1989, a reconciliation between the Egyptian and Israeli textile unions and championing of the rights of expatriate Egyptian labourers in Iraq before the Gulf War. The ETUF is slowly evolving towards a more independent posture, and is unlikely again to revert to the position before 1987 when the posts of Minister of Manpower and Federation President were held simultaneously by one person. Union density in Egypt was estimated at 25 per cent in 1989, a percentage largely accounted for by public sector membership.

Egyptian Trade Union Federation (ETUF)

Address. 90 El Galaa Street, Cairo
Phone. 740362; 740413
Telex. 93255 EGLAB-UN
Cable. MISRLAB CAIRO
Leadership. Ahmed El Ammawi (president); Mukhtar Abd Al-Hamid (vice-president), Mohamed Khaisi Hachem (general secretary).
Membership. 3–4,000,000.
History and character. The ETUF was founded in 1957 as the unifying body for 1,300 separate unions (now reduced to 23). A Workers' University was inaugurated under ETUF auspices on May 1, 1983. For 11 years until 1987 the head of the ETUF was the former Minister of Manpower Saad Mohamed Ahmed who firmly opposed links between affiliates and the ICFTU.
Affiliates. The membership of the ETUF is organized in the following 23 national occupational unions: General Trade Union of Agricultural Workers; Textile Workers; Commercial Workers; Banks, Insurance and Financial Institutions; Railway Workers, Telecommunications Workers; Public Utilities; Educational Services; Health Services; Food Industries; Workers of Engineering, Metal and Electrical Industries; Construction and Wood Industries; Land Transport; Marine Transport; Air Transport; Chemical Workers; Mines and Quarries; Press, Printing and Information; Administrative and Social Services; Tourism and Hotels; Civil Workers in Military Industry; Petroleum Workers; Postal Workers.
Publication. Al Omal (weekly, in Arabic).
International affiliations. OATUU. The ICATU suspended the ETUF from membership "due to the stand taken by its leadership supporting the treasonous Sadat regime and its policy" but it was restored in 1989. Five unions — Telecommunications, Textiles, Agricultural, Chemicals and Petroleum—defied the ETUF charter by affiliating to the ICFTU in the 1980s. Under the Ammawi presidency however the ETUF has accepted invitations from ICFTU-affiliated national unions abroad and has sent observers to conferences of the WFTU.
Structure. A committee of the 23 national unions elects the ETUF leadership. Its executive elects the president, who must be the chair of one of the affiliated unions. Elections were held for a new executive and president in 1987.

El Salvador

Capital: San Salvador   **Population: 5,330,000**

Political System. After 30 years of military rule and a further 20 years of elected Presidents, all from the conservative National Reconcilition Party (PCN), a civilian-military junta seized power in 1979 and one of its members, José Napoleón Duarte of the Christian Democratic Party (PDC), was sworn in as President in December 1980. During the 1970s there had been increased guerrilla activity on the part of left-wing elements, allegedly in receipt of Cuban and/or Soviet support; this intensified after 1979, while the United States gave its backing to the Duarte government. Following elections to a Constituent Assembly in 1982 a centre-right coalition government of national unity was formed, while in 1984 Duarte was elected President; in elections to a unicameral Legislative Assembly in March 1985, the PDC won a narrow overall majority, but it lost this in further elections in 1988. Meanwhile guerrilla action continued, and this was matched by activities on the part of right-wing "death squads" (allegedly including the unofficial involvement of government forces). In June 1989 the National Republican Alliance (ARENA) candidate Alfredo Cristiani was elected President to the great concern of labour organizations who had backed his Christian Democrat opponent. Assassinations of union leaders and attacks on their premises continued throughout the year. The Cristiani administration immediately began implementation of a liberal economic programme and opened talks with the insurgent FMLN. A state of emergency, prompted by the civil war, was declared at one point but the discussions with the FMLN resumed in 1990.

Economy. El Salvador's principal export crop is coffee, but production has latterly been severely affected by disease, by the internal unrest and by the associated large-scale movements of population; moreover, the international market for coffee has been extremely depressed, resulting in particularly low export revenues. An agrarian reform was instituted in 1980 by the ruling junta, but implementation of successive phases of this has been drastically modified and delayed.

Also in 1980 the government took majority holdings in domestic banks and credit institutions and, furthermore, took control of foreign trade in the principal export commodities. Although El Salvador is among the most industrially developed of the Central American countries, the flight of capital due to the disturbed political situation has limited private investment.

Public-sector employment was affected by serious strike action on repeated occasions in the mid-1980s, in support of wage demands and the observance of collective bargaining settlements and against austerity measures introduced by the government; the government for its part, accused the trade unions concerned of being "manipulated" by the main left-wing guerrilla movement, the FMLN, and its political wing, the FDR.

When the FMLN renewed its offensive in November 1989, the national economy was badly hit: growth that year was 1 per cent. Inflation was 18 per cent in 1989 but rose sharply in 1990 as the first liberal reforms lifting price controls and introducing privatization were made. However, in April 1990 the first rise in the minimum wage for four years was made, and rises were conceded to public sector workers two months later. In employment terms, the workforce in 1989 in El Salvador divided between industry (15 per cent), agriculture (40 per cent), and services (45 per cent). Unemployment that year was 12 per cent.

System of industrial relations. El Salvador has ratified neither ILO Convention No. 87

134

(Freedom of Association and Protection of the Right to Organize, 1948) nor No. 98 (Right to Organize and Collective Bargaining, 1949). Although El Salvador ratified Convention No. 105 (Abolition of Forced Labour, 1957) in 1958, it has failed (according to the *Report of the Committee of Experts on the Application of Conventions and Recommendations of the ILO (1988)* to uphold articles of the Convention dealing with the practice of compulsory labour for those deemed to be political prisoners or those workers imprisoned for participation in strikes in what the government (but not the Committee) considers to be "essential" services (namely transport and public utilities). Trade unions currently operate with some freedom, although strikes are banned, but the personal security of trade unionists has been adversely affected by the prevalence of terrorism and political assassination in the country. According to J. Francisco Acosta, the international representative of the UNTS (see below), in March 1986, more than 5,000 trade unionists had been killed since 1979, while there were over 60 documented cases of labour leaders who had "disappeared" or had been arrested, tortured or killed since January 1985. Appreciable labour unrest was recorded in 1985–86, especially in the public sector, and a strike of public health employees in 1985 was ended on June 2 with the use of troops, with five people being killed in the San Salvador general hospital.

In the year to June 1990 the Labour Ministry resolved seven strikes, but many of long duration continued. Despite promises, the Cristiani administration took no steps to update the Labour Code in line with the 1983 Constitution. It requires exhaustive procedural steps before industrial action may be taken. During the state of emergency of 1989–90 union rights were curtailed.

The new President met the unions in June and December 1989, and they are represented in the tripartitie Socio-Economic Commission which discussed possible reforms to the Labour Code in detail from June 1990. The Ministry of Labour oversees the implementation of agreements in the private sector and state agencies. The unions fear that some agencies may be converted to direct government-controlled status, in which case union representation as such will cease by law. The military intervened in three strikes in El Salvador in the year to June 1990.

Trade unionism. The first trade union federation was formed in 1922 and a degree of trade union activity persisted throughout the period of military rule. Centres affiliated to the ICFTU, WCL and WFTU appeared from 1958–65. The history of El Salvador's unions is bound up with politics.

Popular Democratic Unity (Undidad Popular Democratica, UPD, also referred to as the Unión Democrática Popular, UDP) was founded in 1980 with ties to the Christian Democratic Party (PDC) (and the support of the AFL-CIO in the United States), and to counter leftist forces linked to the Revolutionary Democratic Front (FDR), the political wing of the FMLN guerrilla movement, which were active in the trade unions at that time. The alliance claimed 500,000 members, but the true figure was probably nearer 100,000 (although this represented the core of the labour movement in the country), including 50,000 in the rural Unión Comunal Salvadoreña (UCS). The UPD supported Duarte's victorious presidential campaign in 1984, but increasing dissatisfaction with the government's record led to the break-up of the UPD and the creation in February 1986 (with the support of the WCL/CLAT affiliate, the Central de Trabajadores Salvadoreños—CTS—the major urban manual workers' union in the UPD) of the National Unity of Salvadorean Workers (Unidad Nacional de Trabajadores Salvadoreños, UNTS). The UNTS at its formation claimed to respresent over 300,000 workers and 46 unions, many of them not recognized by the Duarte government. Unions involved in the UNTS included both Christian Democratic-aligned unions from the UPD and independent radical unions grouped in the Comité Primero de Mayo (May 1st

135

Committee). One factor in the formation of the UNTS was a desire to create a front independent of the AFL-CIO and the American Institute for Free Labor Development (AIFLD), which were accused of meddling in union affairs. The major centre standing outside the UNTS was the ORIT-linked Democratic Workers' Centre (Central de Tabajadores Democráticos, CTD).

The defection of union support from the government was seen as reflecting in part Duarte's neglect of his previous power base and his emphasis on conciliating the army, in combination with the impact of economic austerity measures. Commencing with a major demonstration in San Salvador on Feb. 21, 1986, the largest in the capital since 1980, the UNTS throughout 1986 demanded both a revision of government economic policies and a resumption of negotiations with the FMLN-FDR guerrilla movements in an attempt to end the civil war. On Feb. 25 the government stated that the UNTS was linked with the armed insurgency, and a hitherto unknown group, the Christian Democrat Workers' Movement, on Feb. 24 made similar claims, which were denied by the UNTS executive. Government supporters in the unions were involved in a counter-demonstration on March 15, which attracted up to 20,000 people.

Following large demonstrations of public sector workers in July 1987, the government again attempted to link the UNTS to the FMLN. In mid-June 1987, the decapitated body of Jesús Hernández Martínez, secretary-general of the National Association of Agricultural Workers (ANTA) was discovered. Between March and August 1988, the number of trade union activists claimed to have been killed by right-wing paramilitary groups, was put by the UNTS at 300, including, on April 29, Adrian Chavarría Girón, international secretary of the General Confederation of Labour (CGT). The leader of the UNTS, Julio Portillo, said in July 1988, that the social and political crisis could only be solved through national dialogue and implementation of the Guatemala accords, reached by five countries of Central America. He also called on the United States to call "a total halt" to its interference in the country's internal affairs, which, he claimed, was ultimately responsible for the "climate of terror and horror" now persisting. A call for the US government to suspend military aid had been made in January 1988 by Lane Kirkland, president of the AFL-CIO following the release of two former guardsmen gaoled "for life" in 1986 for the murder of two AFL-CIO officials. In July 1988, the government proposed to create an emergency law that would "militarize" public agencies and institutions held to be vital to state security. Opposed by the UNTS, the move was thought to be provoked by a strike by power workers at the Río Lempe hydroelectric plant, which coincided with FMLN attacks on the electricity system.

The intensity of intimidation of the trade union movement increased following the 1989 Presidential elections. Unions complained that the November state of emergency was aimed as much against them as against the guerrillas. All year FENASTRAS was the target of kidnappings, torture and imprisonments, culminating in a bomb attack which killed nine people and injured 36 others at its offices in October. In January 1990 armed police raided the offices of the CTD and detained 15 union leaders. In November and December 1989 many union leaders fled the country to escape assassination.

By 1990, the largest union organization in El Salvador was clearly the National Union of Workers and Peasants (UNOC) though it suffered the disaffiliation of the CGT. In May 1990 UNOC joined with the United Worker's Front (FUT), the National Union of Salvadorean Workers (UNTS, which has strong sympathies with the FMLN), some smaller federations and some independent unions to form the "Intergremial". This is a co-ordinating body united around peaceful criticims of the government's economic policies. CGT's withdrawal from UNOC was to register disagreement with criticism of the government, but the move cost it dear in influence and membership. Public sector unions formed their own co-ordinating body, the "Interestatal", in June 1990.

Umbrella organizations

Unidad Nacional De Trabajadores Salvadoreños (UNTS)
National Union of Salvadorean Workers

Membership. Approx. 55,000

History and character. Founded in February 1986. UNTS, since the withdrawal of the UPD (*see below*) is a labour alliance judged to be broadly sympathetic to the FMLN-FDR. Among its chief constituents are COACES (*see below*), the CST (a coalition of almost all the left-led unions in El Salvador), the FUSS and the CGS (*see below*). The most prominent affiliate of UNTS is FENAS-TRAS, the chief union target of terror attacks by gun squads and the military. UNTS also includes some organizations which are popular rather than union in character. It joined with UNOC and FUT to launch the Intergremial in May 1990.

Unión Nacional De Obreros y Campesinos (UNOC)
National Union of Workers and Peasant Farmers

Membership. Around 200,000

History and character. Founded in 1986 the UNOC is a broad coalition whose principal members were the CGT and the CDT. It had close links with former President Duarte, and prominently backed the Christian Democratic candidate in the 1989 Presidential elections. It was not conciliated by government approaches after ARENA came to power and in May 1990 launched the Intergremial with UNTS and the FUT to attack national economic policies. This step cost it the affiliation of the CGT.

United Workers Front (FUT)

History and character. FUT was formed in 1987 by the merger of two public sector unions, the CTS and the General Association of Municipal and Public Employees (AGEPYM), on a Social Christian philosophy. In 1988 it claimed a membership of 40,000. It joined with UNOC and UNTS in May 1990 to launch the Intergremial.

Trade union centres

Central de Trabajadores Democráticos (CTD)
Democratic Workers' Centre/Confederation

Address. 6 Av. Sur y 8 Calle Oriente No. 438, San Salvador

Phone. 215-405

Leadership. Salvador Carazo (president)

History and character. The CTD was formed in the mid-1980s with the backing of the AFL-CIO in the United States, and in the view of its critics was under the control of foreign and anti-democratic elements.

International affiliations. ICFTU; ORIT.

Central de Trabajadores Salvadoreños (CTS)
Salvadorean Workers' Confederation

Address. Calle Dario Gonzáles No. 616, Barrio San Jacinto, San Salvador

Leadership. Miguel Angel Vásquez (secretary general)

Membership. 35,000.

History and character. This powerful centrist organization was formed in 1966 and was first known as UNOC and later as the Consejo Sindical Salvadoreño (CONSISAL). The CTS as a Christian Democrat organization was formely a supporter of the government of President Duarte, but by 1988 was criticizing it for its failure to end the civil war and prosecute those responsible for political assassinations, and had joined the opposition alliance, the UNTS. The CTS organized public sector strikes in November 1985, which won wage increases for almost all public employees, subsequently not honoured by the government. However, a four-day strike the CTS called in July 1986 was a failure and led to a change of leadership in November 1986. On Oct. 21, 1987, the CTS and the General Association of Municipal and Public Employees (AGEPYM) merged to form the public employees umbrella organization, the United Workers' Front (FUT). It left the UPD in August 1985.

International affiliations. WCL; CLAT.

Confederación de Asociaciones Co-operativas de El Salvador (COACES)
Confederation of Co-operative Associations of El Salvador

Leadership. Marco Tulio Lima (president)
Membership. Approx. 15,000 (in four federations)
History and character. Founded in 1984, it is a member of UNTS.

Confederación General de Sindicatos (CGS)
General Confederation of Unions

Leadership. Anibal Somoza Penate
Membership. Approx. 7,000
History and character. The CGS was expelled from ORIT in 1979. Some unions, although nominally members of the CGS, have affiliated to the CTD.

Confederación General del Trabajo (CGT)
General Confederation of Labour

Address. 9a Calle OTE. y 2a Av. Norte 618, Edificio San Francisco, 2a planta, San Salvador
Leadership. Jose Luis Grande (secretary general)
History and character. The CGT which once claimed 70,000 members declined after its withdrawal from UNOC in 1990.
International affiliation. CLAT

Federación Unitaria Sindical Salvadoreña (FUSS)
United Trade Union Federation of El Salvador

Address. Apartado Postal 2226, Centro de Gobierno, San Salvador
Phone. 215-911
Leadership. Juan Edito Genovez (secretary general)
History and character. This left-wing organization was founded in 1965. Its secretary general, Rafeal Aguinado, was assassinated by a right-wing death squad in 1975.
International affiliations. WFTU; CPUSTAL.

Fenastras

History and character. FENASTRAS was formed in 1975 and claims more than 35,000 members in 61 affiliates. Its militant opposition to government economic policies has cost it dear in lives, limbs, torture and property at the hands of the security forces and the death squads. It is affiliated to UNTS.

Unidad Popular Democrática (UPD)
Popular Democratic Unity

Leadership. Jesús Pérez Marroquín (secretary-general)
Membership. approx. 1,000
History and character. Formerly the most powerful alliance of unions, the UPP was severely weakened by internal struggles in 1985, losing most of its union affiliates. It helped to found UNTS but withdrew from it in 1986 due to "ideological differences". Further internal disputes in 1987

effectively split the UDP into two factions, one led by Ramón Mendoza and Jesús Marroquín the other.

Unión Comunal Salvadoreña (UCS)
Salvadorean Communal Union

Address. 4a Calle Oriente 6–4, Nueva San Salvador
Phone. 28-20-23
Leadership. Samuel Maldonado Mezquita (secretary general)
Membership. Claims 165,000.
History and character. Founded in 1966, this was a pro-government peasants' organization, organized with the assistance of the American Institute for Free Labor Development (AIFLD), and was associated with the UPD alliance (see above). Now claiming to be independent, the UCS affiliated to the ICFTU in 1983, and helped to found the CTD and UNOC both of which it is also affiliated to.

Equatorial Guinea

Capital: Malabo

Population: 397,000
(1988)

Political system. The former Spanish overseas provinces of Fernando Pó and Río Muni achieved autonomy in 1963 and independence in 1968. Over the next 10 years the Macías Nguema regime banned all existing parties and merged them into the sole National (Workers') Party; large numbers of refugees and foreign workers left the country; competent administration effectively collapsed; and accusations were made of gross violations of human and civil rights. Under a new Constitution introduced after the overthrow of President Francisco Macías Nguema in 1979 by Obiang Nguema, a unicameral National Assembly was established to which elections were held in 1983 and 1988, although with only a single list of official candidates. A new ruling "party of government" was launched in 1987. Under the Obiang Nguema government Spain, and more recently France, have replaced the Soviet Union as the main provider of financial assistance.

President Obiang Nguema was re-elected for a seven-year term in June 1989. In December 1990 the arrests were reported of a group favouring the introduction of a multi-party system.

Economy. Although Equatorial Guinea has important unexploited mineral reserves, and petroleum and natural gas potential, agriculture is practically the only economic activity. Since independence production of the main crops of cocoa and coffee have declined drastically, and, moreover, the international markets for these commodities and for bananas and timber have been severely depressed. The Constitution envisages a basically free market economy, with certain utility services and the mineral wealth reserved for the public sector. Service for the public external debt is equivalent to almost the whole of export revenue, although some of the debt has been rescheduled.

System of industrial relations. Equatorial Guinea (which has been a member of the International Labour Organization since 1981) has ratified neither ILO Convention No. 87 (Freedom of Association and Protection of the Right to Organize, 1948) nor Convention

No. 98 (Right to Organize and Collective Bargaining, 1949). It has also failed to ratify Conventions No. 29 (Forced Labour, 1930) and No. 105 (Abolition of Forced Labour, 1957), and reports by the Anti-Slavery Society in London in 1976 and by the International Commission of Jurists in 1978 stated that conditions of forced labour and slavery existed in mines and on cocoa plantations under President Macías Nguema.

Trade unionism. A National Trade Union Centre (NTUC), based in the Ministry of Labour, was formerly reported and the OATUU records an affiliate under the name of the Union Nationale des Travailleurs de Guinée Equatoriale, but there is currently no indication of any development of trade unionism. Under the 1982 Constitution, employees of the state and of essential public services may not strike.

Ethiopia

Capital: Addis Ababa

Population: 43,350,000
(estimated mid-1985)

Political system. Emperor Haile Selassie was deposed in 1974 by a military committee which suspended parliament and which in the following year abolished the monarchy. Ethiopia was declared to be a socialist state, and all major sectors of the economy were rapidly brought into state ownership, including the land which hitherto had been held largely on a feudal basis. Lt. -Col. Mengistu Haile Mariam became head of state in 1977 following a series of struggles within the ruling military leadership, and the Workers' Party of Ethiopia (WPE) was formally inaugurated in 1984 as a Marxist-Leninist formation and as the country's sole political party under the leadership of Lt.-Col. Mengistu. A new Constitution approved in 1987 provided for a state system based on "democratic centralism", with the WPE as the leading force of state and society. Elections were held to a unicameral national legislature, and the ruling Provisional Military Administrative Council was dissolved. Ethiopia has received considerable economic assistance from other socialist countries; the Soviet Union and also, notably, Cuba have provided large-scale military support for its efforts to contain and defeat secessionist movements, particularly in Eritrea, Tigre and the Ogaden.

By early 1991, large parts of Ehtiopia were under rebel control and in May President Mengistu fled the country.

Economy. Ethiopia's economy is largely agricultural and pastoral, and has suffered not only from the internal upheavals of the secessionist struggles but also from prolonged periods of almost total drought and widespread famine; both of these factors have led to mass migrations (and also removals of population). International prices for commodity exports have been low, and the level of exports has been sharply reduced by climatic conditions, disruption and disease. Much of the small manufacturing capacity lies in Eritrea which is largely outside the control of the central government. Some 80 per cent of all workers are employed in the agriculture sector, which accounts for more than 50 per cent of GDP, but government policy has not succeeded in boosting this sector, the output of which has suffered from two severe droughts in 1984–85 and 1987–88. Promulgation of liberal economic reforms in November 1988 brought little tangible success in the way of inward investment. In March 1990 the Central Committee of the Workers' Party declared that it favoured movement towards a mixed economy with some state enterprises being put into a competitive environment and privatization or closure facing the rest. The transfer of land ownership (illegal since 1975) would also be allowed.

System of industrial relations. Ethiopia ratifed ILO Convention No. 87 (Freedom of Association and Protection of the Right to Organize, 1948) and No. 98 (Right to Organize and Collective Bargaining, 1949) in 1963. The ILO has noted a number of discrepancies between national legislation and the Convention's provisions, including the right to organize and strike, the rights of association of rural workers, the rights of public servants, and other matters.

Trade unionism. The first clandestine trade unions were formed after 1947, and the basis of a trade union centre known as the Ethiopian Labour Union (ELU) was formed in 1954. After the liberalization of 1962, the ELU was reorganized as the Confederation of Ethiopian Labour Unions (CELU), linked to the ICFTU. The CELU was abolished in 1975 and reformed in 1977 as the All-Ethiopian Trade Union (AETU) and in 1986 as the Ethiopian Trade Union (ETU).

A hierarchial single-trade-union system, organized by the ETU, is in operation, with a parallel system for peasants' organizations co-ordinated by the All-Ethiopia Peasant Association (AEPA), which is described by the government as being "not a trade union organization . . . but a mass organization of independent peasants, established voluntarily by them". The role and tasks of the ETU are embodied in law. Unions are legally obliged to spread knowledge of the development plans of the government and Marxist-Leninist theories among the workers, and to implement the decisions and directives of the authorities. Collective bargaining agreements are conditional on their approval by the Ministry of Labour, which must verify that such agreements conform with the basic policies of the government. Any strike which has not been submitted to the labour division of the High Court for final binding arbitration is illegal.

Ethiopian Trade Union (ETU)

Address. P.O. Box 3653, Addis Ababa
Phone. 157749
Telex. 21618 ETU ET
Leadership. Tadesse Tamerat (chairman, re-elected May 1, 1986).
Membership. 320,000.
History and character. Following the fall of Haile Selassie in 1974, the leadership of the Confederation of Ethiopian Labour Unions (CELU, formed in 1963 and developed with the assistance of western unions) was purged by the provisional military council in May 1975; the new leadership declared that there was a need for a new labour law based on the principles of "Ethiopian socialism" and broke off relations with the ICFTU and the AFL-CIO in the United States. In September 1975, however, the CELU demanded the restoration of democratic rights and civil liberties and threatened a general strike, and after sporadic strikes and disturbances, the government announced the dissolution of the CELU in November 1975. A new All-Ethiopian Trade Union (AETU) was inaugurated by Lt.-Col. Mengistu Haile Mariam in January 1977. The first leader of the AETU, Ato Tewodros Bekele, was killed in office in February 1977 amid a wave of assassinations and counter-assassinations occasioned by power struggles within the country, and his successor Temesgen Madebo suffered a similar fate later the same year. In May 1978 the entire executive committee was dismissed for "political sabotage, corruption and misuse of power", having apparently favoured the return to power of the Marxist All-Ethiopian Socialist Movement (NMAESON), whose influence had been progressively eliminated by the military regime.

At its third congress, which concluded on May 1, 1986, the federation changed its name to the Ethiopian Trade Union. The ETU chairman, Tadesse Tamerat, was elected a member of the new State Council in September 1987, a reflection of the role of the unions in the government.

Affiliated unions. Nine industrial unions and 16 regional unions.

Publication. *Voice of ETU.*
International affiliations. OATUU; WFTU.

Other organization

A National Union of Eritrean Workers and Students, linked to the Eritrean secessionist movement, has been reported; this body was founded in 1977.

Fiji

Capital: Suva

Population: 720,000
(1989)

Political system. Fiji became a fully independent member of the Commonwealth in 1970 with an appointed Senate and elected House of Representatives. Elections to the House are on the basis of both national (cross-voting) and communal rolls, reflecting the fact that the population is almost equally divided between persons of indigenous and of Indian origin, together with a small proportion of persons of Chinese and other (including European) origin. From independence until 1987 the government was formed continuously by the predominantly Melanesian Alliance Party. In that year a multi-racial alliance led by the predominantly National Federation Party came to office, but was almost immediately removed in a military coup amidst increasing racial violence. A temporary constitutional settlement was reached, but a further military *coup* led again by Lt. -Gen. Sitiveni Rabuka took place later that year, a republic was proclaimed and Fiji's Commonwealth member- ship lapsed. Shortly afterwards Rabuka's administration relinquished power and an almost wholly Melanesian government was formed, most of whose members belonged to the Alliance Party.

Economy. Agriculture is predominant in the Fijian economy, with sugar as the principal cash and export crop. However, the severely depressed state of the international markets for sugar and also for copra, and the effects of successive cyclones, have reduced the export revenue from this sector. The government is encouraging diversification not only into other crops and livestock but also into the development of a small-scale manufac- turing base. Tourism has increased. After 1987 the government pursued a course of intro- ducing market disciplines into Fiji, including privatization of state assets.

System of industrial relations. Fiji ratified ILO Convention No. 98 (Right to Organize and Collective Bargaining, 1949) in 1974 but has not ratified Convention No. 87 (Freedom of Association and Protection of the Right to Organize, 1948).

In the aftermath of the May 1987 military *coup*, trade union rights appeared to have been severely curtailed. In protest, ICFTU affiliates in Australia and New Zealand imposed a ban on shipping and maritime links with Fiji. In October 1987 the unions threat- ened to extend the ban to include air traffic as from Nov. 1. A few days prior to the imple- mentation of the airline boycott, the military regime opened negotiations with the ICFTU-affiliated FTUC. During talks, the authorities gave assurances that trade union rights would soon be restored; these assurances led Australian and New Zealand unions to drop their threatened air traffic ban. In mid-January 1988 an ICFTU delegation led by John Vanderveken (the ICFTU general secretary) visited Fiji. Following a meeting with the Fijian Minister of Employment and Industrial Relations, Taniela Veitata, and extensive consultations with the FTUC, the delegation concluded that present circumstances did not warrant the reimposition of the transport ban. In June 1988 the FTUC national secretary, Mahandra P. Chaudhary, was arrested and interrogated by police in connexion with the attempted shipment of arms from Australia by elements of Fiji's Indian community.

Union activity after 1987 was continued under difficult legal conditions and in spite of detentions of leaders and an arson attack on the FTUC head office. At the end of May 1989 the Fijian TUC (FTUC) called a general strike to protest against the failure of government to lift restrictions of union rights imposed by the military after the *coups* of 1987 and against a wage freeze. Continuing concern led to a further ICFTU visit to Fiji in October 1989, resulting in another report critical of the government's failure to recognize the FTUC or to re-establish the country's Tripartite Forum. Continued representations from the FTUC itself for re-establishment of formal industrial relations institutions were made without effect, and the government proceeded towards the establishment of racially based unions.

Trade unionism. Union activity developed following the Industrial Associations Ordinance of 1942, but was affected by racial divisions between Fijians, Indians and Europeans. Racially based unionism declined in the 1960s, however, and the Fiji Trades Union Congress (FTUC) emerged as the dominant central organization.

Fiji Trades Union Congress (FTUC)

Address. 32 Des Voeux Road, P.O. Box 1418, Suva
Phone. 315377; 315402.
Fax. 300306
Cable. FIJICONG
Leadership. Michael Columbus (president); Mahandra P. Chaudhary (national secretary)
Membership. Claims 45,000 in 35 affiliated unions, i.e. about half of the total employed workforce.

History and character. The FTUC originated in 1952 as the Fiji Industrial Workers' Congress, and sugar workers' unions were its main affiliates in the early days. The present name was adopted in 1966, and the FTUC has since then steadily broadened its base among Fijian unions. Following the unilateral imposition by the government of a wage freeze in November 1984, the FTUC withdrew from the Tripartite Forum (established in 1977), where it had conferred with government and employers on economic policy issues. Subsequently, during 1985, the FTUC launched a political party, the Fiji Labour Party, to challenge government policy (the FTUC having previously been politically unaffiliated). This party was nominally a separate organization, but Robert Kumar, the FTUC treasurer, was appointed treasurer of the Labour Party and the FTUC assistant national secretary, Mahendara P. Chaudhary, (who was subsequently elected FTUC national secretary) became its assistant secretary general, while FTUC vice-president Krishna Dutt became the party's secretary-general and Public Service Association president, Timori Bavadra, the party's president. The Labour Party recruited mainly among the Indian section of the population. In September 1985, after extended discussions, all parties agreed to the reactivation of the Tripartite Forum on a reorganized basis. In late 1986 the Labour Party agreed to form a coalition with the opposition National Federation Party (NFP), and in April 1987 the coalition defeated the Alliance Party in the elections, Bavadra becoming Prime Minister while senior FTUC officials also joined the government. The following month, however, the government was overthrown in a military *coup* led by Lt. -Col. Sitiveni Rabuka.

Though civilian government was restored the FTUC operated from 1987 onwards under severe curtailment of its activities. Its offices were burned down and a number of union leaders were imprisoned. On several occasions the FTUC appealed to the ICFTU for support, and the International sent delegations to Fiji in 1988 and 1989 to obtain assurances from government ministers. At the FTUC's third Biennial Conference in June 1990 bitter criticisms of government policy were voiced of the restrictions on union activity and collective bargaining; of the government objective of registering racially based unions; and of the furthering of the interests of a narrow élite through deregulation, privatization and the establishment of tax-free zones. The FTUC called for consultation and discussion to achieve a democratic framework, proper application of ILO conventions in Fiji, a tripartite consultative forum for industrial relations and the restoration of wages to pre-devaluation levels. Michael Columbus, General Secretary of the Transport and Oil Workers' Union was elected as president.

Affiliated Unions.

1. **Air Pacific Employees' Association**.

2. **Association of USP Staff**

3. **BP & WR Carpenter Group Salaried Staff Association**
4. **Building Workers' Union**
5. **Federated Airline Staff Association**
6. **Fiji Air Employees Union**
7. **Fiji Bank Employees' Union**
8. **Fiji Electricity Authority Hourly Paid Employees' Union**
9. **Fiji Electricity Authority Staff Association**
10. **Fiji Foreign Going Seamen's Union**
11. **Fiji Garment Workers Association**
12. **Fiji Local Government Officers' Association**
13. **Fiji Mine Workers' Union**
14. **Fiji National Training Council Staff Association**
15. **Fiji Nurses' Association**
16. **Fiji Public Service Association**
17. **Fiji Sugar Clerks & Supervisors Association**
18. **Fiji Sugar & General Workers' Union**
19. **Fiji Sugar Tradesmen's Union**
20. **Fiji Teachers' Union**
21. **Fijian Affairs Board & Provincial Council Employers**
22. **Housing Authority Employees' Association**
23. **Insurance Officers' Association**
24. **Maritime Officers' & Seamen's Union**
25. **National Farmers' Union**
26. **National Union of Factory & Commercial Workers**
27. **National Union of Hotel & Catering Workers**
28. **National Union of Municipal Workers**
29. **National Union of Timber Workers**
30. **Security Employees Union of Fiji**
31. **Sugar Milling Staff Officers' Association**
32. **Suva City Council Staff Association**
33. **Telecommunications Employees' Association**
34. **Transport & Oil Workers' Union**
35. **USP Staff Union**

Publications. Fiji Labour Sentinel (six per year).
International affiliations. ICFTU/APRO; PTUC.

Finland

Capital: Helsinki **Population: 4,970,000**

Political system. Finland, which became independent from Russia in 1917, has a unicameral parliament, while under the Constitution the President has wide powers, especially in respect of foreign relations. From 1979 there has been a series of centre-left coalitions, led by the social democrats until 1987 and since then by the (Conservative) National Coalition Party. Finland has been a full member of EFTA since the beginning of 1986, having been an associate member since 1961; a special relations agreement was concluded with the European Communities in 1973 (effective 1974); and also in 1973 a co-operation agreement was signed with the Council for Mutual Economic Assistance (CMEA or Comecon). Since the late 1940s, while remaining neutral in foreign policy, Finland has had a close relationship with the Soviet Union, particularly as embodied in the 1948 Treaty of Friendship, Co-operation and Mutual Assistance (as successively extended).

Economy. Around 7 per cent of the Finnish workforce is engaged in agriculture, 41 per cent is in the secondary sector (including transport) and the rest in services. In 1989 unemployment fell to a rate of 3.5 per cent while the rate of inflation rose to 6.6 per cent. The government is pursuing a policy of shifting some public services to the private sector and of cutting public expenditure.

System of industrial relations. Finland has legislated to provide every citizen with the right to work and the possibility of some form of economic activity. The legislation, in force since 1 January 1988, streamlines labour market information, training and placement services, sets up voluntary employment grants for those who fail to find a job in the normal market, and puts the onus on the local authorities, Government agencies and other institutions to take up the residue of the long-term unemployed and of those young job-seekers who have failed to find work through the normal channels. Those between 18 and 20 are to be found work immediately.

Government funds are to be deployed to correct regional imbalances in employment opportunities and to bring assistance to any areas where economic forces have forced the closure of workplaces. A range of grants is available to both local authorities and individual employers. Attention in 1988 was focused on how this far-reaching legislation would work out in practice.

Finland also legislated in 1986 to introduce a flexible system of individual early retirement for persons of 60 and 64 to be taken at a reduced rate and a special invalidity pension for those whose capacity for working is reduced. Surveys from 1988 show that Finnish men tend to enter the workforce late and leave it early. Less than half remain in employment after the age of 55.

Finland ratified ILO Convention No. 87 (Freedom of Association and Protection of the Right to Organize, 1948) in 1950 and Convention No. 98 (Right to Organize and Collective Bargaining, 1949) in 1951.

Since 1968, comprehensive incomes policy agreements — usually of two years' duration — have been negotiated in tripartite meetings. Industrial action is usually obviated during the lifetime of the agreement. The 1990–91 settlement was signed in January 1990 and aims to guarantee an increase of 4.5 per cent in real wages up to 1992; pay increases will be triggered if inflation passes a certain level. In exchange for this and for an increase in welfare benefits, the unions conceded a tripartite committee to examine work schedules with a view to increasing productivity. Restiveness over central wage settlements was already apparent in the later 1980s; on this occasion, ratification by the individual unions was not automatic. It took a personal appeal by President Koivisto in his New Year's message for 1990 to secure acceptance by three of the union centres, but the largest—STK—would not be moved; with strident dissent apparent among some of the STK's major affiliates, the system of central framework agreements—like that of Sweden—is under increasing strain.

Trade unionism. The Finnish labour movement is generally built on the industrial union principle, whereby all workers in one workplace, regardless of occupation, belong to the same union. However, craft unionism exists in some trades. Finnish trade unionists enjoy a wide range of guarantees and benefits, including the eight-hour day and 40-hour week, health insurance, minimum wages, holiday and sick pay, maternity leave and free paid time for shop stewards. Many of the key benefits were first introduced in the 1960s.

Finland is one of the most highly unionized countries in the world. The two major confederations are the (mainly blue-collar) Suomen Ammattiliitojen Keskusjärjestö (Central Organization of Finnish Trade Unions—SAK), with 1,066,790 members, and the (mainly white-collar) Toimihenkilö-ja Virkamiesjärjestöjen Keskusliitto (Confederation of Salaried Employees — TVK), with 360,000 members. There is also a smaller Confederation of Technical Employees' Organizations in Finland (STTK), with about 115,000 members, and a Finnish Central Organization of Professional Workers (AKAVA) with about 240,000 members. The TVK and SAK estimate that 80–90 per cent of potentially organizable workers are in unions, which have an aggregate membership of about 1,750,000. There are a few small unions which operate independently of any of the central confederations.

Political activity is very evident in Finland's major union centres. The STK has a Social Democratic leadership, but five of its affiliates are under Communist leadership. The SDP is also influential in the TVK though the organization itself is politically independent. While STTK stands in the same case, AKAVA which rests on organizations that are as much professional as trade union, is rigorously non-partisan. The STK is in many ways the key to Finland's central bargaining system, facing as it does employers who are as highly associative as the workforce. Its difficulties in securing endorsement of the 1990–91 agreement were therefore especially significant, and acknowledged as such by former President Viinanen who did not seek re-election in November 1990. During 1989 discussion of STK reorganization centred on a proposition that the number of its affiliates might be reduced to four, but the central difficulty seems to be a growing inability to command support for constituent organizations.

Suomen Ammattiliittojen Keskusjärjestö (SAK)
Central Organization of Finnish Trade Unions

Address. Siltasaarenkatu 3A, P.O. Box 157, 00531 Helsinki 53
Phone. 358 0 7721
Telex. 122346 SAK SF
Cables. SAK HELSINKI
Fax. 0 772 1447
Leadership. Laura Ihalainen (president); Aarno Aitamurto, Raimo Kantola (vice-presidents); Pekko Ahmavaara (secretary).
Membership. 1,092,405 (55 per cent male and 45 per cent female), in 24 affiliated sectorally based unions. One of these affiliates, the Virkamiesten ja Työntekijäin Yhteisjärjestö (Central Committtee of Public Servants—VTY) is in turn an umbrella organization for seven public sector unions, four of which are also affiliated directly to SAK. The SAK estimates that there are 2,051,000 wage earners in Finland, 85 per cent of whom are organized. The Municipal Workers' Union overtook the Metalworkers' Union as the largest affiliate in 1982. The third and fourth largest are the Commercial Workers and the Construction Workers.

History and character. The SAK traces back its origins to the Congress of Trade Unions in Finland (SAJ), formed in 1907 with the support of 18 unions with a total of 25,000 members. This organization, which was dominated by Marxists, was dissolved by the government in 1930 but reorganized the same year (purged of communist influence) as the Confederation of Finnish Trade Unions (SAK). For some years thereafter the unions were adversely affected by the world economic depression, the influence of right-wing political formations, and finally by the onset of war. The unions recovered in the aftermath of World War II, but in 1959–60 the movement split with the formation of the rival Finnish Trade Union Federation (SAJ); after a decade of fragmentation the SAJ and the SAK reunited in 1969 as the Central Organization of Finnish Trade Unions (also known as SAK), and membership in this reorganized body increased from 560,000 in 1969 to over 1,000,000 by 1980, when the increase in membership began to level off.

Under Finland's system of centralized agreements on wages and conditions the SAK has enjoyed substantial economic and political influence. Its status has, however, been adversely affected in recent years by the growing importance of unaffiliated white-collar unions. Following the conclusion of a separate central two-year pay and conditions agreement by the white-collar unions with government and employers, 250,000 members of SAK unions staged a 58-hour strike in mid-March 1986, the most extensive industrial action in Finland since 1956, and won somewhat greater concessions than those gained by the white-collar groups.

The SAK stands independent of political parties, and is divided politically between supporters of the Social Democratic Party (constituting about 65 per cent of those on SAK decision-making bodies), and the Left Wing Alliance (ex-communist left-wing Socialists and People's Democrats).

Structure. The ruling body is the congress, composed of elected delegates from the affiliated unions in proportion to their memberships, which convenes every fifth year. Between congresses the ruling body is the general council, which is made up of union representatives on the basis of their

Name	Membership
Automobile and Transport Workers' Union	45,225
Finnish Hotel and Restaurant Workers' Union	49,037
Air Transport Union	2,765
Chemical Workers' Union	22,651
Finnish Caretakers' Union	10,768
Rubber and Leather Workers' Union	14,508
Finnish Municipal Workers' and Salaried Employees' Union	200,000
Finnish Glass and Porcelain Workers' Union	5,130
Union of Workers in the Commercial Field	117,213
Finnish Rural Workers' Union	21,551
Metalworkers' Union	148,921
Paperworkers' Union	49,073
Woodworkers' Union	39,304
Construction Workers' Union	101,395
Finnish Foodworkers' Union	39,425
Finnish Bookworkers' Union	31,474
Ships Officers' Union	330
Finnish Seamen's Union	8,209
Finnish Musicians' Union	3,079
Social Democratic Journalists' Union	346
Electric Workers' Union	30,738
Technical and Special Trades Union	11,075
Finnish Textile Mechanists' Union	845
Textile and Clothing Workers' Union	34,683
Editors' Union	152
Central Committee of Public Servants	93,590
General Union of Journalists	296

numerical strength and meets annually with extraordinary sessions as required. The administrative council, or executive committee, implements the decisions of the general council and the congress and attends to the day-to-day business of the federation. Local SAK organizations—of which there are some 150—unite all the branches of different affiliates within particular localities, typically at the municipality level. These local organizations play a role in training, thereby influencing local government decisions. The SAK is financed from the membership dues from members of the affiliates.

Publications. SAK Palkkatyöläinen (periodical in Finnish); *Löntagaren* (periodical in Swedish).

*International affiliations.*ICFTU; ETUC; TUAC; NFS.

Affiliated unions. At the end of 1989 SAK affiliates were as shown in the table.

Toimihenkilö-ja Virkamiesjärjestöjen Keskusliitto (TVK)
Confederation of Salaried Employees

Address. Asemamiehenkatu 4 SF 00520 Helsinki 52

Phone. 358 0 1551

Telex. 12-2505 TVK ST

Fax. 358 0 143 058

Leadership. Matti Kinnunen (president) and Riitta Prusti (co-president)

Membership. 382,792 (March 1990), 81 per cent of members are women, reflecting a wide recruitment among nurses, shop workers, bank, insurance and clerical employees, etc. Two thirds of the Confederation's members work in the public sector and the remainder in the private sector. There are 13 affiliated unions.

History and character. The TVK was founded in 1922 during the post-World War I inflation, when salaried employees failed to match the increases in wages enjoyed by blue-collar workers in the SAK. Unlike the SAK, the TVK did not align itself with the labour parties. In 1944 (when World War II ended for Finland), the organizational structure was remodelled, and new affiliations increased the membership in that year from 15,000 to 61,000. A further reorganization was

Name	Membership
Public Sector	
Municipal Employees' Union (KVL)	63,673
Finnish Union of Assistant Nurses (SuPer)	34,200
Union of Finnish Police Officers (SPL)	7,915
The Union of Health Professionals (TeHy)	83,523
Union of Civil Servants (VL)	62,187
Total	251,498
Private Sector	
Federation of Salaried Employees of Automobile and Machine Trade (ATH)	5,046
Federation of Agricultural Employees (MTJL)	953
Federation of Storemongers (MEL)	3,625
Federation of Bank Employees (PtL)	40,500
Finnish Federation of Industrial Employees (STL)	45,500
Federation of Insurance Employees (Vvl)	10,171
Federation of State-owned Institutions and Companies (VLTL)	13,924
Federation of Employees in Special Trades (ErTo)	11,575
Total	131,294
TOTAL PUBLIC AND PRIVATE SECTORS	382,792
Co-operative Member	
Union of Graduates of Commercial Institutes	14,000

carried out in 1956. Collective bargaining developed rapidly in the post-war period, and in 1970 civil servants and local government employees achieved rights to strike and bargain almost equivalent to those enjoyed by workers in the private sector. The TVK participates in centralized bargaining on wages and conditions, the central agreement normally providing the framework within which its affiliated unions conduct their own negotiations. The TVK is politically independent.

Structure. The supreme body is the statutory congress which meets every fourth year and is made up of about 400 delegates elected from unions in proportion to their size. The congress elects the general council, the executive committee, the president and co-president. Between congresses, the general council (of about 100 members), which meets at least twice a year, is the decision-making body. Executive power and day-to-day decision-making resides with the executive committee, consisting of the president and co-president and twelve members. Practical and routine work is carried out by a secretariat headed by the president and co-president; the secretariat works in co-operation with advisory committees appointed by the executive committee. The TVK is financed by a proportion of the membership dues paid by the workers to the affiliated unions.

Publication. *TVK-TOC* (12 times per year; circulation 30,000).

International affiliations. ICFTU; NFS; ETUC; TUAC.

Affiliated unions. For 1990 the membership figures for affiliated unions are shown in the table.

Other Organizations

The Confederation of Unions for Academic Professionals in Finland (AKAVA)

Address. Rautatieläisenkatu 6, 00520 Helsinki

Phone. (09) 141 822

Fax. (90) 142 595

Leadership. Raimo Lehtinen (president); Voitto Ranne, Alari Kujala, Markku Äärimaa and Pekka Rinne (vice-presidents)

Membership. 267,613 AKAVA has 35 affiliated unions comprising a wide range of academically trained professionals, the largest of which is the Teachers' Trade Union in Finland (membership 74,174).

Publications. The *AKAVA* magazine.

International affiliation. The Nordic Academic Council.

Affiliated unions. The table below gives facts and figures relating to AKAVA's 35 member organizations.

Name	Membership
Association of Agronomists	3,743
Central Union of Special Branches within AKAVA	5,314
AKAVA's General Group	775
Association of Swedish-speaking Engineers	2,174
Union of Geophysicists	162
Union of Geologists	598
Association of Finnish Engineers	32,690
Central Union of Librarians	2,028
Union of University Assistants and Researchers	2,852
Central Union of Graduate Engineers and Architects	32,650
Kindergarten Teachers' Association	10,679
Teachers' Trade Union Finland	74,174
Finnish Association of University Professors	1,371
League of Social Workers	6,129
Association of Finnish Architects	2,008
Finnish Association of Graduates of Schools of Economy and Business Administration	25,337
Finnish Veterinary Association	1,080
Union of Finnish Pharmacists	6,394

Name	Membership
Finnish Dental Association	5,749
Association of Church Musicians	784
Union of Finnish Chemists	3,243
Union of Ministers of the Church of Finland	3,311
Union of Sisters in the Church of Finland	1,061
Union of Finnish Lawyers	11,043
Union of Finnish Air Hostesses and Stewards	1,335
Finnish Medical Association	14,025
Society of Finnish Foresters	2,214
Union of Finnish Psychologists	2,647
Union of Finnish Speech Therapists	704
Association of Finnish Political Scientists	1,047
Occupational Health Nurses' Association	1,492
Union of Finnish Military Officers	4,805
Association of Employees in Government School Administration	179
Trade Union for Environment Experts	753
The Nurse Administrator Association	420

Suomen Teknisten Toimihhenkilöjärjestojen Keskusliitto (STTK)
Confederation of Technical Employees' Organizations in Finland

Address. Pohjranta Str. 4A, 00170 Helsinki
Phone. (90) 625 871
Leadership. Esa Swamljung (chairman)
Membership. 155,000 in 16 organizations at the end of 1989.
Affiliated unions. STK's member organizations are:

Name	Membership
Union of Ships Captains	3,000
Union of Technicians	70,000
Federation of State-Employed Technicians	21,000
Union of Salaried Employees within Forestry	9,200
Federation of Municipal Technicians	11,000
Federation of Finnish Salesmen	13,000
Union of Construction Technicians of the Private Sector	7,000
Union of Ship Engineers	4,400
Union of Public-Health Nurses	4,000
Union of Swedish-speaking Technicians and Foremen	2,400
Union of Dairy Technicians	2,900
Union of Printing Plant Foremen	2,600
Union of Radio Telegraphists	900
Union of Construction Engineers of the Private Sector	300
Union of Professional Engineers	600
Union of Finnish Docker Foremen	900
Total	155,000
Co-operative members:	
Union Ships' Pilots	600
Union of Opticians	650

France

Capital: Paris   **Population: 56,000,000**

Political system. France has a bicameral parliament with a directly elected Chamber of Deputies and an indirectly elected Senate; the directly elected president has extensive executive powers. From the establishment of the Fifth Republic in 1958 France had centre-right governments and presidents. In 1981, however, the Socialist François Mitterrand won the presidential election, and shortly afterwards the Socialists secured a commanding majority in the Chamber of Deputies (although the Senate remained predominantly non-socialist). In their 1981 election manifesto the Socialists had put forward a far-reaching programme of nationalization and social reform (various sections of the economy having already come under public control in the mid and late 1940s), and the left-wing government formed in that year extended the public sector particularly through the nationalization of a number of banks, certain major industrial groups and two large financial holding companies. In legislative elections in 1986 the centre-right parties (RPR and UDF) gained a narrow overall majority, resulting in a period of "cohabitation" between a president and a government of different political groupings. The new government immediately sought to reverse many of its predecessor's policies and carried through far-reaching privatizations.

In 1988 however President Mitterand was re-elected and appointed a new Socialist-led administration under Michel Rocard. The parties of the Right lost ground in the 1988 Assembly elections shortly after though the Socialists were left short of an overall majority. Rocard, who had observed the President's instruction in economic policy—"neither nationalization nor privatization"—was replaced as Prime Minister in May 1991 by Edith Cresson who had been identified with a more interventionist (but pro-Community) policy.

France was a founder-member of the three components of the European Communities. In the sphere of defence it is a member of NATO but has not participated in the integrated military structure since 1966.

Economy. The 1988 workforce in France numbered 21,510,000, of whom 6,330,000 were employed in industry, 1,550,000 in agriculture, and 13,530,000 in services. The Rocard government which came to power in 1988 pursued an even tighter monetary policy than had his Right-wing predecessor Chirac. Corporate tax was cut in 1989 while public spending was pegged to the rate of inflation. Intervention was more likely to be through the local rather than the central state, and increasingly was directed towards small rather than big business.

By 1990 growth was a robust a 3 per cent but France still had substantial unemployment of 2,600,000. In a report published in March 1990, the OECD forecast that France would out-perform the OECD average in terms of inflation and output for the first time since 1970. Its weaknesses were perceived to be longstanding inadequate industrial investment (though corporate spending on this was rising fast), an obstinate current account deficit, and a shortage of skilled workers.

France still has one of the largest state-owned sectors in Europe: approximately one third of French industrial turnover is accounted for by Government-controlled companies but governments have yet to resolve the thorny problem of how to organize their finances. While wishing the public sector to grow by acquisition, governments also have to be wary of EEC and (increasingly) national rules prohibiting excessive intervention. France's most notorious subsidy, the celebrated write-off of FF 12,000 million at Renault drew an EEC penalty. In 1989 some FF 4,000 million went in state contributions to capital—one quarter of it to one company, the acquisitive Pechiney. Many firms in the state sector broke out of the straitjacket by borrowing on the stock market. It has been estimated that 15–20 per cent of the equity of larger quoted companies is owned by nationalized shareholders. In her first programmatic statement Mme Cresson reaffirmed the approach to economic policy of Rocard.

System of industrial relations. France ratified ILO Conventions No. 87 (Freedom of Association and Protection of the Right to Organize, 1948) and No. 98 (Right to Organize and Collective Bargaining, 1949) in 1951.

Government promotion of collective bargaining was inaugurated under Mauroy in 1981, but by the end of the 1980s it was apparent that it only covered France to a very patchy extent. The "Auroux" laws, named after the Socialists' first Minister for Employment, extended employee and union rights. While apparently strengthening the unions' position, the laws may, by institutionalizing representatives, have hastened their decline. Moreover, a right like that to "expression" (used to establish committees in the mid-1980s), was eventually used by sophisticated employers to avoid communication through the unions. Under Rocard, little was done to extend union rights except make union contributions tax-deductible. France participated in the international tendency to bargain at the enterprise level. The National Council for Collective Bargaining disclosed that in 1989 sectoral agreements declined by 5 per cent while those concluded at company level rose by 14 per cent; the number of central agreements remained unchanged.

The Commission aims at full contractual coverage of the whole labour force, which may inhibit employers' freedom of action though this depends on the type of agreement made. Thus in France, an "accord" is an agreement on one question which affects those firms in membership of an employers' association which belongs to the signatory employers' organization. By contrast a "convention" may, with Commission agreement, be extended by the Minister of Labour to an entire industry. The original agreement, be it an accord or a convention, may arise from the departmental, regional or national level.

Despite falling trade union membership, there was a revival of industrial militancy late in the 1980s, sometimes organized by informal activist groups. A large number of public or state sector enterprises have experienced industrial action since 1988. Moreover the leaderships of all unions were displeased by the proposals in the draft budget of M. Bérégovoy for 1991 to restrict public spending, cut taxes and boost defence expenditure. Nor was their temper improved by the government proposal to move the funding of social security out of general tax into a new Pay As You Earn tax of 1.1 per cent on taxes and dividends. The first programmatic statement of Edith Cresson drew little enthusiasm from the unions.

Trade unionism. Trade union organizations were given legal recognition in 1884 and the oldest confederation still in existence, the Confédération Générale du Travail (CGT), was founded in 1895. The CGT was dominated by socialist, anarcho-syndicalist and communist factions and in 1919 unions influenced by social Catholicism founded the Confédération Française des Travailleurs Chrétiens (CFTC). The CGT was weakened in the inter-war period by the creation of the breakaway Confédération Générale du Travail Unitaire (CGTU), in which communists took control, in 1921; the CGTU rejoined the CGT in 1936 but the majority of its adherents were expelled in 1939 following the Nazi-Soviet pact. Existing union centres were dissolved by the Vichy government under the Nazi occupation in 1940, but in 1943 the underground leaders of the CGT and CGTU agreed to the formation of a united centre. The CFTC, however, refused after the war to accept a merger with the CGT, which in turn was split again by the formation of the ICFTU-affiliated, CGT-Force Ouvrière (FO) in 1947. The CFTC broke into two in 1964, a minority faction retaining the old name and the majority reorganizing as the Confédération Française Démocratique du Travail (CFDT).

Under the labour code the basic criteria involved in the recognition of a confederation as nationally representative are defined as sufficiency of members, independence (from employers), automatic and regular payment of membership dues, experience and length of existence, and patriotic attitude during the occupation. The CGT, FO, CFDT, CFTC and CGC were designated "nationally representative" in 1966, and governments have generally favoured this system as it simplifies the task of dealing with the unions (although the "monopoly" of the "club of five" has recently been attacked from the political right). Unions affiliated to such a recognized centre enjoy a range of privileges including the right to conclude collective bargaining agreements or to form an enterprise branch union without proving that they have representative status in the workplace or industry concerned, and the automatic right to present candidates in elections to various public administrative boards. However, recent years have seen some growth of "independent" and "autonomous" unions, despite the practical difficulties faced in obtaining recognition. The five major centres do not in most cases hold a monopoly on elected works councils, where non-unionized worker candidates won 21.1 per cent of the votes in 1987, and about half of enterprises with from 50 to 149 employees do not have a trade union branch.

Ideological controversies have played a more significant role in the French union movement than in most western industrial countries, a fact reflected in the division of the labour movement and the lack of a clear leading trade union centre. Furthermore, workers are generally less firmly organized than in other industrial countries, membership figures are commonly inflated or imprecise, and dues paid irregularly. Collective bargaining developed weakly in France, partly because since the Matignon Accord of 1936 recognition has been extended to all "representative" unions, rather than a sole bargaining agent, in collective bargaining situations; in addition, the union movement has relied on state intervention and government legislation to ensure gains which in the UK and West Germany have been associated with the independent activity of the trade unions themselves. The emphasis on political pressure as a technique in industrial relations had been further encouraged by the recurrent instability of French governments. This has been most dramatically illustrated in recent times by the events in 1968, when, at the peak, up to half of French workers were on sit-down strikes, and also by the fact that the main confederations—except to some extent the CFDT—have made less progress in the private sector than in areas where the state itself is the employer. The organizational weakness of the unions is also reflected in the fact that major strike waves can originate independently of the unions among unorganized workers, as in 1968 and in the last weeks of 1986.

A major constraint on such national initiatives is low union density: in 1989 only around 13 per cent of the French workforce belonged to trades unions and the decline since the 24 per cent peak of 1975 has been almost unrelenting. The unions did not even benefit in membership terms from the nationalizations of the early 1980s because these were followed by rationalization. Rising unemployment clearly reduced membership during the 1980s, but falling density is better explained by structural shifts in the French economy away from manufacturing towards the service sector. Sub-contracted labour, women, and young people, all of whom are to be found in large numbers in France's peripheral workforce, have tended to find trade unionism unattractive.

French trade unionism has always been confounded by divisions, though this has not prevented it mounting major social challenges. Moreover, even in a climate conducive to the strengthening of plant bargaining such as that produced by the Auroux laws of 1982, all unions have found it difficult to consolidate their position.

The largest union federation is the General Federation of Labour (CGT) which is increasingly disengaged from the PCF. Its smaller rival the Democratic Federation of Labour (CFDT) is not party-aligned though many of its militants are PS activists. The third centre, Force Ouvrière, originated from Post-War divisions in French politics and has the backing of the RPR. The Confédération Générale des Cadres (CGC) has a membership of 297,000 while the Confédération Françaisc des Travaileurs Chrétiens (CFTC) has a membership of around 200,000 (figures are for 1988). Standing apart from the federations is France's largest single union, the Fédération de L'Education Nationale (FEN) whose membership stands at 351,000.

In the 1987 works council elections, the Federations received support as follows: CGT 26.8 per cent, CFDT 21.3 per cent, FO 11.3 per cent, CGC 5.9 per cent, CFTC 4.8 per cent. At that time votes were held in 11,502 establishments which employed 2,500,000 employees eligible to vote. Votes are also held for social security administration councils, and in these the FO tended to poll more impressively. The years 1989–1990 brought increasing calls for a re-alignment. Talks were held between the Socialist-inclined CFDT and FEN and the two jointly organized their celebration of May Day 1990. But the CGT was not invited to join the talks and FO hostility towards what it perceives as undue PS influence in trade unions continues although the CFDT has now joined it as an ICFTU affiliate. The CFDT, FO and CFTC are all affiliated to the European TUC.

Confédération Française Démocratique du Travail (CFDT)
French Democratic Confederation of Labour

Address. 4 Boulevard de la Villette, 75955 Paris, Cédex 19.

Phone. 42-03-80-00

Telex. 240832 F

Fax. 42-03-80-74

Leadership. Jean Kaspar (secretary-general); Nicole Notat (national secretary)

Membership. The CFDT records 539,000 members, of whom 30 per cent are women. In the 1987 Prud'homme elections the CFDT received 23.05 per cent support against the CGT's 36.35 per cent and the FO's 20.5 per cent.

International affiliations. TUAC; ETUC; the CFDT left the WCL in 1978 and joined the ICFTU in 1989 following an 81 per cent vote in favour of making an application at its November 1988 Congress.

Publications. *Syndicalisme* (weekly, 32,000 copies); *CFDT Magazine* (monthly, 320,000 copies); *CFDT Aujourd'hui* (every two months, 3,450 copies); *Action Juridique* (eight times per year, 6,000 copies).

History and character. The CFDT was formed in 1964 by the majority faction of the Confédération Française des Travailleurs Chrétiens (CFTC), the minority retaining the previous name (for origins of the rift, see entry for CFTC). The founders of the CFDT sought to restrict the religious influence within the federation and to reshape it as a democratic socialist centre. The CFDT played a significant role in the industrial unrest surrounding the May-June political crisis of 1968, leading to a period of "politicization" of the confederation. From 1978, however, a process of "resyndicalization"—i.e. emphasizing closely defined trade union issues—has taken place, with the emphasis on union adaptation to economic change. This approach has been criticized by a minority as "pragmatism without a programme". However, Edmond Maire, the leading exponent of the pragmatic approach, was re-elected for a further three-year term as secretary general at the 40th congress in June 1985. The CFDT has been affected by the general relative decline of French trade unionism since the late 1970s, after years of growth from 1964. Official membership slipped below 1,000,000 in 1980, while in the 1983 elections for administrators of the health insurance and family allowance funds, the CFDT lost its previous second place (behind the CGT) to the FO, taking only 18.36 per cent of the votes. The CFDT has lost an estimated 25 per cent of its effective membership since its peak year of 1976, with particular losses in the private sector, where it has traditionally been the strongest of the centres.

Policies. The 1985 (triennial) congress set the following priorities: the reduction of working hours; negotiated agreements on the introduction of new technology; measures to assist in providing better opportunities for the young; reduction in social and economic equalities and recognition of the equal rights of women; and modification of hierarchical relationships in the workplace.

Edmond Maire emphasized that the trade union movement, weakened by the decline of the old industrial sectors, the effects of international competition, and unemployment, must avoid the temptations of a withdrawal into "conservatism". It is, he has argued, in the interest of the workers to embrace the opportunities provided by technological change to acquire diversified skills and to "leave behind hierarchically organized, low-skilled highly compartmentalized work, with all the harmful effects it has on workers.... Changing work means making workers more highly skilled, more autonomous and creative and more responsible. It also means modifying work organization to make it more flexible using workers with a degree of occupational mobility". Unions, according to Maire, must involve themselves in such change as co-partners: "the transformation of work and control over technology represent a great ambition for trade unionism: an extension of the scope of contractual negotiation to everything concerning and affecting work".

The CFDT stresses its entire independence in respect of the state, political parties, the churches and all other organizations but in practice became closely associated with the Socialist Party, an association which has weakened since 1988.

In 1988 the CFDT abandoned the reference to socialism in its Statutes. That year's Congress which was held in November saw the retirement of Edmond Maire, Secretary General since 1971 and his replacement by Jean Kaspar. The Congress set three priorities for the CFDT: action on the changing pattern of work, especially by negotiating the introduction of new technology; a social wage for all workers; the establishment of job security in the face of employer manipulation. It also heard and debated a report on attracting new members and expelled Trotskyists from its executive committee.

Affiliated Unions: 2300 local branches and 19 national industrial federations (with two national unions): 22 regional branches.

The national industrial federations are as follows, and unless otherwise indicated, they are located at 47 avenue Simon Bolivar, 75950 Paris Cedex 19 (Phone: 42-02-42-52; Fax: 42-02-50-53).

1. **Fédération de l'Agroalimentaire (FGA)**.
   Leadership: Jean Alegre (secretary-general).

2. **Fédération des Anciens Combattants, 37 rue Bellechasse, 75007 Paris**.
   Leadership: Nicole Delvaux (secretary-general).

3. **Fédération de la Banque**.
   Leadership: Jean-Luc Wabant (secretary-general).

4. **Fédération Unie Chimie**.
   Leadership: Jacques Kheliff (secretary-general).

5. **Fédération Construction Bois (FFNCB)**.
   Leadership: Michel Salmain (secretary-general).

6. **Fédération de l'Enseignement Privé (FEP)**.
   Leadership: Jacques André (secretary-general).

7. **Fédération des Etablissements et Arsenaux de l'Etat (FEAE)**.
   Leadership: Pierre-Henri Guinet.

8. **Fédération des Finances et des Affaires Economiques**.
   Leadership: Philippe Le Clezio.

9. **Fédération du Gaz Electricité (FGE)**.
   Leadership: Bruno Lechevin (secretary-general).

10. **Fédération de l'Habillement, du Cuir de Textile (HACUITEX)**.
    Leadership: Yvonne Delemotte.

11. **Fédération des Travailleurs de l'Information, du Livre de l'Audiovisuel, de la Culture (FTILAC)**.
    Leadership: Michel Mortelette (secretary-general).

12. **Fédération Personnel du Minstére de l'Intérieur et des Collectivités Locales (INTERCO)**.

13. **Fédération de la Justice**, 25–27 rue de la Fontaine au Roi, 75012 Paris.
    Leadership: Yves Rousset (secretary-general).

14. **Fédération de la Métallurgie et des Mines (FGMM).**
    Leadership: Gerard Cantin (secretary-general).

15. **Fédération Protection Sociale, Travail, Emploi (PSTE).**
    Leadership: Michel Weissgerber (secretary-general).

16. **Fédération Démocratique Unifiée des PTT.**
    Leadership: Jean-Claude Desrayaud (secretary-general).

17. **Fédération des Services de Santé et Services Sociaux.**
    Leadership: Marc Dupont (secretary-general).

18. **Fédération des Services.**
    Leadership: M. Jouan.

19. **Fédération Générale des Transports – Equipements (FGTE).**
    Leadership: Michel Pernet (secretary-general).

20. **Syndicat Général de l'Education Nationale (SGEN).**
    Leadership: Jean-Michel Boullier (secretary-general).

21. **Union Confédérale des Ingénieurs et Cadres (UCC).**
    Leadership: Garnier Croquette (secretary-general).

22. **Union Confédérale des Retraités (UCR).**
    Leadership: Marc Gonin (secretary-general).

23. **Union des Fédérations de Fonctionnaires et Assimilés (UFFA).**
    Leadership: Roselynne Vieillard (secretary-general).

Confédération Française des Travailleurs Chrétiens (CFTC)
French Confederation of Christian Workers

Address. 13 rue des Ecluses Saint Martin, 75483 Paris, Cédex 10
Phone. (1) 42-40-02-02
Telex. 214 046
Fax. (1) 42-00-44-04
Leadership. Guy Drilleaud (president); Alain deleu (secretary-general).
Membership. Claims 255,000 compared with 265,000 in 1987.
History and character. Unions influenced by social Catholicism developed from the mid-1880s, and the CFTC itself was formed in November 1919 at a constituent congress of 321 unions with nearly 100,000 members. The CFTC participated the same year in the establishment of the International Federation of Christian Trade Unions, the predecessor of the WCL. The CFTC, like the CGT, recruited many new members in 1936 (see CGT entry), and lost fewer of them in the rest of the decade. The Vichy government dissolved the CFTC in 1940; activity resumed in August 1944 when the underground leaders of the CFTC and the CGT formed an interconfederal committee of understanding, but the CFTC rejected CGT proposals for a merger after the war. In its early period the CFTC was fundamentally Catholic, rather than primarily working class, in emphasis, but after the war a fraction known as the *minoritaires*, grouped around the journal *Réconstruction*, pressed to release the federation from the religious strait-jacket to permit it to challenge the CGT and the FO and move to a Christian-influenced but non-denominational, independent, and democratic socialist position. In 1946, in repudiation of the acceptance of ministerial posts in the French government by communist CGT officials, the CFTC in its first post-war congress approved a resolution declaring that political office was incompatible with trade union office, and in 1947 the CFTC began the process of weakening its links with the Catholic church by abolishing a constitutional provision whereby its activities were to be based on the papal encyclical *Rerum Novarum*. By 1964 the reformers were in the majority, and a special congress voted to change the name of the organization to the Confédération Française Démocratique du Travail (CFDT—*see separate entry*). A minority, composed largely of miners' and white-collar unions, consequently separated themselves, retaining the previous name as the CFTC. The CFTC today maintains its social Christian orientation, empha-

157

sizing as fundamental the primacy of the individual and the inalienable rights (and duties) of each individual; the defence of the family; the rejection of the class struggle; the development of contractual relations between free and independent organizations; and the rejection of the politicization of trade unions. Such beliefs were reiterated at the 43rd CFTC Congress held at Versailles in November 1987.

In recent years the CFTC has stepped up its international contacts, including those in Latin America, the Caribbean, Africa and the Far East. To help in this work, the CFTC has set up the Centre for International Co-operation, whose Secretary General is Armel Gourmelon. The CFTC's 44th Congress was held in November 1990 at Lille.

Affiliated unions and structure. There are 1,729 workplace union branches; 32 national sectoral federations; 333 local branches; 101 departmental branches (which also cover overseas members); 22 regional branches.

Publications. CFTC Syndicalisme Magazine (monthly); *La Lettre Confédérale* (bi-monthly); *Informations Confédérales* (monthly).

International affiliations. WCL; ETUC.

Confédération Générale des Cadres (CGC)
Confederation of Executive Staff

Address. 30 rue de Gramont, 75002 Paris

Phone. (1) 42-61-81-76

Leadership. Paul Marchelli (president); Jean De Santis (delegate general)

Membership. Claims 300,000 managerial, professional and technical staff, but the true fully paid-up membership was estimated by the metal industry employers' association, the UIMM, as only 150,000 in 1983.

History. Founded in 1944. The CGC emphasizes the themes of "economic citizenship" and "new trade unionism", and that unions must progress beyond the advocacy of workers' sectional interests to assume a role as "co-managers of society". The CGC argues that its membership of managers, supervisors and technicians, constitutes the driving force of economic progress and is thereby uniquely placed to encourage capital and labour to operate towards common goals. Such co-operation is seen as essential if French industry is to withstand the challenges imposed by new technology and the constant increase of international competition. The CGC argues that the relative decline of trade unionism in the industrial world in recent years has reflected the failure of the trade unions themselves to adapt to changes in the structure and expectations of the workforce, and advocates a conception of workers undergoing a process of continual training to adapt to technological change.

International affiliation. TUAC.

Confédération Générale du Travail (CGT)
General Confederation of Labour

Address. 263 rue de Paris, 93516 Paris, Montreuil Cédex

Phone. 48-51-80-00

Telex. 235069

Fax. 48-57-15-20

Leadership. Henri Krasucki (secretary general).

Membership. 797,662 (1988). At one point in the 1970s, the CGT claimed 2,250,000 members and had the ambition of reaching 3,000,000. However the CGT also has nearly 250,000 retired members, bringing its gross total to 1,030,843.

History. The CGT was founded at Limoges in 1895 and from the beginning was affected by ideological divisions between socialists, syndicalists and others. Pre-1914 the CGT adopted an anti-militarist posture, but during the First World War the CGT secretary, Léon Jouhaux, served as a "commissioner of the nation", mobilizing the CGT behind the war effort. Membership, which was only about 400,000 of an industrial workforce of 6,000,000 in 1914, grew rapidly in the 1918–1920 period to about 2,500,000 but tensions generated by conflicting responses to the example of the Russian Revolution led to expulsions of members of the revolutionary minority, and the formation in

1921 of the Confédération Générale du Travail Unitaire (CGTU), in which communists took control. The CGTU and the French Communist Party (PCF, formed 1920) to which it was linked subsequently engaged in a bitter struggle with the CGT and reformist "social fascists". However, in accordance with a switch in policy ordered by Moscow, the communists after 1934 moved to create a "popular front" with socialists and the "liberal bourgeoisie" and the CGTU was readmitted to the CGT, predominantly on the latter's programme, in March 1936. The election of a reforming Popular Front government under Léon Blum in May 1936 and a wave of strikes and popular euphoria encouraged a massive surge in CGT membership, which increased several-fold to as high as 4,000,000–5,000,000 by the end of 1936, before declining to only a quarter of this figure by 1939 in the decreasingly favourable political conditions following the fall of the Popular Front government in June 1937. The communist faction was strident in its calls for unity against Nazi aggression but immediately endorsed the Nazi – Soviet pact of Aug. 23, 1939, and following the declaration of war by France against Germany on Sept. 3, the communists were purged from the CGT. The communists sabotaged war production before the collapse of France but completed a further abrupt switch of policy following the German invasion of the Soviet Union in June 1941, whereafter adherents of the PCF became a major factor in the Resistance. The CGT was liquidated by the Vichy government in November 1940 but some leaders within the CGT were recruited into the new Vichy labour organization, including René Bélin, who became Minister of Labour responsible for the implementation of a corporatist Labour Charter. In May 1943 the communists were readmitted to the (clandestine) CGT, with three of the eight seats on the executive board.

In September 1945, in step with a surge of post-war support for the PCF (which participated in the post-war de Gaulle government) Benoît Frachon, a communist, was appointed a co-equal CGT secretary general with Jouhaux, and during 1946–47 the communists achieved control of most of the CGT apparatus. Communist policies stressed the demands of economic recovery, including a wages standstill backed by the CGT, and confrontation between the different wings of the CGT was initially avoided. Membership in 1946 stood at more than 5,000,000. However, the onset of the Cold War in 1947, the removal of the communists ministers from the government in May of that year, and the switch of the communists to a strategy of industrial confrontation later in the year, precipitated the break-up of the CGT, the socialist minority led by Jouhaux forming the CGT-Force Ouvrière in December (see separate entry). Many non-communists remained loyal to the CGT, however, and the confederation retained its leading position in the labour movement.

Membership of the CGT began to fall steadily after 1977, provoking considerable alarm within the confederation. All the main French trade union centres have lost membership during this period but the disproportionate losses of the CGT have been variously attributed to realignment in French politics (with a decline in the Communist Party), the decay of heavy industries in which the CGT was strong, unemployment, the image of the CGT as having ideological and bureaucratic inflexibility and subservience to the political programme of the Communist Party at the expense of trade union issues, and its failure to respond to social and economic modernization and to recognize the importance of organizing white-collar employees in the small business sector. The CGT's position was also compromised to some extent by the participation of the Communist Party in the socialist government of the early 1980s, and following the withdrawal of communists from office the CGT involved itself in opposition to aspects of government policy, isolating the socialist minority (although the election of a conservative government in 1986 permitted a reconvergence of views within the CGT). Recently it has been the most resistant of the confederations on the issues of flexibility in working hours and labour practices. The Communist Party has retained its dominance over the CGT, although not holding undivided power. The 18-member confederal bureau (the effective ruling body) elected in November 1985 comprised nine communists (including seven members of the central committee of the Communist Party) and nine non-communists, including two members of the Socialist Party (PS), and the executive committee comprised 30 non-communists and 95 communists. Nearly all the leaders of the departmental unions and industrial federations are Communist Party members.

CGT Metallurgie. In September 1988 M. André Sainjon resigned from his post as General Secretary of the Metalworkers affiliate of the CGT. In his resignation statement he said that he had resigned over disagreements with the union over its policy and political direction. He was succeeded by M. Jean Demaison.

Quality circles. As is the case with other Western countries, quality circles have been introduced into French enterprises by the employers. In an interview on the subject published in the *World Trade Union Movement* No. 2 in 1988, the Head of the Economic Department of the CGT maintained that the CGT's participation in quality circles would depend first and foremost on the union's strength in the enterprise concerned and whether such quality circles can be used to increase the union's influence on management.

1987 Conseils de Prud'homme Elections. In the December 1987 elections the CGT maintained its dominant influence; it obtained the highest result of all the trade union confederations with 36.4 per cent of the votes (only down 0.47 points on 1982). M. Henri Krasucki reacted to the results by stating that "despite de-industrialization and the increased repression by employers, the CGT had obtained increased votes to compensate for those lost as a result of redundancies".

Flexibility. The CGT argues that modernization and new technology should lead to shorter working hours and a higher standard of living, to training and qualifications which will result in higher quality products and the satisfaction of economic and social needs. However, the CGT maintains that employers use new technology to raise profits to the maximum level by keeping machinery going round the clock, seven days a week. In addition, employers seek to impose mobility and flexibility of working hours and wages, which result in inhuman working conditions which often jeopardize the economic viability of the companies in question. The CGT vigorously opposed the legislation of the Chirac government in 1987 which allowed night work for women. The CGT attacks the position of other trade union confederations such as the CFDT and the CGT-FO for agreeing to de-regulation and increased flexibility.

Structure. The CGT is organized on a base of tens of thousands of workplace branches, forming 17,211 local unions as of 1983; these are in turn organized by occupational classification into 46 national industrial federations and geographically into 950 local unions, 97 departmental unions, and 21 regional committees. There are in addition special organizations for certain broad categories of members: the UGFF (Union Générale des Fédérations de Fonctionnaires), for officials; the UGICT (Union Générale des Ingénieurs, Cadres et Techniciens), for engineers, managers and technicians; the UCR (Union Confédérale des Retraités), for pensioners; the CCJ (Centre Confédéral de la Jeunesse) for young people; and the Comité National des Chômeurs, for the unemployed. There is a triennial delegate congress (last held in May 1989). Between congresses authority is exercised by a national confederal committee (CCN, normally meeting every six months), composed of the general secretary and the secretaries of the industrial federations and departmental unions; this CCN elects the confederal bureau and the executive committee (*commission exécutive*, CE).

Publications. La Vie Ouvriére (weekly, 385,000 copies); *Le Peuple* (bimonthly, 32,000); *Options* (bimonthly, 55,000); *Tribune* (8 times per year, for immigrant workers, 25,000).

International affiliation. WFTU. A CGT representative held the post of WFTU secretary general continuously from 1947 until in 1978 the CGT failed to offer a candidate, criticizing the insufficient autonomy of the trade unions of the Soviet bloc countries. The CGT remained within the WFTU, however, as its most important affiliate in the Western world, and relations between it and the Soviet bloc unions appeared to improve during 1985–86. Henri Krasucki is a WFTU vice-president. The CGT has tried without success to join the ETUC.

Confédération Générale du Travail-Force Ouvriére (FO)
General Confederation of Labour-Workers' Strength

Address. 198 Avenue du Maine, 75680 Paris, Cedex 14

Phone. 45-39-22-03

Telex. 203405 F

Fax. 45-45-54-52

Leadership. Marc Blondel (secretary-general)

Membership. In 1988, claimed 1,150,000 members in 16,000 local union branches; the metal industry employers' association, the UIMM, in 1985 estimated the real paid-up membership at 600,000.

History. The CGT-Force Ouvrière was formed in April 1948, with the secession from the CGT of a large number of trade unionists who opposed the communist methods and policies of the CGT. At the time of the breakaway the CGT had an estimated 5,000,000 members. The new group was led by Léon Jouhaux, who had been secretary general of the CGT from 1909 to 1946 until compelled to accept a division of his authority, as co-secretary, with the communist Benoît Frachon, himself a former official of the CGTU. The immediate cause of the secession was a wave of communist-led strikes and violent disturbances in November-December 1947, viewed by the Force Ouvrière as a co-ordinated attempt to threaten the stability of the new post-war French Republic, which was governed by a centre-left alliance of popular republicans and socialists. A further source of division between the CGT and the Force Ouvrière was the issue of US economic aid to Europe: the CGT executive (in accordance with Soviet policy) denounced the Marshall Plan (announced in June 1947) as a "war machine of American imperialists against the liberty and independence of other nations", but the Force Ouvrière favoured acceptance of such aid. (This issue was also of significance in the break-up of the WFTU after 1947 and the formation of the ICFTU, to which the FO affiliated.) Most of the strength of the new FO was in the white-collar and public services sectors.

Perhaps the main reason for the secession of nearly 1,000,000 CGT members to form the CGT-FO was the belief that the policies of the CGT were controlled not by the members themselves but by the French Communist Party. Indeed, the CGT-FO retains the title "CGT" in its name because it claims that it remains true to the fundamental democratic principals which characterised the CGT from 1906 right up to 1945 which were based on the original 1906 *Charter of Amiens*. That Charter affirmed the principle of trade union links not only with political parties, but also with the government, employers and various religious groupings.

The FO, despite being the sole ICFTU-affiliated centre in France, has failed to achieve the dominant status enjoyed by ICFTU affiliates in most other western industrial countries, partly reflecting the continued (if declining) strength of the CGT, but also in part as a result of the existence of the CFDT as a major democratic socialist alternative. It has, however, in recent years regained much of the ground lost to the CFDT in the decade or more after the creation of the latter in 1964. In the 1987 Prud'homme elections, the CGT-FO was the only trade union confederation to increase its share of the vote—up 2.71 points on 1982 figures.

The FO emphasizes that it stands independent of any political party and, unlike the CGT and the CFDT, it declined to participate in the socialist government elected in 1981, "believing that it is not possible to be the ruler and the ruled at the same time". It also rejected the conception of the "social compromise", involving wage restraint, advanced by that government. FO organs are, however, controlled by individual supporters (who include Bergeron) of the "SFIO maintenue" element of the Socialist Party (PS). Adherents of both the (Gaullist) Rally for the Republic (RPR) of Prime Minister Jacques Chirac and the small (Trotskyist) International Communist Party (PCI) have been reported as attempting to infiltrate FO branches in recent years, both with some local success.

Structure. Congress is held every three years and the National Confederal Committee is the key body between congresses. This Committee (CCN—Comité Confederal National) serves as the representative body for all the CGT-FO affiliated unions and departmental unions. The CCN has an executive commission and a confederal bureau which runs the overall administration for the union. There are 102 departmental unions (95 in the departments of metropolitan France, and in Réunion, French Guiana, Matinique, Guadeloupe, St Pierre and Miquelon, New Caledonia and for French civilian workers in Germany). The 28 national occupational federations include one for the retired which is 150,000-strong.

1. **Action Sociale**, 8 rue du Hanovre, 75002 Paris.
   Phone: 42-68-08-01.
   Secretary: Michel Pinaud.
   Publication: *Bulletin Federal* (monthly).

2. **Administration Générale**, 46 rue des Petites Ecuries, 75010 Paris.
   Phone: 42-46-40-19; Fax. 42-46-19-57.
   Secretary: Francis Lamarque.
   Membership: 20,000.
   Publication: *Réalités Force Ouvrière*.

3. **Agriculture et Alimentation et Tabac** (agriculture, food and tobacco), 198 Avenue du Maine, 75680 Paris, Cédex 14.
   Phone: 45-39-22-03.
   Secretaries: Gérard Fossé and Alain Kerbriand (agriculture); Daniel Dreux (tobacco).

4. **Bâtiment-Travaux Publics-Bois-Céramique-Papier-Carton-Matériaux de Construction** (building and allied trades), 170 Avenue Parmentier, 75010 Paris.
   Phone: 42-01-30-00. Fax: 42-39-50-44.
   Secretary: Alain P. Emile.
   Membership: 70,000.
   Publication: *Des Faits, des Idées*.

5. **Cheminots** (railway workers), 60 rue Vergniaud, 75640 Paris, Cédex 13.
   Phone: 45-80-22-98.
   Secretary: Jean-Jacques Carmentran.
   Membership: 16,500.
   Publication: *Le Rail Syndicaliste*.

6. **Coiffure-Esthétique et Parfumerie** (hairdressing, beauticians), 130 avenue Palmentier, 75011 Paris.
   Phone: 43-57-31-80.
   Secretary: Michel Bourlon.
   Membership: 1,200.
   Publication: *Spécial Fo Coiffure*.

7. **Cuirs-Textiles-Habillement** (leather and textiles), 8 rue du Hanovre esc. B 2ième étage, 75002 Paris.
   Phone: 47-42-92-70.
   Secretary: Francis Desrousseaux.

8. **Education et Culture**, 4 Boulevard de Strasbourg, 75010 Paris.
   Phone: 42-06-27-87.
   Secretary: François Chaintron.

9. **Employés et Cadres** (white collar staff), 28 rue des Petits Hôtels, 75010 Paris.
   Phone: 42-46-46-64.
   Secretary: Yves Simon.

10. **Energie Electrique et Gaz**, 60 rue Vergniaud, 75013 Paris.
    Phone: 45-88-91-51.
    Secretary: Gabriel Gaudy.
    Membership: 25,000.
    Publication: *Lumiére et Force*.

11. **Finances**, 46 rue des Petites Ecuries, 75010 Paris.
    Phone: 42-46-75-20.
    Secretary: André Roulet.
    Publications: *Finances Informations*.

12. **Fonctionnaires** (civil servants), 46 rue des Petites Ecuries, 75010 Paris.
    Phone: 42-46-48-56.
    Fax: 42-46-97-80.
    Secretary: Roland Gaillard.
    Membership: 100,000.
    Publication: *La Nouvelle Tribune*.

13. **Industries Chimiques** (chemical industries), 60 rue Vergniaud, 75640 Paris, Cédex 13.
    Phone: 45-80-14-90.
    Secretary: François Grandazzi.
    Membership: 15,000.
    Publications: *Le Syndicaliste FO; Le Syndicaliste Militant FO*.

14. **Livre** (book, print trades), 198 Avenue du Maine, 75680 Paris, Cédex 14.
    Phone: 45-40-69-44.
    Secretary: Roger Carpentier.

15. **Métaux**, 9 rue Baudoin, 75013 Paris.
    Phone: 45-82-01-00. Fax. 45-83-78-87.
    Secretary: Michel Huc.
    Membership: 50,000.
    Publication: *Fo Métaux*.

16. **Mineurs, Miniers et Similaires** (miners), 169 Avenue de Choisy, B.P. 325, 75624 Paris, Cédex 13.
    Phone: 45-87-10-98.
    Secretary: René Mertz.

17. **Personnels Civils de la Défense Nationale** (civilian employees in national defence), 46 rue des Petites Ecuries, 75010 Paris.
    Phone: 42-46-00-05.
    Secretary: Jacques Pe.

18. **Personnels des Services des Départements et des Régions**, 46 rue des Petites Ecuries, 75010 Paris.
    Phone: 42-46-50-52.
    Secretary: Michèle Simmonnini.
    Membership: 10,000.

19. **Pharmacie**, 198 Avenue du Maine, 75680 Paris, Cédex 14.
    Phone: 45-39-97-22.
    Secretary: Bernard Devy.

20. **Police**, 6 rue Albert Bayet, 75013 Paris.
    Phone: 42-46-74-12.
    Secretary: Jean-Louis Cerceau.

21. **PTT** (post, telegraphs, telephones), 60 rue Vergniaud, 75640 Paris, Cédex 13.
    Phone: 45-89-89-59. Telex: 200644. Fax. 40-78-30-58.
    Secretary: Jacques Marçot.
    Membership: 60,000.
    Publication: *PTT Syndicaliste*.

22. **Services Publics et de Santé** (public services and health), 153–55 rue de Rome, 75017 Paris.
    Phone: 46-22-26-00. Fax. 42-27-21-40.
    Membership: 70,000.
    Joint secretaries: Guy Millan, René Champeau.

23. **Arts, Spectacles-Presse-Audiovisuel** (theatre and cinema, press and broadcasting), 2 rue de la Michodière, 75002 Paris.
    Phone: 47-42-35-86. Fax. 40-07-04-41.
    Secretary: Georges Donaud.

24. **Transports**, 198 Avenue du Maine, 75680 Paris, Cédex 14.
    Phone: 45-40-68-00.
    Secretary: Gilbert Doriat.

25. **L'équipement des transports et des services**, 46 rue des Petites Ecuries, 75010 Paris.
    Phone: 42-46-36-63. Telex: 643115. Fax. 48-24-38-32.
    Secretary: René Valladon.

26. **Union des Cadres et Ingénieurs**, 2 rue de la Michodière, 75002 Paris.
    Phone: 47-42-39-69.
    Secretary: Hubert Bouchet.
    Publications: *La Lettre de L'Uci* (monthly); *Cadres et Ingénieurs* (quarterly).

27. **Union des Retraités**, 198 Avenue du Maine, 75680 Paris, Cédex 14.
    Phone: 45-39-22-03. Telex: 203405 F. Fax: 45-45-54-52.
    Secretary: Marc Blondel.
    Membership: 150,000.

28. **Voyageurs-Représantants-Placiers** (travelling salesmen), 198 Avenue du Maine, 75680 Paris, Cédex 14.
Phone: 45-40-40-99.
Secretary: Henri Dupille.

Publications. Force Ouvrière Hebdomadaire (25,000 copies); *Force Ouvrière* (monthly magazine, 800,000 copies).
International affiliations. ICFTU; ETUC; TUAC.

Other major trade union organizations

Confédération Autonome du Travail (CAT)
Autonomous Labour Confederation

Address. 19 Boulevard de Sébastopol, Paris 75001
Leadership. Jean Fraleux (secretary general)
Membership. 60,000 (50 per cent women) in affiliated federations and individual unions in both the public and private sectors. Members are in government ministries, including the Ministry of Defence, and in local government.
History and character. Broke away from the CGT in 1953 in rejection of the communist domination of that federation. Is without formal political affiliations but favours the free economy and "keeping government out of business".
Publications. Actualité Autonome (10,000 copies); *L'Echo des Communes* (50,000); *La Gazette de la Défense Nationale* (10,000); *Bulletin Confédéral* (1,500).
International affiliation. None.

Confédération des Syndicats Libres (CSL)
Confederation of Free Trade Unions

Address. 13 rue Péclet, 75015 Paris
Phone. (1) 45-33-62-62
Telex. 201390
Leadership. Auguste Blanc (secretary general)
Membership. Claims 250,000.
History and character. Founded 1959 and rightist in orientation. Formerly known as the Confédération Française du Travail.

Fédération de l'Education Nationale (FEN)
National Education Federation

Address. 48 rue La Bruyére, 75440 Paris, Cédex 09
Phone. (1) 42-85-71-01
Telex. 648356
Leadership. Yannick Simbron (secretary general)
Membership. 361,000 in 49 unions.
History and character. Founded 1948 by secession from the CGT, the FEN held its 31st Congress in February 1988 at La Rochelle. The union promotes a dynamic, modernistic image and expects its membership to rise rapidly as a result of increased recruitment of secondary school teachers, its promotion of the well-being of pupils, acceptance of new working patterns and its close relations with parent organizations of schoolchildren.

In the 1980s FEN achieved considerable success in persuading the government to make eduction its lead budget, but it also began to suffer a decline in membership which reduced its membership by some 200,000 from its 1981 peak of 550,000. The disappearance of the Cold War in which it originated led to questions being raised about its continued purpose and internal disputes have prevented it gaining ground from extensive teacher recruitment. At its triennial congress in February 1991 the leadership had to work hard to avoid a break-up of the Federation.

Publications. Enseignement Public (monthly); *FEN-HEBDO*.

International affiliations. IFFTU.

FRENCH OVERSEAS POSSESSIONS

In the French overseas departments (French Guiana, Guadeloupe, Martinique and Réunion), overseas territorial collectivities (Mayotte, St Pierre and Miquelon), and overseas territories (French Polynesia, French Southern and Antarctic Territories, New Caledonia and Wallis and Futuna Islands), the metropolitan French confederations generally maintain local branches.

The following unions are reported as affiliated directly to the world trade union international organizations.

French Guiana

Centrale Démocratique des Travailleurs de la Guyane (CDTG)

Address. 113 rue Christophe Colomb, Cayenne 97300
Leadership. René Syidalza (secretary general)
International affiliations. WCL; CLAT.

Union des Travailleurs Guyanais (UTG)

Address. 7 Avenue Ronjon, B.P. 265, Cayenne 97326
Phone. 312642
History. The UTG is left-wing and pro-independence and its list of candidates in elections to the French Guiana Assembly in February 1983 won three of the 31 seats.
International affiliation. WFTU.

Guadeloupe

Union Interprofessionelle de la Guadeloupe (UIG)

Address. Logement TEFT no 14, Bergevin, 97181 Pointe-à-Pitre
Leadership. A. Mephon (secretary general)
International affiliations. WCL; CLAT.

Confédération Générale du Travail de la Guadeloupe (CGTG)

Address. 4 Cité Artisanalle-Bergevin, B.P. 779, 97173 Point-à-Pitre
Phone. 823461
Telex. CGTC 919061-GL
Leadership. Claude Morvan (secretary general)
International affiliation. WFTU.

Martinique

Centrale Démocratique Martiniquaise des Travailleurs (CDMT)

Address. Maison des Syndicats, Jardin Desclieux, 97200 Fort de France
Phone. 70-19-86
Leadership. Line Beausoleil, Denis Lange (secretaries)
International affiliations. WCL; CLAT. Co-operates with French CFDT.

Confédération Générale du Travail de la Martinique (CGTM)

Address. Maison des Syndicats, Jardin Desclieux, 97200 Fort de France
Phone. 70-25-89
Leadership. Philibert Dufeal (secretary general)
International affiliation. WFTU.

New Caledonia

Confédération Syndicale de Nouvelle Caledonie (CSNC)

Address. Maison des Syndicats, 1ère valée du Tir, B.P. 241, Noumea
Phone. 272028.
Leadership. Gaillard Didier (secretary general)
History. Was founded in 1951 as the Union des Syndicats Autonomes Caledoniens, and was subsequently known as Confédération Générale du Travail de Nouvelle Caledonie. Has 2,000 members, and is politically unaffiliated.
International affiliation. WFTU.

Union des Syndicats des Travailleurs Kanaks et Exploités (USTKE)

Address. B.P. 4372, Noumea
Leadership. Uregei Kotra Louis (secretary general)
International affiliation. WFTU.

Réunion

Confédération Générale du Travail de la Réunion (CGTR)

Address. 74 bis, rue Maréchal Leclerc, 97400 Saint Denis
Phone. 916652.
Leadership. Georges Marie (secretary general)
International affiliation. WFTU.

St Pierre et Miquelon

Union Intersyndicale CGT

Address. Place du Lieutenant-Colonel Pigeaud, B.P. 4243, 97500 DOM, North America
Phone. 594-141-86
Leadership. Michel Malvaux (secretary general)
International affiliation. Associated organization of the WFTU.

Gabon

Capital: Libreville   **Population: 1,105,000**

Political system. Gabon became a self-governing republic within the French Community
in 1958 and gained full independence in 1960. Albert-Bernard (Omar) Bongo succeeded to
the presidency in 1967, and in the following year a one-party system of government was
formally established with the newly created Gabonese Democratic Party (PDG) as the sole
permitted party. There is a unicameral parliament, comprising 111 elective seats (all held
by the PDG) and nine members nominated by the President. Since independence Gabon
has maintained close relationships with France. The country became a full member of
OPEC in 1975.

A national conference of April 1990 acceded to popular demands for the introduction of
a multi-party system and 13 opposition parties were made legal the following month.
Seven of these gained representation in the National Assembly following phased elections
in September, October and November though the PDG retained a majority. A new coalition government was formed in November by the PDG and five other parties, but the PDG
had three-quarters of the positions.

Economy. Gabon has one of the highest per capita incomes in Africa, with its wealth
being based largely upon its petroleum resources. However, the economy has been
adversely affected by the decline in international demand for oil and in prices, and Gabon
is, moreover, faced with a rapid depletion of its oil reserves. Timber, formerly the major
export, still remains second in importance despite generally falling world demand, and the
availability of both timber and minerals (principally manganese, iron ore and uranium)
has increased with the development of the Trans-Gabon Railway from the coast to
both the northeast and the southeast. Agriculture is largely subsistence, while exports
of most of the main cash crops are subject to wide fluctuations in world market
conditions.

As a result of rapid economic growth and infrastructural investment at a time of buoyant
petroleum revenues, Gabon accumulated considerable external debt (amounting to some
$2,000 million by 1987), and in the light of declining oil revenues concluded a number of
rescheduling arrangements in the mid-1980s. While maintaining a generally liberal
economic system, the government has followed a series of austerity programmes since the
late 1970s. A high proportion of the budget is devoted to development expenditure (as well
as to debt servicing); efforts are being made to diversify the country's economic base and
to expand the industrial sector (currently little developed) in anticipation of the eventual
exhaustion of petroleum reserves.

Of the Gabonese labour force in 1985–87, 75.5 per cent are employed in agriculture,
10.8 per cent in industry, and 13.7 per cent in services.

The 1985 fall in oil prices precipitated an economic crisis in Gabon and the late 1980s
saw more than 200 factory closures and the loss of around one third of the 150,000 jobs in
the private sector.

System of industrial relations. Under French rule a pluralistic system of trade unionism
developed on the French model, but a single-trade-union structure has existed since 1969.
Gabon ratified ILO Convention No. 87 (Freedom of Association and Protection of the
Right to Organize, 1948) in 1960 and Convention No. 98 (Right to Organize and

Collective Bargaining, 1949) in 1961. In reference to the observance of these Conventions, the ILO *Report of the Committee of Experts on the Application of Conventions and Recommendations* (1985) noted that the Gabonese labour code institutionalized a trade union monopoly for the single central organization, COSYGA, and that this was in violation of the Conventions even if, as claimed by the government of Gabon, such a monopoly had arisen at the request of the trade union organizations themselves. Under provisions of the labour code the legal establishment of occupational organizations is dependent on affiliation to COSYGA, and only one union may be recognized for a given occupation or region. The *Report* also observed that the effect of the mandatory conciliation and arbitration procedures laid down by the labour code is such as to practically prohibit any resort to strike action (although the government claimed that 20 strikes had occurred in the previous four years and that no action had been taken against the instigators). It also noted that under legislation of 1980 employers are required to deduct a mandatory trade union solidarity tax from the pay of all workers for the benefit of COSYGA. Workers in various forms of public service may not join trade union organizations. Gabon ratified Convention Nos 29 and 105 on forced labour in 1960 and 1961, but the ILO has noted that compulsory labour can be exacted as a punishment for misdemeanours by seafarers. Late in 1988, as part of government economic reform, the working week was reduced from 48 to 40 hours.

Trade unionism. The Gabonese Trade Union Confederation (COSYGA) is the sole trade union centre in Gabon, whose main concerns at the end of the decade were the deterioration of the social security system and the inadequate diet of much of the population. Despite its official status, in February 1990 the Prime Minister Leon Mebiame received complaints from independent groups of workers who claimed to have lost confidence in the official union channels.

Confédération Syndicale Gabonaise (COSYGA)
Gabonese Trade Union Confederation

Address. B.P. 14017, Libreville

Phone. 721498; 761333; 761330

Telex. 5623 GO

Leadership. Martin Allini (secretary general). The post of president was abolished at an extraordinary council in late 1985, with Allini, the former president, becoming secretary general.

Membership. 89,700.

History and character. A single union centre, the Fédération Syndicale Gabonaise (FESYGA), was created in 1969 from the amalgamation of the three main existing centrals as an organ of the ruling PDG. It changed its name to COSYGA at its 1978 congress. The organization affirms "responsible participation" in economic and social development of the country, has launched various production and consumer co-operatives, and is involved in workers' education.

Affiliated unions. There are 12 affiliated unions covering the following sectors: Agriculture and Forests; Banks, Insurance and other financial institutions; Public Works; Timber; Commerce; Energy; Hotels, Restaurants and Domestic Service; Industry and Processing; Mines and Cement; Parastatals; Oil; Transport.

Publication. Echo du Travailleur.

International affiliation. OATUU.

The Gambia

Capital: Banjul   **Population: 848,000**

Political system. The Gambia became independent as a full member of the Commonwealth in 1965 and adopted a republican Constitution in 1970. Since the early 1960s the majority in parliament has been the People's Progressive Party. The unicameral House of Representatives comprises 36 directly elected members, five chiefs elected by the Chiefs in Assembly, eight nominated (and non-voting) members and the Attorney General. An unsuccessful left-wing *coup* attempt was made in 1981, but this was suppressed with assistance from neighbouring Senegal. The ruling Progressive People's Party had 31 seats in the House of Representatives following the 1987 elections.

A "Senegambia" confederation was established effective early 1982 whereby, although both The Gambia and Senegal retained full independence and sovereignty, provision was made principally for integrated armed and security forces, customs and monetary union, and co-ordination of policies relating to external affairs and communications. However the Senegambia Confederation dissolved in September 1989 to be replaced by a new framework of formal links in January 1991.

Economy. The Gambian economy is heavily dependent upon the growing of groundnuts, around the processing of which, moreover, most industrial activity is centred. However, in recent years production has been severely affected, in particular by drought conditions, and international prices have been depressed. Other cash crops include cotton and palm oil. Development plans initiated in 1976 have sought to diversify the economy and expand its base by increasing the fishing sector and rice cultivation as well as encouraging tourism (which is largely financed and controlled by external interests).

The deteriorating economic situation has led to a rise in the rate of inflation and the adoption of austerity measures proposed by the IMF, as well as to increasing external debt, the accumulation of payment arrears and the subsequent rescheduling of portions of this debt.

System of industrial relations. The Gambia has ratified none of the Conventions of the ILO.

Trade unionism. Trade unionism is nonetheless relatively well developed by African standards, and there are three reported central organizations; the Gambia Labour Congress (GLC, affiliated to the WFTU), the Gambia Trades Union Congress (affiliated to the WCL) and the Gambia Workers' Union (affiliated to the ICFTU); the GLC is the most significant of these.

Gambia Labour Congress (GLC)

Address. 6 Albion Place, P.O. Box 508, Banjul
Phone. 27641
Cables. LABUNION GAMBIA
Leadership. B. B. Kebbeh (president); Mohamed Ceesay (general secretary)
Membership. 45,000.
History and character. The Gambia Labour Union (later the Gambia Labour Congress) was founded by Edward Francis Small in 1929 and was immediately involved in the first organized strike in Gambian history, against 50 per cent wage cuts imposed by the major employers. The 82-day strike ended when the employers conceded recognition to the union and a minimum wage. The GLU was registered under the 1932 Trade Union Act in 1935, making it the first officially recognized national trade union in Africa, and in 1945 it participated in the founding conference of the World

Federation of Trade Unions (WFTU) in London. The GLC is affiliated to the ruling People's Progressive Party.

Affiliated unions. Vehicles and Allied Workers' Union; Hotels, Restaurants, Cooks and Catering Workers' Union; The Gambia General Transport Workers' Union; Petty Contractors and Paint Workers' Union; Women's Section of the GLC; Farmers' Branch of the GLC; Youth and Young Workers' Branch of the GLC.

Publications. *The Worker* (a newspaper).

International affiliations. WFTU; OATUU.

Gambia Trades Union Congress

Address. P.O. Box 307, Banjul

Leadership. Sam Thorpe (secretary general)

International affiliations. WCL; OATUU.

Gambia Workers' Union (GWU)

Address. 16 Lancaster Street, P.O. Box 979, Banjul

Leadership. Amadou Araba Bah (secretary general)

Membership. 3,000 (June 1983).

History. Founded 1958.

International affiliations. ICFTU; OATUU; CTUC.

Note: this organization has also been reported as the Gambia Workers' Confederation (GWC).

Germany, Federal Republic of

Capital: Bonn (seat of government)   **Population: 77,000,000**

Political system. The Federal Republic of Germany was formally established in September 1949 from the former US, British and French zones of occupation, and achieved full sovereignty in 1955; Saarland was politically integrated in 1957.

From 1949 to 1966 the Christian Democratic Union (CDU) and its Bavarian counterpart, the Christian Social Union (CSU), dominated the federal government, although the (liberal) Free Democratic Party (FDP) participated until 1956 and again from 1961; other smaller parties were also within the government until 1960. Since 1966 there have been successively coalitions of the CDU, CSU and Social Democratic Party (SPD)—the "grand coalition"—from 1966 to 1969; of the SPD and FDP from 1969 to 1982; and of the CDU, CSU and FDP since 1982.

The political, economic and social systems of the united Germany closely resemble those of the former West German state. The Basic Law of the Federal Republic defines it as a democracy ruled by law, a "social state", and a federation. The franchise is based on proportional representation, with half the candidates directly elected and half elected from lists drawn up by the parties. The new Germany has a bicameral legislature. Its lower house (*Bundestag*) has 656 deputies elected for a four-year term. Half of them are directly elected and half are elected by a proportional list system. There are 256 constituencies in West Germany and 72 in the East.

To gain entry to the *Bundestag*, parties normally have to pass a threshold of 5 per cent of the total vote cast. However, in the all-German elections of 1990 this threshold was applied separately in the territory of the former GDR, a provision which allowed the former communists now known as the Party of Democratic Socialism (PDS) to enter the House. The upper house is the *Bundesrat* which consists of representatives of the *Lander* (state governments which number 16 after unification). Their votes are cast according to the wishes of *Land* executives which select them. When the opposition SPD captured a state from the CDU early in 1991 it gained as a consequence control of the *Bundesrat*. The 16 *Lander* (of which five are in the territory of the former GDR) are important economic actors.

On Oct. 3, 1990 77,000,000 people in the two Germanies were united under the terms of a 900-page State Treaty. On Dec. 2, 1990 the first all-German elections resulted in increased support for the Christian and Free Democrats and setbacks for the Social Democrats and the Greens. The parties' share of votes (with seats in brackets) following the all-German elections was as follows: CDU 36.7 per cent and CSU 7.1 per cent (319 seats); SPD 33.5 per cent (239); FDP 11 per cent (79); PDS 2.4 per cent (17); Greens (West) 3.9 per cent and Alliance '90/ Greens (East) 1.2 per cent (8). This result allowed the CDU-FDP coalition to remain in office. The right-wing Republicans gained 2.1 per cent of the vote, and so failed to gain entry to the *Bundestag*. Despite this result the first half of 1991 which saw important Opposition gains at elections and a great deterioration in the anticipated cost of unification (as well as a worsening economic outlook) brought a sharp drop in CDU popularity, bringing doubts whether Herr Kohl, the Chancellor since 1982, could continue in office.

Economy. By 1988, the Federal Republic's position as the economic giant of Europe was unquestioned. Some 40.5 per cent of the West German workforce was employed in industry, manufacturing trades and construction, 36.3 per cent in other sectors, primarily services, 18.1 per cent in commerce and transport, and 5.1 per cent in agriculture and forestry. The female participation rate of 51.4 per cent however was the lowest among large West European states indicating substantial labour reserves even though the number of foreign workers was in decline.

In 1989 (the last complete year before unification) West Germany's GNP grew DM 1,769 trillion, dwarfing the DM 353,000 million national income of the GDR; the trading surplus of the West with the East doubled during the year to DM 896m. The DM was the strongest major currency in Europe, and at 4 per cent its growth rate was the best for a decade and employment was at a record level by the end of the year.

As unification approached West German demand boomed to service an East starved of goods. Wages rose by 5.6 per cent, the fastest annual rate of increase since 1981. The trading surplus even outstripped 1989. Bankruptcies in May 1990 hit their lowest level since September 1981. Economic growth hit 4.6 per cent, its fastest rate since 1976. Investment rose by 12.1 per cent, and in construction this was the fastest rate for 20 years. During 1990 private consumption advanced by 4.4 per cent, sharply up from the 1.7 per cent of the previous year, and clearly boosted by 700,000 migrants from the East, higher wages and tax cuts. Strong domestic growth boosted imports and cut the country's trade surplus.

Monetary union and the costs of Unification. Monetary Union of East and West Germany took place on July 1, 1990. East Germans were offered parity for their Ostmarks up to a ceiling of 4,000 savings, and the overall average price was DM 1.8. This rate of exchange was considerably more generous than that desired by the Bundesbank President Karl-Otto Pohl, who was constitutionally bound to give prime consideration to checking inflation. Nevertheless early forecasts of the prospects for union made by the Federal Economics Ministry and the OECD were optimistic.

By the end of 1990 however concern was rising over the impact of unification on

Federal borrowing. There were forecasts that the federal deficit might reach 5 per cent in 1991. It became apparent that the state of East German industry was far more dilapidated than had been realized and that the costs of financing unemployment in the East would be very great. Though far behind Western levels, Eastern wages rose fast, yet the Eastern economy fell back: its GNP contracted by 15 per cent in 1990. The generous rate offered to the Ostmark in 1990 now became a handicap, over-pricing and making uncompetitive East German goods. Most Eastern consumers bought goods from the West, giving a further boost to unemployment. The ambitious programme of privatizations intended to return 8,000 state businesses to the private sector took place far slower than expected and was rocked by the assassination of its Director in the Spring of 1991. In the Spring of 1991 Herr Pohl, shortly before his resignation as Chairman of the Bundesbank pronounced monetary union "a catastrophe".

The agreed four-year programme of the government elected in December 1990 reflected the enhanced position of the FDP in its commitment to contain Federal borrowing to DM 70,000 million during 1991 as part of an overall public sector borrowing requirement of DM 140,000 million. Savings in the Budget would be achieved by savings in defence spending, higher national insurance contributions and increased phone charges. The FDP failed to achieve its aim of making East Germany a tax-free zone but secured agreement on an increased tax-free allowance of DM 1,200 monthly for married people.

System of industrial relations. West Germany ratified ILO Convention No. 87 (Freedom of Association and Protection of the Right to Organize, 1948) in 1957 and Convention No. 98 (Right to Organize and Collective Bargaining, 1949) in 1956. The basic framework for collective bargaining, which is highly developed and binds the members of the contracting parties, was created by the Collective Agreements Act of 1949 (revised in 1952). Collective bargaining occurs at all levels from the individual enterprise through the regional level (the most common) to (in the case of public employees) the whole federal republic. Arbitration and mediation procedures exist to supplement bargaining. The right to strike is constitutionally protected but the level of industrial conflict has been persistently low in the post-war period and strikes are normally called only after approval by at least 75 per cent of the union membership in a special ballot. Civil servants may not strike. In September 1983 the Federal Labour Court (the highest court for labour law cases) upheld the legality of "warning strikes", used while negotiations were still in progress, but also said that such strikes could be staged only when the parties were not bound by a statutory or contractual obligation to maintain industrial peace.

Under legislation passed in 1986 workers laid off as an indirect consequence of a strike (or lock-out) elsewhere in their industrial sector will no longer be able to claim unemployment benefits, provided a major claim by the strikers is the same "in kind and extent" as one supported by those being laid off, a condition to be determined by a neutral committee. (Workers were previously unable to claim benefit only if the strike was in both their own industrial sector and their own regional collective bargaining area.) The new restriction, amending paragraph 116 of the Employment Promotion Act, was introduced as a consequence of a 1984 dispute where the DGB-affiliated metalworkers' union, IG Metall, called out workers in key factories supplying automobile components (the union supporting the strikers from its own strike funds) and thereby brought most of the automobile industry to a standstill, with laid-off workers receiving state benefits. The changes provoked intense union opposition led by the DGB, including a series of massive demonstrations and strikes.

Berufsverbote. Those engaged in "activities against the Constitution" or involved in organizations (of the right or left) regarded as hostile to the Constitution have been subject since 1972 to *Berufsverbote* ("work bans")—barring access to jobs, or involving insecurity of tenure or even dismissal—in the public sector (including teaching and work in local government services). By 1985 proceedings had been started or bans imposed in 7,000 such cases, generally involving leftists. The WFTU made representations to the ILO in 1984 concerning the alleged non-observance by the FRG of ILO Convention No. 111 (Discrimination-Employment and Occupation-Convention, 1958, ratified by the FRG in 1961) involved in such bans, and the 231st session of the ILO governing body in 1986 decided to establish a commission of inquiry to investigate the complaint. The FRG justified such bans as arising from the obligation of faithfulness to the free basic democratic order imposed on public servants.

The ILO Commission of Inquiry reported in February 1987; it concluded that several of the cases which had been presented to it for consideration fell outside the limitations allowed by the Convention and the Federal government should re-examine its policy in relation to such work bans on public servants. The Federal government, in response to the Commission's report, saw no reason to alter its previously stated legal position (namely, that legislation and practice were in conformity with the Convention), and refused to allow the matter to be considered by the International Court of Justice. By July 1988, following the example of local government in Bremen, Hamburg, Rheinhausen and the Saar, the SPD-controlled state government of Schleswig-Holstein decided to abolish the *Berufsverbote*. Such job discrimination continues to be practised in other states governed by the CDU or CSU, such as Lower Saxony, Bavaria, Hesse, Baden-Wurttemburg and Rheinland-Pfalz.

Berufsverbote cases continued into 1989, in which year the ILO Conference denounced the German government for its continuing violation of Convention 111 and re-affirmed the findings of the 1986 Commission. The DGB has challenged the government to cease ignoring the ILO view and to challenge it openly at the International Court of Justice.

Shorter hours. A notable success of the West German trade union movement in recent years has been in negotiations leading to cuts in the length of the standard working week. In particular, the giant 2.6 million strong metal trades union IG Metall signed an agreement on Feb. 26, 1988 which provided for a reduction in the working week for a large group of metalworkers from 38.5 to 36.5 hours without any corresponding loss of earnings. The reduction was due to take effect in November 1988. The agreement also provided for wages to be increased by 2 per cent from March 1, 1988 and by a further 2 per cent from Aug. 1, 1989. The agreement covered some 140,000 workers in the northwestern collective bargaining area, mainly in the heartland of the steel industry, Rhineland-Westphalia, but set the pattern for agreements in other parts of the country.

In the public sector, following a number of strikes in February 1988, 4,500,000 workers won a cut in their working week to 39 hours in April 1989 and 38.5 hours in April 1990. In 1990 IG Metall achieved a commitment to a 35-hour week for metal-workers in 1995; the postal workers' union DPG mounted industrial action with a similar objective; and the new media union IG Medien gained an agreed two-hour cut in the working week in 1995.

The legal background. Potentially the German system of Works Councils and Supervisory Boards offers an alternative channel to trade unions, though in practice they have a strong influence on representation of employees. Under Acts of 1952 and 1972 all firms with five employees or more have elected Works Councils which have a right to be informed, consulted and to participate in company decisions. In large firms there is "co-determination" (*Mitbestimmungesetz*) under an Act of 1976, which allows labour onto the Supervisory Board of firms with more than 2,000 employees in numbers equal to those representing stockholders; firms below this size have one third labour representation on the Supervisory Board. In the coal and steel industries there is labour/management partity. While trade unionism in the decades after the War was characterized mainly by co-operation, there have been major strikes in the 1980s, notably in engineering and steel.

Even the system of industrial relations in Germany is juridically determined. The country has a complex system of labour and social courts at the local, *Land* and Federal level. Two new laws of the GDR, passed in March 1990, established a new legal basis for the development of trade unionism and industrial relations. They came under criticism from employers in the Federal Republic for extending co-determination rights and banning lock-outs, while unionists in the West expressed reservations about the statutory role of unions in the legislative process and the functions of proposed enterprise union committees. In July 1990, in advance of Unification, the GDR adopted a new Labour Code which omitted socialist principles and dealt exclusively with employment. Essentially the Code facilitated Social Union with the Federal Republic. The Unification Treaty laid the groundwork for an industrial relations system, based on that of the West, but it was recognized that there would be an interval before the mechanisms of bargaining would be in place.

Industrial relations in the five Eastern Lander. In the first weeks after monetary union there were sporadic strikes in the East in pursuit of job security and higher wages. Prices of consumer goods and food rose dramatically. While growth continued in the West, prospects in the East tended to deteriorate. Faced with low wages and impending unemployment, 250,000 railway workers struck for pay rises to 60 per cent of Western levels in East Germany in the last week of November 1990 and succeeded in obtaining a small wage rise and talks about job security. By November 1990, unemployment in the East had reached a new official high of 589,200 and there were 1,770,000 on short time. In the same month West German unemployment fell in November for the first time ever: the employed labour force for the country as a whole stood at a new peak level of 28,810,000 boosted by immigration and commuting from the East.

In 1991 a growing divergence between East and West arose. In January 750,000 Easterners were unemployed and nearly 2,000,000 were on short time. With almost the entire trade with the former Eastern bloc lost there were forecasts of half the workforce (4,000,000) becoming unemployed and there were new fears attached to the prospect of 700,000 former state employees losing their job security on July 1, the anniversary of monetary union. In March 100,000 Easterners demonstrated at the "uncaring" Bonn government, yet that same month unemployment in the West fell to 6.5 per cent.

In March 1991 Ursula Engelen-Kefer, Vice-President of the DGB condemned inadequate investment in the East at a meeting of the ILO. The DGB also demanded a DM 60,000 million aid programme. She declared that West German workers were prepared to make a financial contribution, but that the costs should be shared by the whole of society. The DGB later estimated that around DM 6,000 million could be raised for a special fund to help the East if workers voluntarily gave up 1 per cent of their 1991 wage increase. It later complained that its suggestion had been ignored and tax increases had been imposed instead.

1991 also saw a considerable increase in the number and extent of strikes in West and East. Powerful unions like IG Metall argued that lower settlements would not release more money for infrastructural spending in the East and declined to moderate their pay claims.

Trade unionism. Trade unionism developed strongly in pace with industrial development in Imperial Germany, despite various restrictions, and as of 1914 there were 2,500,000 members of social democratic unions, 340,000 members of Christian unions and 105,000 in "liberal" or "yellow" Hirsch-Duncker unions. The unions were a powerful industrial and political factor in the Weimar Republic following World War I, but were abolished and co-ordinated into the German Labour Front (Deutsche Arbeitsfront) after Hitler came to power in 1933.

German unions were reorganized after the War on the principle of one union per industry. The division of sectors of that time has lasted well, with only one adjustment being needed. At the end of 1989 there were 9,462,996 trade union members in the Federal Republic. The bulk of them were organized by the German Trade Union Federation (DGB) whose federations had 7,861,120 members. The German Salaried Employees Union (DAG, 503,528 members) and the German Civil Servants Union (DBB, 793,607 members) competed with DGB affiliates. The only rival confederation to the DGB was the Christian Trade Union Federation (Christlich Gewerkschaftsbund, CGB) whose membership is comparatively small—304,741. Both major political parties maintained support organizations for their union members, the loosely structured AfA for the SPD and the autonomous CDA for the CDU.

The West German unions were relatively little affected by the general decline of the labour movement in western Europe in the past decade. Among the suggested factors behind this success are: (i) the avoidance of fragmentation on political or religious lines; (ii) the positive public image of unionism conditioned by the unions' role in the rebuilding of the German economy since World War II; (iii) the acceptance by management of unions as a co-determining factor in the running of industry, an acceptance institutionalized in labour representation on company boards and in company decision-making; and (iv) the acceptance by unions of the need to engage in responsible industrial relations, reinforced by the legal requirement on unions to ensure that their members fulfil their contractual obligations. As a consequence of the environment in which the unions were restructured after World War II, union policies have been heavily pragmatic and cautious in character, and intended to assist the rebuilding of the economy while stabilizing the institutions of democracy. Radical and authoritarian political currents have been absent at all levels in the leadership to a marked degree. It was estimated that union density in 1988 was 38.3 per cent.

Trade unionism and industrial relations in the former German Democratic Republic. Trade unions were co-ordinated by the Free German Trade Union Confederation (Freier Deutscher Gewerkchaftsbund—FDGB), and they served to mobilize the labour force behind productivity goals, develop socialist consciousness, participate in the formulation and achievement of economic targets, and administer welfare schemes. There were no trade unions outside the structure of the FDGB. The GDR ratified ILO Conventions No. 87 (Freedom of Association and Protection of the Right to Organize, 1948) and No. 98 (Right to Organize and Collective Bargaining, 1949) in 1975. In respect of the GDR's conformity to the standards of Convention No. 87 the ILO *Report of the Committee of Experts on the Application of Conventions and Recommendations* (1985) observed that the FDGB was explicitly established in both Article 44 of the national Constitution and section 6 of the labour code as the sole central organization, and that such establishment was in violation of Article 2 of the Convention whether or not, as maintained by the government, the unification of the trade union movement was a "manifestation of the will of the workers themselves and the consequence of historical circumstances". The *Report* also noted that members of collective farms were excluded from trade union membership, and were represented by the Peasants' Mutual Assistance Association (VDGB), although workers employed by co-operatives might join the Agricultural, Food Processing and Forestry Workers' Union, a component of the FDGB. The law neither prohibited nor allowed the right to strike, but in practice disputes were settled within the context of union participation in the co-management of enterprises, and strikes were unknown.

The FDGB at its peak claimed a membership of 9,600,000. This figure included pensioners, students, etc., and was stated by the FDGB to comprise "97.7 per cent of all production workers, office employees, intellectuals and professional people", although membership was nominally not compulsory. Members of production co-operatives in agriculture and crafts were excluded from membership.

The FDGB was founded on June 15, 1945, in the Soviet zone of occupation. In the early stages, non-communists, including social democrats and Christian democrats, participated in its executive bodies, and the FDGB sought to establish itself as the central organization for all of Germany, holding conferences involving unionists from all the zones of occupation. Following the creation of the GDR in October 1949, however, the FDGB at its third congress in 1950 formally adapted the principles of scientific socialism as the "ideological foundation of its activities", and has since functioned on the pattern of other Soviet bloc trade union centres.

Under Article 44 of the national Constitution the "free trade unions, organized in the Confederation of Free German Trade Unions", were "the all-embracing class organizations of the working class". The unions were constitutionally allocated a role in the shaping and management of the economy and social policies, and (under the FDGB's own constitution) enjoined to disseminate Marxism-Leninism, the ideology of the working class. The FDGB shall consider this to be a fundamental task in its endeavour to enhance socialist consciousness and develop socialist personalities".

The trade unions participated at all levels in the preparation of the national five-year and annual economic plans, and the labour code required that the unions "shall encourage working people's sense of initiative for the overfulfilment of state plan targets in certain major fields", a requirement met through the organization of productivity ("socialist emulation") drives. The principle of co-participation also existed at the enterprise level, where trade union branch committees participated with management in formulating work production plans and union agreements setting out targets for output, costs, wages, labour needs, the provision of welfare services and other matters. Such plans were submitted directly to the workforce for further consideration and amendment. The unions also ran the GDR's social insurance funds, and had an extensive role in providing workers with subsidized holidays, housing, and in ensuring the observance of health and safety standards. There were 1,614 trade union libraries, 365 trade union-sponsored "houses of culture", and thousands of union-organized musical, dramatic and other cultural groups. In addition to monthly dues, most unionists contributed to "solidarity funds"; in 1985 the FDGB allocated DM 174,700,000 in solidarity funds (including DM 107,000,000 handed over to the solidarity funds of the DRG) for such purposes as the provision of care for elderly trade unionists and assisting foreign trade unionists. Between 1959 and 1985, 3,451 trade unionists from 89 countries graduated from the FDGB's Fritz Heckert Trade Union College in Bernau.

The FDGB congress was convened every five years and was the supreme body; between congresses activities were guided by the elected FDGB national executive. Beneath this there were two chains of organization: by locality (county delegate conferences, county executive; district delegate conferences, district executives) and by industry (central delegate conferences of industrial and other unions, central executives; county delegate conferences of industrial and other unions, county executives; district delegate conferences of industrial and other unions, district executives). Trade union branches existed in enterprises, institutions, schools and other facilities where there were at least 10 FDGB members, and trade unionists in small enterprises without branches were enrolled in local branches. Organization was on the industrial union principle so that within enterprises all workers, regardless of occupation, belonged to the same industrial union. There were also 336,000 trade union groups, led by elected shop stewards, which are formed out of "work teams", so that all workers under one supervisor or otherwise forming a natural working unit constituted a trade union group. In addition to shop stewards there were elected cultural representatives, sports organizers, and social insurance and industrial safety representatives. There were 2,500,000 elected representatives at all levels.

In the East the approach of unification stimulated reorganization. The Trade Union Confederation (FDGB) debated a vote of no-confidence in Harry Tisch, its leader since 1975. In November 1989, Herr Tisch told the FDGB Politburo that the movement had lost the trust of the workers and that it would hand over luxury guest houses to the membership.

(Tisch was subsequently imprisoned for one year for financing holidays for himself and his colleague Gunter Mittag from union funds, though acquitted of embezzlement).

In October 1989 an independent union "Reform" was proclaimed by workers at the Wilhelm Pieck electronics factory in Teltow, East Berlin, its members resigning wholesale from the FDGB. Their spokesmen claimed that the Communist Party did not enjoy the confidence of the workers and that factories needed to be independent. It called for restructuring of the state economy. Another movement, the Initiative for Labour Union Reform was active by January 1990, when it claimed 70,000 adherents.

Despite this, at the start of 1990 the FDGB unions still claimed 8,600,000 members, higher than the total membership of the DGB in the much larger Federal Republic, but this figure already registered a 10 per cent decline over the previous year. The FDGB met in Extraordinary Congress in February 1990 and abolished its centralized structure, replacing it with a confederation to which industrial unions or federations might affiliate voluntarily; effectively union members would join a union rather than the FDGB. By this step the 16 industrial unions were freed to formulate their own statutes but they moved slowly in the following months to shift the basis of their organizations, though during this time they faced increasing competition both from independent unions and from the existence of the powerful DGB.

Finally the Presidents of the FDGB's affiliates concluded that the Federation itself was not viable. It met in Extraordinary Congress on Sept. 14, 1990 and dissolved at the end of the month, dismissing all its employees. A year later it was announced that the FDGB paper *Tribune* (the circulation of which had fallen from 280,000 to 100,000) was to shut down during 1991. For the most part the constituent unions were themselves dissolved during the remainder of 1991. In April 1991 it was estimated that some 3,000,000 former affiliated FDGB members had joined a DGB affiliated union.

The DGB faces a major challenge in establishing an efficient structure in the five new *Lander* of the former East German state. While some affiliates moved swiftly to capitalize on the membership opportunities presented there—IG Metall which already claimed to be the largest union in the Western World quickly confirmed an unchallenged position in this respect—they also collided with different expectations of unions among prospective recruits. There were early indications that prospective union members regarded this creation of job opportunities as a union responsibility whereas the newly arrived DGB affiliates regarded their priorities as the negotiation of better wages and conditions.

Christlicher Gewerkschaftsbund (CGB)
Christian Workers' Union

Address. 5300 Bonn 2, Konstantinstrasse 13
Phone. (228) 357061
Membership. This organization has little practical strength, and the German churches have generally not actively supported religious-based unionism since World War II. Its membership numbered 304,741 in 1989.

Deutsche Angestellengewerkschaft (DAG)
German Salaried Employees' Union

Address. 2 Hamburg 36, Karl-Muck-Platz 1
Phone. (040) 349150
Telex. 021 1642 aghv
Fax. (040) 34915400
Leadership. Roland Issen (chairman)
Membership. 574,000 clerical, technical and administrative workers.
History. The DAG, which began organizing in 1945, was formed on a national basis in April

1949, after the formative DGB decided that white-collar staff should be organized in industrial unions, on the one plant, one union, basis, rather than given separate representation.

Publications. Die DAG Journal.

International affiliation. FIET.

Deutscher Beamtenbund (DBB)
German Civil Servants' Federation

Address. 5300 Bonn 2, Dreizehnmorgenweg 36, Postfach 205005

Phone. (228) 8110

Telex. 2283701 DBB

Fax. 811171

Leadership. Werner Hagedorn (national chairman)

Membership. 900,000 (1990).

History and character. The DBB, which traces its origins back to 1918, represents both white-collar and wage-earning public employees, as well as civil-servant-status employees, and by law must be involved in the formulation of legislation and regulations relating to civil service matters. Members include teachers, policemen, employees and civil servants of the armed forces, and railway and post office officials. There are 49 member associations (12 state federations, 14 federal civil servants' associations, and 23 sectoral associations).

Deutscher Gewerkschaftsbund (DGB)
German Trade Union Federation

Address. 4000 Dusseldorf 30, Hans Bocklerstrasse 39, Postfach 2601

Phone. (0211) 43010

Telex. 8584822 A DGB D

Fax. (0211) 4301 324

Leadership. Heinz Werner Mayer (president); Ursula Engelen-Kefer (vice-president). Both elected at the May 1990 Congress.

History and character. The General German Federation of Trade Unions (Allgemeiner Deutscher Gewerkschaftsbund—ADGB) was founded in 1868 by delegates representing 142,000 workers. Bismarck's Anti-Socialist Law of 1878 sharply curtailed union activity, but when this law expired in 1890 a new and overwhelmingly social democratic confederation, the General Kommission der Gewerkschaften (General Commission of Trade Unions), was formed. After World War I this was in turn succeeded by a reborn ADGB, set up in 1919 and the largest confederation in the Weimar period. The ADGB, in common with other trade union organizations, was abolished after the accession to power of Hitler in 1933, when the unions were co-ordinated into the Labour Front (Deutsche Arbeitsfront—DAF).

Following the surrender and allied occupation of Germany in 1945, trade unions were at first permitted only on a *Land* (state) or zonal basis, and in April 1947 the Deutscher Gewerkschaftsbund (DGB) was set up in the British zone (which included the Ruhr). After initial resistance from the French military government, however, the three western occupying powers (i.e. the USA, Britain and France) agreed to the establishment of a tri-zonal federation and at a conference held in Munich in October 1949 a trizonal DGB was formed by 101 unions with a total of more than 4,800,000 members. Workers in the Soviet zone (which became the GDR in October 1949) were by this time organized entirely separately in the Free German Trade Union Confederation (FDGB), and the constitution of the DGB provided that only unions operating within the territory of the West German Federal Republic (i.e. excluding the former Soviet zone and Berlin) would be admitted to membership. The DGB also operated in West Berlin. Sixteen industrial federations (at one point 17, following the admission of a police union) were created on the industrial union principle (i.e. whereby all the workers in one plant would be represented by the same union); these federations are autonomous and bargain separately (the DGB as an umbrella organization neither negotiates nor concludes collective bargaining agreements), but must accept the DGB constitution. The form of organization adopted in the 1940s reflected a compromise between those advocating a highly centralized structure, with co-ordinated industrial sector unions, and those who advocated a central

178

organization on the model of the British TUC, where the individual unions were freely associated bodies with total autonomy. In practice the larger unions, such as IG Metall, enjoy a degree of autonomy, arising from their industrial strength, virtually comparable with that of the major British unions.

Among the principles adopted at the founding convention were: (i) the participation of organized labour in economic planning; (ii) the nationalization of key industries such as mining, iron and steel, large chemical, and power industries and major credit banks; (iii) freedom for unions to engage in collective bargaining with employers. The evolution of public policy in the newly formed FRG after 1949 led for some years to strained relations between the (Christian Democratic) coalition government and the DGB, and the ultimate enactment of legislation providing a framework for modified forms of co-determination, while the issue of nationalization waned in significance. In general the DGB has been associated with the main outlines of policy of the Social Democratic Party (SPD), although it is politically unaffiliated.

Neue Heimat scandal. The DGB and its affiliated unions through a holding company, Beteiligungsgesellschaft für Gemeinwirtschaft (BGAG), have controlling of dominant interests in a range of companies in the banking, insurance, consumer co-operation, construction and other fields, and constitute a significant force in the German economy. The DGB has been adversely affected since 1982 by scandal surrounding the affairs of its housing concern Neue Heimat (New Home). Founded in 1954, Neue Heimat, which reinvested all but 4 per cent of its profits in building in return for tax concessions, had built 260,000 housing units and was regarded as a model of the concept of *Gemeinsirtschaft* (social economy), which sought to achieve socialist aims within a capitalist framework. In March 1982 Alois Pfeiifer withdrew as president-elect of the DGB (Ernst Breit being instead elected president in May of that year) after reports that he and the retiring DGB president, Heinz Oskar Vetter, and the then IG Metall president, Eugen Loderer, had abused their positions to invest privately in tax-preferred building projects undertaken by Neue Heimat. Further scandals developed surrounding allegations that members of the Neue Heimat board had engaged in property speculation and other mismanagement. Debt liabilities accumulated to the level of DM 17,000 million, and in September 1986 the BGAG announced that it would transfer the majority of the Neue Heimat homes and most of the debt to an entrepreneur, Horst Schiesser, for one Deutschmark and the remainder to two (socialist-controllled) state (*Land*) governments. This plan fell through in November 1986, however, when the creditor banks refused to accept the rescue plan proposed by Schiesser, and had been variously viewed in Germany as a "betrayal" of socialist principles by the DGB or as an indictment of the competence of socialist economic management.

The 7,861,190 membership of the DGB at the end of 1989 represented an increase of 64,043 over a year earlier. They were organized into 16 unions which varied in size from the Metalworkers (2,679,237 members) to the Entertainment Workers (43,817). Eleven of the 16 affiliates recorded membership gains. Five returned losses (construction, clothing and textiles, leather, mining, and railways), mostly due to a declining total workforce in their sectors. Their members were again reduced to 16 following the formation of IG Medien *(see below)*.

The DGB has an Executive Board (of which the president is a member) elected by a Delegates Convention every four years (most recently in May 1990). Its numbers were reduced to eight at the 1990 Congress. A Federal Executive Committee is formed by the Executive Board and the Presidents of the 17 member unions. However the highest decision-making body between Conventions is the Federal Council, which is composed of the Executive Committee, the presidents of the regions of the DGB and representatives of the DGB's affiliates. In May 1990 Ernst Breit was succeeded by Heinz Werner Meyer, and the DGB gained its first woman vice-president Ursula Engelen-Kefer. The traditional presence of two CDU members on the executive was confirmed but the DGB generally has policy positions close to those of the SPD.

Apart from its income from affiliation fees, the DGB has controlling interests in a significant range of companies. It also uses the extensive union membership of supervisory boards to fund the Hans-Bockler-Stiftung Foundation: the general requirement is for 12 per cent of fees up to DM 3,000 to go to the Foundation and everything above DM 6,000. The payments are policed by individual unions, such as IG Metall, which publishes an annual blacklist of defaulters.

Affiliated unions. There are 16 industrial organized affiliates of the DGB. These are given below, where possible, with their post-Unification (1990) membership. The grand total does not therefore correspond with the gross (end 1989) affiliated figure for the DGB itself, given above.

Deutsche Postgewerkeschaft (DPG) (postal workers) 6000 Frankfurt a. M. 71, Rhonestrasse 2.
Phone. (069) 66950. Telex: 412112. Fax: (069) 6695 6941
Leadership: Kurt van Haaren (president).
Membership: Like other unions the DPG had to make internal changes to accommodate unification. In August 1990 it was the fourth largest affiliate with a membership of 476,763, at which point it estimated that there were around 130,000 East German employees eligible to join. In February 1991 it claimed 570,000 members. The DPG extended its structure to cover the five new *Lander* and lengthened the period between Congresses from three years to four.

Gewerkschaft der Eisenbahner Deutschlands (railwayworkers), 6000 Frankfurt a. M. 17, Beethovenstrasse 12–16.
Phone: (069) 75360. Telex: 411715. Fax: (069) 747892 and (069) 7536222.
Leadership: Rudi Schafer.
Membership: 520,000.

Gewerkschaft Erziehung und Wissenschaft (GEW) (education and sciences), Postfach 90 04 09, Reifenburger Strasse 21, 6000 Frankfurt am Main 90.
Phone: (069) 789 730. Telex: 4 12989. Fax: (069) 78973-201.
Leadership: Dieter Wunder (president).
Membership: 330,000.
History and Character: The GEW was founded by the teachers' associations of the immediate post-War period and was thus one of the founding organizations of the DGB.
Publication: *Erziehung und Wissenschaft* (monthly review).
Affiliated unions and structure: The GEW has 16 branches.

Gewerkschaft Gartenbau, Land-und Forstwirtschaft (horticulture, agriculture and forestry), 3500 Kassel 1, Druseltalstrasse 51, Postfach 410180.
Phone: (561) 34060. Telex: 099749.
Leadership: Guenther Lappas (president); Heinz Hauk (vice-president).
Membership: 125,000.

Gewerkschaft Handel, Banken und Versicherungen (commerce, banks and insurance), 4 Düsseldorf 30, Tersteegenstrasse 30.
Membership: 360,372.

Gewerkschaft Holz und Kunststoff (wood and plastic) 4000, Düsseldorf, Sonnenstrasse 14.
Phone: (211) 786461.
Membership: 149,724.

Gewerkschaft Leder (leatherworkers), 7000 Stuttgart 1, Willi-Bleicher-Strasse 20.
Phone: (0711) 295555. Fax: (0711) 293345
Leadership: Werner Dick (president).
Membership: 46,000.
Publications: *Leder-Echo*.

Gewerkschaft Nahrung-Genuss-Gaststätten (food processing and catering workers), 2000 Hamburg 50, Haubachstrasse 76.
Phone: 040 38013-0. Telex: 2161884 ngg d. Fax: 040 3892637.
Leadership: Heinz-Günter Niebrügge (president); Jutta Kaminsky (vice-president).
Membership: 400,000.

Gewerkschaft Öffentlich Dienste, Transport und Verkehr (public services and transport workers), 7000 Stuttgart 1, Theodor-Heuss-Strasse 2.
Membership: 1,173,525.

Gewerkschaft der Polizei (police), 4010 Hilden, Forststrasse 3A.
Phone: (211) 71040. Telex: 0858/1968.
Membership: 167,572.

Gewerkschaft Textil-Bekleidung (textiles and clothing), 4 Düsseldorf 30, Ross Strasse 94.
Phone: (0211) 4309-0. Fax: (0211) 3403505.

Leadership: Willi Arens (president).
Membership: 249,880.
Publications: *Textil-Bekleidung Informationen*.

Industriegewerkschaft Bau-Steine-Erden (building and construction workers), 6000 Frankfurt a.
M., Bockenheimer Landstrasse 73–77.
Phone: (069) 7437-0. Telex: 04-12-826. Fax: (069) 7437278.
Leadership: Konrad Carl was due to be replaced as President at the October 1991 Congress.
Membership: 775,000 (including 314,000 members in East Germany).
Publications: *Der Grundstein; Zeitschrift der Industrie-Ggewerkschaft Bau-Steine-Erden* (monthly).

Industriegewerkschaft Bergbau und Energie (mining and energy), 463 Bochum, Alte
Hattingerstrasse 19.
Phone: (234) 3190. Telex: 82-58-09.
Leadership: Hienz-Werner Meyer (president).
Membership: 350,000.

Industriegewerkschaft Chemie- Papier- Keramik (chemical, paper and ceramics), 3 Hanover,
Konigsworther Platz 6.
Phone: (0511) 76310. Telex: 9-22 608 IGCHE D. Fax: (0511) 708473.
Leadership: Hermann Rappe (president).
Membership: 674,105.
Publications: *GP Magazin* (monthly).

Industriegewerkschaft Medien, Druck und Papier, Publizistik und Kunst (IG MEDIEN)
(media, printing, paper and publicity), Freidrichstrasse 15, 7000 Stuttgart 1.
Phone: (0711) 20180. Fax: (0711) 2018-262.
Leadership: Erwin Ferleman.
Membership: 220,000, of which 75 per cent are in the printing and paper processing industries while
nearly 20 per cent are journalists on papers, TV and radio. There are also several thousand writers,
musicians and artists.
History and character: This new union emerged from the unification of the German printers' journalists and artists' unions at a Hamburg congress in April 1989. It was founded in response to what its
constituent unions called an "increasing concentration of power in the media sector". It achieved an
early success when its printer members won a battle to avoid the introduction of regular weekend
work.
Publications: *Kontrapunkt*: *Publizistik und Kunst*.

Industriegewerkschaft Metall (metalworkers), 6 Frankfurt a. M., Wilhelm-Leuschner-Strasse
79–85.
Phone: (069) 26471. Telex: 04-11-115.
Leadership: Franz Steinkuhler (president).
Membership: Approximately 3,600,000. IG Metall is the largest single union in the Western world.
History and character: IG Metall unites workers in metal manufacturing, metal processing and
engineering. In the 1980s it led a determined fight to achieve a shorter working week, at one point (in
1984) mounting a sustained national strike which shattered the German reputation for industrial
relations peace. Though its success at that time was a qualified one, the Union finally won its point in
1990 when the employers finally conceded the introduction of a 35-hour week by 1995.

Herr Steinkuhler was re-elected as leader at the October 1989 Congress where he moderated his
criticisms of the environmentalist policies of the SPD. Even jobs, he advised, could not take prece-
dence over the environment. Congress defied him by strengthening the Left faction on the Union
Executive and there were criticisms of its failure to give proper support to striking steelworkers in
the Ruhr.

IG Metall moved fast as German Unification approached. It invested in equipment for offices and
in low cost housing and in a membership drive covering part of 1990 and 1991 spent some DM
30,000,000 to build a base in the East. Some 150 IG Metall officials were sent to the East to organize
a ballot for employees there on joining the union. This was largely successful and IG Metall's
membership rose by around 1,000,000. Membership does not yet imply parity of treatment however:

the 35-hour agreement will not apply in the East until 1998. In the spring of 1991 IG Metall called protests in the East in support of demands for workers to receive 65 per cent of West German pay with parity to come by the end of 1993.

In June 1991 IG Metall marked its centenary with celebrations in Frankfurt which were attended by Helmut Kohl and Jacques Delors, President of the European Commission. Herr Kohl urged the unions to play the same role in uniting Germany as they had in building the Federal Republic, calling on them to make their contribution to making the East a success. In his response, Herr Steinkuhler (who had defied some of his members by inviting Herr Kohl) asserted the positive use of union power in a democracy: "we are neither the social partners of capital nor the junior partners of government", he declared.

Publications. The numerous periodicals and newspapers published by the DGB and its affiliates have a combined monthly circulation of 13,000,000.

International affiliations. ICFTU; ETUC; TUAC. Most DGB unions are affiliated to the appropriate ICFTU international trade secretariat.

Ghana

Capital: Accra   **Population: 14,900,000**

Political system. Ghana became an independent member of the Commonwealth in 1957 and a republic in 1960 under the leadership of Kwame Nkrumah. During the 15 years following the overthrow of Nkrumah in 1966 a series of mainly military administrations were formed, while at the end of 1981 Flt.-Lt. Jerry Rawlings (who had already been head of state in 1979) again took power as Chairman of a Provisional National Defence Council (PNDC), and parliament was dissolved. People's defence committees, established as the basic unit of the state structure, together with workers' defence committees, were reorganized in 1984 into committees for the defence of the revolution. A number of attempts were made to overthrow the Rawlings regime, but all were unsuccessful.

Economy. The Ghanaian economy is based principally on agriculture, which represents around 40 per cent of gross domestic product. Cocoa has traditionally accounted for some 60 per cent of export revenue, but there has been a sharp reduction in recent years principally because of exhaustion of plantations, a continuing and rapid decline in international prices and difficult infrastructure and administrative problems, and also recurrent adverse weather conditions. In an effort to rectify this situation the government introduced a major programme to encourage the development and revitalization of the industry.

The Rawlings government in 1982 introduced austerity measures combined with price controls, and also made efforts to stem large-scale cross-border smuggling (especially of cocoa). A major four-year economic recovery programme (ERP) was launched at the end of that year, to include the establishment of a state monopoly of all foreign trade, the encouragement of joint ventures in manufacturing and extractive industries, and a doubling (to 80 per cent) of the state's shareholding in foreign-controlled retail, banking and insurance enterprises, while the second ERP (1986–88) aimed in particular to stimulate export growth. During the period of these programmes, the currency was drastically devalued, and debt rescheduling arrangements were concluded. In 1987–88 the government announced that it was to dispose of holdings in many of the state-owned or state-controlled enterprises, including a large number of coffee and cocoa plantations. The implementation of this programme led to some 12,000 being displaced from civil service employment annually, though a programme to mitigate some of the social impact of restructuring was introduced.

System of industrial relations. The key statute governing employment relations in Ghana is the *Industrial Relations Act* 1958. Legislation is prepared by the National Advisory Council on Labour which was entrusted with consolidation of amendments to the 1958 Act. The Tripartite Council (composed of 10 representatives each from the TUC, the employees, and the government) negotiates wages and working conditions and recommends the minimum wage. There is also a Government–TUC Standing Committee to discuss the impact of public policy on labour.

Ghana ratified ILO Convention No. 87 (Freedom of Association and Protection of the Right to Organize, 1948) in 1965, Convention No. 98 (Right to Organize and Collective Bargaining, 1949) in 1959. Unions are free to engage in collective bargaining in the public and private sectors but national strikes are rare. Most open disputes are at company level and very occasionally they may lead to government intervention. Two strike leaders were briefly imprisoned, without being charged, in 1989.

Trade unionism. Ghanaian trade unionism has a long history stretching back before World War II, by which time there were a number of well-established unions. Provision for the registration of trade unions was made under British rule in 1941, and the organized labour movement subsequently became linked to the political movement for independence. The Trade Union Congress has been the sole central organization since its creation in 1945 but has been reorganized on a number of occasions in response to political developments. There are four national unions which are not affiliated to it. Trade union affairs are monitored for the government by the Ministry of Mobilization and Social Welfare whose secretary in 1989 was a seconded TUC official.

Trades Union Congress of Ghana (TUC)

Address. Hall of Trade Unions, P.O. Box 701, Accra
Phone. 227721
Telex. 2644 PTWV. GH
Fax. 772621
Leadership. D.K.Y. Vormawor (chairman); A.K. Yankey (secretary-general)
Membership. 707,610 in 17 unions.
History and character. The TUC of Ghana was founded in 1945 as the Gold Coast Trades and Union Congress. It became closely linked to Nkrumah's Convention People's Party and was reorganized following the fall of Nkrumah in 1966; it was dissolved in 1971 and reorganized again in 1972. Following the military coup of Dec. 31, 1981, which restored Flt.-Lt. Rawlings to power, the TUC secretary general Alhaji A. M. Issifu was forced to resign and a radical faction within the TUC supporting the new regime announced that all the senior officials of the TUC member unions had been dismissed. The union movement remained in turmoil in 1982–84, as workers' defence committees vied with the radicalized unions for the representation of Ghana's workers. However, following the reorganization of the defence committees in 1984, the labour movement was restored to its former structure. The TUC committed itself to the PNDC government's basic goals, but criticized aspects of government policy, including changes to the minimum wage, retrenchment, and other moves made without consultation through the tripartite committee of government, employers and unions. The TUC also charged the government with attempting to drive a wedge between the workers and the peasants, and its affiliated Agricultural Workers' Union modified its constitution to enable it to organize among the self-employed peasant farmers, a move which the government accepted.

The TUC's principal concern has been to maintain living standards threatened by the ERP and it achieved some success when the government introduced the Programme to Mitigate the Social Costs of Adjustment (PAMSACD), a re-training initiative for the redeployed. The TUC argues that real wages have been eroded by inflation and succeeded in 1989 and 1990 in persuading its Tripartite Commission Partners to increase the national minimum wage. A legislative instrument to make payment of this minimum mandatory awaits enactment. At the March 1989 Quadrennial Congress the Chairman and General Secretary were re-elected.

Affiliated unions. Construction and Building Workers' Union, General Agricultural Workers' Union, General Transport, Chemical and Petroleum Workers' Union, Health Service Workers' Union, Industrial and Commercial Workers' Union, Local Government Workers' Union, Maritime and Dockworkers' Union, Mineworkers' Union, National Union of Seamen, Post and Telecommunications Workers' Union, Private Road and Transport Workers' Union, Public Services Workers' Union, Public Utility Workers' Union, Railway Enginemen's Union, Railway and Port Workers' Union, Teachers' and Educational Institutions Workers' Union, Timber and Wood Workers' Union. There is an associated Ghana labour college, founded in 1967.

Publication. TUC News. (monthly)

International affiliation. OATUU. Has good relations with the ICFTU, OUSA, WCL and WFTU. All 17 national unions are believed to affiliate to various international trade secretariats.

Other trade union bodies

Ghana National Association of Teachers (GNAT)
Civil Servant Association
Ghana Registered Nurses' Association
Ghana Merchant Navy Officers' Association

Greece

Capital: Athens   **Population: 10,010,000**

Political system. Following a military *coup* in 1967, Greece formally became a republic in 1973, but the next year the military/civilian administration effectively disintegrated. A new republican Constitution was adopted in 1975, with a unicameral parliament which in turn elects the President. The (conservative) New Democracy government elected in 1974 and re-elected in 1977 was succeeded in 1981 by an administration of the Pan-Hellenic Socialist Movement (Pasok), which was re-elected in 1985.

There were two elections in 1989 and one in 1990 and PASOK was eventually replaced in power by a New Democracy government under Constantine Mitsotakis.

The New Democracy government had negotiated Greek membership of the European Communities (effective January 1981), and although Pasok had in the 1981 electoral campaign undertaken to renegotiate the terms of accession it did not include any comparable undertakings in its 1985 manifesto.

Despite membership of NATO, Greece did not participate in the military structure of the alliance between 1974 and 1980 in protest at the Turkish invasion of northern Cyprus in 1974, and it again withdrew from exercises in 1983.

Economy. Of a civilian labour force numbering 3,900,000 in 1988, industry employed just over 28 per cent and the primary sector 28.5 per cent. Services accounted for 43.7 per cent. Though declining in relative importance within the domestic economy, agriculture still accounts for most of the primary sector; together with the very large retail sector it explains the great numbers of self-employed in Greece. In the 1980s the workforce grew steadily, in sharp contrast to the 1970s when it fell; partly as a result, Greece has a persistently high unemployment rate which has stayed above 7 per cent since 1983 and rose each year at the end of the decade.

On taking power Pasok pursued an expansionist policy, relaxing fiscal and income controls. By 1985 these had precipitated a balance of payments crisis, causing the government to introduce a two-year stabilization programme which included income restrictions. In 1986 and 1987 there was a fall in real incomes, but incomes policy was progressively relaxed in the following years, both under Pasok and its successor governments. From 1987 Pasok bagan to liberalize the economy and the New Democracy governments pursued a similar policy, but the public sector remained large.

The Law of July 31, 1990 was the centrepiece of the new government's approach to economic recovery, providing for investment incentives and modernization of public administration. It proposed privatizing viable public sector companies and closing others down, provoking huge trade union opposition. Other provisions included a choice of provision for those losing their jobs as a result of restructuring, and the first ever regulations on part-time work, as well as measures to relax restrictions on shift work and the arrangement of working time.

System of industrial relations. Greece ratified ILO Conventions No. 87 (Freedom of Association and Protection of the Right to Organize, 1948) and No. 98 (Right to Organize and Collective Bargaining, 1949) in 1962. Trade union rights were severely curtailed under the rule of the junta from 1967 to 1974, and although trade union freedoms were restored thereafter and given formal expression in Article 12 of the 1975 Constitution, the New Democracy government in 1976 enacted restrictive legislation and maintained the practice of state intervention in union affairs. The Pasok government introduced various reforms in 1982 (including guarantees against dismissal for trade union activities and a prohibition against lock-outs) but trade unions are still largely financed by compulsory dues paid by workers and employers, which are channelled through the Ministry of Labour, and the Pasok government itself actively intervened in the affairs of the unions in favour of its own supporters.

The traditional Greek model is one where turbulence accompanies heavy state intervention, primarily through the Ministry of Labour which had extensive compulsory arbitration powers which it was rarely reluctant to use. However, the February 1990 law on free collective bargaining (No. 1876/1990) marked the withdrawal of the state from regulation of incomes, repealing a statute of 1955 and thus ending the long-standing system of compulsory arbitration.

Though Greece ratified ILO Convention 98 in 1962, this Law was the first explicit acknowledgement of the principle of voluntary negotiation. It still provided for arbitration on request, but for the first time brought mediation to the centre of the stage through the good offices of a Mediation and Arbitration Board. This Board is partly funded by the Workers' Centre (which exists under law and is financed by the contributions of employers and employees). Its 11-member board contains three union representatives, three from the employers' associations, three academics, a Ministry of Labour representative and one person of authority in labour relations to be elected by the other 10.

The Act had a further significance by its introduction of two new types of agreement to supplement the already existing national collective agreements and occupational agreements. These were sectoral agreements (which, like occupational agreements may be concluded at the national, regional or city level), and enterprise agreements. Under the terms of the Act national agreements apply automatically to all employees without further Ministry of Labour intervention while more limited agreements have legal standing provided they improve on the minimum laid down in the national agreements.

Works Council Law. Legislation on works councils in companies with at least 50 employees (20 if there is no trade union) was passed by the Greek Parliament on April 6, 1988. The law ratifies ILO Convention No. 135 of 1971, entitled "Convention concerning protection and facilities to be afforded to workers' representatives in the undertaking". Under the law, the size of the works councils varies according to the size of the company—three members in companies with up to 300 employees, five in companies with between 301 and 1,000 and seven in those with over 1,000 employees. Subsidiary companies are considered as separate entities provide they have 50 employees. If they have less than 50 people, they are represented by the nearest plant with the requisite workforce. The first category will be the most common under the law, as Greek industry is weighted heavily towards a proliferation of small companies.

The 1980s did not lack for industrial relations legislation, including law on the democratization of the trade union movement (1982), on workers' participation in company decisions (1983), on the socialization of public enterprises (1983) and on works' councils (above). However Greek governments have not yet successfully tackled the problem of implementation and since some of this earlier legislation is not fully in force, doubts persisted as to the extent of the impact of the 1990 law. These were amplified in December 1990 when more than 1,000,000 Greek workers struck for 48 hours against a bill of the governing New Democracy party to permit the dismissal of employees involved in illegal strikes.

The National Collective Agreements of 1988 and 1989 were concluded without compulsory arbitration, an achievement assisted by the relaxation of incomes' policy from the end of 1987 (though government continued to regulate civil service wages). The GSEE however mounted general strikes while the negotiations were in progress. Real incomes rose by 3.3 per cent in 1988 helped by indexation of wages and a special allowance for working married women. In 1989 there was a further movement of wages in line with prices, though a number of public sector unions mounted strikes and achieved increases higher than the norm. A large number of strikes occurred however in early 1990 in the public and private sectors most of which achieved increases above the indexation level, and (in the case of civil servants) brought an improvement in status.

Trade unionism. The first unions were formed at the end of the nineteenth century and the GSEE (General Confederation of Greek Labour) was founded in 1918.

Split in Greek labour movement. The introduction of a package of austerity measures by the Pasok government in October 1985, including a programme of wage restraint (prohibiting for two years any wage increases beyond new highly restricted limits set under the system of automatic wage indexation—ATA—introduced by Pasok in 1981, i.e. effectively suspending collective bargaining), precipitated a split in the GSEE, which has enjoyed good relations with the Pasok administration from 1981 to mid-1985. Georgios Raftopoulos, the GSEE president, endorsed the austerity package; seven of the 26 Pasok members of the 45-member GSEE governing council (administrative board), however, representing public sector unions, announced their opposition to the package and were expelled from Pasok (preluding the expulsion of numerous other trade unionists from the party in the following months). On Oct. 29, 1985, the 26 opponents of the government measures on the governing council (i.e. the seven Pasok rebels, the 17 members of the pro-Soviet Communist Party of Greece-Exterior—KKE-Exterior—and the two members of the Eurocommunist Communist Party of Greece-Interior—KKE-Interior) announced the dismissal of Raftopoulos and called a 24-hour general strike for Nov. 14. A meeting of the larger GSEE general council on Oct. 31–Nov. 1, however, backed Raftopoulos, and an Athens court on Dec. 5 ordered the appointment of a new governing council with a pro-Raftopoulos majority. There were numerous anti-government strikes, of varying degrees of impact, during the late autumn and winter of 1985/86, and dissident unionists on Feb. 9,

1986, set up the Socialist Trade Union Movement of Workers and Employees (SSEK), which supports "the 26" (i.e. the 26 excluded members of the governing council, as opposed to the pro-government group of 19). The SEA (Struggle Co-ordinating Committee) was formed at the time of the congress staged by the pro-government group in April 1986 to unite the different factions opposed to the pro-government controlling group. The GSEE held its 23rd congress on April 5–7, 1986, and elected a new governing council controlled by the pro-government trade union faction PASKE. According to the dissidents (who boycotted the congress and recognized only the executive bodies elected by the 22nd congress in December 1983), this 23rd congress included illegal delegates, fake "rubber stamp" organizations, and individuals and groups subsidized by the Ministry of Labour. Only 287 of 609 registered delegates attended. Those boycotting the 23rd congress included members of the leftist United Trade Union Anti-Dictatorship Movement (ESAK-A), supporters of the newly formed SSEK, and the right-wing DAKE faction. The direct government and judicial intervention in the GSEE has also been criticized by the European Trade Union Confederation (ETUC). Talks between the pro- and anti-government labour groupings aimed at agreeing on a procedure for the election of a new governing council for a united GSEE ended in failure in early January 1987. However, an Athens court of appeal overturned the previous judicial intervention in the GSEE and on Jan. 10, 1987, the dissenting trade union factions formed a committee to co-ordinate policy.

The pro-government trade union faction which controlled the GSEE executive announced on Aug. 5, 1988 that it was planning to organize a "transitional" Congress on Oct. 21–23, 1988. This was the fourth time within a period of approximately one year that such a Congress had been announced. The dissenting trade union factions were bitterly opposed to this manoeuvre and they claimed that it was being organized against the wishes of the overwhelming majority of its member organizations. The ESAK-A decided to boycott the Congress, claiming that it was fraudulent. The GSEE executive also refused to abide by the agreement signed by the trade union groupings PASKE, ESAK-A, AEM and SSEK in January 1988.

A five-member delegation of Greek trade unionists consisting K. Maragoudakis, M. Kehayias, G. Papamichail, G. Stephanou and K. Goutzmanis attended the 75th Session of the International Labour Conference on June 13–14, 1988, on behalf of 47 of the largest federations and labour centres in Greece, and filed an appeal against the Greek government for its interference in GSEE. Representatives of the ILO expressed the hope that the irregular situation in GSEE would rapidly be ended by a genuine, representative Congress.

The GSEE was restored to better functioning under new leadershp in 1989 *(see below)*, though its factions continue in existence. That year it mounted general strikes against the drift of negotiations for a new National Collective Agreement. In December 1990 it led a strike of more than 1,000,000 workers against the prosposed New Democracy "anti-strike" law. The new GSEE President Lambros Kanellopoulos declared that the Bill "virtually imposed a state of continuous civil mobilization and undermines the working class's right to strike".

General Confederation of Greek Labour (GSEE)

Address. 69 Patison Street, Athens
Phone. (21) 88-34-611
Leadership. Lambros Kanellopoulos
Membership. 618,498
History. The GSEE held its founding congress in 1918. Following the eighth congress in 1946 the government deposed the elected executive and imposed one in its favour, and the GSEE remained subject to government intervention. Following the end of the dictatorship in 1974 the GSEE retained

a semi-official character and was opposed by a significant proportion of the labour force organized in independent unions which were unrecognized by the government and did not receive funding from the Ministry of Labour. A congress (the 22nd) broadly representative of the organized labour movement was held for the first time since military rule in December 1983, and elected a governing council with a Pasok majority and a large communist minority. The 23rd congress, held in April 1986, followed the rupture of the GSEE and was boycotted by a large section of the membership (*see above*), leaving the executive organs of the GSEE in the hands of government supporters from the PASKE group. The 24th Congress, coinciding with the 70th anniversary of the founding of the GSEE, was held in Athens on Oct. 21–23, 1988. It was again boycotted by ESAK-A, and many delegates refused to take part, claiming that it was fraudulent.

The boycotted Congress elected only PASKE members to its administration, and was immediately confronted with further claims of fraud by the Opposition. A petition to the Court of First Instance which pleaded that the new GSEE administration was illegal was upheld in November and Georgios Raftopoulos was unseated. In January 1989 a new GSEE administration was installed by the Court representing all five factions in the Confederation in the following proportions: PASKE 21 seats, DAKE 7, ESAK 14, AEM 1, and SSEK 2. This new administration organized the 25th Congress and opened negotiations for a new Collective Agreement.

This Congress which was held on April 14–15, 1989 was the first for an extended period in which all factions had participated. It seated 573 delegates representing 69 unions and 60 federations claiming to represent some 563,000 workers between them. As a measure of progress, the new Administrative Board comprised 18 PASKE, 17 Left Alliance (including ESAK), 8 DAKE and 2 SSEK, and it elected an Executive Board representative of all factions. Lambros Kanellopoulos, former President of the caretaker administration, continued in office.

Structure. The congress elects the 45-member governing council (administrative board), and this elects a bureau of eight officials (including the president and the general secretary) and an executive committee of 15 (comprising the bureau and seven others). The governing council itself comprises the 15 members of the executive committee and 30 others. The governing council also elects the secretaries for the eight sectors (education, international relations, etc).

Publications. GSEE News.

International affiliations. ICFTU; ETUC; TUAC.

Affiliated unions. The GSEE claims the adherence of 82 affiliated federations and 86 "labour centres". The most significant of these is the Labour Centre of Athens which organizes 230,000 workers. Its October 1989 Congress elected a Board composed of PASKE, Left Alliance and DAKE representatives, and Panayiotis Ploumis of ESAK-S became President. The Labour Centre of Athens jointly organized the GSEE strikes for a new Collective Agreement in 1989, and broke new ground the same year by commissioning a poll to ascertain the characteristics of the Athenian labour force.

GSEE opposition factions

SEA
Struggle Co-ordinating Committee

Address. 8 Ippokratus Street, Athens
Phone. 3636-5888; 3609-534
Telex. 225989
Membership. Includes the federations of unions of construction workers, bank employees, electricity, telecommunications, and industrial workers, and large labour centres including ones in Athens and Salonika.
History and character. The Struggle Co-ordinating Committee was formed on April 5, 1986, specifically to "restore legitimacy to the GSEE", with its term of existence to be no longer than required for the achievement of that objective. The SEA complains that Greece is in violation of ILO Conventions 87 and 98 because of the unseating of the GSEE executive elected by the 22nd congress, the appointment of individuals controlled by the government, and the effective abolition of ATA's and collective bargaining.
Publications. INFO Bulletin (in English).

SSEK
Socialist Trade Union Movement of Workers and Employees

Address. 13-15 Solomas Street, Athens

Phone. 3611321

History and character. Some 1,200 expelled Pasok members and other left-wingers formed the SSEK at a conference held on Feb. 9, 1986; the new organization's programme was based on the "September 3rd manifesto" issued at the founding of Pasok in 1974.

Other organizations

Civil Servants' Confederation (ADEDY)

Leadership. Spyros Giatras (president)

Membership. ADEDY claims 240,000 members who are organized in 59 federations and 1400 branches.

International affiliations. ADEDY has a loose relationship with the PSI.

History and character. At its 27th (November 1989) Congress ADEDY elected a general Council dominated by PASKE and DAKE representatives in roughly equal measure. The President Spyros Giatras is from the PASKE faction.

Because it does not have the legal right to negotiate on behalf of civil servants, whose wages are determined unilaterally by the Ministry of the Presidency, ADEDY concentrates on other forms of representation. It seeks the removal of restrictions on the political rights of civil servants, and the extension of permanent status to those on temporary contract or doing seasonal work. It succeeded in achieving a legal change requiring consultation with the unions when civil servants are transferred between agencies.

ESAK-A
United Trade Union Anti-Dictatorship Movement—Associates

Address. 44 Menandrou Street, Athens 114 31

Phone. 52-37-312; 52-43-949; 52-40-605

Leadership. Giannis Epitropou (President); Kostas Papachristodoulou (general secretary)

History. ESAK—Associates was established in 1968 in order to rally democratic trade unionists within its ranks and fight to restore trade union liberties which had been abolished when the military dictatorship seized power on April 21, 1967.

During the junta regime, ESAK-A developed significant anti-dictatorial activities both within Greece and abroad. With the collapse of the dictatorship in 1974, ESAK—A continued its activity to restore democratic legitimacy to the labour movement and to protect the unity and organizational independence of the trade unions from interference by management, the state and governments. It is well represented in a number of federations, including the federation of construction workers, the largest federation in the GSEE.

Policy. ESAK—A claims that it is not an official trade union with members and statutes, but a grouping of trade union staff workers. It has a "guiding and co-ordinating role without in any way replacing the role or jurisdiction of the trade unions".

ESAK—A believes "in the principles of class trade unionism and seeks to maintain relations with all trade union organizations in Europe and in other continents, to promote the interests of working people, democracy and peace. Through its programmes and action, it supports struggles and just claims for economic, social and statutory improvements to benefit the working class and safeguard national independence, for a Greece without foreign military bases and nuclear weapons, for our country's disengagement from the NATO alliance, and to promote progressive policies and social transformations and the building of a socialist society".

Publications. *ESAK—A Bulletin* (English); *Ergatoipaliliki* (in Greek).

Grenada

Capital: St George's   **Population: 102,000**
                                                        (1988)

Political system. Grenada (a former West Indies associated state) became an independent member of the Commonwealth in 1974. In a *coup* in 1979 a left-wing People's Revolutionary government took power; the (bicameral) parliament was dissolved and the Constitution suspended; and close diplomatic and economic links were established with Cuba and countries of the Soviet bloc, while relations with the United States deteriorated. In the course of violent dissension within the government in October 1983 a Commonwealth Caribbean force together with some 2,000 US troops landed on the islands and imposed order, following which an interim advisory council was appointed and the 1974 Constitution restored. Elections to the House of Representatives in December 1984 were won overwhelmingly by the New National Party (NNP) which also accordingly secured a large majority in the nominated Senate. The last foreign military personnel were withdrawn in September 1985.

Economy. Grenada's main exports are cocoa, nutmeg, bananas and mace, but agriculture was severely hit by floods in 1979 and a hurricane in 1980. Moreover, the international markets for Grenada's principal crops have been particularly depressed. Agriculture currently accounts for about 30 per cent of gross domestic product, and there is only a limited manufacturing sector.

The new interim administration sought in 1984 to secure external support for the country's economic development. US assistance included finance towards the completion of an international airport under construction at Port Salines; this opened for commercial flights in October 1984, and it was hoped that it would make possible the exploitation of Grenada's tourism potential (tourism having been adversely affected in the early 1980s both by the US attitude to the then left-wing government and by falling US tourism generally).

The NNP government has sought to "restructure" the economy and stimulate "free enterprise" through a fiscal reform programme; as a result of severe budgetary and external financial difficulties it has found it necessary to make substantial cuts in investment and infrastructural expenditure.

Unemployment at the end of the 1980s was high, despite an increase in employment, with agriculture, construction, light manufacturing and tourism all contributing.

System of industrial relations. Grenada ratified ILO Convention No. 98 (Right to Organize and Collective Bargaining, 1949) in 1979. There are local affiliates to both the ICFTU and WCL.

There is a tripartite committee entrusted with compiling a Labour Code, but up to 1989 progress was slow. The New National Party proposed early in 1989 to introduce legislation to abolish the right to strike in 12 industrial sectors it deemed essential, but was forced to withdraw due to popular opposition. During the year it faced strikes at the LIAT airline and at the Grenada Rocks Corporation. Talks held by three unions and the government in the spring of 1989 to agree a settlement for the public sector were prolonged and acrimonious.

Trade unionism. Two trade union leaders, Vincent Noel and Fitzroy Bain, were among those killed at the time of the overthrow of the Bishop government by a rival faction within the New Jewel Movement in October 1983. Chester Humphrey, the vice-president of the Technical and Allied Workers' Union (TAWU) and a former official of the New Jewel Movement, was released from prison in January 1986 after the Grenadian courts refused a request for his extradition to the USA on charges of having illegally purchased in the USA arms which were used in the *coup* which brought the New Jewel Movement to power. Other union leaders were implicated and faced serious charges.

A legal ruling in September 1988 upheld the claims of the deposed president of the TAWU, Wilfred Hayes (elected in March 1986) to the effect that the membership of the union was not properly determined. The government froze the union's bank account and instructed employers not to negotiate with the union's representatives, whose salaries were stopped. However, Chester Hunter and the other leaders of TAWU continued to have the support of a majority of the union's general council.

There were a large number of leadership changes in Grenada's unions at the end of the decade. Lauret Clarkson of the Public Workers' Union (PWU) became its third leader in two years in 1989; the Grenada Union of Teachers' President Dawn Lett died in 1988 and was replaced by Hudson McPhail; the Seamen and Waterfront Workers Union (SWWU) replaced Arthur Ramsey with Stanley Roberts. In this picture of change the leadership of the country's national centre the GTUC was an exception.

Grenada Trade Union Council (GTUC)

Address. P.O. Box 411, Tanteen, St George's
Phone. 440 3733
Leadership. Anselm de Bourg (president); Clasis Charles (secretary/treasurer)
Membership. 7,532.
History and character. The GTUC was founded and registered in 1955.
Affiliated unions.

1. **Bank and General Workers' Union**

2. **Commercial & Industrial Workers' Union**

3. **Public Workers Union**

4. **Grenada Union of Teachers**

5. **Seamen and Waterfront Workers' Union**

6. **Taxi Owners and Drivers' Association**

7. **Technical and Allied Workers' Union**

International affiliation. ICFTU; CCL

The Grenada Public Workers' Union

Address. P.O. Box 420, St George's, Grenada
Phone. 1-809-440-2203
Leadership. Lauret Clarkson (president)
Membership. Approx. 1,000.
History and character. The Public Workers Union was founded in 1931 under the official name of the Grenada Civil Service Association. In March 1980, the name of the organization was changed to the Grenada Public Workers' Union.
Publications. The Public Worker.
International affiliation. PSI.

Guatemala

Capital: Guatemala City   **Population: 8,700,000**

Political system. Under a new Constitution introduced in 1965 a civilian President was elected in 1966, followed by three successive military heads of state. A further military candidate declared elected in 1982 was prevented from taking office by a *coup* led by Gen. Efraín Ríos Montt, but the latter was himself removed from office in 1983, after opposition particularly from within the Roman Catholic Church. A new Constitution was drawn up, under which a Christian Democratic President was elected in 1985 and sworn in early in 1986. Also elected was a unicameral Legislative Assembly, in which the Christian Democrats had a bare overall majority.

Guatemala has been subject to persistent internal unrest and guerrilla activities, accompanied frequently by harsh measures of suppression by the army and security forces. There has been a long-standing dispute over territorial claims on neighbouring Belize, but the first direct bilateral talks between the two countries with a view to reaching a bilateral settlement took place in April 1987.

President Cerezo, elected in 1986, survived an attemped *coup* by sections of the military in May 1988, and his term of office ended in January 1991.

Economy. Agriculture, forestry and fisheries represent the major economic activity and export sector, although there is also a relatively well-developed industrial and manufacturing sector based largely on the processing of agricultural products. A strong influence on the economy is exercised by the private-sector Co-ordinating Committee of Agricultural, Commercial, Industrial and Financial Associations. Agricultural production has been disrupted by the internal security situation and output is also liable to be adversely affected by severe climatic conditions; moreover, most of the main products are subject to wide demand and price fluctuations on the international markets. Receipts from tourism have declined in recent years.

The government formed in 1986 introduced programmes of austerity measures and fiscal reform designed both to stimulate the economy and to reduce the high level of unemployment (which affected nearly half of the labour force).

By 1988 the official unemployment rate was 6.3 per cent, but a Household Survey found that in the same year nearly 57 per cent of the workforce was underemployed. More than half of the 2,640,000 workforce was employed in agriculture.

System of industrial relations. Trade unionism developed strongly in the period of reformist civilian government preceding the 1954 coup, and Guatemala ratified ILO Convention No. 87 (Freedom of Association and Protection of the Right to Organize, 1948) and No. 98 (Right to Organize and Collective Bargaining, 1949) in 1952. Union activities since then, however, have been held back by tactics of repression (including the assassination of union activists), blacklisting and corruption. Under the labour code and other legislation trade unions have been prohibited from participating in party politics, the right to strike has been limited in all sectors and denied to agricultural workers at harvest time and to workers in the public service (with heavy penalties prescribed for violators), and public servants have been forbidden to organize (although a National Union of Public Employees of Guatemala—ANTEG—linked to CLAT, was reported to be in formation at the time of the transition to civilian government in early 1986, this being described as the first national organization of public servants with a federal structure). Such formal restrictions have been less significant in practice than the general climate of fear and violence in which industrial and political relations have been conducted. The disappearance and assassination of trade unionists have been the subjects of complaints to the ILO by both the

WFTU and the ICFTU. The ICFTU in *Trade Union Rights: Survey of Violations 1985–86* noted that reports continued throughout 1985–86 of cases of arrest, torture, assassination and disappearance of trade unionists, and that these acts "were primarily perpetuated by members of the armed forces or by death squads operating under their protection". The *Survey* stated that the election of a democratically elected civilian government, which came to power in January 1986, had not thus far altered the situation. However, a significant change came with the formation of the Popular Labour Action Unity (USAP) in January 1988, which represents several labour federations. On Jan. 13, it was able to mobilize 50,000 people on a demonstration in support of wage increases, a minimum daily wage and price controls, and, following the threat of a general strike, drew concessions from the government by negotiating a "social pact" on March 8. However, following the attempted military *coup* of May, the government reversed its commitment to maintain wages, and controls on the prices of basic commodities were lifted in June and July. In August the UASP broke off talks with the government and called for progressive work stoppages which culminated in a general strike on Aug. 22. Confidence in the government's intentions was further eroded in some union circles due to its advocacy of "solidarism", a paternalistic mutualist movement initiated three years before by conservative elements in the Catholic Church and supported by multinational companies and local firms. In June 1988, Juan Alfaro, secretary general of the CUSG, called on the government to take effective action against "death squads" which, he said, it had failed to do since coming to office.

The following year there were 2,000 deaths according to official sources as well as hundreds of disappearances. In the first nine months of 1990 there were over 160 illegal executions. The ICFTU denounced Guatemala at the ILO and cited it in its annual survey of union rights violations for 1990.

There were other important developments on the Guatemalan labour scene in 1988. President Cerezo made an agreement with the newly formed union confederation UASP in March, but under pressure of the abortive May *coup* government leaders drew back from their commitments at that time, provoking unrest and a somewhat unsuccessful general strike in August. A farm workers' strike hit the sugar industry at the beginning of the year after which the employers also agreed to talks with UASP. Later in the year UASP had formal consultations with the employers' organization UNAGRO, the first such talks in the country's history. Guatemala's new National Reconciliation Commission met for the first time in February 1989 bringing together government representatives, the representatives of some employers' organizations and representatives of all union confederations.

Trade unionism. Unions in Guatemala are legalized under complicated regulations within the country's Labour Code. By May 1989, their number had risen by 10 per cent, (67 in 1988 and a further 29 in the first four months of 1989). Union density in Guatemala in 1988 was 9 per cent. There are three major union centres, CUSG—much the largest with 180,000 members, CGTG—which is affiliated to the WCL and claims 90,000, and the loosely associated UNSITRAGUA, some of whose members are affiliated to the WFTU. In 1988 CUSG and UNSITRAGUA joined with the University Students' Association (AEU) to form the co-ordinating body UASP whose breadth allowed it to initiate the dialogue with farmers and Guatemalan employers (CACIF) in 1989.

FENASTEG is a newly formed federation of public sector workers uniting unions from competing confederations. FASGUA is an independent union affiliated to the WFTU. Like all Gautemalan union organizations it faces rivals. The law allows the formation of new unions in a company if they can recruit 26 members, a useful device for employers seeking to foster disunity within the firm but also not unknown in the public sector. The

Solidarismo movement of Costa Rica is also present in Guatemala, though the government does not acknowledge its associations as trade unions. By 1990, however, the movement was growing in strength with 280 member associations and 80,000 affiliates.

Confederación de Unidad Sindical de Guatemala (CUSG)

Address. 4a, Av. 5-12, Zona 1, 2do. Nivel Oficina 1, Guatemala City
Phone. (2) 26-515
Leadership. Juan Francisco Alfaro (secretary general)
History and character. Founded in 1983, with social democratic orientation. Claims to have 180,000 members, mainly rural workers. Receives support from the Inter-American Regional Workers' Organization (ORIT) and the American Institute for Free Labour Development (AIFLD). Consists of federations rather than individual unions.
International affiliations. ICFTU; ORIT.

Co-ordinadora General de Trabajadores de Guatemala (CGTG)

Address. 8A, AV. 3-38, Zona 1, Guatemala City
Phone. 21105, 538159
Leadership. José E. Pinzón (secretary general)
Membership. Claims 90,000.
History and character. Is the renamed Central Nacional de Trabajadores (CNT), which operated clandestinely from mid-1980 after the "disappearance" of 21 of its leaders arrested on June 21. Its leader, Julio Celso de Leon, was abducted and tortured during four days of detention during September 1985. The CTCG was founded in 1987, with 25,000 members organized into five federations. Affiliated with the Christian Democrat-oriented Latin American Workers Central (CLAT). Dropped out of the UASP and formed the main organization of the Unitary Union Coordinate (COSU), created to act as a pro-government counterbalance to the UASP. The CGTG did not support the labour protest of 1988.
Publication. Organo Informativo de la CGTG.
International affiliations. WCL; CLAT.

Federación Autónoma Sindical Guatemalteca (FASGUA)

Address. c/o CPUSTAL, Ribera de San Cosme No. 22, Despacho 105, México 4 D.F., Colonia San Rafael, Mexico
Leadership. Miguel Angel Solis (general secretary)
History and character. FASGUA was formed in May 1955.
International affiliations. WFTU; CPUSTAL.

Guatemalan Workers Labour Unit (UNSITRAGUA)

History and character. Founded in 1985. Has some 13,000 members in 40 private sector unions. Self-defined as a class-based expression of workers' unity. Has no international affiliation, although it maintains ties with the Social Democrat-oriented International Union of Food and Allied Workers (IFU). UNSITRAGUA opposed the UASP decision to call for work stoppages, and only 10 of its member unions participated briefly.

International Food and Beverage Workers' Union (IFU/UITA)

Character. Militant affiliate of UNSITRAGUA.

National Federation of State Workers (FENASTEG)

Character. Social Democrat orientation. The majority of FENASTEG's member unions are participating in the strikes.

194

Guinea

Capital: Conakry

Population: 6,641,000
(1988)

Political system. Guinea became fully independent in 1958, after declining to accept self-governing status within the French Community. For over 25 years the government was dominated by President Sekou Touré, as leader of the socialist and nationalist Parti Démocratique de Guinée (PDG, which was constituted as the sole legal political party). Upon his death in 1984, a military *coup* took place, a military-civilian administration was set up under Lansana Conté at the head of a Military Committee of National Recovery, the Constitution was suspended and the PDG and the unicameral National Assembly were dissolved. During most of the period of Sekou Touré's rule, official policy was applied with considerable severity; in the early 1980s, however, there was some relaxation of this political centralism, while at the same time the international isolation into which Guinea had withdrawn was also relaxed under a policy of "positive neutrality".

During 1990 the military drew up a draft constitution which was approved by popular referendum in December. Opposition groups in exile objected to its five year time-scale for creating a two party system, called for a boycott of the referendum and advocated an immediate conference of all political forces.

Economy. The main export crops are bananas and other fruit, groundnuts, oil palm and coffee. However, this sector has been severely affected by adverse climatic conditions and also widely fluctuating world market conditions. The programme of establishing collective farms has been modified by the Lansana Conté government and encouragement has been given to the expansion and diversification of agricultural production. Most export revenue derives from mining, notably of bauxite (partly processed into alumina), iron ore and diamonds, although all of these have faced depressed world markets.

The economy was almost wholly socialized under the Sekou Touré regime; private trade was largely prohibited in 1975, but this policy was subsequently partly relaxed. At the end of 1985 there was a major restructuring of Guinea's public financial and industrial sector, including the ending of state commercial banking activities and the dissolution or sale to private interests of certain state manufacturing and processing industries. In 1986 and again in 1987 the IMF approved support for Guinea's economic, financial and administrative adjustment programmes aimed at reversing more than two decades of steady economic decline, and the substitution of a generally market-oriented economy for a state-controlled economy. This followed a major currency reform designed to narrow the wide margin between the official and blackmarket exchange rates.

In 1985-87, 80.7 per cent of the Guinean labour force was engaged in agriculture, 9 per cent in industry and 10.3 per cent in services.

System of industrial relations. Following independence in 1958 Guinea ratified ILO Conventions No. 87 (Freedom of Association and Protection of the Right to Organize, 1948) and No. 98 (Right to Organize and Collective Bargaining, 1949) in 1959.

Under a decree of 1964 (which the government maintained had never been applied but repeatedly refused to repeal) all persons aged between 16 and 25 were placed at the service of the Organization for Work Centres of the Revolution, which was aimed at directing labour to overcome problems of under-development (the decree contravening ILO Convention No. 105, Abolition of Forced Labour, which Guinea had ratified in 1961).

A new labour code was drafted with the assistance of the ILO, updating the code of

1960 which incorporated the main ILO conventions. The new code claims to promote higher productivity, to give workers more protection, and to revive the role of trade unions and collective bargaining. The code makes 16 years the minimum age for entering the labour market, the establishes a 40-hour working week; there are also provisions covering apprenticeship, fixed term contracts, training levies, accidents at work, maternity leave, dismissal, collective bargaining and settlement of disputes. The ILO Committee of Experts on the application of Conventions and Recommendations welcomed the adoption of the new labour code, but noted some shortcomings, principally the power of compulsory arbitration under certain circumstances by the Ministry of Labour.

Trade unionism. From 1958 until his death in 1984, however, Sekou Touré combined the position of President of the country with that of leader of the sole trade union organization, the Confédération Nationale des Travailleurs de Guinée (CNTG). Following Touré's death, the new regime which came to power in the *coup* of April 3, 1984, announced that free trade unions would be permitted. The CTG remains the only trade union centre.

Confédération des Travailleurs de Guinée (CTG)
Confederation of Workers of Guinea

Address. B.P. 237, Conakry

Leadership. Dr Mohamed Samba Kébé (secretary general)

History and character. Sekou Touré became leader of the Guinea branch of the French Confédération Générale du Travail (CGT) in 1948, by which time he had also founded the Parti Démocratique de Guinée (PDG), which demanded independence from France. When Touré became the first President of independent Guinea in 1958 his union (renamed as the Confédération Nationale des Travailleurs de Guinée—CNTG—in 1956) became the sole trade union organization and was integrated into the structure of the PDG (the sole legal party). Following Touré's death and the change of regime in 1984 the CNTG was restyled as the CTG. In November 1985 its new leader, Samba Kébé, stated that there had been a "certain liberalization" in the mass organizations since the 1984 *coup*, "in particular, the trade union movement, which since then has not been responsible to a party or affiliated to a party". Kébé stated that the trade union movement was now free and had good relations with the Military Committee of National Recovery, but was not yet in a position to make "demands" in view of the poor state of the economy. An ordinance of August 1986 confirmed the legal independence of the CTG from the state.

Structure. There are affiliated organizations for the various sectors of the economy, but not for agriculture.

International affiliation. OATUU. The CTG has since 1984 also established contacts with the ICFTU.

Guinea-Bissau

Capital: Bissau   **Population: 960,000**

Political system. Guinea-Bissau became formally independent of Portugal in 1974 (its independence having been proclaimed unilaterally in 1973). Initially the governments of both Guinea-Bissau and Cape Verde (the latter independent from 1975) were formed by the African Party for the Independence of Guinea and Cape Verde (PAIGC) with a view at that stage to the eventual integration of the two countries. Under a new constitution adopted in May 1984, which defined Guinea-Bissau as an anti-colonialist and anti-imperialist republic with a policy of national revolutionary democracy, the PAIGC, as the sole and ruling party, was described as the leading political force in society and in the state, and as defining the bases for state policy in all fields. There is a unicameral National People's Assembly, elected indirectly by the eight regional councils; this in turn elects a Council of State to which powers are delegated between sessions.

In June 1989 President Vieira was elected unopposed as President, but during the course of 1990 pressure mounted for the establishment of democracy. In January 1991 the ruling PAIGC approved formally a plan to introduce a multi-party system.

Economy. The economy of Guinea-Bissau is largely agricultural, with rice as the staple food and with groundnuts, coconuts and palm kernels providing nearly half of export revenue, while the other main export is fish; agriculture and fisheries between them account for three-quarters of the economically active population. However, agricultural output has been depressed as a result both of persistent drought conditions and of the effects of massive disruption in the period leading to independence. Overall direction of the economy lies with the state, which also controls foreign trade, but under the 1983–86 and 1988–91 development plans there has been a liberalization of trade, and encouragement has been given to the growth of private-sector activities.

Guinea-Bissau has experienced chronic trade and also budgetary deficits, leading to high rates of inflation and to rapidly growing external debt. It is a desperately poor country, with the lowest life expectancy and GNP per head (US$160) in West Africa.

System of industrial relations. Guinea-Bissau ratified ILO Convention No. 98 (Right to Organize and Collective Bargaining, 1949) and Convention Nos. 29 and 105 on forced labour in 1977. The ILO has noted discrepancies between labour law and the conventions ratified, in particular provisions covering freedom of organization and collective bargaining. A new Labour Code came into effect in May 1986 which met in law, if not in implementation, some of the ILO criticisms.

Trade unionism. Trade union activities were severely restricted under Portuguese colonial rule, and since independence the União Nacional dos Trabalhadores de Guiné (UNTG) has been the sole trade union organization. It is closely tied to the ruling party, the PAIGC, but development has been restricted by the small industrial base.

The decision to introduce multi-party democracy must have implications for the UNTG which has held a monopoly position since the 1970s.

União Nacional dos Trabalhadores de Guiné (UNTG)
National Union of Workers of Guinea-Bissau

Address. Caixa Postal 98, Bissau
Phone. 2094; 27755
Telex. 96900
Leadership. Mario Mendes Correa (secretary general)
History and character. The UNTG when in exile was affiliated to the ICFTU, but since independence has transferred its affiliation to the WFTU. The UNTG, as an arm of the ruling party, emphasizes the need to mobilize the workers to achieve greater productivity and overcome problems of backwardness.
International affiliations. OATUU; WFTU.

Guyana

Capital: Georgetown

Population : 799,000
(1988)

Political system. Guyana (formerly British Guiana) became a fully independent member of the Commonwealth in 1966 and adopted republican status in 1970. There is a unicameral National Assembly (principally comprising directly elected members, together with 12 members elected indirectly by the organs of local government). Under the current 1980 Constitution the leader of the majority party in the National Assembly holds the office of executive president. Since 1964 the government has been formed by the People's National Congress (PNC), which is based predominantly on the section of the population of African rather than Asian descent and which adheres to a Marxist-Leninist ideology. The 1980 Constitution declares that the principal objective of the state's political system is to extend socialist democracy. The national economy is based on the social ownership of the means of production, with national economic planning being the basic principle of the development and management of the economy. Co-operativism in practice is the dynamic principle of socialist transformation, although the existence of privately owned economic enterprises is recognized within certain constraints.

Under President Desmond Hoyte, who succeeded Forbes Burnham in 1987, Guyana began to move towards more market-oriented policies.

Economy. Over three-quarters of the economy is socialized, although there has during the 1980s been an increase in private-sector activity. Agriculture is the principal productive sector in terms of employment. Sugar is the main export crop, but earnings have been severely reduced as a result of adverse climatic conditions, of industrial unrest, and of depressed world market prices, and the government has sought to restructure the industry and to diversify crops grown on the cane plantations. The bauxite sector (nationalized in 1971–75) is the principal export earner, but here also low world prices have had a serious effect on revenue. Industry is centred largely on the processing of minerals and of agricultural produce. Guyana has a relatively high external debt. Support for the economy was received until the early 1980s from the IMF, but in 1985 Guyana was declared ineligible for further use of the Fund's general resources owing to its failure to maintain adequate repayments of interest and capital from previous drawings.

Out of a workforce of approximately 265,000, a quarter are employed in public services and a quarter in public industries, with the balance employed or self-employed in the private sector. The standard of living in Guyana fell again in 1989 and there were extended protests against the government's Economic Recovery Programme. The 1989 budget entailed a 70 per cent devaluation, a 20 per cent wage rise and privatization. In 1990 the government provoked further union anger by refusing to negotiate the public sector minimum wage with the GTUC, and instead imposing increases periodically.

System of industrial relations. Guyana ratified ILO Convention No. 87 (Freedom of Association and Protection of the Right to Organize, 1948) in 1967 and Convention No. 98 (Right to Organize and Collective Bargaining, 1949) in 1966. (Presently, Guyana is not allowed to vote at the ILO annual conferences because of arrears in membership dues.) Although Guyana does not have a legal minimum wage, the government and the TUC agreed a wage package for public employees biennially, which includes a minimum daily wage (estimated to rise from GY10.80 to GY23.75 (GY10 = US$1) in a two-year agreement made in August, 1987). This minimum is generally reflected in the private sector but most wage levels are higher than those of public employees. The bargaining monopoly of the TUC, legally endorsed in 1984, was finally abolished by a Court of Appeal decision in

October 1987, despite government opposition which might still take the form of a constitutional change to nullify the court's decision.

The state's involvement in Guyanese industrial relations is made inevitable by the fact that the government employs nearly half the nation's workforce, and shaped in part by the close links between the ruling PNC and the GTUC. In 1988 most strikes that occurred were in the Sugar industry where the main union (GAWU) is an affiliate of the opposition PPP. In 1989 however the government had to face a seven-week strike led by the breakaway union centre FITUG in opposition to its austerity programme.

Trade unionism. Unions have existed since the establishment of the British Guiana Labour Union (BGLU) by Hubert Critchlow in 1922, and the Guyana Trades Union Congress (TUC) had its origins in 1941. The unions have been divided in their allegiances between the PNC and the People's Progressive Party (PPP), with the division (as of the two parties) largely on racial lines; the TUC is affiliated to the ICFTU and is generally aligned with the ruling PNC while the other centre, the FITUG, groups unaffiliated or PPP-supporting unions.

Trade union density in Guyana is high at 25 per cent. However the monolithic structure of Guyanan trade unionism was shaken in September 1988 when there was a walk-out from the GTUC Annual Conference. Six unions, all of them either politically independent or affiliated to opposition parties, covering about 45 per cent of the unionized workforce launched the Federation of Independent Trade Unions of Guyana (FITUG). Though rivals, the GTUC and FITUG came together to oppose the austerity programme in 1989, but FITUG went further in launching a seven-week protest strike in the sugar industry.

The action of 1989 brought government retaliation against FITUG, several of whose leaders were de-recognized, and a number of whose affiliates had their check-off facilities withdrawn. The FITUG affiliates GAWU and NAACIE dominate the sugar industry and the bauxite industry, the two principal dollar earners. The GTUC on the other still holds the affiliation of unions representing the vast majority of the public sector. There is one small independent union, the National Workers' Union (NWU) which is affiliated to the Democratic Labour Party.

Federation of Independent Trade Unions in Guyana (FITUG)

Membership. Around 30,000.

Affiliated unions and structure. Six unions mainly in the private sector, including the two main organizations in sugar, the National Association of Agricultural, Commercial and Industrial Employees (NAACIE) which has no political ties, and the 14,000 strong Guyana Agricultural and General Workers' Union (GAWU) which is affiliated to the Opposition PPP and the WFTU; and the two major organizations in bauxite, the 5,800 strong Guyana Mine Workers' Union (GMWU) and the Guyana Bauxite Supervisors' Union (GBSU).

History and character. FITUG was formed following the walk-out of six unions from the GTUC Annual Conference in September 1988 and has since behaved in line with the independent or oppositional stance of its member unions (all of which joined it). FITUG led a seven week strike against the government's austerity budget in 1989, but moderated its opposition in 1990 in favour of talks with the GTUC and the administration.

Affiliated union.

Guyana Agricultural and General Workers' Union (GAWU), 104–106 Regent Street, Lacytown, Georgetown

Leadership: Kamal Chand (general secretary)

History and character: The GAWU, with 14,000 members is the biggest union in Guyana and a founder member of FITUG. Its membership is predominantly Asian and it is affiliated to the PPP and the WFTU.

Guyana Trades Union Congress (TUC/GTUC)

Address. Critchlow Labour College, Woolford Avenue, Non Pareil Park, Georgetown
Phone. 2-61493
Cable. UNICO Georgetown
Leadership. Joseph H. Pollydore (general secretary)
Membership. Around 35,000.
History and character. The TUC originated in 1941 as the British Guiana Trades Union Council. In recent years the PNC government (while disavowing an intention to control the TUC) has generally retained a dominant influence in it, in part by the creation of small PNC-controlled unions which make exaggerated membership claims to secure a disproportionate representation at TUC congresses. According to anti-government unionists, some of these unions are in effect state enterprise company unions, which are readily sanctioned by the government in exchange for their political support. At the 1984 congress anti-government candidates were elected with the assistance of delegates from some normally pro-government unions (voting was by secret ballot). At the 1986 congress, however, the PNC regained control after bitter controversy over the seating of certain pro-PNC delegates, notably the representatives of9the General Workers' Union, whose membership had allegedly been artificially inflated. Dissident unions within the TUC (who oppose the PNC aligned unions) called for more democracy within the TUC at the latter's 34th annual conference in September 1987. The GAWU and other TUC affiliates want both the composition of TUC bodies to be determined by proportional representation as well as the verification of membership figures of affiliated unions to guarantee that they are what they claim to be. Such demands were resisted by the TUC leadership. In a statement of June 1988, the president of the TUC, George Daniels, said there had been a 50 per cent drop in real wages since 1977, which also meant that unions were not able to meet increasing running costs, particularly those of their educational programmes.

In September 1988 the GTUC suffered the defection of six important unions—all politically independent or affiliated to the Opposition PPP—which were unwilling to continue support for government economic policy. These unions formed the Federation of Independent Trade Unions of Guyana (FITUG) but in 1990 began talks to open the possibility of re-unification.

The TUC is represented on numerous official bodies; the State Planning Secretariat, Guyana State Corporation, Bauxite Industry Development Company, Guyana Management Institute, Guyana Mortgage Finance Bank, Guyana Mines Commission, Forest Commission, Kuru Kuru Co-operative College, University of Guyana Board of Governors, National Insurance Scheme, National Transport Advisory Board, Guyana School of Agriculture.

Affiliated unions and structure: There are 17 affiliates, the largest of which are the Guyana Public Service Union (GPSU), 11,600 members; the General Workers' Union (GWU), 8,000 members; the Guyana Teachers' Association (GTA), 6,000 members; and the Guyana Labour Union (GLU), 6,000 members.
International affiliations. ICFTU; CCL; AIFLD.
Publications. *Voice of Labour* (irregular); weekly radio programme.

Other organization

National Workers' Union (NWU)

Address. Critchlow-Edun House, 88 Alexander Street, Lacytown, Georgetown
Leadership. Claudius N. London (president); Paul N. Tennassee (secretary, international relations)
Membership. 2,000.
Publication. *Workers Action.*
History and character. The NWU was founded in 1986 and held its first Biennial Conference in 1987. It has members in the transport, sugar, farming and security sectors and is the union arm of the Democratic Labour Movement, an opposition party.
International affiliations. WCL.

Haiti

Capital: Port-au-Prince

Population: 6,300,000
(1988)

Political system. Haiti was from 1957 to early 1986 ruled by the Duvalier family. Following increasing internal unrest, and in the face of effective withdrawal of US support, Jean-Claude Duvalier left the country in February 1986 when a civilian-military council assumed power, the Constitution was suspended and the National Assembly was dissolved. Under a new Constitution approved by referendum in March 1987, controversial presidential and legislative elections were held in January 1988, but amidst continuing widespread violence and intimidation two successive military *coups* took place later in that year.

Under popular pressure military rulers yielded to civilians in March 1990 and a caretaker government prepared for free elections, which were held in December 1990. These returned an administration led by a priest active on behalf of civil rights, despite a final *coup* attempt in January 1991 by a Tonton Macoute leader which collapsed due to lack of military support.

Economy. Over half to the workforce is engaged in agriculture. Coffee represents the main export crop, but this sector was drastically affected by a hurricane in 1980 and also by generally depressed world market prices. Traditionally the other main export has been bauxite, but mining was suspended in 1983 because of low international demand for aluminium. Industry includes manufacturing for the domestic market together with processing and the assembly of electronic and other goods for the exports market (principally the USA which accounts for over half of Haiti's exports). Efforts have been made to develop tourism, but uncertain internal conditions have hampered expansion in this field. During the 1980s Haiti has had high trade deficits, and foreign aid has met not only the bulk of the external deficit but also much of the government's own budgetary deficit. Haiti is the poorest country in the Western hemisphere.

In 1986 the new post-Duvalierist government announced its intention to encourage competition in the economy, and in this context it closed inefficient public enterprises and maintained stringent controls over public expenditure. However, the severe political instability caused a widespread breakdown of economic activity.

1989 saw a contraction of the economy while inflation rose to 11 per cent.

System of industrial relations. Haiti ratified ILO Convention No. 98 (Right to Organize and Collective Bargaining, 1949) in 1957, shortly before Duvalier came to power, and Convention No. 87 (Freedom of Association and Protection of the Right to Organize, 1948) in 1979. Haiti also ratified ILO Conventions No. 29 (Forced Labour, 1930) and No. 105 (Abolition of Forced Labour, 1957) in 1958 (as did the Dominican Republic in 1956 and 1958, respectively). However, throughout the period of Duvalier rule Haitian labourers were employed in large numbers on a seasonal basis in the sugar plantations of the Dominican Republic in conditions of near-servitude, the Haitian government receiving fees for "recruiting expenses"; such work was sought in many cases, however, by Haitian labourers in view of the extreme poverty prevailing in their own country and large numbers remained permanently in the Dominican Republic. *The Report of the Committee of Experts on the Application of Conventions and Recommendations of the ILO* (1988) in early 1988 had failed to receive notification from the government that it was complying with Convention No. 105 in relation to further evidence of the forced migration of labour to Dominican Republic plantations. (The government had assured an ILO mission in October 1986 that such migration would not be officially organized.) The ILO's Committee on Freedom of Association reported to the ILO in February–March 1988 on repressive measures imposed on trade unions including the arrests of trade union leaders, anti-union dismissals and the dissolution, by administrative authority, of the Autonomous Confederation of Haitian Workers (CATH) on June 23, 1987 (*see below*), although this was subsequently rescinded. Both Committees deplored the lack of co-operation from the government and asked it to send a report on the application of Conventions Nos. 87 and 98 as well as to facilitate their implementation in law. In January 1989 *Free Labour World*, noting that trade union rights were "repeatedly abused" and that the Labour Code was a "dead letter", stated that the free trade union movement was "still very young" and that "its ideas and structures have yet to be defined and strengthened". Only a few collective bargaining agreements had been signed. The chief legal framework governing industrial relations is the 1984 Labour Code, under which the government issued two important decrees in 1986. One established a mixed commission for overseeing wage levels while the other defined the circumstances in which a strike is legal. In 1989 a new Tripartite Commission was formed to revise the Code, but it collapsed amid the wave of popular unrest which terminated military rule in 1990. The later 1980s saw an increase in the number of disputes as unions responded to the post-Duvalier atmosphere. Where the Labour Court was called on to intervene, it frequently decided in favour of the unions.

Trade unionism. Several trade union centres functioned in the period from 1946–1957, but following the assumption of power by François Duvalier in 1957, unions were either eliminated or brought under government control. During the 1970s, rank-and-file labour organization occurred at plant level, with strikes occurring in some sectors despite vigorous repression, but there were no federations inside the country. The Union National d'Ouvriers d'Haïti (UNOH), the principal centre before 1957, existed in exile as an ICFTU/ORIT affiliate but this has since disbanded and there is currently no ICFTU/ORIT affiliate in Haiti. The WCL/CLAT afffiliated is the Central Autonome des Travailleurs Haïtiens (CATH). There is no WFTU affiliate, although a Union Intersyndical d'Haïti (UISH), associated with the WFTU, was active at one time. Figures for union membership in Haiti are unreliable since members do not pay contributions and because unions also act as peasants' organizations. There are five chief centres whose relative importance is difficult to gauge.

Central Autonome des Travailleurs Haïtiens (CATH)
Autonomous Confederation of Haitian Workers

Address. Rue Mgr. Guilloux No. 134, Guilloux, Port-au-Prince

History and character. The CATH was founded in 1959 inside Haiti as the Fédération Haïtienne des Syndicats Chrétiens (FHSC) but was quickly suppressed and re-established in exile in Venezuela under the protection of the WCL/CLAT. It was permitted to return to Haiti under Jean-Claude Duvalier and according to the CLAT in 1984 the CATH represented "huge sectors of the population". In March 1988 CATH claimed 76 member unions and a membership of 5,000. In November 1989 three CATH members were killed by paramilitary forces during a strike, while in January 1990 its offices were raided and a leader detained. There was a major change in CATH leadership in 1990.

Centrale Des Travailleurs Haïtiens (CTH)
Haitian Workers' Centre

Leadership. Former President was Georges Fortune of the political party RDNP.

Membership. Claimed to have 180 member organizations in May 1990; outside estimates put its membership at 7,000 in May 1988.

History and character. Predominantly an industrial union which spent its years of exile in Venezuela.

International affiliations. CLAT; WCL.

Confédération Ouvriere Des Travailleurs Haitiens (KOTA)

Address. CNPC 186, Cité de l'exposition, Port-au-Prince, Haiti
International affiliation. WFTU (ratified October 1987).

Federation Des Ouvriers Syndique (FOS)
Federation of Union Workers

Membership. Claimed 25,000 members in 85 unions at April 1990 but outside estimates put the figure at nearer 3,000.

History and character. Predominantly non-political.
International affiliations. Links with the ICFTU and ORIT.

Organisation Générale Indépendante Des Travailleurs Haïtiens (OGITH)
Independent Organization of Haitian Workers

Membership. 42 unions, of which 17 were legally registered with the government in 1990. It also claims the affiliation of eight agricultural co-operatives.

History and character. Formed in February 1988.
International affiliations. None but informal links with several.

Other organization

Outside the centres is the National Confederation of Haitian Teachers (CNEH), formed in 1986, and claiming 10,000 members.

Honduras

Capital: Tegucigalpa   **Population: 5,103,772**
                                                                    (1989)

Political system. Honduras has remained for much of the past 50 years under military control, although periodically having a nominally civilian administration. General elections held under a new Constitution in 1981 were won by the Liberal Party (PLH). In November 1985 the PLH (which like the right-wing National Party was divided into competing factions) was again successful, and its leading candidate, José Azcona (generally regarded as strongly anti-communist, pro-US and a fiscal conservative) was sworn in as President in January 1986; elections held at the same time to the unicameral National Assembly resulted in exactly half the seats being won by the various PLH factions.

The Ancona government was suceeded by an administration under the National Party's Leonardo Callejas following the November 1989 presidential elections, at which time a number of union leaders were also elected as Congressional deputies. However despite the existence of civilian administrations, there seems little doubt that the army is still the dominant influence on Honduran institutions. The internal situation is markedly affected by the presence in Honduras of refugees from the guerrilla war in El Salvador. Honduras has been in receipt of considerable military aid from the USA, which has counter-insurgency training facilites within the country, and joint military manoeuvres are carried out.

Economy. The economy is largely dependent on agriculture, with bananas, coffee, timber and sugar as the main exports, However, the banana crop has been severely affected by climatic conditions; coffee revenue has been reduced by depressed world market prices, by disease and by the internal security situation; and forestry revenue has been reduced by serious fires. Agrarian reform launched in 1975 has remained largely unfulfilled. Industrial potential is little exploited, and has suffered from a lack of both financial resources and demand in the region. A programme was initiated in 1982 to encourage foreign invest-ment, and to reverse the considerable capital outflow experienced in the previous few years as a result of political instability.

Growth of 2.1 per cent in 1989 was not enough to keep pace with the expansion of the workforce, and the worst performing sectors tended to be the largest, notably agriculture. The official estimate of inflation for 1989 of 9.8 per cent must be set against other estimates which put it as high as 20 per cent. Unemployment may have been only 9 per cent for the same year but underemployment afflicted more than one third of the workforce.

System of industrial relations. Widespread strikes and unrest in 1954 led to the first major advance of the Honduran labour movement when the US-owned United Fruit Company was forced to negotiate with its employees. In 1955 the government extended legal recognition and the right to strike to trade unions, and Honduras ratified ILO Conventions No. 87 (Freedom of Association and Protection of the Right to Organize, 1948) and No. 98 (Right to Organize and Collective Bargaining, 1949) in 1956. Since then trade unionism has remained alive in Honduras despite the assassination of many union activists (especially in peasant unions), the use of blacklisting, intimidation and corruption by employers, and waves of organized repression.

The ILO Report of the Committee of Experts on the Application of Conventions and Recommendations (1985) noted in respect of the observance by Honduras of ILO Convention No. 87 that there were various restrictions on trade union freedoms imposed by the national labour code: thus only one union could exist in any workplace; federations and confederations could not call strikes; government approval or six months' notice was required prior to strike action in non-essential public services; and the Labour Minister was empowered to enforce binding settlements in the case of disputes in the petroleum industry. Adalberto Discua Rodriguez, Minister of Labour and Social Security (in a direct communication to *Trade Unions of the World* on October 7, 1988) confirmed that the Labour Code "contained some norm that do not exactly coincide with the broadly spirited interpretation of the referred code (No. 87)". Honduras was studying the Committee's recommendations and was about to make an official announce-ment. In the meantime, the study of the problem had been charged to a Tripartite Commission (formed by the Minister of Labour) which included a representative of the Hondurian Council of Private Business (Consejo Hondureno de la Empresa Privada—COHEP) and the secretary of the ICFTU-affiliated CTH; this Commission had expressed itself opposed to a reform of the Labour Code which would allow more than one union in a workplace. This, the Minister stated, reflected the view of the Honduran union movement which recognized the danger of many small and underfinanced unions coexisting in the same workplace. In relation to Convention No. 29 (Forced Labour, 1930) ratified, 1957, ILO's *Report of the Committee of Experts* (1988) hopes that the government will take the necessary measures, especially in relation to section 274 of the National Constitution, to guarantee that only in emergency situations "may non-military work be required of persons performing their compulsory military service". "Disappearances" of union activists have continued in recent years, and in 1983 four organizers of a banana plantation workers' union were killed by men in military uniforms whose actual identity was disputed. Victor Velasquez, a trade union official (arrested in 1988) has not been seen since, despite government claims that he has been released.

The lives of Honduran trade unionists became no more secure as the 1980s passed into the 1990s. There were a number of killings and bombings in 1989. In May 1990 Francisco Bonilla, President of the Social Security workers' trade union was shot dead, and in June R. A. Brisero, former leader of the bank workers suffered the same fate at the hands of the "Triple A" death squad.

A series of strikes in 1989 were held by members of the public health workers' union and also by municipal workers' union members. There were 37 major strikes in all during the year, 31 of them in the public sector. President Azcona's last months in office were greatly occupied by interventions in disputes, including his eventual success in persuading the country's teachers to return to work, but only after they had staged the longest (81-day) strike in Honduran history.

Trade unionism. There are three major centres of Honduran trade unionism. The largest is the Honduran Workers' Confederation (CTH) with perhaps 160,000 members. The second largest is the General Confederation of Labour (CGT) which is closely linked with the Nationalists, and had two major leaders elected to the Congress as a result of the swing to that party in November 1989. Estimates of its size diverge widely from 65,000 to twice that number. The United Federation of Honduran Workers (FUTH) claims a membership of 25–30,000, and is affiliated to the WFTU. There are two smaller centres, the Federation of Honduran Workers (FITH) formed by FUTH dissidents, the Federation of Co-operatives of Agrarian Reform of Honduras (FECORAH) and the Co-ordinating Council of Peasant Organizations (COCOCH).

Central General de Trabajadores (CGT)
General Confederation of Labour

Address. Ba. La Ronda, No. 815, 9a Av. (a dos cuadras del Hotel la Ronda contiguo a Imprenta Morazán), Tegucigalpa DC

Leadership. Oscar Escalante, Marco Tulio Cruz (joint secretaries-general)

Membership. 65,000.

History and character. The Federación Auténtica Sindical de Honduras (FASH) was founded in 1963 with the backing of the regional Christian trade union organization CLASC (now known as CLAT), and the CGT developed from this in 1972 (with FASH as a component of the organization). The CGT is closely linked to the Nationalists who assumed power after the 1989 elections. In those elections, both secretaries-general obtained Congressional seats. Though it still includes among its members the National Peasants' Union (the 40,000 strong UNC), this organization has acted independently following a split between the Nationalist-oriented Marcial Caballero and a dissident movement headed by Lucas Aguilera.

Affiliates. The CGT includes among its components the Federación Auténtica Sincidal de Honduras (FASH), the Unión Nacional de Campesinos (National Peasants' Union, UNC), the Trade Union Federation of the South (Federación Sindical del Sur, FESISUR), the Federación Nacional de Pobladores (shanty dwellers), and various occupational federations. The Unión Nacional de Campesinos Auténticos de Honduras, a peasants' organization, is closely linked to the CGT.

International affiliations. WCL; CLAT.

205

Confederación de Trabajadores de Honduras (CTH)
Honduras Workers' Confederation

Address. Aptdo. Postal 720, Tegucigalpa
Phone. 22-42-43
Cables. CTH HONDURAS
Leadership. Mariano de Jesús González (president); Andrés Víctor Artiles (secretary general)
Membership. Claims 160,000.
History and character. The CTH is the largest union centre in Honduras and was founded in 1964. Its largest constituent federations are the Federation of Trade Unions of Northern Honduras (FESINTRAH), the country's most powerful federation led by Mario Quintanilla with perhaps 50,000 members, many of them employed by American fruit companies; the Central Federation of Unions of Free Workers of Honduras (FECESITLIH) with 16,000 members, a mainly public sector organization; the Federation of National Maritime Unions of Honduras (FESIMANH); and the National Association of Honduran agricultural workers (ANAHC) which claims 80,000 members. In the 1989 elections the CTH President González was elected as a Congress Deputy for the Nationalist Party, while the leader of ANAHC is a Deputy for the social democratic Innovation and Unity Party (PINU-SID).
International affiliations. ICFTU; ORIT.

Federación Unitaria de Trabajadores de Honduras (FUTH)
United Federation of Honduran Workers

Address. Av Cervantes N 1219, Aptdo. Postal 1663, Barrio la Plazuela, Tegucigalpa DC
Phone. 226-349
Leadership. Hector Hernández (president); Roger Barbados (general secretary).
Membership. 25–30,000
History and character. FUTH was founded in 1981 and had links with the left-wing electoral alliance of the Frente Patriótico Hondureño. It is strongly opposed to the pro-United States orientation of the government, and participates in radical politics through the Co-ordinating Committee of Popular Organizations (CCOP).
Affiliated Unions:

1. **Brewery Workers (STIBYS)**

2. **Council for the Development of Women Agricultural Workers (CODIMCA)**

3. **Electricity Workers (STENEE)**

4. **National Central of Farm Workers (CNTC)**

5. **Organization of Honduran Farmers** (OCH, which split from the CNTC and held its first Congress in July 1989)

6. **Organization of Honduran Farmworkers (CNTC)**

7. **Professional Association of Honduran Educators (COPEMH)**

8. **Professional Association of Honduran Teachers (COLPROSUMAH-AUTENTICO)**

9. **University Workers (SITRAUNAH)**

10. **Water Workers (SITRASANAA)**

International affiliation. WFTU.

Smaller organizations

Independent Federation of Honduran Workers (FITH)

Leadership. Israel Salinas.

Membership. 10,000 members in 14 unions.

History and character. FITH was formed by a breakaway from FUTH and aspires to form an umbrella confederation of labour, the Unitary Confederation of Workers (CUTH), though it has not yet obtained legal recognition of this.

Federation of Co-operatives of Agrarian Reform of Honduras (FECORAH)

Leadership. Nahum Calix
Membership. 22,000.

Co-ordinating Council of Peasant Organizations (COCOCH)

History and character. COCOCH evolved in 1988 from the National Council of Workers and Farmers (CONOCH).

Hungary

Capital: Budapest

Population: 10,375,000
(1990)

Political system. Hungary became a republic in 1946, and after the Communist Party (later merged into the Hungarian Worker's Party) gained control in 1947, a people's republic was declared in 1949, with a Constitution vesting all power in the working people. In the early to mid-1950s there was a partial political and economic liberalization. However, increasing internal unrest in 1956 culminated in October of that year in Soviet and other Warsaw Pact military intervention. After a period of consolidation there has more recently again been both political and economic reform. Since 1983 a choice of candidates has been mandatory in parliamentary and local council elections, although all have to accept the programme of the Patriotic People's Front (PPF) which unites social organizations behind the policies of the Hungarian Socialist Workers' Party (HSWP—the successor to the Hungarian Workers' Party).

Political change and economic liberal reforms accelerated in the middle 1980s, and when the communist structures collapsed in other Eastern European countries, Hungary's reform process was well advanced. Nevertheless, like them it dismantled many structures in 1989 and 1990, including that of the trade unions. Hungary is expected to be the first Eastern European country to join the European Community.

Economy. Under the 1949 Constitution (as amended) most means of production and most of the arable land were owned by the state, by public bodies or by co-operative organizations, and all natural resources, means of communications, banks, mines and major industrial plants were the property of the state. However, means of production could be privately owned (although private enterprise was not allowed to run counter to the public interest) and members of co-operative farms were permitted to cultivate household plots.

Agriculture accounts for about 15 per cent of net material product and industry for about 50 per cent. Around half of Hungary's foreign trade is with other countries of Comecon, while West Germany is the major Western trading partner. Tourism is an important source of foreign exchange.

A "new economic mechanism" was introduced in 1968 designed to reduce centralized planning, increase freedom for individual enterprises and relate earnings more directly to the profitability of enterprises. Further measures became effective in 1982 increasing the scope of activity of small enterprises, particularly in the private and co-operative sectors, and in 1985 measures were introduced which aimed at developing economic self-management, including the election of managers within enterprises. Among features of a stabilization programme approved in 1987 were a planned expansion of the private sector and the encouragement of competition among private and state companies.

Since 1989 Hungary has made rapid progress towards a market economy, and has a far-reaching programme of privatization. Ministers proclaim their intention to sell off 60 per cent of the state's businesses in the three years to 1993, accelerating a process which began with the sale of state bonds in 1983, and this in turn has forced unions to re-organize, for example in Posts and Telecommunications. A Stock Market has been established under 1990 legislation. In May 1991 the government opened up state industry to hostile bids in order to speed its return to market. Inflation remained a problem the same year, running at 35 per cent and inhibiting convertibility of the *forint*. Hungary joined GATT in 1973 and the IMF and the World Bank in 1982. .

System of industrial relations. Hungary ratified ILO Conventions No. 87 (Freedom of Association and Protection of the Right of Organize, 1948) and No. 98 (Right to Organize and Collective Bargaining, 1949) in 1957, i.e. shortly after the suppression of the independent workers' councils formed outside the single trade union structure. However, Hungary's Constitution did not prohibit the formation of trade unions outside this structure, provided that they undertook to protect the socialist society and to pursue its construction. Much of the industrial relations' framework of the communist era has been dismantled.

Trade unionism. Trade unions developed from the 1860s onwards under the Austro-Hungarian Empire despite episodes of repression, and in 1891 the Social Democratic Party established the first Central Trade Union Council (which was put on a permanent basis in 1899, and from which the Central Council of Hungarian Trade Unions, SZOT, claimed descent). Following World War I and the abortive declaration of a communist republic in 1919 (which was followed by some months of a social democrat Provisional Trade Union Government), left-wing influence in the trade unions was crushed by the government of Nicholas Horthy between 1920 and 1944, and unions were banned from many sectors of the economy. After World War II communist control was progressively consolidated in the unions as in the state and in October 1948 the Trade Union Council became the Central Council of Hungarian Trade Unions (SZOT) and basic trade union structure was established. Independent workers' councils sprang up briefly in 1956, when there was a general strike against the Soviet-led intervention. The economic reforms of 1968 were not reflected in changes in the trade unions, the government fearing any repetition of the events of 1956, but substantial changes occurred in the 1980s even before the collapse of communism.

The role of trade unionism changed from the early 1980s to complement the general liberalizing and decentralizing of the economy and also partly to pre-empt any such development as Polish Solidarity. In broad terms the effect of the various changes appears to have been to reduce the administrative and quasi-governmental powers of the unions but to have more clearly defined their role as a separate social force concerned with the representation of worker's interests.

According to SZOT, its affiliates operated as "organizationally autonomous organizations under the principled and political guidance of the revolutionary, Marxist-Leninist party of the working class (i.e. the HSWP)", both to give expression to the workers' demands and to "organize work movements to promote the achievement of economic aims". Under this definition the trade unions were not "independent" of the Party or the government but were "autonomous" and were to play a critical role. Before 1956 the Party in practice exerted total direct control over the unions, but the relationship had now become more complex, and the trade unions could influence policy within limits.

The multi-centred trades unionism of Hungary in 1991 reflects the greater length of its reform process. An ILO Mission to the country reported in 1984 that they had the impression of "a country in the process of rapid change". The trades unions, far from being immune to this process, were in a competitive situation at least a year before the old East European régimes had begun to collapse, and had already embarked on a process of internal change.

In place of the monopolistic SZOT there now stands the Confederation of Hungarian Trade Unions (MSzOSz), the strongest centre, with 100 affiliates, 3,600,000 members, and controlling most of SZOT's assets. The Democratic League of Independent Trade Unions (FSzDL) was initiated by the Democratic Trade Union of Scientific Workers (TDDSZ) in 1988. It had 130,000 members in 1991. The March 1990 Congress which formed MSzOSz in place of SZOT was not, however, attended by all of SZOT's affiliates. About 10 unions stayed out and formed the Co-operation Forum, comprising some 500,000 workers; their objection was to what they saw as continuity between SZOT and MSzOSz while they suspected that the FSzDL had political links with the Free Democratic Party. As in 1956 workers' councils emerged during the events of 1989: they have formed a federation and have sympathetic contacts with the governing Democratic Forum. A further centre, with the title Workers' Solidarity, has also been formed. Moreover some unions, among them the Chemical Workers' Federation, have declined to affiliate to any centre.

Confederation of Hungarian Trade Unions (MSzOSz)

Address. 1068 Budapest 6, Dózsa György utca 84/B
Phone. 228-016
Telex. 22-58-61
Leadership. Lazslo Sandor (president); Sandor Nagy (general secretary)
Membership. 3,600,000.
History and character. MSzOSz derives its organizational base from SZOT which traced its origins back to the Trade Union Council formed in the 1890s (*see above*).

There were 19 industrial unions affiliated to the SZOT. Organization on the "one enterprise, one union" principle, so that membership included the whole workforce including managers (who commonly participate actively in union affairs). The basic unit was the trade union section (typically at the workplace level) and its supreme body was the meeting of shop stewards (or the assembly of all members where the branch is small) and the executive body was the trade union committee (elected by the shop stewards). Shop stewards were elected by subgroups of employees within the enterprise. The basic trade union bodies formed district trade unions bodies and these combined nationally to form the 19 industrial unions. These 19 unions in turn formed a confederation whose two main bodies were the Hungarian Trade Union Congress. The principles of "democratic centralism" applied, i.e. the trade union organs were elected at all levels (with practices varying as to whether voting is secret), and subordinate bodies were bound by the decisions of superior bodies. This latter principle, also applied in other eastern European countries, effectively invested supreme power in the central council, SZOT. Representatives other than the "official" nominees were sometimes elected at lower levels, but such occurrences were not usual at high levels.

The role of the 19 affiliated national industrial unions was weakened by the process of decentralization of powers, particularly in the area of collective bargaining. Tibor Baranyai stated in June 1986 that many of the previous functions of the national unions were to be reduced or abolished, and they would play a new role of providing local unions with information, assistance and advice. Furthermore, some additional occupation trade unions would be set up as quasi-independent organizations within the structure of the existing 19 unions, as was already the case with the Federation of

Art Workers' Unions (which united seven unions), and prototype representative bodies on these lines had already been elected by the congresses of the national trade unions.

The SZOT worked directly with government in the detailed discussion and formulation of social and economic policies, and in cases of severe disagreement the Party acted as arbiter. This relationship was conditioned by the assumption that the SZOT was not "independent" of the government or the HSWP, but was "autonomous". SZOT officials attended sessions of the Council of Ministers and the State Planning Committee and had consultations rights.

From the beginning of 1988 disillusionment with the impotence of the SZOT in the face of rising unemployment and falling living standards caused by the government's stabilization policies, together with the introduction from Jan. 1 of the check-off system for union dues, prompted many resignations from the official unions; over 300,000 members left between January and March 1988 alone. Trade unionists were reported to be particularly aggrieved by the failure of the SZOT to make an effective protest against the rise in inflation and the fall in real wages arising from the stabilization programme, and by its failure to challenge a legal loophole which allowed enterprises to avoid paying severance pay to redundant workers; redundant workers received severance pay only if at least 10 workers were dismissed at a time, so enterprises were simply announcing redundancies in batches of nine. New regulations closing this loophole took effect on April 1, 1988.

Far-reaching changes in Hungary's political leadership were reflected in the SZOT. Sándor Gáspár was removed as the SZOT chairman and Tibor Baranyai as the SZOT general secretary in June 1988, shortly after Gáspár had relinquished his membership of the HSWP politburo in a purge of conservatives from the party leadership. Previously, conflicts within the political leadership over economic reforms were assumed to be behind reshuffles and suspected power struggles at the top of the SZOT, notably in the period between December 1983, when Gáspár was replaced as SZOT general secretary by Lajos Méhes (hitherto Minister of Industry) and given the largely honorary title of chairman, and March 1985, when Méhes was replaced by Baranyai and the office of chairman was declared pre-eminent in leading the work of the SZOT council. Upon the removal of Gáspár and Baranyai, Sándor Nagy was named as general secretary and the pre-eminence of this office was restored (Gáspár was not replaced as chairman); but the SZOT leadership was no longer represented at the highest levels of the HSWP.

In 1989, under its new leaders, SZOT strived for further reform. The constitution was suspended in March in line with the wishes of a December 1988 conference. The old branch structures were dismantled, trade union elections were held, and the central leadership became a provisional council whose task was to organize an extraordinary congress. Some outside forces such as the FSzDL wished to radicalize SZOT's affiliates. When workers' councils reappeared they did so entirely outside the SZOT structure. Some SZOT affiliates decided their atttitude to it would depend on the outcome of the Congress but other affiliates doubted the reform process and were unwilling to participate in the preparation of the Congress. In this respect, FSzDL went further, and challenged SZOT's right to continue in sole control of the movement's assets.

The Congress met in March 1990 with substantial, but not comprehensive attendance. It decided to dissolve SZOT and create MSzOSz and to finish SZOT's affiliation to the WFTU. The leadership remained unchanged and the new organization, with about 100 affiliates, claims the adherence of 3,600,000 workers.

Affiliated unions and structure: Approximately 100 affiliates including:

Association of Art Workers' Unions, 1068 Budapest 6, Gorkij Fasor 38.
Phone: 1428-372.
Leadership: Tibor Simó (general secretary).

Confederation of Foodworkers' Unions (EDOSZ), 1068 Budapest 6, Gorkij Fasor 44.
Phone: (1) 228 090. Telex: 22 32 41. Fax: 142 5374.
Leadership: Bela Vanek (general secretary).
Membership 16 affiliated organizations holding 230,000 members.
History and character: The Union held its 48th Congress on Jan. 25, 1991.
Affiliated organizations: Union of Poultry, Wine Industry, Sugar Industry, Tobacco Industry, Sweets Industry, Corn and Milling Industry, Canned Food Industry, Vegetables Oil Industry, Baking

Industry, Brewing Industry, Distilling Industry, Educational Institution, Milk Industry, Refreshing Industry Workers.

International affiliation: IUFAW.

Federation of Trade Unions of Hungarian Posts and Communications Workers, 1146 Budapest 14, Cházár András utca 13.

Phone: 1428 777. Telex: 221912. Fax: 1214 018.

Leadership: Enikó Gricser (president).

Membership: 69,650 in four unions.

Publication: *Journal of Posts and Communications Employees.*

Affiliated unions: Trade Union of Postal Employees (56,270 members); Free Trade Union of Telecommunications Employees (8,140); Trade Union of Broadcasting Employees (1,660); Trade Union of Infrastructural Units (3,570).

History and character: At the beginning of 1990 the Hungarian PTT was split into three independent companies: Hungarian Telecommunications Co., Hungarian Posts Co. and Hungarian Broadcasting Co. This change was followed by the re-organization of the unified trade union as well: independent unions were formed, which held their congress in June. On June 16, 1990 the Federation of Trade Unions of Hungarian Posts and Communications Employees was established as a legal successor of the former Union of Postal Workers. Its main goals are to represent and defend the interests of the affiliated unions' membership in conditions of imminent privatization and market competition in Hungary.

Hungarian Graphical Workers' Union, 1085 Budapest 8, Kölcsey utca 2.

Phone: (36) 1 1142 413. Telex: 20 2612. Fax: (36) 1 11342 524.

Leadership: Andras Barsony (president).

Membership: 22,790 in 57 local branches.

Publication: *Typographia* (montly).

International affiliation: IGF.

Hungarian Union of Teachers, 1068 Budapest 6, Gorkij Fasor 10.

Phone: 228-099.

Leadership: Dr József Voksán (general secretary).

National Mineworkers' Union, 1068 Budapest 6, Gorkij Fasor 46–48.

Union of Agricultural, Water Supply and Forestry Workers, 1066 Budapest 6, Jókai utca 2–4.

Union of Civil Servants, 1088 Budapest 8, Pushkin utca 4. (*see also* entry for the Democratic Trade Union of Scientific Workers, TDDSZ).

Phone: 188-900; 382-651.

Leadership: Dr Enclre Szabó (general secretary).

Union of Clothing Workers, 1077 Budapest 7, Almássy Tér 1.

Union of Health Workers, 1051 Budapest 5, Münnich Ference utca 32.

Union of Leather Workers, 1062 Budapest 6, Bajza utca 24.

Union of Railway Workers, 1068 Budapest 6, Benczur utca 41.

Phone: 1424 184. Telex: 2268 19. Fax: 1 228 818.

Leadership: Papp Pal (president).

Membership: 170,000.

Publication: *Hungarian Railway Worker* (fortnightly).

Union of Road Haulage and Transport Workers, 1428 Budapest 8, Köztársaság Tér. 3.

Phone: 139-046.

Leadership: Gyula Moldován (general secretary).

Union of Textile Workers, 1068 Budapest 6, Rippl-Rónai utca 2.

Phone: (36) 1428 196.

Leadership: Tarmas Keleti (secretary-general).

Membership: 100,145 in 168 branches.

Publication: *Textile Worker.*

Union of Workers in Building, Wood and Building Materials Industries, 1068 Budapest 6, Dózsa György utca 84/B.

Union of Workers in Commerce, Finance and Catering Industries, 1066 Budapest 6, Jókai utca 6.

Union of Workers in Iron, Metal and Electrical Energy Industries, 1086 Budapest 8, Koltói Anna utca 5-7.
Phone: 135-200. Telex: 224791 vfszh.
Leadership: Laszlo Paszternak (general secretary).

International affiliation: The affiliation of the SZOT lapsed with its dissolution.

Independent League of Democratic Trade Unions (FSzDL)

Address. 45 Gorkis' Fasot, Budapest 1071
Phone. (361) 142 6957
Fax. (361) 142 8143
Leadership. Pal Forgacs (president)
Membership. Claimed 130,000 in January 1991.
Affiliated unions and structure. One hundred and twenty-eight unions with 30 applications pending (January 1991).

Tudományos Dolgozók Demokratikus Szakszervezete (TDDSZ)
Democratic Trade Union of Scientific Workers

Address. P.O. Box 526, Budapest 114, 1538 Hungary
Phone. (361) 142 8438
Fax. (361) 142 8438
Membership. 5,500.
History and character. The TDDSZ was formed on May 14, 1988, by 1,028 academics and research scientists who had left the SZOT-affiliated Union of Civil Servants in disillusionment at the latter's failure to take action against cuts of up to 25 per cent in state funding for scientific research announced at the end of 1987. At the same time one of the main goals of the TDDSZ was to make an example in how to organize an independent trade union in Hungary. The TDDSZ was taking part for the struggle to define the new strike law in Hungary, and since then has been active to influence the new legislature to build up the social dimension of the new Hungarian state. The main means for that is lobbying (TDDSZ has more than 50 members in the parliament in different parties), and with expertise using the tripartite negotiations with the government and the employers. In the crisis situation, during which the whole Hungarian system is being restructured the TDDSZ is trying to defend the interest of its members and the interests of research as such.
Structure. The TDDSZ is non-hierarchical and has a 45-member national assembly and a seven-member executive board. For the separate fields of organization it has an academic assembly (co-ordinating the work of the members who are employed by the Hungarian Academy of Sciences), a higher education board, a public collection board, and a board co-ordinating the work done at private enterprises.

In 1990 FSzDL formed some of its affiliates into federations for transport, health and mines. In 1991 regional offices were established.

International affiliations. None, but in 1991 FSzDL acknowledged financial help from the American Free Trade Union Institute, ICFTU, CISL and the Friedrich Ebert Stifturng.

Co-operation Forum

Membership. Around 500,000 affiliated workers.
History and character. Formed in 1990 by 10 mostly white collar unions from the public service sector. They preferred to stay aloof from MSzOSz, seeing in it a contiuation of SZOT.

Independent Unions

Pedagogusok Demokratikus Szakszervezete
Democratic Trade Union of Teachers

History and character. Established at a meeting in Budapest attended by some 300 teachers on Nov. 26, 1988, the unions aims "to carry out comprehensive reform in education and to achieve autonomy for schools". It declared its independence from the SZOT-affiliated Hungarian Union of Teachers, but provided for dual membership.

Hungarian Press Union

Address. 1085 Budapest, Berkocsis 1
Phone. (00) 11141 407
Telex. 202 612
Fax. (00) 134 2524
Leadership. Janos Berenyi (president); György Lepies (general secretary).
Membership. 9,500.
History and character. The SAJTÓSZAKSZERVEZET (Hungarian Press Union) is an independent union founded by a congress in May 1989. (Formerly it was together with the printers' and paperworkers' union.) It is a country-wide organization with 9,500 members. About 1,500 out of them are professional journalists working in the printed media. Even though, the number of the journalist members is growing rapidly, the majority of members are office clerks, typists, and other workers in editorial offices and publishing firms. Therefore the HPU is not a pure journalist organization.

The main scope of activity of the HPU is bargaining over collective agreements. The HPU made a model contract. It helps its members at negotiations with the employers.

Affiliated unions. The HPU has no affiliated unions but in January 1991 three independent unions (HPU, Hungarian Broadcasting Workers Union and Union of the Hungarian Television Workers) founded a federation called the Federation of Hungarian Media Unions. The postal address is the same as the HPU. The Media Unions' first elected president is Dr. György Lepies.

Mozgókép Demokratikus Szakszervezete (MODESZ)
Motion Picture Democratic Trade Union

Membership. 500 (October 1988).
History and character. The MODESZ held its inaugural meeting on Oct. 4, 1988. This followed the publication of a declaration at the beginning of September by 88 professionals in the film, television and video industries who were "aggrieved by the continuous deterioration of their professional and working conditions" and by the "formal and inefficient" pay bargaining system within the SZOT-affiliated Association of Art Workers' Unions. The MODESZ defines itself as a grass-roots, democratic, autonomous trade union. At the inaugural meeting it was decided to seek relations with the other sectoral trade unions and the SZOT.

Structure. The MODESZ is made up of autonomous units, whose work is co-ordinated by the Board, which cannot, however, pass binding decisions.

Union of Chemical Workers

Address. 1068 Budapest 6, Benczur utca 45
Membership. 140,000.
History and character. This former affiliate of SZOT refused to join the MSzOSz.

Union of Municipal Workers and Local Industries

Address. 1068 Budapest 6, Benczur utca 43.
Affiliated unions.

Union of Communal Building Management Enterprise Workers, 1319 Budapest 62. Pf. 201.
Secretary: Mrs. László Hornyák.

Union of Communal Workers, 1319 Budapest 62. Pf. 201.
Secretary: Dr. Zsolt Pék.

Union of Public Service Workers in Water Supply, 1319 Budapest 62. Pf. 201.
Secretary: Sándor Zsiros.

Union of Settlement, Industrial and Service Workers, 1319 Budapest 62. Pf. 201.
Secretary: Zoltán Szikszai.

Union of Workers in the Co-operative Industry, 7107 Szekszárd, Beloiannisz u. 9–11.
Secretary: Mrs. Lajos Krasznai

Union of Workers in Industrial Co-operatives, 1319 Budapest 62. Pf. 201.
Secretary: Mrs. Béla Szücs.

Iceland

Capital: Reykjavik   **Population: 240,000**

Political system. Iceland is a multi-party presidential republic, currently governed by a coalition of the liberal-conservative Independence Party (IP), the centrist Progressive Party (PP) and the Social Democratic Party (SDP). It is a member of NATO.

Economy. Iceland's economy is heavily dependent on the fishing industry which in the late 1980s generated over 70 per cent of export earnings. In 1987, a series of austerity measures were introduced, including tax reform and a succession of devaluations, aimed at reducing inflation (which in 1983 had reached over 80 per cent), budget deficit and foreign debt.

Trade unionism. Iceland has a highly organized workforce. The largest organization of trade unions in Iceland is the Icelandic Federation of Labour (ASÍ), to which 63,000 workers are affiliated either directly or through their unions, including nearly all private sector employees. The largest union organization outside the ASÍ is the Federation of State and Municipal Employees (BSRB) which had just over 15,000 members in early 1991. Apprentices are represented by the Icelandic Federation of Apprentices; collective bargaining for apprentices, however, is conducted through the ASÍ. Iceland ratified ILO Convention No. 87 (Freedom of Association and Protection of the Right to Organize, 1948) in 1950 and Convention No. 98 (Right of Organize and Collective Bargaining, 1949) in 1952. Angered over the government's interventions in industrial relations, the ASÍ reported it to the ILO Committee on Freedom of Association in 1991.

System of industrial relations. In Iceland two large centralized organizations face each other, the ASÍ normally having a counterpart in the shape of the Confederation of Icelandic Employers (CIE). Until 1988 the normal pattern of wage regulation was for these two to negotiate a national framework agreement to be followed by federation level bargaining. But in the years immediately before this, dissatisfaction mounted. There was alarm in government circles at the way in which wage drift was taking increases far above the settlement level. There was concern among the unskilled that they had accrued little benefit from wage drift which permitted differentials to stretch to their disadvantage. Meanwhile the ASÍ leadership was criticized from the Left for settling at too low a level in the national framework talks.

These combined pressures led to the withdrawal of the ASÍ from national framework talks early in 1988 in order to allow federation level negotiations to the consternation of the CIE which (unusually for an employers' central) preferred national bargaining. Disaggregation led to separate agreements being reached for the unskillled, though not without a series of strikes, at which the membership registered their dissatisfaction. The CIE found it more difficult to reach agreements with the skilled workers' unions and federations, and the government intervened in May 1988 with a labour relations law which prohibited strikes for 11 months and impelled unions to make an agreement. Later in the year further laws froze wages and prices over a temporary period, leading to the ASÍ being moved to complain to the ILO Committee on Freedom of Association.

Althydusamband Íslands (ASÍ)
Icelandic Federation of Labour

Address. Grensásveg 16A, 108 Reykjavík

Phone. 91-83044

Leadership. Ásmundur Stefánsson (president); Ragna Bergmann; Oln Fritriksson (vice-presidents).

Membership. Represents about 63,000 workers (including 27,000 women). Approximately 30,000 employees belong to organizations not affiliated to the Federation.

History and character. The ASÍ was established on a permanent basis in 1916, after an attempt to create a central organization in 1907 had foundered after three years; the federation was organizationally part of the Social Democratic Party until 1940, when it became (as it remains) an independent trade union federation without political ties.

The ASÍ established a Workers' Educational Association in 1969, and it also has its own art gallery and travel bureau, and a share in a co-operative trade union bank.

Structure. The supreme authority is the quadrennial congress, to which each union and federation sends delegates on the basis of its numerical strength. The congress elects a president, two vice-presidents and 18 other members of the executive council and 18 other members to sit on the national council. The national council is the supreme authority between congresses, and consists of the 18 members elected by the congress, members of the executive council, and representatives from the national federations and larger individual unions outside the national federations. The executive council comprises the president, vice-presidents and 18 others and runs the day-to-day affairs of the ASÍ. The federation is financed mainly by pro rata contributions from the member unions, but receives government funding to support some of its cultural, educational and other activities. At the 1988 Convention its president was re-elected for his third consecutive term.

Affiliated federations. Construction Workers' Federation; Federation of Electrical Industry Workers; Federation of Icelandic Seamens' Unions; Federation of Industrial Workers; Federation of Lorry Drivers; Icelandic General and Transport Workers' Federation; Icelandic Metal Workers' Federation; Icelandic Shop and Office Workers' Federation; Hotel and Restaurant Federation.

Originally individual trades unions were direct members of the ASÍ; after about 1950, however, unions in a number of sectors organized their own national federations, and now have indirect membership in the ASÍ through those federations. Some 25 unions remain directly affiliated to the ASÍ; these unions are found particularly in the services sector like the Union of Women Assistants in Hospitals, and the Air Hostesses' Union, and others.

Publications. *Vinnan* (10 times per year, circulation 10,000); *ASÍ News Letter* (about 20 per year, circulation 2,000).

International affiliations. ETUC; ICFTU; TUAC; NFS; North Atlantic Labour Movement.

Bandalag Starfsmanna Rikis og Baeja (BSRB)
Federation of State and Municipal Employees

Address. Grettisgata 89, 105 Reykjavík

Phone. 354 1 626688

Fax. 354 1 629106

Leadership. Ogmundut Jonasson (chairman and general secretary)

Membership. 15,068 (1991).

History. Founded 1942. At its 1988 Convention the BSRB elected TV reporter Ogmundun Jonasson to replace Kristjan Thorlacius who had held the post of chairman for nearly 30 years.

International affiliations. ICFTU; ETUC; TUAC; NFS.

Publications. Newsletter every two months.

India

Capital: New Delhi   **Population: 844,000,000**

Political system. The Union of India, comprising 25 self-governing states and seven union territories, is under its Constitution (with amendments which came into force in 1977) "a sovereign socialist secular democratic republic". The legislative field is divided between the Union and the states, the former possessing exclusive powers to make laws on foreign affairs, defence, citizenship and trade with other countries. Central legislative power is vested in parliament, consisting of the President (who appoints a Prime Minister and a Council of Ministers), the indirectly-elected Council of States (*Rajya Sabha*, the upper house) and the directly elected House of the People (*Lok Sabha*). Elections to the *Lok Sabha* were held in December 1984 and resulted in an overwhelming majority for the Congress (I) Party, which held power under Prime Minister Rajiv Gandhi until 1989. In that year's elections Congress (I) left office after losing more than half its seats and was succeeded by a Janata Dal coalition government under V. P. Singh. When Singh himself lost office following a split in his party, there was a brief and unstable government under Chandra Shekhar with Congress (I) support. After its collapse in March 1991 new elections were called for May but were postponed following the assassination of Rajiv Gandhi during the campaign.

Economy. Some two-thirds of India's working population are in the agricultural sector (including tea, rubber and coffee). Despite the prominence of its agricultural sector, India ranks among the 10 leading industrial nations in the world. The main emphasis of the seventh five-year plan (1985–90) was on improving the energy sector, the inadequate performance of which has contributed towards industrial production shortfalls. India has the fourth largest coal reserves in the world as well as considerable reserves of bauxite and other ores, while about half of total petroleum needs are met from domestic sources. The government of Rajiv Gandhi pursued an economic liberalization policy with the aim of modernizing existing industries, introducing new electronic and computer-based industries and curbing the "black economy".

Towards the end of his term of office the Indian economy recovered substantially in 1988 and 1989 and growth for the decade as a whole exceeded an annual average of 5 per cent the best achievement since Independence. However performance across the economy was uneven: industrial production only picked up half way through 1988 as the demand from the agricultural sector for machinery began to revive: in rural areas some 160,000 units were classified as "sick" (heavily in debt) by the official Economic Survey.

The low figure for India's civilian employment (25,300,000 in 1988) reveals the huge extent of the country's informal economy. Nearly 13,000,000 worked in industry that year, 1,400,000 in agriculture, and 11,200,000 in services; services accounted for more than 40 per cent of GNP, a larger contribution than agriculture which is, of course, mainly subsistence. The real proportion of Indians relying on some form of agriculture for their income, though falling, is still not far below 70 per cent; a majority of the workforce on a broad definition works in the countryside. Inflationary pressures are a major fear, and India—though its credit is good—has a large and growing foreign debt.

System of industrial relations. India has ratified neither ILO Convention No. 87 (Freedom of Association and Protection of the Right to Organize, 1948) nor No. 98 (Right to Organize and Collective Bargaining, 1949). However, freedom of association has existed since the Trade Union Act of 1926 and collective bargaining and the right to strike both exist, although these have been increasingly restricted.

Protest against the Industrial Relations (Amendment) Bill. The Gandhi government's

217

Trade Unions and Industrial Relations (Amendment) Bill, which generated widespread protest, was seen by trade unions to be part of a systematic programme of "anti-union legislation". In August 1987, a National Campaign Committee of Trade Union Centres which included the All India Trade Union Congress (AITUC), the Bharatija Mazdool Samgh, the Hind Mazdoor Sabha (HMS) and the Centre of Indian Trade Unions (CITU), organized nationwide demonstrations against the government's proposed labour laws. Protests were voiced against the move "to restrict trade union rights" and appeals were made for the introduction of a minimum wage. In June 1988, members of the Upper House of Parliament, including the secretary-general of the All India Trade Union Congress, staged a walk-out in protest against the provisions of the Bill. In July 1988, Indian affiliates of both the WFTU and the ICFTU once again participated in a National Convention against the government's "Anti-Working Class Bills". Delegates at the Convention opposed the proposal to increase the minimum number of workers from seven to 10 before a union could be registered on the grounds that it infringed the right of associ- ation. The imposition of heavy penalties, including imprisonment, for "illegal" workers and for those who took part in "go slows", was also singled out as "an attack on the right to strike". The government's Industrial Disputes (Amendment) Bill was also criticized by international labour organizations. In August 1988, the WFTU secretariat, in a telegram to the Indian Prime Minister, described the government's Bill as "limiting the right of associ- ation and collective bargaining". It drew attention to the "excessive powers" granted to the authorities to "impose compulsory adjudication and restraints on the right to strike", and called upon the government to uphold international labour standards.

Unofficial strikes and demonstrations, often of a highly political nature, are frequent. These involve both white and blue collar workers, although the latter are reported to enjoy better union discipline and be capable of abiding more closely to agreements with employers. Most issues revolve around parity of pay, promotional opportunities and status.

India is a signatory of ILO Convention No. 100 on Equal Remuneration. The ILO's *Report of the Committee of Experts on the Application of Conventions and Recommendations* (1988) observed that although the Government had done something towards implementing the principles of the Convention, equal remuneration, particularly for women employed in traditional industries, still remained to be achieved in full. Indeed, the percentage and position of women in the workforce, both urban and rural, suggests that there is much room for improvement. Although there has been a slight increase in the overall proportion of women in the total workforce, the employment of women in mines, plantations and factories has declined. Their proportion of "marginal work", however, remains high. Generally, women workers earn about 50 per cent of what their male colleagues do in both urban and rural areas.

Nearly all agricultural workers (except in tea and other plantations), as well as domestic and casual workers are unorganized. The influence of organized labour generally is weakened by the high levels of unemployment and under-employment and availability of non-union casual labour. There are, however, some signs of the growing power of organized unions. In March 1987, the All India Overseas Bank Employees Union succeeded in obtaining significant amendments to an agreement on the introduction of technology in the Indian banking sector. These provide, among other things, a guarantee against staff redundancies incurred as a result of new technology and the right of pregnant women to refuse to work at computerized stations.

In general, the organized workers constitute a comparative élite, and the unions have done little to ameliorate the plight of the non-union masses in sweatshops, the informal economy and on the land. The plight of rural workers in particular is, however, now being taken up more vigorously not only by well-established organizations like the Indian National Trade Union Congress (INTUC), but also by lesser known bodies like the

Confederation of Indian Rural Workers' Unions (Hind Keth Mazdoor Sabha—HKMS) which is affiliated to the HMS. The Confederation has appealed for rural poverty and unemployment to be relieved not so much by aid and food hand-outs, but by the creation of job opportunities for the needy through a programme of extensive public works. India ratified ILO Convention No. 141 on Rural Workers' Organizations in 1977.

In March 1989 242,532 workers—mostly on the land—were reported to be bonded labourers, bound to work for their creditor until a debt is settled; the effect of a low rate of pay and high interest rates is such that bonded status is commonly life-long or even hereditary. Some of the worst cases are reported to occur in the northern states of Bihar and Uttar Pradesh where significant numbers of labourers are bonded as agricultural and construction workers. In western India, bonded labour exists in the tribal and semi-tribal belts of north Maharashtra, eastern Madhya Pradesh and in the sugar industries of south Gujarat. Although legislation in 1976 outlawed the practice of bonded labour, and the government itself claimed to have released and "rehabilitated" some 217,816 bonded labourers, it is clear that its eradication is as yet nowhere is sight.

The problem of child labour appears to be equally intractable. Although government legislation in 1986 prohibited the use of child labour, its enforcement has proved to be extremely difficult. A 1981 survey estimated that the use of child labour was higher in the state of Tamil Nadu than anywhere else in India. Latest official estimates suggest that there could be as many as 17,500,000 child labourers working in factories throughout the country. Widespread poverty and unemployment, both in urban and in rural areas, have ensured that children under the age of 15 continue to be employed. Urban child employment tends mostly to be concentrated in hotels and restaurants, building construction sites, automobile workshops, fireworks, match factories, and children are also widely used as domestic servants. In rural areas children are used in agriculture, herd-tending and the handloom industry. Children are also bonded. Statistics on child labour are virtually impossible to establish as much of it is either not recorded to avoid detection by the authorities, or escapes notice as in instances where a child is deemed not to be formally employed but simply "helping out". More recently, the government has come under increasing pressure to monitor the use of illegal child labour and to provide for more stringent regulation where it is known to exist. In response, the government has appointed a committee to monitor implementation of the 1986 Act, and introduced a programme designed to provide better educational training facilities for children, align children's wages with those of adults so as to reduce the incentive to employ children at lower wages, and to cover families of child workers under income and employment generating schemes.

Employer-union attitudes are commonly adversarial, and the government frequently acts as mediator, a role encouraged by the close association of many unions (notably those of INTUC) with the governing Congress Party. In recent years the Supreme Court of India has also sought to mediate between employers and workers as in the case of the Prakash Cotton Mills, where the Court ruled that the closure of the Mills did not, in itself, entitle employers to withhold compensation from employees.

Worker participation. The Industrial Disputes Act of 1947 made provision for the creation of works committees in every industrial establishment of more than 100 workers, and there have been other ventures in worker participation, including joint councils set up in 1975 during the Emergency (when normal trade unionism was suspended), and the recent establishment of "quality circles", based on Japanese concepts, in a few enterprises. Further initiatives were taken by the election of workers' representatives in public corporations like the Steel Authority of India, and in November 1987, by the election of workers' directors, representing executives, supervisors, skilled and unskilled workers, to the board of Coal India Limited.

The success of all such ventures has been very limited, however, reflecting: (i) the lack of effective powers given to such bodies in respect of the basic issues of wages, hours and conditions; (ii) the contrary tradition of management authoritarian-paternalism; (iii) the attitude of many unions that such participation was "class collaboration" and designed only to increase productivity; and (iv) the diversity—and often mutual hostility—of unions at plant level, particulary in places like Bombay where it has erupted in violence.

The 28th tripartite Indian Labour Conference was held in 1985, 14 years after the previous conference. Appeals to revive the Indian Labour Conference (ILC) and the Standing Labour Committee came from the All India Organization of Employers (AIOE) which sought an "effective forum" where employers may express their views and contribute to the solution of industrial and labour disputes. (India ratified ILO Convention No. 144 of 1976, providing for tripartite consultations, in 1978.)

In April 1990 the government finally convened the ILC and it appointed a bipartite committee to suggest a new industrial relations law. Its recommendations were submitted to the government in October but no action was taken before the national elections were called in March 1991. Two other government-sponsored measures, the *Participation of Workers in Management Bill* and a proposal for workers to share in the equity of undertakings were similarly stalled.

There was a decline in militancy in 1988 as compared to 1987 with 70 per cent of the days lost to disputes occurring in four states: West Bengal, Maharashtra, Tamil Nadu and Andhra Pradesh. The number of disputes was provisionally estimated at 1,502 for the year involving 1,010,000 workers and costing 30,500,000 days. This is a decline in days lost compared to the early 1980s, but the duration of disputes clearly increased over the decade.

Trade unionism. Illiteracy, caste and religious animosities inhibited the early development of trade unions. Such development was all the more slack as existing unions tended, at least until World War I, almost always to recruit members from a narrow labour aristocracy. The seasonal and migratory nature of much industrial labour as well as the control of workers through company housing, also contributed to a relatively weak trade union movement. In 1920, however, the All-India Trade Union Congress (AITUC) was formed; this remained the principal centre until after independence in 1947 when it became the focus of intense conflict between nationalists and communists. This stemmed from differences which had surfaced during the War when the Communist Party chose, against nationalist opinion, to support Britain's war effort. Having done so, its members were able not only to escape imprisonment, unlike their nationalist colleagues, but also effectively to gain control of the AITUC. The war-time split led the ruling Congress Party in 1947 to favour and sponsor the creation of a rival Indian National Trade Union Congress (INTUC).

The unions are highly-politicized, and the INTUC and AITUC both supported the Emergency declared from 1975–77 (despite the suspension of trade union rights and ban on strikes), in line with the position of the political parties with which they are associated, i.e. the Congress Party and the Communist Party of India (CPI). The high level of politicization, the lack of a sound mass base in many sectors, the looseness of ties between local and central unions, and the lack of adequate financial resources have reduced the organizational strength of the unions. Furthermore, there is no institutionalized system for the recognition of union, which in effect depends on union strength in a given plant and the attitude of the employer. The Industrial Relations (Amendment) Bill made few changes in this respect. Its recommendations for ascertaining which unions may be recognized as bargaining agents at workplaces based on membership figures drawn from "check-off" records, have been criticized by trade union leaders as "open to abuse" by employers.

National unity. All the national trade union centres took part in a "National Convention of Trade Unions Against Communalism" in New Delhi in May 1986. The convention, said to be the first time all the centres had ever united on a common platform, unanimously voted to hold a National Solidarity Day on Aug. 9, 1986, and adopted a resolution opposing the "growth of communal and fundamentalist organizations of various shades" and warned "the working class of the dangers posed by religious, casteist, linguistic, chauvinist and all other parochial elements", as seen in the extreme in the Punjab "where secessionist elements are trying to destroy the unity of the country".

The most recent estimate of trade union density, which put it at 24 per cent was made in 1985. Unfortunately there was no official trade union membership verification process between 1980 and 1989, and the impartiality of the procedure at the earlier date was challenged by the AITUC and CITU. It must be pointed out nonetheless that in every case the official figures put the numbers of unions and members affiliated to each centre below the centre's own claims. The results of the 1989 verification are expected at the end of 1992, but in the meanwhile membership continues to be a hotly contested matter. Nevertheless the broad trends are clear.

The Indian National Trade Union Congress (INTUC) is thought by many observers to be the largest union centre, claiming more than 5,000,000 members. It has strong and longstanding links with Congress (1) and is ICFTU-affiliated. The Bharatiya Mazdoor Sangh (BMS) is the second largest centre, claiming just over 4,000,000 members in 1989. It is inspired by the nationalist Hindu party RSS and disputes the membership base of the INTUC, claiming to have a larger following itself. Unusually for an Indian union centre, the BMS bars politicians from holding union office. The third largest centre is the Hind Mazdoor Sabha (HMS) claiming 2,800,000 members and founded by Socialists opposed to government domination of INTUC. It has a very strong industrial base and is also affiliated to the ICFTU.

The All-India Trades Union Congress (AITUC) was the national centre until Independence when Congress inspired the foundation of the INTUC: it is linked to the Communist Party of India (CPI) and has an WFTU affiliation. Much of its strength is among white collar workers. The Centre of Indian Trade Unions (CITU) is linked to the Chinese-oriented Communist Party of India the CPI(M). Dissidents in its ranks attempted a re-formation of the national centres under the title All-India Centre of Trade Unions (A-ICTU) but this appears not to have made progress. The National Labour Organization (NLO) originated in the Textile Labour Association founded by Mahatma Gandhi in Ahmedabad and is no longer a national force. The United Trades Union Congress (UNTUC) is marxist-oriented and split between two opposed factions.

There are also unaffiliated unions. Thus in 1972 the Indian Self-Employed Women's Association (SEWA) was formed: by 1989 its membership had grown to 40,000 and it had members in six states. Many other unions are not aligned to any centre.

All-India Centre of Trade Unions (A-ICTU)

Leadership. Mohan Punamia

History and character. The A-ICTU was formed in June 1986 under the leadership of former activists of the Centre of Indian Trade Unions (CITU), to "organize the most exploited and unorganized workers". The founding convention was attended by representatives of 300 unions claiming a membership of 1,400,000; those attending included a former CITU secretary and nine former members of the CITU's national committee. The convention denounced the leadership of the CITU for "wavering" as "attacks on the workers' struggles by the government and capitalists intensified", and accused the CITU of acting like a "government-sponsored union".

All-India Trade Union Congress (AITUC)

Address. 24 Canning Lane, New Delhi 110001
Phone. (11) 38-73-20; (11) 38-64-27

Telex. 3165982 CNS IN

Cables. AITUCONG NEWDELHI

Leadership. Chaturanan Mishra, MP (president); Indrajit Gupta, MP (general secretary; also a vice-president of the WFTU)

Membership. The 33rd congress in December 1986 was attended by delegates representing 3,622 affiliated unions with 3,470,000 members.

History and character. The AITUC was founded in 1920 and was the primary trade union centre until independence in 1947 and the formation of the INTUC. Since then it has been closely linked to the Communist Party of India (CPI), and states that it strives to "unite the entire working class and the working masses in their unions irrespective of caste, creed, religion, language" with policies based on "class struggle, anti-imperialism and international trade union solidarity". Its strongholds are Karnataka, Andhra Pradesh, Bihar, Gujarat, Delhi, and Punjab.

Discussion at the 1986 congress emphasized the need for a united approach by Indian trade unions (the congress being attended by representatives from the two ICFTU affiliates, the HMS and INTUC and other centres) to various questions, including the preservation of national unity, i.e. in the face of separatist movements in the Punjab and Assam. An All-India Convention of Public Sector Unions, held under AITUC auspices in late 1986, opposed steps by the government towards privatization of public sector enterprises as opening the way for trans-national corporations to compete with the public sector; the convention also opposed attempts to reduce bipartite bargaining in the public sector.

Publications. *Trade Union Record* (a fortnightly journal, in English); *ANTUC News* (a monthly journal in Hindi). Various state branches publish journals in their regional languages. Recent publications include *Trade Union Education* and *Defeat the Black Trade Union Bill.*

International affiliation. WFTU.

Bharatiya Mazdoor Sangh (BMS)

Address. Ram Naresh Bhavan, Tilak Gali, Paharganj Ganj, New Delhi

Telephone. (011) 523644

Leadership. Raman Bhai Shah (president); R. K. Bhakt (general secretary)

Membership. 4,079,449 in 2,821 affiliated unions (1989).

History and character. The Bharatiya Mazdoor Sangh (BMS) was founded in July 1955. It is said to have been closely associated at various times with the Indian People's Union (Jan Sangh) party, the Bharatiya Janata Party and the Hindu communalist organization, the Rashtriya Swayamsevak Sangh. The union's constitution, however, specifically bars politicians and the BMS itself has formally denied any political affiliations. Its general secretary has declared that the "BMS is not aligned with any political party and believes that the Trade Union movement should be above party politics". A Government of India survey in 1984 established the BMS as the second largest union in the country after the INTUC. The BMS played a prominent role in the opposition to the declaration of a state of Emergency in 1977, and since 1984, has been regularly included as part of the Indian delegation to the International Labour Conference. The BMS aims, among other things, "to establish ultimately a Bharatiya order of society"; "full employment"; "replacement of profit motive by service motive"; "labourization of industry" and "maximum industrialization". It has established the Vishwakarma Shramik Shiksha Sanstha, an institute for workers' education; Shram Shod Mandal, for Labour Research; Mahila Vibhag, a Women's Section; Akhil Bharatiya Krishi Mazdoor Sangh, for agricultural and rural workers; and the Government Employees' National Confederation. The BMS has adopted Sept. 17, the birthday of Vishwa Karama, a personality from the Hindu epics, as National Labour Day.

Affiliated Unions. (Figures relate to 1986):

1. **Bharatiya Railway Mazdoor Sangh (BRMS)** (14 unions).

2. **Bharatiya Pratiraksha Mazdoor Sangh (BPMS)** (civilian defence, 87 unions).

3. **National Organization of Bank Workers (NOBW).**

4. **National Organization of Insurance Workers (NOIW).**

5. **Bharatiya Post and Telegraph Employees' Federation (BPTEF)** (14 unions).

6. **Akhil Bharatiya Khadan Mazdoor Sangh (ABKMS)** (coal).

7. **Akhil Bharatiya Vidyut Mazdoor Sangh** (ABVMS) (72 unions, electricity).

8. **Bharatiya Parivahan Mazdoor Mahasangh** (11 federations, road transport).

9. **Bharatiya Engineering Mazdoor Sangh** (230 unions).

10. **Bharatiya Ispat Mazdoor Sangh** (iron and steel).

11. **Bharatiya Jute Mazdoor Sangh** (40 unions).

12. **Bharatiya Vastrodyog Karmachari Mahasangh** (textiles).

13. **Bharatiya Cement Mazdoor Sangh** (36 unions).

14. **Akhil Bharatiya Sugar Mill Mazdoor Sangh** (95 unions).

15. **Akhil Bharatiya Krishi Mazdoor Sangh** (landlesss agricultural labourers, 16 unions).

16. **Bharatiya Port and Dock Mazdoor Sangh.**

17. **Akhil Bharatiya Kendriya sarvajanik Pratisthan Mazdoor Maha Sangh** (72 public sector unions).

18. **National Organization of Bank Officers (NOBO).**

19. **Bharatiya Swayathshasi Karmachari Mahasangh** (local government, 200 unions).

20. **Akhil Bharatiya Bidi Mazdoor Sangh.**

21. **Akhil Bharatiya Khadan Mazdoor Sangh** (non-coal mines, 33 unions).

Publications. BMS Samachar (fortnightly, in Hindi); *Bhartiya Mazdoor* (monthly, in English).
International affiliations. None.

Centre of Indian Trade Unions (CITU)

Address. 6 Talkatora Road, New Delhi 110001
Phone. (11) 38-40-71
Cables. CITUCENT
Leadership. B. T. Ranadive (president); Samar Mukherjee (general secretary)
Membership. 1,800,000 in 3,000 affiliated unions.
History and character. The CITU was formed in 1970 and is closely linked to the Communist Party of India (Marxist). Many members and officials of the CITU were driven from their homes or killed in attacks by supporters of the Congress Party and other factions in the early and mid-1970s. A breakaway group formed the All-India Centre of Trade Unions (A-ICTU) in June 1986. The secretary, P. K. Ganguly has described the break as follows: "because of its consistent struggle against the anti-labour policy of the Congress Government, a semi-fascist offensive has been launched against the CITU and its cadres at Tripura after the Congress-TUJS alliance captured power from the left-front Government in the State in early February this year [1988] through a highly manipulated election. Its cadres are being murdered, the unions captured by anti-

socials and Congress supporters, houses of workers burned and unions are being deregistered". Jyoti Basu, the Chief Minister of West Bengal since 1977, is a CITU vice-president.

Publications. The Working Class (monthly, in English); *CITU Mazdoor* (monthly; in Hindu); *The Voice of Working Woman* (bimonthly, in English). Eight other journals in regional languages.

International affiliation. None.

Hind Mazdoor Sabha (HMS)
Indian Labour Association

Address. Nagindas Chambers, 167 P. D'Mello Road, Bombay 400038
Phone. (22) 26-21-85
Cables. HINDMAZDUR BOMBAY
Leadership. Samarendra Kundu (president); Umraomal Purohit (general secretary)
Membership. 2,800,000 in 1,800 affiliated unions.

History and character. The HMS was founded on Dec. 29, 1948, in rejection of the communist domination of the AITUC and the control of the INTUC by the Congress Party. It defines its ideals as "secularism, socialism, democracy, free trade unionism and nationalism", and favours free collective bargaining by sole bargaining agents elected by secret ballot. Its position was one of extreme difficulty during the Emergency from 1975–77 when the HMS leadership was divided over the issue for acquiescence in the suspension of trade union rights.

The HMS believes in the "overall development of its members", and many of its affiliates run schools, community halls, and medical and family planning facilities. It has encouraged workers education, has its own education and research institute, the Maniben Kara Institute, and its Rural Workers' Federation not only organizes rural workers but assists them in establishing self-employment programmes.

The HMS identifies the rise of communalism, unemployment, privatization, and the attitude of the organized towards the great mass of unorganized casual and contract workers as among the principal problems facing the Indian trade union movement. It favours an extension of worker participation in industrial management, a concept which has had little practical result in India despite numerous experiments since 1947.

In March 1990 Samarendra Kundu was elected as President of the HMS.

Publication. Hind Mazdoor (monthly, in English and Hindi).

International affiliation. ICFTU/APRO.

Indian National Trade Union Congress (INTUC)

Address. 1B Maulana Azad Road, New Delhi 110011
Phone. (11) 30-18-150
Cables. SHRAMIK NEWDELHI
Leadership. G. Ramanujan (president); M. P. Gopeshwar (general secretary); H. N. Trivedi (treasurer; an ICFTU vice-president)
Membership. 5,174,765 in 26 State branches and 29 Industrial Federations. INTUC has 4,427 affiliated unions.

History and character. INTUC was founded on May 3, 1947, inspired by Gandhian principles and is probably the largest trade union centre in India. It is closely linked to the Congress Party and this has allowed it to stay at the centre of trade union affairs and be influential in all industrial relations legislation. It has committees to co-ordinate its activities in workers' education, organization, the public sector, productivity, social security, safety and health, international relations, women workers, young workers, and child labour.

Affiliates.

Indian National Bank Officers' Congress, 12-A, Prerana, Tilak Road, Borivli, Bombay-400 092.
Leadership: Mr Gopeshwar (president); Mr K. K. Nair (general secretary).

Indian National Bank Employees' Federation, Ground Floor, Kasturi Apartment, J. P. Avenue, Dr. Radhakrishnan Salai, Madras-600 004.
Leadership: Mr Gopeshwar (president); Mr R. P. K. Murgesan (general secretary).

Indian National Building and Construction Workers' Federation, 1-B, Maulana Azad Road, New Delhi-110011.
Leadership: Mr Tara Singh Viyogi (president).

Indian National Cement Workers' Federation, Mazdoor Karyalaya, Congress House, Bombay-400 004.
Leadership: Mr H. N. Trivedi (president); Mr N. Nanjappan (general secretary).

Indian National Chemical Workers' Federation, Tel-Resayan Bhavan, Tilak Road, Dadar, Bombay-400 014.
Leadership: Mr Raja Kulkarni (president); Mr R. D. Bhardwaj (general secretary).

Indian National Food & Drink Workers' Federation, LIGHE, Block M/4, 49, Narikeldanga North Road, Calcutta-700011.
Leadership: Mr R. N. Choubey (president); Mr Chander Prakesh Singh (general secretary).

National Federation of Government of India Press Workers, A/290, New Friends Colony, New Delhi-110065.
Leadership: Mrs Usha Malhotra (president); Mr Mohan Lal (general secretary).

All Indian National Life Insurance Employees' Federation, 127/M/3, Manicktola Main Road, Calcutta-700054.
Leadership: Mr Raja Kulkarni (president); Mr K. P. Chakravorty (general secretary).

Indian National Metalworkers' Federation, 26 K. Road, Jamshedpur-831001.
Leadership: Mr V. G. Gopal (president); Mr Gopeshwar (general secretary).

Indian National Shop and Commercial Employees' Federation, 28/29, Old Rajinder Nagar, New Delhi-110060.
Leadership: Mr P. S. Khera (president); Mr M. P. Padmanabhan (general secretary).

Indian National Defence Workers' Federation, 25/19, Karachi Khana, Kanpur-208001.
Leadership: Mr Madan Sen Gupta (president); Mr R. N. Pathak (general secretary).

Indian National Electricity Workers' Federation, H S 29, Kailash Colony Market, New Delhi-110048.
Leadership: Mr D. P. Pathak (working president); Mr S. L. Passey (general secretary).

Indian National Mineworkers' Federation, Michael John Samriti Bhavan, Rajendra Path, Dhanbad-826001.
Leadership: Shri Bindeshwari Dubey, MP (president); Mr S. Das Gupta (general secretary).

Indian National Municipal & Local Bodies Workers' Federation, Kamgar Karyalaya, Topiwala Lane, Lamington Road, Bombay-400007.
Leadership: Mr Ratilal Shah (president); Mr S. V. Gole (general secretary).

Indian National Paper Mills Workers' Federation, 6/B, LIGH Barkatpura, Hyderabad-500027.
Leadership: Mr G. Sanjeeva Reddy (president); Mr M. N. Dorairajan (general secretary).

Indian National Port & Dock Workers' Federation, 15, Coal Dock Road, Calcutta-700043.
Leadership: Mr Janaki Mukherjee (president); Mr G. Kalan (general secretary).

National Federation of Petroleum Workers, Tel-Rasayan Bhavan, Tilak Road, Dadar, Bombay-400 014.
Leadership: Mr Raja Kulkarni (president); Mr S. N. Surve (general secretary).

Indian National Plantation Workers' Federation, 25-A, Park Street, Suit No. 125, Calcutta-700016.
Leadership: Mr Jagan Nath Sinha (president); Mr Pran Dey (general secretary).

National Federation of Indian Railwaymen, 3, Chelmsford Road, New Delhi-110001.
Leadership: Mr Keshav H. Kulkarni (president); Mr Ch Shashi Bhushana Rao (general secretary).

Indian National Rural Labour Federation, Shram Shibir, Devi Ahilya Marg. Indore-452003.

Leadership: Mr M. L. Giani (president); Mr C. Jambu (secretary general); Mr Subhash Sharma, Mr A. K. Sarmah, Mr Jashwant Sinh Chouhan (general secretaries).

Indian National Sugar Mills Workers' Federation, 19, Lajpat Rai Marg. Lucknow-226001.
Leadership: Mr Chander Bhan Gupta (president); Mr Ram Yash Singh (general secretary).

Indian National Textile Workers' Federation, 'Mazdoor Manzil', G. D. Ambekar Marg, Parel, Bombay-400 012.
Leadership: Mr P. L. Subbiah (president); Mr Haribhau Naik (general secretary).

Indian National Transport Workers' Federation, L/1, Hathital Colony, MP Housing Board, Jabalpur-482001.
Leadership: Mr Laxmi Narain (president); Mr K. S. Verma (general secretary).

Federation of National Postal Organizations, T-24, Atul Grove, New Delhi-110001.
Leadership: Mr K. Ramamurthy (general secretary).

Congress of Central Government Employees' Organizations, 3, Chelmsford Road, New Delhi-110001.
Leadership: Mr Keshav H. Kulkarni (president); Mr Madan Sen Gupta (general secretary).

National Organisation of Government Employees, 90/72, Malviya Nagar, New Delhi-110017.
Leadership: Mr Yash Pal Kapoor (president); Mr Tirath Ram Sharma (general secretary).

Indian National Jute Mills Workers' Federation, 177/B, Acharya Jagdish Bose Road, Calcutta-700014.
Leadership: Mr Subrato Mukherjee, MLA (president); Mr Ganesh Sarkar (general secretary).

Indian National Glass & Potteries Workers' Federation, 1-B, Maulana Azad Road, New Delhi-110011.
Leadership: Mr Damodar Pandey (president); Mr Lal Bahadur Singh (general secretary).

Indian National Press Workers' Federation, Shivraj Bhawan No. 2, Shop No. 5, Balshet Madhukar Marg, Behind Elphinston Road Rly Station, Bombay-400013.
Leadership: Mr Ram Mahadik (president)

Publications. The Indian Workers (weekly, in English); *Mazdoor Sandesh* (weekly, in Hindi).
International affiliations. ICFTU/APRO; CTUC.

Rashtriya Mazdoor Sangh
National Labour Organization (NLO)

Address. Textile Labour Association, Gandhi Majoor Sevalaya, P.B. No. 110. Bhadla, Ahmedabad 380 001

United Trades Union Congress (UTUC)

Is split into two tendencies, the UTUC and the UTUC (Lenin Sarani), the second being an affiliate of the WFTU.

Indonesia

Capital: Jakarta   **Population: 179,000,000**

Political system. According to its 1945 Constitution, the Republic of Indonesia is a unitary state with a government comprising the sovereign People's Consultative Assembly, an executive branch headed by a President, and an elected legislature, the

House of Representatives. The government-sponsored *Golkar* grouping has captured an absolute majority of seats in elections to the House of Representatives, held every five years, since 1971. Despite the existence of the necessary elements of constitutional government, the state has been dominated since the installation of the New Order regime in 1966 by President Suharto, whose power is based largely on the continued support of the Armed Forces.

Economy. The Indonesian economy is predominantly agricultural and this sector employs over 40 per cent of the working population and accounts for 25 per cent of Gross Domestic Product. Rice self-sufficiency was achieved in 1985 and crop diversification is now encourged. Oil and gas continue to dominate the country's export sector, despite a dramatic fall in earnings as a result of the world oil glut. They are however being challenged by the non-oil and gas industrial sector which grew by 12.2 per cent in 1989. Foreign investment surged in the late 1980s and the financial sector expanded. Since 1986 the government has emphasized deregulation and the development of weak sectors to absorb the fast-growing workforce of 76,000,000. The Fifth Development Plan was inaugurated in 1989 and government projections were that the economy would have to create 2,300,000 jobs a year to absorb new entrants to the workforce during its span.

System of industrial relations. The Development of Manpower (Depnaker) administers an extensive framework of employment law and regulations. Minimum wages are set for a large number of industries by quadripartite bodies of employer, labour, government and academic representation, but a survey by the country's main union centre SPSI in 1989, discovered that these were ignored in many cases. In 1990 (Depnaker) promised stricter employment.

Collective bargaining is guaranteed by law. Employers must negotiate with unions who request it, or consult the workforce where no union exists. All companies employing more than 25 staff are covered by the main industrial relations regulations.

Indonesia ratified ILO Convention No. 98 (Right to Organize and Collective Bargaining, 1949) in 1957 but has not ratified Convention No. 87 (Freedom of Association and Protection of the Right to Organize, 1948).

Pancasila development policy. The unions are required to carry out the Pancasila development policy (which under legislation passed in 1985 has become the "sole ideological foundation" of all mass organizations). According to this philosophy—which involves belief in a deity but endorses no particular religion, and officially stand for humanitarianism, nationalism, democracy and social justice—industrial relations are to be based on tripartism (involving government, employers and unions) and to be non-confrontational. In practice the Department of Manpower—its former head—plays the dominant role. Adml. Sudomo has said that in Pancasila philosophy "there is no concept of the strike, because strike action represents force from one side upon the other". Thus although strikes are nominally still lawful, permission for strike action is required from the Department of Manpower, and in 1989 there were only 19 official strikes, involving 6,168 workers, and a loss of 29,257 working hours (although there may be as many as five times this number of unauthorized strikes. Civil servants and public sector workers may not join trade unions and there is extensive government interference in collective bargaining. Equally, however, the powers of employers to dismiss workers are strictly limited, and the Department of Manpower has obliged managers to retain workers regardless of business conditions.

The ruling Golkar alliance is heavily represented in the SPSI, although other partles are also represented. The national employers' union is also dominated by the ruling party.

Trade unionism. The first Indonesian federation, Persatuan Pergerakan Kaum Buruh (United Workers' Movement) was formed in 1919, but lasted only two years; union activities continued, however, and were heavily influenced by nationalist and communist politics, until suppressed under the Japanese occupation in World War II. The Barisan Buruh Indonesia (Indonesian Workers' Front—BBI) was established in 1945 as a united trade union centre, but this almost immediately fragmented. Some unions were actively involved in communist agitation and insurgency in the 1950s and 1960s and these were suppressed after an attempted *coup* in 1965. In 1973 the All-Indonesian Labour Federation (FBSI) was created under government auspices as a central co-ordinating body; the existing trade union centres remained in existence, however. In 1985 the FBSI was reorganized as the All-Indonesia Union of Workers (SPSI) and its affiliated industrial unions brought under tighter central control. In 1990 they were reorganized again, this time into 13 industrial sectors. The SPSI and PGRI are the country's only two registered unions, a status achieved only by those who organize and gain representation in 20 of Indonesia's 27 provinces. Most often unions which attempted to stay outside the SPSI after 1985 have lost ground, but some maintain an association, SEKBER.

Public employers in 21 industries deemed vital to the national interest do not have the right to strike. Public sector employees are co-ordinated in a separate association, the Corps of Civil Servants (KORPRI) (set up by the government in 1971 and whose central board is chaired by the Minister of Internal Affairs), and rural workers in a Farmers' Association.

Indonesian Seafarers' Union (KPI)

Membership. 16,000 including merchant marine officers.
International affiliations. The KPI is an independent union within the SPSI. It is also affiliated to the Asian Seafarers' Union and hosted that body's 1990 meeting
History and character. The KPI grew rapidly from 1989–90 following its success in obtaining recognized seamen's certificates for seafarers.
Publication. Media Pelaut.

Indonesian Teachers' Association (PGRI)

Membership. 1,300,000.
History and character. In 1990 PGRI became Indonesia's second registered union because it had secured representation in all 27 provinces, easily passing the legal threshold.
Publication. Teacher's Voice.
International affiliations. WCOTP; IFFTU. PGRI hosted the Ninth Council of the ASEAN Council of Teachers in 1987.

SEKBER

History and character. SEKBER is a loose association of the former members of the industrial unions abolished during the 1985 restructuring of SPSI. Its main activities are in training, but it ventured into a new field in January 1990 when it hosted a well attended national seminar on deregulation and conglomerates.

Serikat Pekerja Seluruh Indonesia (SPSI)
All Indonesia Workers' Union

Address. JL. M. H. Thamrin No. 20 LT VI. Jakarta Pusat
Phone. (21) 323872
Fax. 3107868
Leadership. Imam Soedarwo (general chairman); Dr H. Bonner Pasariku (general secretary)
Membership. 900,283.
History and character. National union leaders on Feb. 20, 1973, formed the Federasi Buruh Seluruh Indonesia (FBSI—All-Indonesia Labour Federation), with government backing. At its

second congress in November 1985 several major changes were made to the FBSI: (i) it was given its present name (i.e. the SPSI), the change being reported to reflect the distaste of the Manpower Minister Adml. Sudomo for the "communist" overtones of the word *buruh* (labour)—which was replaced by *pekerja* (workers)—while the removal of the word meaning "federation" was intended to assert the unitary, rather than federal, nature of the organization; (ii) the previous 21 national industrial unions were reduced to nine "departments", with the apparent intention of bringing them under tighter central control; (iii) all but the lowest-level officers were henceforth to be appointed, rather than elected as previously; (iv) Agus Sudono, the executive president of the organization since its formation, was replaced by Imam Sudarwo; and (v) the executive board was reduced from 33 to 27 members, including the chairman, the secretary-general and the appointed chiefs of the nine "departments".

The third national congress, held in 1990 transformed the nine industrial departments into 13 sectoral unions covering: textile and governments; trade, banks and insurance; plantation and agriculture; metals, electronics and machinery; timber; food, drinks and cigarettes; hotels and tourism; transport; building and construction; chemicals and mining; printing and publishing; seafaring; hospitals and clinics.

In the late 1980s the SPSI intensified its efforts to improve organisation and secure international recognition. There was an increase in training programmes and some 50 per cent of the Union's local branches made collective agreements in 1989. In 1989 and 1990 it gained considerable publicity for disclosing, through an American-funded survey, the extent of non-compliance with minimum wage regulations.

The SPSI defines its policies as being to improve the conditions of workers, participate actively in national development; create and maintain social stability and industrial peace; strive for equitable distribution of wealth; and to co-operate with international workers' organizations. It is represented nationally on the Tripartite Body, Consultative Council, Productivity Council, Population and Family Planning Board, and the Labour Disputes Settlement Committee.

Publications. SPSI News; *Media Pekerja* (tabloid).

International affiliations. None. ICFTU connections with Indonesia ceased at the time of the SPSI's 1985 restructuring but the Union has pursued training and organizational programmes with APRO and the ICFTU which are seen as preliminary to affiliation.

Iran

Capital: Tehran   **Population: 48,555,000**
                                                                          (1988)

Political system. Government authority in the Islamic Republic of Iran (established in 1979 after the overthrow of Shah Reza Pahlevi) is vested in a President (directly elected), Prime Minister and Cabinet. A 12-member Council of Guardians ensures that all legislation conforms with the (1979) Islamic Constitution and has the power to veto candidates to high elected office on the same grounds. There is a 270-member parliament (*Majlis*), elected by direct universal suffrage. Elections were last held in April–May 1988. The Speaker of the *Majlis*, *Hojatolislam* Hashemi Ali Akbar Rafsanjani, was chosen as President following the death of Iran's spiritual (and actual) leader the Ayatollah Ruhollah Khomeini. While opposed to the presence of United States and other Western forces in the Region, Iran remained neutral in the 1991 Gulf War following Iraq's invasion of Kuwait.

A ceasefire in the Gulf War between Iran and Iraq, which had broken out in September 1980, came into effect on Aug. 20, 1988, over a month after the Iranian government had announced its willingness to agree to a ceasefire under the terms of UN Security Council Resolution 598 passed in August 1987.

Economy. The Gulf War and the 1984–86 collapse in world oil prices adversely affected the Iranian economy, which is heavily reliant on the revenue earned from oil exports. Nevertheless, at the time of the ceasefire agreement with Iraq in mid-1988, the government's position was better than expected after eight years of war, particularly in the case of foreign exchange reserves.

System of industrial relations. Iran has ratified neither ILO Convention No. 87 (Freedom of Association and Protection of the Right to Organize, 1948) nor No. 98 (Right to Organize and Collective Bargaining, 1949). The ILO Committee of Experts on the Application of Conventions and Recommendations has expressed its deep concern at the failure of Iran to apply Convention No. 111 on Discrimination in Employment and Occupation which Iran ratified in 1964. This has applied particularly to the treatment of members of the Baha'i community, the Freemasons and to members of organizations whose constitutions imply atheism.

An Act of January 1985 provided for the establishment of an Islamic labour council, made up of representatives of the workers and one representative of management, in every enterprise or industrial, agricultural or services unit of more than 35 employees; the number of worker representatives was to vary from 3 to 11 depending on the size of the enterprise. Candidates to become workers' representatives (who would be elected for two-year terms by the workers' general assembly for the unit) were required to be: (i) at least 22 years old; (ii) of Iranian nationality; (iii) to have worked in the same unit for at least one year; (iv) to be a member of the Islamic faith or, in the case of Christian, Jewish or Zoroastrian minorities, faithful to the Constitution of the Islamic Republic of Iran; and (v) not connected to the former régime or to have a criminal record. The eligibility of candidates was to be vetted by a committee made up of officials of government ministries and a member of the workers' assembly.

These councils, which were required to report back to the workers' general assembly at least every six months and which would be financed by workers' contributions, were: (i) to encourage co-operation between workers to enhance productivity; (ii) to represent the problems of the workers to management and to co-operate with management in devising methods to improve working conditions; and (iii) to co-operate with the unit's Islamic association. In turn each council was to be consulted by management on issues affecting wages, working hours and conditions, and would appoint a (non-voting) delegate to represent it on the enterprise's board of directors. A tripartite body would be set up in every district, composed of representatives of the Islamic councils, enterprises and the Ministry of Labour and Social Affairs; these bodies would have powers to supervise and dissolve the labour councils and to rule on disputes between the councils and management (although with further recourse to the courts).

Trade unionism. Trade unions organized vigorously and openly after World War II until the Shah assumed full powers after the overthrow of the government of Dr Mohammed Mussadeq in 1953 in a *coup* supported by the western powers. The Shah thereafter suppressed independent trade unions and promoted the government-controlled Workers' Organization of Iran (WOI), although unofficial strikes contributed to the instability of the régime in the late 1970s. There has been no development of trade unionism since the fall of the Shah in 1979.

There is no ICFTU or WCL affiliate, but there is a WFTU-affiliated union in exile, the Trade Union Liaison Committee of Iranian Unions (Commission de Liaison des Syndicats Iraniens) (address: c/o CGT, 263 rue de Paris, 93516 Montreuil, France), led by Hossein Nazari. This publishes a bulletin, *Ettehad*, opposes the Islamic regime and the war with Iraq, and states that workers laid off in mass redundancies because of the country's economic crisis are providing manpower for the war. Other reports suggest that spontaneous strikes have occurred and have been violently suppressed.

The WFTU reported in 1989 a large number of summary executions of trade unionists held in Iran's jails and it "denounced and condemned these new acts of terror". A Trade Union Liaison Committee of Workers of Iran (TULCWI) began in that year to publish a list of executed trade union activists. Later that year it was reported that five members of another organization Workers' Unity had been arrested and in 1990 20 more. Those arrested in 1989 confessed under torture to "stealing and murder" and were sentenced to death.

Iraq

Capital: Baghdad

Population: 16,110,000
(official estimate as at mid-1986)

Political system. The Republic of Iraq was declared in 1958 following the overthrow of the monarchy by left-wing officers. Power is concentrated in the hands of the Revolutionary Command Council (RCC), which elects the President from among its own members. The President (Saddam Hussein) appoints a Council of Ministers. Legislative authority is shared between the RCC and a 250-member National Assembly, the latter elected every four years by universal adult suffrage. Following general elections in October 1984, the Arab *Baath* Socialist Party holds the majority of the Assembly seats. A leading political role is also played by the *Baath* Party's most senior body, the 17-member Regional Command.

Following Iraq's defeat in the Gulf War and the occupation of substantial tracts of its territory by American and Allied forces, senior ministers declared their intention to move towards a more pluralistic society.

Economy. Iraq suffered growing economic problems between 1985–88, due largely to a shortage of foreign exchange as a result of falling oil prices and the war with Iran, which led to delays with a series of debt servicing payments. The government announced extensive economic restructuring plans following the end of the war with Iran. However, the invasion of Kuwait, triggered by a dispute over oil revenues, led to the Gulf War and considerable loss of life and industrial capacity. In May 1991 Iraq pleaded that it was unable to pay even the first instalment of reparations.

Under a privatization programme announced in 1988, more than 87 state enterprises were sold by the summer of the following year. By the end of 1989 it was reported that Iraq had more than 1,000,000 co-operators in 244 societies.

Repression of opposition trade unionists intensified after 1978, with many imprisoned or forced into exile. Conscription of labour has occurred since the beginning of the war with Iran in 1980. On March 19, 1987, the Iraqi government passed a decree (No. 150) making all workers in the state sector civil servants without rights of association. The ICATU condemned the move saying that it contravened the rules of the Arab Labour Organization as well as ILO Convention No. 87 (Freedom of Association and Protection of the Rights to Organize, 1948) which Iraq has not ratified. Iraq ratified ILO Convention No. 98 (Right to Organize and Collective Bargaining, 1949) in 1962. The *Baath* dominated

GFTU did not protest against the withdrawal of trade unions rights. Though the right to strike existed it was only exercised once in the 20 years to 1990, when Egyptian workers protested for one day against excessive hours. Considerable harassment of immigrant workers occurred before and after that date.

Trade unionism. The first unions formed in the 1920s were violently suppressed. At the end of World War II 16 unions were formed to cover workers in all sectors except the oil industry, but in the following decade these were broken up or severely curtailed. Following the overthrow of the monarchy in 1958 the first oil workers' union was formed and the General Federation of Trade Unions established. Since 1968 the unions have been instruments of the ruling *Baath* Party.

In 1979 the general secretary and the president of the Federation were executed after being accused of conspiring against the security of the state.

General Federation of Trade Unions of Iraq (GFTUI)

Address. P.O. Box 3049, Tahrir Square, Rashid Street, Baghdad
Phone. 8870820/8870810
Telex. 212457 IK GFTUI
Leadership. Fadhil Mahmoud Gharib (president)
Membership. Claims 1,250,000. Peasants are organized separately in the General Federation of Peasant Societies.
History and character. Founded 1959. The GFTUI is the instrument of the ruling *Baath* Party.
Affiliates. Six national unions: agricultural and foodstuff workers, textile and leather workers, transport workers, building and wood-workers, public servants and mechanics, printing and metal workers. In addition, 18 local trade federations are affiliated.
Publication. Wayulomal (*Workers' Consciousness*) in English and Arabic (monthly).
International affiliations. ICATU; WFTU.

Ireland

Capital: Dublin   **Population: 3,650,000**

Political system. Ireland is a multi-party republic with a bicameral parliament (*Oireachtas*) and a president as Head of State. It is a member of the EC but not of NATO.

Economy. Ireland's economy developed rapidly after entry to the EC in 1973 though structural weaknesses presisted. These were addressed by the Programme for National Recovery inaugurated by the Fianna Fail government in conjunction with the social partners from 1987. By 1990 Ireland had enjoyed several years of high growth, cut inflation and interest rates, but still suffered a high national debt and persistent unemployment. Irish agricultural employment in 1988 was 14.9 per cent of the labour force, industrial employment 27.5 per cent and service employment 57.6 per cent.

System of industrial relations. Ireland ratified ILO Conventions No. 87 (Freedom of Association and Protection of the Right to Organize, 1948) and No. 98 (Right to Organize and Collective Bargaining, 1949) in 1955. There is a network of tripartite institutions including the Labour Court, which may hear disputes referred to it by management or labour; its findings are not binding.

Under the Programme for National Recovery, a Programme for Economic and Social Progress was agreed by the ICTU, employers' organizations and the government. One feature was the *Industrial Relations Act* 1990 which provided an improved framework for the resolution of disputes and established the Labour Relations Commission with overall responsibility for promoting good industrial relations through conciliation and advisory services and the preparation of codes of practice. The *Workers Participation (State Enterprises) Act* 1988 provided for the setting up of participative structures in 35 state enterprises and there have been discussions between the ICTU and the Federation of Irish Employers about the development of employee involvement in the private sector.

Trade unionism. An Irish Trade Union Congress was founded in 1894 and unions developed strongly under British rule. Total trade union membership in the Republic and Northern Ireland is estimated at 718,000 of which (at the end of 1989) 679,000 were in organizations affiliated to the Irish Congress of Trade Unions. Trade Union density in 1988 was estimated at 45 per cent. The following year a number of mergers were agreed including: Association of Inspectors of Taxes and the Irish Tax Officials Unions with the Union of Professional and Technical Civil Servants; Irish Customs and Excise Association with the Civil and Public Services Union; Irish Customs and Excise Union with the Public Services Executive Union; Postal and Telecommunications Workers' Union with the Communications Union of Ireland to form the Communication Workers' Union; Irish Transport and General Workers' Union with the Federated Workers' Union of Ireland to form the Services, Industrial, Professional, Technical Union; Association of Professional, Executive, Clerical and Computer Staff with the General Municipal Boilermakers and Allied Trades Union.

In 1991 the Local Government and Public Services Union amalgamated with the Union of Professional and Technical Civil Servants to form the Irish Municipal, Public and Civil Trade Union (IMPACT).

Irish Congress of Trade Unions (ICTU)

Address. Congress House, 19 Raglan Road, Dublin 4

Phone. 680641

Fax. 609027

Leadership. Chris Kirwan (president, 1990–91); Peter Cassells (general secretary)

Membership. 679,000: 455,500 in the Republic and 223,500 in Northern Ireland.

History and character. The Irish Trade Union Congress was founded in 1894. This body split in two in 1945 with the formation of the breakaway Congress of Irish Unions (which rejected the inclusion of British-based unions), but was reunited under the present name in 1959. The principle of a united Irish trade union centre persisted through the period of British rule to the separation of the North from the rest of Ireland. The ICTU is politically non-aligned.

Affiliated unions. There are 78 affiliated unions; 38 of these have members only in the Irish Republic and 21 have members only in the North of Ireland. All but six of the 40 affiliated unions with members in Northern Ireland have their head offices in Britain; this is also true of 13 of the 57 affiliated unions with members in the Republic. The two general unions in the Republic account for a membership of 215,600 which is nearly half of union membership in the country; in Northern Ireland, three general unions account for one-third of total membership.

Partly as a result of a rash of amalgamations, nearly 80 per cent of affiliated members in the Republic are in the 11 unions with more than 10,000 members; the 23 unions with less than 2,000 members hold around 3 per cent of affiliated membership in the Republic. In 1990 the ICTU gained an important new affiliate in the shape of the Irish Nurses Organization. Women make up 37 per cent of the ICTU's affiliated membership, compared to 33 per cent in 1988–89; the figure for Northern Ireland is 38 per cent. The following ICTU affiliates had membership in excess of 10,000 in 1990 (R = Republic of Ireland; NI = Northern Ireland); asterisked affiliates have their headquarters in Great Britain.

1. **Amalgamated Engineering Union***, 26–34 Antrim Road, Belfast BT15 2AA.
   Phone: 743271.
   Irish representative: J. Blair.
   Membership: 4,000 (R); 12,000 (NI).

2. **Amalgamated Transport and General Workers' Union***, Transport House, 102 High Street, Belfast BT1.
   Phone: 232381.
   Irish representatitve: J. Freeman.
   Membership: 20,000 (R); 50,000 (NI).

3. **Association of Secondary Teachers, Ireland**, 36 Lower Baggot Street, Dublin 2.
   Phone: 607444.
   Fax: 607403.
   General secretary: K. Mulvey.
   Membership: 12,032 (R).

4. **Civil and Public Services Union**, 72 Lower Leeson Street, Dublin 2.
   Phone: 765394/5.
   General secretary: J. O'Dowd.
   Membership: 12,003 (R).
   The CPSU merged with the Irish Custom and Excise Association in January 1990 but the two unions continue to affiliate separately to the ICTU.

5. **Communication Workers' Union**, Aras Ghaibreil, 575 North Circular Road, Dublin 1.
   Phone: 366388.
   General secretary: S. De Paor.
   Membership: 20,100 (NI).
   The Communication Workers' Union was formed in November 1989 by a merger of the Postal and Telecommunications Workers' Union and the Communications Union of Ireland.

6. **Confederation of Health Service Employees***, 27 Ulsterville Avenue, Belfast BT9 7AS.
   Irish representative: W. J. Jackson.
   Membership: 20,000 (NI).

7. **Electrical Trades Union**, 5 Cavendish Row, Dublin 1.
   Phone: 747047.
   General secretary: F. O'Reilly.
   Membership: 10,425 (R).

8. **General Municipal and Boilermakers and Allied Trade Union (GMB)***, 102 Lisburn Road, Belfast BT9 6AG.
   Phone: 681421.
   Irish representative: T. D. Douglas.
   Membership: 162 (R); 15,001 (NI).
   Though the GMB merged with the British-based APEX in March 1989, the two continue to affiliate separately to the ICTU.

9. **Irish Distributive and Administrative Trade Union**, O'Lehane House, 9 Cavendish Row, Dublin 1.
   Phone: 746321.
   General secretary: J. Mitchell.
   Membership: 20,010 (R).

10. **Irish Municipal, Public and Civil Trade Union (IMPACT)**, 9 Gardiner Place, Dublin 1.
    Phone: 728899. Fax: 728715.
    General secretaries: P. Flynn, G. Maxwell.
    Membership: 25,000.
    The Union was formed by the merger of the 18,000-strong Local Government and Public Services Union with the 6,700 strong Union of Professional and Technical Civil Servants in January 1991.

11. **Irish National Teachers' Organization**, Address: 35 Parnell Square, Dublin 1.
    Phone: 746381.
    Fax: 722462.
    General secretary: E. G. Quigley.
    Membership: 19,026 (R); 5,314 (NI).

12. **Irish Nurses Organization**, Address: c/o 11 Fitzwilliam Place, Dublin 2.
    Phone: 760137.
    General secretary: P. J. Madden.
    Membership: 10,000 (R).

13. **Manufacturing, Science and Finance***, 15 Merrion Square, Dublin 2.
    Phone: 761213.
    Joint national secretaries: B. Anderson and J. Tierney.
    Membership: 20,800 (R); 9,200 (NI).

14. **National Union of Public Employees***, 523 Antrim Road, Belfast BT15 6BS.
    Phone: 370684/370971.
    Irish representative: I. McCormack.
    Membership: 12,054 (NI).

15. **Northern Ireland Public Service Alliance**, 54 Wellington Park, Belfast BT9 6BZ.
    Phone: 661831.
    General secretary: J. McCusker.
    Membership: 32,000 (NI).

16. **Services Industrial Professional Technical Union**, 10 Palmerston Park, Dublin 6.
    Phone: 973361.
    General secretaries: C. Kirwan and T. Garry.
    Membership: 195,599 (R); 9,401 (NI).
    SIPTU was formed in January 1990 by a merger of the Irish Transport and General Workers
    Union and the Federated Workers' Union of Ireland. It is easily the biggest union in Ireland.

17. **Union of Construction, Allied Trade and Technicians**
    Address: 56 Parnell Square West, Dublin 1
    Phone: 731599.
    Regional Secretary: N O'Neill.
    Membership: 8,179 (R); 6,353 (NI).

There are eleven unions in the Republic which are not affiliated to the ICTU, representing perhaps
5 per cent of the country's total union membership. Of these the largest is the Irish Bank Officials'
Association (13,845). There are three main unions in Northern Ireland which are not affiliated to the
ICTU: their total membership is 16,500.

Israel

.

Capital: Jerusalem   **Population: 4,588,000**
(although not recognized as such
by the international community)

Political system. The state of Israel declared its independence in 1948, since when it has been involved in three wars with its Arab neighbours, in 1956, 1967 and 1973. It is a unicameral parliamentary democracy; the *Knesset* (parliament) is elected for a four-year term under a pure system of proportional representation. Elections to the *Knesset* held in November 1988 resulted in a deadlock between the two main party blocs, the *Likud* front and the Labour-dominated alignment, which had hitherto been partners in a coalition government formed following the last, similarly inconclusive elections in 1984.

Until June 1990 a national unity government ruled the country as Labour and *Likud* formed a coalition under the *Likud* leader Yitzhak Shamir. However Labour left the government in June 1990 and Mr Shamir continued as Prime Minister with religious minority party support.

Economy. Of a civilian labour force numbering 1,461,000 in 1989, virtually 1,000,000 were employed in services, 385,000 in industry and 68,000 in agriculture. These numbers however exclude West Bank and Gaza Strip residents and do not take account of rapid Jewish immigration from Russia, which increased six-fold in 1989. Labour wastage also results from the dedication of 40 per cent of the country's budget to defence, including the commitment of every man under 55 to 40 days reserve training a year. Unemployment reached a 20-year peak of 9.3 per cent in the first quarter of 1990, apparently driving large numbers of women and Israeli Arabs out of the labour market. Israel's traditionally high inflation rate was cut in the 1980s but rose again in 1989.

System of industrial relations. A new law introduced in March 1987, fixed for the first time a national minimum wage (of 45 per cent of the average wage) applicable to all branches of the Israeli economy. An agreement between Histadrut and the government valid from April 1987 provided for a five day working week in the public sector to be phased in from April 1988. In addition, equal opportunities for men and women at work were guaranteed under a law which came into force in April 1988.

Israel has a tradition of national tripartite framework agreements, though this does not prevent national disputes, including industrial action. In February 1989 the government, Histradut and the Manufacturers' Association of Israel made a cost of living agreement which in February 1990 was extended for a further two years. Public and private wage agreements are also centrally made, but in 1990 the employers manifested greater reluctance to sign a master agreement preferring that wages should reflect the viability of plants. A major issue that year was the "Sussman" reform which would introduce performance evaluation into the civil service and whose introduction the *Likud* government required as the price of an agreement. In June, Histradut dissatisfaction bubbled over in a 24-hour strike.

Israel ratified ILO Conventions No. 87 (Freedom of Association and Protection of the Right to Organize, 1948) and No. 98 (Right to Organize and Collective Bargaining, 1949) in 1957. A wide range of labour laws, mostly passed in the 1950s, provides the framework for the regulation of hours, holidays, youth and women's employment, disputes, national insurance, etc.

Trade unionism. The Histadrut, the dominant labour organization in Israel, was formed in Palestine in 1920 as an expression of both trade union and Zionist aspirations, and played a major role in building the state of Israel. It is unique in the non-communist world in the wide role it plays in the direction and development of much of the Israeli economy. The Histadrut is affiliated to the ICFTU.

The origins of the peculiar character of Histadrut lie in the quarter century during which it was effectively the Jewish state in embryo, a microcosm rather than simply an employees' organization. After the proclamation of the State of Israel, Histradut continued its economic activities. Its "workers" company—effectively the employer arm—Hevrat Ha'ovdim controls 30 per cent of industrial output. Histradut's health insurance system covers around 80 per cent of the population. In 1989 however the financial problems of

236

Koor, the largest group in the Hevrat Ha'ovdim, became unmanageable and led to a series of redundancies which in some instances were met by strikes. The Labour leadership of Histradut is under increasing pressure to turn its vast enterprises over the market disciplines.

Though the Histradut dominates Israeli trade unionism, there is a small number of independent trade unions. The Palestinian Trade Union Federation (GFTU) maintains an affiliation to the WFTU, while several wings of the General Federation of West Bank Trade Unions applied in 1989 for ICFTU membership. An ICFTU Executive Board meeting of November 1989 heard a report from a fact-finding mission to the West Bank: it urged the Israeli government to lift restrictions on union activity there, called on the West Bank unions to rationalize and exhorted Histradut to engage in dialogue with *bona fide* West Bank and Gaza union leaders. This course of action was endorsed by Histradut at its 1990 Convention.

Hakistradut Haklolit Shel HaOvdim BeEretz – Israel Histradut General Federation of Labour in Israel

Address. 93 Arlosoroff Street, 62098 Tel-Aviv
Phone. (3) 431111
Fax. (3) 269349
Telex. 342488 HISTD IL 269906
Cables. OVDIM TEL-AVIV
Leadership. Israel Kessar (secretary general)
Membership. 1989 membership was 1,640,440, including housewives, while an additional 100,000 were in the Working and Student Youth Organization. About 50 per cent of the membership was female. Some 106,000 workers and 36,000 housewives connected with labour organizations outside the Histadrut have joined its Trade Unions and Sick Fund. About 290,000 workers are members of unions standing outside the Histradrut. The Histadrut constitution defines membership as being open to "all men and women workers 18 years of age and above who live on the earnings of their own labour without exploiting the labour of others..." and the membership includes the unemployed, students, pensioners, self-employed, professionals and housewives. The Histadrut is open to all ethnic groups and three-quarters of the Arab and Druze workers in Israel are members.

History. The Histadrut was founded in December 1920 at a meeting in Haifa, Palestine, of representatives of 4,400 (Jewish) members of different trades, at which it was decided to create a single organization to represent all trades and professions. As Jewish settlers came in increasing numbers to Palestine, the Histadrut took on a broad role in developing housing, social services, and education and in training workers and developing the economy. Similarly, the Histadrut fostered the development of co-operative enterprises and settlements, creating an entire network of enterprises and communities. As part of its work, the Histadrut oversaw the creation of trade unions. The Histadrut today is not only the major union federation in the country but also, through the *Hevrat Ovdim* (Labour Economy), a major employer.

Structure. The Histadrut is not a federation of autonomous unions; a worker joins directly, and through this membership becomes a member of the appropriate trade union. A unique feature is that members' wives, even if solely engaged as housewives, are entitled to full membership and voting rights. Women workers automatically become members of the Histadrut Women's Organization (*Na'amat*), which elects its own governing bodies and operates independently; it runs nurseries, daycare centres, vocational and educational centres, and promotes the rights of women. Those under 18 are members of the Histadrut through its Working and Student Youth Organization (*Hano'ar Ha'oved Ve'halomed*).

General elections are held every four years, at which candidates stand for local labour councils, *Na'amat*, and the general convention. (Elections to the national trade unions are held separately.) Every member has the right to a personal vote, by secret ballot, for the list of his choice. Delegates are elected on a proportional basis and most lists correspond to national political parties. There is a 3 per cent threshold for representation.

The 1,501-member general convention elects the Histadrut council (501 members), which serves as the highest authority between conventions and meets approximately every eight months. The council elects a 189-member executive committee from within its own ranks; this body, which meets every four to six weeks, elects the general secretary and a 45-member executive bureau, which usually convenes weekly, under the chairmanship of the general secretary. The bureau is responsible for the day-to-day implementation of policy. At the grass-roots level the basic unit is the works committee in every enterprise. All Histadrut members in each district elect the local Histadrut branch—the labour council—and each union is governed by a council elected by the union membership.

The 16th Histadrut national convention met in April 1990, marked by greater rank and file representation than was the case hitherto. It approved a platform of support for Soviet–Jewish immigration, advance for the peace process, Jewish–Arab co-exisistence, and a dialogue with legitimate Palestinian unions.

Judicial control of the elected bodies is exercised by the court of honour, which is elected by the Histadrut council. Local courts, elected by local labour councils, hear claims by individual members or institutions relating to the affairs off the organization. However, these courts may not try criminal cases.

A central control committee, elected by the Histadrut council, and local control commissions, elected by local labour councils, supervise the conduct and budgetary management of the various Histadrut institutions.

Relationship to political parties. Political parties receive funding from the Histadrut budget in proportion to their representation on its elected governing bodies. The Labour Parties have always had an absolute majority within the Histadrut, and in the national elections of November 1989 the Labour list—headed by Israel Kessar and No'amat Secretary-General Masha Lubelsky—were returned with 55.1 per cent support. The *Likud* share rose to 27.5 per cent but fell short of the Party's own 30 per cent target. Mapam came third with 9 per cent, a joint Arab-Jewish list led by the Communist-sympathising Hadash fourth with 4.5 per cent, and the Citizen's Rights Party fifth with 4 per cent. Labour captured most local councils.

Trade union department. The Histadrut's trade union department represents 43 national professional and occupational unions. One responsibility of the department is to ensure that Histadrut policies are implemented by the individual unions. All Histadrut members automatically have membership in the appropriate occupational or professional union. Within the various unions are works committees (at plant level) and local unions (members of the same trade in the same locality); these are linked to other trades through the local labour councils (multi-union local bodies). Each national union has a council, elected by secret ballot on party political lines, as its governing body; the council elects a national secretary, who represents the national union at the Histadrut headquarters.

In June 1989 the Central Committee approved a report of Professor Avraham Friedman which recommended restructuring the Department by reorganization of national unions to reduce them to 17 industrial-based bodies, democratization of negotiations to local unions (except for pensions, cost of living adjustments and other national issues). The merger plan was due to be implemented within a year of the June 1990 Convention.

Collective bargaining. At the national level collective agreements are negotiated between the Histadrut executive committee and employers, and specific agreements between the national trade unions and employers in their industries. A high degree of wage standardization exists throughout the economy, and the wage policy set by the Histadrut executive committee is binding on the unions, no matter how strong their individual bargaining power. Collective agreements are legally recognized under the Collective Agreement Law of 1957, which also empowers the Minister of Labour to extend the work standards set in such agreements to non-signatory enterprises. The Settlement of Labour Disputes law of the same year sets up machinery for mediation and arbitration in the event of disputes, but does not impose compulsory arbitration or curtail the right to strike.

Productivity councils. In an attempt to increase productivity, in 1952 an agreement was signed between the Histadrut and the Employers' Association providing for the creation of joint productivity councils in every plant with over 50 workers. These provide forums for the discussion of productivity issues; they operate in *Hevrat Ovdim* enterprises, the private sector and, increasingly, in the public sector. At the national level, the Histadrut co-operates with the Ministry of Labour and the

238

Employers' Association in the Israel Productivity Institute, which organizes educational campaigns for employers and workers.

Education. In conjunction with the Ministry of Labour and the trade unions, Histadrut operates a nationwide network of vocational training schools and apprenticeship classes. *Mishlav* (the Israel Institute for Education through Correspondence) offers day and evening classes at secondary school level. The Histadrut's Department for Higher Education conducts university-level courses in management and the Culture and Education Centre conducts a wide range of activities, reaching the whole community, including the Arab and Druze populations.

Histadrut benefit schemes. The *Kupat Holim* (Workers' Sick Fund) is the main mutual aid institution of the Histadrut. In its early years it played a key role in combating epidemics and raising the health standards of immigrants, many of whom came from developing countries. Today it employs 22,000 personnel, who provide medical care to about 75 per cent of the population, including the Arab and Druze minorities. Membership of the Histadrut automatically ensures membership of *Kupat Holim*, and 72 per cent of membership dues are allocated to this. The Histadrut pension funds deal with pensions, and various other benefits such as holiday and compensation payments. *Mish'an*, established in 1931, provides loans for a variety of purposes, and operates old age homes and pensioners' clubs, and programmes for children and orphans. *Dor le Dor* provides financial aid for the elderly, and Lev Zahav offers them nursing services on behalf of the National Insurance Institute.

Hevrat Ovdim (General Co-operative Association of Labour in Israel). Every member of the Histadrut is simultaneously a member of *Hevrat Ovdim*, which is in turn open only to members of Histadrut. It is an autonomous establishment operating under the overall supervision of Histadrut. Enterprises belonging to *Hevrat Ovdim* supply 87 per cent of Israel's agricultural produce, carry out more than 7 per cent of all building activity and produce about 22 per cent of the total industrial domestic product. Consumers' co-operatives cater for about one-third of the population. The Histadrut is also a major factor in transportation, insurance and finance; the Bank Hapoalim, which belongs to the Histadrut, is the largest in the country. In all, about 20 per cent of the total labour force is employed through the *Hevrat Ovdim*. Most of the collective and co-operative agricultural settlements (*kibbutzim and moshavim*) are affiliated to *Hevrat Ovdim* through their own organizations, and all 215,000 members of these settlements are direct members of the Histadrut (and therefore of *Hevrat Ovdim*).

In the mid-1960s, the Histadrut council decided to introduce labour participation in management and profit-sharing in Histadrut enterprises. After some resistance, management executives have become more responsive to the philosophy of industrial democracy, which has been implemented in an increasing number of Histadrut enterprises, with workers' representatives on joint management boards.

Na'amat (Working Women's Movement in Israel). This organization has 800,000 women members, and every woman member of the Histadrut is a member of *Na'amat*. It has its own governing bodies, the highest of which is the convention, elected every four years at the same time as the general Histadrut elections. *Na'amat* operates child care, nursery school, vocational training and adult education programmes. *Na'amat* also lobbies for legislation of specific interest to women.

Hano'ar Ha'oved Ve'halomed is the youth organization, with about 100,000 members and its own elective bodies. Its trade union department provides professional direction to youths serving apprenticeships, while also supervising their conditions of employment and protecting their wages.

Representation on government bodies. The Histadrut is represented on all government councils with labour and social welfare responsibilities, and in many cases the Minister of Labour is required to consult the Histadrut on the application of the laws.

Affiliated unions. There are 37 affiliated national unions, which are themselves the creation of the Histadrut.

Publications. Davar (daily newspaper, first published 1925); *Labour in Israel* (journal, three to four times per year, in English, French, German, Spanish; circulation 22,000). The Histadrut's publishing house, *Am Oved*, is the largest in Israel, publishing about 100 new titles per year, of all types, and *Sifri* is a Histadrut-owned chain of bookshops.

International affiliations. ICFTU/APRO; ICFTU trade secretariats; TUAC. *Hevrat Ovdim* is a member of the International Co-operative Alliance. The Histadrut had friendly relations with the national labour movements of many countries including those of countries which do not maintain diplomatic relations with Israel.

In 1958 the Histadrut established the Afro-Asian Institute for Labour Studies (now the International Institute for Development, Co-operation and Labour Studies) to provide courses in trade union, economic and social matters for trade union and community activists from Africa and Asia. Students from more than 100 countries have completed courses at the Institute. A parallel Latin American Centre—Centre for Co-operative and Labour Studies for Latin America, Spain and Portugal—was founded in 1962.

At the end of 1990, the Eastern and Central European Foundation was set up for the purpose of offering labour education facilities to the trade union movements of the former Eastern bloc countries.

Histadrut Haovdim-Haleumit
The National Labour Federation in Eretz-Israel (NLF)

Address. 23 Shprintzak Street, Tel-Aviv 64738
Phone. (3) 258351-4
Fax. 972-3-261753
Cables. OVED LEUM TEL-AVIV
Leadership. Shalom Cohen (secretary general)
Membership. Claims 180,000 but some estimates put the figure as low as 40,000.

History and character. The National Labour Federation in Eretz-Israel was founded in Jerusalem on April 9, 1934, to unite those workers who believed in solving the country's social and economic problems on the basis of the teachings of Herzl, Nordau and Jabotinsky.

The NLF is committed to the principles of Zionism, and has as its banner the national flag. It believes in the separation of the functions of employers and trade unions, and in this is opposed to the Histadrut, which is both the largest trade union in Israel and a major employer. (The NLF is not opposed, however, the workers' co-operative enterprise). Likewise, it stands in opposition to the unification of all trade unions in a single political labour organization. The NLF favours the nationalization of basic social services and supports state retirement and unemployment insurance and the nationalization of health insurance. It maintains a separate sick fund (Kupat Holim Leumit).

The NLF opposes the solution of labour disputes by strike or lockout and has requested the establishing of a National Compulsory Arbitration Body in labour conflicts especially in vital public and state services.

The NLF advocates that the elections to the Labour organizations and Trade Unions should be non-political, and that decisions taken should be by bodies elected by the trade unions, only. Though disclaiming political affiliations, the NLF supports the compulsory arbitration platform of *Likud*. It is the only Israeli federation which is completely independent of the Histadrut.

The Health Fund (Kupat Holim Leumit) has 330,000 members in over 200 medical centres and operates a complete range of health services. The Federation runs convalescent and vacation centers in Tiberias and the Dead Sea areas.

Structure. A national conference, which elects officers and committees, is held ever four years. The NLF operates a wide range of enterprises on behalf of its members, including insurance and pension funds, unemployment funds, settlement activities, a housing company, convalescent and vacation centres, savings and loan funds, mutual help funds and a disablement fund. The health fund has 300,000 members and accepts any citizen of Israel; it operates a complete range of medical services. The NLF Youth Section is organized as a "National Working and Learning Youth Movement". There are separate students' and women's organizations.

Publications. Three periodicals: *Hazit Haoved* (circulation 25,000); *Yaad* (circulation 15,000); *Briut la'Kol* (circulation 15,000).

Other organizations

There are three autonomous unions, the High School Teachers Union, a doctors' union and a union for university professors. From time to time they co-operate with Histadrut professional unions.

Italy

Capital: Rome   **Population: 57,000,000**

Political system. Italy is a multi-party republic "founded on labour" with a bicameral Parliament and a President acting as head of state. The system of proportional representation has resulted in frequent changes of government despite an underlying continuity of policy. It is a member of both the EC and NATO.

Economy. Out of total employment of 21,100,000 in January 1990, 6,860,000 were employed in industry, 1,880,000 were employed in agriculture, and 12,360,000 in services. The 11.5 per cent unemployment rate at that date was the lowest since early 1987, and it was noticeable that the rate of employment creation was higher in the south than the north, suggesting that many years of development policy might finally be paying off. GDP increased 3.2 per cent in 1989 and indeed there was sustained economic growth in every year from 1983. The 1990 rate of inflation was 5.5 per cent.

There is a persistent economic division between the industrial North and the predominantly agricultural South. Not well-endowed with natural resources, Italy is dependent on manufacturing industry. Despite strong GNP growth rates in recent years, attributable largely to a depreciation of the US dollar and falling commodity prices, there are significant structural problems, including rising unemployment and a persistent budget deficit.

System of industrial relations. Italy ratified ILO Conventions No. 87 (Freedom of Association and Protection of the Right to Organize, 1948) and No. 98 (Right to Organize and Collective Bargaining, 1949) in 1958. Freedom of association has prevailed since the end of World War II.

In June 1990 Parliament passed a landmark law preventing strikes in a wide array of sectors from crippling essential services. It had been pending since 1988 and was the first post-War restriction on strikes in Italy.

Collective bargaining. Collective bargaining in Italy has developed since World War II in line with the process of industrialization and modernization of the economy; adverse factors—such as the acute under-development of the south, the prevalence of casual, home and informal work, and high unemployment levels—have been considerably offset by the fairly high level of union organization (with about 6,700,000 members of trade unions, compared with a total employed workforce of 14,640,000), the generally dynamic character of Italian industry since the war, and the movement to trade union unity of action from the 1960s which led to the formation of the CGIL-CISL-UIL federation in 1972. Bargaining at national level (involving the CGIL, CISL and UIL, the public and private employers' organizations and where appropriate the government) occurs irregularly and is concerned with issues of universal concern, notably the system of wage indexation (*see below*). Sectoral negotiations, involving industry level unions and employers' organizations and typically occurring on a three-yearly basis, set agreements covering all aspects of labour relations and apply to all workers whether unionized or not. At workplace level, shop stewards' committees—factory councils (*consigli di fabbrica*) or councils of delegates (*consigli dei delegati*)—have been established in large numbers since the late 1960s, as part of the development of policies of unity between the CISL, UIL and CGIL, and extend a form of organization known since the 1920s, the *commissione interne*, which had involved only a small minority of the workforce. These bodies, which are elected by all the workers, union and non-union, further define and modify the content of sectoral agreements and they, rather than the unions separately, conduct all intra-plant negotiations. Bargaining in general is relatively decentralized, and this has allowed for considerable flexibility in adapting to technological change in some sectors. The UIL has complained that some workplace councils have in some cases arbitrarily excluded white-collar employees from participation or been affected by a climate of intimidation where extremists were in control.

Scala mobile. A dispute over modification of the system of wage indexation (the *scala mobile*), first introduced in 1975, contributed to the collapse of the CGIL-CISL-UIL federation in 1984. A draft comprehensive incomes policy agreement, involving wage restraint in combination with measures to create jobs, control rents and combat tax evasion, was in early 1984 accepted by the CISL, the UIL and the socialist minority of the CGIL (these groups arguing that the control of inflation was essential to combat unemployment), as well as by the employers, but not by the CGIL communist majority. CGIL opposition to the draft centred on the proposal to set a fixed ceiling to wage increases provided by the *scala mobile*, but also reflected apparent doubts in the Communist Party (PCI), to whose policies the CGIL normally closely adheres, about the developing role of the CGIL-CISL-UIL federation as an independent political force. The draft agreement was subsequently passed by parliament as a decree, in the face of bitter PCI opposition and strikes and disturbances led by the CGIL. On June 9–10, 1985, a national referendum was held on a PCI proposal to abrogate a single item of the 1984 agreement, i.e. that relating to wage policy. The referendum resulted in a narrow defeat for the communist proposal, partly because inflationary pressures had eased in 1984 (from an annual rate of over 12 per cent in January 1984 to under 9 per cent by December) with the result that real wages kept pace with inflation.

The breakdown of the CGIL-CISL-UIL federation was never total, however, Thus in December 1984 the three centres jointly signed an agreement on union participation in policy-making in the Institute for Industrial Reconstruction (IRI), a state-run holding company controlling the principal public sector undertakings. This agreement provided for the establishment of joint advisory committees (whose recommendations would not be binding) at every level of the IRI, and was considered a major advance in Italian industrial relations. Within a month of the June 1985 referendum, the CGIL-CISL-UIL had again agreed a joint programme of demands for bargaining purposes (thus pre-empting the employers' demand that the incomes question should be settled directly by legislation), and in December 1985 the three confederations reached a framework agreement with the government concerning all aspects of pay and conditions in the public sector. This agreement included modifications to the *scala mobile*, greater workers' participation in policy-making, provisions to reduce hours and increase employment, and a voluntary code of conduct for regulating strikes. This agreement was immediately extended unilaterally to the private sector by the employers' confederation, Confindustria. In its new form the *scala mobile* provided for pay adjustments on a six-monthly basis (rather than quarterly as formerly); the first L 580,000 of monthly pay was to be fully indexed, but only 25 per cent of the balance exceeding this amount. The framework agreement of May 1987 governing the private sector along with the changes in the *scala mobile* aimed at securing the self-regulation of strike activity without state intervention and at restoring the wage differentials and status of middle management (*quadri*) which had been significantly eroded under the previous system of automatic wage indexing.

The call of the main union confederations in November 1987 for the first one-day general strike in six years to protest against government economic measures to reduce the budget deficit met with greater success in the industrial sector than in public services. The rapid spread of the Cobas in public services and their resort to frequent and disruptive wildcat strikes, especially in transport, also undermined the authority of the main unions and led to demands for legal restrictions on the right to strike. The unions responded by proposing a compromise involving legislation covering certain essential services and the revision of the voluntary codes of conduct to ensure the provision of minimum services, appropriate periods of notice of strike action, bans on strikes during holiday periods, and conciliation procedures. A bill passed through the Italian parliament in 1988 with widespread union and political support incorporating these features as well as greater sanctions against non-compliance and the creation of a "watchdog" Commission for Industrial Relations in the Public Services to assess the adequacy of the new voluntary codes.

Hours lost to strikes in 1989 were just over 29,000,000, an increase over the amount for 1988 of nearly one third. Most stoppages occurred as part of the tactics to bring pressure to bear in negotiations. Strikes tended to be brief and locally called. Despite this increase, the years from 1985 to 1990 saw no general strikes. However, following the breakdown of negotiations with the employers' organization Confindustria, the main union centres called a general strike on July 10, 1990. The two flashpoints were the refusal of the employers to negotiate a new contract for engineering until the unions agreed a change in the structure of the pay bargaining system, and their threatened unilateral withdrawal from the *scala mobile*.

On the eve of the threatened strike, government intervention secured a settlement based on one year's more life for the *scala mobile* with a union commitment to negotiate a new structure in June 1991, and an agreement in engineering followed. In 1991 the three main union centres tabled far-reaching proposals for the reform of bargaining in the private sector, in advance of the talks scheduled for June. The three centres also secured government acceptance of their proposals to apply private sector rules to industrial relations in the public sector, replacing civil service law and regulations.

Trade unionism. The (socialist) Confederazione Generale di Lavora (CGL) and the (Catholic) Confederazione Italiana dei Lavoratori (CIL) were founded in the first decade of the twentieth century; both faced intense opposition from employers, with especially violent conflict in the agrarian sector where the unions recruited many agricultural labourers. In the period of political upheaval and labour unrest following the end of World War I, the claimed membership of the CGL increased to 2,000,000 and that of the CIL to over 1,000,000. Under Mussolini, however, fascist unions were accorded monopoly representation in 1925 and by 1927 all other unions were abolished. In June 1944 (i.e. when Italy was effectively divided between German and Allied occupying forces), socialist, communist and Christian democrat trade unionists in the "Pact of Rome" agreed on the formation of a unified national centre, the Italian General Confederation of Labour (Confederazione Generale Italiana del Lavoro—CGIL). Under the Pact, each of the three political tendencies was to have equal representation on the CGIL executive bodies. However, the CGIL progressively disintegrated and by 1950 the present basic tripartite division of the trade union movement had developed, with the CGIL dominated by communists, the Confederazione Italiana dei Sindacata Lavoratori (CISL) dominated by Christian democrats (but with some socialist influence) and the Unione Italiana del Lavoro (UIL), the smallest of the three, led by social democrats and republicans. Both the CISL and the UIL are ICFTU affiliates; the CGIL was formerly a WFTU affiliate but broke away in 1978. There is no WCL affiliate, although the WCL has a collaborative relationship with the Associazione Cristiane Lavoratori Italiana (ACLI).

The industrial organization of the various centres has tended to be weak and underfunded, reflecting the relatively recent development in Italy of "trade" as opposed to "class" unionism and the disunity of the trade union movement, and the central organizations have dominated their industrial affiliates (i.e. in contrast to the situation in Britain, West Germany and the USA). Local chambers of labour, linked directly to their respective trade union centres and uniting workers regardless of industry, have been of more significance than the industrial unions. The numbers of members claimed by the various organizations undoubtedly overstates the dues-paying membership and are inflated partly because of competitiveness between the different centres.

Throughout the 1960s, aided by the increasing acceptance by the CGIL of the European Economic Community and also by the strength of the liberal movement in the Roman Catholic Church under Pope John, relations between the main three trade union centres markedly improved, and a CGIL-CISL-UIL working alliance was formed in 1972, although the federations retained their separate identities. The creation of the CGIL-CISL-UIL federation embodied an agreement that to achieve a unitary policy the confederations must be independent of the government and the political parties, and the three confederations accepted that it was incompatible for trade union officials to be at the same time union officials and leaders of political parties, members of parliament, senators or town, provincial or regional councillors. This agreement was included in the statutes of the three confederations. The CGIL-CISL-UIL federation collapsed in 1984, but has since been partly restored (*see below*).

The model of Italian trade unionism institutionalized in the 1970s (involving a synthesis of political or class unionism with a strong if decentralized base of plant organization and worker militancy) entered a period of crisis in the 1980s. At the top the involvement of the confederations in political bargaining with the state came under increasing strain with the worsening economic situation and ultimately, if temporarily, fractured their political unity. At the base the unions faced, first, a decline in rank-and-file militancy with the number of working hours lost due to industrial disputes falling from nearly 193,000,000 in 1979 to 39,000,000 in 1986. Second, mainly as a result of the egalitarian wage policies pursued through neo-corporatist bargaining, union organizations outside the three main confederations emerged to challenge their hitherto dominant position. In the public sector localized and sectionalist *sindicati autonomi*, independent unions of mainly professional employees, developed or revived in areas such as state and local government, the service sector, the health service and the airways in order to contest the erosion of income differentials and status of highly skilled workers. In response to the same trends, associations of *quadri* (cadres) emerged among middle level employees, such as foremen and technicians, at primarily the company level. Since 1986 even more localized *comitati di base* (grass-roots committees), known popularly as "Cobas", have formed in areas such as teaching and essential public services in opposition to not only the main union confederations but the autonomous unions themselves.

Union density in Italy is hard to assess, and estimates range from 39 per cent for 1986 to 15 per cent for 1989. The comparable ratio for 1977 to the 1986 figure is 48.4 per cent. There are major problems in assessing the membership of individual unions and confederations, for example double counting. There is less dispute over the trend however; indeed, there is considerable concern that further decline may result from what the communist daily *L'Unita* called "a crisis of representation". All union centres appear to face factional and disciplinary problems, even the famously well organized CGIL. Under the "Workers' Statute" (Law 300 of May 20, 1970) the three centres have status as "most representative unions", giving them legal rights to workplace representation. By Section 111 the most representative unions at enterprise level have certain rights, usually used to establish a factory council (*consiglia di fabbrica*) which represents the interests of the entire workforce.

In 1972 the three centres established a unitary *Federazione* which survived until 1984 when it collapsed in an inter-union dispute over the *scala mobile*. The *Federazione* had harmonized the centres' approach to factory councils. Lacking common regulations they came together in 1989 to form a Works Council of Trade Union representatives (CARS) but this has failed to build links anew between the centres and those they claim to represent. An inter-confederal commission of 1989 failed to produce a constructive way forward for enhancing representation. While the centres had their own individual proposals no significant steps had been taken in advance of the talks with Confindustria in June 1991.

Meanwhile, all three centres face a threat from the Base Committees (COBAS) which have explicitly called for the abolition of the Workers' Statute. The COBAS held a delegate conference in September 1990 to consider the formation of a national organization and have achieved considerable success at the expense of the confederations in some areas of high union density; other autonomous unions have also gained ground.

The various independent or autonomous unions have a combined membership, estimates of which range from 1,800,000 to 4,000,000. Like the *cobas*, to which they have almost certainly lost membership, they reject the partisan or macro-economic orientation of the confederations. They are to be found in some strength in transport, health, public administration, public utilities and finance. Because they are sectionally motivated, the autonomous unions have been slow to confederate despite the use of the term confederation by two of their number, CISAL and CISNAL. The *quadri*, or "grey collar" movement is in philosophy opposed to sectionalism, seeking to represent all employees, regardless of status. It came into being in opposition to the FIAT strike mounted by the three confederations in 1980, organizing a famous "march of the 40,000". In 1985 the *quadris* received a major boost when Law 190 granted them equal status with other unions in negotiations.

Comitati Di Base (COBAS)
Base Committees

History and character. The origins of the COBAS lie in rank-and-file revolts during 1987 and 1988 against the leadership of the three confederations. COBAS members are normally disgruntled members of the confederations whom they believe to have neglected bread and butter issues in their pursuit of overall economic and partisan political objectives. Quite frequently they are skilled or professional groups which feel that their interests are neglected in negotiations where the demands of large unskilled groups are to the fore.

On several occasions they rejected agreements reached by the confederations in the public sector, and gained enough support to mount many strikes for the re-opening of agreements. Their first success in 1988 was in the schools, where with the backing of only 7 per cent of the workforce they secured a wage increase for more than a quarter of teachers. In 1989 the COBAS called strikes primarily in the public transport sector; they claim the support of as many as 20,000 railway trade unionists and also have a significant following among airline employees and social security.

By 1990, 20 years after the Workers' Statute, the COBAS had determined to work for its repeal. Though their aims are sectional they have resolved to establish a national dimension to their influence. In September 1990 they held a delegates' conference which decided to found a national organization and to initiate a petition to abolish the concept of "most representative unions" which it entails.

Confederazione Generale Italiana del Lavoro (CGIL)
Italian General Confederation of Labour

Address. Corso d'Italia 25, 00198 Rome
Phone. (6) 84761
Telex. 623083
Leadership. Bruno Trentin (general secretary)
Membership. At the end of 1989 the CGIL claimed to have passed 5,000,000 members for the first time. However it is thought that 40 per cent of the membership consists of retired members.
History and character. The CGIL was formed by agreement between socialists, communists and

245

Christian democrats in the "Pact of Rome" of June 1944 as a unified trade union centre. The CGIL at first functioned only in southern and central parts of Italy controlled by the Allies, but was accepted as nationally representative at a conference with the chambers of labour from the industrialized north in June 1945 after the surrender of German forces in that area. Under the Pact of Rome, socialists, communists and Christian democrats were to enjoy equal representation on the CGIL executive bodies, but tensions between the different factions were encouraged after 1945 by the emergence of the Christian democrats as the major political party and by the intensification of the ideological division of Europe, which was reflected in a campaign of strikes and violent unrest led by communists within the CGIL in 1947–48. By 1950 most socialists and Christian democrats had withdrawn from the CGIL (see CISL and UIL), and the confederation has since then been dominated by supporters of the Communist Party (PCI), although with a socialist minority, with close financial and other ties to the party.

The CGIL was for many years closely associated with the policies of the Soviet Union and its allies, but a modification of its position enabled the formation of the CGIL-CISL-UIL federation in 1972. In 1974, in step with the move to advocacy by the PCI of "Eurocommunism", it downgraded its relationship with the Soviet bloc-led World Federation of Trade Unions (WFTU), of which it had previously been the largest western European affiliate, to that of associate, and withdrew altogether in 1978. In 1987 the CGIL vociferously demanded union pluralism in Poland.

The unopposed election of Antonio Pizzinato, a career trade unionist, as secretary general in March 1986 in succession to Luciano Lama, was seen as marking a healing of the internal divisions within the CGIL caused by controversy over the *scala mobile* (above). However, Pizzinato's reign proved to be brief as he was increasingly blamed for the CGIL's lack of direction and the growing strength of the Socialist minority in the union. He was dismissed in October 1988 and replaced by Bruno Trentin, a left-wing intellectual and former leader of the metalworkers union, who was thought by his supporters to be more capable of promoting a modern image and coping with the continuing problems of the union.

The CGIL still contains a large socialist faction whose leader is the Deputy General Secretary Ottaviano Del Turco. It has advocated a new legislative framework for workplace representation, and at a Council in July 1990 resolved to finance a major programme of workplace reform. The centrepiece of its proposals is elections in the enterprise for works' committees rather than allocation of places by size of confederation. Its most recent congress was in November 1990.

International affiliation. ETUC. In May 1989 the CGIL (with CISL and UIL support) became the first West European communist union to enter the TUAC.

Confederazione Italiana dei Sindacati Lavoratori (CISL)
Italian Confederation of Workers' Unions

Address. Via Po 21, 00198 Rome
Phone. (6) 84731
Telex. 614045
Leadership. Franco Marini (secretary general)
Membership. Claims 3,379,028.

History. The CISL was founded in 1948 as the Libera Confederazione Generale Italiana dei Lavoratori and took its present name in 1948. In its early years it received direct support from both the Roman Catholic Church and the US AFL-CIO and (indirectly) the US Central Intelligence Agency (CIA), which were alarmed at the communist domination of the CGIL. It has remained predominantly Christian democratic (i.e. supporting what has been the dominant political party in Italy since World War II), but with some socialist influence.

Prof. Enzo Tarantelli, the president of the CISL Research Institute, was murdered by "Red Brigades" terrorists on March 27, 1985.

The CISL has proposed legally regulated triennial workplace elections of worker representatives to coincide with bargaining rounds. All workers, including non-members, would be entitled to vote. In the view of Sergio D'Antoni more frequent elections will strengthen the confederation's representative status.

International affiliations. ETUC; ICFTU; TUAC.

Unione Italiana del Lavoro (UIL)
Italian Labour Union

Address. Via Lucullo 6, 00187 Rome

Phone. (6) 49731

Telex. 622425

Fax. 4973208

Leadership. Giorgio Benvenuto (general secretary)

Membership. Claimed membership of 1,560,436 in 1990.

History and character. The UIL was founded in 1950 and named after an earlier organization which had split from the USI (Anarcho-Syndicalist Federation) in 1918, and opposed the fascists until banned under Mussolini. The UIL was created, with predominantly republican and social democrat leadership, in opposition to the communist domination of the CGIL and the Christian democratic control of CISL, and was expressly non-confessional. In the post-war ideological division of the trade union movement, the UIL was partly funded by the American Federation of Labour (and indirectly by the CIA).

The UIL describes itself as socialist, non-confessional and politically independent, and as being an advocate of full internal union democracy rather than adherence to ideological positions influenced by outside forces (i.e. in contrast to the CGIL and CISL). The UIL emphasizes the need for unions to adapt to the challenges of technological change, and to adopt a positive rather than backward-looking and negative approach. This includes the requirement that the labour movement should enter a sustained dialogue with other social classes and in turn be accepted as a co-partner in planning, in rejection of the "sterile antagonism" of institutionalized class conflict. The UIL strongly favours the extension of tripartism to encompass an incomes policy involving a "macro-economic agreement to fight inflation and foster employment", but has criticized the working of the *scala mobile* as having eroded differentials. It has also campaigned against tax evasion and the growth to major proportions of the black economy in Italy.

The UIL favours an extension of the powers and influence of the European Trade Union Confederation (ETUC) to meet common European problems such as unemployment and the influence of monetarist theories, and global action to meet the problem of Third World indebtedness and under-development (although not advocating wholesale debt repudiation). It describes itself as a pacifist organization but advocates multilateralist rather than unilateralist positions on disarmament.

At its March 1990 Congress the UIL proposed a pact of the three Italian confederations to strengthen European trade unionism. Its preferred solution to the representational problem is a dual structure of works' committees with exclusive negotiating rights elected by union members only, and works councils elected by the whole workforce with participation rights and the duty to monitor the implementation of agreements.

Organizations created by the UIL to provide various services to its members include ITAL (Institute for the Protection and Welfare of Workers; this operates both in Italy and in many countries to which Italians have emigrated); ENFAP (National Vocational Training Agency); OTIS (Italian Organization for Social Tourism); UNIAT (National Union of Tenants); CREL (Centre for Economic and Labour Research); and Instituto "Progretto Sud" (to develop co-operation with the unions of "the South", i.e. the Third World).

Structure. The basic unit is the branch workplace union (the "company group"); these federate both regionally and industrially and the UIL as the national confederation is formed by the national industrial and regional unions.

Affiliated unions. There are 30 affiliated unions, including a pensioners' union: *Agriculture*: UIMEC (sharecroppers and farmers), UISBA (farmhands); *Industry*: UILIAS (food and sugar industries); UILTA (textile, clothing and shoe workers); UILM (metalworkers); UILPEM (petrol and gas industry workers); UILCID (chemical and diverse industries); MONOPOLI (employees of state monopoly agencies); FENEAL (building and wood industry workers); UILSP (public service workers); RICERCA (research workers); FILSIC (federation of press, information and cultural workers); *Services*: UILTUCS (tourism, commerce and services); UIB (bank employees); FILE (tax collectors), UILPOST (post office workers); UILTES (state telephone workers); UILASS (insurance workers); UILTCA (autonomous municipal treasury workers); UILTE (telephone workers); *Transport*: UIL TRASPORTI (transport workers); *Civil Service*: SANITA (health federation);

UILDEP (employees of public authorities); UIL-SCUOLA (schoolworkers); UNDEL (local authority workers); UIL-STAT (state employees); UILEM (workers for authorities in the south); UIL ORGANI CONSTITUZIONALI (constitutional agency workers); UILP (retired workers); UILGIO-VANI (youth association).

There is in addition a Confederal Union of Cadres (UCQ), which is defined as being an "inter-trade union body in which UIL members whose job definition is that of technician, cadre, or similar, are given special room for union consideration and proposals".

Publication. Lavorosocieta (weekly); *Polis.*

International affiliations. ETUC; ICFTU; TUAC. Has good relations with the Yugoslav trade unions and some limited contacts with Soviet bloc unions.

Other central organizations

Associazione Cristiane Lavoratori Italiana (ACLI)
Christian Association of Italian Workers

Address. Via Guiseppe Marcora 18–20, 00153 Rome
Leadership. D. Rosati (president)
International affiliation. Collaborates with the WCL as an "extraordinary member".

Confederazione Italiana dei Sindacati Autonomi Lavoratori (CISAL)
Italian Confederation of Autonomous Workers' Unions

Address. Via Cavour 310, 00184 Rome
Phone. (6) 6785402/6785877/6785405
Fax. 3220087
Leadership. Dr Constantino Gilco (secretary general)
Membership. Claims 1,800,000.
History and character. CISAL was founded in November 1957. It strongly supports trade union pluralism and opposes any political or outside intervention in union affairs.
Affiliated unions. 65 affiliated unions.
Publications. CISAL Notizie.
International affiliations. None.

Confederazione Italiana dei Sindacati Nazionali dei Lavoratori (CISNAL)
Italian Confederation of National Workers' Trade Unions

Address. Via Principe Amedeo 42, 00185 Rome
Phone. 4817919
Fax. 482266
Leadership. Fedele Panipo (general secretary)
Membership. Claims 2,269,224 but in reality appears to be concentrated in a few state enterprises.
History. Founded in March 1950.
Publications. Cisnal Notizie; Lameta Sociale; Pagine Libere.
Affiliated unions. There are 27 CISNAL affiliates:

Cisnal Alimentazione, Via Principe Amedeo 42 Rome.

Cisnal Carta e Stampa, Via Principe Amedeo 42 Rome.

Cisnal Chimici, Via Principe Amedeo 42 Rome.

Cisnal Costruzioni, Via Principe Amedeo 42 Rome.

Cisnal Energia, Via Iside 12 Rome.

Cisnal Metalmeccanici, Via Principe Amedeo 42 Rome.

Cisnal Spettacolo, Via Principe Amedeo 42 Rome.

248

Cisnal Telecomunicazioni, Via Volturno 40 Rome.

Cisnal Tessili, Via Marchese De Rosa 41 Foggia.

Cisnal Coltivatori, Via Principe Amedeo 42 Rome.

Cisnal Lavoratori Agricoli, Via Principe Amedeo 42 Rome.

Cisnal Autoferrotranvieri, Via Sommacampagna 29 Rome.

Cisnal Ferrovie, Via Iside 12 Rome.

Cisnal Mare, Via Principe Amedeo 42 Rome.

Cisnal Trasporti, Via Iside 12 Rome.

Cisnal Terziario, Via Principe Amedeo 42 Rome.

Cisnal Sicurezza Civile, Via Principe Amedeo 42 Rome.

Cisnal Assicuratori, Via Principe Amedeo 42 Rome.

Cisnal Credito, Via Carlo Emanuele I, 48 Rome.

Cisnal Enti Locali, Via Cialdini 14 Rome.

Cisnal Enti Pubblici, Via del Corea 13 Rome.

Cisnal Poste, Via Principe Amedeo 42 Rome.

Cisnal Sanita, Via Principe Amedeo 42 Rome.

Cisnal Scuola, Via Principe Amedeo 42 Rome.

Cisnal Statali, Via Principe Amedeo 42 Rome.

Cisnal Vigili del Fuoco, Via Principe Amedeo 42 Rome.

Cisnal Pensionati, Via Principe Amedeo 42 Rome.

Federazione fra le Associazoni e i Sindacati Nazionali dei Quadri Direttivi dell'amministrazione dello Stato (DIRSTAT)

Address. Via Ezio 12, 00192 Rome.
Phone. (06) 3211535.
Fax. (06) 3212690.
Leadership. Dr Eduardo Mazzore (secretary-general).
Membership. 9,500.
Publication. Riforma Administrativa (monthly).
Affiliated unions. There are 33 unions and associations of civil service executives and officers.
International affiliations. Confédération Internationale des Fonctionnaires (CIF).

Jamaica

Capital: Kingston   **Population: 2,340,000**

Political system. Jamaica achieved full independence within the Commonwealth in 1962. The British monarch (represented by a Governor-General) is the head of state, and the country has a bicameral legislature, the lower house of which is popularly elected and the upper house appointed. The political system has been dominated since independence by the Jamaica Labour Party (JLP) and the People's National Party (PNP). After a violent election campaign in 1980 the DLP under Edward Seaga won a decisive victory, and was re-elected in 1983, winning all seats in the legislature after the PNP boycotted the election as a protest against the use of outdated electoral lists.

The JLP stayed in power until 1989, when Michael Manley's PNP returned to power. Unlike its previous term of office however, the PNP's new spell was marked by the continuation of the free market policies of the JLP.

Economy. The Jamaican economy (based principally upon sugar, bauxite and tourism) suffered from a prolonged recession during the 1970s, causing increasing unemployment and social unrest. The deflationary policy of the Seaga government received substantial support from the USA and the IMF, but economic recovery was hampered by depressed world bauxite and sugar prices.

The Manley government reached a new standby agreement with the IMF, the core of which was a wage increase guideline of 10 per cent in 1989 and 12.5 per cent in 1990, following the period 1986–88 when wages outstripped inflation. Economic growth was resumed in 1989 and 1990 but Jamaica still suffers a persistent balance of payments problem and has failed to overcome a high unemployment rate of 17.5 per cent in 1989. It also had to overcome the effects of Hurricane Gilbert which struck the island in September 1988. As a guide to the structure of the workforce, there were 877,000 in civilian employment in 1988, of whom 199,000 were in industry, 240,000 in agriculture, and 435,000 in services.

System of industrial relations. Jamaica ratified ILO Conventions No. 87 (Freedom of Association and Protection of the Right of Organize, 1948) and No. 98 (Right to Organize and Collective Bargaining, 1949) in 1962, and there has been significant trade unionism activity since the 1940s. The *Report of the Committee of Experts on the Application of Conventions and Recommendations of the ILO (1988)* noted "with regret" that for the third year running, the government had failed to reply to queries on its application of Convention No. 122 (Employment Policy, 1964, ratified 1975). Regarding Convention No. 87, the Committee also regretted the denial of the right to negotiate collectively in the case of workers in a bargaining unit, "when these workers do not amount to more than 40 per cent of the unit". It calls on the government to amend section 5 of the Labour and Disputes Act No. 14 of 1975 in order to ensure that the union with the greatest number of workers in a bargaining unit (even if it does not have 40 per cent of the workers in that unit) is entitled to negotiate, collectively, conditions of employment, at least on behalf of its own members. The Committee also requests the government to amend sections 9 and 10 of the above Act which allows the compulsory arbitration and termination of any strike in the essential services; this power should be narrowed to cover strikes which endanger life, personal safety or health of the whole or part of the population, or in the event of a national crisis. In a report received by the Committee in April 1987, the government stated that the national minimum wage would be applicable (in correspondence to Convention 100, Equal Remuneration, 1951, ratified 1975) to all workers irrespective of sex. The Committee, in reply, stated that this should cover all men and women performing work of equal value. The right to strike is prohibited in a range of "essential services" including banking, transport, the docks and oil refining under the Labour Relations and Industrial Disputes Act of 1975 (as amended), and the Labour Minister is empowered to refer all disputes to compulsory arbitration. Collective bargaining is developed, and supplemented by government conciliation services.

Jamaica has a number of bi-partite and tripartite institutions including the Labour Advisory Council and the National Planning Council. Unions are consulted about industrial relations matters and assist in the development of social programmes. There is a predisposition to collective bargaining, the status of which is upheld in law; where bargaining breaks down the Ministry of Labour may arbitrate. In 1989 there was a marked fall in the number of disputes over the previous year.

Trade unionism. Jamaican trade unionism has its origins in the development of the country's party system in the 1930s, with one wing (BITU) being the outgrowth of the JLP and the other (NWU) being founded by the PNP. These two remain Jamaica's largest unions, but they are being challenged by the fast-growing UAWU which has communist links, and is recruiting sugar and part-time workers in competition with the two older bodies. Some unions remain unaffiliated to a major centre. Union density is 24 per cent and there are also well-organized employee associations which bargain collectively for nurses, teachers, police, junior doctors, and civil servants.

Bustamante Industrial Trade Union (BITU)

Address. 98-100 Duke Street, Kingston
Phone. 922 2443
Cables. BITU, KINGSTON, JAMAICA
Leadership. Hugh Shearer (president); Edith Nelson (general secretary)
Membership. 114,000.
History. The BITU was founded in 1938 by Alexander Bustamante. In 1943 Bustamante created a political arm for the union, the Jamaica Labour party, and relations between the union and the party (which is the more right-wing of the two principal Jamaican parties, and free-enterprise in orientation) have remained close. In June 1985, however, the BITU joined a four-day general strike, supported by all the main unions on the island, in protest against the JLP government's policy of wage restraint and the impact of austerity measures backed by the IMF. BITU opposed the 12.5 per cent IMF wage guideline for 1990 as "totally unworkable".
International affiliation. ICFTU.

Independent Trade Unions Action Council (ITAC)

Address. 2 Wildman Street, Kingston
Phone. 92-25266
Leadership. Christopher Lawrence (general secretary); Roderick Francis (president)
Membership. 12,000.
History and character. Founded in 1968, the ITAC was established as a federation of trade unions (currently 11) and is affiliated to neither the JLP nor the PNP. All the affiliated unions share the same headquarters and in 1982 a Trade Unions Co-operative Credit Union was organized, with 6,000 shareholders and assets of US$3,000,000.
Publications. Independent Trade Unionism; Forward to Freedom.
International affiliation. WFTU/CPUSTAL.

National Workers' Union of Jamaica (NWU)

Address. 130-32 East Street, P.O. Box 344, Kingston
Phone. (92) 21150 4
Leadership. Lloyd Goodleigh (general secretary); Derrick Rochester (president)
Membership. 20,000.
History and character. The NWU was founded on April 2, 1942, as an affiliate of the People's National Party (PNP—itself an affiliate of the Socialist International); its status was formally changed to that of a PNP "associate" in 1983. The orientation is to democratic socialism.
Affiliates. There are three affiliated unions: Union of Clerical, Administrative and Supervisory Employees; Carreras Staff Association; Jamaica Enrolled Nurses Association.
Publication. *NWU News* (quarterly newspaper).
International affiliation. ICFTU.

Trades Union Congress of Jamaica (TUCJ)

Address. P.O. Box 19, 25 Sutton Street, Kingston
Phone. (809) 922 5313; 922 3292; 922 5468
Leadership. Edward Smith (president); Hopeton Caven (general secretary)
Membership. 20,000.
History and character. Formed in 1948 by unions opposed to the Bustamante Industrial Trade Union. Independent, leftist, acts as an umbrella union.
International affiliations. CCL; ICFTU.

University and Allied Workers' Union (UAWU)

Address. 50 Lady Musgrave Road, Kingston 10
Phone. 92-77968
Leadership. Muriel Johnson (general secretary); Trevor Munroe (president)
Membership. 21,000.
Character. Founded in 1971, it originally organized workers in the University of the West Indies and other educational institutions in Jamaica before its influence spread to include workers in the public, private and agricultural sectors. Some members of the leadership of the union are in the leadership of the pro-Soviet Workers' Party of Jamaica (WPJ). The UAWU has quadrupled its membership in recent years.
International affiliation. WFTU.

Japan

Capital: Tokyo **Population: 123,220,129**
(1989)

Political system. Japan is a constitutional monarchy within which legislative power resides in a bicameral legislature known as the Diet. The conservative Liberal Democratic Party (LDP) has governed since its formation.

Economy. Although almost bereft of natural energy sources Japan has enjoyed spectacular economic success since 1945 in the manufacture and export of engineering and consumer goods and, most recently, the production of microprocessor technology. Although some progress has been made towards liberalizing Japanese financial markets, removing import restrictions and stimulating domestic demand, Japan's continuing surplus with its major trading partners has remained the cause of international friction.

In the five years to 1990 Japan experienced uninterrupted growth: in 1989 the rate was 5 per cent. Inflation was below 1 per cent and unemployment less than 2.5 per cent. The 1988 workforce of 61,660,000 was distributed between industry (33.6 per cent), agriculture (7.9 per cent) and services (58 per cent). A growing worry for Japan at the start of the 1990s was the shortage of labour; various options were being considered including raising the retirement age and measures to encourage more women to return to or take up paid work. There was strong resistance to meeting the shortages by increasing the number of foreign workers in Japan. By the end of 1989 shortages were being felt right across industry and services: a Ministry of Labour Survey disclosed that no single sector claimed to have enough workers.

System of industrial relations. The basic rights of private sector workers—comprising 75 per cent of all organized workers—are guaranteed by the Trade Union Law of 1945 and the Labour Relations Adjustment Law, but public sector employees are covered by separate legislation, principally the Public Corporation and National Enterprise Labour Relations Law, the Local Public Enterprise Labour Relations Law, the National Public Service Law and the Local Public Service Law. In addition Japan ratified ILO Convention No. 98 (Right to Organize and Collective Bargaining, 1949) in 1953 and Convention No. 87 (Freedom of Association and Protection of the Right to Organize, 1948) in 1965. The closed shop is legal in the private sector, but where more than one union exists in an enterprise the employer cannot choose to bargain collectively with only one. The employer is obliged to engage in collective bargaining with workers' representatives unless there are fair and appropriate reasons to do otherwise. "Yellow-dog" contracts and interference by employers in union affairs are unlawful, as is discrimination against trade unionists on the grounds of their legitimate union activities. Relief may be obtained both through the courts and through the Labour Relations Commission. Employees covered by the National Public Service Law, with the exception of employees in the police, maritime defence and prison services, are permitted to organize and may not be discriminated against for so doing; such organizations may negotiate with the employer within limits but may not take industrial action.

Sanrokon (the Industry and Labour Round Table Conference) has since 1975 provided a tripartite national forum for the discussion of industrial and labour issues, under the sponsorship of the Minister of Labour; similar to this body is Korokon (Round Table Conference for the Public Corporation and National Enterprises). There are numerous forums for bilateral consultation between employers and unions at confederal and federal level, and the unions are also involved in the work of deliberative and advisory councils within the Ministry of Labour, etc.

Labour Standards. Under the amended Labour Standards Law in force since April 1, 1988, statutory annual leave has been increased from six to 10 days and annual holidays of at least five days' consecutive leave are required. A recent survey showed that less than 20 per cent of firms were at present putting this into practice.

The present maximum working week is set at 46 hours and is planned to be reduced to 40 hours in the 1990s. The recommendation on model rules governing hours of work and conditions of service is particularly important in the medium and small firms not covered by unionization, collective bargaining or the practice of joint consultation which is carried out in an estimated 77 per cent of establishments with more than 100 employees.

Sex equality. A law on occupational equality between men and women came into effect in April 1986, but this embodied a series of guidelines without effective sanctions. Japan has not ratified ILO Convention No. 111 (Discrimination—Employment and Occupation —Convention, 1958), and there is substantial resistance within the country to equality of opportunity at work (although equal pay is required for the same work). The Equal Opportunity Law prohibits discriminatory treatment of workers by reason of sex in policies and practices involved in employees' basic training, welfare provisions, retirement age provisions and discharge decisions. It also calls on employers to make effort to ensure equal treatment in recruitment, employment promotion and job assignment decisions. In addition, the Law revised some provisions of the Labour Standard Law and abolished or drastically eased restrictions originally designed to protect women workers. These concerned overtime arrangements for women, late night work and holidays. In November 1985, when the Labour Ministry announced guidelines in respect of the legislation, the then existing four National Centres all critized the Law and the guidelines arguing that they only provided an "infrastructure" and failed to lay down actual steps to improve working standards for women.

Spring Labour Offensive. More than 80 per cent of organized labour in Japan is involved in the Spring Labour Offensive (the *shunto*), in which co-ordinated annual wage demands are presented to all employers in a concentrated period, with a peak in April. The agreements reached through the Offensive affect wage determination for all workers, including those denied true collective bargaining rights and non-union workers. The Offensive—which in effect co-ordinates what would be the otherwise limited bargaining power of Japanese enterprise unionism—was first employed on a significant scale (under Sohyo leadership) in the mid-1950s and was encouraged thereafter by the rapid development of the Japanese economy and labour shortages, with Domei unions (which had initially opposed the practice) joining in the 1960s. Traditionally the different central organizations formulated their respective proposals separately (although Churitsuroren worked with Sohyo on a Joint Struggle Council for the Spring Labour Offensive). In 1984, however, the four national centres and the IMF-JC established the Chingintoso Renraku Kaigi (Wage Struggle Liaison Council) to formulate a uniform bargaining position; this basic position is refined at confederal and federal congresses held early in the year and then detailed claims are presented at enterprise level, where collective bargaining agreements are in almost all cases actually negotiated and concluded (an exception occurs notably in the case of Kaiinkumiai, the All Japan Seamen's Union, which itself negotiates an industry-wide agreement). This process is reinforced at the national level by the actions of the two national centres and their co-ordinating committees, which lobby the government and the *Diet* over labour-related issues in the budget (the fiscal year commencing on April 1) and stage demonstrations. Kokumin Shunton Kyoto Kaigi (People's Spring Labour Offensive Joint Struggle Council) has often backed this strategy with selective strikes, principally of transport workers, although this practice has declined in recent years. Tekkororen (Japan Federation of Steel Workers' Unions), followed by other unions in the automobile, electrical machinery and shipbuilding industries organized in the IMF-JC, have traditionally served as pace-setters in the bargaining process, and settlements in other sectors normally follow quickly after agreement in those industries. Simultaneously with negotiations in the private sector, settlements for labour in public corporations and national enterprises are reached through mediation by the Public Corporation and National Enterprise Labour Relations Commission and are embodied subsequently in an arbitration award; in practice, the Commission normally links public sector awards closely to those in the private sector. The same is true of awards for public service employees reached later in the year through the National Personnel Authority, and for local public service employee awards made at municipality level, although from 1981, in an effort to curtail public budget deficits, public service award recommendations were not fully implemented. Overall the impact of the Spring Labour Offensive has weakened somewhat since the early 1980s because of slower economic growth and increased unemployment, and individual enterprise agreements have shown more variation related to the particular circumstances

254

and ability to pay of the company concerned. Since the mid-1970s wage settlements have generally not exceeded the employers' target figures and real wages have lagged behind increases in productivity.

However, the average wage increase in the 1989 Shunto was 5.17 per cent compared to the 1988 increase of 4.5 per cent, the biggest rise in real terms since 1974, which followed on from large summer and winter bonuses (each of them the largest since 1980). Expectations in 1990 were shelved following turmoil in Japanese financial markets in the spring, though the minimum level sought by New-rengo was 6 per cent. A 1987 law calls for the reduction of the working week from 48 hours to 40, and in 1989 for the first time since 1975 the upward trend in the number of hours worked a year was halted.

Disputes. The number of days lost in industrial disputes has tended to decline since the high inflation of the mid-1970s, and Japan typically has fewer days lost per worker per annum than any industrial country other than West Germany (only 252,000 workdays were lost in total in 1986). Most disputes occur at the time of the Spring Labour Offensive, and Sohyo unions are most frequently involved. Lockouts are considered lawful but are rare. The right to strike is guaranteed in the private sector, but employees in national and local government, and the national enterprises (postal service, forestry service, government printing and the mint) are prohibited from striking, and the right to strike is restricted in the electric power and coal mining industries, the merchant marine, and in the public utilities generally. Political and sympathetic strikes (which are rare) are generally considered unlawful, as are wildcat strikes, strikes involving sabotage or a threat to safe workplace practices, and strikes violating industrial peace clauses of existing collective bargaining agreements. Unions engaged in legitimate strikes are exempt from civil and criminal liabilities; where strike action is considered illegitimate, employers generally seek to dismiss or discipline the strike leaders and rarely seek damages from the union, or to impose sanctions on those who merely followed the strike call. The Labour Relations Adjustment Law provides for conciliation, mediation and arbitration, which may be carried out through the Labour Relations Commission; this body (which is structured at both national and local levels) is tripartite in composition, comprising representatives of labour, employers and the public interest. In practice, however, most disputes are settled directly between employer and unions. A Public Corporation and National Enterprise Labour Relations Commission exists to adjust disputes in the national enterprises (where industrial action is prohibited), and this is supplemented by a Grievance Handling Joint Adjustment Council. Local public enterprises are excepted from certain areas of the Trade Union Law and Labour Relations Adjustment Law, but disputes in this field are adjusted by the Labour Relations Commission. The ILO Committee of Experts on the Application of Conventions and Recommendations has noted that the present denial of the right to strike to public servants is in violation of the Conventions, under which the right to strike may be denied only in the case of narrowly-defined essential services, and even then only when other guarantees of speedy, impartial and binding arbitration and conciliation procedures exist. Cases where the government seeks to penalize public sector strike leaders directly are rare, although prior to the privatization of JNR (the National Railways) management did act frequently to "punish" strikers.

The number of disputes in 1988 was 1,879 involving 1,240,000 workers. This represented an increase in the number of disputes over 1987 of 2.2 per cent and of workers involved of 14.2 per cent. The number of hours lost to disputes declined however. In 1989 there were no major strikes.

Privatization. In April 1985 the former public corporations, the Japan Monopoly Corporation and the Nippon Telegraph and Telephone Corporation, became private corporations and their employees were brought under the Trade Union Law rather than the Public Corporation and National Enterprise Labour Relations Law. The privatization and break-up (with heavy job losses) of the public corporation, Japan National Railways, took effect in April 1987; the privatization was bitterly opposed by the Sohyo-affiliated railway union, Kokuro, which had traditionally been one of the strongest and most militant of unions, notwithstanding the nominal legal ban on strike action by public railway workers.

Trade unionism. The first unions were formed in the 1890s but these were effectively suppressed by the Law for the Maintenance of Public Peace of 1900. A Workers' Fraternity Association (Yu-ai-kai) was established in 1912; this became the Japan Confederation of Labour (Nihon-Rodei-Sodomei) in 1921, and by 1936 there were 420,000 trade union members. Trade union activities in the 1920s were powerfully influenced by communist and other radical tendencies; by 1940 however, Nihon-Rodei-Sodomei had been dissolved by the government, and until the defeat of Japan in World War II workers were mobilized in Sangyo Hokoku (Service to the State through Industry). Following World War II the Trade Union Law of December 1945 for the first time formally guaranteed workers the right to form trade unions, and Article 28 of the 1946 Constitution guaranteed workers the right to organize, bargain collectively and to strike. Sodomei was re-established in 1945 but the trade union movement was divided by intense ideological conflict over the following decade against a background of appreciable industrial unrest and underwent a complex process of fragmentation. Until 1987 there were four national trade union centres: Sohyo (General Council of Trade Unions of Japan), which was the largest, Domei (Japanese Confederation of Labour), the second largest, and two smaller organizations, Churitsuroren (Federation of Independent Unions of Japan) and Shinsanbetsu (National Federation of Industrial Organizations). Of these, only one was affiliated to one of the three international trade union centres of the ICFTU, WFTU and WCL (i.e. Domei, to the ICFTU). On Nov. 20, 1987, a new National Centre, the Japanese Private Sector Trade Union Confederation (Rengo), was set up, comprised of the affiliated union federations of Domei and Chiritsuroren and a number of private sector federations from Sohyo. Domei and Chiritsuroren were merged into Rengo. A year later, in October 1988, Shinsanbetsu was also dissolved and its union federations also joined Rengo. Rengo itself affiliated to the ICFTU, which also still has three public sector direct Japanese affiliates (the Municipal Traffic Workers' Union Toshiko, the Postal Workers' Union Zentei, and the Japan Confederation of Public Sector Trade Unions, Zenkanko). After intense negotiations the most significant structural development in Japanese trades unionism since World War II occurred on Nov. 21, 1989, when the Rengo and Sohyo merged to form the third largest trade union centre in the ICFTU. The new Rengo, with eight million affiliated members, represents around two thirds of organized labour in Japan. The other centres are the National Union Confederation (Zenroren) which is linked to the Japan Communist Party, and the National Union Consultative Council (Zenrokyo) which has links with the Left of the Japanese Socialist Party. These centres are very small by comparison with the new Rengo.

The reasons for this major shift in the structure of the Labour Movement in Japan are complex. Over the last decade, there has been considerable collaboration between the previous four National Centres over the annual wage round (the Shunto) (*see below*) and other issues, and the old ideological split between the Left (Japan Socialist Party) and the Right (Democratic Socialist Party) has cooled. Factions in both Left and Right continued to resist the formation of a single national centre, however, and the Japan Communist Party has been opposed to it consistently. The drive to privatize the National Corporations, particularly the Japan National Railways which was split into a number of private companies in 1987, seems to have convinced many public sector unions, who were mainly affiliated to Sohyo, that it was necessary to ally with the more thriving private sector federations. The process of forming the new national centre has been a slow and cautious one and it has taken place whilst the overall membership of unions in Japan has been declining slowly as a percentage of the employed population. This crisis of membership seems to have been a further reason for persuading union leaders that a new union structure and strategy was necessary.

Union membership in 1989 fell to 25.9 per cent of the workforce, continuing the decline which had taken it down from 56 per cent in the 1950s and 33.9 per cent in 1974. During that 15-year span, the number of employees has risen by 10,500,000 but the number of union members has fallen back from 12,462,000 to 12,227,000. In 1988 unionization rates by broad sector were as follows: all industries 26.8 per cent; agriculture, forestry and fishing 11.7 per cent; mining 41.9 per cent; construction 17.4 per cent; manufacturing 32.6 per cent; wholesale and retail 8.8 per cent; finance, insurance and property 50 per cent; transport and telecommunications 57.4 per cent; utilities 65.6 per cent; services 16.3 per cent; government 71.9 per cent. The new Rengo is committed to a membership drive among small businesses; in 1986 the rate of unionization in firms employing less than 30 staff was 0.4 per cent. As may be seen, organization is much more robust in the public sector than it is in the private sector. It is also determined to end the unchallenged rule of the Liberal Democratic Party and looks towards the creation of a centre-left alliance. In 1989 private sector Rengo fielded 12 candidates in the Senate elections and 11 of them were elected.

Enterprise unionism. The basic form of trade union organization in Japan, in contrast to all other western industrial countries, is the single-enterprise union, which is either workplace-based or federates the different workplaces of a single company, and organizes all full-time workers regardless of job classification. (A parallel system exists in the public sector, based on individual offices, corporations, etc.) The characteristic of this form of unionism is the close relationship between the two sides of industry, involving a high degree of both formal and informal consultation. The system has been widely seen as having greatly assisted Japan's economic development by encouraging workers to view their interests as being best served by promoting the health of the company for which they work; conversely, it has somewhat weakened the overall union movement by creating a sense in each enterprise that "the union exists because the company exists". Japan's consistently strong economic performance since World War II has enabled the large employers in effect to guarantee a job for life, and school leavers and university graduates typically make "career plans" involving a commitment to a particular firm (rather than type of occupation); furthermore, salary levels are tied to length of service, so that loyalty of itself brings a constantly increasing reward. In these circumstances, Japan has found issues of retraining and job flexibility less difficult than most of its industrial competitors. Many so-called "part time" workers (including full-time workers), however, who are not entitled to company benefits because hired on short-term contracts, are excluded from enterprise unions; women are especially affected by such exclusion. Union closed shop agreements, under which employees may in some cases be dismissed for failure to join the union, exist in many enterprises in the private sector (such agreements are illegal in the public sector), although rival enterprise unions sometimes co-exist within the same enterprise, divided on policy issues or their central trade union affiliation. The practical significance of worker involvement in the enterprise varies from informal consultation solely on issues directly relevant to labour through to (in rare cases) extensive co-participation in management. Rengo-affiliated unions favour full worker participation, with co-determination of basic management strategies, but Sohyo unions commonly have been cautious, fearing to dilute the identity of the union as a separate force, and the Japanese employers' federation Nikkeiren, while favouring joint consultation, does not greatly favour worker directorships or co-determination on the West German model. Dues for unions in the private sector average 2 per cent of income and are usually collected by the check-off; the unions are well-staffed at all levels with both career officials and elected worker officials (with enterprise employees receiving unpaid extended leave during their period of service as union officers), and this facilitates a close familiarity with the problems of the workers and the business. Upper industrial and central federations and confederations—which are poorly funded relative to the enterprise unions—have negligible control over their affiliated enterprise unions, and the role of the industrial federations has often been peripheral. This role has tended to increase in recent years, however, as the industrial federations have become involved in such issues as the establishment of uniform standards for the introduction of new technology, problems of depressed areas and industries, etc., and an increase in job mobility may ultimately weaken the dominance of enterprise unionism.

Nihon Rodokumiai Sourengokai (JTUC, New-Rengo)
Japanese Trade Union Confederation

Address. Denkiroren kaikan, 10–3, 1-Chome, Mita, minato-ku, Tokyo 108
Phone. 03 3769-6545
Telex. J25908
Fax. 03 3454-6206
Leadership. Akira Yamagishi (president); Seigo Yamada (general secretary)
Membership. 8,000,000.
History and character. New-Rengo is the product of the fusion of the former private sector Rengo, and the mainly public sector Sohyo. Private sector Rengo was formed in November 1987 as Japan's unions took their first step towards unification of the labour movement. At that point it embraced some 5,500,000 affiliated members and was already the largest union centre in the country. It comprised the affiliates of Domei, Churitsuroren and Shinsanbetsu (brief descriptions of these now defunct centres are provided below) as well as most of the private sector affiliates of Sohyo. It replaced the loose association of private sector unions Zenminrokyo and affiliated to the ICFTU in December 1987. Sohyo was the largest centre until the formation of Rengo for it had 4,360,000 members in 1987. It originated in July 1950 as a major breakaway from the Japan Communist Party-dominated Zen-Nihon-Sanbetsu-Kaigi (All Japan Congress of Industrial Unions, itself formed in 1946 and which folded in 1958). Sohyo initially intended to affiliate to the ICFTU (which was formed in December 1949); however, after a struggle between rival factions through the early 1950s Sohyo ultimately resolved not to affiliate to the ICFTU, principally because the ICFTU supported the position of the non-communist countries on the Korean War, the 1951 Japan-US security treaty and related issues. Following this a number of unions left Sohyo and combined with the rightist group from Sodomei to form Zenro (Japanese Trade Union Congress) in 1954; this subsequently evolved into Domei. In the mid-1950s, however, a faction within the leftist leadership of Sohyo emphasizing economic demands, rather than conflict with the USA, gained the ascendancy, and in 1956 Sohyo and other unions initiated the full Spring Labour Offensive. Since that time radical politics and class struggle ideology declined as a feature of Sohyo's policies, in step with the decline of radicalism in the Japanese working class, and during the 1980s Sohyo emphasized its wish to modernize its approach to industrial relations in order to take account of the changed realities of Japanese economic and political life. Sohyo joined TUAC in 1989 and its relations with the ICFTU warmed.

Throughout its history Sohyo was linked to the Japanese Socialist Party, and in 1985, 65 of the 111 Socialist members of the House of Representatives and 29 of the 43 Socialist members of the House of Councillors were former officers of Sohyo or its member unions.

On Nov. 21, the New-Rengo was inaugurated at a unification conference. It is the third largest ICFTU affiliate in the world. It intends to build on the growing political interest shown by the old Rengo which fielded candidates for the Senate in the 1989 elections, 11 of whom were elected. The New-Rengo aims to contribute towards building a centre-left challenge to the LDP which has dominated Japanese politics since the War.

Affiliated unions. The following lists all more than 50,000 members, ranked by order of size of membership.

1. **JICHIRO**
   All-Japan Prefectural and Municipal Workers' Union, 6-Bancho 1, Chiyoda-ku, Tokyo 102
   Phone: (3263) 0263. Fax: (3230) 1386.
   Leadership: Takemitsu Yamada (president); Huruo Sato (general secretary).
   Membership: 1,110,400.

2. **JIDOSHASOREN**
   Confederation of Japan Automobile Workers' Union, Kokuryu Shobakoen Bldg, 6–15, Shibakoen 2-chome, Minato-ku, Tokyo 105.
   Phone: (3434) 7641. Fax: (3434) 7428.
   Leadership: Teruhito Tokumoto (president); Tadayoshi Kusano (general secretary).
   Membership: 720,234.

3. **DENKIROREN**
   Japanese Federation of Electrical Machine Workers' Unions, Denkiroren Kaikan Bldg, 10–3, Mita 1-chome, Minato-ku, Tokyo 108.
   Phone: (3455) 6911. Fax: (3452) 5406.
   Leadership: Yasuo Iwayama (president); Katsutoshi Suzuki (general secretary).
   Membership: 693,013.

4. **ZENSENDOMEI**
   Japanese Federation of Textile, Garment, Chemical, Mercantile, Food and Allied Industry Workers' Unions, 8–16, Kudan Minami 4-chome, Chiyoda-ku, Tokyo 102.
   Phone: (3865) 9051. Fax: (3865) 9062.
   Leadership: Jinnosuke Ashida (president); Tsuyoshi Takagi (general secretary).
   Membership: 518,165.

5. **NIKKYOSO**
   Japan Teachers' Union, Nihon-kyouiku Kaikan, 2-6-2 Hitotsubashi, Chiyoda-ku, Tokyo 101.
   Phone: (3265) 2171. Fax: (3230) 0172.
   Leadership: Shoju Ohba (president); Hiromu Hata (general secretary).
   Membership: 518,000.

6. **SEIHO ROREN**
   National Federation of Life Insurance Workers' Union, Tanaka Bldg, 3-19-5 Yushima, Bunkyo-ku, Tokyo 113.
   Phone: (3837) 2031. Fax: (3837) 2037.
   Leadership: Yotarou Kohno (president); Koichiro Watanabe (general secretary).
   Membership: 438,368.

7. **ZENKINRENGO**
   Japanese Federation of Metal Industry Unions, Yuai Kaikan, 2-20-12 Shiba, Minato-ku, Tokyo 105.
   Phone: (3453) 5377. Fax: (3453) 5379.
   Leadership: Tohru Eguchi (president); Kurami Nakajo (general secretary).
   Membership: 315,349.

8. **JOHO-TSUSHIN-ROREN**
   The Japan Federation of Telecommunications, Electronic Information and Allied Workers, Zendentsu-Rodo Kaikan, 3–6 Kanda-Surugadai, Chiyoda-ku, Tokyo 101.
   Phone: (3219) 2231. Fax: (3253) 3268.
   President: Akira Yamagishi (president); Masaki Morikawa (general secretary).
   Membership: 289,040.

9. **DENRYOKUSOREN**
   Confederation of Electric Power Related Industry Workers' Unions of Japan, Denryokurodo Kaikan, 7–15, Mita 2-chome, Minato-ku, Tokyo 108.
   Phone: (3454) 0231. Fax: (3798) 1470.
   Leadership: Shizuka Katayama (president); Yuji Fukuda (general secretary).
   Membership: 222,381.

10. **TEKKO ROREN**
Japan Federation of Steel Workers' Unions, Tekko Roren Kaikan Bldg, 23–4, Shinkawa l-chome, Chuo-ku, Tokyo 104.
Phone: (3555) 0401. Fax: (3555) 0407.
Leadership: Etsuya Washio.
Membership: 201,724.

11. **KINZOKU-KIKAI**
National Metal and Machinery Workers' Union of Japan, 6–2, Sakuraoka-cho, Shibuya-ku, Tokyo 150.
Phone: (3463) 4231. Fax: (3463) 7391.
Leadership: Akikazu Ikeda (president); Kazuo Shimada (general secretary).
Membership: 200,000.

12. **SHITETSU-SOREN**
General Federation of Private Railway Workers' Unions, Shitetsu Kaikan, 3–5, Takanawa 4-chome, Minato-ku, Tokyo 108.
Phone: (3473) 0166. Fax: (3447) 3927.
Leadership: Makoto Tamura (president); Kanju Suzuki (general secretary).
Membership: 192,158.

13. **ZENTEI**
Japan Postal Workers' Union, 2–7, Kouraku l-chome, Bunkyo-ku, Tokyo 112.
Phone: (3812) 4260. Fax: (3816) 4762.
Leadership: Satoru Kawasuzaki (president); Mototaka Ito (general secretary).
Membership: 165,000.

14. **J.R. SOREN**
Japan Confederation of Railway Workers' Union, Meguro-Satsuki Kaikan, 2–13, Nishi-Gotanda 3-chome, Shinagawa-ku, Tokyo 141.
Phone: (3491) 7191. Fax: (3491) 7192.
Leadership: Fukutaro Fukuhara (president); Shibata (general secretary).
Membership: 130,445.

15. **ZOSENJUKI ROREN**
Japan Confederation of Shipbuilding and Engineering Workers' Union, Yuai Kaikan Bldg, 20–12, Shiba 2-chome, Minato-ku, Tokyo 105.
Phone: (3451) 6783. Fax: (3451) 6935.
Leadership: Sukesada Ito (president); Yoshii (general secretary).
Membership: 120,120.

16. **IPPAN DOMEI**
National Federation of General Workers' Union, Yuai Kaikan Bldg, 20–12, Shiba 2-chome, Minato-ku, Tokyo 105.
Phone: (3453) 5969. Fax: (3769) 3738.
Leadership: Akashi Ohki (president); Yoshio Tsujimura (general secretary).
Membership: 113,408.

17. **SHOGYO ROREN**
Japan Federation of Commercial Workers' Unions, New-State Mena Bldg, 23–1 Yoyogi 2-chome, Shibuya-ku, Tokyo 151.
Phone: (3370) 4121. Fax: (3370) 1640.
Leadership: Mamoru Shibata (president); Mitsuo Nagumo (general secretary).
Membership: 106,335.

18. **KOTSU ROREN**
Japan Federation of Transport Workers' Union, Yuai Kaikan Bldg., 20–12, Shiba 2-chome, Minato-ku, Tokyo 105.
Phone: (3451) 7243. Fax: (3454) 7393.
Leadership: Motoji Fujiwara (president); Kazuo Hirokawa (general secretary).
Membership: 103,932.

19. **ZENKA DOMEI**
Japanese Federation of Chemical and General Workers' Union, Yuai Kaikan Bldg, 20–12, Shiba 2-chome, Tokyo 105.
Phone: (3453) 3801. Fax: (3454) 2236.
Leadership: Hiroichi Honda (president); Yoshikazu Ueno (general secretary).
Membership: 101,038.

20. **GOKA ROREN**
Japanese Federation of Synthetic Chemistry Workers' Union, Senbai Bldg, 26–30, Shiba 5-chome, Minato-ku, Tokyo 108.
Phone: (3452) 5591. Fax: (3454) 7464.
Leadership: Takeshi Sasaki (president); Toshikazu Minami (general secretary).
Membership: 91,527.

21. **UNYU ROREN**
All Japan Federation of Transport Workers' Union, Zennittsu Kasumigaseki Bldg, 3–3, Kasumigaseki 3-chome, Chiyoda-ku, Tokyo 100.
Phone: (3503) 2171. Fax: (3503) 2176.
Leadership: Tetsuya Akita (president); Kiyoshi Oyama (general secretary).
Membership: 79,720.

22. **ZENKOKU IPPAN**
National Council of General Amalgamated Workers' Union, Zosen Kaikan Bldg, 5–6, Misaki-cho 3-chome, Chiyoda-ku, Tokyo 101.
Phone: (3230) 4071. Fax: (3230) 4360.
Leadership: Ikuo Tomioka (president; Yasuhiko Matsui (general secretary).
Membership: 75,584.

23. **KAGAKU SOREN**
Japanese Federation of Chemical Workers' Union, Tamachi Annex Bldg, 7–7, Shiba 4-chome, Minato-ku, Tokyo 108.
Phone: (3454) 2491. Fax: (3454) 2492.
Leadership: Masahiko Takabe (president); Sunao Washida (general secretary).
Membership: 70,981.

24. **ZEN YUSEI**
All Japan Postal Labour Union, 20–6, Sendagaya 1-chome, Shibuya-ku, Tokyo 151.
Phone: (3478) 7101. Fax: (5475) 7085.
Leadership: Yoshihisa Matsuda (president); Kazuyuki Kaho (general secretary).
Membership: 70,255.

25. **KAIIN**
All Japan Seamen's Union, 15–26, Roppongi 7-chome, Minato-ku, Tokyo 106.
Phone: (3403) 6251. Fax: (3478) 0023.
Leadership: Shosiro Nakanishi (president); Shinji Ohsawa, Tetsuji Kobatake (vice-presidents).
Membership: 70,000.

26. **SHOKUHIN ROREN**
Japan Federation of Food and Allied Workers' Union, Hiroo Office Bldg, 3–18, Hiroo 1-chome, Shibuya-ku, Tokyo 150.
Phone: (3446) 2082. Fax: (3446) 6779.
Leadership: Ken-ichi Tamura (president); Eiji Takada (general secretary).
Membership: 59,470.

27. **ZENJIKO ROREN**
National Federation of Automobile Transport Workers' Unions, 7–9, Sendagaya 3-chome, Shibuya-ku, Tokyo 151.
Phone: (3408) 0875. Fax: (3497) 0171.
Leadership: Osamu Mimashi (president); Akira Kurozawa (general secretary).
Membership: 56,123.

28. **KAMIPA RENGO**
Japanese Federation of Pulp and Paper Workers' Unions, 12–4, Kita-Aoyama 2-chome, Minato-ku, Tokyo 107
Phone: (3402) 7656. Fax: (3402) 7659.
Leadership: Yasuhiro Kakugo (president); Aritomi Doi (general secretary).
Membership: 54,262.

29. **KOKKO SOREN**
Japan Central Federation of National Service Employees' Unions, 2–1, Kasumigaseki 1-chome, Chiyoda-ku, Tokyo 100.
Phone: (3508) 4990. Fax: (3580) 8038.
Leadership: Kiyoshi Fujinama (president); Tatsuo Shima (general secretary).
Membership: 50,434.

Publications. Monthly Rengo.
Affiliated Unions and Structure: 81 unions (*see above*).
International affiliations. ICFTU.

Major independent unions (Private Sector)

Independent unions with more than 50,000 members:

Zenkensoren
National Federation of Construction Workers' Unions, 7–15, Takadanobaba 2-chome, Shinjuku-ku, Tokyo 169.
Phone: 03 3200 6221. Fax: 03 3209 0538.
President: Tadayoshi Kato.
Gen. secretary: Tadaki Yata.
Membership: 543,229.

Shiginren
Federation of City Bank Employees' Unions, Ida Bldg, 3–8, Yaesu 1-chome, Chuo-ku, Tokyo 103.
Phone: (274) 5611.
President: Terufumi Hiroshima.
Gen. secretary: Keiichi Ando.
Membership: 149,000.

Kirokaigi
Machinery Labor Union Council, c/o Nihon Seiko Roso, Yusen Bldg, 2–3–2 Marunouchi, Chiyoda-ku, Tokyo 100.
Phone: (284) 1657-8.
President: Masaoki Kitaura.
Gen. secretary: Takayuki Hirai.
Membership: 114,000.

Zennokyororen
National Federation of Agricultural Mutual Aid Societies Employees' Unions, Shinjuku Nokyo Kaikan Bldg., 5–5, Yoyogi 2-chome, Shibuya-ku, Tokyo 151.
Phone: (370) 8327.
President: Hideo Goto.
Gen. secretary: Yoshiharu Nakazawa.
Membership: 89,000.

Major independent unions (Public Sector)

Independent unions with more that 50,000 members:

Tororen
The Federation of Tokyo Metropolitan Government Workers' Unions, 3-8-1, Marunouchi,

Chiyoda-ku, Tokyo 100.
Phone: (212) 6931.
President: Tamio Miyabe.
Gen. secretary: Hiroshi Kimura.
Membership: 200,000.

Zenkanko
Japanese Confederation of Public Sector Trade Unions, Yuai Kaikan Bldg., 20–12, Shiba 2-chome, Minato-ku, Tokyo 105.
Phone: (451) 7963.
President: Yoshihiro Matsuda.
Gen. secretary: Yoichi Ishii.
Membership: 124,000.
Note: Zenkanko is directly affiliated to the ICFTU.

Zen-yusei
All Japan Postal Labor Union, Zen Yusei Bldg., 20–6, Sendagaya 1-chome, Shibuya-ku, Tokyo 151.
Phone: 03 3478 7101.
President: Yoshio Matsuda.
Gen. secretary: Kazuyuki Kato.
Membership: 71,000.

Liaison Councils for ICFTU affiliates

FIET—Nihon Kameisoshiki Renraku Kyogikai
FIET—Japanese Liaison Council (FIET-JLC)

Address. Nyusuteitomena Bldg., 23–1, Yooyogi 2-chome, Shibuya-ku, Tokyo 151
Phone. 03-3370-4121
Fax. 03-3370-1640
Leadership. Tadashi Miura (general secretary)
Membership. 366,000.
Affiliates. There are six, as follows:

1. **Japan Federation of Commercial Workers' Unions**.

2. **Japanese Federation of Textile, Garment, Chemical Distributive and Allied Industries Workers' Unions**

3. **Federation of Non-Life Insurance Workers' Unions**

4. **Confederation of Japan Automobile Workers' Unions**

5. **Japanese Confederation of Aviation Labour**

6. **Chain Store Labour Unions' Council**

ICEF—Japanese Affiliates Federation (ICEF-JAF)

Address. Denryokurodokaikan Building, 7–15, Mita 2-chome, Minato-ku, Tokyo 108
Phone. 03-3454-8521
Fax. 81 3-3454-8516
Leadership. Koichi Honda (president); Tetsuya Iwata (general secretary)
Membership. 673,000.

ICFTU—Nihon Kameishoshiki Renraku Kyogikai
ICFTU—Liaison Council (ICFTU-LC)

Address. Oikawa Bldg., 7th Floor, 12–18, Shinbashi 2-chome, Minato-ku, Tokyo 105
Phone. (508) 1351
Leadership. Tadanobu Usami (also acting president of Rengo) and Tadashi Kubo (co-presidents)
Membership. 4,771,000.

IUF—Kemeikumiai Renraku Kyogikai
IUF—Japan Co-ordinating Council (IUF-JCC)

Address. Ajinomoto Takaramachi Bldg., 15–1, Kyobashi 1-chome, Chuo-ku, Tokyo 104
Phone. (561) 4540
Leadership. Shigeo Shiina (president); Koichi Maeda (general secretary)
Membership. 165,000.

Zennihon-Kinzokusangyo-Rodokumiai-Kyogikai
Japan Council of Metalworkers' Unions (IMF-JC)

Address. Santoku Yaesu Building, 2-6-21, Yaesu, Chuo-ku, Tokyo 104
Phone. 03-274-2461
Telex. 02222534 IMFJC J
Fax. 03-274-2476
Leadership. Tesuhito Tokusnoto (president); Shiro Umehara (general secretary)
Membership. 2,418,200.
Affiliates.

1. **Japanese Federation of Electrical Machine Workers' Unions (Denki Roren).**

2. **Confederation of Japan Automobile Workers' Unions (Jidosha Soren).**

3. **Japanese Federation of Steel Workers' Unions (Tekko Roren).**

4. **Japan Confederation of Shipbuilding and Heavy Engineering Workers' Unions (Zosen Juki Roren).**

5. **Japanese Federation of Metal Industry Unions (Zenkin Rengo).**

6. **National Metal and Machinery Workers Union of Japan (Kinzoku Kikai).**

7. **National Machinery and Metal Workers Union (Zen Den Sen).**

8. **Japanese Metal Mine Workers' Union (Hitetsu Kinzoku Roren).**

9. **Eight enterprise-based unions directly affiliated with the IMF-JC.**

Recently dissolved federations.

1. **Chiritsuroren** (Federation of Independent Unions of Japan) was founded in 1956 by independent unions seeking to avoid entanglements in the polarization of the labour movement between Sohyo and Zenro (the predecessor of Domei). It was dissolved in 1987 on the formation of Rengo. In 1985–86 it had 1.5 million members in 10 affiliated industrial federations, nearly all in the private sector. Key federations were Denkiroren, (Japanese Federation of Electrical Machine Workers Unions), Zenseikiyu, (All Japan Oil Workers Union) and Zenkokugasu, (National Council of Gas Supply Workers Unions).

2. **Shinsanbetsu** (National Federation of Industrial Organizations) was founded in December 1949 as a split from Zen-Nihon Sanbetsu-Kaigi (All Japan Congress of Industrial Unions, the predecessor of Sohyo) by unions opposed to the Communist domination of that organization. There were five affiliated industrial federations, four of them in the private sector, accounting for 95 per cent of total membership (61,000). It merged with Rengo in October 1988.

3. **Domei** (Japanese Confederation of Labour) was founded in 1962 in opposition to Sohyo when Sohyo unions decided not to affiliate to the ICFTU. It was an important supporter of the Democratic Socialist Party (DSP) founded by right-wing defectors from the Socialist Party in 1960. In 1985, 12 of the 38 Democratic Socialist members of the House of Representatives and five of the 13 in the House of Councillors came from former officers of Domei and its affiliated unions. It was estimated that 50 per cent of the voters for the DSP in the 1983 election came from families of Domei union members.

There were 29 affiliated industrial federations, 23 in the private sector, with 2,000,000 members, and six in the public sector, with 144,000 members, in 1985. It was dissolved in 1987 on the formation of Rengo.

Unions affiliated to trade union internationals of the WFTU.

1. **Japan Council of Medical Workers Unions** (Public Service Related Workers—TUI).
   Membership. 152,000.

2. **All-Japan General Construction Day Workes' Union** (Construction—TUI).
   Membership. 47,000.

3. **All-Japan Construction Workers' Union** (Construction—TUI).
   Membership. 10,000.

4. **National Federation of Automobile Transport Workers' Union** (Transport, Dockworkers and Fishing—TUI).
   Membership. 55,000.

5. **All-Japan Transport and General Workers' Union** (Transport, Dockworkers and Fishing—TUI).
   Membership. 15,000.

In addition, the Hitotsubashi branch of the Japan Senior High School Teachers' Union (Nikkokyo-Hitotsubashi, 30,000 members) has observer status in the WFTU Teachers' Union. The Japan Federation of National Service Employees (138,000 members) has observer status in the Public Service Related Workers—TUI.

Jordan

Capital: Amman   **Population: 3,247,000**

Political system. The Hashemite Kingdom of Jordan is a constitutional monarchy in which the King exercises considerable power; no political parties are permitted. In July 1988 it renounced its claim to the Israeli-occupied West Bank. The general election of 1989 appeared to herald a phase of liberalization.

Economy. Although Jordan itself has no readily exploitable oil reserves, its economy is affected by oil prices which in turn affect the Arab states' ability to meet aid commitments.

In 1988 572,000 of the civilian population were engaged in paid work—231,000 in industry, 40,000 in agriculture and 269,000 in services. While the government recorded unemployment at 8.9 per cent for the same year, unofficial estimates put the rate much higher. The government (including the armed forces) is the largest employer: it has pursued a policy of persuading Jordanians to accept employment normally taken by foreign workers and encouraging migration of labour.

System of industrial relations. Jordan ratified ILO Convention No. 98 (Right to Organize and Collective Bargaining, 1949) in 1968, but has not ratified Convention No. 87 (Freedom of Association and Protection of the Right to Organize, 1948).

Informal consultations are regularly held with the JFTU, both by employers and the government. Strikes rarely occur, and are forbidden to government employees. However, the liberalization process which began in 1989 may lead to greater activity and a strike did occur at the Petra Bank early in 1990.

About 40 trade union activists sympathetic to the Democratic Front for the Liberation of Palestine (DFLP) were arrested in the winter of 1985–86, apparently because of DFLP attempts to control trade union activity on the West Bank.

Trade unionism. The main union centre is the Jordan Federation of Trade Unions (JFTU) which has traditionally taken a pro-government stance though this is now under challenge from within.

Jordan Federation of Trade Unions

Leadership. Abdul Khaddam

International affiliations. IAATU.

Affiliated unions and structure. The Federation now has 17 unions affiliated, having lost two following Jordan's withdrawal of administrative responsibility for the West Bank in 1988.

History and character. The government has for decades exercised indirect control over the Federation and Jordanian unions rarely involve themselves in politics, concentrating on workplace issues. In April 1990 however, 10 Federation unions formed a "democratic unionist bloc" and boycotted the Executive Committee elections, demanding reforms in the handling of finance and the proportional representation of individual unions. In defiance of this challenge the remaining unions elected an establishment candidate, Abdul Khaddam as Secretary General of the Federation.

Kenya

Political system. Kenya became an independent state within the Commonwealth in December 1963, and a Republic in December 1964. President Daniel arap Moi, who succeeded Kenya's first President, Jomo Kenyatta, after his death in August 1978, was returned to office unopposed in 1983. Following a constitutional amendment of June 1982, the Kenya African National Union (KANU) became the sole legal party.

Economy. Agriculture is the basis of the economy, accounting for over 60 per cent of exports, 24 per cent of which comes from tea, grown in plantations, and over 80 per cent of employment. Although the industrial sector is one of the most advanced in Africa it contributed only 11 per cent of gross domestic product in 1985 and 13 per cent of employment.

The expansion of the public sector allowed it to surpass the private sector in size in 1987, with more than 660,000 workers. Inflation in 1988 was 10.7 per cent and rising and there was an unemployment rate in excess of 11 per cent and tending to grow as Kenya's workforce rapidly expanded. The waged workforce is comparatively small, and the government hopes to absorb greater numbers of new workers in small scale informal enterprises.

System of industrial relations. Kenya ratified ILO Convention No. 98 (Right to Organize and Collective Bargaining, 1949) and Convention Nos. 29 and 105 on forced labour in 1964. However, there are compulsory procedures for government conciliation and arbitration, compulsory communal labour may be exacted, and compulsory labour may form part of punishment for political dissidence and for participation in some strikes.

The number of registered wage agreements rises most years, and reached 384 in 1988. From 1973 onwards the Kenyan government monitored all wage agreements and by the later 1980s they were permitted to increase rates at only 75 per cent of the pace of inflation. Higher increases have been obtained by public sector workers, who are not subject to these guidelines. The minimum wage was raised in 1989.

The 1962 Industrial Charter (revised in 1980) established tripartite machinery in which COTU joins the powerfully interventionist Ministry of Labour and Kenya's well organized employers, the FKE. Nevertheless the number of recorded trade disputes both in 1987 and 1988 was close to 1,000—forcing the opening of a second industrial court in 1989, and the number of strikes near to 100. These were normally of short duration however.

Trade unionism. Trade unions developed after World War II under British colonial labour legislation, and were closely linked to nationalist politics.

The unions are closely identified with the ruling party, but clashes between the government and sections of the labour movement have nevertheless occurred from time to time. In 1980 the Nairobi University Staff Union and the Kenya Civil Servants' Union were banned because of their "over-indulgence in politics", and from 1985 all civil servants were required to be members of the ruling KANU party.

The Central Organization of Trade Unions (COTU) is the sole national centre for unions and is recognized as such by its place in the country's tripartite machinery. It was unenthusiastic about Daniel Arap Moi's 1988 announcement that it would be affiliated to the ruling party, but it opposes the more radical orientation of other African union centres. The only substantial union outside it is the Kenya National Union of Teachers (KNUT).

Central Organization of Trade Unions (COTU)

Address. Solidarity Building, Digo Road, P.O. Box 13000, Nairobi
Phone. 761375/6/7
Leadership. P. Mwangi Kibiribiri (chairman general); J. J. Mugalla (secretary general)
Membership. Approximately 300,000 in 1988, which represents a decline of one quarter over the figure for the late 1970s.

History and character. The COTU was founded in 1965 in succession to the Kenya Federation of Labour and the African Workers' Congress, which were dissolved. It is the only trade union centre in Kenya and most unions are affiliated to it. In conjunction with the ICFTU, COTU prepared a report in 1987 which reviewed the Kenyan economy to 1986, and made proposals to raise the purchasing power of wages, increase employment, and improve productivity and working conditions. Among the proposals was another call for a five-day working week. More recently COTU has become increasingly critical of the austerity measures associated with the government's IMF-backed economic reform programme.

In 1987 and 1988 COTU began an ambitious restructuring programme to improve administration and consolidate member unions where members had been lost. It also redesigned the curriculum of Tom Mboya College and increased its staff, though in 1988 the financial support the College had received from the African-American Labour Centre (AALC) was reduced. The professional staff of COTU itself was also expanded to include experts in women's affairs, computing, accounts and economic research and in some of these areas continued to receive AALC support.

Affiliated unions and structure.

1. **Amalgamated Union of Kenya Metal Workers**, Avon House, Mfangano Street, P.O. Box 73651, Nairobi.
   Phone: 23190.
   Leadership: Samuel Oyongo (chairman); Hon. F. E. Omido (general secretary); M. Tindi (treasurer).

2. **Bakers, Confectionery, Manufacturing and Allied Workers' Union**, Lengo House, Tom Mboya Street, P.O. Box 57751, Nairobi.
   Phone: 333628.
   Leadership: John Alukwe (chairman); George M. Muchai (general secretary); M. Mugli (treasurer).

3. **Dockworkers' Union**, Dockers House, Kenyatta Ave., P.O. Box 98207, Mombasa
   Phone: 491490, 491427.
   Leadership: G. Vuja (chairman); Juma K. Mbarak (general secretary); Rabu Justin (treasurer).

4. **Kenya Airline Pilots' Association**, Quaran House, Mfangano Street, P.O. Box 57509, Nairobi.
   Phone: 25859.
   Leadership: S. Rapuoda (chairman); E.A. Wanyama (general secretary); A. Ahmed (treasurer).

5. **Kenya Building, Construction, Civil Engineering and Allied Trades Workers' Union**, Munshi Ram Building, Mfangano Street, P.O. Box 49628, Nairobi.
   Phone: 23434, 336414.
   Leadership: E.G. Karagita (chairman); John Murugu (general secretary); Francis Wareru (treasurer).

6. **Kenya Chemical and Allied Workers' Union**, Hermes House, Tom Mboya Street, P.O. Box 73820, Nairobi.
   Phone: 338815.
   Leadership: J.A.C. Bondi (chairman); Were Ogutu (general secretary); W. Otiti (treasurer).

7. **Kenya Engineering Workers' Union**, Simla House, Tom Mboya Street, P.O. Box 73897, Nairobi.

Phone: 333745.
Leadership: W. Gathogo (chairman); Justis Mulei (general secretary); M. Muriuki (treasurer).

8. **Kenya Game Hunting and Safari Workers' Union**, Comford House, Diwani Road, P.O. Box 47509, Nairobi.
Leadership: Samson Kioko (chairman); J.M. Ndolo (general secretary); J. Kilonzo (treasurer).

9. **Kenya Jockey Workers' Union**, P.O. Box 55094, Nairobi.
Leadership: Samuel Wanjori (chairman); S.G. Kobogo (general secretary); Opiri Okwang (treasurer).

10. **Kenya Local Government Workers' Union**, Dunbee House, Country Road, P.O. Box 55827, Nairobi.
Phone: 726352.
Leadership: Makua Nguku (chairman); G.W. Ndombi (general secretary); S. Kibaya (treasurer).

11. **Kenya National Union of Fishermen Workers**, Pirbhi House, Turkana St., P.O. Box 90082, Mombasa.
Leadership: N. Onyango (chairman); S.P. Nyakanga (general secretary); O. Amayo (treasurer).

12. **Kenya Petroleum and Oil Workers' Union**.
Leadership: J. Onyango (chairman); J. Ochino (general secretary); B. Mbatia (treasurer).

13. **Kenya Plantation and Agricultural Workers' Union**, P.O. Box 1161, Nakuru.
Phone: 45167, 42007.
Leadership: M. Karanja (chairman); Phillip Mwangi (general secretary); William Ojuka (treasurer); S.K. Mathuki (assistant general secretary).

14. **Kenya Quarry and Mine Workers' Union**, Radab Menzil Building, Tom Mboya St., P.O. Box 48125, Nairobi.
Phone: 332120.
Leadership: S. Ojunga (chairman); Wafula la Musamia (general secretary); D. Kivuva (treasurer).

15. **Kenya Railways and Harbours Workers' Union**, P.O. Box 72029, Nairobi
Phone: 765318.
Leadership: J.O. Kadiri (chairman); R. Okanga (general secretary); W. Mutemi (treasurer).

16. **Kenya Shoe and Leather Workers' Union**, Simla House, Tom Mboya St., P.O. Box 49629, Nairobi.
Phone: 336911.
Leadership: J. Odewo (chairman); J. Bolo (general secretary); E. Lugawa (treasurer).

17. **Kenya Tailors and Textile Workers' Union**, Consulate Chambers, Racecourse Rd., P.O. Box 72076, Nairobi.
Phone: 338836.
Leadership: D. Osore (chairman); J.A. Ogendo (general secretary); H. Kikami (treasurer).

18. **Kenya Transport and Allied Workers' Union**, Coffee Plaza, Haile Selassie Ave., P.O. Box 45171, Nairobi.
Phone: 23618.
Leadership: M. Bohero (chairman); J. Ngie Malii (general secretary); T. Kasyoko (treasurer).

19. **Kenya Union of Commercial, Food and Allied Workers**, Comford House, Diwani Rd, P.O. Box 46818, Nairobi.
Phone: 25049.
Leadership: B. Nzioka (chairman); Hon. Sammy Muhanji, MP (general secretary); Mrs R. Nyathogora (treasurer); J.J. Mugalla (deputy general secretary).

20. **Kenyan Union of Domestic and Hotels, Educational Institutions, Hospitals and Allied Workers**, Kiburi House, Kirinyaga Road, P.O. Box 41763, Nairobi.
Phone: 338836, 21191.

Leadership: Joseph Nyabiya (chairman); Duncan Mugo (general secretary); Peter M. Kitaka (treasurer).

21. **Kenya Union of Entertainment and Music Industry Employees**, Solidarity Building, Digo Rd., P.O. Box 75776, Nairobi.
Phone: 761375/6/7.
Leadership: Geoffrey Ngao (chairman); James Yongo (general secretary); John Kioko (treasurer).

22. **Kenya Union of Journalists**, P.O. Box 47035, Nairobi.
Leadership: P. Mulami (chairman, acting); George Odiko (general secretary); H. van der Laan (treasurer).

23. **Kenya Union of Printing, Publishing, Paper Manufacturing and Allied Workers**, Meru South House, Tom Mboya St., P.O. Box 72358, Nairobi.
Phone: 338554.
Leadership: John Kilonzo (chairman); Rajab Mwondi (general secretary); P.M. Majiga (treasurer).

24. **Kenya Union of Sugar Plantations Workers**, P.O. Box 36, Kisumu.
Leadership: J. Wanjala (chairman); Paul Omanga Abuto (general secretary); C. Olang (treasurer); Linus Onyango (assistant general secretary).

25. **National Union of Seamen of Kenya**, P.O. Box 8123, Mombasa.
Phone: 312106.
Leadership: J.H. Badole (chairman); I.S. Abdalla (general secretary); Mussa Jama (treasurer).

26. **Union of Posts' and Telecommunications' Employees**, Hermes House, Tom Mboya St, P.O. Box 48155, Nairobi.
Phone: 338703.
Leadership: E. Egesa (chairman); Ali Mohammed (general secretary); A. Njagi (treasurer).

27. **Union of Scientific, International, Technical and Allied Workers**, Hermes House, Tom Mboya St., P.O. Box 55094, Nairobi.
Phone: 339964.
Leadership: J. Kangethe (chairman); Samson Kubai (general secretary); A.H. Karumba (treasurer).

The Kenya Timber and Furniture Workers' Union was deregistered on June 28, 1988. The Minister of Labour recommended that former timber workers join the Building and Construction Workers' Union. Deregistration proceedings are pending against the Banking, Insurance and Finance Union.

International affiliations. OATUU. Relations between COTU and the more radical OATUU leadership were strained in the later 1980s, and the Kenyans explored closer links with centres in neighbouring countries such as Tanzania and Uganda. By government decree COTU is free to affiliate only to African organizations, but its member unions may affiliate to International Trade Secretariats. Contacts between COTU and the WFTU have declined since 1986.

Kenyan National Union of Teachers (KNUT)

Address. Knut House, Mfangano Street, P.O. Box 30407, Nairobi
Phone. 220387/338768
Leadership. J.M. Katumanga (national chairman); A.A. Adongo (secretary general)
Membership. 145,700.
History and character. KNUT was founded in December 1957 with the aim (under its 1958 constitution) of uniting teachers in Kenya regardless of race, tribe, colour or grades; to struggle for the improvement of teachers' pay; to protect their rights; to involve them in co-operatives, education and professional activity. KNUT is not affiliated to COTU.
Publication. The Kenya Teacher; The KNUT Constitution; Study Circle Handbook.
International affiliations. WCOTP; AATO.

Kiribati

Capital: Tarawa   **Population: 68,200**

Political system. The Republic of Kiribati, formerly the Gilbert Islands, became an independent state within the Commonwealth in July 1979. It has an elected executive president.

Economy. Over 90 per cent of the population is occupied in fishing or subsistence farming.

System of industrial relations. Kiribati is not a member of the International Labour Organization.

Trade unionism. A national trade union centre was formed in 1982, affiliated to the ICFTU, and has campaigned to become a participant in discussion with government and employers on a tripartite basis.

However the KTUC proposal that there should be a permanent consultative council for government employees leading to more formal industrial relations has been rejected. Employers are still encouraged to bypass trade unions by means of Joint Consultative Committees. By 1988 all 12 unions in Kiribati had affiliated to the KTUC.

Kiribati Trade Union Congress (KTUC)

Address. P.O. Box 40, Bairiki, Tarawa
Phone. 21267
Leadership. Kabwebwenibeia Yee-on (president); Iote Malua (general secretary)
Membership. 2,500.
History and character. Founded in 1982, the unions and associations affiliated to the KTUC include the Teachers' Union, the Seamen's Union, the Fishermen's Union, the General Workers' Union, and the Co-operative Workers' Union. All unions are affiliated to the KTUC. The KTUC has been active in promoting self-help and educational projects, with help from Japanese unions, APRO and other trade union sources.
International affiliation. ICFTU/APRO.

North Korea

Capital: Pyongyang   **Population: 22,521,223**
                                                                                      (1989)

Political system. The Democratic People's Republic of Korea (North Korea) was established in 1948 and has been led throughout its history by President Kim Il Sung. Under its 1972 constitution the country has a unicameral legislature, the Supreme People's Assembly, consisting of representatives drawn almost exclusively from the communist Korean Workers' Party (KWP) which appoints the President who governs with the assistance of an Administrative Council. The KWP Central Committee (elected by the Party Congress) elects a politburo to direct policy, which in turn selects a five-member presidium.

In May 1991 North Korea announced its intention to apply for membership of the

United Nations, a move from which it had recoiled previously on the grounds that it would lead to South Korean admission and affirmation of the division of the country.

Economy. Although it has no oil North Korea has substantial mineral and hydroelectric resources and meets 90 per cent of its energy needs. Industry, like land, is nationalized, with production centred upon steel, cement, chemicals and machine building rather than consumer products. Since 1954 the economy has been subject to the guidelines laid down in a series of centrally directed economic plans aimed at achieving autarchy.

System of industrial relations. North Korea is not a member of the International Labour Organization.

Trade unionism. A single-trade-union system is in force, co-ordinated by the General Federation of Trade Unions of Korea, and unions function on the Soviet bloc model, with responsibility for mobilizing workers behind productivity goals and state targets, and for the provision of health, educational, cultural and welfare facilities.

General Federation of Trade Unions of Korea (GFTUK)

Address. P.O. Box 333, Pyongyang

Cables. ZIKCHONG PYONGYANG

Leadership. Kim Bong Ju (chairman of the GFTUK central committee, also general secretary of the Supreme People's Assembly); Shim Hong Gyu (vice-chairman)

Membership. 1,600,000.

History and character. Founded on Nov. 30, 1945, the GFTUK is described as a "revolutionary political organization of the working masses". It conducts ideological education to ensure its members fully understand the revolutionary ideas of President Kim Il Sung and to enable them to contribute towards the socialist construction and management of the economy.

Affiliates. There are nine member unions, for the following sectors: metallurgy and engineering; transport and fishing; education and culture; construction and forestry; chemical industry; commerce; light industry; mines and energy; public administration.

Publications. *The Korean Trade Unions* (bi-monthly).

International affiliation. WFTU.

South Korea

Capital: Seoul   **Population: 42,380,000**

Political system. The Republic of Korea (South Korea) was established as an independent state in 1948. All political parties were banned following the 1979 military *coup*. Since the resumption of political activity in 1980, the right-wing Democratic Justice Party (DJP) has held power. After widespread popular unrest, a new constitution was adopted in 1988 and a senior member of the DJP, Roh Tae Woo, became the first President of the newly consti- tuted Sixth Republic. In legislative elections held in early 1988 the DJP won most seats but failed to achieve an overall majority.

Disillusionment set in rapidly with Roh Tae Woo due to his failure to make rapid civic and democratic reforms, and the years of his presidency have been marked by a succession of popular uprisings — often sparked by heavy-handed police behaviour — which sometimes included self-immolation by individual protesters. As a result of one of these in the spring of 1991 a new Prime Minister Chung Won-Shik was installed who immediately promulgated an amnesty for political prisoners.

Economy. The agricultural sector, which provides employment for up to 30 per cent of the population (principally producing rice, wheat, barley and sweet potatoes) contributes only about 16 per cent towards the country's gross domestic product. The manufacture of textiles, electronics, motor vehicles, steel and petrochemicals have provided the basis of the South Korean economy, with its shipbuilding yards accounting for up to 20 per cent of world orders. Since 1980, however, the emphasis of manufacturing has shifted from heavy industry towards the production of electronic components. The country's huge trade surplus and its maintenance of strict import controls has continued to cause friction with the USA and its Western European trading partners.

From 1986 to 1988 Korea had one of the highest growth rates in the world at 12 per cent, though this fell by almost half in 1989. Inflation however is rising, and some Korean companies, unused to wage increases of the kind now being gained by employees have moved their operations offshore in search of cheaper labour. By 1989 the country had a 17,500,000 civilian workforce, of which 4,900,000 were in industry, 3,400,000 in agriculture, and 9,200,000 in services.

System of industrial relations. The adoption of a revised Constitution and the inauguration of a Sixth Republic on Feb. 24, 1988, under President Roh Tae Woo did little to quell the country's volatile labour situation. According to press reports, almost 400 industrial disputes broke out in the period from January to April 1988. Massive and violent disputes were reported at Hyundai, Daewon and Kyonggi factories in, respectively, Ulsan, Kuro and Inchon. On the whole, the disputes reflected intra-union discord as well as labour-management conflict. At least two workers committed suicide as a form of protest at Daewon in Inchon during March. However, the attempt to fragment the trade union movement was only partly successful and union membership recovered to about 1,000,000 by 1985.

An increase in anti-government political activity in 1985 was reflected in an increase in strikes, which the government stated was a consequence of activist students infiltrating workplaces, and in November 1986 the Labour Minister ordered the dissolution of 14 dissident unions in the Seoul-Inchon area by the end of the year. Throughout 1986 the government had been under persistent pressure, particularly from the student population, to institute wholesale constitutional reforms. In April 1986, President Chun Doo Hwan agreed to amend the Constitution, but after a year of talks and consultations he broke off negotiations on constitutional reform, a decision publicly supported by the FKTU. Under the continuing pressure of opposition protest Chun's decision was effectively reversed in late June 1987 and proposals for major reforms were outlined. The government's apparent concession to opposition demands led to a dramatic increase in labour disputes. In July and August 1987, there were almost 3,000 separate disputes involving lock-outs and strikes, more than the combined total for the previous 10 years. The principal demand of the workers was for pay increases commensurate with rising profits and labour productivity which, since 1980, were estimated as having grown at least twice as fast as wages. The other major demand was for the right to engage freely in trade union activities. Although not strictly illegal, the complex procedural impediments prohibiting a strike (which included advance notification and mandatory arbitration) in practice made it difficult for them to be called legally without the agreement of employers.

The explosion of labour unrest in July and August challenged not only employers and the government, but also the FKTU leadership, whose deferential attitude towards the Chun regime had been seen in April 1987. At the height of the unrest in mid-July a Committee for the Democratization of Trade Unions was formed by delegates from some 50 unions, in an effort to make the FKTU more representative and to replace its leadership.

These so-called "democratic unions" had their support base amongst the white-collar financial workers and by early 1988 they were thought to number around 300. During the unrest these unions maintained a close relationship with the country's wider dissident movement, in contrast with the majority of the so-called "company unions". Despite the technical illegality of the strikes, the authorities displayed a relatively high degree of tolerance towards those involved and it was estimated that in over 50 per cent of the disputes workers won concessions on pay and conditions. On Aug. 18, the Ministry of Labour intervened in a violent dispute involving the massive Hyundai company in Ulsan, and forced management recognition of newly formed independent trade unions. Some estimates suggest that over 1,200 new trade unions were formed during the July–August period, with a total membership of up to 400,000. Many of these new unions subsequently found it difficult to remain operational, largely as a result of the inexperience of many new leaders.

Though Korea is not a member of the ILO, the Ministry of Labour claims that Korean employment law satisfies 105 of the ILO's 115 Conventions, while the Domestic Labour Code infringes 11 of the 47 statutes classified as major basic statutes by the ILO. Korea wishes to join the ILO but as a non-member of the UN would find difficulty in doing so. However it has sent tripartite delegations to the ILO, for example in 1988.

Newly amended labour legislation was passed by the National Assembly on Oct. 30, 1987. Most significantly, the amendments abolished compulsory arbitration. Nonetheless, unions remained banned from any political involvement. On Jan. 1, 1988, a minimum wage law, the country's first, came into operation. The law established basic monthly wages of Won 111, 000 and Won 117,000, depending on the industry's competitiveness. A national pension system, legislated in 1973, was enforced in January 1988.

Despite these changes, the practice of industrial relations tended to continue unshaped by legislation, causing the government to resort more frequently to the use of strikes in 1989 than it had in either of the two previous years. There was evidence of increased toughness in the government stance when in intervened to sack 1,500 members of a teachers' union which it said was illegal under legislation prohibiting them from the public sector. While the number of strikes fell in 1989 to 1,616 from 1,873 the previous year, their average duration (18 days in 1989) has more than trebled.

In February 1989 the Assembly amended three key employment laws, but President Roh vetoed all these changes except that to the Labour Standards Law which cut the standard working week by four hours (the average Korean worked more than 50 hours a week in 1988), increased annual leave and prohibited blacklisting. The hand of the unions was strengthened by a Supreme Court opinion early in 1989 that unions might be active in the defence industries.

Despite its paternalist traditions Korea does not lack for tripartite structures. There are no Labour Courts, but there are tripartite Local and Central Labour Committees which together provide a dispute-resolving procedure which can lead on to the civil courts. All firms with more than 100 employees must have a Labour-Management Council, meeting at least quarterly with equal representation from each side. After some disagreement the government accepted in the autumn of 1989 an FKTU proposal that there should be a broad tripartite committee to discuss a wide range of employment issues.

Trade unionism. The first Korean trade union was the Song-Jin Dockers' Union organized in May 1898, and unions began to develop after the annexation of Korea by Japan in 1910, becoming a centre of opposition to Japanese rule. Following the end of Japanese rule and the establishment of US military government in the south of Korea at the close of World War II a General Council of Korean Trade Unions was formed under communist control and this led general strikes in 1946 and 1947; in 1946, however, the General Federation of Korean Trade Unions was created with US backing (this becoming a founder member of the ICFTU in December 1949), and communist organizations were banned in 1947.

Following the 1961 military *coup*, all labour organizations were dissolved and were replaced by the Federation of Korean Trade Unions (FKTU). After industrial unrest in the late 1960s, trade union rights were restricted by a series of measures brought into force in the early 1970s; these measures were justified by the government as necessary for Korea to appear a stable market for foreign investors and as being in the interest of national security, but were only partly effective in curbing labour disputes.

The present status of trade unionism is defined by legislation enacted in 1980 following the *coup* which brought Chun Doo Hwan to power. Under the 1980 legislation only one union is permitted in each enterprise; only enterprise-level unions may negotiate with employers, without any intervention by third parties (i.e. seriously weakening the rule of industry-wide federations); and there are restrictions on the dues which unions may collect from their members. Disputes are to be settled directly between union and employer, under the authority of tripartite labour committees representing the interests of employers, workers and the government but whose members are nominated by the government. The immediate effect of the 1980 legislation was to reduce total union membership from 1,200,000 to 820,000 and to severely weaken the position of the FKTU (the only officially recognized federation) and the Christian activist Urban Industrial Mission.

By the end of 1989 trade union density in Korea was 22 per cent. The FKTU, which has not yet fully established itself as an independent force in the eyes of the population, remains the largest and only truly national centre but its position is not unchallenged. The new unions founded after 1987 which stayed aloof from it have formed 14 regional councils and a number of industrial councils, but they are prevented by law from forming an alternative centre. A total of 602 (with a membership approaching 200,000) formed such a centre nonetheless in January 1990 but it was immediately suppressed. There is in addition a further group of unions organizing more than half a million workers which maintain a semi-detached relationship with the FKTU while not affiliating to the independent unions.

Federation of Korean Trade Unions (FKTU or NOCHONG)

Address. 35, Yiodo-dong, Youngdeungpo-ku, Seoul
Phone. 782-3884
Telex. 29682
Fax. (02) 784-6396
Cables. NOCHONG SEOUL
Leadership. Lee Si-Woo (acting president); Lee Sung-Sik (vice president); Min Yo-Ki (general secretary)
Membership. As of May 1988 the FKTU claimed to have 1,526,452 members of whom 465,312 were women. Approximately 23 per cent of the country's total unionizable labour force are FKTU members.

History and character. The Korean Labour Federation of Independence Promotion (KLFIP), the former structure of the FKTU, was established in March 1946. In May 1961 all KLFIP affiliates were dissolved by military decree, to be reformed in April of that year under a "committee to re-establish trade unions", constituted by the military authorities. Four months later the FKTU was created. It is the sole trade union centre in South Korea; it had no representation on government bodies. The FKTU was severely weakened under the 1980 legislation which excluded it from direct involvement in industrial disputes and collective bargaining, leaving it only a generalized role of representing the interests of organized labour to government.

The role of the FKTU in the widespread movement for constitutional reform in 1985–87 is open to various interpretations. In its official publications, the FKTU places itself at the heart of the movement and outlines its support of the reforms gained. However, the federation's close ties to the

Chun regime were most vividly demonstrated in April 1987, when it supported the President's decision to suspend talks on constitutional revisions. A number of "democratic unions" formed in mid-1987 during a period of widespread labour unrest, derided what they perceived to be the FKTU's tendency to compromise too quickly. In an attempt to gain legitimacy amongst workers whose democratic aspirations had been raised by the constitutional reforms adopted in February 1988, the FKTU pledged to adopt a more political role. In late February the leadership resolved to establish a political-education committee and called for an end to restraints on the political activities of unions. The FKTU also decided to support pro-union candidates, whether from opposition parties or from the ruling Democratic Justice Party, in legislative elections held in late April 1988.

Under pressure of criticism, the FKTU held a special convention in November 1988 and elected a new reformist leadership pledged to increase its independence. However at the Federation's February 1990 Convention the new leadership barely retained its position.

Affiliated unions. Affiliated to the FKTU are 16 industrial federations, four national unions and 4,729 local unions. Membership figures relate to 1988 unless otherwise stated.

1. **Korean Railway Workers' Union**, 40, Hangangro-3-ga, Yongsan-ku, Seoul.
    Phone: 795-6174.
    General Secretary: Oh Jae-Sik.
    President: Lee Jong-Rak.
    Membership: 30,305.

2. **Federation of Korean Textile Workers' Unions**, 382–31, Hapjung-dong, Mapo-ku, Seoul.
    Phone: 393-3111.
    Fax: 335 1810.
    General Secretary: Kim Jeong Hwang.
    President: Song Soo-il.
    Membership: 130,436 (1990).

3. **Federation of Korean Mine Workers' Unions**, 78, Changsin-dong, Chongno-ku, Seoul.
    Phone: 763-3157.
    General Secretary: Hwang Kyung-hwa.
    President: Hong Keum-Woong.
    Membership: 66,302.

4. **Korean National Electrical Workers' Unions**, 167, Samsung-dong, Kangnam-ku, Seoul.
    Phone: 550-4381.
    General Secretary: Chung Ik-Soo.
    President: Lee Jong-Wan.
    Membership: 19,548.

5. **Federation of Foreign Organization Employees' Unions**, 175–9, Huam-dong, Yongsan-ku, Seoul.
    Phone: 757-2355.
    General Secretary: Cha Won-Ik.
    President: Kim Kyu-Ho.
    Membership: 28,820.

6. **Korean Federation of Postal and Telecommunication Workers' Unions**, 21, Choongmuro-1-ga, Joong-ku, Seoul.
    Phone: 756-1502.
    General Secretary: Kim Duk-Kon.
    President: Park Soo-Keun.
    Membership: 43,842.

7. **Korean Federation of Port and Transport Workers' Unions**, 118, 7-ga, Bomun-dong, Sungbuk, Seoul.
    Phone: 923-5743.
    General Secretary: Kim Ki Seo.
    President: Kim Joon-Sang.
    Membership: 39,112.

8. **Federation of Korean Seafarers' Unions**, 44–16, Dohwa-dong, Mapo-ku, Seoul.
Phone: 718-4541.
Fax: 701 7991.
General Secretary: Lee Sang-Woo.
President: Kim Boo-Woong.
Membership: 77,491 (1990)

9. **Korean Federation of Bank and Financial Workers' Unions**, 88, Da-dong, Joong-ku, Seoul.
Phone: 756-2339.
General Secretary: Lee Sun-Kyu.
President: Yoon Wan-Sup.
Membership: 125,358.

10. **Korea Monopoly Workers' Union**, 112, Inui-dong, Chongro-ku, Seoul.
Phone: 763-8850.
General Secretary: Cho Hong-Tae.
President: Hong Sam-Heui.
Membership: 10,816.

11. **Federation of Korean Chemical Workers' Unions**, 35, Yoido-dong, Youngdeungpo-ku, Seoul.
Phone: 783-2441.
General Secretary: Kim Yoo-Kon.
President: Chung Choon-Taek.
Membership: 216,390.

12. **Federation of Korean Metal Workers' Unions**, 1570–2, Sinlim-dong, Kwanak-ku, Seoul.
Phone: 864-2901.
General Secretary: Kim Sung-Moon.
President: Park In-Sang.
Membership: 297,225.

13. **Federation of Korean Printing Workers' Unions**, 35, Yoido-dong, Youngdeungpo-ku, Seoul.
Phone: 782-7969.
General Secretary: Kim Yoon-Eung.
President: Hwang Tae-Soo.
Membership: 8,951.

14. **Korea Automobile and Transport Workers' Federation**, 678–27, Yoksam-dong, Kangnam-ku, Seoul.
Phone: 554-0890.
General Secretary: Lee Kap-Chong.
President: Lee Si-Woo.
Membership: 83,006.

15. **National United Workers' Federation**, 39–7, Dongja-dong, Yongsan-ku, Seoul.
Phone: 757-1567.
General Secretary: Kim Dong-Chul.
President: Kim Rak-Ki.
Membership: 146,121.

16. **Korean Tourist Industry Workers' Federation**, 749, 5-ga, Namdaemun-ro, Seoul.
Phone: 779-1297.
General Secretary: Han Ki-IL.
President: La Woon-Suk.
Membership: 15,908.

17. **Korea Communications Workers' Union**, 154–1, Seoulin-dong, Chongno-ku, Seoul.
Phone: 732-2291.

General Secretary: Park Kyu-Hyun.
President: Lee Joo-Wan.
Membership: 22,564.

18. **Korea Federation of Insurance Labour Unions**, 21–9, Cho-dong, Choong-ku, Seoul.
Phone: 274-3280.
General Secretary: Hwang Won-Rae.
President: Kwun Se-Won.
Membership: 6,944.

19. **Federation of Korean Taxi Transport Workers' Unions**, 217, Sukchon-dong, Songpa-ku, Seoul.
Phone: 416-8325.
General Secretary: Kang Kil-Ho.
President: Lee Kwang-Nam.
Membership: 87,500.

20. **Federation of Korean Rubber Workers' Unions**, 35, Yoido-dong, Youngdeungpo-ku, Seoul.
Phone: 783-2194.
General Secretary: Yang Hyo-Suk.
President: Kim Man-Ho.
Membership: 55,000.

Publications. *FKTU News* (monthly, in English); *Foreign Labour News* (monthly, in Korean).
International affiliation. ICFTU/APRO.

National Council of Labour Unions (CHONNOHYOP)

Leadership: Dan Byong Ho (chairman)
Membership: Claims an initial membership approaching 200,000.
History and character. Founded in January 1990 by 602 independent unions formed since 1987 and launched in defiance of legislation forbidding the establishment of an alternative centre. Its chairman was arrested in February 1990 following the detention of 150 other union leaders.

Some independent unions outside the FKTU

1. **Seoul Area Labour Union Association** (31,000).

2. **Masan-Changwon Union Coalition** (27,000).

Kuwait

Capital: Kuwait City   **Population: 1,872,000**
(pre-invasion estimate)

Political system. Kuwait is a semi-constitutional hereditary monarchy, governed by an Amir from the Sabah family who rules in conjunction with senior family members, through an appointed Cabinet. The country's legislature (*Majlis al-Umma*), elected by adult, literate, male Kuwaiti citizens, was dissolved in 1986, since when the Amir ruled by decree. The Amir defied street demonstrations to restore the Constitution in 1989.

Following the end of the Gulf War undertakings were given by the restored Sabah family that the 1962 Constitution would be restored. However, an Amnesty International report in April 1991 documented substantial human rights abuses by vigilantes against Palestinian and Kuwaiti opponents of the regime.

Economy. The Kuwaiti economy (which had suffered during the early 1980s as a result of falling oil prices) was strengthened during 1987 by increased oil exports, the revenue from which accounts for most of the country's income. In May 1988 the government announced that the country's unofficial stock market (*Souk el-Manakh*) would close in the near future. The market's collapse in 1982 had adversely affected the country's non-oil sector.

The Kuwaiti economy was devastated by the Iraqi invasion of August and the Gulf War and the oil wells set alight in February 1991 were still burning in May of that year.

System of industrial relations. The ILO *Report of the Committee of Experts on the Application of Conventions and Recommendations* (1985) noted as among restrictions contained in the 1964 labour law applicable to the private sector that: (i) a certificate of good reputation and conduct is required before any individual may be admitted to trade union membership; (ii) the Minister of the interior must certify that there is no objection to any of the founding members before a trade union may be established; (iii) only one trade union may be formed for any establishment or activity; (iv) the authorities have extensive powers to supervise the internal affairs of unions; (v) unions may not engage in any political or religious activity; (vi) trade unions may only federate if involved in the same occupation or industry with only one federation for such an industry; (vii) there can be no more than one general confederation; (viii) at least 100 members (of whom at least 15 must be Kuwaiti) are required to form a trade union; (ix) foreigners of less than five years residence in Kuwait may not join trade unions, and those eligible to join may not vote in union affairs other than to elect a non-voting representative to express their views; and (x) all assets of a trade union become the property of the Ministry of Social Affairs and Labour in the event of its dissolution. All these restrictions were defined by the Committee of Experts as being in contravention of ILO Convention No. 87 (Freedom of Association and Protection of the Right to Organize, 1948), which Kuwait ratified in 1961. A draft revised labour code prepared by the government ended many of these restrictions, but left in place the system of trade union monopoly and provided for unions to follow model rules laid down by the government. Restrictions on expatriate labour were imposed in 1985 as part of a series of measures intended to ensure that Kuwaiti nationals should total 50 per cent of the country's population by the year 2000.

A report of the American State Department in 1989 commented that foreign—and especially domestic—workers were subject to numerous abuses.

Strikes were legal, but rare, since the bulk of union members were employed in the public sector where employment was virtually guaranteed. The great majority of trade union members are Kuwaiti. Under pre-occupation legislation, expatriate workers became entitled to join a union after five years' residence but could not vote or hold office. A new union might be formed only if it contained at least 100 Kuwaitis.

Trade unionism. Trade unions were first accorded legal recognition under legislation of 1964 and a single-trade-union system co-ordinated by the Kuwait Trade Union Federation is in place. Before the Iraqi invasion of 1990, the Kuwait Federation of Trade Unions (KFTU) held affiliations from 12 of the country's 13 unions, the exception being the bank workers' union. Nine of the KFTU affiliates represented civil and public servants while the other three organized petrol and chemical employees. Total union membership, at 27,000, represented 4 per cent of the total workforce.

KFTU joined with the democratic opposition during the Gulf War to demand restoration of the 1962 Constitution, with guarantees of freedom of expression and women's equality.

Kuwait Federation of Trade Unions (KFTU)

Address. P.O. Box 43005, 43100 Hawalli
Phone. 5616055
Leadership. Hayef al Agami (president)

History and character. The KTUF, which was founded in 1968, is the sole permitted central organization of trade unions, and it identifies with the WFTU trade union bloc. Its fourth congress, held in November 1986, received trade union delegations from Iraq, Syria, South Yemen, Sudan (Trade Union Front), the WFTU and the ICATU. Resolutions adopted at the congress included a call for increased numbers of Kuwaiti workers in the oil sector, the strengthening of the ICATU, an immediate end to the Iran–Iraq war, opposition to US policy in the Middle East, and support for the "peace initiatives" of the Soviet Union.

Two former presidents of the KFTU, Nasser al Faraq and Mliehan al Harbi, were arrested and tortured by the Iraqi forces during the occupation. Both died within days of their release. Their successor Hayef al Agami escaped from Kuwait shortly after the invasion and rallied to the democratic opposition in Kuwait. Though he received some financial support from the government in exile, the Federation had to borrow against money frozen in the Kuwaiti National Bank.

Structure. There are 12 member trade unions, divided into two sectors (state and oil), and a 15-member executive committee, led by the president and the general secretary, elected by the congress.

International affiliations. WFTU; ICATU.

Laos

Capital: Vientiane

Population: 3,935,786
(1989)

Political system. The Lao People's Democratic Republic was established in 1975 following the victory of the communist *Pathet Lao* forces. Laos has no constitution and the dominant political force is the Lao People's Revolutionary Party. National elections (at district and provincial level) were held in June and November 1988, the first elections since 1975.

Economy. The government's principal economic aim is to develop agriculture and forestry as the basis for future industrial development. Over 70 per cent of the population is involved in agricultural production, the main crops being rice, maize, cassava and coffee. Industrial production is limited and the sale of electricity to Thailand is the country's main source of foreign exchange. A series of economic reforms introduced in 1987–88 is designed to cut government subsidies and give producers increased incentives.

Trade unionism. A single-union system prevails.

Federation of Lao Trade Unions (FLTU)

Address. B.P. 780, 87 ave. Lane Xang, Vientiane
Phone. 5353
Leadership. Thitsoi Sombatdouang (president); Sinsa Keomanivong (secretary)
History and character. This organization absorbed the few small existing unions after the establishment of the present regime in 1975. One of five popular or mass organizations (the principal one being the Lao Front for National Construction), the FLTU held its first national congress in December 1983.
International affiliation. WFTU.

Lebanon

Capital: Beirut

Population: 2,830,000

Political system. Central authority in Lebanon progressively decayed following the outbreak of civil war in 1975. The war, fought out by militias largely organized on religious lines, disrupted the frail compromise on which the state had been established since the National Covenant of 1943. On his resignation in 1988 President Gemayel appointed the (Maronite Christian) Gen. Michel Aoun as head of an interim government. The Aoun régime never commanded international acceptance, and in 1990 President Hrawi (himself a Maronite Christian, and elected in November 1989) invited the Syrian forces to drive the former out of territory he had occupied during an internal battle among the Christian forces. After this a number of steps were taken to restore peace during the latter part of 1990. Finally, in 1991, under the Taif Peace Accords sponsored by the Arab League, a Government of National Unity was formed and all militias were ordered to be dissolved.

Economy. Formerly the financial centre of the Middle East, Lebanon's economy has been severely damaged by the continuing civil strife. In 1987, a high level of inflation coupled with a depreciation of the local currency effectively reduced the value of the statutory minimum monthly wage to US$15, from an average of US$120 in 1975. Following the emergence of two rival governments in the Moslem west and Christian east sections of Beirut in September 1988, the central bank indicated that it would continue to guarantee the public debt, issue treasury bills and finance oil and wheat imports.

System of industrial relations. Lebanon ratified ILO Convention No. 98 (Right to Organize and Collective Bargaining, 1949) in 1977 but has not ratified Convention No. 87 (Freedom of Association and Protection of the Right to Organize, 1948).

Trade unionism. The first trade unions appeared under French rule, and at one point the Lebanon offered the unusual spectacle of Muslim and Christian confederations in peaceful competition. The labour movement tended to remain fractured on craft, religious or political lines as it came under pressure from the same forces that destroyed the country's unity. Nevertheless the ICFTU-backed and pro-national unity CGTL claims to be the only social organization of any kind uniting workers irrespective of religious or political affiliation, and certainly is the only national trade union centre.

The CGTL President Antoine Bechara received threats in 1990 from the quondam dictator General Aoun who was reported to wish to establish a corporatist trade union. A further clear illustration of the baneful effect of the civil war on Lebanese trade unionism may be had from the experiences of the CGTL-affiliated commercial workers' federation LFCTU which once had 18,000 members and now has 4,000.

Confédération Générale des Travailleurs du Liban (CGTL)
General Confederation of Lebanese Workers

Address. P.O. Box 4381, Beirut

Leadership. Antoine Bechara (president)

Membership. Uncertain, comprises 18 federations involving most of the country's trade unions, including the WFTU affiliate FENASOL.

History and character. Founded 1958. In July 1986, the CGTL called a one-day national strike to "save Lebanon from war and famine", calling for the removal of all Israeli troops from Lebanese soil and for a "national dialogue" to find a political solution to the civil war. This was followed by a three-day strike in April, 1987, in support of an end to the fighting, improved conditions for workers and social and economic reforms. The CGTL held two national union congresses in 1987 which resulted in more specific demands being made. These included an end to speculation against the Lebanese pound by private banks; subsidies for basic necessities, schoolbooks, medicines etc. and reform of the social security system. Further strikes ensued in 1988, including a one-day strike in April involving workers in factories, educational establishments, transport, small enterprises and the public sector. The CGTL began to complain of a new anti-union alignment of middle-class and communal groups which they said were seeking to break union power by intimidation.

Affiliated unions. The following are some of the CGTL affiliates with latest membership figures, as available. With the national situation uncertain, the ICFTU permitted individual affiliation.

1. **Ligue des Syndicats des Employés et des Ouvriers dans la République Libanaise**
   ICFTU affiliate; 13,000 members (1983).

2. **Fédération des Syndicats-unis des Employés et Ouvriers au Liban (SYNDICATS-UNIS)**
   ICFTU affiliate; 10,000 members (1983).

3. **Fédération Ouvrière des Offices Autonomes et des Enterprises Publiques et Privées au Liban (OFFICES AUTONOMES)**
   ICFTU affiliate; 13,000 members (1983).

4. **Federation of Petroleum Trade Unions in Lebanon (PETROLEUM)**
   ICFTU affiliate: 1,700 members (1983).

5. **Fédération des Syndicats des Employés de Banques au Liban (BANQUES)**
   ICFTU/FIET affiliate; 2,000 members (1983).

6. **Federation of Insurance Sector Employees in Lebanon (INSURANCE)**
   ICFTU affiliate; 1,000 members (1983).

7. **Fédération des Syndicats des Employés du Commerce au Liban (COMMERCE)**, P.O. Box 5208/116, Beirut.
   President: Nicola Berbari.
   Publication: *The Economic Worker* (monthly).
   ICFTU/FIET affiliate; 4,000 members (1990).

8. **Federation of Syndicates of Health and Education Sector in Lebanon** (Health and Education)
   ICFTU affiliate; 2,500 members (1983).

9. **Workers' Syndicates Federation of Sea Transport in Lebanon (SEA TRANSPORT)**
   ICFTU affiliate; 8,000 members (1983).

10. **Federation of Airlines Companies' Employees and Labourers of Lebanon (AIRLINES COMPANIES)**
    ICFTU affiliate; 4,000 members (1983).

11. **Fédération Syndicale des Employés et Ouvriers des Offices Autonomes et Services Publics au Liban (OFFICES AUTONOMES & SERVICES PUBLICS)**
    ICFTU affiliate; 9,000 members (1983).

12. **Fédération des Syndicats des Ouvriers des Imprimeries et de l'Information au Liban (IMPRIMERIES)**
    ICFTU affiliate.

13. **Fédération des Employés des Hôtels, Restaurants, et Lieux de Loisirs au Liban (HOTEL)**
    ICFTU affiliate.

14. **Fédération Nationale des Syndicats des Ouvriers et des Employés du Liban (FENASOL)**, B.P. 733, Beirut.
    Phone: 816165. Telex: CTTD 23308 LE FENASOL. Cables: FENASOL BEYROUTH.
    President: Elias Habre (a WFTU vice-president).
    WFTU affiliate.

283

Lesotho

Capital: Maseru   **Population: 1,722,000**

Political system. Lesotho became an independent member of the Commonwealth in 1966 as a constitutional hereditary monarchy, with legislative power vested in a bicameral parliament and executive power in the Cabinet under the Prime Minister. In 1970 the Constitution was suspended by the Prime Minister, Chief Leabua Jonathan. Chief Jonathan's government was overthrown by a Military Council under the Chairmanship of Maj.-Gen. Justin Lekhanya in January 1986. Legislative and executive powers were returned to the king in conjunction with the Military Council.

But after four years' domination of Lesotho politics, the Military Council took effective power from the King in 1990. After disagreements with the Council over the nature of the transition to democracy—Lesotho is committed to establishing it in 1992—he went into exile and was replaced in November by his son.

Economy. Lesotho is economically dependent on South Africa, which surrounds it on all sides. Around 40 per cent of Lesotho's food needs are met by imports principally from South Africa. Manufacturing accounted for 10 per cent of GDP in 1985. Remittances from over 100,000 migrant Lesotho workers employed in the South African mines are a major source of foreign exhange, and constitute some 50 per cent of GDP.

Like Botswana, Lesotho has experienced a sharp drop in the extent to which agriculture provides an income for its employed population. The percentage employed in agriculture fell from 92 per cent in 1965 to 23.3 per cent in 1985–87, industry accounted for 33.1 per cent and services for 43.6 per cent. In June 1990 the IMF announced a new loan for Lesotho under the structural adjustment facility which opened in 1988.

System of industrial relations. Lesotho ratified ILO Conventions No. 87 (Freedom of Association and Protection of the Right to Organize, 1948) and No. 98 (Right to Organize and Collective Bargaining, 1949) in 1966, when Convention No. 29 on forced labour was also ratified.

Trade unionism. The first trade unions were established prior to independence.

Lesotho Council of Workers (LCW)

Address. P.O. Box MS 727, Maseru 100
Phone. 22768
Membership. 11,000 (1983).
International affiliations. ICFTU; OATUU.

Lesotho Federation of Trade Unions (LFTU)

Address. P.O. Box 266, Maseru 100
Phone. 326251
Leadership. M.A. Limema (secretary-general), S.M. Moreke (president)
Membership. 16,000.
History and character. The Basutoland Federation of Labour was formed by two national trade unions in 1962, and was renamed as the Lesotho Federation of Trade Unions after independence. A merger with the LCW has been considered but was opposed by the AFL-CIO's African-American Labour Centre and the ICFTU on the grounds that the government of Chief Jonathan was thought to favour the LCW. The formation of a single union centre has nevertheless continued to be a burning issue. The LFTU is wary of government legal and other intervention, and is concerned that it is being rendered increasingly impotent.
Affiliated unions. Lesotho Union of Clothing and Textile Employees (LUCTE); Typographical

Workers' Union (LTWU); Union of Hotel, Food and Allied Workers (LUHFAW); Union of Masons and Allied Workers (LUMAW); General Workers Union (LGWU); Union of Guards and Allied Workers (LUGAW). The LFTU has recently lost the affiliation of the Transport and Telecommunications Workers' Union and the Lesotho Pharmaceutical and Allied Workers' Union, but has gained the affiliation of the LUCTE, LUMAW and LUGAW.

Publication. Workers' Voice.

International affiliation. ICFTU.

Liberia

Capital: Monrovia   **Population: 2,360,000**

Political system. President (then Master-Sergeant) Samuel K. Doe seized power in a bloody *coup* in April 1980, and ruled through a military People's Redemption Council (PRC). A new Constitution was approved by referendum in July 1984 and presidential and legislative elections followed in October 1985. President Doe won over 50 per cent of the vote and his National Democratic Party of Liberia won a substantial majority, amid allegations of widespread electoral malpractice. A three-sided civil war culminated in the overthrow of the Doe regime in early 1991.

Economy. Around 80 per cent of the Liberian workforce is engaged in subsistence agriculture, but the country traditionally is a source of primary commodities: iron ore, timber and rubber and these account for around 85 per cent of GDP. The exploitation of these tends to be in the hands either of the state or of multinationals. Falling export earnings led the economy into decline in the later 1980s while foreign backers showed diminishing confidence in the economic competence of the government.

System of industrial relations. A 1982 decree prohibited strike action in all sectors of the economy. The government has had plans to declare all workers civil servants and to compel them to join a government-controlled staff association, though this seems unlikely to be successfully implemented. Liberia ratified ILO Conventions No. 87 (Freedom of Association and Protection of the Right to Organize, 1948) and No. 98 (Right to Organize and Collective Bargaining, 1949) in 1962. The ILO has for long raised objections to breaches of the conventions ratified, in particular with regard to interference in collective bargaining, freedom of organization, and the ban on strikes. A new Labour Code is reported to be under preparation.

Liberia ratified Convention No. 29 on forced labour as long ago as 1931 and No. 105 in 1962, but use of compulsory labour has been a controversial issue ever since Firestone's system of labour recruitment came under heavy criticism in the late 1920s. The new Constitution that came into force in January 1986 prohibited use of forced labour, but the ILO noted that it could still be legitimately levied for local public works and could be used as part of the punishment for some misdemeanours.

The Constitution also guaranteed the right of association but in practice the government denied this right to civil servants or public corporation employees (where it did permit professional associations to form). A draft Labour Code was published in 1986 roughly in correspondence to ILO standards, but by 1990 it had only passed through the lower house of the legislature.

Trade unionism. Efforst to establish trade unions early in the century were unsuccessful until the late 1950s when the Labour Congress of Liberia was formed, succeeded in 1959 by the Congress of Industrial Organizations. Trade unions have had legal status since 1963 but there has been only modest development and activity in the agricultural and public services sectors and they have been subjected to numerous restrictions.

The main union centre is the LFLU which has ten affiliates with which its relations are sometimes fraught but which gained new adherents in the later 1980s. It assisted the Firestone Agricultural Workers' Union (FAWUL) in negotiations in 1989. Agricultural workers are mostly organized by NAFAPAW, and there are a number of independent unions and professional associations, of which the National Teachers' Association of Liberia is the most prominent. NAFAPAW was never able to regain recognition at Firestone—Liberia's biggest company—after its suspension, and now co-exists with its successor as an LFLU affiliate.

Liberian Federation of Labour Unions (LFLU)

Address. J. B. McGill Labor Center, Gardnersville Freeway, P.O. Box 415, Monrovia.
Leadership. Amos Gray (general secretary); J. N. Davies (executive vice-president)
Membership. 10,000 (1983).
History. Formed in 1980 by amalgamation of the United Workers' Congress and the Liberia Federation of Trade Unions (the latter formed in 1977 by merger of the former Congress of Industrial Organizations and Labour Congress of Liberia). The second quadrennial congress of the LFLU was held in 1988 and endorsed the current leadership against protests from the losing candidates. They took their case to law and the union's effectiveness was reduced by the dispute until the Supreme Court of Liberia rejected it in August 1989.
Affiliated unions and structure. Firestone Agricultural Workers; National Union of Plantation, Agricultural and Allied Workers; Maritime, Seamen, Ports and General Workers Union; Domestic, Commercial, Clerical and General Services Union; National Timber, Wood, and Construction Workers Union; LIMCO/Bong Workers Union (merged in June 1989, bringing the Bong Workers Union into affiliation for the first time).
International affiliations. ICFTU; OATUU.

National Federation of Peasant Farmers, Agriculture and Plantation Workers (NAFAPAW)
(formerly the National Agriculture and Allied Workers' Union of Liberia—NAAWUL)

Address. P.O. Box 3403 Bushrod Island, Monrovia
Leadership. David White (secretary general), Alexander Daylee (president)
Membership. 45,000 claimed in 1988.
History and character. The NAFAPAW was formed in December 1986 from an amalgamation of the NAAWUL and five smaller unions and associations (*see below*). NAAWUL was founded in May 1980 by David White, shortly after the seizure of power by Samuel Doe. The new regime lifted the embargo on trade unionism among agricultural workers who had been denied the right to organize despite Liberia's ratification of ILO Conventions 87 and 98. The union was recognized by the government in September 1980, and won representation in the two largest rubber plantations of US company Firestone, the country's main employer. The union subsequently negotiated a substantial pay rise for 13,000 Firestone workers, arbitrated by the Ministry of Labour and effective from 1982. However the NAAWUL subsequently fell foul of the government and was suspended between November 1982 and October 1984; secretary general David White was arrested and detained for a total of 15 months. Firestone meanwhile would only recognize its house union, the Firestone Agricultural Workers' Union, and did not implement the new pay agreement. Since its suspension was lifted NAAWUL and its successor NAFAPAW have been active in workers' education, agricultural projects, and the promotion of production and consumer co-operatives.
Affiliated unions. The NAFAPAW comprises six unions and associations: NAAWUL (membership 25,000 claimed in 1988); the Workers' Educational Association; the Utility and General

Workers' Union; the National Seamen's Ports and General Workers' Union of Liberia; the Brewery Workers' Union, and the People's Swamp Development Community [sic].

Libya

Capital: Tripoli   **Population: 4,395,000**

Political system. The Socialist People's Libyan Arab *Jamahariyah* is a revolutionary "state of the masses", with overall leadership exercised by Col. Moamer al Kadhafi, who came to power in 1969 as a result of a bloodless military *coup*. Since 1979 Kadhafi has held no official post and is commonly referred to as "the leader of the revolution". Officially, authority is vested in the Libyan people, with local "basic people's congresses" forming an electoral base for the General People's Congress, which is serviced by a Secretariat. The Congress exercises a degree of control over the General People's Committee, which is broadly equivalent to a Council of Ministers.

Economy. The oil price slump in the early 1980s had a serious effect on Libya's petroleum-based economy, necessitating the postponement or abandonment of several large infrastructural projects. However, the ambitious US$3,300 million "great man-made river" irrigation project, signed with a South Korean construction firm in 1983, is scheduled for completion in the early 1990s.

System of industrial relations. Libya ratified ILO Convention No. 98 (Right to Organize and Collective Bargaining, 1949) in 1962 (i.e. under the monarchy) but has not ratified Convention No. 87 (Freedom of Association and Protection of the Right to Organize, 1948). Mass expulsions of Tunisian workers occurred in 1985.

Trade unionism. A single-trade-union system is in force, organized by the General Federation of Producers' Trade Unions, created in 1972.

General Federation of Producers' Trade Unions (GFPTU)

Address. P.O. Box 734, Tripoli
Leadership. Hamid Abu Bakar Jallud (secretary general)
Membership. 275,000 in 18 unions, including the General Union for Oil and Petrochemicals.
International affiliations. ICATU; OATUU.

Liechtenstein

Capital: Vaduz   **Population: 27,399**
                                                              (estimated December 1986)

Political system. The Principality of Liechtenstein is a constitutional and hereditary monarchy, controlled under its 1921 constitution by a unicameral parliament (*Landtag*).

Economy. With GNP per capita of around US$15,000 in 1984, Liechtenstein is one of the richest countries in the world. In 1986, 43.8 per cent of the workforce was involved in industry, construction or commerce, of which the metal, machinery and precision instruments industry was by far the most important single sector, employing 5,025 workers in 1986. Much of the labour for industry is provided by the one third of the population who are resident foreigners, while some 4,900 workers come from neighbouring Switzerland and Austria each day to work in Liechtenstein. The other major sector of the economy is the banking and services sector with employs nearly 45 per cent of the workforce.

System of industrial relations. Liechtenstein is not a member of the International Labour Organization and the Employees' Association does not face a clearly designated employer organization.

Trade unionism. Apart from the Employees' Association there is also an Artisans' and Tradespeoples' Association.

Liechtensteiner Arbeitnehmer-Verband
Liechtenstein Employees' Association

Address. 9490 Vaduz
Phone. (075) 24255
Leadership. Alfons Schädler (president); Eugen Büchel (secretary)
International affiliations. WCL.

Luxembourg

Capital: Luxembourg-Ville   **Population: 370,000**

Political system. The Grand Duchy of Luxembourg is a constitutional, hereditary monarchy. It is a member of the EC and of NATO.

Since 1921 it has been in monetary union with Belgium. Although the Christian Social and Socialist Parties lost ground in the 1989 election they were strong enough to form a coalition government under the Prime Minister Jaques Santer. His deputy is the socialist leader Jaques Poos.

Economy. The economy was traditionally based on iron and steel, but since the 1970s an extensive process of diversification has been carried out, especially into financial services.

Steel accounted for 34 per cent of GDP in 1952 but less than 10 per cent in 1990. The financial services on the other hand now account for more than 15 per cent of Duchy employment.

System of industrial relations. Luxembourg ratified ILO Conventions No. 87 (Freedom of Association and Protection of the Right to Organize, 1948) and No. 98 (Right to Organize and Collective Bargaining, 1949) in 1958.

Luxembourg has a tripartite Economic and Social Committee and six professional chambers—three each for the employers and for labour—which are consulted on all laws affecting them. During the painful crisis over the restructuring at Arbed steel works, the governing parties, in concert with the social partners, developed a "Luxembourg Model" of change by agreement.

Trade unionism. Despite nationalization in the late 1970s the union centres have been unable to establish a single organization as counterpart to the powerful and comprehensive Luxembourg Industrialists' Organization, FEDIL.

Confédération Générale du Travail du Luxembourg (CGT-LUX or CGT) Luxembourg General Confederation of Labour

Address. 60 Boulevard J.F. Kennedy B.P. 149, L-4002-Esch/Alzette
Phone. 54 05 45
Telex. 1368 OGB-LU
Fax. 54 16 20
Leadership. John Castegnaro (president); Josy Konz (general secretary)
Membership. 44,000 (20 per cent women). Membership of non-affiliated unions is estimated at 40,000.
General. The General Confederation of Labour of Luxembourg (CGT-LUX) consists of three trade union organizations: the Confederation of Independent Trade Unions (OGB-L—*see below*), the National Federation of Railway Workers, Transport Workers and Officers (FNCTTFEL), and the Luxembourg Federation of Publishing and Printing Workers (FLTL) with a total of 42,000 members. The President of the CGT-LUX is John Castegnaro who is also the President of the OGB-L. The General Secretary is Josy Konz, who is also the President of the FNCTTFEL.

In 1978 the trade union Letzebuerger Arbechterverband (the precursor of the present Confederation of Independent Trade Unions—OGB-L) took the initiative to form a united trade union movement based on the Austrian or West German model. The Christian trade unions in Luxembourg organized in the LCGB (*see below*) refused to become part of this new model organization, but nevertheless the majority of members of another organization, the Federation of the Self-employed (FEP), decided to affiliate to the OGB-L.

The FGIL (the General Federation of Luxembourg Institute Employees—FGIL) which was a member of the CGT before 1979, allowed its members to choose which trade union confederation they wanted to belong to. The majority joined the OBG-L. Nevertheless the FGIL is still in existence and it also serves as a vocational co-operative organization.

The FNCTTFEL is not an affiliate of the OGB-L, following a negative vote taken amongst its members. The FLTL no longer affiliates to the OGB-L.

In essence, the CGT-LUX is a loose and pragmatic federation which acts as one united organization in order to deal with major social and economic problems. It is politically independent.

Affiliated unions. OGB-L (see separate entry); Fédération Luxembourgeoise des Travailleurs du Livre (FLTL—printers' union); Fédération Nationale des Cheminots, Travilleurs du Transport, Fonctionnaires et Employés Luxembourgeois (FNCTTFEL—railway, transport, officials and salaried employees).
Publications. Two affiliates have publications: *Aktuell* (OGB-L); *Signal* (FNCTTFEL)
International affiliations. ICFTU; ETUC; TUAC.

Lëtzebuerger Chrëschtleche Gewerkschafts-Bond (LCGB) Luxembourg Confederation of Christian Trade Unions

Address. 11 rue du Commerce, B.P. 1208, 1012 Luxembourg
Phone. 49-94-24-1
Telex. 2116 LCGB LU
Fax. 49-94-24-49
Leadership. Marcel Glesener (president); Robert Weber (general secretary)
Membership. 20,000 (one-third women).
History and character. The LCGB was formally created in 1921, although it traces its origins back to the nineteenth century. In 1978 it declined to affiliate to CGT-LUX. Its orientation is social-Christian, and it gives no financial aid to political parties and is not involved in party politics. It provides a range of welfare and similar services and conducts collective bargaining.
General. In late 1987 the LCGB held its 53rd Congress in Dummeldingen. This Congress, attended by 420 delegates, was the first National Congress to be held since the change in its statutes

in 1984. Marcel Glesener was re-elected for a new four-year term with more than 90 per cent of the votes. The focus of the Congress was on the fight against unemployment and the systematic introduction of Sunday work. It was also revealed that the membership had increased by 150 per cent in the previous decade; in 1987, 2,000 new members were registered.

Structure. The LCGB has about 25 local offices and three regional offices throughout Luxembourg. There is a national congress, central committee, executive committee and a secretariat. The 14 secretaries of the affiliated unions and associations are responsible for professional issues and for collective bargaining issues affecting their members.

Affiliated unions. Steelworkers' Union; Metalworkers' Union; Steel and Metal Private Employees' Union (SESM); Trade Workers, Bank and Insurance Workers' Union; Healthworkers' Union; Union of Small- and Medium-Sized Industry; Public Services Union; Private Employers' Union; Young LCGB; Pensioners' LCGB.

Publication. Soziale Fortschrett (21,000 copies).

International affiliations. WCL; ETUC; TUAC.

Onofhängege Gewerkschaftsbond Lëtzebuerg (OGB-L) Confederation of Independent Trade Unions

Address. 60, Boulevard J.F. Kennedy, B.P. 149, L-4002 Esch-Alzette

Leadership. John Castegnaro (president)

Phone. 54-05-45

Telex. 1368 OGB-LU

Fax. 54-16-20

Membership. 13 unions with 34,000 members.

History and character. The OGB-L was formed in January 1979 as the successor organization to LAV (Lëtzebuerger Aarbechterverband), founded in 1916, and is a confederation within the CGT-LUX (*see above*).

Madagascar

Capital: Antananarivo   **Population: 11,250,000**

Political system. The Democratic Republic of Madagascar (the former Malagasy Republic), which became independent from France in 1960, has been under military rule since 1972. Didier Ratisraka, who came to power in 1975 as chairman of the Supreme Revolutionary Council, was returned for a seven-year term in presidential elections in 1982 and 1989. Until 1990 all parties were obliged to belong to the National Front for the Defence of the Revolution (FNDR) but in March a decree was promulgating the free formation of political parties. A large number were then formed which pressed demands for further reform.

Economy. Agriculture — mainly coffee, vanilla and cloves — accounts for almost 80 per cent of export revenues. Industry, the sector targeted for growth in the years immediately following independence, contributes 16 per cent of GDP. Under the 1986–90 public investment plan, prepared in conjuction with an International Monetary Fund (IMF) restructuring programme, the government has sought to revitalize agriculture, diversify exports and, in the context of economic liberalization, promote foreign investment. High inflation and constraints on government expenditure have led to a steady fall in the standard of living and widespread discontent.

In 1985–87, the Madagascan workforce was divided between agriculture (80.9 per cent), industry (6 per cent) and services (13.2 per cent).

System of industrial relations. Madagascar ratified ILO Convention No. 87 (Freedom of Association and Protection of the Right to Organize, 1948) in 1960 but has not ratified Convention No. 98 (Right to Organize and Collective Bargaining, 1949). Public servants may not form independent trade unions but may join "Malagasy Revolutionary Organizations" (ORMs), under the supervision of the government. Under the Charter of Socialist Undertakings of 1978 workers' committees were established, but preferential access to these was extended to the members of trade unions belonging to one of the ORMs of the National Front for the Defence of the Revolution.

Madagascar ratified Convention No. 29 on forced labour in 1960, but the ILO has noted that compulsory labour may be levied in prison and for some economic and social development work within the framework of compulsory national service.

Trade unionism. Five federations have been identified in Madagascar and two separate unions. SEREMA — one of the unions — is the largest organization, and is linked to President Ratsiraka's ruling AREMA party.

Cartel National des Organisations Syndicales de Madagascar (CARNOSYAMA)

Address. B.P. 1035, Antananarivo
International affiliation. OATUU.

Fivondronamben'ny Mpiasa Malagasy (FMM)
Confederation of Malagasy Workers

Address. B.P. 1558, 3 Avenue Lénine, Ambatomitsanga, Antananarivo

Phone. 24565
Leadership. Jean Rasolondraibe (secretary general)
Membership. 30,000 (1983).
History and character. Founded 1957.
International affiliations. ICFTU; OATUU.

Fédération des Syndicats des Travailleurs de Madagascar (FISEMA)
Malagasy Workers' Federation

Address. B.P. 172, Lot III, Rue Pasteur Isotry, Antananarivo
Cables. FISEMA ANTNANARIVO
Leadership. Desiré Ralambotahina (president); Razakanaivo (general secretary)
Membership. 60,000 (20 per cent women) in eight affiliates.
History and character. The FISEMA was established in 1956 when the previous Madagascan branch of the French Confédération Générale du Travail (CGT) became an independent organization. It generally opposed the government until 1975, but has since then (i.e. since the institution of the Socialist Revolutionary Charter and the naming of the country as the Democratic Republic of Madagascar) supported the government and sought to consolidate the revolution, although it is not formally linked to the ruling party. The FISEMA is opposed to (western) imperialism in Africa in the form of the presence of transnational corporations in the country. It also opposes the IMF-supported programme of economic reform currently being implemented by the government. At its Seventh Congress in October 1987, the FISEMA demanded effective application of ILO Conventions 87 and 98, the abolition of privileges given to trade unions, political parties and groups in the ruling National Front, and greater democracy. It was the largest trade union confederation until the early 1970s, but now ranks behind the SEREMA (see below).
Publication. *Feon'ny Mpiasa* (3,000 monthly).
International affiliations. WFTU; OATUU.

Fédération des Travailleurs Malagasy Révolutionnaires (FISEMARE)
Federation of Revolutionary Trade Unions of Madagascar

Address. B.P. 1128, Lot IV N 77, Ankadifots, Antananarivo-Befelatanana
Phone. 21989
Leadership. Paul Rabemananjara
History and character. Held its second congress in August 1986.
International affiliations. WFTU; OATUU.

Sendika Kristianina Malagasy (SEKRIMA)
Christian Confederation of Malagasy Trade Unions

Address. Lot IVE Soarano Antananarivo – 101. BP 1035 Madagascar
Phone. 23174
Leadership. Marie Rakotoanosy (president); Raymond Rakotoarisaona (vice-president); Andre Silamo David (secretary general)
Membership. 2,079.
History and character. Formed in 1938 as a section of the French CFTC, the organization became the CCSM in 1956 and adopted the name SEKRIMA in 1964. From 100,000 members in the mid-1950s, the confederation declined in importance during the 1960s under the first republic. Political changes in 1972–75 meant that the confederation almost stopped functioning, but it revived in the 1980s. Recruitment drives were launched in 1984–85 and a programme of development projects was set in motion; in 1986 the SEKRIMA was reorganized as the agricultural, industrial and public service workers' organizations were restructured. Further reorganization is under way.
Affiliated unions. Fédération Chrétienne des Agriculteurs (FEKRITAMA); Fédération Chrétienne des Travailleurs des Industries Malagasy (FEKRIMI); Fédération Chrétienne des Employés des Services Divers Malagasy (FEKRISAM). The Fédération des Enseignants, la Fédération du Secteur non Structuré and the Fédération des Artisans Pêcheurs are said to be in process of affiliation.

International affiliations. WCL, FOPADESC, which are reported to have provided significant assitance in the re-launch of SEKRIMA.

Sendika Revolisakionera Malagasy (SEREMA)
Revolutionary Malagasy Trade Union

The SEREMA is the trade union organization of President Didier Ratsiraka's Vanguard of the Malagasy Revolution (AREMA) party, the majority party of the regime. As of 1983 the SEREMA held 37 per cent of the seats allocated for labour representatives on works committees, the other seats being distributed among the FISEMA (with 28 per cent) and six smaller pro-government unions.
International affiliation. OATUU.

Union Syndicale des Travailleurs et Paysans Malagaches

Address. B.P. 1635, Antananarivo
International affiliation. OATUU.

Malawi

Capital: Lilongwe

Population: 8,155,000
(1988)

Political system. Malawi became a republic within the Commonwealth on July 6, 1966, on the second anniversary of its independence from the United Kingdom. Dr Hastings Kamuzu Banda, who had been Malawi's first Prime Minister prior to independence, and became President in 1966, was appointed President for Life in 1971. The Malawi Congress Party (MCP), of which Dr Banda is the President, is the sole legal party and nominated candidates for the 1987 elections. All Malawi citizens are party members.

Economy. Agriculture provides about 45 per cent of GDP, 80 per cent of export revenue, about half of which is earned tobacco, and nearly 50 per cent of employment. Poor in natural resources, Malawi's industry is largely based on food processing. In 1985 industry accounted for about 12 per cent of GDP and employs 13 per cent of the working population.

System of industrial relations. Malawi ratified ILO Convention No. 98 (Right to Organize and Collective Bargaining, 1949) in 1965 but has not ratified Convention No. 87 (Freedom of Association and Protection of the Right to Organize, 1948).

Trade unionism. Trade unions developed under British rule and the Trades Union Congress of Malawi was formed in 1964 in succession to the Nyasaland Trades Union Congress. Like most Malawian organizations, the union movement is strongly integrated into the ruling regime. The Teachers' Association is reported to be unaffiliated to the Trades Union Congress of Malawi.

Trades Union Congress of Malawi (TUCM)

Address. P.O. Box 5094, Limbe
Leadership. W. C. Chimphanga (chairman); L. Y. Mvula (general secretary)
Membership. 14,600 (1983).

International affiliations. ICFTU; OATUU. The most important affiliates are reported to be the Building, Construction, Civil Engineering and Allied Workers' Union (general secretary, G. Sitima) and the Railway Workers' Union of Malawi (general secretary, A. M. G. Kapahdamoyo-Dhuwa).

Malaysia

Capital: Kuala Lumpur   **Population: 16,920,000**

Political system. Malaysia is a federation of 13 states and a parliamentary monarchy. It has a Supreme Head of State (*Yang di-Pertuan Agong*) who appoints a Cabinet headed by a Prime Minister. The country's bicameral legislature comprises a 69-member indirectly elected Senate and a 177-member directly elected House of Representatives; residual legislative power rests with the states. The governing multi-racial National Front coalition embraces 13 political formations (the leading party being the United Malay National Organization).

Economy. The New Economic Policy (NEP), adopted in 1970 with the intention of raising the economic status of the ethnic Malay majority (the *bumiputras*) to that of the wealthier Chinese minority, has been the cornerstone of the economic policy of successive National Front governments. However, by 1986 *bumiputra* ownership of corporate assets had reached only 18 per cent of total equity (against a target of 30 per cent for 1990). Shortages of capital obliged the government to announce in 1986 that 100 per cent foreign ownership of Malaysian companies would henceforth be permitted. Real economic growth averaged 7.9 per cent in the late 1970s with the world commodity boom, but since 1980 declining prices for rubber (the main export crop), tin and crude oil have depressed the economy and a consistent trade deficit has been recorded. The budget for 1988 imposed restraints on government expenditure and aimed to increase revenue by selling the government's shares in the national airline and shipping line to the central bank.

Malaysia is still the leading rubber and a major tin producer but, in a triumph for the policy of diversification, manufacturing supplanted agriculture as the largest sector of the economy in 1987 and accounted for 48 per cent of export earnings. The 6,090,000 civilian employees of the country in 1988 were apportioned between industry (1,450,000), agriculture (1,910,000), and services (2,730,000). The late 1980s brought a strong recovery from the flat output of the middle 1980s, with economic growth passing 8 per cent. However, with a rapid increase in the size of the workforce this did not bring the expected benefits in terms of unemployment, which fell only slightly to 8.1 per cent. There is no minimum wage, but pay is high by the standards of South-East Asia.

System of industrial relations. There are restrictions on collective bargaining in the public sector under the Industrial Relations Act of 1967 and amendments; the Trade Unions Act of 1959 as amended in 1981 gives the Registrar of Trade Unions wide discretionary powers to deny recognition to new unions or to suspend existing unions; and workers in the free-trade zones, in an attempt to encourage investment by foreign capital, have not been permitted to form unions. Significant strikes are rare, most disputes being settled by conciliation with the assistance of the Ministry of Labour or in the Industrial Court, and the government has powers to impose compulsory arbitration making strikes illegal and punishable by imprisonment. ILO Convention No. 98 (Right to Organize and

Collective Bargaining, 1949) was ratified by Peninsular Malaysia in 1961 and by Sabah and Sarawak in 1964. Peninsula-based unions may not have members from Sabah and Sarawak, and vice versa.

Attempts by the government to tighten Malaysian law still further in respect of trade unions were dropped in 1986 in the face of union and employer opposition. In 1988 the tripartite Labour Advisory Council (NLAC) was presented with 12 proposed amendments by the government and some of them became law in February 1989. The changes to the Trade Union Act extend government powers to dub a government department or statutory body an "essential service", but they relax the employment requirement for union office. The changes to the Industrial Relations Act permit the use of secret ballots to check representation claims; double the time unions must wait between claims, bar legal representation from conciliation cases and independents from Industrial Court panels, and make Industrial Court awards enforceable by the regular courts (with the effect of allowing unions to approach the High Court directly for enforcement).

Strikes in Malaysia are relatively rare and usually do not last long. In 1988 5,784 days were lost to strikes, little more than half the total for the previous year, though they included a major dispute in the plantations with the National Union of Plantation Workers, the country's biggest union. There were 988 disputes of all kinds during the year, according to the Ministry of Labour. In June 1988, the AFL-CIO applied for Malaysia's preferences under the United States General System of Preferences to be suspended because the government did not respect international union rights standards. Extended hearings followed and it was only in April 1989 that Malaysia was deemed to have taken steps to respect these rights.

Trade unionism. Chinese *hongs*, or guilds, were predecessors of trade union organizations before World War II, and there was also some organizational activity among immigrant Indian workers, under the influence of trade union developments in the subcontinent. Immediately following the war and the Japanese occupation, the Malayan Communist Party (MCP) formed the General Labour Union (GLU), which later became the Pan Malayan Federation of Trade Unions (PMFTU). To counteract this influence the British encouraged the development of "free" trade unions, and trade union officers came from Britain to assist in the education of union officers. Following widespread industrial unrest from 1946–48, a State of Emergency was declared, the MCP was outlawed and the PMFTU was deregistered.

Trade unionists were among more than a hundred public figures—including opposition and government politicians, intellectuals and community activists—who were arrested in October and November 1987 under Malaysia's Internal Security Act. The government claimed the arrests had been made to calm rising racial tension. Dr V. David, secretary general of the MTUC and the Transport Workers' Union, was arrested immediately on his return from a convention in the USA in November. While abroad he had publicly criticized conditions in Malaysia's free-trade zones and had spoken of the denial of trade union rights to some 100,000 workers, mostly young Malay women in the electronics industry. In December 1987 Dr David and two other trade union leaders were served with detention orders of up to two years and were sent to a political detention camp for "rehabilitation". The ICFTU reported in June 1988 that Dr David had recently been conditionally released from detention.

Malaysia's Minister of Labour and Manpower, Datuk Lee Kim Sai, announced on Sept. 22, 1988, that electronics workers would henceforth be allowed to form a national trade union. The announcement ended a 15-year ban which, together with generous tax concessions, had been a major factor in attracting many foreign manufacturers to Malaysia. The decision had been widely linked with the hearing in mid-November 1988 of a petition to the US government by the American Federation of Labour Congress of

Industrial Organizations (AFL-CIO), seeking the removal of Malaysia from the United States' generalized system of preferences on the grounds that Malaysia had violated workers' rights. However, on Oct. 17, Datuk Lee announced what appeared to be a reversal of his original decision; electronics workers, he said, would only be allowed to form in-house unions, and not independent national trade unions. The reversal provoked protests from the MTUC and from the Geneva-based International Metalworkers' Federation.

The "free" trade unions formed the Malaysian Trade Unions Congress (MTUC) in 1950, and it has been the main trade union centre since that time. The Congress of Unions of Employees in the Public and Civil Services (CUEPACS) represents unions organizing around 110,000 public sector staff members. For many years there were regular attempts made to merge these two centres into a United Malaysian Labour Movement (UMLM) and harmonize representation at the ILO but they were bedevilled by CUEPACS fears over the loss of its identity and controversy over the leadership of the new organization. Moreover in 1989 there were the first moves—instigated by the National Union of Newspaper Workers (NUNW)—to form a rival centre grouping private sector unions, the Congress of Unions in the Private Sector (CUPS). A number of unions do not affiliate to either of these bodies and some of them also had discussions in 1989 about establishing an alternative national union centre. The National Union of Bank Employees, the National Union of Commercial Workers, the National Union of Petroleum and Chemical Workers, and at least one of the state-based textile workers' unions was reported to be involved.

At the end of 1988 there were 392 individual unions in Malaysia with 616,626 members, an increase of 10,000 over 1987. Under the 1959 Act unions are not allowed to organize outside their primary industry and so unions tend to be organized along company lines. Where more than one union is present at a company, they usually represent different classes of employees.

Union density on this basis in 1988 was just over 10 per cent. However, what complicates matters is the widespread existence of company or "in-house" unions. At the end of 1988 there were 224 of these with membership of 200,200, divided almost two and a half to one in favour of the public sector: 138,997 to 61,203. This was in sharp contrast to the division of public and private sector union members overall which was roughly equal: 299, 156 to 317,761.

Congress of Unions of Employees in the Public and Civil Services (CUEPACS)

Leadership. A. Ragunathan (president); Mohamed Abas bin Isa (secretary-general)
Membership. 110,000 members organized in 55 unions.
Affiliated unions and structure. Major affiliates of CUEPACS include:

1. **Amalgamated National Union of Local Authorities Employees Peninsular Malaysia** (19,707 members).

2. **Independent Unions** (over 10,000 members in 1988).

3. **Malay Teachers Union** (15,391 members).

4. **National Union of Bank Employees** (20,051 members).

5. **National Union of Commercial Workers** (11,979 members).

Kongres Kesatuan Sekerja Malaysia
Malaysian Trades Union Congress (MTUC)

Address. 19 Jalan Barat, P.O. Box 38, 46700 Petaling Jaya, Selangor
Phone. (03) 7560224; 7567713

Cables. MALTUC, PETALING JAYA

Leadership. Zainal Rampak (president); Dr V. David (secretary general); P. P. Narayanan (president of the ICFTU since 1975, stood down as president of the MTUC in 1986, but remained an honorary life president with the title of "Father of Malaysian Workers")

Membership. 350,000 in 136 affiliated unions. The largest individual union affiliated to the MTUC is the National Union of Plantation Workers (NUPW), with over 100,000 members.

History and character. The MTUC, founded in 1950 by the "free" trades unions, was initially known as the Malayan Trades Union Council; in 1958 it became the Malayan Trades Union Congress, and took its present name with the formation of Malaysia. The MTUC is represented on government wages councils and a range of other governmental bodies.

The MTUC secretary general, Dr V. David, was one of a number of people placed in detention by the Malaysian government in October and November 1987. His conditional release was reported in June 1988. In December 1988 the MTUC held its 29th Biennial Delegates' Conference. The President and General Secretary were re-elected.

Affiliated unions. MTUC affiliated unions include:

1. **National Union of Plantation Workers**, 2 Jalan Templer, 46700 Petaling Jaya.

2. **All Malayan Estate Staff Union**, P.O. Box 12, Taman Universiti, 46700 Petaling Jaya.

3. **Transport Workers Union**, 21 Jalan Barat, 46200 Petaling Jaya.

4. **Construction Workers Union**, 13 (2nd floor) Jalan 14/20, 46100 Petaling Jaya.

5. **Metal Industry Employees Union**, 5 Lorong Utara Kecil, 46200 Petaling Jaya.

6. **Electricity Industry Workers Union**, 55-2 Jalan SS 15/8-A, Subang Jaya, 47500 Petaling Jaya.

7. **Timber Employees Union**, 10 Jalan AU 5-C/14 Ampang, Ulu Leleang, 54200 Kuala Lumpur.

8. **National Union of Commercial Workers**, 98-A Jalan Masjid India, P.O. Box 12509, 50780 Kuala Lumpur.

9. **Amalgamated Union of Employees in Government Clerical and Allied Services**, 32A Jalan Gajah, Jln Yew, 55100 Kuala Lumpur.

10. **National Mining Workers Union**, Bangunan KKPLN, 84-1A Jalan Sungai Besi, 57100 Kuala Lumpur.

11. **Railwaymen's Union of Malaya**, 9-A (Tingkat 1) Bangunan Tong Nam, Jalan Tun Sambanthan, 50470 Kuala Lumpur.

12. **Union of Post Office Workers**, c/o Pejabet Pos Besar, 50670 Kuala Lumpur.

13. **National Union of Journalists**, 30-B, Jalan Padang Belia, 50470 Kuala Lumpur.

14. **National Union of Teaching Profession**, 13-B Jalan Murai 2, Komplex Batu, 51100 Kuala Lumpur.

The largest MTUC affiliate — indeed the largest union in the country — is the National Union of Plantation Workers which had 83,992 members in 1988, a loss of more than 6,000 from the year before. The NUPW General Secretary D. P. Narayanan is a noted figure in international trade union circles. The second largest is the National Union of Telecoms Employees with 18,593 members in 1988, and only two more unions — the Transport Workers Union, Peninsular Malaysia (10,831) and the National Electricity Board Employees Union (10, 409) — have more than 10,000 members. The General Secretary of the Transport Union is Mr V. David, the MTUC General Secretary.

Publication. Suara Buruh.

International affiliations. ICFTU; ICFTU-APRO; CTUC.

National Union of the Teaching Profession, Peninsular Malaysia

Address. 13-B, Jalan Murai Dua, Batu Complex, 51100 Kuala Lumpur

Phone. 6210621/3

Fax. 6211060
Leadership. Tuan Hj. Salleh Yusof (President); N. Siva Subramaniam (secretary-general)
Membership. Claims 40,000 members.
History and character. The Union is CUEPAC's largest affiliate and the biggest civil service union in Malaysia and was formed in 1954.

Maldives

Capital: Malé   **Population: 200,000**
                                                                                    (1988)

Political system. The Republic of the Maldives has an executive President (currently Maumoon Abdul Gayoom) elected for a five-year term by universal adult suffrage, a Cabinet presided over by the President, and a Citizens' Council (*Majlis*). There are no political parties.

Indian troops went to the Maldives at the invitation of the government when it faced the threat of a *coup* in late 1988.

Economy. The fish industry is the largest element in the Maldivian economy. During the 1980s tourism has steadily increased and it now constitutes the principal source of export earnings. Fishing employs 35 per cent of the workforce and accounts for nearly 20 per cent of GDP.

System of industrial relations. Maldives is not a member of the International Labour Organization.

Trade unionism. Trade Unions do not exist in the Maldives, partly due to the deferential nature of society.

Mali

Capital: Bamako   **Population: 7,989,000**
                                                                                    (1988)

Political system. Mali is a one-party unitary state with a mixed military-civilian government. The ruling body is the Military Committee for National Liberation, in power since 1968 when the current President, Gen. Moussa Traoré, came to power in a *coup d'état*. Gen. Traoré was elected President without opposition in June 1979 and was re-elected in June 1985.

From December 1990 to March 1991 major strikes and demonstrations were held in support of calls for an end to President Traoré's rule and the introduction of political pluralism.

Economy. The economy is largely subsistence, and the country is heavily dependent on foreign aid. Some 85 per cent of the population is engaged in farming and fishing; 10 per cent of the population are nomadic livestock-herders. Cotton is the main cash crop and provided approximately 40 per cent of export revenues in 1985. A series of droughts have devastated the agricultural and pastoral sectors since 1980 and there have been frequent food shortages. Industry, which accounted for only 7 per cent of GDP in 1984 and 5 per cent of employment in 1982, has also been affected because over half the enterprises are agro-industrial and textiles plants. Under an International Monetary Fund (IMF) restructuring programme the government encouraged private enterprise and tried to phase out unprofitable state-owned corporations whilst holding down expenditure on civil service salaries.

Recent surveys have shown that very large numbers of new graduates are without work in Mali and this may have been a powerful factor impelling them to support the Association of Pupils and Students (AEEM) in its participation in the oppositional activities of 1990–91.

System of industrial relations. Mali ratified ILO Convention No. 87 (Freedom of Association and Protection of the Right to Organize, 1948) in 1960 and Convention No. 98 (Right to Organize and Collective Bargaining, 1949) in 1964. Although recognized in Mali's constitution, the right to strike has been seriously circumscribed, and was for long banned among public servants. However, following strikes by teachers and health workers late in 1986, two acts were passed in July 1987 recognizing the right of civil servants to strike. Strict limits were nevertheless maintained, requiring advance notice and mandatory recourse to a conciliation board. Emergency regulations cover the provision of minimal services in the event of a strike. Mali ratified Convention Nos. 29 and 105 on forced labour in 1960 and 1962.

Trade unionism. Branches of the metropolitan French confederations existed before independence in 1960, but trade union activity was subsequently co-ordinated in a single-trade-union system organized by the Union Nationale des Travailleurs du Mali (UNTM). But from May 1990 the UNTM began to shift to an oppositional position and organized a general strike on Jan. 8–9, 1991.

Union Nationale des Travailleurs du Mali (UNTM)
National Union of Workers of Mali

Address. Bourse du Travail, Boulevard de l'Indépendence, B.P. 169, Bamako

Phone. 222031

Leadership. Bakary Karambé (general secretary). There is an executive bureau of 19 members.

Membership. 130,000 (15,000 women) in 12 affiliated national industrial sector unions. There are no unaffiliated unions.

History and character. Founded 1963. At the sixth congress, held in October 1985 and presided over by the President of Mali, Moussa Traoré, the UNTM attacked the IMF and multinationals and called for a raising of the minimum wage and the monthly payment of old age pensions. President Traoré spoke of the need to raise the minimum wage but told the congress that "logically we can only share out what we have produced" and attributed Mali's economic problems to the continuing drought. The congress excluded Bidia Toucour, the retiring deputy general secretary, who was charged with having brought about the dismissals of public sector employees while being minister responsible for nationalized industries. The UNTM receives financial support from the government, has a policy of "responsible participation" in the development of the country, and is represented in the Ministry of State Companies and Enterprises. However, it is not formally affiliated to the ruling party, and has indeed been one of the few voices critical of the regime. The UNTM has warned of serious civil unrest as a result of rising food prices, delays in the payment of public sector wages, and the fall in real value of pay since it was last increased in 1985. These grievances led to numerous work stoppages early in 1988. The teachers' union, the Syndicat National de l'Education et de la

Culture (SNEC), went on strike for a week in protest at delayed pay and allowances. While pressing for the resolution of workers' grievances, the UNTM criticized the SNEC for "indiscipline" since settlement of such disputes was the responsibility of the central union body, it claimed.

The UNTM National Council in May 1990 called for the introduction of a multi-party system. When the first marches and demonstrations against the Traoré régime were suppressed, the UNTM called a two-day general strike in January 1991. The UNTM had long been concerned about the impact of the privatization programme on the low-paid and especially upon women workers, and had established a women's committee. In February 1991 it reported that it had been conceded a role in the privatization of state enterprises and would play a part in a conciliation board intended to facilitate negotiations between the government and the opposition.

Publications. Baarakela-Travailleurs (monthly, circulation 50,000); *Educateur* (for teachers).

International affiliation. OATUU. The UNTM has no other international affiliation but there are good relations with the WFTU and the ICFTU supports a number of agricultural co-operatives run by the UNTM.

Malta

Capital: Valletta

Population: 348,000
(1988)

Political system. Malta is an independent republic within the Commonwealth and a member of the non-aligned movement. The conservative Nationalist Party (NP) has formed the government since elections in May 1987, when it defeated the incumbent Labour Party.

Economy. Malta's economy is based on the export of manufactured goods, tourism, and shipbuilding, all of which were badly affected by the global recession in the early 1980s. In July 1986 a major three-year development plan was introduced to tackle infrastructural problems, provide support for manufacturing and tourism and create jobs.

System of industrial relations. Malta ratified ILO Conventions No. 87 (Freedom of Association and Protection of the Right to Organize, 1948) and No. 98 (Right to Organize and Collective Bargaining, 1949) in 1965.

The responsible minister may under the Industrial Relations Act of 1976 compulsorily refer disputes to the Industrial Tribunal for binding settlement (i.e. in effect limiting the right to strike). The 1976 Act provided for the creation of a joint negotiating council for the public sector, to take unanimous decisions, but this has not yet been formed, in part because of disagreements between the two national trade union confederations.

Trade unionism. Trade unions before World War II had the predominant character of workers' beneficial guilds, but the General Workers' Union was formed in 1943 as a full trade union, with its early strength among white-collar workers and skilled workers in the British naval dockyards. There are two trade union organizations recognized under the 1976 Industrial Relations Act as being representative at the national level, the Confederation of Trade Unions, (CMTU), a WCL affiliate, and the General Workers' Union (GWU), which is affiliated to the ICFTU.

Confederation of Trade Unions (CMTU)

Address. 13/3 South Street, P.O. Box 467, Valletta.
Phone. 220847; 222663

Telex. 1593 EXPRESS MW

Fax. 246091; 236320

Leadership. Salvino Spiteri (president); Charles V. Naudi (general secretary)

Membership. 28,018 at June 1990 representing 40 per cent of unionized labour.

History and character. The CMTU was founded in 1959 and is open to all unions in Malta. The number of affiliated unions has been halved since the mid-1970s, as a consequence of mergers of public sector unions and the closure of the UK military base in 1979, which led to the dissolution of unions representing workers employed by the British government. However, the total membership of the affiliates has increased by one-third since 1982. The federation was known as the Malta Confederation of Trade Unions until 1978 when the Labour government, which has a close association with the GWU, put through legislation which prohibited the use of the word Malta in the name (although the federation now uses the acronym CMTU). The CMTU makes no financial contributions to political parties and is politically non-aligned. While Labour held office the CMTU campaigned for the establishment of a joint negotiating council and industrial tribunal for government employees as required by the 1976 legislation, and accused the GWU of supporting the government in its failure to implement the law.

Affiliated unions. United Workers' Union (Union Haddiema Maghqudin—UHM); Malta Union of Teachers (MUT); Movement of United Bank Employees (MUBE); Drydock Senior and Executive Staff Union (DSESU); Lotto Receivers' Union (LRU); MAM—The Medical Union; Chamber of Pharmacists; Casino Employees' Union.

Publication. CMTU Review.

International affiliations. WCL; CTUC; ETUC.

General Workers' Union (GWU)

Address. Workers' Memorial Building, South Street, Valletta

Phone. 624300; 620505

Telex. MW1307

Fax. 243454

Leadership. Lawrence Lautier (president); Angelo Fenech (general secretary)

Membership. 38,190.

History and character. The GWU was founded in 1943 and has a membership distributed throughout the major sectors of the economy. Politically it is identified with the Malta Labour Party, with which it was officially amalgamated in 1978, to the extent that the union's president and general secretary have participated in Cabinet meetings.

Since the electoral victory of the conservative Nationalist Party in May 1987 ended 16 years of Labour rule, the GWU has engaged in a series of actions opposing government plans for the running of the important parastatal sector, especially over moves towards privatization. Conflict reached a peak in June 1988. Drydock workers belonging to the GWU blockaded the main port by anchoring a tanker across the mouth of the breakwater, preventing a visit by four British warships. Later, arrests of union members for interrogation about the incident led to further demonstrations.

Structure. The GWU is organized in nine trade sections, which are organized on an industrial basis, with each section having its own executive committee, and the national council of the GWU fulfilling functions similar to those of a trade union federation. The supreme body is the national conference, composed of delegates from the nine trade sections, which elects the national council and formulates policy. The nine trade sections are: drydocks (metal) workers' section; metalworkers' section; port and transport workers' section; hotels, restaurants and food workers section; parastatal and people's industries workers' section; chemicals and general workers' section; textiles, garments and leather workers' section; public services employees' section; supervisory, technical and professional staff association.

Publications. L'Orrizont (daily, in Maltese); It-Torca (weekly, in Maltese); Labour Post (fortnightly, in English).

International affiliations. ICFTU; ETUC. Several of the trade sections are affiliated to the appropriate international trade secretariats of the ICFTU.

Mauritania

Capital: Nouakchott   **Population: 1,954,000**

Political system. The Islamic Republic of Mauritania was constituted in 1960, as a parliamentary democracy, in practice as a one-party state. It has been ruled since 1978 by military administrations. A bloodless *coup* in December 1984 brought to power the former Armed Forces Chief of Staff, Col. Taya, who took over from former President Haydalla as head of state.

The dominant political events in Mauritania in 1990 were related to the ethnic conflict between the Moorish majority and the minority of black Francophones and the worsening situation on the border with Senegal. One group of (illegal) opposition forces is waging an armed struggle on their behalf, and the other consists of opposition groups in exile. A *coup* attempted from within the armed forces failed in November but a number of those alleged to be implicated were released from prison the following March.

Economy. Drought and locust plagues led to a steady fall in agricultural production from the early 1970s and in 1983–4 cereal production covered only 5 per cent of Mauritania's food needs necessitating substantial food imports. Exports of iron ore, which provided half the country's foreign exchange in 1985, have fallen since the 1970s due to declining world demand and in 1984 they were lower than exports of fisheries products, the only other significant export. As a result the current account, in surplus till 1980, has moved into deficit.

Traditionally, slavery was common among the black or mixed-race descendants of freed slaves (*haratin*) of the south. In 1980 Mauritania officially abolished slavery and in 1984 a report to the UN recorded that slavery had been virtually eradicated.

Mauritania is more urbanized than some West African countries and since the 1960s has experienced a growth of industry, and especially services, at the expense of agriculture. While agriculture still accounted for 69.4 per cent of the labour force in 1985–87, 8.9 per cent was in industry and 21.7 per cent in services.

System of industrial relations. Mauritania ratified ILO Convention No. 87 (Freedom of Association and Protection of the Right to Organize, 1948) in 1961 but has not ratified Convention No. 98 (Right to Organize and Collective Bargaining, 1949).

Trade unionism. There is a single-trade-union system in operation.

Union des Travailleurs de Mauritanie (UTM)

Address. B.P. 630, Bourse du Travail, Nouakchott
Leadership. Elkoli Himelty (secretary general)
Membership. 10,000.
History. Founded 1961.
International affiliations. OATUU; ICATU.

Mauritius

Capital: Port Louis

Population: 1,002,178

Political system. The former British colony of Mauritius became an independent state within the Commonwealth in 1968. The British monarch is head of state and is represented by a Governor-General, who appoints the Prime Minister, and on his advice, Cabinet ministers. There is a unicameral Legislative Assembly, elected by direct universal adult suffrage for five years.

The Mauritius Labour Party (MLP) held office from 1967 until it was defeated in the election of 1982 by an alliance between the (Marxist) Mauritian Militant Movement (MMM) and the Parti Socialiste Mauricien (PSM) whose leader, Aneerood Jugnauth, became Prime Minister. Following the break-up of the coalition in 1983, Jugnauth set up a new party, the Mouvement Socialiste Mauricien (MSM), which as a coalition with the MLP and the Conservative Party, defeated the MMM. Jugnauth remained Prime Minister but relations within the coalition were strained.

Economy. The government has sought to reduce the economy's dependence on sugar, which provided 43 per cent of exports in 1985 and employed 25 per cent of the workforce, by reducing production by 80 per cent during the 1980s and encouraging farmers to diversify. Industry has seen rapid growth since independence, accounting for 22 per cent of GDP in 1986 and employing one third of the workforce, largely due to the success of export processing zones (EPZ) in attracting foreign investors. Mauritius is now the third largest producer of woollen knitwear in the world and the clothing industry employs 85 per cent of those in the industrial sector and provides 40 per cent of exports.

Unemployment, standing at 20 per cent in 1984, has been a serious problem in recent years and has fuelled industrial discontent. Employment opportunities in the industrial sector are considerably better for women than men. The total number of paid workers was 200,442 in 1984. However the years 1982–1990 saw very rapid economic development, stimulated by the successful application of Export Processing Zones. It has been claimed that these zones now employ 88 per cent of the country's manufacturing employees and 31 per cent of the total workforce. Growth has stayed between 5 and 7 per cent and inflation is running at 8 per cent. Following an IMF recommendation, the government imposed a one year wage freeze in July 1988 in the teeth of popular protest.

System of industrial relations. Mauritius ratified ILO Convention No. 98 (Right to Organize and Collective Bargaining, 1949) in 1969, but has not ratified Convention No. 87 (Freedom of Association and Protection of the Right to Organize, 1948). Labour legislation has been modified in the EPZ, which has expanded rapidly in recent years. The unions have been pressing for an increase in the basic wage in the EPZ, regulation of overtime, and the harmonization of working conditions there in line with national legislation and other sectors.

Wages in Mauritius are low and so there was widespread support for a national strike when the government froze wages for one year in July 1988. Some 300,000 workers took part. The government arrested several union leaders for their part in the strike. Since that time annual tripartite negotiations have failed to lift the minimum wage to the levels sought by the unions. The government is in fact empowered by law to summon an Advisory Labour Council but has declined to do so.

Trade unionism. There are six main union organizations in Mauritius, of which the largest is probably the ICFTU-affiliated Mauritius Labour Congress (MLC). National employment law allows new organizations to be set up with a minimum of seven members

303

however, and this has encouraged proliferation to the point where the Island (of little more than 1,000,000 people) has 300 unions.

Fédération des Syndicats des Corps Constitués (FSCC)
Federation of Civil Service Unions (FCSU)

Address. 33 Corderie Street, Port Louis
Phone. 26621
Leadership. Dipnarainsingh Bhuruth (president); Ramlacksing Sungkur (secretary)
Membership. 16,000.
History and character. The FSCC was created as a federation for unions of workers in parastatal (semi-governmental) organizations in 1973, and was officially registered in 1975. Some of its affiliates were previously members of the Mauritius Labour Congress. There are 43 affiliated unions, representing most sectors of public employment. The FSCC favours worker participation and has secured the involvement of workers' representatives on the boards of various public bodies. It is the sole recognized bargaining agent for employees in parastatal bodies and local authorities.
Publication. Quarterly newsletter.
International affiliation. FOPADESC (WCL).

General Worker's Federation (GWF)

Address. 19 B, Poudrière Street, Port Louis
Leadership. Georges G. Candassamy Pillay
International affiliations. WFTU; OATUU.

Mauritius Labour Congress (MLC)

Address. 8 Louis Victor de la Faye Street, Port Louis
Phone. 24343
Telex. 4611 AFAM LAB 1W
Leadership. C. Bhagirutty (president); Khemraze Cunniah (general secretary)
Membership. 55,000.
History, structure, policies and character. The MLC was formed in 1963 as a result of a merger of the Mauritius Trades Union Congress and the Mauritius Confederation of Free Trade Unions. It claims to be the largest recognized central organization of workers in the country, grouping 47 unions covering the main sectors of the economy: sugar, tea, transport, docks, aviation, banks, insurance, construction, textiles, public service, parastatals and local authorities. The president of one of the MLC affiliates, the Mauritius Textile and Garment Workers' Union, and two other union leaders were arrested in July 1988 for their part in a textile workers' strike in the EPZ. The workers demanded an increase in pay up to the EPZ legal minimum, which the company refused. The government invoked labour legislation to order a return to work, resulting in the subsequent arrest of the three men.

The MLC General Secretary Khemraze Cunniah announced early in 1991 that his union was modernizing its services and stepping up training of officers in order to cope with the accelerated scale of Mauritian development.
Publication. MLC News Bulletin.
International affiliations. ICFTU; OATUU.

Organization of Artisans Unity (OAU)

Address. Bureau de la Fédération des Travailleurs Libres, 42 Sir William Newton Street, Port Louis
Phone. 24557
Leadership. Auguste Follet (president); Tristan Monvoisin (secretary)
Membership. 2,804 (1988)
History and character. Founded June 1973. Members work in the tea and sugar industries,

predominantly in rural areas, and the OAU negotiates with employers on their behalf. The OAU's policy-making body is the Annual General Assembly which elects a 25-member executive committee. The OAU favours worker participation, is campaigning for a 40-hour week, and is politically non-aligned. It is represented on the Sugar Industry Labour Welfare fund.

Publication. News bulletin for members.

International affiliation. WCL.

Mexico

Capital: Mexico City   **Population: 79,800,000**

Political system. Mexico is a federal republic comprising 31 states in which the presidency is the strongest branch of government. The dominant political institution is the Partido Revolucionario Institucional (PRI), the political orientation of which depends largely on the faction represented by the incumbent President. President Carlos Salinas de Gortari took office following a disputed election in 1988 for a six year period.

Economy. Government macro-economic policy is shaped within the tripartite Economic Solidarity Pact of 1987 and its successor of January 1989, the Pact for Stability and Economic Growth (PECE). The principles of Phase II of the PECE (which began in June 1989) are tight fiscal and monetary policy, price and wage controls. Its effectiveness seems to have declined over time as sharp prices came into view in 1990. Mexico's high inflation—it passed 100 per cent in 1986—was reined back in 1989 to 19 per cent. Partly as a result real wages grew substantially for manufacturing workers in 1989 and 1990, though the value of the minimum wage fell in 1990 for the eighth consecutive year. In November 1990, PECE was extended to the end of 1991.

Nevertheless unemployment—officially 8–9 per cent but in the view of many 18–20 per cent—had not been overcome by the end of the decade. In May 1989 the Mexican government enacted new legislation intended to liberalize the economy, particularly aimed at relaxing constraints on foreign participation. This move was a response to the plan of US Secretary Brady to cut the country's debt, but other measures associated with it have taken Mexico in the direction of a North American Free Trade Area (formed by the United States, Mexico and Canada) which the Bush administration submitted to Congress for approval in May 1991.

A major contributor to economic and employment growth is the maquiladora (sub-contract assembly) sector launched in 1966. By the middle of 1990 it had grown to some 2,000 plants close to the United States border employing around 500,000 workers. The competitive advantage of the *maquiladora* sector is cheap labour for exported products: one estimate assessed its share of Mexico's electric and electronic equipment sector at 44 per cent. The firms concerned—often US-owned multinationals—exhibit a much greater growth rate than that shown by the Mexican economy as a whole. US unions have expressed their growing concern at the use of the maquiladora sector—which began as a zone to give work to migrants denied entry into the United States—to undercut domestic activity and labour standards. The AFL-CIO and CTM meet annually to discuss the problems posed for both by the maquiladora sector and hope to raise the level of unionization there.

System of industrial relations. Mexico ratified ILO Convention No.87 (Freedom of Association and Protection of the Right to Organize, 1948) in 1950 but has not ratified Convention No. 98 ((Right to Organize and Collective Bargaining, 1949). There are restrictions on the trade union rights of public servants, notably that: (i) no more than one union is permitted in any state body; and (ii) state employees may not leave the unions to which they belong and their unions may not join organizations of workers and peasants. These limitations have been held by the ILO's Committee of Experts on the Application of Conventions and Recommendations to be in violation of the Conventions.

Following an economic crisis in 1973, it became government policy to adjust minimum wages more frequently than before in recognition of soaring inflation, and a national tripartite board was set up (of workers', employers' and government representatives). From 1975, due to the continuing economic crisis, it became government practice to review wages on a yearly basis; and from 1982 onwards, there was the possibility of changing them within the current year if the economic climate justified this. Despite elaborate machinery in the private sector to set wage levels, there are frequent discrepancies between minimum wages and those resulting from collective agreements, the latter provoking frequent strikes (a political decision of 1982 separated the review of minimum wages from the scales set by collective bargaining agreements, thus opening the way for inequalities). There is no "official" collective bargaining in the public sector though unions have bypassed official structures, transforming "general working conditions" discussions into actual collective bargaining agreements.

In December 1987, the government, leading employers and unions signed a "Social Pact" in the face of a deepening economic crisis. It provided for (alongside state utility price increases, cuts in public expenditure and the privatization of some 50 State enterprises) a 15 per cent increase in minimum wages in December and a further 20 per cent increase in January 1988. From March 1988, monthly wage "adjustments" would be made in line with the price of basic foodstuffs and other commodities. CTM president, Fidel Velázquez, stated that the unions had signed the pact solely in the national interest, not because it met the needs of workers. It was estimated that there had been a 60 per cent drop in real wages since 1982. This "Social Pact", extended in late March for a further two months, drew criticism from political and labour opponents of the ruling PRI party. Instead of wage rises, the pro-government union leadership accepted tax cuts and a private sector commitment to lower prices. On Nov. 3, 1988, the Labour Congress (Congreso del Trabajo—CT), the umbrella organization of all unions, indicated its general hostility to the government's austerity programme and the year's pay freeze, by calling for a 50 per cent increase in the purchasing power of wages. This was on a day when supporters of two of the confederations with close ties to the PRI (the CTM and the CROC) clashed physically in a five star hotel in Mexico City, in an old inter-union dispute as to which union should represent a quintet of musicians. Two people were reported killed and fifteen injured after a gun battle involving an estimated 400 workers broke out in the Hotel President de Chapultepec. And on November 9, 1988, following tense state elections in Tabasco between the PRI and the National Democratic Front, Lenin Falcón, leader of the Union of Oilworkers of the Mexican Republic (STPRM) was shot dead. Leaders of oil workers in the state company (PEMEX) had presented evidence to the Mexican Chamber of Deputies on Oct. 21, 1988, alleging a US$49,000,000 fraud.

During 1989 strike activity increased while remaining at a low level. More than 4,600 notices of intent to strike were posted compared with some 3,700 in 1988 and 100 were declared legal (88 in 1988). Most strikes were of brief duration but in the case of longer disputes the government sometimes intervened heavy-handedly. There was, unusually, strike activity in the maquiladora sector in 1989, in the state of Tamaulipas.

Trade unionism. Workers' rights were given recognition in the Constitution of 1917, which gave expression to the objectives of the 1910 revolution. The Confederación Regional Obrera Mexicana (CROM) was formed in 1918, and a breakaway anarchist-led group, the Confederación General de Trabajadores (CGT), in 1921. Since the 1930s, however, the dominant force has been the Confederación de Trabajadores de Mexico (CTM—founded in 1936), which is closely allied with the PRI, the party of government continuously since 1929. Union density in Mexico is between 25 and 30 per cent. The CTM's dominance, though not unchallenged, remains massive. It is easily the largest union centre and its nonagenarian Secretary General Fidel Velázquez is regularly consulted by President Salinas. Its support for successive government policies is probably a major factor explaining the surprisingly low level of union unrest in Mexico. Discontent with its stance is growing at rank-and-file level, but has not yet reached the point where its orientation will be changed. Other established confederations include the revolutionary Confederation of Workers and Farmers (CROC) and the Mexican Regional Workers' Confederation (CROM). These and other confederations and unions—36 in all—are co-ordinated by the Congress of Labour.

Congreso del Trabajo (CT)
Congress of Labour

Address. Ricardo Flores Magón 44, Col. Guerro, México 13, DF

Leadership: Rafael Rivapalacio Pontones (rotating president)

History and character. The CT was founded in 1966 to provide a unifying voice for labour, each organization having one vote, on the principle that only unanimous decisions would be binding.

There are 36 PRI—affiliated confederations or independent unions affiliated to the Congress of Labour, including the CTM, CROC, CROM and COR. Estimates of the size of its affiliated membership range as high as eight million of Mexico's 9.5 million workers, but this figure depends on the accuracy of CTM membership claims. The CTM's influence is paramount in the Congress.

Confederación Regional Obrera Mexicana (CROM)
Mexican Regional Workers' Confederation

Membership. Estimated at 250,000.

Confederación Revolucionaria de Obreros y Campesinos (CROC)
Revolutionary Confederation of Workers and Farmers

Address. San Juan de Letrán 80, 6°, México, DF

Leadership. Alberto Juárez Blancas (president); Eleazar Ruiz Cerda (secretary)

Membership. 600,000. Strong in textile, food, hospital and transport unions, and the state of Jalisco.

History and character. Founded 1952. At its 34th General Ordinary Congress, held in late March 1988, it was agreed that preparatory work must begin to establish the conditions for a single trade union centre for all Mexican workers, but CROC activity continues to be shaped for the present by its rivalry with the much larger CTM.

Confederación de Trabajadores de México (CTM)
Confederation of Mexican Workers

Address. Vallarta 8, Piso 7, 06030, Mexico, DF

Phone. 546-99-86; 546-58-27

Leadership. Fidel Veláquez (general secretary)

Membership. Is put variously at between 2,000,000 and 5,000,000. Strong among unskilled workers.

History and character. The CTM is by far the largest and most influential Mexican federation, and is tied to the ruling PRI. It was formed in 1936, and soon became the dominant force in Mexican trade unionism, its power surviving a series of breakaways by factions critical of the relationship with the PRI. The dominant figure in the CTM is the 87-year old Fidel Velázquez (Don Fidel), who has been the general secretary for 40 years and also exercises significant influence over parts of the labour movement outside the CTM. CTM officials hold numerous political offices, including seats in Congress and as state governors for the PRI, and the relationship has been seen as a major factor in the relative quiescence of Mexican labour. The CTM has played a key role in the development of the social security system and in creating housing schemes for the low-paid; its critics maintain that it is bureaucratic and has prevented the development of union democracy and effective plant- and industry-level collective bargaining.

Inflation is regarded as the nation's leading problem by the government, and the CTM has accepted increases in the minimum wage which is received by many of its members, at levels below price inflation in an attempt to assist government counter-inflationary policy.

The discontent of some CTM members surfaced in 1989–90 when large numbers of them employed by Ford at Cuautitlan threatened to defect to COR. The situation was resolved by Ford's insistence that it would bargain only with the CTM.

After the general elections in 1988, the PRI embarked on an internal inquiry into its own structure, a move which had important implications for the CMT which holds a privileged and incorporated position therein. The 14th Assembly of the PRI in September 1988 eliminated union representation from the National Central Executive Committee, though unions continue to attend the new National Political Council of the Party.

Confederación de Trabajadores Y Campesinos (CTC)
Confederation of Workers and Peasants

Leadership. Leonel Dominguez (secretary general)
Membership. 100–200,000.
History and character. The CTC is affiliated to the PRI but rivals other affiliated centres for members. In Mexico state it has been particularly successful in persuading former CTM members to join it.

Federación de Sindicatos de Trabajadores al Servicio del Estado (FSTSE)
Federation of Government Employee Unions

Membership. Possibly 1.8 million, all civil servants and government workers.
Affiliated unions. The chief affiliate of the FSTSE is the teachers' union SNTE with around one million members. The SNTE has a dissident movement in its ranks, the CNTE which has led militant actions in a number of districts and agitated for more democracy in the SNTE. In 1989 some of these efforts led to success and with the election of a new SNTE leader, Elba Ester Gordillo, prepared to open greater dialogue with the CNTE.

Other Congress of Labour confederations

Confederación General de Trabajadores (CGT)
General Confederation of Workers

Confederación Obrera Revolutionaria (COR)
Revolutionary Workers Confederation

Leadership. Angel Olivio Solis (Solis and his colleague Jose de Jesus Perez were reported in 1990 to be taking legal action to hold their positions against CTM and government moves to displace them).

Confederación Revolutionaria de Trabajadores (CRT)
Revolutionary Confederation of Workers

Independent unions inside the Congress of Labour

Apart from the confederations there are more than 20 PRI-affiliated but non-confederated unions in the Congress. They include:

Mexico City Electricians Union (SME)

Leadership. Jorge Sanchez (secretery general)
Membership. 35,000 members.

National Union of Mining and Metallurgical Workers

Membership. 100,000.

The Railway Workers Union of the Mexican Republic

Membership. 150,000.

Sole Union of Workers in the Nuclear Industry (SUTIN)

Leadership. Arturo Whaley Martínez (secretary general)
History and character. SUTIN, whose leader was a member of the former Mexican Communist Party is the most Marxist-oriented and independent union in the Congress.

Union of Telephone Workers of the Mexican Republic

Leadership. Hernández Suárez (secretary general)
Membership. 20,000
History and character. The Union of Telephone Workers has traditionally taken a leftist stance, but with the election of Suárez this seems to have changed and it supported the privatization of Telmex, the state telecommunications arm. The union led the founding of a new confederation in 1990, under the title of the Federation of Unions in Businesses Providing Goods and Services (FESBES), but in 1990 it had not been recognized by the government or the Congress of Labour.

Independent unions outside the Congress of Labour

Mesa de Concertación Sindical
Trade Union Harmony

History and character. The Mesa is a loose organization, and includes among its ranks not only trade unions but also parties and local organizations. Its chief inspiration was the old Communist Party, but it backed the candidacy of Cardenas in the 1988 Presidential elections.

Of independent unions outside the Congress there are a large number, holding in aggregate perhaps one million members. Some are company unions, "sindicatos blancos", but others are independent either because their concerns are entirely industrial or because of their revolutionary political stance. Some of the more Conservative unions are members of the National Federation of Independent Unions (FNSI) which claims 200,000 affiliated members, mostly in the Monterrey region.

Frente Auténtico del Trabajo (FAT)

Address. Calle Gordad No. 20, Col. Guadalupe Victoria, C.P. 07780, Deleg. Gustavo A. Madero, México, DF

Phone. 556 93 75
Fax. 556 93 16
Membership. Claims 50,000.
History and character. Founded 1960. Is strong in the automobile industry.
International affiliations. WCL; CLAT—the only such affiliate in Mexico.
Publications. Resistencia Obrera.

Movimiento Proletario Independiente (MPI)
Independent Proletarian Movement

History and character. The MPI was founded in 1972 under the name United Independent Workers (UOI) but changed its name in 1987. It is a loose co-ordinating body of highly independent unions, most of whom have a Trotskyist orientation, and oppose both the PRI and the Communist Party. While most of these are small, they do include SUTUAR—100, the Union of Workers of the Route 100, which has 20,000 members who staged illegal strike action in 1989.

Monaco

Capital: Monaco-Ville   **Population: 27,063**

Political system. The Principality of Monaco is a hereditary monarchy. There are no political parties as such though the National and Democratic Unions support established policy.
Economy. Light and medium industry, real estate and tourism contribute 40 per cent, 30 per cent, and 25 per cent of business turnover respectively in the Principality. Nationals of Monaco and foreign residents do not pay income tax, and taxation on company profits is low. There is also an important banking and insurance sector.
System of industrial relations. Trade unions participate in Monaco's Tripartite Economic Council along with the Employers' Federation of Monaco.
Trade unionism. Freedom of association and the right to strike are guaranteed by the 1962 Constitution. Monaco is not a member of the International Labour Organization.

Union des Syndicats de Monaco (USM)

Address. 2 rue Saige, Monaco, MC 98000
Phone. (93) 30-19-30
Leadership. Charles Soccal (president); Angele Braquetti (secretary general)
Membership. 5,000 in 35 unions.
History and character. The USM was founded in 1944 and has no political affiliation.
Publication. Unité Syndicale (monthly).

Other organizations

There are three unaffiliated unions: Syndicat Autonome des Fonctionnaires, Syndicat Antonome des Infirmières, Syndicat Autonome du LOEWS.

Mongolia

Capital: Ulan Bator

Population: 2,086,000
(1988)

Political system. Until 1990 the Mongolian People's Republic was a "sovereign democratic state of working people" in which effective political power was held by the (communist) Mongolian People's Revolutionary Party, the sole legal political formation. Popular unrest was manifested in Mongolia in 1990 and the transition to a multi-party system was peacefully made. In 1991 the Small Hural (Parliament) published a draft constitution envisaging a separation of powers and regular parliamentary elections. The country is to be renamed Mongolia.

Economy. Industry, trade and agriculture are state-owned and directed by plan. Although agriculture (particularly animal herding) is the dominant economic activity, the eighth five-year plan (1986–90) placed great emphasis on industrial development.

Under plans of economic reform the state will retain ownership of key industries such as railways and power, but it is intended to sell off 2,200 of the country's 2,600 public businesses. In June 1991 some small businesses and shops were put up for auction; Mongolians and foreigners will be entitled to acquire shares in former state assets. Privatization plans also extend to the agricultural co-operatives, but the mode of sale is to be decided by them. By 1993 it is envisaged that 57 per cent of the state holding will have been sold off. However Mongolia's immediate problems have their roots in the loss of Soviet aid: rationing and shortages are endemic and the country is seeking emergency assistance.

System of industrial relations. Mongolia ratified ILO Conventions No. 87 (Freedom of Association and Protection of the Right to Organize, 1948) and No. 98 (Right to Organize and Collective Bargaining, 1949) in 1969.

Trade unionism. Trade unions were established in the 1920s following the establishment of the People's Republic, although there was little development until after World War II.

Until 1990 the unions functioned in accordance with the Soviet Bloc model: there were not organizations outside the single structure of the Central Council (later the Federation) of Mongolian Trade Unions; the Council's constitution named the Mongolian People's Revolutionary Party as the leader and guide of the working masses.

Discontent with the union structure had been apparent as early as 1987, and an Extraordinary Congress of the Federation in June 1990 changed its statutes.

Federation of Mongolian Trade Unions

Address. Sukhbaataryn Talbai 3, Ulan Bator 11
Leadership. Shiilegiin Batbayar
Membership. Claims 620,000.
History and character. The Mongolian trade union movement began life in 1927 as the Central Council of Mongolian Trade Unions. At its 13th Congress in 1987 dissatisfaction began to be expressed at the way in which union reform was failing to keep pace with economic change. Delegates strongly criticized the centre for being too bureaucratic and out of touch with the membership. In June 1990 the Federation (as it now was) held an Extraordinary Congress and adopted a new action programme and constitution.
Publication. Khudulmur.
Affiliated unions and structure. The Federation has 11 affiliated unions.
International affiliations. WFTU.

Morocco

Capital: Rabat   **Population: 24,600,000**

Political system. The Kingdom of Morocco is a constitutional monarchy, the present King, Hassan II, having ascended to the throne in 1960. The unicameral parliament, the Chamber of Representatives, is composed of 306 members, two thirds of whom are directly by universal adult suffrage. The principal political party is the centre-right Union Constitutionelle, but all legal parties support the monarchic constitution as well as the government's position on the Western Sahara. The national election scheduled for 1990 was postponed until 1992.

Economy. The highest percentage of Moroccan workers is accounted for by agriculture and mining, though the proportion employed in services and industry continues to rise. The fast growing workforce (of which women comprised a quarter by the end of the 1980s) partly accounts for a rate of unemployment close to 13 per cent, though the King has indicated that there may be negative employment consequences as a result of his government's privatization programme (*see below*).

Unlike most Arab countries, Morocco is not a major oil producer, and its economy benefited from the slump in oil prices in the mid-1980s. Morocco is the world's leading exporter of raw and refined phosphates, sales of which increased in 1987 after a relatively long period of depressed world demand. The government receives substantial assistance from the IMF and the World Bank. King Hassan opened the Spring parliament session in April 1988 by outlining a major government privatization programme.

By the end of 1989 the National Assembly had determined on almost 120 enterprises in virtually all sectors to be privatized by 1994 and they were so promulgated in a Law of April 8, 1990.

System of industrial relations. Morocco ratified ILO Convention No. 98 (Right to Organize and Collective Bargaining, 1949) in 1957 but has not ratified Convention No. 87 (Freedom of Association and Protection of the Right to Organize, 1948). While the right to strike exists in law and open disputes are not uncommon, government agencies tend to intervene in disputes on an *ad hoc* basis. In sectors where national security is deemed to be at stake, strikes are outlawed. At the end of 1990 two union centres called a one-day strike which was severely repressed in support of doubling the legal minimum wage. In January 1991 the King offered a 15 per cent rise in wages and some benefits as part of a social peace pact which would be updated annually but this failed to appease the unions who staged further actions at the end of the month which merged with general opposition on the streets to the government's participation in the anti-Iraq coalition.

Trade unionism. Morocco's trade union movement is mostly dispersed between three centres probably of comparable size which sometimes compete at one workplace. There are however some 10 smaller unions which are not aligned with any one of these three. Though union density is only about 12 per cent, organized unionism is probably the strongest independent social force in Morocco. The political orientation of the centres, each of which has links to a political party, is significant and 10 places are reserved in the Chamber for workers' representatives which are filled by special election between the centres. Despite their rivalry the centres may unite, as they did to protest against their exclusion in 1989 from an ALO Conference and from a delegation to the ILO that year. In December 1989 they jointly complained that they were not allowed to attend the founding congress of the Maghreb Trade Union Organization (USTM).

Confédération Démocratique du Travail (CDT)
Democratic Confederation of Labour

Address. 51 rue Abdallah Médiouni, B.P. 576, Casablanca
Phone. 31-34-32; 31-34-08
Leadership. Noubir El Amaoui (secretary general)
Membership. 300,000 (50,000 women).
History and character. The CDT was founded in November 1978 by six national unions, and has campaigned against government and employer repression of trade union activists. The CDT is linked to the Union Socialiste des Forces Populaires (USFP); this in elections in 1984 took 36 of the 306 seats in the Chamber of Representatives, while the CDT took three seats (all of them indirectly elected) in its own right. A general strike called by the CDT in 1981, and attendant demonstrations, resulted in incidents in which dozens died in clashes with the security forces.

The CDT held its second national congress in November 1986, delegates attacking the government for corruption, emphasis on short-term prestige projects, lack of respect for trade union freedoms, the absence of a proper framework for collective bargaining, and dependence on external forces such as the International Monetary Fund. The congress decided to further the creation of small companies on a co-operative basis.

In the late 1980s the CDT concentrated increasingly on industrial issues, and scored some success on behalf of workers at the government-owned Jerada coal mines. Most of its strength is concentrated in the public sector. It joined the UGTM in organizing the December 1990 general strike for a higher minimum wage.

But it did not neglect political activity. General Secretary Amaoui was elected to the USFP central committee in 1989, and the Federation used the threat of a general strike to force a government dialogue with it the following year. In January 1991, the CDT firmly opposed the participation of Moroccan troops in the anti-Iraq coalition, having earlier suspended criticism in the belief that they were being despatched to protect the Saudi royal family. Mr Amaoui declared that "the people don't want their persons allied to American imperialism". The CFDT has three parliamentary deputies.

Affiliated unions. Syndicat National des Travailleurs du Phosphate, Syndicat National des Postes et Télécom, Syndicat National du Sucre et Thé, Syndicat National des Cheminots, Syndicat National de la Santé Publique, Syndicat National del l'Enseignement, Syndicat National du Pétrole et Gaz, Syndicat National d'Eau et Electricité, Syndicat National du Tabac, Syndicat National des Travailleurs des Municipalitiés et Préfectures, Syndicat National du Transport, Syndicat National de l'Agriculture.

Publications. *Démocratie Ouvriére* (banned in June 1981); internal bulletin.

International affiliation. OATUU. Maintains friendly relations with the WCL, WFTU and socialist-bloc, leftist and Third World unions.

Union Générale des Travailleurs Marocains (UGTM)
General Union of Moroccan Workers

Address. 9 rue du Rif, Angle Route de Médiouna, Casablanca
Phone. 28-21-44
Leadership. Abderrazzaq Afilal (secretary general)
Membership. Probably around 300,000.
History and character. Founded in 1960, the UGTM is linked with the Independence Party (Istiqlal), which following the 1984 elections was the fourth largest party in the Chamber of Representatives, with 41 of the 306 seats. The UGTM itself took two seats in the Chamber.

While the UGTM has public and private sector members, its real strength is among agricultural workers. In the past it has been less militant than the other federations, but it supported the CDT's 1989 Jerada strike and jointly organized the December 1990 minimum wage general strike. The UGTM responded to the King's January 1991 offer of improved wages and benefits by declaring that partial solutions would be inadequate. General Secretary Abderrazzaq Afilal is a Parliamentary Deputy.

International affiliation. OATUU.

Union Marocaine du Travail (UMT)
Moroccan Workers' Union

Address. 232 Avenue des Far, Casablanca
Phone. 30-22-92
Telex. 27825M
Leadership. Mahjoub Ben Seddiq (general secretary)
Membership. In 1990 the UMT reported 438,000 members to the ICFTU.

History and character. The UMT was founded in 1955 and is associated with the socialist Union Nationale des Forces Populaires (UNFP). The UMT took five seats (all indirectly elected) in the 1984 elections to the Chamber of Representatives. The UMT has strongly opposed the government's IMF-backed economic austerity programme. Mahjoub Ben Seddiq has alleged that the imprisonment of workers and trade union representatives is becoming common practice.

The UMT is equally strong in the public and private sectors and specialized in the 1980s in making progress on the social welfare front both by industrial means and through its Parliamentary deputation (the biggest single union group). The UMT did not participate in the organization of the December 1990 minimum wage general strike and cautiously welcomed the King's January 1991 offer of improved benefits. In 1960 it suffered the secession of the UGTM and three years later it left the ICFTU after the formation of the All-African Trade Union Federation. However in 1990 it re-affiliated to the ICFTU after its General Secretary Mahjoub Ben Seddiq (Morocco's best-known trade unionist who has led it since its inception) declared that the UMT could not afford to remain isolated from the world.

International affiliations. OATUU; ICATU; ICFTU.

Mozambique

Capital: Maputo   **Population: 14,967,000**
                                                    (1988)

Political system. Mozambique achieved independence in 1975 after more than a decade of guerrilla war against Portuguese colonial rule. A people's republic was declared, with Marxist-Leninism as the official ideology, and the Front for the Liberation of Mozambique (Frente da Libertação de Moçambique—Frelimo) became the sole legal party. Samora Moîses Machel led Mozambique from independence until his death in an aircraft crash in October 1986. He was succeeded in November of that year by Joaquim Alberto Chissano. The Resistência Nacional Moçambicana (MNR or Renamo), with support from South Africa, waged a guerilla war against the government which cost more than 100,000 lives and caused the flight from their homes of more than 2,600,000 people by the end of the 1980s. In July 1989 the Frelimo Congress renewed President Chissano's mandate until 1994.

Economy. Real economic growth declined by 30 per cent between 1981 and 1984. Agriculture, mainly at subsistence level, occupies about 84 per cent of the population. Despite the priority given to food production and improved incentives for peasant farmers the country remains dependent on food aid. The government estimated that about 4,000,000 people—one quarter of the population—were destitute in 1987.

Mining and manufacturing account for about 25 per cent of GDP but only 6 per cent of the employed workforce. Mozambique's principal source of foreign exchange is in the form of remittances from migrant workers, of whom over 61,000 were employed on short-term contracts in South Africa's mines in 1986. However, relations with South Africa were poor and in October 1986 the South African government introduced strict controls on the use of Mozambican labour. The reduction of freight from land-locked "front line states", due to anti-government guerrilla activity, has been a further blow to the economy.

In 1984, as part of a strengthening of ties with Western bodies, Mozambique became a member of the World Bank, International Monetary Fund and a signatory to the Lomé III convention. It has since received financial assistance from these sources. A system of communal villages with farmers' co-operatives is operated and state farms have been established—the state and co-operative sectors together accounted for an estimated 40 per cent of marketed agricultural output in 1985.

In 1987 Mozambique launched an economic recovery programme with IMF and World Bank support. While it led to an economic revival in urban areas, most of the population were still afflicted by under-development and the effects of RENAMO activity. The Fifth (July 1989) Frelimo Congress resolved nevertheless to continue the programme and to develop the private sector in industry, health, education and housing.

System of industrial relations. Mozambique joined the International Labour Organization in 1976 but has not ratified Convention No. 87 (Freedom of Association and Protection of the Right to Organize, 1948) or No. 98 (Right to Organize and Collective Bargaining, 1949). However, in 1977 Mozambique ratified Convention Nos. 101 and 111 on equal remuneration and discrimination, which have since been covered by a new general Labour Act of 1985.

In January 1990, President Chissano presented a new draft constitution for Mozambique which included the right to strike and freedom of association. In fact although strikes were technically illegal before 1990, there were strikes by students and teachers in 1989 against low pay and by manual workers over the same cause the following year.

Trade unionism. Trade union activities were closely circumscribed under Portuguese rule, and a single-trade-union system is now in place. The eighth session of the Central Committee of Frelimo in 1976 instituted the creation of an "embryonic organization of the working class", the Comissão Nacional de Implementação dos Conselhos de Produção (National Commission for the Implementation of Production Councils—CNICP). This was the forerunner of the OTM, the country's first trade union federation.

Organização dos Trabalhadores de Moçambique (OTM)
Mozambique Workers' Organization

Address Rua Manuel António de Sousa 36, Maputo
Phone. 28300; 26477
Telex. 6116 MO
Leadership. Augusto Macamo (secretary general)
Membership. 225,000.

History and character. The OTM was created at a Trade Unions Constitutive Conference held in 1983, following a decision of the fourth congress of the ruling Frelimo party to create trade unions on the basis of the pre-existing production councils. The OTM describes its aims as being to "develop socialist consciousness among the workers", to mobilize the workers to raise their productivity, to improve working conditions and to help to develop the country and combat famine and poverty. According to its constitution the OTM is to be guided and led by the single party, Frelimo. In a speech to the constituent congress, President Samora Machel stated: "Taking into account the class nature of our party and state, the socialist trade unions are not instruments of confrontation. They are aimed at carrying out the fundamental objectives of the worker-peasant alliance. They keep a watch on the correct implementation of the party policy... the first task of the Mozambique trade unions must be a deep study of their contribution to the fight against famine and nakedness and the liquidation of armed bandits .... The trade unions will perform a central role in the mobilization of workers towards the correct and permanent application of the principles of self-reliance. The fight for discipline, punctuality, organization and efficiency is also an immediate task. The permanent concern of the trade unions must be the organization of workers and the political, ideological, technical, cultural and scientific formation of the Mozambican man.... That is the only way the trade unions will be a reservoir of cadres for our party and revolution."

Structure. National conference; central committee; secretariat; committee of control and discipline. OTM central committee members are also members of people's assemblies at national, provincial and district levels. The OTM also sponsors the creation of scientific, cultural, professional and other associations.

Publication. Boletim dos Trabalhadores de Moçambique (quarterly).
International affiliation. OATUU.

Myanma (Burma)

Capital: Rangoon   **Population: 37,610,000**

Political system. Burma became an independent republic outside the Commonwealth in 1948. In 1962 the Constitution was suspended and full powers were assumed by Gen. Ne Win at the head of a Revolutionary Council. In 1964 all political parties were banned except the governmental Burma Socialist Programme Party (BSPP). A new Constitution effective from January 1974 laid down that within the Socialist Republic of the Union of Burma the BSPP was the "only political party leading the state", while in 1976 the BSPP was given the special status of leadership over the Council of State, the central organs of power, and people's councils at subordinate levels. However, a rapid succession of events in mid-1988 led to the assumption of power by the military in September of that year and to the withdrawal of the BSSP's special status.

In 1989 Myanma was shaken by massive pro-democracy demonstrations which were put down by the military. However the ruling State Law and Order Restoration Council resolved to hold elections in May 1990. These were won overwhelmingly by the opposition National League for Democracy (NLD) but the military refused to transfer power to it and declared that it was no longer a legal party.

Economy. Following the 1962 assumption of power by Gen. Ne Win, many of the major sectors of the economy—notably industry, transport, internal and external trade, communications and finance—were brought into public ownership and control. Burma embarked on a general policy of self-sufficiency, but in the 1970s this policy was to some extent liberalized and foreign aid and investment have since been accepted. Under the 1974 Constitution the state was named as the ultimate owner of all natural resources, which it exploited in the interests of the people, and although private enterprise was permitted, it operated within limits and in clearly defined areas.

System of industrial relations. The ILO *Report of the Committee of Experts on the Application of Conventions and Recommendations* (1985) observed that there was a trade union monopoly, in contravention of Articles 2, 5 and 6 of ILO Convention No. 87 (Freedom of Association and Protection of the Right to Organize, 1948), ratified by Burma in 1955. Noting the statement by the Burmese government that there were no legal provisions prohibiting workers' and employers' organizations from establishing or joining federations or confederations, and that the government claimed that the unification of the trade union movement arose from the wishes of the workers themselves, the Committee stated that it did not believe workers could in fact establish any union outside the government-created structure. During August and September 1988 a general strike was in force throughout Rangoon and other areas of Burma in support of demonstrators' demands for the installation of a democratically elected government. The Armed Forces, who had taken control of the country on Sept. 18, ordered a return to work, warning that anyone preventing workers from doing so would be dealt with sternly. Burma has not ratified Convention No. 98 (Right to Organize and Collective Bargaining, 1949).

Trade unionism. Trade unions first developed in the 1920s in reaction to the then widespread use of immigrant Indian and Chinese labour and union activities subsequently became closely linked to nationalist politics, with many strikes in the 1945–48 period. Following independence in 1948 (which led to the emigration of most non-Burmese workers), trade union rights granted in 1926 under British rule were incorporated in the constitution. Unions remained active both politically and industrially and although in 1961 the total membership of the 173, mainly one-shop, registered unions then in existence was put at only 64,000 of an urban labour force of 1,000,000, there were many unregistered unions. Union centres in operation at that time were the Burma Trades Union Congress (BTUC), affiliated to the WFTU, the Free Trades Unions of Burma (FTU-B), affiliated to the ICFTU, and the Trades Union Congress (Burma) (TUC-B) and the Union of Burma Labour Organizations (ULO), these having no international affiliations but being linked to rival internal political fractions. In 1964, however, Gen. Ne Win abolished all trade unions. In 1968 Ne Win set up a new system for workers' representation, consisting of local workers' councils at factory and township level, and a central *asiayone* (union) presided over by the minister of labour and controlled by BSPP officials. The representatives of these councils have seats on joint committees with management in every workplace. Wages, working hours and other labour conditions are determined by the government. By the beginning of 1985, 293 township workers' councils with more than 1,800,000 workers had been formed. The primary task of the workers' councils is to ensure labour discipline and explain government policies and targets.

Workers' Asiayone

Address. Central committee headquarters, 6th Storeyed Building, Strand Road, Rangoon

Leadership. U. Ohn Kyaw (chairman); U. Thura Tin Myat (secretary)

History. The Workers' Asiayone, or Council, was set up in 1968 (*see above*); a parallel peasant organization was created the following year.

International affiliation. None.

Namibia

Capital: Windhoek   **Population: 1,550,000**
                                                              (1989)

Political system. Namibia became independent on March 21, 1990 following 75 years of South African rule and 23 years of guerrilla war. Under a constitution drawn up by all parties in the Constituent Assembly elected the previous November, Namibia has a liberal constitution with a limited executive presidency. The South West African People's Organization (SWAPO) won 41 of the 72 seats in and 57 per cent of the votes for the Constituent Assembly. Its leader, Sam Nujoma became the country's first President.

Economy. Mining is the principal economic activity, providing 80 per cent of export earnings and 26 per cent of GDP in 1984 (a decline from 50 per cent of GDP in 1980, largely attributable to a fall in world market prices for Namibia's minerals). High quality diamonds provide 60 per cent of the revenue from mineral sales, uranium 40 per cent.

Agriculture, based largely on livestock production, and fishing together contributed 8.2 per cent of GDP in 1986. Manufacturing, mostly meat and fish processing, employed about 10 per cent of the workforce and contributed 5 per cent of GDP. Levels of unemployment rose from 12 per cent of the labour force in 1975 to 20 per cent in 1986.

SWAPO is committed to extending the role of the state in the economy while maintaining a role for private profit. It has the longer term aims of reducing dependence on South Africa and redistribution of the land.

System of industrial relations. Under its constitution, the new state has the objective of becoming a member of the ILO and observing its conventions. Article 21 of the Constitution proclaims freedom of association and other articles forbid child labour and promulgate equal opportunity.

Trade unionism. The development of trade unionism in Namibia has very much reflected developments in South Africa. Labour began to assert itself in 1971 when a three-month general strike over wages and working conditions involving 12,000 people was organized with the help of SWAPO activists. A further strike wave occurred in 1973. Although the protest eventually won the abolition of the contract labour system, one of its principal targets, this labour unrest did not consolidate into a formal union movement.

Nevertheless, trade unionism was legalized for all races in July 1978; previously it had been legal only for white and coloured workers and only for branches of lawful South African unions.

However, 1985 regulations prohibited activity by non-Namibian trade unionists in order to prevent links between black unions in South Africa and Namibia. While some of the unions registered under the Wages and Industrial Conciliation Ordinance 1988 are still functioning, the status of others is unclear. The new Namibian Constitution proclaims the policy aim of independent trade unionism which may have implications for the National Union of Namibian Workers (NUNW), which is affiliated to the liberation movement SWAPO, and which was suppressed by the authorities after a short existence in 1978–79 and went into exile in Angola. It was re-launched in the mid 1980s, began to reorganize in Namibia, and was instrumental in the formation of a number of new unions after 1987.

National Union of Namibian Workers (NUNW)

Address. P.O. Box 953, Luanda, Angola
Phone. 39234
Telex. 3069 AN
Leadership. John G. Yaotto (secretary general, also Secretary of Labour of the South West African People's Organization SWAPO); Reinhold Eino Muremi (deputy general secretary).

History and character. The NUNW was organized by SWAPO on April 24, 1971, with the aim of promoting trade unionism among Namibian workers, and is open to workers of all categories. After its collapse in 1978–79, the NUNW was re-launched by SWAPO in the mid-1980s. Its primary immediate objective is to work torwards the liberation of Namibia, within the framework provided by SWAPO, and until recently it operated from exile in Angola. Influenced by developments in South Africa, the NUNW decided to change from being a general union and established industrial affiliates in the main sectors of the Namibian economy. The Mineworkers' Union of Namibia, with about 7,000 members, and the Namibia Food and Allied Workers' Union, with 6,000 members were organized under the NUNW umbrella in late 1986 and operate openly within Namibia. A shop steward training programme and a recruiting drive were launched.

On May 1, 1987, the NUNW demonstrated its new strength by organizing mass rallies involving 35,000 workers, followed by strikes in many sectors of the economy. By early 1988 membership was estimated at 32,000, and two more affiliates, the Metal and Allied Namibian Workers' Union (8,000 members) and the Namibian Public Workers' Union (5,000 members), had joined the grouping. The Namibia Allied and Transport Workers' Union affiliated in mid-1988. The setting up of the commission of enquiry into labour legislation chaired by Professor Wiehahn was thought by the NUNW to be part of an effort to bring the burgeoning labour movement more firmly under state control. Police actions, detentions, and other official harassment of the unions continued. The NUNW's offices were raided and seriously damaged by the South African authorities in mid-1987. Since independence the NUNW has been able to work unhindered.

Affiliated unions. Namibian Food and Allied Workers' Union (NAFAU; general secretary: John Pandeni); Mineworkers' Union of Namibia (MUN; general secretary: Ben Uelenga); Metal and Allied Namibian Workers' Union (MANWU; general secretary: Barnabas Tjizu); Namibian Public Workers' Union (NAPWU; general secretary: Lamek Ithete); Namibia Allied and Transport Workers' Union. The NAFAU, formed in September 1986, was registered in mid-1987; it held its second national congress shortly afterwards. The MUN, formed in November 1986, held its second national congress early in 1988, when resolutions on unemployment, political policy and the right to strike were passed; membership had by then tripled to 9,000 at 12 mines, and the union has recently won important recognition agreements with several mining companies. The NAPWU held its founding congress at the end of 1987, by which time it had organized 5,000 of Namibia's 17,000 public sector workers. The MANWU was formed in May 1987 and the NATW in July 1988.

Publication. The Namibian Worker.

International affiliations. OATUU; WFTU. The NUNW organized a seminar "Facing the Future" jointly with the ICFTU in February – March 1990.

Other organizations

The following unions were reported by the government to be registered under the Wages and Industrial Conciliation Ordinance as of September 1988:

1. **Association of Government Service Officials**, P.O. Box 2300, Windhoek.
   Phone: 36289.

2. **Association of Officials of Financial Institutions**, P.O. Box 2998, Windhoek.
   Phone: 222887.

3. **Automobile and Metal Workers' Union**, P.O. Box 5658, Windhoek.

4. **Drivers', Transport and Allied Workers' Union**, P.O. Box 20557, Windhoek.

5. **Fishermen's Union of Lüderitz**, P.O. Box 383, Lüderitz.

6. **Food Products and Associated Workers' Union of Namibia**, P.O. Box 1169, Windhoek. Phone: 61361.

7. **Metal and Allied Namibian Workers' Union**, P.O. Box 217, Okahandja. Phone: 63100.

8. **Mineworkers' Union of Namibia**, P.O. Box 22391, Windhoek.

9. **Namibia Building Workers' Union**, P.O. Box 22679, Windhoek. Phone: 212828.

10. **Namibia Food and Allied Workers' Union**, P.O. Box 7404, Windhoek. Phone: 63108.

11. **Namibia Wholesale and Retail Workers' Union**, P.O. Box 378, Windhoek. Phone: 228173.

12. **Public Service Union of Namibia**, P.O. Box 21662, Windhoek. Phone: 228848

13. **Rössing Mine Workers' Union**, P.O. Box 3199, Swakopmund.

14. **SWA Mineworkers' Union**, P.O. Box 71, Tsumeb. Phone: 2328.

15. **SWA Municipal Staff Association**, P.O. Box 22060, Windhoek. Phone: 34625.

16. **Typographical Union**, P.O. Box 56, Windhoek.

17. **Union of the National Transport Corporation**, P.O. Box 4, Windhoek. Phone: 34625.

Nauru

Capital: Domaneab (de facto)

Population: 9,000
(July 1989)

Political system. The Republic of Nauru became independent in 1968 as a special-status member of the Commonwealth.

Economy. The Nauruan economy is almost wholly dependent on the extraction of phosphate rock derived from the country's substantial guano deposits. Poor quality agricultural land has resulted in the island's heavy dependence upon imported food.

Trade unionism. A Nauruan Workers' Association was created in 1953.

Nepal

Capital: Katmandu

Population: 18,699,884
(1989)

Political system. The Kingdom of Nepal is a constitutional monarchy, with executive power vested in the King who presides over a unicameral legislature, the *Rashtriya Panchayat*. The 1962 Constitution established a tiered, party-free system of elected village and provincial councils (*panchayats*). Limited reforms to this system were approved in a 1980 national referendum, which also rejected the restoration of a party system (abolished in 1961).

In May 1991 after social unrest the first free elections for three decades were held in Nepal. The victors were the Nepali Congress who took 110 of the 205 seats in the New Parliament which took over from King Birendra.

Economy. Agriculture is the largest economic sector, although tourism is an important earner of foreign exchange. The seventh five-year plan (1985–90) aims to initiate a shift in the economic base of the country from agriculture to small-scale and cottage industry.

System of industrial relations. Nepal became a member of the ILO in 1966 but has ratified neither Convention No. 87 (Freedom of Association and Protection of the Right to Organize, 1948) nor No. 98 (Right to Organize and Collective Bargaining, 1949). Indeed, it has ratified just four conventions.

Trade unionism. A Nepal Labour Organization (NLO) was created under the 1962 Constitution, to embody the principles of *panchayat* democracy; local units of the NLO were permitted to bargain collectively and to elect district committees, from which the King would nominate four representatives to the National Assembly. Although workers' associations exist at local level they are severely restricted in their right to strike and have no national negotiating rights. Such associations appear to fulfil a mutual welfare function and possess little political power. A major problem hampering the growth of trade unionism is that, with few exceptions, workers tend to be spatially fragmented. The only large concentrations of urban workers occur in the jute mills of Biratnagar, and pockets within the Katmandu valley and the plains of Nepal. Most protracted labour disputes have only reached the zonal level of official action; nevertheless, in a number of cases improvements in working conditions and pay have been won. A limited right to strike was given legislative recognition in 1974 and a royal statement delivered in parliament in June 1979 committed the government to a policy of establishing workers' welfare organizations and expanding the scope of protection given to workers by law. Between January and May 1985, hundreds of teachers and students were arrested following strikes and demonstrations on the issue of teachers' pay and conditions and recognition of the Nepal Teachers' Association. A general strike was held in the Katmandu valley in January 1986 in protest against the devaluation of the Nepali rupee (against the Indian rupee) and consequent rise in prices.

Nepal Labour Organization (NLO)

Membership. Claims 200,000.

History and character. The NLO was created under the 1962 Constitution, and is the only union with legal status in Nepal. In 1987 and 1988 the NLO organized some education programmes to aid recruitment, and in December 1988 called on the government to discourage the entry of foreign labour and help local people to get employment. It has called on the government to ratify ILO Convention No. 87.

Publications. *Majdoor* (*Worker*, monthly).

Affiliated unions and structure. The NLO's officers are elected quinquennially, the last such occasion being in 1987. The Central Executive of 15 meets quarterly.

International affiliations. The NLO is negotiating for affiliation to the ICFTU.

Other unions

Nepal Teachers' Association (NTA)

History and character. The NTA has been denied registration by the Nepalese government. The police prevented it from holding its third national conference in June 1987.

Other unions are active in transport, tourism and hotels.

The Netherlands

Capital: Amsterdam   **Population: 14,900,000**

Political system. The Kingdom of the Netherlands is a constitutional and hereditary monarchy and comprises three parts (the Netherlands in Europe, the Netherlands Antilles, and Aruba). The country in Europe is a multi-party democracy currently governed by a coalition of the Christian Democratic Appeal (CDA) and the Labour Party (Partij van de Arbeid—PvdA) led by the CDA leader Ruud Lubbers with the Socialist leader Wim Kok (a former union leader) as Finance Minister. This coalition followed seven years of a CDA coalition with the right-wing Dutch Liberals. The Netherlands is a member of the EEC and of NATO.

Economy. The civilian workforce of the Netherlands in 1989 stood just below 5,000,000, of which more than 3,500,000 were employed in services. Nevertheless manufacturing industry enjoyed a surge in growth during the 1980s which saw great economic expansion. Growth slowed to 2 per cent in 1990 and the CDA – PvdA coalition became engulfed in a controversy over the budgetary implications of continuing to fund social welfare programmes, especially those for the disabled.

System of industrial relations. Support for the collaborative Dutch industrial relations system unites the CDA and the PvdA as well as most employers' organizations. The result is a network of institutions which draws trade unions into economic discussions and which, during the 1980s, successfully gained their agreement for low wage increases to bolster economic growth. In 1990 tripartitism was extended to the local level when the Netherlands' state-run employment exchanges were hived off from government to 28 regions for job placement purposes. Each region has a labour board with representation from local unions, employers, and local government.

The Stichting van de Arbeid (Foundation of Labour) is a consultative body on which both sides of industry have an equal number of seats; it is a non-binding forum for the discussion of industrial issues. The Social and Economic Council, created in 1950, comprises 15 representatives of the employers, 15 of the unions, and 15 independent experts nominated by government, and is the main advisory board to the government on social and economic issues. The CNV and FNV are represented on this and other government bodies with responsibilities for social welfare. A rotation scheme for the nomination of the annual delegate to the ILO has been agreed between the FNV and the CNV.

The Netherlands ratified ILO Convention No. 87 (Freedom of Association and Protection of the Right to Organize, 1948) in 1950, but has not ratified Convention No. 98 (Right to Organize and Collective Bargaining, 1949). There are restrictions on collective bargaining in the subsidized public sector, which were made permanent by legislation adopted in 1985 and are designed to enable the government to retain control over its financial obligations in this area.

Trade unionism. Before World War II trade unionism in the Netherlands was divided into three main streams, represented by the general confederation, the Netherlands Federation of Trade Unions (Nederlands Verbond van Vakverenigingen—NVV), and Roman Catholic and Protestant federations. In the post-war period these organizations increasingly co-operated, and from the late 1950s they sought to co-ordinate their policies through a formal consultative framework. In January 1976, the Netherlands Trade Union Confederation (Federatie Nederlandse Vakbeweging—FNV) was formed by the NVV and the Netherlands Catholic Federation of Labour (Nederlands Katholiek Vakverbond—NKV), the NVV accepting the NKV's condition that special recognition should be accorded to the role of religious inspiration in the new confederation. The (Protestant) Christian National Federation of Trade Unions (Christelijk Nationaal Vakverbond—CNV), however, proved unwilling to surrender its sovereignty, and did not join the federation.

Trade union membership in the Netherlands was hit particularly hard in the first half of the 1980s. In March 1980 trade union density stood at 39 per cent and had decreased to 29 per cent by March 1985.

By 1989 it had fallen to 24 per cent. However, from the later 1980s union membership, especially that of the affiliates of the FNV began to grow again, and lower density persisted principally as the result of a quickly growing workforce. A contributory factor to this growth was female entry as the Netherlands' traditionally low level of female participation began to rise. However, the FNV succeeded in recruiting them to such an extent that women accounted for more than half of its 1989 membership growth.

Christelijk Nationaal Vakverbond (CNV)
Christian National Federation of Trade Unions

Address. Ravellaan 1, Postbus 2475, 3500 GL Utrecht
Phone. 30-913911
Telex. 40646
Leadership. Henk Hofstede (chairman).
Membership. 308,000. Includes pensioners and unemployed.
History and character. The CNV was founded in June 1909 as an inter-confessional (Christian) organization, but in practice quickly became a Protestant federation. After the formation of the FNV in 1976 some Catholic organizations affiliated and the CNV, which espouses social Christianity, is independent of any church or political party. The Actie Kom Over is a CNV organization which assists trade union organizations in the Third World; there is a CNV youth organization; a women's union; a study institute; and the CNV has its own holiday resorts and travel organization.
Structure. Ruling general assembly; executive council; executive board. There are local branches composed of representatives of the affiliated organizations.
Affiliated unions. There are 16 affiliated unions. Certain categories—such as clergymen or students—may also affiliate personally to the CNV.

1. **Catholic Teachers' Union**, P.O. Box 5826 2280 HV Rijswijk.
   Phone: 070-3981100. Telex: 31779 NL. Fax: 070-988579.
   Leadership: Dr C. van Onerbeek (chairman).
   Membership: 38,000.
   Publications: *Het Katholieke Schoolblad.*

2. **Centre for Christian Journalists**, A. v.d. Neerstraat 67, 8932 BK Leeuwarden.
Phone: 58-120528.
Membership: 150.

3. **CNV Organization of Sextons in Holland**, Grutkolaan 19, 2261 ET Leidschendam.
Phone: 070-3275811.
Membership: 875.

4. **CNV Union for Government, Health, Wealth and Job Procurement Scheme**, Zeekant 35, 2586 AA's-Gravenhage.
Phone: 070-3582582. Fax: 070-3512444.
Membership: 84,000.
Leadership: L.G.L.M.Poell (president).
International affiliations: EUROFEDOP; INFEDOP.
Publications: *CFO Magazine*.

5. **General Christian Organization for Professional Soldiers** (ACOM), P.O. Box 960, 3800 AZ Amersfoort.
Phone: 33-621414. Fax: 33-653613.
Membership: 15,000.
International affiliations: EMANIL; EUROFEDOP.
Publication: *ACOM Journal*.

6. **General Christian Police Union**, Liedseweg 65c, 3531 BD Utrecht.
Phone: 02481-2444. Fax: 03481-2425.
Leadership: M. Blyleve (chairman).
Membership: 20,500.
International affiliations: INFEDOP; EUROFEDOP.
Publication: *Politiebericht*.

7. **Industrial and Agricultural Union CNV**, Rietgors 1, 3435 CB Nieuwegein.
Phone: 3402-44124.
Membership: 48,000.

8. **Printing Union** (Grafische Band CNV), Valeriusplein 30, 1075 BJ Amsterdam-Zuid.
Phone: 20-6713279. Telex: 18695. Fax: 20-751331.
Leadership: R. E. van Kesteren (president).
Membership: 7,500.
International affiliations: International Graphical Federation (WCL); European Graphical Federation.
Publication: *Grafisch Orgaan*.

9. **Protestant–Christian Teachers Union**, P.O. Box 87868, 2508 DG's-Gravenhage.
Phone: 70-352-2541.
Membership: 18,000.

10. **Services Union CNV**, Hobbemastraat 12, 1070AA Amsterdam.
Phone: 20-764771. Telex: 10471. Fax: 020-750001.
Leadership: J. Kos (president); R.J. Potshuizen (secretary-general).
Membership: 16,500.
International affiliations: WCL, WVB, WVA.
Publications: *Akkoord* (about 10 times a year).

11. **Transport Union** (Veluoeisband CNV), P.O. Box 2129, 3440 DC Woerden.
Phone: 03480-20014. Telex: 710545. Fax: 03480-23488.
Membership: 16,000.

12. **Wood and Construction Union CNV**, Kromme Nieuwegracht 22, 3512 HH Utrecht.
Phone: 30-332531. Telex: 40603.
Membership: 39,000.

13. **Women's Organization CNV**, P.O. Box 2475, 3500 GL Utrecht.
    Phone: 30-913911.

14. **CNV Youth Organization**, P.O. Box 2475, 3500 GL Utrecht.
    Phone: 30-913911.
    Publications. De Gids (fortnightly); *CNV Opinie* (monthly).
    International affiliations. WCL; ETUC; TUAC.

Federatie Nederlandse Vakbeweging (FNV)
Netherlands Trade Union Confederation

Address. Postbus 8456, 1005 AL Amsterdam
Phone. 20-5816300
Telex. 16660 FNV NL
Fax. 20-6844541
Leadership. Johan Stekelenburg (president); A.J. Groen (general secretary)
Membership. 1,024,599.
History. The FNV was founded on Jan. 1, 1976 by a partial merger of the social democratic NVV and the Roman Catholic NKV. The NVV had sought a total merger, while the NKV had wished for a looser arrangement, and the FNV constitution embodied a compromise position, laying down that unity would be aimed at and a total merger not excluded. The two head offices were combined in mid-1976. By the end of 1981 all affiliated trade unions of NVV and NKV had merged or federated with their corresponding unions in the other federation, and on Jan. 1, 1982, the NVV and NKV were formally liquidated and the merger completed.

Structure. A delegate congress is the supreme policy-making body, and it meets at least once per year in an ordinary one-day session and triennially for a three-day session. The congress elects the executive board, and the president of the executive board also serves as president of the council and the congress. The confederation council is composed of members of the executive board (without voting rights) and representatives of the affiliated unions. The council takes policy decisions and supervises the activity of the board. The executive board is responsible for the day-to-day affairs of the federation. There are also a number of specialized policy groups, advisory councils, and secretariats: there are secretariats for ethnic minorities, women, people drawing state benefits, and "outlook on life". This last group was established in 1979 and "organizes activities ... for members who wish to reflect critically on trade union policy, on the basis of their conception of life", whether religious or otherwise. There is additionally a network of local offices, information and advisory teams on matters such as social services, law, etc., a legal aid service, training and educational scheme, and a youth movement.

Policies. The FNV is independent of political parties, but reflecting the role of the Catholic federation in its creation, its constitution also recognizes the place of religion as an "inspiration for trade union activities".

In mid-1985, the FNV set in train a wide-ranging policy review. It was alarmed at the dramatic decline in union membership in the first part of the 1980s, where not only did total union membership in the country as a whole decline, but there was also a longer term decline in the share of the FNV total Dutch trade union membership from 64.5 per cent in 1971 to 58.3 per cent in 1985. The FNV was failing to keep pace with the changing composition of the Dutch workforce and was faced with a continued decline in membership unless swift action was taken. The final review report *FNV 2000*, was published in June 1987 and contained a comprehensive set of recommendations which were designed to make trade unionism more relevant to members and potential recruits for the rest of the 20th century. The Report's findings are now integrated into FNV practice and membership rose between 1988 and 1991 by over 100,000.

The FNV is "internationalist" in character and is keen to assist other less fortunate union movements in other parts of the world.

Affiliated unions. (Membership as of January 1991).

1. **AbvaKabo** (civil servants), Bredewater 16, 2715 CA Zoetermeer.
   Phone: 79-536161. Telex: 34513. Fax: 79-521226.
   Membership: 281, 992.

2. **Algemene Bond van Onderwijzend Personeel** (teachers), Herengracht 54, 1015 BN Amsterdam.
   Phone: 20-5206700. Telex: 17118. Fax: 20-6274205.
   Membership: 43,219.

3. **Bouw- en Houtbond FNV** (building and wood workers), Houttuinlaan 3, 3447 GM Woerden.
   Phone: 3480-75911. Telex: 47610. Fax: 3480-23610.
   Membership: 157,167.

4. **Dienstenbond FNV** (shop assistants, clerical workers), Houttuinlaan 3, 3447 GM Woerden.
   Phone: 3480-75922. Fax: 3480-31498.
   Membership: 80,174.

5. **Druk en Papier FNV** (typographers), Jan Tooropstraat 1–3, 1062 BK Amsterdam.
   Phone: 20-6143105. Telex: 12623. Fax: 20-6151091.
   Membership: 48,267.

6. **Federatie van Werknemersorganisaties in de Zeevaart** (seamen), Heemraadssingel 323, 3023 BH Rotterdam.
   Phone: 10-4771188. Telex: 25526. Fax: 10-4773846.
   Membership: 6,135.

7. **Horecabond FNV** (hotel and restaurant workers), Stadhouderskade 126, 1074 AV Amsterdam.
   Phone: 20-6794105. Fax: 20-6752706.
   Membership: 14,156.

8. **Industriebond FNV** (industrial workers), Slotermeerlaan 80, 1064 HD Amsterdam.
   Phone: 20-5110511. Telex: 18160. Fax: 20-6130623.
   Membership: 217,961.

9. **Jongeren FNV** (youth), Standerdmolen 8, 3995 AA Houten.
   Phone: 3403-51590. Fax: 3403-51203.

10. **Kappersbond** (hairdressers), Nachtegaalstraat 37, 3581 AC Utrecht.
    Phone: 30-314221. Fax: 30-317136.
    Membership: 4,738.

11. **Kunstenbond FNV** (artists), Arie Biemondstraat 111, 1054 PD Amsterdam.
    Phone: 20-6837176. Fax: 20-6836821.
    Membership: 5,415.

12. **Nederlandse Politiebond** (police), Naritaweg 12, 1043 BX Amsterdam.
    Phone: 20-6820301. Telex: 11627. Fax: 20-6868146.
    Membership: 17,385.

13. **Nederlandse Vereniging van Journalisten** (journalists), Joh. Vermeerstraat 55, 1071 DM Amsterdam.
    Phone: 20-6766771. Telex: 18227. Fax: 20-6624910.
    Membership: 5,119.

14. **Vereniging van Contractspelers** (soccer professionals), Harderwijkweg 5, 2803 PW Gouda.
    Phone: 1820-71172. Fax: 1820-32732.
    Membership: 580.

15. **Vereniging van Dienstplichtige Militairen** (conscripts), Prins Hendriklaan 105, 3584 EK Utrecht.
    Phone: 30-540694. Fax: 30-540564.
    Membership: 11,077.

16. **Vervoersbond FNV** (transport workers), Goeman Borgesiuslaan 77, 3515 ET Utrecht.
    Phone: 30-738222. Telex: 40693. Fax: 30-738313.
    Membership: 63,810.

17. **Voedingsbond FNV** (agricultural and food workers), Goeman Borgesiuslaan 77, 3515 ET Utrecht.
    Phone: 30-738333. Telex: 40693. Fax: 30-738313.
    Membership: 57,817.

18. **Vrouwenbond FNV** (women's union), Naritaweg 10, 1043 BX Amsterdam.
    Phone: 20-5816300. Fax: 20-6844541.
    Membership: 9,032.

19. **Werknemers in de Sport** (workers in sport), Herenstraat 35, 3512 KB Utrecht.
    Phone: 30-316207. Fax: 30-332708.
    Membership: 555.

Publications: *FNV Magazine* (fortnightly); *FNV Bulletin* (11 per year); *IZ Bulletin* (4 per year); *FNV News* (4 per year in English); *ATA* (information on South Africa; 3 per year); *Nieuwsbrief* (each FNV-secretariat publishes its own newsletter; 4 per year).

International affiliations. ICFTU; ETUC; TUAC. The NVV had historically been an ICFTU affiliate, while the NKV was affiliated to the WCL. The NVV and NKV jointly sought a restructuring of the international trade union movement aimed at a linking of the ICFTU and WCL. This was not forthcoming (in the NVV-NKV view because of the lack of the will to do so on the part of the WCL), and the NKV withdrew from the WCL as of Jan. 1, 1981 (i.e. one year before the completion of its merger with the NVV).

Other organizations

Vaksorganiatie van Middelbaar en Hoger Personneel (VHP)
Netherlands Federation of Managerial Personnel

Address. Randhoeve 223, P.O. Box 300, 3990 DH Houten
Phone. 03403 94811
Fax. 03403 79825
Leadership. E. Nypels (president); Th. M. Peperkamp (manager)
Membership. 30,000.
History and character. The VHP is a managerial trade union which is independent of all political parties and religious affiliations. Its acronym was changed from NCHP in January 1990.
Publication. *Het VHP Journaal*.

There are two unaffiliated unions at the national airline KLM, one for employees and one for flight personnel. Civil servants have an unaffiliated Civil Servants Centre.

ARUBA

Capital: Oranjestad

Population: 60,312
(estimated 1981)

Political system. On Jan. 1, 1986, Aruba achieved *status aparte* in preparation for full independence from the Netherlands in 1996: in doing so it separated from the other islands of the Netherlands Antilles but retained loose ties with them at ministerial level. Defence and foreign policy interests remained the responsibility of the Netherlands.

Economy. With the closure of the island's oil refinery in 1985, tourism was the sole remaining major industry, and Aruba is heavily dependent on aid from the Netherlands.

Trade unionism. The FTA has traditionally been the dominant organization on the island. The ICFTU also formerly recorded an affiliate, the Independent Oil Workers' Union of Aruba, which had 860 members in 1980.

Federación Di Trahadornan Di Aruba (FTA)
Aruban Workers' Federation

Address. Bernardstraat No. 23, San Nicolás.
Phone. 55448, 45376, 41531.
Fax. 45504
Leadership. Anselmo Pontilius (president).
Membership. 3,300.
History and character. Founded in July 1964 by leaders of the Independent Oil Workers Union, to represent workers within the oil refineries, the FTA lost membership after 1984 following the decline of the oil industry. However, it is slowly regaining its strength with members in the construction, hotel and catering, industrial, commercial, banking and insurance sectors. It is politically independent, and membership will swell with the re-opening in 1991 of the largest refinery on the island.
Publication. Boletin informativo FTA.
International affiliations. WCL/CLAT.

NETHERLANDS ANTILLES

Capital: Willemstad　　　　　　　　　　　　　　　　　　**Population: 171,620**
(estimated 1981, excluding Aruba)

Political system. The Netherlands Antilles has since Jan. 1, 1986 comprised the islands of Curaçao (with 147,388 inhabitants in 1981), Bonaire, St Eustatius, Saba and St Maarten, and is (with the Netherlands and Aruba) one of the three members of the Kingdom of the Netherlands. A multi-party coalition government, formed following elections to the parliament (*Staten*) in November 1985, is led by Don Martina of the Curaçao-based social-democratic New Antillean Movement (MAN).

Economy. The economy is based on oil refining, tourism, and offshore financial activities (these based in Willemstad). The Antilles have traditionally been among the most prosperous of Caribbean territories, but have been adversely affected since the early 1980s by difficulties in the oil industry and by changes in US tax laws relating to the taxation of bonds issued by US subsidiary companies in the Antilles, and unemployment reached 35 per cent in 1985.

Trade unionism. Trade unionism is highly developed but fragmented, with some unions operating only on individual islands and others throughout the Antilles (including Aruba).

Sentral di Sindikatonan di Korsou (SSK)
Central Trade Union of Curaçao

Address. Schouwburgweg 44, P.O. Box 3036, Willemstad, Curaçao
Membership. 6,000 (1983)
International affiliation. ICFTU/ORIT.

Windward Islands Federation of Labour (WIFOL)

Address. P.O. Box 418, W.A.J. Nisbeth Rd No. 91, Pondfill, St Maarten
Phone. 22797
Leadership. Egbert W. Richardson (president); Theophilus Thompson (general secretary)
Membership. 2,000. WIFOL represents the majority of workers on the island of St. Maarten, most of whom are employed in tourism.
Publication. WIFOL Newsletter.
International affiliations. CLAT/WCL.

New Zealand

Capital: Wellington   **Population: 3,356,000**

Political system. New Zealand, an independent member of the Commonwealth, is a parliamentary democracy with the British monarch (represented by a Governor-General) as head of state. The Labour Party, led by David Lange, came to power in 1984 and held it until 1990 when, weakened by division and Lange's resignation, it was defeated at a general election under the leadership of Mike Moore.

Economy. New Zealand has a developed market economy based on agriculture, small-scale industry and services. The Labour government of Mr Lange carried out a radical restructuring of the economy designed to combat its weaknesses, notably its external debt which accounted for 60 per cent of GNP in 1985. The deregulatory programme included a severe restriction of government spending, privatization, a shift from direct to indirect taxation and a major reform of industrial relations legislation. In the short term, the policies resulted in high inflation, increased unemployment and high interest rates.

Civilian employment in New Zealand in 1988 was 1,496,000, of whom 270,000 were employed in industry, 160,000 in agriculture, and 938,000 in services. Unemployment was 6.3 per cent and rising in 1988, while inflation was 4 per cent and falling. Under Labour the budget deficit was reduced as a proportion of GDP to 1.6 per cent: nevertheless GDP actually fell by 1 per cent that year.

System of industrial relations. New Zealand is a member of the ILO and the right to organize is recognized in law and in practice. The Labour Relations Act 1987 completely revised the law relating to labour relations. The government claimed that its overall objective was to encourage the development of "effective unions and employer organizations which: (i) can operate independently of legislative support; and (ii) can negotiate relevant awards and agreements which are adhered to". In an extensive three-part document comprising 373 sections the resulting legislation covered registration of unions and employers' organizations, internal affairs of unions, union membership, change of union coverage, union ballot and elections, dispute settlement, the tri-partite wage conference, negotiation of wages and working conditions, personal grievances, strikes and lockouts, mediation and arbitration. The changes introduced by the new legislation included the following: (a) *minimum union membership*—a union must have at least 1,000 members before it can be registered. In the case of an existing union, where its membership falls below 1,000, it is given one year to take remedial action before its registration is cancelled; (b) *union membership*—the insertion of a union membership clause can be negotiated by both sides but, if not settled by negotiation, the matter can be determined by a secret ballot of all workers covered by the agreement. The insertion of a provision for compulsory union membership depends on attainment of a simple majority of valid votes cast. Exemptions may be made on grounds of conscience or other deeply held personal conviction; (c) *union rules criteria*—the rules of unions and employers' organizations may not be unreasonable, undemocratic, unfairly discriminatory or prejudicial, or contrary to law. Unions must have an acceptable degree of internal democracy and accountability to members; all officials with power to vote on union business must be elected to office; (d) *scope of negotiations*—the state should have no role in direct negotiations between unions and employers. The scope of negotiations should be determined by both sides to the agreement. The previous definition of "industrial matters" has been deleted and bargaining can take place on subjects as diverse as the introduction of new technology, superannuation schemes and the provision of childcare facilities. Questions of the introduction of new technology had been the prerogative of management under previous legislation; (e) *freedom to strike and lockout*—strikes and lockouts are deemed illegal where they occur during a dispute which: i) falls within the jurisdiction of a disputes or grievance procedures; ii) occurs in an essential industry and the notice requirement has not been fulfilled; iii) is over an issue of union membership or union coverage or cancellation of union registration; or iv) is over a dispute of interest. The powers available to employers to suspend striking and non-striking workers are maintained, but the appeals procedure will be strengthened by enabling classes of workers as well as individuals to appeal against suspension; (f) *personal grievances*—the scope of personal grievances has been extended beyond unfair dismissal to cover discrimination, duress and sexual harassment. There is a new obligation for an employer to give written reasons for dismissal if asked; and reinstatement is emphasized as the primary remedy; (g) *labour court*—a new Labour Court was established to take over the high court's jurisdiction over torts, injunctions and judicial review relating to industrial disputes and institutions and the tasks of specialized industrial bodies; (h) *tri-partite wage conference*—an annual tri-partite wage conference was scheduled for the end of each year. Each conference will receive an economic briefing from the government and consultations will cover the economic environment within which the wage negotiations take place in relation to the government's stated economic policies.

The New Zealand Employers' Federation submitted a complaint to the ILO Committee on the Application of Conventions and Recommendations against the new legislation. The Federation objected to the 1,000-member rule and complained that compulsory union membership undermined workers' rights to freedom of choice. The Federation also claimed that the legislation failed to put enough emphasis on the industry or business of the employer as a basis of bargaining structures.

As in Australia, the floor for union membership has had the effect of accelerating amalgamations. In the brief period from September 1988 to May 1989 (which spanned the implementation date) the number of unions dropped from 245 to 166. Ending compulsory arbitration did not lead to an increase in the incidence of strikes: indeed 1988 saw less days lost through disputes than in any of the previous three years. Employers have so far moved cautiously to take advantage of their right to sue unions over illegal strikes. On the other hand the impact of an unregulated environment has been more apparent in the structure of collective bargaining. Employers moved swiftly to end national bargaining in several sectors and the unions, enfeebled by unemployment, found resistance difficult to organize. Strike action over this issue was mounted in 1988 by the Air New Zealand Pilots' Association and by the Clerical Workers' Union, while in the public sector unions faced attempts to deal with them department by department.

Privatization also precipitated a dispute when the Shipping Corporation attempted to alter staffing levels in anticipation of being sold. In the ports, the unaffiliated Watersiders'

Federation was found by the Labour Court to be entitled in law to exclusive membership rights, a ruling which cuts out its rival the Harbour Board Workers. In this muddled post-legislative scene, the new NZCTU General Secretary Ken Douglas proposed a compact which would draw government into employer–employee relations and stimulate new management thinking about involvement in the company. Douglas negotiated the compact with Minister of External Relations and Trade Mike Moore and it was introduced in September 1990. By this date however, Moore had succeeded to the position of Premier and shortly afterwards the Labour Party was defeated in the general election.

Trade unionism. Under amendments to the Industrial Relations Act which came into force on July 1, 1985, and were introduced by the Labour government elected in July 1984, a system of compulsory trade union membership was imposed. Under this system unions were granted compulsory membership rights which would be confirmed provided that they voted within 18 months to retain the rights. By January 1987 (i.e. at the expiry of the 18 months' time limit on union ratification of compulsory membership), 193 of the country's 230 unions had voted to retain compulsory membership and only two (representing commercial travellers and optical technicians) had voted against. Some 35 unions, predominantly small unions representing professional or supervisory staff, had held no ballots and were consequently to be considered voluntary. Union density in New Zealand was assessed at 64 per cent in 1988 but unionists were apprehensive that ending the closed shop would result in a severe reduction in their numbers.

The first federation was formed in 1909 and became known as the "Red Federation"; its history was one of industrial turmoil, and in 1913 the United Federation of Labour, which was linked to the newly formed Social Democratic Party, was formed and became the leader of organized labour. This was superseded by the Alliance of Labour in 1919. Following the election of a Labour government in 1935 the New Zealand Federation of Labour (NZFL) was formed in 1937. Fifty years after its foundation, in October 1987, the NZFL merged with the public sector group, the Combined State Unions, to form the New Zealand Council of Trade Unions (NZCTU). Approximately half of all unions and three quarters of all union members are affiliated to the NZCTU. Its major affiliates are the Service Workers' Federation, the Public Service Association, the Engineers' Union, the Food and Chemical Workers' Union, the Post Office Union, and the Clerical Workers' Union. The number of affiliates has dropped to 50 because of amalgamations. The fall in the number of affiliated members from 530,000 in 1988 to 460,000 in 1991 is however considered the direct result of privatization and high unemployment. The NZCTU General Secretary Ken Douglas is President of the Socialist Unity Party (SUP), but no unions in New Zealand are affiliated to the WFTU. At its 1989 biennial conference the NZCTU reaffirmed its affiliation to the ICFTU.

The most prominent non-affiliated union is the Waterside Workers' Union, followed by the Carpenters' Union, the Electricians' Union, the Seamen's and the Workers' Unions. One railway union is also unaffiliated.

New Zealand Council of Trade Unions (NZCTU)

Address. 6th Floor, Union House, Cnr Willis and Dixon Streets, P.O. Box 6645, Wellington 1

Phone. 851 334; 851 843

Fax. 856 051

Leadership. Ken. G. Douglas (president); Angela Foulkes (vice president); Ron Burgess (secretary).

Membership. 530,000 (mid-1988).

History and character. The NZCTU held its founding conference in Wellington in late October 1987. It was formed out of the merger of the New Zealand Federation of Labour (NZFL), and the Combined State Unions (CSU). At the time of the NZFL's disestablishment, over 150 unions had been affiliated to it, the majority representing private sector workers. The CSU, on the other hand, had been an amalgam of public sector unions. Several other unions, including the Bank Officers' Union, which had hitherto stood outside the two large formations, joined the NZCTU.

Publications. Minutes and proceedings of Biennial conference; Trade union directory; Research publications.

International affiliations. CTUC; PTUC; ICFTU; APRO.

Nicaragua

Capital: Managua   **Population: 3,503,103**
                                                                                          (1989)

Political system. The Frente Sandinista de Liberación Nacional (FSLN or Sandinistas) came to power in July 1979 following the overthrow of the right-wing Somoza régime which had ruled Nicaragua since 1933. The Sandinistas began their rule militarily, then in November 1984 held presidential and legislative elections which returned them with a substantial majority. However the stability of the Sandinista government of President Daniel Ortega was progressively undermined by the hostility of the United States and insurgency mounted by the contra guerrillas, largely drawn from former Somoza forces. In February 1990 new elections led to a victory over the Sandinistas by the opposition UNO party led by Violeta Chamorro to whom they and Ortega peacefully transferred power.

Economy. The Nicaraguan economy, which is based on agriculture, with coffee, cotton, sugar and bananas as the principal crops, has been in crisis since the devastation of civil war which has been sustained since 1979 by the counter revolutionaries (contras). In 1979, the FSLN nationalized the banks, but also encouraged private enterprise. The trade embargo imposed in 1985 by the USA, historically the principal market for Nicaraguan products, had a severe effect on the economy. In September 1988 hurricane Joan devastated the Caribbean coastal region. There is hyperinflation, an acute fuel shortage, a critical balance of payments deficit and a flourishing black market.

In 1987 total employment in Nicaragua was 843,000, of whom 365,000 worked in agriculture. Of the workforce as a whole some 33 per cent worked in services, a similar number in agriculture and around 8 per cent in manufacturing. Unemployment at that date was more than 25 per cent. The later 1980s saw the Nicaraguan economy contract while falling export earnings made it progressively more difficult to purchase necessary capital goods.

By the end of 1990 unemployment was thought to have reached 40 per cent with a further 25 per cent underemployed. The Chamorro government's programme of cutting government spending had already begun to bite, with redundancy being handed out to 15,000 civil servants and 10,000 army personnel. In the face of an inflation rate of 3,200 per cent purchasing power had on some estimates fallen by 80 per cent.

System of industrial relations. The right to strike, with various restrictions, was re-established in August 1984. However, measures announced on Oct. 15, 1985, declaring a state of emergency, suspended the right to strike, to protest and to hold meetings. Members of opposition trade union organizations have been detained from time to time for relatively brief periods. Nicaragua ratified ILO Conventions No. 87 (Freedom of Association and Protection of the Right to Organize, 1948) and No. 98 (Right to Organize and Collective Bargaining, 1949) in 1967. The Committee of Experts on the Application of Conventions and Recommendations (1988), while expressing awareness of the gravity of the situation through which the country was passing, was concerned that the suspension of the right to strike and of freedom of association, due to proclamations of states of emergency over several years, constituted "extremely serious" restrictions of workers' rights in contravention of conventions 87 and 98. The government, in reply, confirmed that the current state of emergency had been suspended in January 1988. The Committee, in return, wished for confirmation that this meant a "return to normal trade union life" (viz. freedom of communications, right of independent organizations for employers and workers without interference, right to hold trade union meetings on union premises) and asked that Decree Law No. 530, which subjects collective agreements to the prior approval of the Ministry of Labour, be repealed.

In its last two years the Sandinista régime faced considerable trade union opposition. In February 1988 it used the Somoza-era Labour Code to declare a strike of car and building workers illegal, and the strikers were replaced in their employment by prisoners. It controlled appointments to ILO meetings to represent both employers and trade unions for which it received fierce criticism, and it refused to negotiate with non-Sandinista unions in the public sector.

Industrial relations difficulties did not however disappear after the change of government. In July 1990 a 10-day general strike was held by the National Federation of Workers (FNT) accompanied by occupations of factories and skirmishes with right-wing gunmen. The strike only ended when the government conceded a 43 per cent wage rise, linking of pay to a new "gold córdoba" monetary standard, repeal of a privatization decree affecting state farms and a guarantee of job security for state employees, but the loyalty of the armed forces and the police to the new Chamorro administration was thought to be a significant pointer to the future.

Trade unionism. The first national trade union organization—the Organized Labour of Nicaragua (OON)—was formed in 1924, but faltered because of its support for Gen. Sandino (assassinated in 1934), who led opposition to the US military presence in the country. The position of trade unions was difficult under the rule of the Somozas, although unions independent of the government managed to retain a degree of organizational identity for much of that period. Substantial anti-government industrial unrest occurred in 1978–79, but the fall of Somoza was a result of military action. Following the Sandinista revolution, union membership increased rapidly, reaching over 100,000 by 1982, as compared with 27,000 in July 1979.

The trade union movement within the country is divided in its international affiliations and in its attitude to the policies of the Sandinistas. Such opposition reached a high point in April 1988 when several thousand workers (most prominently in the construction trade) were on strike, demanding that their wages be at least returned to the level of buying power before the monetary reforms of February 1988, which in particular had led to steep declines in the real incomes of many workers. The government response had been to declare such strikes illegal and dismiss workers. In May 1988 the ICFTU reported that several union leaders had been detained and the leaders of the ICFTU-affiliated CUS, Alvin Guthrie and José Espinoza, threatened with arrest. In August 1988, however, the Sandinista government allowed the CUS and the CTN to receive US$200,000 from the National Endowment of Democracy (NED) an agency sponsored by the US government. At the end of September 1988, the ICFTU denounced the killing of a member of the CUS, Carlos Garcia Velásquez on July 3 in the city of Mindiri (which it claimed was carried out by a policeman) and the abduction of Miguel Valdivia, a CUS union leader of rural workers, on July 1, allegedly by members of the Sandinista army. A demonstration called by the CPT (*see below*) on July 17 to protest against anti-union repression and rising prices, had, according to the ICFTU, been forbidden. On July 21, the CST's general secretary, Lucio Jiménez Guzmán, affirmed that the majority of Nicaragua's workers supported measures to safeguard national security and sovereignty. Following the 5th Assembly of the Eduardo Contreras unions in Managua (December 1987) the pro-government CST called for, (in line with the plans of the National Labour and Wages Organization System—SNOTS) the defence of peace, the safe-guarding of public ownership and the right to work. Better wages and working conditions would be in line with what the country (given the internal emergencies and continuing international economic blockade) could afford. However, there would be equal rights and opportunities for workers of both sexes, remuneration according to the quality and quantity of work done and the development of a united trade union approach, as a factor fundamental to unity.

On the eve of the Sandinistas' fall from power the political geography of Nicaraguan trades unionism was as follows. The FSLN received support from the CSN and CST, to whom a large number of unions, active in different sectors of the economy, were affiliated. In varying degrees of opposition to it and the Sandinistas, were the CTN-A, the CUS, the CGT-I, and CAUS, each aligned with a different political party and ideologically diverse. They were co-ordinated through the Permanent Congress of Workers (CPT) which was formed in April 1988. The CTN, from which the CTN-A broke away in 1982, did not join the CPT.

Asociación Nacional de Educadores de Nicaragua (ANDEN)
National Association of Educators of Nicaragua

Address. Contiguo al Parque de las Madres, Managua
Phone. 661471-662394-664733
Leadership. Guillermo Martínez (president)
Membership. 22,500 claimed in 1988. This union controls 75 per cent of all school teachers.

Asociación de Trabajadores del Campo (ATC)
Farm Workers' Association

Address. de la Casa Morales, 7 C. al Sur, 1 C. Arriba, Managua
Phone. 23338-22779-26976
Leadership. Edgardo García (secretary-general)
Membership. 70,000 claimed in 1987.
History and character. The ATC was founded in 1976 and assisted the Sandinistas in the civil war in ensuring food supplies in areas under their control. It backed the government's agrarian policy, although nominally autonomous of the FSLN. It is the leading organization representing workers on public and private farms in the coffee, cotton, beef, and rice sectors.
Publication. *El Machete.*

Central de Acción y Unidad Sindical (CAUS)
Labour Action and Unity Central

Address. de los Semaforos del Colonial 1 C. Abajo, 1 C. al Lago, Managua
Phone. 42587
Leadership. Roberto Moreno (secretary-general)
Membership. 2,000.
History and character. Marxist movement critical of Sandinista labour policies. Founded after the 1967 schism in the Socialist Party. Traditionally strong in the Managua textile industry.
Affiliations. Communist Party of Nicaragua (PCdeN) and Permanent Congress of Workers (CPT).

Central Sandinista de Trabajadores (CST)
Sandinista Workers' Centre

Address. Calle Colón, Iglesia del Carmen, 1c Abajo y 1/2 al Sur, Casa del Obrero, Managua
Phone. 24121; 74953; 74973
Leadership. Lucio Jiménez Guzmán (general secretary)
Membership. 150,000 claimed in 1987.
History and character. The CST was founded immediately following the 1979 revolution, growing out of the workers' insurrectionist committees and their later form, the comités de defensa de trabajadores Sandinistas, and rapidly became the dominant labour organization in the country. It is closely linked to the FSLN and in the view of opposition unions is favoured by the government as a central vertical structure. The CST stated in July 1986 that it would "defend the revolution and production; continue to make constant efforts in the economic sector and, if necessary, work more than eight hours a day, so as to be able to survive", and also that it would intensify the "ideological struggle" in the workplace to ensure the preservation of the gains of the Sandinista revolution.
Publication. El Trabajador.
International affiliations. WFTU; CPUSTAL.

Central de Trabajadores de Nicaragua (Autónoma) (CTN-A)
Autonomous Nicaraguan Workers' Central

Address. de la Iglesia Santa Ana, 1-1/2 C. Abajo, Managua
Phone. 25981
Leadership. Antonio Jarquin (secretary-general)
Membership. 18,000.
History and character. Product of 1982 split in the CTN. Strongly committed to social christian communitarianism and militantly anti-Sandinista. Organized among Managua urban workers and peasants in Nueva Guinea, Nueva Segovia, and Chinandega. Key unions include rural transport workers (SITRARU) and Union of Campesino Workers of Nueva Guinea (nearly half of CTN-A membership).
Affiliations. Popular Social Christian Party (PPSC) and Permanent Congress of Workers (CPT).

Central de Trabajadores de Nicaragua (CTN)
Nicaraguan Workers' Central

Address. de las Delicias del Volga, 1/2 C. Arriba, Managua
Phone. 22917
Cable. CTN Managua
Leadership. Carlos Huembes (secretary-general)
Membership. 35,000.
History and character. In 1962 the Christian-inspired Nicaraguan Autonomous Trade Union Movement (MOSAN) was formed, recruiting several thousand members principally in rural areas, and in 1972 this became the CTN. The CTN did not join the pro-Sandinista Nicaraguan Labour Union Co-ordination (CNS) founded in 1981. Members of the CTN were subjected to periods of detention without charge by the Sandinista government.

Largest independent union before losing FETSALUD to the Sandinistas in 1980 and splitting with CTN-A in 1982. Active in Managua, Chinandega, Leon, Masaya, and Granada, mostly among employees of private farms and factories. Key unions include bus drivers (SIMOTUR), cooking oil factory workers (SITRIAM), banana workers (STB), gasoline station attendants (SITEGMA), and *La Prensa* newspaper employees (STLP). It supports the Social Christian Party (PSC).
International affiliation. WCL. The WCL and CLAT criticized the Sandinista government for infringements of human and trade union rights, but opposed US aid to the *contra* rebels.

Confederación de Asociaciones de Profesionales "Heroes y Mártires" (CONAPRO "Heroes y Martires")
Heroes and Martyrs Confederation of Professional Associations

Address. de la Casa Morales 1 C. Abajo, 3–1/2 C. al Sur, Managua
Phone. 23765
Leadership. Freddy Cruz (president)
Membership. 13,000 claimed in 1987.
Character. Created as a parallel organization to the private sector CONAPRO.

Confederación General de los Trabajadores (independiente) (CGT-I)
Independent General Confederation of Labour

Address. KM. 4, Carretera a Masaya, Managua
Phone. 70615-75570
Leadership. Carlos Salgado (secretary-general)
Membership. 31,000.
History and character. The CGT-I was formed in 1963 as a split from the Confederación General de Trabajo, CGT (itself founded in 1949, and controlled by the Somoza government). The more right-wing elements of the CGT subsequently allied with the CSN formed in 1964 (see Confederación de Unificación Sindical), the old CGT collapsing. Under the Somozas the CGT-I (which was affiliated to the WFTU) became a principal centre of illegal opposition to the régime and the pro-government unions. Before the revolution the CGT-I was a member of UDEL, the Democratic Union of Liberation, and in 1980 joined the National Inter-Union Commission (CNI) along with other pro-Sandinista unions including the CST. It is allied with the Marxist-Leninist Partido Socialista Nicaragüense (PSN), and remained independent of the CST while co-operating with it. The CGT-I was opposed to Sandinista wage controls. Based on the Managua Construction Workers' Union (SCAAS). Also active among construction workers, artisans, and farm workers in Granada, Masaya, Carazo, Rivas, and Leon.
Affiliations. Nicaraguan Socialist Party (PSN), Permanent Congress of Workers (CPT), and World Federation of Trade Unions (WFTU).

Confederación de Unificación Sindical (CUS)
Confederation of Labour Unification

Address. Ciudad Jardin q-3, Managua
Phone. 42039
Leadership. Alvin Guthrie, (secretary-general)
Membership. 35,000.
History and character. The CUS was formed as the Nicaraguan Trade Union Council (CSN) under the auspices of ORIT in 1964, absorbing independent and pro-government unions including part of the CGT. The CUS describes itself as the "labour arm of the Socialist International" in Nicaragua, but following the revolution it declined rapidly as a consequence of its accommodation with the previous regime. It is partly funded by the American Institute for Free Labour Development (AIFLD) of the US AFL-CIO. Leaders and members of CUS were detained for periods in 1985–86. It is a democratic labour movement with regional organizations in Managua, Chinandega, Leon, Carazo, Nueva Segovia and Bluefields. Key unions include auto mechanics (Simaresisa) and restaurant workers (FETRAHOMESIMA) in Managua, Chinandega farm workers (FETRACAMCHI), Carazo farm workers (FETRACAMCA), and miskito workers in Managua (SITRAMIS). CUS also has influence among Leon market vendors, Corinto port workers and at the San Antonio sugar mill.
Publication. *Solidaridad* (reported as banned in early 1986).
National and international affiliations. Social Democratic Party (PSD), Nicaraguan Democratic Co-ordinator (CDN), Permanent Congress of Workers (CPT), Intern-American Regional Organization of Workers (ORIT), International Confederation of Free Trade Unions (ICFTU), and American Institute for Free Labor Development (AIFLD). The ICFTU has opposed US aid to the *contra* guerrillas and also the US economic embargo of Nicaragua imposed in 1985, and has argued

that the USA should maintain relations with Nicaragua linked to the observance of human and trade union rights.

Coordinadora Sindical de Nicaragua (CSN)
Labour Coordinator of Nicaragua

Membership. Over 300,000 claimed in 1987.

History and character. Umbrella organization for FSLN-controlled labour organizations. Formerly included the CGT-I, CAUS, and FO non-Sandinista Marxist labour groups.

Affiliated organizations. All the following organizations backed the FSLN during its period of government.

Federación de Trabajadores de la Salud (FETSALUD)
Health Workers' Federation

Address. Shell Cuidad Jardin, 1/2 C. Arriba. Managua

Phone. 26482

Leadership. Gustavo Porras (secretary-general)

Membership. 15,000.

Character. Government-controlled union of workers in the public health care industry.

Frente Obrero (FO)
Workers' Front

Address. del Puente "el Paraísito" 20 vrs. Arriba, Managua

Phone. 23787

Leadership. Fernando Malespin (secretary-general)

Membership. Small.

History and character. Radical leftist group with Maoist and anarchist elements that split with the FSLN in the early 1970s. Agitates against Sandinista labour policies and demands complete abolition of private property.

Affiliations. Popular Action Movement—Marxist–Leninist (MAP–ML). Supports platform of the CPT.

Unión Nacional de Agricultores y Ganaderos (UNAG)
National Union of Farmers and Ranchers

Address. del Banco Inmobiliario las Palmas, 1 C. al Lago, 1/2 C. Abajo, Managua

Phone. 660632-664110-661482

Leadership. Daniel Núñez (president)

Membership. 138,400 claimed in 1988.

Character. Union of Sandinista co-operative members and small landowners benefiting from the agrarian reform programme. Also attempts to co-opt larger private sector producers away from the Nicaraguan Union of Agricultural and Livestock Producers (UPANIC).

International affiliation. WFTU.

Unión Nacional de Empleados (UNE)
National Union of Employees

Address. Casa de la CST, Managua

Phone. 22720-27082

Leadership. José Angel Bermúdez (secretary-general)

Character. Government white collar employees' union.

337

Unión de Periodistas de Nicaragua (UPN)
Union of Journalists of Nicaragua

Address. del Hospital Velez Paiz, 4 C. Arriba, Managua
Phone. 51642
Leadership. Lily Soto (secretary-general)
Membership. 900 claimed in 1988.

Niger

Capital: Niamey

Population: 7,250,000
(1988)

Political system. Niger gained independence from France in 1960. It has been governed by a Supreme Military Council and a largely civilian Council of Ministers since a *coup* in 1974. In 1983 the National Council for Development, formerly an advisory body, was reconstituted as part of an elective system. Colonel Ali Seibou became President in 1987 after the death of his predecessor and cousin, General Seyni Kountché.

The President and his ruling party, the Mouvement National pour la Société de Développment (MNSD) have faced increasing opposition in recent years and have lost the support of the country's trade union movement. Leaks from a 1990 report by the World Bank suggested the possibility of corruption in government circles.

Economy. Niger's main export is uranium, which accounted for 81 per cent of exports in 1981, making Niger the fifth largest producer of uranium in the non-communist world. Although only 10 per cent of the land is cultivated, drought, desertification and pests mean that agriculture employs 89 per cent of the working population and accounts for 45 per cent of GDP.

Compulsory military service was replaced for young Nigerans in 1989 with a system of participative training and public works employment.

System of industrial relations. Niger ratified ILO Convention No. 87 (Freedom of Association and Protection of the Right to Organize, 1948) in 1961 and Convention No. 98 (Right to Organize and Collective Bargaining, 1949) in 1962.

Trade unionism. Niger's union centre the USTN has evolved to a position independent and critical of the government and since 1990 has been calling for a multi-party system.

Union des Syndicats des Travailleurs du Niger (USTN)
Union of Workers' Trade Unions of Niger

Address. Bourse du Travail, B.P. 388, Niamey
Phone. 73-52-56
Telex. 5438INEO
Leadership. Iaouali Montari (secretary-general)
Membership. 24,810.

History and structure. A trade union central, the Union Nationale des Travailleurs du Niger (UNTN), was established at independence in 1960. Its name was changed to the Union des Syndicats des Travailleurs du Niger (USTN) in 1978. The USTN's main policy-making body is its congress, which meets every four years. The organization's affairs are run by a general council, a union council and a national executive office.

338

The USTN was a long-standing associate of the country's ruling party the MNSD. However, its support for the pro-democracy movement (which included mounting a general strike against austerity measures) led to police raids on its premises and the detention of General Secretary Laouali Moutari in June 1990. The President told the unions' leaders in October that their role should not extend beyond defending the workers' interests. A further general strike, this time for five days, was mounted in November in support of calls for a conference on the country's political future.

Affiliated unions. There are 26 affiliated unions covering the main sectors of the economy, the public sector, and the major service industries.

Publication. Ma'aykaci (The Worker).

International affiliation. OATUU.

Nigeria

Capital: Lagos   **Population: 114,000,000**

Political system. Nigeria became an independent member of the Commonwealth in 1960, adopting a Constitution which established the Federal Republic of Nigeria in 1963. Maj.-Gen. Ibrahim Babangida took power in a *coup* in August 1985, displacing a previous military ruler, and established an Armed Forces Ruling Council. In 1987 the Council postponed the return to civilian rule from 1990 to 1992.

In 1989 the government established a new two-party structure which was not based on pre-existing political associations.

Economy. Nigeria's economy is dominated by the oil industry which accounted for 97.2 per cent of exports in 1986 and about 20 per cent of GDP, but less than 1 per cent of employment. Agriculture, which provided 27 per cent of GDP and employed about 60 per cent of the population in 1985, and industry, which contributes less than 10 per cent of GDP, have lagged behind the mining sector despite liberalization measures intended to promote investment.

As a result of rising population and the falling price of oil, Nigeria's per capita GDP fell by 18 per cent in 1986. Since 1986, Nigeria has implemented an IMF structural adjustment programme which has led to reduced domestic subsidies and a 60 per cent devaluation of the niara. Falling standards of living and inflation have led to widespread discontent.

System of industrial relations. Nigeria ratified ILO Conventions No. 87 (Freedom of Association and Protection of the Right to Organize, 1948) and No. 98 (Right to Organize and Collective Bargaining, 1949) in 1960, together with Convention Nos. 29 and 105 on forced labour. However the ILO has noted discrepancies between Nigerian legislation and the conventions ratified, in particular with regard to the right to organize and strike, and to the imposition of compulsory labour.

In December 1989 the government ordained (Decree 35) that membership of international trade secretariats was illegal and under it four transport unions were fined in March 1990. The government has also barred public employees from being members of one or other of the two legal political parties. The Nigerian Labour Party, favoured by the Nigeria Labour Congress (NLC), was not one of the two made legal in the 1989 rearrangement, and the NLC has since that time backed the Social Democratic Party. Under pressure of a threatened general strike by the NLC the government established a tripartite committee to consider the possibility of an increase in the minimum wage at the end of 1989.

Trade unionism. This has a long history stretching back to the turn of the century. By the 1930s a number of unions were well established and during World War II the colonial authorities began to register them, giving organized labour official recognition for the first time. Complex and fissiparous groupings of unions and central organizations developed in the 1950s and 1960s, with allegiances to the various world confederations. By the early 1970s there were several hundred unions and four competing trade union centrals. The centrals attempted to merge in 1976 to form the Nigeria Labour Congress, but against a background of four years of industrial unrest, the military government intervened to impose its idea of order on industrial relations. The four centrals were dissolved, their assets seized, 11 union leaders were banned from union activity, and all international organizations except the ILO and OATUU were prohibited from Nigeria. In 1978 a reconstituted NLC was launched by government decree with a large subvention of public funds. The country's several hundred unions and staff associations were rationalized into 42 industry-based unions affiliated to the NLC. Unions were to be recognized by employers and check off of dues was made automatic. Strikes were forbidden in certain industries and procedures were laid down for settling disputes and collective bargaining. The other main pieces of legislation governing industrial relations passed in this period were the Trade Disputes Decree of 1976 and the Trade Unions (Amendment) Act of 1979.

In February 1988 the government intervened in an ideological split at the quadrennial NLC conference. It suspended all officers and placed the whole organization under an administrator. The administrator drew up a joint slate representative of both factions and it was returned unopposed for all offices under the presidency of Paschal Bafyau of the Nigeria National Union of Railwaymen. In early 1990 the administrator made a number of recommendations for the running of the NLC and other unions, most of which were adopted by the government (see below). The NLC itself is examining the possibility of rationalizing its structure, principally by reducing the number of affiliates. By law unions for senior staff are not allowed to affiliate to the NLC; they are in the separate Senior Staff Consultative Association of Nigeria (SESCAN).

Nigerian Labour Congress (NLC)

Address. 29 Olajuwon Street, off Ojuelegba Road, P.O. Box 620, Yaba, Lagos
Phone. 835582/78/71
Leadership. Paschal Bafayu (executive president); Lassisi Osunde (general secretary)
Membership. There are 42 constituent unions.
History and character. Notwithstanding its formation under state sponsorship in 1978, the NLC has enjoyed a substantial degree of autonomy, and has not proved the compliant institution hoped for by the government. The left-wing union leader Hassan Sunmonu won the election for NLC president, and was re-elected in 1981. After a protracted struggle with the civilian government of President Shehu Shagari, including a general strike in 1981, the NLC won a national minimum wage of 125 naira (then about US$125) per month. Public sector wages had hitherto been set by periodic government commissions, the private sector taking its cue from the wage levels they determined.

There have since been frequent confrontations between the unions and government over wages, which were subsequently frozen. Since austerity measures were imposed from 1982, there have also been disputes over mass lay-offs. Other aspects of government policy, notably recourse to the IMF and privatization, have come under attack by the unions more recently, and to support its case the NLC has produced a number of statements of alternative policy, generally recommending reflationary measures.

Confrontation with government has increased in recent years. In 1986 following student unrest, seven unions' leaders were detained, including Ali Chiroma, who succeeded Sunmonu as NLC president in 1985. The NLC has been one of the main sources of opposition to the government's structural adjustment programme launched with IMF backing in mid-1986. The NLC opposed the

340

introduction of the National Minimum Wage Amendment Order of 1986, which exempted employers with less than 500 employees—estimated to account for 80 per cent of workplaces—from paying the minimum wage. The government subsequently backed down over this measure, and as a further reconciliatory gesture the ban on 11 trade unionists imposed in 1977 was lifted. The NLC next came into conflict with the government over its proposed increase in the price of petroleum-product prices to compensate for the four-fold depreciation of the naira—a key demand of the IMF for continued support for Nigeria. After waging an effective campaign against the increase, Chiroma and three other senior leaders were detained for alleged sedition, although they were released shortly afterwards. The 1988 budget did not increase petrol prices; it lifted the wage freeze and allowed free collective bargaining (though increases were limited to 15–20 per cent), for which the NLC had been campaigning for some time. Public sector pay was increased and wage bargaining intensified in the private sector, with the number of industrial disputes rising markedly.

The apparent *rapprochement* with organized labour proved temporary, for late in February 1988 the government dissolved the NLC executive and subsequently the executives of the NLC's 19 state councils. The NLC's affairs were put in the hands of a government-appointed administrator, Michael Ogunkoya. The dissolution prompted widespread protest, including condemnation by the international labour confederations. Ostensibly the government action was taken to halt a bitter conflict between rival "socialist" and "democratic" factions within the NLC. However, a resumption of the labour movement's long history of in-fighting just when the government was about to introduce more painful economic reforms led to allegations that the split was officially engineered to disable the labour movement. The presence of an IMF team in the country to discuss economic reforms and new credits lent credence to this view. Unrest nevertheless continued over pay, and when the government increased petroleum-product prices in April strikes and violent rioting broke out in protests lasting three weeks. There were several deaths, strikers were dismissed, rallies were banned, universities closed and many trade unionists arrested. A truce was eventually negotiated under which the government promised to release detainees, and undertook to speed up implementation of pay rises, though it did not rescind the petroleum-product increases.

Against a background of continuing unrest of pay and allowances, union-government relations have since continued to be uneasy. Three committees were set up to consider union grievances. However detainees continued to be held, and the government announced that an anti-strike division, the Labour Intelligence Monitoring Unit, was to be set up. Subsequently a unit to maintain essential services during strikes was established. A strike of power workers which blacked out the whole country in October was broken by the arrest of 11 strikers, who were charged with economic sabotage.

Meanwhile, re-elections for a reconstituted NLC executive promised by the government for August were postponed, and the tenure of the administrator was extended to the end of 1988. Plans were announced by the administrator to restructure the unions once again, with a view to reducing their number from 42 to 19. A committee was set up to see through the restructuring, but was restrained from proceeding by legal action brought by some unions. The restructuring was subsequently deferred by the government. In December 1988, however, the contending factions within the NLC reportedly came to terms, with Paschal Batyau succeeding Ali Chiroma as president.

Early in 1990 the administrator recommended changes for the operation of the NLC. There should be improved administration of finance with a legal requirement for unions to pay their fees to the NLC (the government accepted this and ordained that the NLC should deposit copies of its budget with the Registrar of Trade Unions). The administrator also recommended that the Congress avoid ideology and called for the General Secretary to be appointed. This too was accepted by the government, but it reserved its position on a further recommendation that affiliation to international bodies other than African ones should not be a matter of law.

The Congress itself stated that most of the 50 recommendations of the administrator were in Labour's interests, but registered its objections to posting its budget, appointing the General Secretary, and non-affiliation, on all of which it sought further discussions with the government.

During 1989 it succeeded in resolving an internal dispute at the National Union of Banks, Insurance and Financial Institutions Employees (NUBIFIE). In February 1990 the number of affiliates of Congress fell from 42 to 41 when the government added customs and excise posts to the list of essential occupations and so dissolved the Customs, Excise, and Immigration Staff Union.

This move was challenged in law by the union, but the NLC itself also returned the following month to the general matter of reducing the number of its affiliates, previously stalled by legal action, and established a technical committee of inquiry.

Most staff associations outside the NLC are grouped in the Senior Staff Consultative Association of Nigeria (SESCAN). There are four professional unions which are unaffiliated.

Affiliated unions.

1. **Agricultural and Allied Workers' Union of Nigeria (AAWUN)**, No. SW8/123A Lagos Bye-Pass, Oke-Ado, Ibadan, Oyo State.

2. **Automobile, Boatyard, Transport Equipment and Allied Workers' Union of Nigeria (ABTEAWOUN)**, 14 Bishop Street, Surulere, Lagos.
   Membership: 17,000.

3. **Civil Service Technical Workers' Union of Nigeria (CSTWU)**, 9 Aje Street, Yaba, Lagos.
   Phone: 01-863724, 01-863722.
   Membership: 100,500.

4. **Customs, Excise and Immigration Staff Union (CEISU)**, 367 Herbet Macaulay Street, P.M.B. 1012, Yaba, Lagos.
   Phone: 01-862471.

5. **Dockworkers' Union of Nigeria (DUN)**, Dockworkers' House, Seriki Street (Miliki Bus Stop), Okokomaiko Town, Badagry Expressway, P.O. Box 3236, Lagos.
   Membership: 30,000.

6. **Footwear, Leather and Rubber Products Workers' Union of Nigeria, (FLRPWUN)** 71, Palm Avenue, Mushin, Lagos.
   Membership: 6,000.

7. **Iron and Steel Workers' Union of Nigeria (ISWUN)**, 11 Oregun Road, Alausa, Ikeja, Lagos.

8. **Medical and Health Workers' Union of Nigeria (MHWUN)**, 2 Jeminatu Buraimoh Close, Opposite Barrack Bus Stop, Western Avenue, P.O. Box 553, Surulere, Lagos.
   Phone: 01-832274.
   Membership: 100,000.

9. **Metal Products Workers' Union of Nigeria (MPWUN)**, 119 Agege Motor Road, Bolade, Oshodi, Lagos.
   Phone: 01-962933.
   Membership: 7,000.

10. **Metallic and Non-Metallic Mines Workers' Union (MNMWU)**, 95/1 Enugu Street, P.O. Box 763, Jos, Plateau State.
    Phone: 073-52401.
    Membership: 20,000.

11. **National Association of Nigeria Nurses and Midwives (NANNM)**, 64 B Oduduwa Way, P.O. Box 3857, Ikeja, Lagos.
    Phone: 01-932173, 932349, 932283.
    Membership: 100,000.

12. **National Union of Air Transport Services Employees (NUATSE)**, Off Medical Road, Ikeja, Lagos.
    Phone: 01-963812.
    Membership: 13,000.

13. **National Union of Banks, Insurance and Financial Institutions Employees (NUBIFE)**, 310 Herbert Macaulay Street, P.M.B. 1139, Yaba, Lagos.
    Phone: 01-863193, 862429.
    Membership: 69,600.

14. **National Union of Chemical and Non-Metallic Products Workers' (NUCANMP)**, 119 Agege Motor Road, Bolade, Oshodi, Lagos.
Phone: 01-934048, 931276.
Membership: 27,000.

15. **National Union of Electricity and Gas Workers (NUEGW)**, 200 Herbert Macaulay Street, P.O. Box 212, Yaba, Lagos.
Phone: 01-860048, 863870.
Membership: 15,500.

16. **National Union of Food, Beverage and Tobacco Employees (NUFBTE)**, 6 Oba Akran Avenue, P.O. Box 3193, Ikeja, Lagos.
Phone: 01-962572, 931116.
Membership: 32,200.

17. **National Union of Furniture Fixtures and Wood Workers (NUFFWW)**, 3 Kunle Akinosi Street, LSDPC Residential Layout, P.M.B. 1095, Oshodi, Lagos.
Membership: 5,000.

18. **National Union of Hotel and Personal Services Workers (NUHPSW)**, 97 Herbert Macaulay Street, P.M.B. 1041, Ebute-Metta, Lagos.
Phone: 01-863803.

19. **National Union of Local Government Employees (NULGE)**, 148 Murtala Mohammed Way, P.M.B. 1042, Ebute-Metta, Lagos.
Phone: 01-844949, 863917.
Membership: 245,000.

20. **National Union of Paper and Paper Products Workers (NUPPPW)**, 15 Oshin Street, Alausa, Ikeja, Lagos.

21. **National Union of Petroleum and Natural Gas Workers (NUPENG)**, 2 Jeminatu Buraimoh Close, Western Avenue, P.O. Box 533, Surulere, Lagos.
Phone: 01-846569.
Membership: 286,000.

22. **National Union of Postal and Telecommunications Employees (NUPTE)**, 12 Gbaja Street, PO Box 284, Surulere, Lagos.
Phone: 01-837620, 831877, 831906.
Membership: 23,000.

23. **National Union of Public Corporations Employees (NUPCE)**, 18 Irepo Street, Challenge, P.M.B. 5124, Ibadan.
Phone: 022-315637.

24. **National Union of Road Transport Workers (NURTW)**, 18A Kayoade Street, Igbobi, Lagos.
Phone: 01-820610, 821296.

25. **National Union of Shop and Distributive Employees (NUSDE)**, 64 Olonade Street, P.M.B. 1050, Yaba, Lagos.
Phone: 01-863536.

26. **National Union of Textile, Garment and Tailoring Workers, (NUTGTW)**, Textile Workers House, B 6/8 Kubi Road, P.O. Box 905, Off Nassarawa Expressway, Kaduna.
Phone: 062-214438.
Membership: 41,300.

27. **Nigeria Civil Service Union (NCSU)**, 23 Tukunbo Street, P.O. Box 862, Lagos.
Phone: 01-635087.
Membership: 205,400.

28. **Nigeria Coal Miners' Union (NCMU)**, 14 A/B Bassey Street, Asata Mine Quarters, Coal Camp, Enugu, Anambra Street.
Membership: 1,500.

29. **Nigeria Ports Authority Workers' Union (NPAWU)**, 117 Osho Drive, Off Kirikiri Road, Olodi, Apapa, Lagos.
Phone: 01-860951.
Membership: 22,500.

30. **Nigeria Union of Civil Service Typists, Stenographic and Allied Staff (NUCSTSAS)**, 8A Bola Street, Ebute-Metta (East), Lagos.
Phone: 01-863502.

31. **Nigeria Union of Construction and Civil Engineering Workers', (NUCCEW)**, 51 Kano Street, P.M.B. 1064, Ebute-Metta, Lagos.
Phone: 01-800261, 800262, 800263.
Membership: 73,000.

32. **Nigeria Union of Journalists (NUJ)**, NUJ Building, 5 Adeyemo Alakija Street, Victoria Island, Lagos.
Phone: 01-613941.
Membership: 3,950.

33. **Nigeria Union of Pensioners (NUP)**, P.O. Box 1911, Ibadan.

34. **Nigeria Union of Railwaymen (NUR)**, 33 Exololu Street, Surulere, Lagos.
Phone: 01-842648.
Membership: 33,000.

35. **Nigeria Union of Seamen and Water Transport Workers (NUSWTW)**, 8 Bolaji Oloro Street, Ajegunle, Lagos.

36. **Nigeria Union of Teachers (NUT)**, 15 Rosamond Street, P.M.B. 1044, Surulere, Lagos.
Phone: 01-833443.
Membership: 250,000.

37. **Non-Academic Staff Union of Educational and Associated Institutions (NASU)**, NW 8/673 Orita VI, P.M.B. 8, University of Ibadan Post Office, Ibadan.
Phone: 022-410676.
Membership: 260,000.

38. **Precision, Electrical and Related Equipments Workers' Union (PEREWU)**, 21 Sadiku Street, Ilasamaja, Mushin, Lagos.
Phone: 01-520632, 521703.
Membership: 9,000.

39. **Printing and Publishing Workers' Union (PAPWU)**, 60 Old Yaba Road, Ebute-Metta, Lagos.
Phone: 01-860053, 860527, 862205.

40. **Radio, Television and Theatre Workers' Union (RATTAWU)**, SW9/9/927 A Azeez Aina Street, Ring Road, P.O. Box 3156, Mapo Post Office, Ibadan.

41. **Recreational Services Employees' Union (RSEU)**, 238, Second East Circular Road, P.O. Box 1244, Benin-City, Bendel State.
Phone: 052-223716.
Membership: 17,000.

42. **Union of Shipping, Clearing and Forwarding Agencies Workers of Nigeria (USCFAWN)**, 9 Agard Street, Yaba, Lagos.
Phone: 01-843665.
Membership: 3,900.

Publications. The NLC has produced a wide range of pamphlets setting out its position on economic and social issues.

International affiliations. OATUU, whose current secretary-general is Hassan Sunmonu, former president of the NLC; CTUC.

Senior Staff Consultative Association of Nigeria (SESCAN)

Address. 79, Tejuoso Street, P.O. Box 4526, Surulere, Lagos

History and character. Umbrella group of member senior staff associations in their dealings with government and employers.

Affiliated associations. Eighteen affiliated member associations. They are:

Agricultural and Allied Senior Staff Association
Automobile, Boatyard, Transport Equipment and Allied Senior staff Association (AUTOBATE)
Association of Senior Staff of Bank, Insurance and Financial Institutions
Chemical & Non-Metallic Products Senior Staff Association
Association of Senior Civil Servants of Nigeria
Construction and Civil Engineering Senior Association
Electricity and Gas Senior Staff Association
Food, Beverage and Tobacco Senior Staff Association
Footwear, Leather & Rubber Products Senior Staff Association
Nigeria Merchant Navy Officers and Water Transport Senior Staff
Metallic and Non-Metallic Mines Senior Staff Association
Petroleum & Natural Gas Senior Staff Association of Nigeria
Senior Staff Association of Shipping, Clearing & Forwarding Agencies
Shop and Distributive Trade Senior Staff Association
Senior Staff Association of Statutory Corporations and Government Owned Companies
Senior Staff Association of Universities, Teaching Hospitals, Research Institutions and Associated Institutions
Textile, Garment & Tailoring Senior Staff Association
Water Transport Senior Staff Association

SESCAN affiliates who supplied further information:

1. **Association of Senior Civil Servants of the Federation of Nigeria (ASCSN)**, 1–3, Odunlami Lane, Off Kakawa Street, P.O. Box 9908, Lagos.
   Phone: 01-635503.

2. **Association of Senior Staff of Banks, Insurance and Financial Institutions**, 64 Olonade Street, P.M.B. 2040, Yaba, Lagos.
   Phone: 01-861784.

3. **Automobile, Boatyards, Transport Equipment and Allied Senior Staff Association (AUTOBATE)**, 53 Western Avenue, Surulere, P.O. Box 253, Yaba, Lagos.
   Phone: 01-841686.

4. **Chemical and Non-Metallic Products Senior Staff Association (CNMPSSA)**, 51 Ijaye Road, Ogba, Ikeja, Lagos.
   Phone: 01-933786.

5. **Food, Beverage and Tobacco Senior Staff Association (FBTSSA)**, 48 Oguntolu Street, Shomolu, Lagos.
   Phone: 01-823905.

6. **Hotel and Personal Services Senior Staff Association (HPSSSA)**, Third Avenue, 'O' Close, House 9, P.O. Box 2032, Festac Town, Lagos.
   Phone: 01-881915.

7. **Senior Staff Association of Statutory Corporations and Government-Owned Companies (SSASSCGOC)**, 42 Ojekunle Street, Off Ladipo Street, Papa Ajao, P.O. Box 8767, Mushin, Lagos.
   Phone: 01-520859.

Professional unions

Academic Staff Union of Universities (ASUU)
National Association of Aircraft Pilots and Engineers
Nigerian Medical Association (NMA)
Nigerian Union of Professions Allied to Medicine

Norway

Capital: Oslo   **Population: 4,200,000**

Political system. Norway is a parliamentary democracy under a constitutional hereditary monarchy. Until September 1989 it was ruled by a minority Labour government. However, a general election in that month brought losses to the Labour and Conservative parties and a minority non-Socialist coalition was formed under the Conservative Prime Minister Jan Supe, to be succeeded in turn by a minority Labour government in November 1990.

Economy. Out of a civilian employment total of 2,110,000 in 1988, 1,430,000 were employed in services, 570,000 in industry, and 13,000 in agriculture. From 1986 Norway's governments pursued tight economic policies which had the effect of restricting domestic demand. In 1988 the New Incomes Regulation Act restricted hourly wage growth to 5 per cent. However, with unemployment rising to more than double its 1987 rate, policy switched to stimulation—through fiscal and labour market measures—in 1989, and growth was resumed that year and in 1990.

System of industrial relations. Norway ratified ILO Convention No. 87 (Freedom of Association and Protection of the Right to Organize, 1948) in 1949 and Convention No. 98 (Right to Organize and Collective Bargaining, 1949) in 1955.

Basic agreement. Relations between the LO and the employers' confederation (the Norsk Arbeidsgiverforening—NAF) are governed by the so-called "Basic Agreement" (*Hovedavtalen*), first drawn up in 1935 and periodically revised since then, which lays down a detailed framework for the conduct of industrial relations and the settlement of disputes. Through this agreement the employers recognize the right of the unions to speak and act for the workers and their own obligation to deal with the unions, while the unions accept the constraints of submitting to highly formalized negotiating procedures. These constraints include the so-called "duty of peace", which implies that the unions will not call strikes or disrupt production in a workplace while a collective bargaining agreement is in force. Since 1975 there has also been a framework agreement on the introduction of new technology, possibly the first agreement of its kind between a labour confederation and employers. There is in addition machinery establihed by the Labour Disputes Act, which provides for a Labour Court (of seven judges, three of whom are independent, with two each appointed by the LO and the NAF) and the office of a State Mediator. Unsuccessful negotiations may be submitted to the Labour Court, which hands down binding judgments. Collective bargaining occurs both between the LO and the NAF and also between the LO and its affiliates and other employers' groups; collective agreements are submitted to referendums of the membership.

The 1990 Central Wage Agreement between the LO and Norway's newly unified employers (NHO) was at first rejected by the LO membership in a ballot. Its final terms allowed for a wage increase of 4.27 per cent for around 350,000 private sector workers and included a clause allowing for re-opening of negotiations if prices exceeded 4.2 per cent during 1990. This agreement was intended to provided a framework for local agreements for a period of two years.

In 1986 Norway experienced its most dramatic upheavals in industrial relations for more than half a century, as strikes occurred for shorter hours and a minimum wage. Union success and political conciliation by Labour led to a subsidence of discontent, though not without the need for compulsory arbitration. In 1990 4,000 offshore workers staged a major strike over wages stimulated by fears that automation on platforms would cost jobs. Output of oil and gas was virtually cut off for the duration of the strike, which ended only when the government imposed compulsory arbitration in a provisional decree.

Trade unionism. In 1988, 60 per cent of Norway's civilian workforce were union members. The oldest trade union still in existence is the Oslo Union of Typographers, founded in 1872. The LO, the Norwegian Federation of Trade Unions, originated in 1899 and developed in effect as the trade union arm of the Labour Party. It is the sole central trade union organization.

By 1988 LO membership had reached a historical peak, matched by its influence with the then Labour government. However its representative position is threatened by the growth of alternative centres. While union density has not fallen, LO's share of the organized workforce dropped from 84.5 per cent in 1958 to 64.1 per cent 25 years later, and its own think-tank projects a 50 per cent share for the year 2006. In other respects changes in the membership of the LO reflect broad economic shifts: by the end of the 1980s, blue collar members—formerly the entire membership—accounted for only one third of it. The LO made administrative changes to stem the weakening of its position including an improved system of transfers, targetting of new industrial sectors and a consciousness-raising campaign among the young. Nevertheless it has not entirely succeeded in projecting a new identity which corresponds to such alterations of composition.

LO's political links, with the Labour Party, are of the strongest. It is represented on the Party's Central Committee, and perceived to wield great political power in its own right. A Co-operation Committee of the two meets weekly, and when Labour is in power the Prime Minister attends. These links can be controversial, as in 1989 when the LO–NHO central agreement was backed up by law to the consternation of many local union leaders who were not prepared to tolerate wage restraint to achieve the then Labour government's aims of reviving economic activity. It remains a very active figure on the international trade unions scene and conducts solidarity programmes with local unions in a large number of developing countries, often through the International Solidarity Committee of the Norwegian Labour Movement (AIS).

The LO's rivals, while gaining ground, do not have—or even aspire to—its coverage. The largest is the determinedly non-political Confederation of Norwegian Professional Associations (AF), though the equally non-partisan Confederation of Vocational Unions (YS) is not far behind it. The Federation of Offshore Oil Workers' Trade Unions, which mounted the 1990 strike is likewise independent and nearly two dozen other unions are unaffiliated to any centre.

Landsorganisasjonen i Norge (LO)
Norwegian Confederation of Trade Unions

Address. Youngsgata 11, 0181 Oslo 1
Phone. (2) 401050
Fax. (2) 401743

Telex. 19861 LONOR

Leadership. Yngve Hågensen (president); Esther Kostal (vice-president); Svein-Erik Oxholm (treasurer)

Membership. 786,000 in 28 unions (1990).

History. The LO (literally the "National Organization in Norway") was founded in 1899 and was initially known as the Arbeidernes Faglige Landsorganisasjon i Norge (Workers' Federation of Trade Unions in Norway). Its status was secured during the inter-war years and entrenched in the first of the Basic Agreements in 1935. Historically, the LO has maintained considerable central power over its affiliates.

Structure. The members of the LO are the national unions, whose representatives attend a policy-making congress every four years. There are inter-union trades councils in each county. Most blue-collar unions are, in accordance with an LO policy adopted in 1923, based on the industrial union principle (i.e. so that all workers in one plant are members of the same union); however, there are exceptions in the white-collar field. The ruling body is a quadrennial congress of 300 elected delegates and the 15 members of the executive board. The general council, which meets at least once a year in years when no congress is held, comprises 100 representatives elected by the national unions, 19 representatives elected from the counties and the 15 members of the executive board; the executive board is composed of the president, vice-president, general treasurer and first secretary and representatives of the national unions, and usually meets on a weekly basis.

Union	*Membership figure*
The Labour Press Union	897
Norwegian Union of Supervisors and Technical Employees	16,091
Norwegian Union of General Workers	34,700
Norwegian Union of Child Welfare Workers	1,954
Norwegian Union of Electricians and Power Station Workers	27,865
The Norwegian United Federation of Trade Unions	174,004
Norwegian Union of Prison Officials	2,254
Norwegian Graphical Union	14,983
Norwegian Union of Employees in Commerce and Offices	57,847
Norwegian Union of Hotel and Restaurant Workers	16,562
Norwegian Union of Railwaymen	21,209
Norwegian Union of Cantors and Organists	772
Norwegian Union of Chemical Industry Workers	36,049
Norwegian Union of Municipal Employees	197,468
Norwegian Union of Locomotivemen	2,470
Norwegian Union of Musicians	2,194
Norwegian Union of Military Officers	4,197
Norwegian Oil and Petrochemical Union	7,625
Norwegian Union of Food and Allied Workers	35,071
The Norwegian Postal Organization ⎫	
Norwegian Union of Postmen ⎭	30,427
Norwegian Seamen's Union	10,265
Norwegian Union of School Employees	3,230
Norwegian Union of Social Workers	4,393
Norwegian Union of Data and Telecommunications Workers	16,761
Norwegian Union of Government Employees	43,160
Norwegian Union of Transport Workers	16,230
Norwegian Union of Woodworkers	5,150
Norwegian Union of Social Care Personnel	2,144

Policies. Broadly social democratic on the western European model, stressing full employment policies, lowering of the retirement age, sexual equality, freedom and independence of the trade union movement. A particular issue in recent years has been equalizing the working hours of blue-collar and white-collar workers (see above). The 1985 congress (the 26th) resolved to introduce "gender-neutral" titles for LO officers and to emphasize the appointment of women to leadership positions within the union movement, but rejected a proposal to introduce a quota for the election of women to the LO governing bodies. (One-third of LO members are women.) The LO has favoured Norwegian membership of NATO but has called for a nuclear weapons-free zone in northern Europe. The emergence of Yngve Hågensen as President at the 27th Congress in 1989 was widely seen as symbolizing an orientation towards private sector trade unionism.

The LO operates a workers' educational association (AOF) and there is a People's Correspondence School, owned jointly by the labour movement and the co-operatives. The LO is a co-owner of an insurance company. The Tiden Norsk Forlag is a publishing house owned by the labour movement and publishing a wide variety of literature. The trade union movement has also for more than 50 years had its own bank, the Landsbanken A/S. The Framfylkingen is a children's organization within the labour movement.

The LO supports the Labour Party (Arbeiderpartiet). Many unions previously took out collective party memberships, and although this practice has declined, the organizational and financial links remain strong. However, the Labour Party's main source of income is not the unions but the state subsidy paid to all parties based primarily on their share of the vote at the previous election. The LO's president always sits on the central board of the Party, and the LO customarily has representation in Labour governments.

Publication. LO Aktuelt.

International affiliations. ICFTU; ETUC; Nordic Trade Union Council; TUAC.

Other national centres

Akademikernes Fellesorganisasjon (AF)
Confederation of Norwegian Professional Associations

Membership: 40 unions representing 194,848 members of which the largest is the Norwegian Nurses Associaton with 38,985 members.

Yrkesorganisatjonenes Sentralforbund (YS)
Confederation of Vocational Unions

Membership: 17 unions representing 172,588 members of which the largest is the National Bank Employees Union with 31,075 members.

Oljearbeidernes Fellessammenslutning (OFS)
Federation of Offshore Oil Workers' Trade Unions

Membership: 4 unions with a total membership of 5,500.

Unaffiliated unions

A total of 23 unaffiliated unions may be indentified. The largest is the Norwegian Teachers Union (Norsk Laererlag) with 58,919 members, but most are much smaller.

Oman

Capital: Muscat   **Population 1,486,000**

Political system. The Sultanate of Oman is ruled by decree of the Sultan. There are no political parties and there is no parliament but in November 1990 the Sultan announced the creation of a new Consultative Council of provincial representatives.

Economy. Oman's economy is almost exclusively dependent on the production and exportation of crude oil. Oman is a net importer of food. Only 1 per cent of the land is cultivated.

Some 50 per cent of the Omani workforce was engaged in agriculture (mostly subsistence) in 1985–87, 21.8 per cent in industry, and 28.6 per cent in services. Under the fourth Five Year Plan (for 1991–95) budget deficits are to be limited to 10 per cent of revenue, funds are to be locally raised, and privatization is to begin.

System of industrial relations. Oman is not a member of the ILO.

Trade unionism. Trade unions are not legal and there is no indication of any significant organizational activity within the country, although the WFTU in the late 1980s did recognize an organization based in Yemen.

National Committee of Omani Workers

Address. P.O. Box 5044, Maala, Aden, Yemen
Leadership. Ahmed Salim Kassim
International affiliations. WFTU.

Pakistan

Political system. With the victory of the centre-left Pakistan People's Party (PPP) led by Benazir Bhutto in the elections of November 1988 Pakistan was set to return to a democratic form of government after 11 years of martial law under General Zia ul-Haq who led the military *coup* in 1977 which overthrew the government of Miss Bhutto's father, Zulfiquar Ali Bhutto.

However, following accusations of corruption, Miss Bhutto was dismissed as Prime Minister late in 1990 by the President of Pakistan in a move backed by the military. A new government under Nawaz Sharif was installed.

Economy. Pakistan's economy is primarily agricultural, with rice and cotton as the main agricultural exports. Since 1979 it has shown strong growth, and in the fifth Five-Year Plan 1983–1988 there has been an increased role for the private sector. However, Pakistan has a severe foreign debt burden and receives aid from the World Bank, the Asian Development Bank and the IMF for infrastructural purposes.

Out of a 1988 civilian workforce of 29,600,000, 5,990,000 were engaged in industry, 14,570,000 in agriculture, and 9,030,000 in services.

Pakistan's problems are aggravated by the rapid expansion of the workforce, growing at perhaps 1,000,000 annually. As a result unemployment probably far exceeds the 3–4 per cent estimated by the government and may be as high as 20 per cent. Meanwhile the number of Pakistanis working abroad probably exceeds 1,500,000. At home there is a lack of job opportunities for graduates and unskilled alike, while the country lacks for literate workers able to fill clerical and administrative posts. The PPP announced in 1989 a programme of support for sick industries and employment creation was the centrepiece of the Seventh Five Year Plan (1988–93). All recent Pakistan governments have looked to the rural areas to promote employment, but Nawaz Sharif also proposes to privatize 115 state firms by 1992.

System of industrial relations. Trade unions have been subject to periods of repression and government intervention throughout Pakistan's history, and were weakened by the loss of East Pakistan (a stronghold of militancy) as Bangladesh in the early 1970s.

Numerous restrictions were placed on trade union activity under martial law from 1977, when strikes and some unions were banned. Regulations were eased following the lifting of martial law in December 1985, but a number of restrictions still remained in force: trade union organization and collective bargaining continued to be prohibited in public sector enterprises such as the Pakistan Television Corporation, Pakistan Broadcasting Corporation, Pakistan International Airlines, hospitals, schools and nationalized banks, while the trade union rights of workers in utilities—including petrol and gas, harbours and transport—remained restricted by the Essential Services (Maintenance) Act of 1952.

Although the 1969 Industrial Relations Act provides for collective bargaining, it is not uncommon for employers to maintain their own controlled unions, and in some cases, to refuse to recognize a bargaining agent. There restrictive practices co-exist with others including unjust contracts and child labour, both of which were singled out for abolition by delegates at the conference of the ICFTU-affiliated All Pakistan Federation of Trade

351

Unions (APFTU) in April 1988. Delegates at the conference also stressed the need to recognize workers' rights to better health and safety standards, retirement benefits and participation in decision-making bodies.

Discrimination against women at work has also commanded the attention of Pakistani trade unions. In September 1987, at a trade union seminar organized by the APFTU participants from a variety of different trade unions called, among other things, for more employment opportunities for women in the industrial and commercial sectors; day-care centres near the workplace, and the provision of low interest loans to rural women to establish income-generating activities. In August 1988, the WFTU-linked All Pakistan Trade Union Federation (APTUF) also joined in the campaign for the repeal of all legislation which discriminated against women.

Trade unions are represented on a range of government bodies, including the National Tripartite Labour Body, and there is an Industrial Relations Commission to hear unfair labour practices cases.

Pakistan ratified ILO Convention No. 87 (Freedom of Association and Protection of the Right to Organize, 1948) in 1951 and Convention No. 98 (Right to Organize and Collective Bargaining, 1949) in 1952.

More recently, however, the ILO's *Report of the Committee of Experts on the Application of Conventions and Recommendation (1988)* has drawn the attention of the government of Pakistan to practices which it deems to be inconsistent with the principles of ILO Convention Nos. 87 and 98. These refer, among other things, to the government's continued restrictions upon the right of certain workers to organize trade unions, bargain collectively, or resort to strikes. In addition, the Committee has also reminded the government of its obligations under Conventions Nos. 29 and 105 on Forced Labour, ratified in 1957 and 1961 respectively, which deny it the right to exercise such discretionary powers as have resulted, in some cases, in imprisonment with compulsory labour, or to allow the use of bonded labour, including that of children, such as has been alleged in the construction of dams and irrigation canals in remote rural areas. The Committee has also called upon the government to amend the Pakistan Essential Services (Maintenance) Act on the grounds that it is in contravention of Convention No. 105 on the Abolition of Forced Labour ratified by Pakistan in 1960. Finally, the Committee has taken strong exception to the Government's Anti-Islamic Activities Ordnance, 1984, which it believes, discriminates against some religious groups like the Quadianis, by denying them equal access to employment in contravention of Convention No. 111 (Discrimination—Employment and Occupation—Convention), ratified by Pakistan in 1961.

The PPP came to power pledged to restore all unions, bring Pakistan into conformity with ILO Conventions, eliminate contract labour, reinstate those dismissed for political reasons, and raise the minimum wage. The reinstatement process began in 1989 and a review of the minimum wage was set in train. On May Day 1989 it was announced that unions would be restored at Pakistan International Airlines, and at the state broadcasting and printing services, but such steps required legislation and in any case fell short of the general liberalization which had been promised. A tripartite consultative process was inaugurated though this was not in itself new: the PPP pledged itself to establish a full national tripartite structure. Nevertheless the ICFTU-affiliated PNFTU called at the start of 1990 for an ILO mission to Pakistan to investigate the behaviour of multinationals which were bypassing the very limited protections afforded employees under the law. In February 1991 a number of union leaders were arrested following their strong opposition to government plans of privatization.

Trade unionism. In 1949 there was founded an All Pakistan Confederation of Labour (APCOL) with affiliates in East and West Pakistan and which adhered to the ICFTU. In 1962 dissatisfied affiliates of APCOL, notably the Petroleum Workers' Federation and the

Cigarette Labour Union, formed the Pakistan National Federation of Trade Unions (PNFTU) with 59 member unions at that time. A further series of splits in APCOL led to it losing its ICFTU affiliation while the PNFTU gained ICFTU affiliated status in 1964. APCOL's component parts each claimed the name West Pakistan Federation of Trade Unions simultaneously until one faction changed its name to the All Pakistan Federation of Trade Unions (APFTU) and it too affiliated to the ICFTU. The third contemporary ICFTU affiliate is the All Pakistan Federation of Labour (APFOL). When its President Rahmatullah Khan Durrani died the Presidency was claimed by his son Auranzeb. This succession was challenged and Auranzeb seceded to found a federation known as APFOL, Durrani Group. The remainder registered under the original name of APFOL, and when the ICFTU upheld its affiliation the Durrani group affiliated to the WFTU.

At the end of the 1980s, trade union density was perhaps 3 per cent in Pakistan. Some 6,000 unions and around 1,000 federations were registered, but of these perhaps only 10 were serious national centres. Attempts at unity between the major national centres have been made from time to time, in 1986 and again in 1988, but these have not succeeded. As a result Pakistan still has three ICFTU affiliates (APFOL, APFTU, PNFTU), three of the WFTU (APFOL Durrani Group, APTUF and PTUF) and one of the WCL (APTUC). APTUF claims to be the oldest federation in the country, founded shortly after partition; APFOL recently defected from its ICFTU affiliation to join the WFTU.

All Pakistan Federation of Labour (APFOL)

Address. Islamabad

History and character. With the secession of the Durrani Group, the rump retained the name APFOL and succeeded in keeping ICFTU affiliation. In 1988, Rahmatullah Chowdry, who had disputed the leadership with Auranzeb Durrani, and assumed the office of general secretary, died.

All Pakistan Federation of Labour (APFOL—Durrani Group)

Address. Labour Hall, Pakistan Hotel, Khyber Bazar Peshawar

Phone. 0521-214530

Cable. APFOL

Leadership. Auranzeb Durrani (president); Sabir Farhat (secretary-general)

Membership. Claims 293,000 in 216 unions and eight federations.

History and character. The APFOL was founded in 1955 under the leadership of Rehmat Ullah Khan Durrani, who remained president until his death on Nov. 21, 1985, when he was succeeded by his son Aurangzai Durrani. The APFOL claim be the largest and most representative labour organization currently in existence in Pakistan. Durrani was elected President of the Pakistan Labour Party at a meeting held at Peshawar in February 1986. Since then, the APFOL has suffered a split resulting in the creation of a minority rival group, also registered as the APFOL.

Publication. Annual Report of Federation Activities.

International affiliation. WCFTU, joined after the ICFTU continued to accept the affiliation of APFOL.

All Pakistan Federation of Trade Unions (APFTU)

Address. Bakhtiar Labour Hall, 28 Nisbat Road, Lahore

Phone. 222192; 229419

Cable. PAKFED

Leadership. Bashir Ahmed Bakhtiar (president); Khurshid Ahmed (general secretary).

Membership. 601,200 in 825 affiliated unions (1988).

History and character. The West Pakistan Federation of Labour was founded on Dec. 20, 1947, following the establishment of Pakistan, and was part of the All Pakistan Confederation of Labour. The organization was subsequently renamed first as the West Pakistan Federation of Trade Unions and then, following the secession of East Pakistan (Bangladesh), as the All Pakistan Federation of Trade Unions. The current president, Bashir Ahmed Bakhtiar, was a co-founder in 1947. The APFTU describes itself as an independent trade union without political links, and seeks to unify the trade union movement to press the government to formulate labour policy in conformity with ILO Conventions No. 87 and No. 98, including the repeal of the Essential Services Act and the restoration of trade union rights to public sector employees. The federation has a workers' education programme for training in collective bargaining and organization, and also has women's and youth sections. The APFTU held its 26th Conference in April 1988, and has recently established Pakistan's first-ever Institute for Education and Training which provides for the training and residence of trade union representatives.

Publication. PAK Workers (fortnightly, in English and Urdu).

International affiliation. ICFTU/APRO.

All Pakistan Trade Union Congress (APTUC)

Address. 1st Floor, Delhi Muslim Hotel, Arambagh Road, P.O. Box 1004, Karachi.
Phone. (21) 210359
Cable. APTUC-PAK KARACHI
Leadership. A. H. Shirazi (president); M. L. Shahani (vice-president)
Membership. 30,715 in 15 affiliated unions (1988).
History and character. The APTUC was founded in 1973. It supports free and independent trade unionism regardless of caste, creed, colour and religion, and emphasizes education activity directed at improving trade union organization and at teaching skills to groups such as women heading one-parent families in self-help schemes. The APTUC established a "Service Centre" in 1980 which provides assistance to workers, regardless of whether affiliated to the APTUC, and its projects include a low-cost housing scheme. A policy report issued at the first national convention (held in 1982) stated that the APTUC has "undeterred faith in the reality that Almighty God created man and this universe and that man has a spiritual as well as material nature, and eternal and temporal purpose.... The APTUC rejects all concepts of man that deny his free and responsible nature, consequently it rejects materialist, determinist and extreme liberal philosophies, specifically dialectical materialism and rugged individualism, as incomplete ...". The report called for "social and responsible onwership of the means of production and distribution; democratic participation in the process of production; just distribution and utilization of the fruits of production and services; democratic planning of the entire political and economic structure", but noted that "the question as to how a movement fully catering to the national requirements of the country could be organized, remains to be answered in the light of the resources at our disposal and the general conditions obtaining in the country". The APTUC has no political affiliation.

Publication. APTUC News Bulletin (monthly).

International affiliations. WCL; BATU.

All Pakistan Trade Union Federation (APTUF)

Address. Peoples Building, Farid Kot Road, Lahore
Leadership. Wali Mohammad (president); Ch. Gulzat Ahmad (general secretary)
Membership. 170,000 claimed.
History and character. APTUF was established soon after partition.
Affiliated unions. Over 100 including two railway unions, the Wyth Laboratories Workers' Union, the Peco Workers's Union, the Beco Workers' Union, the Millat Tractor Workers' Union, the Wasa Workers' Union and the LBA Workers' Union.
Publication. Monthly circular in Urdu.
International affiliation. WFTU (affiliated 1987).

Pakistan National Federation of Trade Unions (PNFTU)

Address. 406 Qamar House, M. A. Jinnah Road, Karachi 27
Phone. (21) 200990; 200535; 628726

Leadership. Mohammad Sharif (president); Rashid Mohammad (secretary-general)

Membership. 150,000 (about 5,000 women) in 216 affiliated unions. Most affiliated unions are based on one enterprise, with a high turnover.

History and character. The PNFTU was founded in September 1962 by 59 unions with a membership of 23,000. Its policy has been that union office holders should themselves be workers in the industry they represent. It is politically independent and pursues the policies of free trade unionism.

The PNFTU called a one-day general strike in March 1986 in protest at the level of cost-of-living allowances and at the remaining restrictions on freedom of association and collective bargaining.

Affiliates.

1. **Pakistan Petroleum Workers' Federation** (four unions).

2. **Chemical and Pharmaceutical Group** (10 unions).

3. **Food and Allied Industries Group** (16 unions).

4. **Pakistan Insurance Employees' Federation** (17 unions).

5. **Pakistan Bank Employees' Federation Lahore** (32 unions).

6. **Automobile, Engineering and Metal Workers' Federation** (45 unions).

7. **Transport and Dock Workers** (13 unions).

8. **Textile, Garment and Leather Workers** (10 unions).

9. **Building and Wood Works** (one union).

10. **General Unions** (13 unions).

11. **Agriculture and Rural Workers' Organization of Pakistan** (14 unions).

The PNFTU also has affiliated to it the Pakistan Teachers' Associations Council (PTOC) which has eight associations in membership. Teachers cannot form unions as such under the 1969 Ordinance.

Publication. PNFTU News.

International affiliation. ICFTU/APRO.

Pakistan Trade Union Federation (PTUF)

Address. KMC Building, Khamosh Colony, Karachi 18

Leadership. Fatima Kaniz (president)

International affiliation. WFTU.

Panama

Capital: Panama City   **Population: 2,250,000**

Political system. Although nominally a parliamentary democracy until the end of military rule in 1987, Panama was ruled until 1989 by the commander of the Panamanian Defence Forces, Gen. Manuel Antonio Noriega Morena, who in February 1988 used his own supporters to overthrow the nominal head of state, President Eric Arturo Delvalle and replaced him with his own appointee.

In December 1989 American forces invaded Panama and deposed General Noriega, who was taken to the United States to face drugs charges. Guillermo Endara, the victor in the May 1989 election (which Noriega had refused to acknowledge) was installed in his place.

Economy. The financial pressure brought to bear on Panama by the USA following Gen. Noriega's *de facto* assumption of power in February 1988 and the government's resulting inability to pay salaries brought it into sharp conflict with public employees and exacerbated the problems of structural change and austerity measures necessitated under the IMF Structural Adjustment Programme for the period 1983–8.

System of industrial relations. Trade unions were recognized under the 1946 Constitution, and Panama ratified ILO Convention No. 87 (Freedom of Association and Protection of the Right to Organize, 1948) in 1958 and Convention No. 98 (Right to Organize and Collective Bargaining, 1949) in 1966. There have been repeated revisions of the labour code in recent years. The code was amended in 1981 to confirm the right to strike. Further amendments adopted in March 1986, and which were opposed by the trade unions, included the exclusion of home workers from the scope of labour laws, restrictions on overtime pay rates, and changes in the method of calculating benefits. Public servants are excluded from the protection of the labour code and thereby denied collective bargaining rights. The *Report of the Committee of Experts on the Application of Conventions and Recommendations (1988)* noted that the government had still to reply to queries on its failure to uphold Convention No. 122 (Employment Policy, 1964, ratified in 1970), Convention No. 105 (Abolition of Forced Labour, 1957, ratified in 1966) and Convention No. 29 (Forced Labour, 1930, ratified in 1966) which cover, respectively, the absence of any official and comprehensive employment plan; the imprisonment and forced labour of seafarers for leaving their vessels before completion of a contract; and the power conferred on police chiefs as administrative authorities to impose penalties, including labour on public works and detention under section 873 of the Administrative Code. The impact of the US economic boycott had resulted in an estimated 50,000 job losses by June 1988. Luis Anderson, general secretary of the ICFTU's Inter-American Regional Organization (ORIT), in April 1988, urged the USA "to allow the Panamanians themselves, using their sovereign rights, to settle their differences and progress towards a democratic regime that is authentically representative and participative".

The arrival of United States forces in December 1989 however brought little relief to Panama's trade unions who continued to complain of the harassment they had suffered under General Noriega. Two leaders of the CNTP, Maurice Maurillo and Gustavo Martinez were arrested, together with Juvenal Jimenez of the Banana Workers' Union on Dec. 29. ORIT also lodged protests against a wave of what it deemed unfair dismissals of CTRP members, notably those employed by the Gran Morrison chain. An ICFTU delegation in February 1990 uttered warnings that the process of rooting out Noriega supporters should not be taken advantage of in order to dismantle unions or exclude them from the reconstruction process. It singled out Decree Nr 1 whereby civil servants alleged to have connived in the Noriega dictatorship might be arbitrarily dismissed.

In the Spring of 1990, the WFTU-affiliated National Federation of State Employees complained of the dismissal of some 1,000 public sector trade unionists; another WFTU affiliate, the National Press Trade Union protested at the continued detention of its General Secretary and other officials. The fears of trade unionists were not assuaged however, and discontent mounted, culminating in a general strike in December. The government retaliated with further public sector sackings and the Panamanian Congress gave consideration to a law which would give official sanction to the dismissal of trade unionists.

Trade unionism. The three national trade union centres have rival affiliations to the ICFTU, WFTU and WCL, but have co-operated with each other in the co-ordinating organization, CONATO. The latter, in March 1988, joined in the formation of the United Popular Front (FPU) with student, peasant and other popular groups to resist what it saw as the threat of US aggression and intervention.

Co-ordinating organization

Consejo Nacional de Trabajadores Organizados (CONATO)
National Council of Organized Workers

Leadership. Norma Múñez Montoto (president); Eduardo Ríos (co-ordinator)

Membership. Is supported by the CIT, CNTP and CTRP.

History and character. The CONATO was established as a central body by the three trade union centres CIT, CNTP and CTRP in 1970 to avert a government-imposed unification of the trade union movement, but its member organizations have retained their autonomy. The CONATO was active in opposing austerity measures and changes to the labour code demanded by the IMF and the World Bank. A general striked called by the CONATO for March 10, 1986, had considerable impact in industry, electricity supply and telecommunications.

Trade union centres

Central Istmeña de Trabajadores (CIT)
Isthmian Labour Confederation

Address. Vía España, No. 16 Oficiana 1, Panamá

Leadership. Julio César Pinzón (secretary-general)

Membership. 19,000 (46 per cent women) in 1984 in eight member federations (FENTIMICOP, FENAT, COS, FITLATEVEC, FITAR, FIT, FNTT, FENATRACAS), which themselves had a total of 46 member unions.

History and character. The CIT was founded on July 24, 1971 (succeeding other Christian trade union centres dating back to 1959), and is social Christian in orientation. It recruits in all fields, emphasizes the autonomy of its member federations, and does not permit the intrusion of party or church politics into its activities.

Publication. Information bulletin.

International affiliations. WCL; CLAT

Central Nacional de Trabajadores de Panamá (CNTP)
National Centre of Panamanian Workers

Address. Av 15-85 Altos, Apartado 3253, Panamá 3

Phone. 627457

Cables. CNTP PANAMA

Leadership. Domingo Barria; Jose Florencio de Gracia Gil (deputy general secretary)

Membership. 22,000.

History and character. The CNTP was founded in 1970 in succession to the previous Trade Union Federation of Workers of Panama (FSTP), itself formed in 1939.

International affiliation. WFTU.

Confederacíon de Trabajadores de la República de Panamá (CTRP)
Conferation of Workers of the Republic of Panama

Address. Calle 31 No. 3-50, Apartado 8929, Zona 5, Panamá

Phone. 250293

Telex. 0378/2216 CTRP PA

Cable. CONTRAPA
Fax. 250259
Leadership. Aniano Pinzón Real (secretary-general)
Membership. 35,000 claimed in 13 federations: FENATRAMET; FENDEPETROSID; FITTTAMPS; FETRACELAP; FENATRACOVAP; FNTD; FISITRPROCEN; FESICIP; FENATRACOMAP; FITABHA; FECHISIO; SINABAN; SINATRATC. These federations cover 56 different unions.
History. Founded 1956.
International affiliations. ICFTU; ORIT.
Publications. *CTRP en Marcha*

Papua New Guinea

Capital: Port Moresby

Population: 3,804,000

Political system. Papua New Guinea is a parliamentary democracy and has been an independent member of the Commonwealth since 1975. Political party allegiances are fluid; a coalition led by Mr Rabbie Namaliu of the *Pangu Pati* is currently in power.

Economy. Mineral extraction accounts for the largest element in Papua New Guinea's GDP, with the exploitation of the newly discovered gold and oil resources expected to compensate for the declining production from existing copper and gold mines. Two-thirds of the population are employed in agriculture, which is mainly at subsistence level.

System of industrial relations. Papua New Guinea ratified ILO Convention No. 98 (Right to Organize and Collective Bargaining, 1949) in 1976 but has not ratified Convention No. 87 (Freedom of Association and Protection of the Right to Organize, 1948).

Trade unionism. Trade unions enjoy legal status and there is a trade union centre, the PNGTUC.

The ICFTU and its regional agency APRO have played an important part in rationalizing the trade union movement in Papua New Guinea. The key development was the transformation of the PNGTUC into a genuine national centre, which inadequate resources prevented before the middle of the 1980s. A new (ICFTU/APRO-drafted) constitution was adopted in 1986 which *inter alia* raised affiliation fees, and in October of that year the 30,000 strong Public Employees' Association joined, bringing a new impetus. Since that date the PNGTUC has developed into a genuine national centre.

Papua New Guinea Trade Union Congress (PNGTUC)

Address. P.O. Box 4729, Boroko
Phone. 256041
Leadership. John Dumit (president); Lawrence Titumur (general secretary)
Membership. 60,000.
History and character. The PNGTUC was formed in 1970 after the failure of several previous attempts to establish a trade union centre. Membership of the PNGTUC increased from 12 affiliates with 17,000 members in 1986 to 30 affiliates with 60,000 members in June 1988. The PNGTUC held its third delegate conference in Waigani in July 1988. At the conference John Dumit, president of the Bougainville Copper Limited National Staff Association, was elected to replace Henry Moses as

PNGTUC president. Rabbie Namaliu, the Prime Minister of Papua New Guinea, addressed the conference. He pledged that he would strengthen workers' pension rights, increase share ownership by workers, and introduce more union representation on statutory bodies. He also said that he would examine the ratification of ILO conventions on maternity leave, rural workers' organizations, and dismissals, and would review the country's labour legislation.

International affiliation. ICFTU/APRO.

Paraguay

Capital: Asunción   **Population: 4,000,000**
                                                                            (1988)

Political system. Nominally a multi-party democracy, the Republic of Paraguay was ruled by the right-wing military regime of General Alfredo Stroessner under a "state of siege" from 1954 until his overthrow in a military *coup* in February 1989.

Economy. The Paraguayan economy is based on agriculture, fisheries and forestry which together account for 40 per cent of the labour force, contributing 30 per cent of the GDP and 99 per cent of all declared exports. It has one of the region's lowest foreign debt levels.

System of industrial relations. The Paraguayan Constitution guarantees the right to meet and associate as does the 1962 Labour Code, and Paraguay ratified ILO Convention No. 87 (Freedom of Association and Protection of the Right to Organize, 1948) in 1962 and Convention No. 98 (Right to Organize and Collective Bargaining, 1949) in 1966. However, by law public sector workers may only associate for social and cultural purposes and strikes are prohibited in a wide range of public services, including banks, transport and fuel distribution. Strikes may not be called in any sector without exhausting protracted conciliation and arbitration procedures, which in the view of the ILO *Report of the Committee of Experts on the Application of Convention and Recommendations (1985)* "appears to prevent all recourse to strikes", and workers who stop work during these procedures may be dismissed without compensation. Government controlled *garroteros* ("clubbers") were used to break a hospital strike in 1986.

Despite the participation of 3,000 MIT trade unionists in a celebratory march following the overthrow of General Stroessner—the first such legal opportunity they had had for many years—his departure did not lead automatically to the relaxation of industrial relations disciplines. A number of trade unionists were arrested during 1989, and in one instance an entire workforce was dismissed for engaging in a strike. The ICFTU collected evidence that the names of those trade unionists dismissed—the *despedidos*—were being circulated on blacklists among employers. In October 1989 it lodged a complaint about Paraguay at the ILO.

Trade unionism. Trade unions faced considerable harassment after Stroessner came to power in 1954, but independent trade unionism developed significantly in the 1980s and the Inter-Trade Union Movement of Paraguayan Workers (MIT-P) was founded in 1985 to unite opposition to the regime. Trade union activists were frequently detained and there were regular reports of torture at the hands of the police and armed forces; the most brutal harassment occurred in the rural areas, as in most Latin American countries. Many trade union activists were exiled following the 1958 general strike (the last general strike in Paraguay) and there is a Paraguayan Movement of Unity and Trade Union Action in Exile (UNASE). According to the WFTU, Antonio Maidana, the exiled leader of the teachers' association and First Secretary of the Communist Party of Paraguay, who was a leading figure in the 1958 strike, was abducted from Argentina to Paraguay by the regime in 1980 and disappeared without trace.

In August 1989, Paraguay's union confederations jointly announced the formation of a United Workers' Centre, the CUT.

Movimiento Intersindical de Trabajadores de Paraguay (MIT-P)
Inter-Trade Union Movement of Paraguayan Workers

History and character. The MIT-P (or MIT) was established on May 1, 1985, to unite trade union opposition to the regime. A priority has been the demand for an increase in the minimum wage. It staged a demonstration on May 1, 1986, which was broken up by the police with several hundred arrests, and another to celebrate Stroessner's overthrow.

Publication. Clandestine monthly magazine.

International affiliation. None, but is supported by both the ICFTU and the WCL. The ILO transferred recognition from the official CPT to the MIT-P in July 1985.

Other unions

Confederacíon Paraguaya de Trabajadores (CPT)
Paraguayan Confederation of Workers

Address. Calle Yegros no 1333, Y Simón Bolívar, Asunción

Phone. 72434; 443184

Leadership. Julio Etcheverry Espinola (executive secretary-general)

Membership. Claimed 83,500 at the end of 1990.

History and character. The CPT was founded in 1951 under the influence of the Colorado Party; independent elements gained control during the 1950s, however, and led a general strike in 1958. Following this many trade unionists were exiled, forming a CPT in exile (CPT-E), while the organization within the country was brought firmly under government control; it was described in the ICFTU's *Free Labour World* in April 1986 as the "government-controlled completely discredited official labour federation". The CPT is now functioning again in Paraguay after its years of exile in Mexico and elsewhere.

Publications. *Revista CPT* (bi-monthly); *Periódico CPT* (monthly); weekly information bulletins.

International affiliation. The CPT was affiliated to the ICFTU/ORIT until 1974, when its affiliation was suspended.

Co-ordinación Nacional de Trabajadores (CNT)
National Workers' Co-ordination

Address. Calle Piribebuy 1078, Entre Hernán Darías y Colón, Asunción

Leadership. Juan Manuel Peralta (secretary-general)

History and character. The CNT originated in 1963 as the Christian Workers' Centre (CCT), taking its present name in 1978. Its associated agrarian leagues were active in the countryside with the support of sections of the clergy, but many of the leagues were broken up by the government in the mid-1970s and in 1977, 21 CNT leaders were arrested and tortured. The CNT is active in the Inter-Trade Union Movement of Paraguayan Workers.

International affiliations. WCL; CLAT.

Peru

Capital: Lima

Population: 20,681,000

Political system. In 1980, the Republic of Peru returned to parliamentary government after 13 years of military rule. It is a multi-party state. The stability of the centre-left Peruvian Aprista Party (PAP) which came to power in 1985 is threatened on the one hand by the subversive activities of the Maoist guerrilla movement, *Sendero Luminoso*, and on the other by economic decline.

Alan García was succeeded as President in July 1990 by Alberto Fujimori who had defeated the candidate of the Fredemo Coalition of the Right, the novelist Mario Vargas Llosa. The new administration proved no more effective in dealing with insurgency than the old, which had been unable to prevent 15,000 Peruvians losing their lives to terror in the seven years to 1990 and 3,000 disappearing. In 1989 alone there had been more than 2,400 killings, but in 1991 Sendero Luminoso (Shining Path) were still able to maintain a regular sequence of terrorist acts.

Economy. Out of the labour force of 5,370,000 in 1989, 770,000 Peruvians found employment in industry, 2,600,000 in agriculture, and 2,000,000 in services. Minerals and fisheries accounted for 66 per cent of the country's export earnings during that year. The García administration adopted an interventionist approach to Peru's economic problems, funding subsidies and public sector employment in preference to servicing Peru's massive external debt. In 1986 Peru was declared ineligible for IMF support because of its overdue obligations to the Fund. The use of price controls to handle inflation turned out to be a failure, and by May 1989 prices were raising at 30 per cent a month. The economy stagnated the same year, and so with a fast expanding workforce it was inevitable that unemployment would rise: the official estimate of 15 per cent unemployed in 1989 must be set against estimates of underemployment in excess of 50 per cent.

Though the election of Fujimori appeared at first to mean that the monetarist proposals of Vargas Llosa would be shelved, the new administration did introduce a severe programme of anti-inflationary policies—after a brief delay—in August 1990. This had the effect of pushing up prices and depressing retail and commercial activity. The new President renewed contacts with the IMF and in March 1991 under its aegis he introduced the most sweeping liberal reforms of the economy for 40 years. Nevertheless Peru's external debt in 1991 amounted to $22,000 million.

System of industrial relations. Peru ratified ILO Convention No. 87 (Freedom of Association and Protection of the Right to Organize,1948) in 1960 and Convention No. 98 (Right to Organize and Collective Bargaining, 1949) in 1964. The *Report of the Committee of Experts on the Application of Conventions and Recommendations (1988)* comments favourably on the application of Conventions Nos. 111 and 29 (Discrimination, Employment and Occupation, 1958, ratified 1970; Forced Labour, 1930, ratified 1960) which, respectively, allow employees redress under the Stable Employment Act (No. 24514, May 31, 1986) for political or trade union, religious or sexual harassment at work, and repeals the Vagrancy Act (No. 4981, Jan. 18, 1924) whereby it was deemed a political offence for people to live in another's house as if it were their own and live off the tolerance and complacence of another.

Further repression followed a move to the right in the military government in 1975, and there was widespread industrial unrest in the late 1970s. The right to organize and to strike was extended to public servants in the 1980 Constitution, with a number of restrictions. Legislation passed in June 1986 and made retroactive to July 28, 1985 (i.e. the commencement of civilian government) strengthened workers' job security; however, relations between the new government and the unions have been affected by the difficult economic situation, and a 24-hour strike was staged by public sector workers in January 1987 in protest against government plans to extend working hours, and to demand an increase in pay and the reinstatement of dismissed workers. The second half of 1987 witnessed long strikes against the government's auterity measures, the CGTP spearheading a campaign to reject government wage offers aimed at ending strikes by 17 public and private sector unions. (The state plays a decisive role in wage fixing in both the public and private sectors.)

Under the García administration there was a general strike in 1987 and four general strikes in 1988, all led by the CGTP with varying degrees of support from other confederations, around a radical political agenda. The 12 months of 1988 were in any case a record strike year for Peru: 38,000,000 working hours were lost by nearly 700,000 people in 619 strikes culminating in miners' strikes at the end of the year and the beginning of 1989. The latter period brought no general strikes but there were major disputes in the public sector.

The Fujimori programme instituted following the changeover of administrations was greeted by union demonstrations and a general strike—declared illegal—in August 1990; each was savagely treated. In the second phase of the programme (March 1991) the long-standing labour stability law was re-framed in order to ease the ability of companies to shed labour.

Trade unionism. Trade union activities gained strength in the 1920s, assisted by the rise of the populist APRA movement, and a Marxist-influenced General Confederation of Peruvian Workers (CGTP) was established in 1929. However, the trade unions were suppressed in the 1930s, a time of violent labour unrest, and remained generally weak until the early 1970s, with intervals of repression.

Today, union density in Peru is a steady 18 per cent, an achievement in the face of the country's economic difficulties, the variable favouritism of the governing parties for different union centres, and the intimidation which has claimed many union lives including those of Saúl Cantoral leader of the Miners' Federation, and the famous rural workers' union leader Hugo Blanco, both in 1989.

The CGTP is the largest union centre in Peru and claims 800,000 members, whose numbers were boosted by the adherence of the National Federation of Mining and Metallurgical and Steel Workers of Peru (FNTMMSP) in 1987. In 1988 it also accepted the affiliation of CITE, the 500,000-strong public sector employees' federation in defiance of legislation which forbids the linkage of public and private sector organizations.

The CTP is the country's second largest centre which, until the arrival of the radical military régime in 1968, enjoyed sole recognition. At the end of 1989 it was split between two factions, one of which was connected to the ICFTU. The much smaller CNT is also afflicted by factionalism; its former links with the WCL have been eroded. The Velasco régime founded the CTRP in 1973 as an alternative to the CGTP, but it failed to establish a mass presence. The centres discussed the formation of a single national centre in August 1990 when pressed by the need to resist the Fujimori programme. There are a number of independent unions, some in the energy sector.

Confederación General de Trabajadores del Perú (CGTP)
General Confederation of Peruvian Workers

Address. Plaza 2 de Mayo 4, Lima
Phone. 231707

Leadership. Isidoro Gamarra Ramírez (president); Valentín Pacho (secretary-general, also vice-president of the WFTU)

Membership. The CGTP claims 800,000 members though other estimates put the figure at nearer 600,000. However this only reflects the legal private sector membership of the CGTP but it has been strengthened by the adherence of the public sector CITE.

History and character. The CGTP was formed in 1968 under the leadership of the Peruvian Communist Party (PCP), and regards itself as the successor to the CGTP formed in 1929.

Principal affiliates of CGTP.

1. **National Federation of Mining and Metallurgical and Steel Workers of Peru (FNTMMSP)**

   Leadership: Moises Palomino (president); Jorge Quesada (secretary-general).

   History and character: FNTMMSP affiliated to the CGTP in 1987 and the following year mounted two major strikes to be followed by a third in early 1988. Its attempts to use the strike weapon to force the introduction of a single industry-wide collective bargaining agreement in 1989 was a failure.

2. **Inter-sectoral Confederation of State Workers (CITE)**

   Leadership: The CITE has a collegiate leadership of four secretaries-general, César Passalacqua, Luis Iparraguirre, Félix Martínez, and Carlos Jiménez.

   History and character: The CITE was founded in 1978 by the coalescence of various unions at Peruvian ministries. By 1988 it had around 500,000 of Peru's 700,000 public sector workers in membership. It mounted two major strikes in 1989 in pursuit of a single integrated civil service pay scale to replace the separate arrangements operated by the individual ministries and succeeded in gaining a promise from the outgoing García government to introduce such a scale from May 1, 1990.

   CITE joined the CTGP in 1988 in defiance of the law which requires public and private federations to stay apart. Both APRA and United Left members are active within its ranks.

International affiliation. WFTU.

Confederación Nacional de Trabajadores (CNT)
National Confederation of Workers

Address. Av. Inca Garcilazo de la Vega No. 1168, Oficina 902, 9 Piso, Lima

Leadership. Secundino Pérez (secretary-general)

History and character. Under the military government of Velasco, CNT received official recognition and some years later severed its connections with the WCL for a closer relationship with the ICFTU-affiliated CTP. This is still the approach of the Secundino Pérez faction which controls the union's head office but it is challenged by factions headed by Victor Sánchez Zapata and Teodosio Torres.

International affiliation. ICFTU/ORIT.

Confederación de Trabajadores del Perú (CTP)

Address. Jirón Ayacucho 173, Casilla 3626, Lima

Phone. 282253; 270470

Cables. CETEPERU, LIMA

Membership. Combined membership of the two factions is put between 120,000 and 150,000

History and character. Founded in 1944 and always linked to the APRA party, the CTP was the only recognized confederation before 1968, incorporating most of Peruvian labour. Its position was eroded after that date by government promotion of rival centres and by factionalism. Internal disputes peaked in 1989 with an open split; the pro-García government faction led by Manuel Ramírez and Bernardino Céspedes maintained an ICFTU affiliation, while the faction led by Julio Cruzado gained control of the head office. The CTP's strengths are among the miners, sugar workers and social security workers.

International affiliations. ICFTU; ORIT.

Confederación de Trabajarodes de la Revolución Peruano (CTRP)
Workers' Confederation of the Peruvian Revolution

Address. Hernan Velarde 240, Lima

History and character. The CTRP created in 1973 by the military to counter-balance the CGTP, but lost most of its membership when official sponsorship ceased. Its main strength lies among fish processors but its total membership is now thought to be small.

Philippines

Capital: Quezon City (Manila)   **Population: 60,200,000**

Political system. After the adoption of the new Constitution in February 1987, President Corazon Aquino, who had come to power in 1986, began dismantling the coercive apparatus of the former Marcos régime, and the institutions of the republic's American-style democracy were reasserted. The stability of the Philippines is constantly undermined by the residual forces of the dynastic, land-owning families and the threat of insurgency from the communist New People's Army (NPA).

The period since President Aquino's assumption of power has also been punctuated by a series of unsuccessful military uprisings.

Economy. The economy of the Philippines is predominantly agricultural. Between 1983 and early 1986, GDP fell by more than 19 per cent; however by 1987 there had been a significant recovery with overall economic growth at 5.5 per cent. Robust growth continued from then on and by the end of 1989 (in which year growth was 5.7 per cent) the Philippines had experienced four successive years of economic recovery. With a fast-growing workforce, unemployment in the first quarter of 1990 defied the growth rate, staying at 8.6 per cent; the underemployment rate was 33 per cent. Those employed in 1989 numbered 21,600,000 and were divided between industry 15.9 per cent, agriculture 46.3 per cent, and services 37.8 per cent. Inflation in 1989 was 10.6 per cent and rising, perhaps boosted by the enactment of minimum wage legislation in July. However pay in the Philippines remains low, even by South-East Asian standards, and is a major motive for inward investment.

System of industrial relations. The Philippines ratified ILO Conventions Nos. 87 and 98 in 1957 and 1953 respectively. The principal limitations on strike action in force in 1985 included: (i) a wide range of circumstances in which the government could on the grounds of the national interest ban a strike, impose compulsory arbitration, and bring about the dismissal and imprisonment for up to six months of strikers; (ii) the possible permanent deportation of foreign workers participating in an illegal strike; (iii) sentences of penal servitude for life for organizers of pickets or other collective actions held to be meetings or demonstrations used for anti-government propaganda purposes, and lesser sentences of imprisonment for participants in such actions; and (iv) the requirement of the approval of a two-thirds majority of workers in a bargaining unit for a strike to be called. (In practice, however, strikes in various public interest sectors had occured without prosecutions, although compulsory arbitration was used to end 33 strikes in 1983). The incoming Aquino government in 1986 introduced radical changes to the country's labour code and established the framework for a more liberal labour relations policy in compliance with

ILO Conventions already ratified by the Philippines. The right of workers to choose their own form of unionization was affirmed by repealing labour code provisions relating to restructuring along one-union one-industry lines. Moreover, where there was no certified bargaining agent at the workplace, the union membership requirement for registration was reduced from 30 to 20 per cent. Where the workforce was already covered by a collective agreement and a petition questioning the majority status bargaining union was received 60 days before the end of the agreement, then an automatic election to confirm the proper bargaining agent was to be held by secret ballot. The changes meant that a strike could be called by a simple majority vote, rather than by the two-thirds majority required under previous legislation, while a lock-out needed a majority vote on the board of directors. In addition, employers could no longer recruit strike-breakers or dismiss workers for failing to comply with return-to-work orders.

The country's new Constitution, adopted in February 1987, contained the following passage on labour relations: "The state shall afford full protection to labour, local and overseas, organized and unorganized, and promote full employment and equality of employment opportunities for all. It shall guarantee the rights of all workers to self-organization, collective bargaining and negotiation, and peaceful concerted activities including the rights to strike in accordance with law. They shall be entitled to security of tenure, humane conditions of work and a living wage. They shall also participate in policy and decision-making processes affecting their rights and benefits as may be provided by law. The state shall promote the principle of shared responsibility between workers and employers and the preferential use of voluntary modes in settling disputes, including conciliation, and shall enforce their mutual compliance therewith to foster industrial peace. The State shall regulate the relations between workers and employers recognizing the right of labour to share in the fruits of production and the right of enterprises to reasonable returns on investments, and to expansion and growth."

A large number of strikes were recorded in mid- and late 1987; particularly affected were the large food processing plants south of Manila. The actions threatened to spoil what had been a general improvement in labour relations under President Aquino. The number of strikes to mid-September 1987 fell to 355 from 494 in the same period of 1986. For 1986 as a whole, the number of strikes had been a record 581, involving 169,000 workers and resulting in a wastage of 3,640,000 man-days. Much of the industrial unrest taking place in late 1987 was blamed on the radical May 1st Movement (Kilusang Mayo Uno—KMU), leading some commentators to suggest that the disputes were ideologically motivated. The *Far Eastern Economic Review* of Oct. 15, 1987, reported that non-economic issues had gained importance in the recent rash of strikes. Of the strikes declared in the first eight months of 1987, only 21 per cent resulted from a breakdown in talks over economic demands, against 29.5 per cent in the same period in 1986. Other non-economic factors increased; discrimination against or harassment of union members was the reason for almost 40 per cent of the strikes, compared to 30 per cent in the same 1986 period.

A wave of protests was triggered by the announcement on Aug. 14, 1987, of an 18 per cent increase in fuel prices. A series of demonstrations were held in Manila on Aug. 21 and three days later the United Association of Transport Workers (involving mainly bus company employees) together with jeepney drivers staged a one-day strike. The following day President Aquino announced a partial reversal of the increases. This failed to satisfy the protesters and on Aug. 26 workers from many sectors of the economy responded to a KMU strike call, which affected about half the country. The day after the strike, which had turned violent in many areas of the country, police arrested 71 people, mostly labour leaders, on charges of "incitement to sedition". Some labour leaders, including the KMU chairman, Crispin Beltran, went into hiding. President Aquino on Oct. 3 requested Congress to increase the minimum wage; her request followed the collapse of tripartite negotiations, involving management, workers and the department of labour and employ-ment (DOLE). Unions had demanded an across-the-board increase of 10 Peso on daily wage rates, while employers had maintained that they could not afford such an increase. The DOLE had proposed an increase of 8 Peso for industrial workers, and 6 Peso for agricultural workers. The KMU called a further series of nationwide strikes in mid-October to protest the deadlock on wage negotiations. A spekesman for the KMU said that the strikes had affected 250,000 workers in 387 factories and businesses. President Aquino warned on Oct. 20 that the government would use force if necessary to break the strikes. The next day police began implementing her order, removing barricades and camps erected by striking workers in front of Manila businesses.

Each years since 1986 the number of strikes has fallen, dropping to 197 in 1989; the number of days lost to strikes in that year was less than half that of 1987. (An upturn in the first half of 1990 may perhaps be explained by a number of agreements expiring during this period.) Notable disputes included two highly effective teachers' strikes in 1989, and stoppages by air traffic controllers (February 1990) and at the Philippines National Railways (June 1990).

Contributing to this improved record have been the country's new industrial relations institutions including the National Conciliation and Mediation Board, established in 1987. The provisions of the Labour Law Reform Act (1989) have also helped to clarify the rules for organizing and certification elections, while the Department of Labour and Employment Secretary has intervened in a series of important disputes.

In January 1990 the government supplemented this framework with the Labour Urgent Emergency Action (LUNAS) facility to provide instant mediation services and emergency strike reaction teams. In May a tripartite Industrial Peace Accord (IPA) was signed by all major union centres except the KMU, affirming their commitment to democracy, free enterprise, shared responsibility, and preference for procedural resolution of disputes. The IPA contains a no-strike clause in return for which President Aquino undertook to activate the regional boards responsible for reviewing the minimum wage (which the unions by this time wished to see raised). The IPA is to be monitored by a new Tripartite Industrial Peace Council.

Trade unionism. Trade unions were first legalized in 1908 and the first labour congress was held in 1913. Following the declaration of martial law by Marcos in 1972 (when many trade union leaders were dismissed) the labour code was revised in 1974 to curb the right to strike and to bring about the unification of the labour movement, leading to the forma-tion of the Trade Union Congress of the Philippines (TUCP).

The Aquino period has witnessed a resurgence of union organization. In 1989 it was 12 per cent, two percentage points advanced from its position the previous year. In govern-ment agencies 62 new bargaining units were established during the year to March 1990, bringing the total to 149, though at 74,300 membership is only a small fraction of 1,500,000 state employees. There is great pressure to put public sector industrial relations on a stable footing and a bill has been introduced to Congress for full associative and bargaining rights for public employees.

In the private sector, progress has been slower but from a position of greater strength. There are 2,400,000 private sector unionists according to TUCP, and the Department of Labour and Employment registered 3,945 unions in 1989, a rise of more than 550.

The largest union centre is the ICFTU-affiliated TUCP, which also receives substantial aid from AAFLI. On May 1, 1990 it launched an alliance with the WCL-affiliated Federation of Free Workers (FFW) and the Workers Strength Labour Centre (LMLC) under the name Labour Unity for Democracy and Peace. The FFW and the LMLC had two years earlier joined the May First Movement Labour Centre (KMU) and three WFTU affiliates (TUPAS, NCW and NATU) in launching a Labour Advisory Consultative

Council (LACC), which was intended to associate non-TUCP centres. There is a dispute as to whether or not the FFW and LMLC had, prior to associating with the TUCP, withdrawn from the LACC. The chief rival to the TUCP is the KMU which adopts a more militant stance, for example on the issue of the level of the minimum wage.

Federation of Free Workers (FFW)

Address. 1943 Taft Avenue, Malate, Metro Manila
Phone. (2) 571511
Leadership. Juan C. Tan (president, also president of the WCL); Ramon Jabar (vice-president)
Membership. 390 affiliated unions, seven industrial federations, 400,000 members.
History and character. The FFW was founded in 1950 and developed with the assistance of the Roman Catholic clergy. At its 16th national convention, held in April 1986, The FFW called for: (i) the right to form unions to be extended to public employees; (ii) full rights to strike and picket; (iii) the promotion of conciliation, mediation and voluntary arbitration and the ending of compulsory arbitration; (iv) restraints on the use of injunctions in labour disputes; (v) removal of barriers to union registration, and the lowering of the requirement that 30 per cent of workers in any bargaining unit must join a union for it to be registered; and (vi) the abolition of clauses in the labour code structuring trade unions on a one-industry, one-federation basis. The FFW favours a managed, co-operative economy, with profit-sharing and extended social benefits.

The FFW joined LACC but in 1990 claimed to have withdrawn before its association with the TUCP in Labour Unity for Democracy and Peace.
International affiliation. WCL.

Kilusang Mayo Uno (KMU)
May First Movement Labour Centre

Address. 3rd Floor, Jopson Building, 510M Earnshaw Street, Sampaloc, Metro Manila
Phone. 0063-2-619369
Telex. 40404
Leadership. Crispin B. Beltran (chairperson); Leto Villar (vice-chairperson); Ernesto Arellano (secretary-general)
Membership. Claims 800,000.
History and character. Formed on May 1, 1980, the KMU describes itself as "an independent labour centre promoting genuine, militant and nationalist trade unionism in the Philippines". At its founding the KMU had some 50,000 members belonging to seven labour federations. By October 1988 it claimed a membership of 800,000 and 11 labour federations, namely:

1. **National Federation of Labor Unions (NAFLU).**

2. **National Federation of Labor (NFL).**

3. **Association of Democratic Labor Organizations (ADLO).**

4. **Alliance of Nationalist and Genuine Labor Organizations (ANGLO).**

5. **National Federation of Sugar Workers-Food and General Trade (NFSW-FGT).**

6. **Southern Philippines Federation of Labor (SPFL).**

7. **United Workers of the Philippines (UWP).**

8. **Genuine Labor Organization of Workers in Hotel, Restaurants and Allied Industries (GLOWHRAIN).**

9. **Drug, Food and Allied Industries Workers Federation (DFA).**

10. **Ilaw at Buklod ng Manggagawa** (IBM-Light and Unity of Workers).

11. **Organized Labor Association in Line Industry and Agriculture (OLALIA).**

The KMU lists as its aims; (i) increasing workers' wages to a "reasonably decent level"; (ii) repealing all anti-labour laws; (iii) halting all repression of trade union and democratic rights; (iv) gaining recognition of the right to unionize, bargain collectively and to strike in government offices and corporations; and (v) the establishment of genuine industrialization and an end to "foreign domination" by the nationalization of basic and strategic industries.

Rolando Olalia, the previous leader of the KMU and also formerly chairman of the newly formed Party of the Nation (Partido Ng Bayan – PNB), was found brutally murdered on Nov. 13, 1986, and party leaders attributed his killing to forces within the military. The Armed Forces had regarded the KMU as a communist front since its formation. The day before Olalia's assassination, the KMU had stated that it would call a general strike in the event of a military *coup* (which was widely expected at the time) to overthrow the Aquino government. The KMU had boycotted the February 1986 elections which brought Aquino to power, but had subsequently given support to the new government while calling for fundamental reforms. The KMU appears to have increased in strength under Aquino, particularly at the expense of the moderate Trade Union Congress of the Philippines (TUCP), which was seen by some workers as a "Marcos union". By late 1987, workers in approximately half of Metro Manila's industrial plants were thought to be KMU-affiliated. In mid- and late 1987, the KMU organized a number of large-scale strikes in protest at rising fuel prices and low wages. There were widespread accusations that the unrest had been provoked by the KMU for ideological reasons.

The KMU was the prime mover in LACC. More recently it spearheaded a general strike for higher wages and in opposition to a petrol price increase in adherence to IMF wishes. The Aquino government threatened to ban the KMU, which for its part complained to the ILO of violations of union rights. It claims to have lost a number of members, killed by government forces. It was the only major union centre not to sign the Industrial Peace Accord.

Publication. KMU Correspondence.

Lakas Manggagawa Labour Centre (LMLC)
Workers' Strength Labour Centre.

Address. Room 401, FEMI Annex Building, A. Soriano Street, Intramuros, Manila
Leadership. Fernando T. Aldaba (secretary for international affairs)
Membership. 100,000 in 140 affiliates.

History and character. The LMLC was founded on December 10, 1986, Human Rights Day, by a group of unions and federations seeking an alternative centre oriented to democratic trade unionism. It emphasizes the autonomy of trade unions from government, political parties and the church and the need to solidarity between the nation's various trade union centres and opposes what it sees as the rightward shift of the Aquino government since 1987. It has no international affiliation but has formed links with the Norwegian Federation of Trade Unions (LO) and ICFTU trade secretariats.

The LMLC joined the FFW and the TUCP in launching Labour Unity for Democracy and Peace, despite its earlier involvement in LACC (*see above*).

National Association of Trade Unions (NATU)

Address. RM 404, San Luis Terraces, T. M. Kalaw Street, Ermita, Manila
Phone. 598705
Membership. Claims 50,000 in 70 unions.
Leadership. Vicente S. Bate (president); Ma. Aniceta M. Pangiliman (secretary)
History and character. NATU was founded in 1954, affiliated to the WFTU in 1962 and established itself as a national centre in 1964.

When martial law was proclaimed in 1972, its founder and president. Atty. Lacsina was detained, suspected of rebellion. The then Executive Vice-President, Pacifico Rosal, acted as president but a power struggle broke out between the latter and another Vice-President, Atty. Marcelino Lontok in 1974.

Disputes over the leadership of the Federation never ceased for certain factions disliked the administration of Atty. Lontok. A petition to hold a national election was filed. A legal battle ensued until ultimately, the Supreme Court ordered NATU to hold a unity convention to determine who would be the proper authority to run its affairs. Hence, the first convention after eight long years was held in October 1980. Vicente S. Bate, the appointed Executive Vice-President since 1978 and then the President of the Philippine Bank of Communication Employees' Association (PBCEA) won the election as president.

In the May 27, 1990 12th Triennial Convention and 36th Founding Anniversary, Vicente S. Bate resoundingly was elected President for the fifth time.

Affiliates.

1. **AEA Employees' Association.**

2. **Affiliated Food Stores Employees' Union.**

3. **Allied Bank Chapter—NATU.**

4. **Almacenes Workers' Union.**

5. **Aristocrat Workers' Union.**

6. **Asia Traders Employees' Association.**

7. **Bagong Alyansa ng Nagkakaisang Guwardiya (BANG).**

8. **Berlimed Employees' Union.**

9. **BPI Family Bank and Subsidiary Workers' Union**

10. **Butch Garments Workers' Union.**

11. **C. Itoh Employees' Association.**

12. **CIGC Employees' Union.**

13. **Carston Workers' Union.**

14. **CCCIC Employees' Union.**

15. **Century Hardwood Workers' Union.**

16. **Chartered Adjusters Employees' Union.**

17. **Citibank Contractual Employees' Union.**

18. **Citibank Phils. Employees' Union.**

19. **Citytrust Organization.**

20. **D.P. Guevarra & Sons Enterprise Employees' Union.**

21. **Everett Steamship Checkers Workers' Union.**

22. **Feltman Employees' Association.**

23. Filcon Employees' Union.

24. Hemisphere Builder Workers' Union.

25. Independent Union of Manila Pavillon.

26. Interbank Employees' Union.

27. Interbank Messengerial & Allied Workers' Union.

28. International Oil Factory Workers' Union.

29. Kanematsu-Gosho Employees' Union.

20. Laseco Trading Workers' Union.

31. Legaspi Tower 300 Employees' Union.

32. Libra Engine Products Workers' Union.

33. Malayang Manggagawa sa Fiesta Resort.

34. Malayang Manggagawa sa Kawsek.

35. Marubeni Corp. Employees' Union.

36. Metropolitan Convenience Employees' Union.

37. Mitsubishi Filipino Employees' Union.

38. Mitsui Employees' Union.

39. Mr. Grocers Equipment & Food Supply Employees' Union.

40. NSR Workers' Union.

41. Nation Automotive Workers' Union.

42. National Foundry Workers' Union (DONGTEK).

43. New India Assurance Employees' Union.

44. Nichimen Filipino Employees' Union.

45. OMIC Union.

46. Pacific Blacksmith Shop Workers' Union.

47. PBCOM Employees' Association.

48. Petron Employees' Association.

49. Phil. British Assurance Co. Employees' Union.

50. Phil. Clearing House Corp. Employees' Association.

51. **Philippine Superfeeds Workers' Union.**

52. **Planters Development Bank Employees' Union.**

53. **PNZ Workers' Union.**

54. **Prudential Guarantee Assurance Labor Union.**

55. **Rempson Employees' Union.**

56. **Republic Planters Bank Employees' Union.**

57. **RPB General Services Employees' Union.**

58. **RPB Supervisory.**

59. **Sandigan at Diwa ng Aping Tanod (SANDATA).**

60. **Shoemart Employees' Union.**

61. **SM-ACA Employees' Union.**

62. **Tabacalera Insurance Labor Union.**

63. **Tikicrafts Workers' Union.**

64. **Traders Royal Bank Employees' Union.**

65. **Union Insurance Society Employees' Association.**

66. **Universal Hats & Bags Workers' Association.**

67. **Viva Footwear Workers' Union.**

68. **Wise & Company Employees' Union.**

69. **W. R. Grace Employees' Union.**

70. **Workers' Union of Dunkin Donuts.**

Publication. NATU News.
International affiliation. WFTU.

National Congress of Workers (NCW)

Address. Room 505, Insurance Centre Building, General Luna, Intramuros, Manila
Leadership. Reynaldo Capa
International affiliation. WFTU.

Katipunang Manggagawang Pilipino (KMP)
Trade Union Congress of the Philippines (TUCP)

Address. TUCP/PGEA Compound, Masaya Street, corner Maharlika Street, Diliman, Quezon City 3008.
Phone. (2) 972829; 922 2185; 921 94 66
Telex. 2364 ALUMLA PU

Leadership. Democrito T. Mendoza (president); Ernesto F. Herrera (general secretary)

Membership. 3,970,000 members, including 2,700,000 agricultural workers in the National Congress of Farmers' Organizations (NCFO), with which the TUCP has a solidarity pact. The TUCP estimates that there are 1,830,000 members of non-affiliated unions.

History and character. The TUCP is the largest trade union centre in the Philippines and includes a number of autonomous general federations. It was formed in 1975 in response to the implementation of the 1974 labour code which emphasized the co-ordination and unification of the trade union movement, reflecting the official view of President Marcos that such unification would both benefit the labour movement and provide a favourable environment for economic development. According to some sections of organized labour the TUCP had been unduly close to the Marcos government; it did, however, mobilize 7,000 volunteers for the watchdog National Citizens' Movement for Free Elections (NAMFREL) which unofficially supervised the February 1986 election. The TUCP's policies as defined in mid-1986 included the extension of collective bargaining to government-owned or controlled corporations and to managerial employees; expanded conciliation and mediation and the creation of a full-time arbitration body; an end to the dominance of government on tripartite agencies; the reorganization and reform of the National Wages Council; an end to restrictions on strikes; and measures to relieve unemployment and underemployment. It has no political affiliation, and emphasizes the improvement of industrial relations.

The February 1990 Triennial Convention of the TUCP re-elected "Kito" Mendoza and "Boy" Herrera. It also heard an address by President Aquino. The Convention took a qualified view over the matter of withdrawal of US bases, influenced by consideration of the presence there of 22,000 members of its affiliate FFCEA. It also received into membership the Lumber and General Workers' Union of the Philippines (ULGWP), a former KMU affiliate.

On May Day 1990 the TUCP successfully launched Labour Unity for Democracy and Peace with the FFW and LMLC and later that month was a signatory to the Industrial Peace Accord.

Affiliated unions. There are 37 affiliated federations, including the Associated Labour Unions (ALU-PHILCONTU), Association of Trade Unions (ATU), Federation of Free Farmers (FFF), Federation of Agrarian and Industrial Toiling Hands (FAITH), National Association of Free Trade Unions (NAFTU), National Labour Unions (NLU), Philippine Federation of Labour (PFL), Philippine Association of Free Labour Unions (PAFLU-GUEVARRA), Philippine Association of Free Labour Unions (PAFLU-SEPTEMBER), Philippine Labour Federation (PLF), Confederation of Labour and Allied Social Services (CLASS), and the Workers' Alliance of Trade Unions (WATU).

Publications. Ang Pilipino (monthly); press releases, reports etc.

International affiliations. ICFTU; Asean Trades Union Council (ATUC).

Trade Unions of the Philippines and Allied Services (TUPAS)

Address. Rooms 203–204, Med-dis Building, corner Real and Solana Streets, Intramuros, Manila

Phone. (2) 493449; 493450

Leadership. Vladimir R. Tupaz (secretary-general); Dioscoro Nunez (national president)

Membership. 475,000 (September 1988).

History and character. The TUPAS was formed in 1971 with its original base in a union of docks security guards dissolved by Marcos after the declaration of martial law in 1972. It now has affiliates in 12 industrial sectors, and the Bicol Federation of Labour, Sarangani Federation of Labour and Mindanao Congress of Labour are affiliated. The TUPAS defines its policies as socialism, proletarian internationalism, and the unity of the labour movement.

Publications. Ang Pandayan; Bandilang Pula.

International affiliation. WFTU.

Poland

Capital: Warsaw

Population: 37,873,000
(1988)

Political system. During 1991 a Commission sat preparing a new constitution for Poland to replace that amended in 1986 which still allotted to the defunct Polish United Workers' Party (PUWP) the primary role of building socialism. The new constitution will acknowledge formally the transition Poland made during the 1980s to a multi-party democracy.

Following the emergence in 1980–81 of the Solidarity free trade union movement, which the government and the PUWP eventually regarded as a threat to the régime, a state of martial law was imposed on Dec. 13, 1981, and remained in force until July 22, 1983. During this period power was exercised by a Military Council of National Salvation headed by Gen. Wojciech Jaruzelski, the PUWP First Secretary who was at that time also Chairman of the Council of Ministers. Solidarity was formally abolished on Oct. 8, 1982, but continued to organize clandestinely and to speak out against official policies. Between 1983 and 1987 popular support for protests declined markedly, and the authorities claimed that the "period of political conflicts" had been an aberrant phase which was being entirely superseded. However, at the end of 1987 the government seriously overestimated the extent to which widespread popular apathy and mistrust had been dispelled when it sought, and failed to get, majority support in a popular referendum for a programme of limited political and economic reform. A resurgence of industrial unrest in 1988 prompted the authorities to agree in August to round-table talks with Solidarity and the Roman Catholic Church on ways to resolve Poland's continuing state of social crisis.

The collapse of Communist government took place in August 1989 under pressure of poor economic performance and industrial unrest. A Solidarity government led by Tadeusz Mazowiecki came to power pledged to tackle Poland's economic troubles by decentralization and a shift to a market economy. The policies of this government were eventually the cause of a split between Mr Mazowiecki and Lech Walesa, the influential founder of Solidarity. In the Presidential elections to succeed General Jaruzelski, both men declared their candidatures, along with Stanislaw Tyminski, a former United States resident. With the Solidarity camp split, the Prime Minister was eliminated in the first round and Lech Walesa emerged as Poland's President in December 1990. He appointed Jan Krzysztof Bielecki as Prime Minister to replace Mazowiecki. General elections were due to take place in October 1991.

Economy. The rise of Solidarity was partly a result of long-standing grievances among the workforce which were brought to a head by government efforts in 1980 to cut extensive food price subsidies because of a developing economic crisis stemming in part from the servicing of heavy foreign currency borrowings in the 1970s and deteriorating export performance. Exacerbated by the industrial unrest, the economic decline worsened in 1981–82, while the proclamation of martial law led non-communist governments and international commercial lenders to impose embargoes on temporary assistance to Poland. A three-year reconstruction plan which was introduced in 1983 achieved an upturn in economic performance, and the restoration of equilibrium was a key element of the plan for 1986–90. The reforms which were put to a referendum at the end of 1987 were designed to regenerate the economy primarily by reducing central control and by eliminating subsidies, and in spite of the lack of majority support a modified version of the reform programme was put into effect on Feb. 1, 1988. Protests began almost immediately against massive price rises caused by the withdrawal of subsidies, and major industrial unrest in April and May and again in August effectively wrecked the reforms and prompted their chief architect, Prime Minister Zbigniew Messner, to resign.

The different economic thrust of Solidarity government was speedily felt. Under a plan introduced in January 1990 by the Finance Minister Leszek Balcerowicz, Poland was rapidly subjected to market principles. There was to be a withdrawal of subsidies, wage restraint and privatization. The immediate results were severe: living standards fell by 40 per cent in the first quarter of 1990 and hundreds of thousands of jobs were lost. The price of coal, heating, housing, electricity and public transport all went up. Under a letter of intent to the IMF wages were allowed to move ahead at only 20 per cent of the rate of inflation, and the zloty was devalued. For later in the year, a series of buy-outs and flotations, and the creation of a Stock Exchange were planned. The IMF provided an immediate bridging loan and made standby credits available early in 1990. Despite significant opposition, including a strike wave affecting the pits, the railways and the ports, the government pressed ahead with its programme; the effect was to introduce splits into the Solidarity trade unions, torn between political and industrial objectives, and stimulate a revival of the old trade unions, now relaunched with a new identity. On the eve of President Walesa's inauguration, the economic changes had brought a deep recession. Unemployment was running at 1,200,000 and purchasing power had fallen by one third, a development sharply criticized by Lech Walesa, as he increasingly parted company with the Prime Minister. Inflation had been halved (though at the end of the year it was still running at some 250 per cent) and the way cleared for strong growth of new businesses, but the privatization programme had fallen substantially short of intent: only five of Poland's 7,000 state businesses (which account for some 90 per cent of the economy) had been sold off. GNP for the year fell by 14 per cent and industrial production by 23 per cent.

In appointing the Bielecki government President Walesa signalled his intention to pursue with vigour the liberalizing path which had brought Poland more than US$13,000 million of foreign credits during 1990. The new government however faced a wave of strikes comparable to that experienced the previous year, mounted by — among others—copper miners, doctors, and dustmen. Like its predecessor however, it persisted with its economic programme, and a "shock therapy" approach to privatization was planned. Much interest centred on the Gdansk shipyard, from which Solidarity originated, a symbolic business for which a private owner had to be found.

In March 1991 Poland conducted a strong campaign to reduce its huge foreign debt and succeeded in having half of this written off. Further IMF funding was also made available.

System of industrial relations. Poland became a member of the International Labour Organization in 1919 and ratified ILO Conventions No. 87 (Freedom of Association and Protection of the Right to Organize, 1948) and No. 98 (Right to Organize and Collective Bargaining, 1949) in 1957. At the 67th session of the International Labour Conference in June 1981 the place of the workers' delegate was attributed to the chairman of the national committee of Solidarity, Lech Walesa. In November 1984 Poland gave notice of its intention to withdraw from the ILO (effective November 1986), following the decision of the ILO governing body to approve a report of an ILO commission established to investigate violations by Poland of Conventions No. 87 and No. 98. However in 1986 the ILO granted Poland a one-year deferral of its withdrawal at the request of the Polish authorities, which had stated that "anti-Polish activities" within the ILO had declined, and the decision to withdraw was formally rescinded in November 1987.

On April 6, 1989 Poland's Working Group on Trade Union Pluralism reached agreement on the need for a pluralist framework for unionism. The agreement called for legislative changes to enact union rights, and these were subsequently incorporated into the country's constitution. This meant established procedures for determining bargaining rights at the enterprise level. There were further procedures governing the reinstatement of victimized workers: here the right of appeal is to a conciliation commission composed of management and union representatives with an impartial chairman.

In May 1989, just before the national elections, the outgoing Parliament passed two laws which also set a legal framework for employer activity. Under the first law, trade associations may now be formed by the retail, catering and allied trades, and in transport. The first group requires the adherence of 50 firms to launch an association while the latter needs 100. The step to establishing a registered national association can be taken once such a body has 10 sectoral associations affiliated. Under the second law regional chambers of commerce may now be set up at local level by 50 or more businessmen; to extend coverage beyond the region, the affiliation of 100 or more businesses is required. On June 1, 1989 the first meeting of a preparatory commission of the Polish Tripartite Committee for Co-operation with the ILO took place with representatives of the new employers' organizations present as well as the trade unions.

But while the formal institutions of industrial relations were being established, the strike pattern in evidence periodically under the communists reasserted itself as a favoured form of protest against austerity. The renewed communist unions in particular discovered an oppositional role rallying discontent as did increasing sections of Solidarity.

Trade unionism. Before 1980 trade unionism in Poland, as in other East European countries, was organized by an official central body, the Central Council of Trade Unions (CRZZ); in that year, however, the independent union Solidarity was created and, following massive popular pressure, accorded recognition by the government. At its height Solidarity had 9,500,000 members (including agricultural wage earners), while the peasants' organization Rural Solidarity had 2,350,000 members and there were 3,000,000 members of branch and autonomous trade unions. For more than a year Solidarity functioned both as a union and as a vehicle for the expression of Polish national, religious and political aspirations, posing an increasingly apparent threat to the role of the PUWP and by implication to the Warsaw Pact alliance. Following repeated rumours in both Poland and the West of the possibility of a Soviet invasion, martial law was declared on Dec. 13, 1981, and Solidarity banned. The Solidarity organization was formally dissolved by the Trade Union Act of October 1982, which also provided for the creation of a new structure of official trade unions which would take over the property of the dissolved unions. The All-Poland Alliance of Trade Unions (OPZZ) was formed in November 1984 to co-ordinate the official unions and amendments to the 1982 Trade Union Act passed by the *Sejm* in July 1985 confirmed a trade union monopoly by prohibiting the establishment of more than one trade union in any enterprise; these amendments also gave the trade unions a legal right to be consulted by factory managements about working conditions and certain other issues.

The Polish experience of political repression and economic collapse created a situation where by February 1989 a communist government had little alternative but to hold talks with Solidarity, a movement it had declared illegal (*see below*). But this recognition of Solidarity's influence also exposed it to influences which threatened to undermine it.

Trade unionism in Poland in 1991 had an established pluralist character. The OPZZ is clearly established as the larger of the two national centres, and has benefited greatly from being able to adopt an oppositional stance against successive government austerity programmes. Its role has been further clarified since the election of President Walesa, indelibly associated with Solidarity. Solidarity's experiences since communism collapsed have been less happy. Its membership may only be a quarter of its peak in the early 1980s and some of its component parts have also mounted industrial action against government policy. With a Solidarity government in 1990, and a Solidarity President in 1991, the movement is in some confusion over whether it has a political or an industrial identity.

NSZZ Solidarnosc
Solidarity

Address. NSZZ Solidarnosc, Gdansk
Leadership. Marian Krzaklewski (chairperson)
Membership. Approximately 2,200,000.
History.

December 1970–January 1971. 44 people were killed in a wave of (illegal) strikes and disturbances concentrated in the Baltic coast cities.

Sept. 23, 1976. Following industrial disturbances in the summer of 1976, precipitated by the effects of inflation on living standards, a group of intellectuals formed *komitet obrony robotnikow* (KOR—workers' defence committee) to assist the families of those dismissed in strikes. (KOR was subsequently renamed the committee for social self defence—KSS.)

May 1978. The committe of free trade unions for the Baltic coast was formed under the leadership of Andrzej Gwiazda.

June 2–10, 1979. The elevation of the Pole Karol Wojtyla to the papacy as John Paul III on Oct. 16, 1978, and his visit to Poland in June 1979, encouraged the fusion of Catholic religious and nationalist sentiments with economic grievances which proved a catalyst in the rise of Solidarity in 1980.

Summer 1980. A rolling wave of strikes began in July 1980 in response to price rises with Lech Walesa (a Gdansk shipyard worker) emerging as the most prominent leader of the movement. Workers struck at the Lenin shipyards in Gdansk on Aug. 14, occupying the yards, which became the centre of the unrest; on Aug. 16 the inter-factory strike committee (MKS) was formed in Gdansk to co-ordinate activity; and as a result of negotiations with the MKS held on Aug. 23–30, the government on Aug. 31 conceded (in the "Gdansk accords") the right of workers to form free unions independent of the monolithic structure organized by the Central Council of Trade Unions, with the right to strike, and ancillary demands such as the broadcasting of Masses, Saturday holidays, and greater civil liberties. On Sept. 5, 1980, the PUWP Secretary, Edward Gierek, was replaced by Stanislaw Kania, with widespread upheavals and dismissals occurring within the party over the following months. On Sept. 15 the government established a procedure for the registration of the new trade unions in the Court of the Voivodship of Warsaw, outside the register kept by the Central Council of Trade Unions, and acknowledged that the Gdansk accords applied to the whole economy.

Sept. 22, 1980. Delegates of 36 regional independent unions met in Gdansk under the name of Solidarity and under the chairmanship of Lech Walesa, and Solidarity applied for registration with the Warsaw Court on Sept. 24.

Oct. 8, 1980. The *Sejm* adopted an Act to amend the Trade Union Act of 1949, thereby giving statutory validity to the procedure established by the Council of State on Sept. 15.

Nov. 10, 1980. The Polish Supreme Court overruled a decision by the Warsaw Court that the charter legalizing Solidarity would be invalid without the inclusion in the union's statutes of recognition of the PUWP as the leading political force in the country (although this recognition was by compromise inserted in the annexes to the statutes), thereby averting a general strike over the issue threatened for Nov. 12.

Jan. 1, 1981. The Central Council of Trade Unions (CRZZ) was dissolved, most of the former official trade unions having by this time dissolved or voted to become autonomous.

Jan. 30, 1981. The government conceded the five-day week, as of 1982.

April 17, 1981. The government agreed to recognize the creation of Rural Solidarity, which had held its first congress on March 9; it was registered on May 12.

September – October 1981. Solidarity held its first delegate conference, in two states (in sessions starting on Sept. 5 and Sept. 26) in Gdansk, revealing splits between moderates (led by Lech Walesa) who, fearing Soviet intervention and alarmed by persistent industrial disorders and the collapse of productivity, wished to pursue a policy of greater accommodation towards the government, and militants who wished to press broad political demands. On Sept. 28, KSS(KOR) disbanded. On Oct. 2 Walesa was elected chairman of Solidarity, but congress elected a radical-dominated national commission. On Oct. 18 Stanislaw Kania resigned and was replaced as First Secretary of the PUWP by the Prime Minister and Defence Minister Gen. Jaruzelski.

Dec. 6, 1981. Warsaw Solidarity called on the national Solidarity leadership to form a force of "permanent worker guards"; strikes were by this time widespread, continuing against the wishes of Walesa.

Dec. 12–13, 1981. The national leadership, contrary to Walesa's advice, voted on Dec. 12 to call a national referendum in which the people would be asked *inter alia* if they favoured the establishement of an interim government and the holding of free elections, and whether they wished to continue to provide "military guarantees" to the USSR. Over Dec. 12–13 the government was put under the direction of a Military Council of National Salvation under Gen. Jaruzelski, martial law declared, strikes banned, Solidarity leaders (including Walesa) arrested and all trade unions suspended; according to government figures, 7,000 persons were interned in detention camps. The representation of the interests of workers was subsequently placed in the hands of social committees set up in January 1982.

According to the Polish government Solidarity had proceeded beyond the limits of the Gdansk accords and its constitution and under the influence of extremist elements had increasingly moved towards an attempt to seize power from the government; the imposition of martial law had been necessary to prevent this and to end a condition of mounting disorder and economic disintegration which posed a threat not just to Poland but to the stability of world peace. Particular concern was expressed at the appeals made by Solidarity to the peoples of other socialist countries and at the questioning of Poland's international alliances. The suspension of the newly formed trade unions was initially represented by the government as a short-term measure. The position and role of the hierarchy of the Church had by this time become ambiguous, the Church supporting the principles of Solidarity but expressing a desire for stability and national unification.

There were no reports of violence or deaths related to the activities of Solidarity in the period from its emergence in the summer of 1980 to its dissolution under martial law, and strikes had been avoided in the health services and some other essential services. Following the imposition of martial law, eight miners died in a confrontation with security forces at the Wujek mine near Katowice (although most protest strikes were ended relatively peacefully), and according to the ICFTU, WCL, and other reports several dozen persons were killed by the security forces in demonstrations, strikes and other incidents in the following months. There was also numerous reports of torture of detainees, dismissals from employment of previous Solidarity activists and the imposition of loyalty oaths requiring disavowal of support for or sympathy with Solidarity. Extensive purges were also carried out of Solidarity supporters in the judiciary, government service, universities and the media. In decisions in May and July 1982 the Supreme Court held that protection against dismissal under the labour code could not be applied while trade union activities were suspended.

Oct. 8, 1982. Under a new Trade Union Act approved by the *Sejm* all existing unions were dissolved, to be replaced by a pattern of enterprise-level representation, with federations and confederations to be introduced on a fixed time scale, which could only be modified by the Council of State. The Act provided that the Council of State could after three years consider the provisions of the Act so as to allow for the existence of more than one trade union in an enterprise, but the Act was amended in July 1985 to eliminate this possibility. Trade unions were required to recognize the principles of the social ownership of the means of production, the leading role of the PUWP in the construction of socialism and the constitutional principles of the foreign policy of the Polish People's Republic. A formal but highly restricted right to strike was restored, with exhaustive mandatory arbitration procedures and leaders of illegal strikes (which included strikes with a political motive) liable to a term of imprisonment of up to one year. Members of the police, armed forces and prison service were to be excluded from trade union membership (an independent policemen's union having been established in 1981). The Act also provided for the eventual transfer of the assets (frozen since the imposition of martial law) of the dissolved unions to the new official unions. A parallel Act dissolved Rural Solidarity and provided for the creation of new organizations which lacked the characteristics of trade unions.

Nov. 12, 1982. Release from detention of Lech Walesa.

Dec. 31, 1982. Martial law was suspended (and lifted in July 1983, when an Amnesty Act—from which many members of Solidarity were excluded—was adopted).

Oct. 5, 1983. Lech Walesa was awarded the Nobel Peace Prize. The Polish government lodged a formal complaint with the Norwegian ambassador.

1983–1987. Following its formal dissolution by the authorities, Solidarity maintained an underground identity through a temporary co-ordinating committee (TKK), while Lech Walesa remained the chairman. However, the effective strength of Solidarity appeared to decline steadily and calls for strikes and demonstrations against price rises in 1985 and 1986 were poorly supported.

Notwithstanding the easing of tension within Poland as compared with the period of martial law, the ICFTU's *Trade Union Rights: Survey of Violations, 1985–86* stated that Solidarity activists remained subject to "physical harassment, denial of employment, discriminatory employment practices, arrests and re-arrests and severe prison sentences". In the course of 1985 and early 1986, according to the *Survey*, "several cases of brutality inflicted on Solidarnosc members by the security forces were reported, resulting in at least 15 deaths".

Several principal leaders of Solidarity were subject to arrest and detention within this period: Zbigniew Bujak, the TKK leader in Warsaw, was arrested in May 1986 (but released later in the year), having been in hiding since the imposition of martial law; in June 1985 Wladyslaw Frasyniuk, Bogdan Lis and Adam Michnik were sentenced to prison terms for planning to foment public unrest and "fulfilling a leading role in an illegal union" (all three being prematurely released in 1986). Proceedings were brought against Lech Walesa following his claim that the official turnout figures in the *Sejm* elections of October 1985 were inflated (Solidarity having called a boycott of the elections), but were abandoned on the opening day of the trial in February 1986 when the government withdrew charges of slander and spreading false information. The ICFTU reported that 500 Solidarity activists were in prison at the end of 1985 (although this figure according to the ICFTU fell to about 100 by the autumn of 1986 as many political prisoners were released). Solidarity sources stated in early 1987 that all leading Solidarity figures had been released.

On Sept. 30, 1986, Walesa and other leading figures in Solidarity announced the formation of an open seven-member Temporary Council of Solidarity (TRS), stating that they were willing to work within the system to improve the country's social, political and economic conditions, and would "seek to ease the transition to legal and open undertakings". It was announced that Walesa would remain the titular chairman of Solidarity, but would not be a member of the TR. Any decision to disband the underground TKK was apparently dependent on the attitude of the government to the TR. In response, however, the Polish authorities stated that the TR was illegal, and the Polish Supreme Court on Nov. 16 rejected an appeal by Baltic shipyard workers to create a union called Solidarity on the grounds that the certain of more than one union in an enterprise is forbidden. By November 1986 temporary councils of Solidarity had sought registration in at least 10 provinces. It was reported that the Solidarity leadership was divided on the question of how far it should seek to co-operate with the authorities.

Three leaders of the banned former Rural Solidarity announced on Nov. 25, 1986, that it would be re-established in the form of a temporary council.

Oct. 25, 1987. A national meeting of Solidarity activists announced the creation of a National Executive Commission (KKW), with Lech Walesa as chairman. This was in response to fragmentation of the leadership between the TRS and the TKK leading to complaints that it was losing touch with grass-roots support. An application for official registration of the KKW was rejected by a Gdansk court on Nov. 9, and in late 1987 and early 1988 courts rejected several other attempts to obtain registration for Solidarity branches in individual enterprises.

Nov. 29, 1987. In a referendum on government proposals for economic reform and limited political liberalization the government only received the backing of around 45 per cent of the electorate after only 67 per cent of eligible voters participated. Solidarity leaders had called for a boycott of the referendum, condemning it as "solely propaganda" and calling on the government to present voters with a genuine choice.

1988. In spite of the lack of majority support the government proceeded with the implementation of its economic reform programme, albeit modified, from Feb. 1, 1988, when retail price rises averaging 27 per cent took effect. The Solidarity leadership announced that it would not call for large-scale protests but would support local stoppages by workers demanding wage rises. Sporadic work stoppages began almost immediately, and a major wave of strikes began on April 25 when transport workers in Bydgoszcz won a 63 per cent wage increase after a 12-hour stoppage. This sparked off a strike at the Nowa Huta steelworks near Krakow on the following day, and workers at the Lenin shipyards in Gdansk began a strike on May 2. The authorities reacted by having nine members of the Solidarity KKW arrested, and on May 5 police stormed the Nowa Huta steelworks and arrested the strike co-ordinators. The strike at the Lenin steelworks was called off on May 10 without any concessions from the authorities. Some of those arrested remained in police custody until May 25, and 19 workers lost their jobs at Nowa Huta.

A further wave of strikes began on Aug. 15–18 with the occupation of mines in the Silesian coalfield, and by Aug. 22 the action had spread to enterprises in several cities, including the Lenin shipyard, prompting the declaration of a curfew in the three worst affected provinces. Following mediation by Roman Catholic Church representatives, Walesa held talks with the Interior Minister, Lt.-Gen. Kiszczak, on Aug. 31, and the strikes were called off after Walesa had received guarantees that the government would involve Solidarity in proposed round-table discussions, and was prepared to consider the union's reauthorization. However, these discussions failed to convene as scheduled in October following arguments about procedure and participants and doubts cast on the sincerity of the government by the emergence of what appeared to be a leaked confidential PUWP document which declared that the re-legalization of Solidarity was the main danger facing the party and would not be permitted. Furthermore, Solidarity interpreted as a deliberate provocation a government decision announced on Oct. 31 to use special powers of intervention in the management of enterprises which it had acquired under a temporary law of May 31 to close the Lenin shipyards on Dec. 1.

After two mass strikes in 1988 which finally shook the communist régime of General Jarulselzki, it was apparent that no economic solution could be found without the consent of Solidarity. The final collapse of communist government was attended by further industrial and political action by local Solidarity unions. In January 1989 alone there were 173 pay disputes and 39 "strike situations". On Feb. 6, against a background of increasing economic chaos, talks opened between Solidarity (supposedly illegal) and government ministers. In April, after two months of talks with an increasingly impotent government, the seven-year ban on it was lifted and elections were announced for June. Solidarity formally applied for registered status, declaring that the National Executive Commission (KKW) would administer the movement until a Congress could be held.

In the (partially) democratic elections of June 1989, few candidates of the PUWP were elected while almost all candidates of the "Solidarnosc Citizens Committee" were. A prolonged government crisis which found the leading communist candidate unable to form a coalition led to his displacement at the head of a new coalition by Tadeusz Mazowiecki, a Solidarity nominee, with another well-known Solidarity figure, Jacek Kuron, as Minister of Labour.

The formation of this government led to new differentiation within Solidarity. Factions appeared such as the "working group" of well-known leaders from 1981 (Andrzej Gwiazda, Jan Rulewski, Seweryn Jaworski) who were opposed to voluntary restrictions on the right to strike, and members of the Polish Socialist Party (Democratic Revolution) who played leading roles in some important localities.

Not until April 1990 did Solidarity finally meet in Congress at Gdansk with membership fallen to 2,200,000 and in confusion over its role because of pressure to support the Solidarity-inspired government of Tadeusz Maziowecki. Objectors to lending support for the government included many within its own ranks, including the "Solidarity 80" faction, and the Congress heard many speeches in criticism of privatization policy, growing unemployment and pay curbs. The following month there were widespread strikes by Solidarity unions on the railways which disrupted the approach to local elections.

In December 1990 Lech Walesa was elected President of Poland. Solidarity met in Extraordinary Congress in February 1991 to review its role in the changed socio-economic circumstances and elect a new leadership. Walesa's successor was Marian Krzaklewski, who had campaigned on a platform of staying free from political entanglements: "I am convinced that the Union chairman should remain outside of political arrangements and pressures by various political centres". President Walesa, in a speech to Congress, adopted a similar view: "The Union should not and will not replace political parties".

International affiliations. The ICFTU and the WCL on Nov. 19, 1986; jointly announced the double affiliation of Solidarity (such double affiliations being extremely rare).

Ogolnópolskie Porozumienie Zwiazków Zawodowych (OPZZ) All-Poland Alliance of Trade Unions

Address. ul. Kopernika 36/40, 00-924 Warsaw 56
Phone. 26-02-31

Telex. PL 813834

Leadership. Alfred Miodowicz (chairman, former member of the PUWP politburo); there are seven deputy chairmen

Membership. Estimated at 6,000,000.

History and character. The OPZZ was founded at Bytom in November 1984 to co-ordinate the new official trade unions. According to Miodowicz, who was elected chairman at the founding meeting, the autonomy of enterprise-level trade unions was to be preserved and strengthened; the OPZZ was not to be an authoritarian but an open representative body, and "striving for unity does not and will not have anything to do with restoring the old organizational structures ... or returning to old mistakes". Statements from the OPZZ since then have consistently emphasized the autonomy of member unions and that the OPZZ cannot take decisions binding the unions. The OPZZ was formally registered on April 12, 1985, and it was subsequently reported that the authorities had turned over to it funds impounded upon the suspension of Solidarity in December 1981.

The OPZZ held its second meeting on Nov. 26–30, 1986, this being declared the first congress to the Polish Reborn Trade Unions. Miodowicz was re-elected as chairman by 879 votes to 159, but the abstention of a significant minority of the 1,480 delegates was viewed as expressing dissatisfaction with Miodowicz's election to the PUWP Politburo in July 1986, which was seen as compromising the asserted independence of the trade union movement. The congress called for the creation of an effective system of consultation between workers and government, and adopted a final resolution which criticized government attempts to centralize control over the labour movement and proposed amendments to the labour code to make dismissals easier, and also called for stable prices for basic goods. The final resolution also reversed a decision taken earlier by the congress to constitute the OPZZ as the sole representative of unionized workers, following protests that this would jeopardize the status of the estimated 4,000 non-affiliated trade unions (mostly organized in single factories or enterprises) and would give the OPZZ a public image akin to that of its monolithic forebear, the Central Board of Trade Unions.

In an interview with the official Polish Press Agency (PAP) in August 1987 Miodowicz stated that the OPZZ considered itself to be the heir to the 1980 "Gdansk accords" between the government and Solidarity and had a moral obligation to ensure their realization. However, he also rejected trade union pluralism in enterprises, commenting that a divided workforce "serves those who manipulate". The OPZZ criticized the decision announced at the end of 1985 to reintroduce a six-day working week (the five-day working week, conceded in 1981, having been the last major surviving accomplishment of the Solidarity era), and during 1987–88 it frequently criticized other aspects of government economic policy. The OPZZ succeeded in winning a reduction in price rises in March 1987 and a general wage increase for state enterprise employees to offset the major price rises of February 1988. It also gave qualified support for the strikes in 1988, but stated officially that the right to strike was a "class weapon of the last resort, especially given Poland's existing economic position" and should not be abused by those seeking to exploit the situation for political ends.

In 1989 OPZZ was increasingly willing to countenance use of the strike weapon for economic goals and appeared to gain support from Solidarity which was compromised by its association with the post-communist governments. Throughout the period OPZZ seems to have retained the bulk of its membership that it had inherited from the CRZZ. It also successfully resisted claims from Solidarity for redistribution of the assets of CRZZ.

In June 1990 OPZZ held its Second Congress in Warsaw and confirmed the leadership of Alfred Miodowicz, with Wojciech Obarski as the new Deputy Chairman. The Congress disclaimed any intention to destabilize the government, claiming that it sought a strong administration. It called for "an institution of social accord", signed by government and unions, and demanded that the new Polish constitution should include the right of unions to make legislative initiatives, an upper chamber of "self-management producers", and the right to strike in solidarity and in defence of democracy. The OPZZ's proclaimed goals reflect a tension between its new identity and the traditional approach of monopolistic communist union centres in a centrally planned economy.

Objectives. These are to: (a) participate in developing new forms of social consultation and agreements as regards all matters of vital importance for employees; (b) support and enforce self-management rights of employees to co-decide about the matters of their work establishments; (c) counteract further decline of the living standard of the working people, fight for a growth of the share of wages in production cost; (d) actively oppose group layoffs, proposing instead changes as regards economic policy; the state, production structures, organization of labor and employment in work establishments, as well as by way of reducing worktime, earlier retirement, etc.; (e) demand properly organized, safe, productive and well paid work; (f) systematically study the level of the social minimum and fight for its being ensured for all families; (g) enforce the inalienable trade union rights to control conditions of work and improvement of its safety; (h) determinedly fight for maintaining and developing enterprise-sponsored social programmes as one of the elements of humanization of labor; (i) undertake initiatives on behalf of providing workers with recreation after work, develop enterprise-sponsored cultural, educational, sports and recreational activities; and (j) be concerned about workers' health, protection of natural environment at places of work and residence.

In December 1990, OPZZ withdrew from the WFTU, the second of the major East European centres to do so. It motivated this decision by its modest resources, the pluralistic nature of its own movement, and the diminished coverage of the WFTU itself. OPZZ also declared a wish to associate with many internationals, and above all the ETUC. Alfred Miodowicz met President Walesa in January 1991 for the first time since the December elections had brought the former Solidarity leader to power.

Structure. Before the collapse of communism there were over 26,000 enterprise trade union organizations, which each had the right to associate into multi-enterprise branch unions. At regional level there were Voivodship Alliances of Trade Unions (WPZZ). An estimated 80 per cent of all OPZZ trade unionists are affiliated through membership of the 23 trade union federations. At national level the leading bodies of the OPZZ are the 242-member Council and the Executive Committee.

Publication. Zwiakowiec (weekly).

International affiliation. None.

Portugal

Capital: Lisbon   **Population: 9,790,000**

Political system. Portugal is a multi-party democracy with a unicameral assembly and a popularly elected head of state. Since 1987 it has been governed by the centre-right Social Democratic Party (SDP) of Prof. Aníbal Caraco Silva. Portugal is a member of the EC.

Economy. For Portugal the late 1980s were years of rapid growth, stimulated by EEC spending and a new-found flexibility in the private sector. Its civilian employment of 4,401,000 was in 1989 divided between services (2,056,000), industry (1,518,000) and agriculture (827,000). Unemployment was at 5.8 per cent. With women joining the labour force in increasing numbers, a high proportion of the country's population is economically active (46.6 per cent as against an EC average of 43.3 per cent).

System of industrial relations. Portugal ratified ILO Convention No. 98 (Right to Organize and Collective Bargaining, 1949) in 1964 and Convention No. 87 (Freedom of Association and Protection of the Right to Organize, 1948) in 1977. There are restrictions on the collective bargaining rights of public servants, but the labour legislation remains generally protectionist, despite 1989 changes.

In the years immediately following the 1974 revolution, there were significant improvements in employees' rights. A 1977 strike law provided that the "right to strike is exercised via trade unions but, in companies where the majority of workers are not represented by unions, strikes will be determined by secret ballot and by a majority"; a secret ballot could be called by 20 per cent of the workforce. The law provided that written notice of a planned strike must be served only 48 hours in advance to the Ministry of Labour and management; allowed picketing; and freed workers from the responsibility of upholding their contracts during a strike. Lockouts were prohibited, but the government was empowered to requisition or conscript workers if a strike endangered essential services.

Industrial unrest rose sharply in 1988 in response to policies initiated by the recently elected majority Social Democratic government of prime minister Aníbal Cavaco Silva in preparation for full intergration into the EC. Government attempts to hold wage increases to 6 per cent, liberalize the country's strict constitutional protections against dismissal and privatize state industries met with strong and continued union protests. In a rare display of unity the two largest union federations called a general strike on March 28, which was heeded by over two million workers or roughly half the workforce. The demonstrations forced some modifications of the liberalization bill and led to president Mário Soares referring the legislation to the constitutional court. In the midst of further protests the court ruled in May that sections of the proposed legislation were unconstitutional, forcing it to be redrafted and resubmitted to parliament and delaying its passage until at least the end of the year.

Labour law change only finally occurred in February and March of 1989 when Cavaco Silva achieved presidential approval for five decrees, the *pacote laboral* which came into force on May 31, 1989. The decrees met in considerable degree the longstanding complaint of Portuguese employers about dismissal procedures and the use of fixed term contracts, each of which was a legislative legacy of the 1974 Revolution. In the government's view, liberalization of dismissals law was essential if the Portugese economy was to be reformed and integration into the Europe of 1993 achieved.

In December 1989 the government announced that it planned to launch a 44-strong Economic and Social Council to replace the tripartite Permanent Council for Social Co-operation (CPCS). The CPCS had met since 1984 but both sides of industry had questioned its effectiveness as a forum for creating a wage framework. The new Council was intended to incorporate the National Planning Council and the National Council of Prices and Incomes but doubts were quickly expressed about the extent to which it would be dominated by Portugal's powerful public sector. Under the threat of abolition employers and unions met at the CPCS and held a number of constructive meetings in the first half of 1990 on pay levels and dismissals procedures.

In October 1989 the Cavaco Silva government implemented its controversial plan to harmonize civil service remuneration scales; one effect was to raise top salary levels to prevent seepage to the private sector. Despite this shift, private sector pay continued to outstrip that in the public sector. Public sector unrest contributed to 1989 being the worst year for incidence of strikes and days lost through strikes since 1986, while the number of workers involved in disputes was the largest for many years.

Trade unionism. In the early decades of the twentieth century the Portuguese labour movement was dominated by revolutionary trade unionism and anarchosyndicalism. Following the creation of the first national confederation in 1914, the União Operária Nacional (National Workers' Union), union activity culminated in the first revolutionary general strike in 1918. The (renamed) Confederação Geral de Trabalhadores (CGT— General Confederation of Workers) was dissolved by the Salazar regime in 1933 and replaced by official trade unions within a fascist corporative structure. A general revolutionary strike in January 1934 led to increased repression and the CGT gradually lost influence among the workforce. After World War II no effective trade union movement, either legal or clandestine, existed in Portugal until the emergence of an informal and politically pluralist trade union structure, intersindical, in 1970. Following the revolution of 1974, a restricted right to strike was granted in 1974 (for the first time in four decades) and on April 30, 1975, the Supreme Revolutionary Council accorded recognition to the communist-led Intersindical Nacional (IN) as the sole national trade union centre (to which all unions were obliged to affiliate), despite the opposition of the Socialist Party, which had emerged as the dominant party in elections to a Constituent Assembly held on April 25. In October 1976, however, the Socialist government formed in July 1976 revoked the status of the IN as the sole legal centre (leading to the development of socialist trade unions) and further legislation adopted in 1977 recognized a more complete right to strike. The Labour Relations Bureau was set up within the Ministry of Labour in 1978 with responsibility for conciliation in collective bargaining disputes. Collective agreements are signed at plant, inter-plant, district and national levels, and are valid for two years (12 months for wage clauses). A 1979 law gave extensive consultative and supervisory rights to workers' committees (which are open to all workers regardless of union membership), although these are found primarily in the larger concerns. The two trade union centres are currently the Confederação Geral dos Trabalhadores Portugueses-Intersindical Nacional (CGT-IN), which is the renamed IN, and the socialist União Geral de Trabalhadores (UGTP-P). These centres (of which the CGT-IN has been generally the stronger, except in the white-collar sector) are ideologically opposed, and have generally not co-operated with each other. Many unions are unaffiliated to either centre. The UGT in particular faces a breakaway faction, the Social Democratic Workers' Organization [TSD] and has expressed concern at the emergence of a Federation of Cadres' Labour Unions (for government managers) which appears closely linked to it.

In 1989 union density in Portugal was 55 per cent. The two national centres continued to compete, but the co-operation evinced in the organization of the March 1988 strike found a tangible continuation in their joint presentation on economic modernization to the CPCS in September 1989 and occasional meetings. But clashes continued, embittered by the UGT call for the CGTP to disown the Communist Party, and the two centres were unable to organize jointly for May Day in 1989 or 1990.

With membership of the WFTU a diminishing asset, the CGTP sought entry to the ETUC but its entry was contested by the UGT. Each organization is politically divided. The UGT Socialist faction (led by its general secretary Torres Couto) is rivalled by the Social Democrats (led by President Jose Pereira Lopes). It has also made links with the Christian Democratic Workers' Federation, a small labour grouping. The CGTP contains a faction composed of socialists and communist dissidents which challenges its orthodox communist leadership.

Confederacão Geral dos Trabalhadores Portugueses-Intersindical Nacional (CGTP-IN)
General Confederation of Portugese Workers

Address. Rua Vitor Cordon, Nr. 1–20, 1200 Lisbon
Phone. 372181
Telex. 16795
Fax. 372189
Leadership. Manuel Carvalho da Silva (Co-ordinator of the Executive Committee)
Membership. 550,000–600,000 (1989 estimate).

History and character. The Confederation was founded illegally in October 1970 under the name Intersindical Nacional. Following the Revolution of 1974, Intersindical, under communist leadership, became the sole national trade union centre. inheriting the assets of the former government-sponsored syndicates. Its first Congress was held in July 1975 and it was recognized as a trade union confederation on 28th October 1975. The Second (1977) Congress changed Intersindical's name to its present one. With the waning of the revolutionary mood, the Confederation (which had supported nationalization and decolonization) lost support and faced a new rival in the UGT—P which was formed in 1978.

In the early 1980s it called unsuccessful general strikes against the Democratic Alliance government, but later in the decade participated in a number of different state bodies, such as the National

Planning Council and the Council for Social Dialogue. At the end of the 1980s industrial militancy revived, and the CGTP's fortunes recovered. It reassessed its attitude to the UGT—P and called a national day of mobilization in February 1989. Recognition by the Constitutional Court of the Union of Civilian Workers in Armed Forces Manufacturing Facilities brought new prestige to the CGTP, which had backed it. The 1989 Congress reaffirmed the Portugese Communist Party's control of the National Council, but on the Executive both Party loyalists and dissidents lost their seats.

Publication. Alavance (monthly).

International affiliations. CGTP—IN is not aligned with any world trade union centre following a decision to stay in contact with the whole international trade union movement. In the early 1980s it suffered a series of reverses over international recognition and was forced to share representation at the ILO with UGT—P. Its applications for membership of the ETUC have hitherto been unsuccessful, but it participates in the Economic and Social Committee of the EEC.

Affiliated unions and structure. CGTP-IN has a triennial Congress (last held in 1989), a General Assembly, and a National Council which has its own Executive Committee. Around 70 non-affiliated unions participate in Congressses and General Assemblies. The Confederation has a central youth organization with financial and administrative autonomy, known as Interjovem. The 152 affiliated unions are grouped in 20 Branch Federations organized along sectoral lines and 22 District Trades Councils.

União Geral de Trabalhadores (UGT – P)
General Workers' Union

Address. Rua de Buenos Aires, 11–1200 Lisbon
Phone. 676503
Telex. 15581
Fax. 674612
Leadership. José Pereira Lopes (president); José Torre Couto (secretary-general)
Membership. Claims 1,040,000 in 60 unions, but outisde estimates range as low as 330,000.

History and character. The UGT–P was founded in October 1978 with the backing of the Socialist and Social Democratic parties, in succession to the Carta Aberta (Open Letter) union grouping which in 1976 had challenged the status of the CGTP–IN as sole centre. It held its first congress in 1979.

The UGT is probably smaller than the CGTP–IN, though there are doubts about the real membership of both. It also resembles the CGTP–IN in that there are political factions within it. In 1989 it established relations with the small Christian Democratic Workers' Federation, and in March 1990 it blessed the conjunction of some of its affiliates with independent unions in a new National Federation of Transports. However, one of these affiliates, the Lisbon Transit Workers' Union (SITRA) nearly seceded from the UGT around the same time in a dispute over the level of support it had received in negotiations. The UGT also faces some competition from the Social Democratic Workers' Organization (TSD) which in 1990 launched a series of rival organizations to its affiliates.

Publications. Info–UGT; *Novos Desafios*; *Trabalho E Ambiente*; *UGT Consumidores.*
International affiliations. ICFTU; ETUC; TUAC; IFWEA.

MACAO

Capital: Nome de Deus de Macao   Population: 262,000

Political system. Macao, comprising a small peninsula in the south of the People's Republic of China and three neighbouring islands, has been under Portuguese administration since the sixteenth century. Under an agreement signed in April 1987, it will revert to China as a Special Administrative Region in 1999.

Economy. The principal economic activities of the territory are textile manufacturing and tourism-related service industries.

Trade unionism. The territory's first ever labour law, which came into effect in May 1984, made the use of child labour illegal, stipulated a maximum six-day working week and established a minimum period of annual leave.

One trade union has been reported in Macao.

Associacão Geral das Associações dos Operàrios de Macau

Address. No. 2 Rua da Ribeira do Patane
Fax. 553110
Affiliates. The organization is claimed to have 36 affiliates.

Qatar

Capital: Doha

Population: 350,000
(1988)

Political system. Qatar, which has neither a parliament nor official political parties, is ruled by decree by the Amir (head of state) who is appointed by the 30-member Advisory Council, and whose term was extended for four years in 1990. There are no political parties and no elections.

Economy. Oil accounts for 94 per cent of exports and 84 per cent of government revenue. Petrochemical industries and refineries have also been developed in order to diversify the economy. Steel, cement works and construction are the main heavy industries.

Qatar had the third highest GNP per capita of all the Gulf States but one of the smallest private sectors.

System of industrial relations. Qatar has been a member of the International Labour Organization since 1972, but has ratified neither ILO Convention No. 87 (Freedom of Association and Protection of the Right to Organize, 1948) nor No. 98 (Right to Organize and Collective Bargaining, 1949).

Trade unionism. Trade Unions are illegal and none have been reported.

Romania

Capital: Bucharest

Population: 23,200,000
(1989)

Political system. Romania was declared a socialist state in 1947 following the abolition of the monarchy, and was officially renamed the Socialist Republic of Romania under the 1965 Constitution. This Constitution also reaffirmed the leading role of the Communist Party, which was then the only legal political party.

The sudden revolution of December 1989 — the last in Eastern Europe that year — overthrew President Ceausescu and he was replaced with a government of the National Salvation Front which won elections in May 1990. Further elections were planned for the autumn of 1991 or 1992.

Economy. Scarcity and low living standards were major driving forces behind the Revolution of December 1989. The initial view of the National Salvation Front was that private enterprise would be allowed to extend its scope but that the economy would remain under central state control. Following the 1990 elections—which it won on a platform of cautious reform—the Prime Minister Petre Roman became more dominant in the government and its economic stance became more liberal. Subsidies on food and other items were cut in order to gain IMF funding. The government also began to reduce the country's industrial base, a Ceausescu legacy, amid predictions that eradicating overmanning would raise the unemployment rate to 20 per cent. The year ended with shortages of power and falling living standards and in February 1991 250,000 industrial workers in 92 plants were laid off on social security pay for two months to conserve energy for the civil population.

System of industrial relations. Romania ratified ILO Convention No. 87 (Freedom of Association and Protection of the Right to Organize, 1948) in 1957 and Convention No. 98 (Right to Organize and Collective Bargaining, 1949) in 1958.

Under Ceausescu, employment was compulsory for all able-bodied persons over 16 years old who were not receiving any form of training or education. This was criticized by the ILO as contravening ILO Convention No. 29 (Forced Labour, 1930), which Romania ratified in 1957.

The country was not without industrial disputes. Strikes were reported in 1977, 1981, 1983, 1986 and 1987. In each case they were savagely repressed.

In 1989, on the eve of Ceausescu's fall, the ILO announced a Commission of Inquiry under Convention 111 into alleged discrimination in employment against members of Romania's ethnic minorities.

In early 1990 there were signs that the National Salvation Front would develop relations with the unions on the Ceasescu pattern. By the summer of 1990 however, it had developed contacts both with the CNSLR and with Fratia (*see below*). It responded to a Fratia demand for a comprehensive law on trade union recognition and to pressure to consult unions during the formulation of all employment legislation. In June 1990, Fratia demanded—and obtained—a six-month moratorium on legislation (in return for a no-strike pledge) while legislation was considered. However June 1990 also saw clashes between anti-government demonstrators and miners supporting the National Salvation Front outside the Fratia office.

Trade unionism. Trade unions were organized on the orthodox socialist bloc model, with responsibility for mobilizing workers behind the achievement of productivity targets and for advancing the social and cultural interests of the workers. There was a single-trade-union system organized by the central UGSR; under the labour code no unions could be established outside this structure, and trade unions were required by section 165 of the code to mobilize the masses for the accomplishment of the programme of the Communist Party.

A small dissident trade union calling itself the Free Union of Romanian Working People (*Sindicatul Liber al Oamenilor Muncii din Romania*—SLOMR) was formed in February 1979 by a group of workers in the Danube port city of Turnu Severin, but was suppressed after only three months by harsh police reprisals against its members. A new clandestine trade union calling itself Freedom (*Libertatea*) emerged in May 1988 with an appeal to the Vienna follow-up to the Conference on Security and Co-operation in Europe (CSCE) calling for freedom of association in Romania and the abolition of the existing labour code. Members of Libertea, whose demands included the right to a living wage, wage protection, and eight-hour day and the right to strike were subjected to arrests, beatings and imprisonment. In June 1988 it was reported that 34 workers at an armaments factory near Brazov had discussed the formation of an independent union, and that a number of them had been punished for it.

The official UGSR was dissolved five days after the fall of Ceausescu, to be replaced at once by a "Provisional Committee for the Formation of Free Trade Unions in Romania" (later the National Free Trade Union Confederation of Romania, CNSLR) which inherited its assets and initially supported the newly governing National Salvation Front. The same month saw the formation of an independent union Fratia (Fraternity), reportedly grouping lorrydrivers, journalists, chemical workers, health and office workers. In March 1990 Fratia mounted a demonstration to challenge the right of the reformed official union to retain the assets of UGSR, though it later shifted its demand to one that the UGSR funds be used for unemployment benefit. By August 1990 Fratia claimed 800,000 members against CNSLR's claimed 3,500,000. Both have good relations with the ICFTU. There are several other federations and groups, the most radical of which appears to be Alpha which in 1991 countered the increasingly pro-market programme of the Front with its own plan to divide the country's wealth equally among the people, and at the time of the subsidies cuts threatened a general strike. The issue rumbled on into May 1991 when 80,000 food industry workers in 1,000 local branches staged a two-hour strike for the continuation of subsidies.

Alpha

Membership. 1,200,000.

Confederatia Nationala a Sindicatelor Libere din Romania (CNSLR)
National Free Trade Union Confederation of Romania

Address. 70109 Bucharest 1, 1–3 Ministerului Street
Phone. 13.65.79
Telex. 10844 CNSLR R
Leadership. Victor Ciorbea (president)
Membership. 3,500,000 (1991).
History. Founded in 1991.
Publication. NewsBulletin (monthly).

Affiliated unions. 16 professional or branch federations in all spheres of the economy (agriculture, food industry, textile and leather industry, wood industry, engineering industry, industrial railways, workers and handicraft co-operatives, Commerce, education, public services, health units etc) and 36 territorial leagues in almost all districts in the country. Not affiliated internationally, sympathizing with ICFTU, however.

Fratia
Fraternity

Leadership. Miron Mitrea

Membership. 800,000.

History and character. Founded in December 1989, and mounted important demonstrations during 1990.

Publication. Argument.

Rwanda

Capital: Kigali   **Population: 6,657,000**
                                                   (1988)

Political system. Rwanda is a one-party state which has been ruled since a *coup* in 1973 by Juvenal Habyarimana.

Economy. Agriculture is the largest sector of the economy, employing 93 per cent of the workforce, and the main cash crop is coffee which employs some 400,000 peasant farmers. Manufacturing industry is based mainly on processing agricultural products and foodstuffs. A law of October 1988 allowed five tax free years to Rwanda's fast-growing co-operative sector.

System of industrial relations. Rwanda has been a member of the International Labour Organization since 1962, and ratified ILO Conventions No. 87 (Freedom of Association and Protection of the Right to Organize, 1948) and No. 98 (Right to Organize and Collective Bargaining, 1949) in 1985.

Trade unionism. Rwanda's only centre is the Centrale Syndicale des Travailleurs du Rwanda.

Centrale Syndicale des Travailleurs du Rwanda
Central Union of Rwanda Workers

Address. B.P. 1645 Kigali

Phone. (250) 84012, 85639

Leadership. J. Ntabanganyimana and A. Rukebesha (joint secretaries-general)

Membership. Claims a membership of around 70,000.

History and character. The Union was founded in August 1985 and is the only national centre in Rwanda.

Publications. Ijwi Ry'Abakozi; Presence Syndicale (forthnightly since March 1991).

Affiliated unions.

1. **Syndicat de Base de l'Administration (SYBAD)**

2. **Syndicat des Enseignements du Secteur Public** (SYNESP)

3. **Syndicat du Personnel de Santé** (SPS)

4. **Syndicat du Personnel Judiciaire** (SPJ)

5. **Syndicat du Personnel Communal** (SPECOM)

6. **Syndicat du Personnel des Services Parastataux** (SEPAR)

7. **Syndicat de Personnel des Travailleurs des Industries, Constructions, Mines et Imprimeurs (STRIGECOMI)**

8. **Syndicat des Banques, Hotels, Compagnies de Transport (STBACHETRA)**

9. **Syndicat des Enseignements, Journalistes, Services Médiaux et Librairies (SENJOUSMEL)**

10. **Syndicat des Travailleurs, Agricoles, Fleureurs et Forestiers du Rwanda (SAEFR)**

International affiliations. OUSA; OCATU.

St Kitts and Nevis

Capital: Basseterre

Population: 43,000
(1988)

Political system. St Kitts and St Nevis, a federation of two islands, is an independent member of the Commonwealth with the British monarch, represented by a Governor-General as head of state. There is a popularly elected unicameral National Assembly. The country is currently ruled by a coalition between the conservative Nevis Reform Party (NRP) and the centre-right People's Action Movement (PAM).

Economy. The state-owned sugar industry is the country's principal source of export earnings. Tourism and the electronics industry for the US market are increasingly important. Infrastructural facilities are relatively well-developed for the region.

System of industrial relations. St Kitts is not a member of the ILO. In the period before the March 1989 elections which confirmed the government in power, substantial pay increases were granted to civil servants; while the government gave rises unilaterally to the sugar workers rather than enter negotiations with the TLU.

Trade unionism. Trade unions were legalized in 1939. The TLU strongly supported the St Kitts Labour Party in the 1989 elections and, following its defeat, Lee Moore—president of both organizations—was forced to resign each position. The National Allied Workers' Union (NAWU) represents dockers in the port of Basseterre but has not been able to spread its influence as it would wish. The United Workers Union (UWU) is linked to the governing People's Action Movement.

St Kitts – Nevis Trades and Labour Union (TLU)

Address. P.O. Box 239, "Masses House", Church Street, Basseterre
Phone. 2229; 2891
Cable. TRALION, ST KITTS
Leadership. Joseph N. France (general secretary)
Membership. 1,322 (1989)
History and character. The efforts of the St Kitt's Workers' League (founded in 1932 and later renamed as the Labour Party) were instrumental in the legalization of trade unionism in 1939, and the consequent formation of the St Kitts–Nevis Trades and Labour Union in 1940. The union's orientation is social democratic and the relationship with the Labour Party (which won all elections from 1937 to 1975 and was in power until 1980) is close.
Publication. The Labour Spokesman (two per week, circulation 6,000).
International affiliations. ICFTU; CCL.

United Workers' Union (UWU)

Address. Fort Thomas Road, Basseterre
Leadership. Nassibou Butler (president)
History and character. Has been associated with the People's Action Movement of Dr Kennedy Simmonds.
International affiliations. WCL; CLAT.

391

St Lucia

Capital: Castries   **Population: 140,000**

Political system. St Lucia is an independent member of the Commonwealth with the British monarch, represented by a Governor-General, as head of state. It is a multi-party democracy with an elected bicameral parliament. The conservative United Worker's Party (UWP) is currently in power.

Economy. The country's main export earnings come from bananas. The tourist and broad-based manufacturing sectors are growing rapidly. St Lucia is still dependent on external aid to underpin the process of economic growth.

The government is actively working to reduce the dependence of St Lucia's economy on bananas, and until it succeeds it is unlikely that unemployment can be overcome.

System of industrial relations. St Lucia has been a member of the International Labour Organization since 1980, and ratified ILO Conventions No. 87 (Freedom of Association and Protection of the Right to Organize, 1948) and No. 98 (Right to Organize and Collective Bargaining, 1949) in that year.

Unions which gain sufficient membership at new firms may demand a ballot for recognition, but gaining this first foothold has proved difficult for them in the country's new Export Processing Zones.

Trade unionism. The three largest unions in St Lucia are the National Workers' Union (now no longer affiliated to the WFTU), the St Lucia Civil Service Association (SLCSA), and St Lucia Teachers' Union (SLTU) which work together in a Committee of Labour Solidarity, though this has not developed into the comprehensive organization which Prime Minister Compton sought. As a result, there are still 10 unions in St Lucia, their numbers recently swollen by the formation of a new Technical and Allied Workers' Union (TAWU), though it has encountered difficulties with the Registrar of Trade Unions. Like a number of other unions the TAWU is closely linked to the opposition St Lucia Labour Party and was founded by its deputy leader.

National Workers' Union (NWU)

Address. P.O. Box 713, 60 Micoud Street, Castries
Phone. 23664
Leadership. Tyrone Maynard (president-general); George Goddard (secretary-general)
Membership. 6,000 in 36 branches.
History and character. The NWU was founded in August 1973 and is a general union with branches for each occupational sector. The union has shifted from its previous leftish stance to a pragmatic position of working with the government.
Publication. Combat (2,500 circulation).
International affiliations. PSI.

St Lucia Seamen Waterfront and General Workers' Trade Union (SWGWTU)

Address. Reclamation Grounds, Conway, P.O. Box 166, Castries
Cable. SEAMEN ST LUCIA
Leadership. Peter Josie (president); Julia Phillips (secretary)
Membership. Claims 2,500.
History. Founded 1945.
International Affiliations. ICFTU; CCL.

St Lucia Workers' Union (WU)

Address. P.O. Box 245, 3 Park Street (Reclamation Grounds), Castries
Phone. 45-22620
Cable. RECLAMATION GROUNDS CASTRIES ST LUCIA
Leadership. George Louis (president); Titus Francis (secretary)
Membership. 1,000.
History and character. Founded 1939 on the recommendation of a Commission (appointed by the British government to investigate labour disturbances throughout the then British West Indies). Is linked to the St Lucia Labour Party and is the oldest union in St Lucia but is now in decline.
International affiliation. ICFTU.

St Vincent and the Grenadines

Capital: Kingstown   **Population: 135,000**

Political system. St Vincent and the Grenadines is an independent member of the Commonwealth with the British monarch, represented by a Governor-General, as head of state. The election in July 1984 was won by the conservative New Democratic Party (NDP).

In May 1989 the NDP renewed its mandate with a 15–0 victory at the polls under Prime Minister James Mitchell.

Economy. The economy of St Vincent and the Grenadines is based on the cultivation and processing of bananas and arrowroot. Tourism plays a significant role in the economy.

Unemployment continues to be a major problem and unofficial estimates put it at a rate above 30 per cent. Agriculture offers the best additional hope to tourism of providing new jobs though an industrial estate is being established. The 1989 rise in the minimum wage was the first since 1982 and seems to have resulted in some private sector job losses.

System of industrial relations. St Vincent and the Grenadines is not a member of the International Labour Organization.

Trade unionism. There is no one centre of unions in St Vincent. Apart from the CTAWU, the National Progressive Workers' Union and the long-established Public Service Union (still hampered by being short of the 50 per cent civil service backing it needs for recognition), there is the St Vincent Union of Teachers (SVUT) led by Joye Browne, and the National Workers' Movement (NWM) which operates in the private sector.

Commercial, Technical and Allied Workers' Union (CTAWU)

Address. P.O. Box 245, Kingstown
Phone. 61525
Cable. DEMLAB
Leadership. Cyril Roberts (president); Colin Williams (general secretary)
Membership. Claims 3,800.
History and character. The CTAWU, which was founded in 1962, normally backed the opposition Labour Party at elections, but 1989 was an exception. Its former secretary Burns Bonadie took

up a post as Labour Attaché to the Organization of Eastern Caribbean States (OECS) and broke with the Party, for which he had once been a candidate.

International affiliations. ICFTU; FIET; PTTI; ITF; IUF; CCL.

National Progressive Workers' Union

International affiliation. WFTU.

St Vincent and the Grenadines Public Service Union

Address. P.O. Box 875, McKie's Hill, Kingstown
Phone. 71801
Leadership. Julian Casuth (president); Glenn Jackson (general secretary)
Membership. 961 (Dec. 31, 1987).
International affiliations. PSI; PTTI; CCL.

San Marino

Capital: San Marino   **Population: 22,000**

Political system. San Marino is a republic in which legislative power is vested in a 60-member, elected Grand and General Council; two Council members are appointed every six months to act as Captains-Regent who, with a congress of State (government) exercise executive power. It is currently ruled by a coalition between Communists and Christian Democrats.

Economy. Traditionally dependent upon tourism and agriculture, San Marino has recently attempted to diversify the economy, expanding the manufacturing sector.

System of Industrial Relations. Trade unions have legal recognition in San Marino, and collective agreements have legal force. San Marino has been a member of the International Labour Organization since 1982 but has not yet ratified ILO Convention No. 87 (Freedom of Association and Protection of the Right to Organize, 1948) or Convention No. 98 (Right to Organize and Collective Bargaining, 1949).

Trade unionism. The Confederazione Sammarinese del Lavoro (CSdL), founded in 1943, was the only recognized union until the recognition of trade union pluralism in 1957 and the formation of the Confederazione Democratica dei Lavoratori Sammarinesi (CDLS). During the 1960s these two groups tended to adopt similar policies, and in 1976 they formed the Centrale Sindicale Unitaire (CSU—Central United Union) with the ultimate objective of creating an organic union. This goal has not yet been achieved although the CSdL and the CDLS share offices. In this they were disadvantaged against the employers who are united in the National Association of San Marino Industry.

Confederazione Democratica dei Lavoratori Sammarinesi (CDLS)
Democratic Confederation of San Marino Workers

Address. Via Napoleone Bonaparte 75, 47031 Republic of San Marino
Phone. (549) 992007/992333
Fax. (549) 992178

Leadership. Mrs Rita Ghironz (secretary-general)

Membership. 2,000.

History and character. Founded in 1957 by promoting committees of workers from all employment categories in San Marino. General orientation is Catholic and socialist, but it believes in trade union autonomy from political organizations. Opened the "Ufficio Studi e Formazione" (Studies and Information Office) in 1987, a branch office which produces the statistic publication, *Grandangolo*.

Affiliated unions. Federazione Pubblico Impeigo (FPI—public administration, 1,000 members); Federazione Industria (FI — industrial workers and craftsmen, 700 members); Federazione Construzioni (FC — construction industry, 500 members), Federazione Pensionat (FP — retired persons, 250 members).

Publication. *Grandangolo* (monthly).

International affiliation. ICFTU.

Confederazione Sammarinese del Lavoro (CSdL)

Address and telephone. As for the CDLS (above)

Leadership. Stefano Macina (secretary-general)

Membership. 2,450 in five affiliated unions.

History and character. The CSdL held its 10th Congress in March 1988. Women constituted 30 per cent of the delegates and one-third of the Confederal Bureau elected by the congress, reflecting the high percentage (half) of women members of the union.

Publication. *Argomenti*; *Notizie Sindicale*.

São Tomé and Príncipe

Capital: São Tomé   **Population: 122,000**

Political system. The Democratic Republic of São Tomé and Príncipe is a *de facto* one-party state, ruled since independence from Portugal in 1975 by the marxist Movement for the Liberation of São Tomé and Príncipe (MLSTP).

A new constitution providing for a multi-party system was approved by referendum in August 1990. In January 1991 the first multi-party elections were held as a result of which the MLSTP government resigned, following its defeat by the opposition Democratic Convergence (PCD). Presidential elections were held in March 1991 and won by the former exile Miguel Trovoada.

Economy. The economy is predominantly agricultural with cocoa as the principal crop. There is a heavy reliance on external aid to cover current payments deficits and to fund capital projects.

System of industrial relations. The country joined the International Labour Organization in 1982 but has yet to ratify either Convention No. 87 (Freedom of Association and Protection of the Right to Organize, 1948) or No. 98 (Right to Organize and Collective Bargaining, 1949).

Trade unionism. Trade unionism was severely curbed under Protuguese rule. In 1982 a national commission was established to prepare the creation of basic trade union structures, and the National Organization of Workers held its first conference in 1988.

Organizaçao Nacional dos Trabalhadores de São Tomé e Príncipe
National Organization of Workers of São Tomé and Príncipe

Address. B.P. 8, São Tomé
Phone. 22388
Telex. 213 st
Leadership. Francisco Pires (president)
International affiliation. OATUU.

Saudi Arabia

Capital: Riyadh

Population: 14,016,000
(1988)

Political system. Saudi Arabia is an absolute monarchy ruled according to the laws and precepts of Islam. The kingdom has no parliament and no political parties though in November 1990 King Fahd promised to set up a Consultative Council, first mooted in 1981.

Economy. Saudi Arabia controls nearly one quarter of all proven oil reserves and has the world's largest crude oil export capacity. In the 1980s, responding to the uncertainty of oil prices, it has sought to diversify the economy and to improve the productivity of the local labour force in order to reduce the Kingdom's heavy reliance on expatriates.

A Saudi businessman's conference held in June 1989 promulgated a four-point plan of economic development including privatization, private sector restructuring, joint venture promotion and labour force development. in 1985–87, 48.5 per cent of the Saudi labour force was engaged in agriculture, 14.4 per cent in industry and 37.2 per cent in services.

A royal decree in 1984 banned women from working. Saudi Arabia has been a member of the International Labour Organization since 1976, but has ratified neither Convention No. 87 (Freedom of Association and Protection of the Right to Organize, 1948) nor No. 98 (Right to Organize and Collective Bargaining, 1949). It has, however, ratified Convention No. 111 (Discrimination, Employment and Occupation, 1958) and No. 29 (Forced Labour, 1930).

According to *Workers' Voice*, the organ of the Workers' Union of Saudi Arabia, strikes do occur occasionally.

Trade unionism. Trade unions are illegal and dismissal, imprisonment or (in the case of foreign workers) expulsion follow attempts at organization. Strikes occurred in the oil industry in 1945 and 1947, following which labour statutes were introduced by royal decree which banned trade unionism. A trade union organization, the Workers' Committee, was established in 1953, but this was repressed; there is currently a WFTU-recognized Workers' Union of Saudi Arabia, based in Syria, but the effective support within Saudi Arabia for this organization is unclear. It claims to have established underground committees in many workplaces. Strikes were reported between 1983 and 1985, and the WFTU stated in 1986 that dozens of workers had been imprisoned.

Workers' Union of Saudi Arabia

Address. P.O. Box 3066, Damascus, Syria
Leadership. Majed Ali Al-Zahrani
History and character. A constitutive committee was set up in 1977, and the Workers' Union (also reported as the Workers' Federation of Saudi Arabia) was founded in 1984.
Publication. Saout Al Omal (Workers' Voice).
International affiliation. WFTU (associated organization).

Senegal

Capital: Dakar   **Population: 7,154,000**
                                                            (1988)

Political system. Senegal is a multi-party democracy with a popularly elected National Assembly and an executive President. It has been ruled by the Socialist Party of Senegal (PSS) since full independence was achieved in 1960.

Confederation with the Gambia, begun in 1982, has collapsed, and 1989 and 1990 saw increasingly open opposition to the rule of President Abdou Diouf. Elections are next due to be held in 1993.

Economy. It is estimated that there are 320,000 workers in the formal economic sector, divided between 65,000 public sector workers. 30,000 in quasi-state bodies, and 225,000 in the private sector. The informal sector however may contain as many as 900,000 people. Here the peanut industry is dominant, accounting for 23 per cent of GDP. 1989 however brought severe economic difficulties for the formal sector with major banking and textile closures, and the decision of the national Assembly to press ahead with reorganization of the National Rail Company against union opposition.

System of industrial relations. Senegal ratified ILO Convention No. 87 (Freedom of Association and Protection of the Right to Organize, 1948) in 1960 and Convention No. 98 (Right to Organize and Collective Bargaining, 1949) in 1961.

In 1987 the government introduced amendments to labour legislation which would have reduced workers' security of employment and entitlements to social security benefits and pensions. Unions opposed the amendment and it was withdrawn. There have also been continuing protests against austerity measures and redundancies associated with the IMF and World Bank-backed economic reform programme.

Simultaneously with reorganization of the Rail Corporation, the government introduced amendments to the investment code which were also resisted by the unions because they permitted the employment of workers on limited contracts. This has the effect of bypassing other procedures laid down in the Labour Code to govern dismissals.

Strikes and industrial unrest in Senegal were prevalent in 1989, notably in education—where two independent teachers' unions and the students—went on strike. There was also a major bank strike, but this was in order to improve redundancy terms and resulted in no gains for SYTBEFS, the union concerned. A large number of workers in the food industry lost their jobs during the year and there was widespread social unrest.

Trade unionism. Trade unions developed under French rule, but in 1969 the Confédération Nationale des Travailleurs Sénégalais was established as the sole trade union centre, with affiliation to the sole legal party, the Union Progressiste Sénégalaise (UPS, now known as the Parti Socialiste du Sénégal—PS). Political and trade union pluralism was re-established after 1976. At different times there have been three rival centres but all now appear to be defunct.

Like other African union centres which have links with the ruling party, the CNTS has come under pressure to oppose government policies which undermine the living standards of its members. In 1989 and 1990 it was the scene of a robust struggle between its leadership which is still aligned to the ruling Socialist Party (PS), and backers of the Opposition Alliance. There are a number of independent unions of which the largest is the Democratic Union of Senegalese Workers (UDTS) with 6,000 members.

Confédération Nationale des Travailleurs Sénégalais (CNTS)
National Confederation of Senegalese Workers

Address. 15 rue Escarfait, B.P. 937, Dakar
Leadership. Madia Diop (secretary-general)
Membership. 65,000 in 62 unions.
History and character. Founded 1969, and affiliated to the ruling Parti Socialiste du Sénégal (PS). There is a 47-member executive. At its 1985 congress the CNTS called on the government to associate the confederation closely with its policy-making, and to curb speculation, which had led to inflation in basic foodstuffs. The CNTS has opposed recent amendments to labour legislation and austerity measures (*see above*), but has come in for criticism from some sections of the labour movement for its ineffectiveness and alleged corruption.

The CNTS's inability to resist legal changes which weakened organized labour's position contributed to undermining the position of its leaders. In the period leading up to and including the March 1990 Confederal Congress of the CNTS, a fierce factional battle developed between supporters of the PS and the opposition Alliance. In the pre-Congress period, the Alliance took control of the Sugar Workers' Union, the Senegalese River Development Agency, and the Telephone Company Union. At the Congress seven Alliance members were elected to the policy-making Confederal Bureau, among them four members of the Independence and Labour Party (PIT).
International affiliation. OATUU.

Other organizations

Democratic Union of Senegalese Workers (UDTS)
Democratic Union of Teachers (UDEN)
Independent Democratic Union of Senegalese Teachers (SUDES)
Independent Union of University Professors (SAES)

Seychelles

Capital: Victoria   **Population: 68,000**
(1988)

Political system. Seychelles is an independent republic within the Commonwealth. The left-wing Seychelles People's Progressive Front has since 1979 been the country's sole legal political party. The last general election was held in 1987.

Economy. Seychelles is heavily dependent upon tourism, which accounts for about one-fifth of GDP, one-third of employment and over 90 per cent of foreign exchange earnings. In 1987 over 35 per cent of the total budget expenditure was allocated to servicing the country's debt.

System of industrial relations. Seychelles has been a member of the International Labour Organization since 1977, and ratified ILO Convention No. 87 (Freedom of Association and Protection of the Right to Organize, 1948) and Convention Nos. 29 and 105 on forced labour in 1978.

Trade unionism. All previously existing trade unions were co-ordinated in 1978 in the National Workers' Union (Seychelles) (NWUS). According to the constitution (incorporated into the national Constitution in 1979) of the ruling Seychelles People's Progressive Front, the NWUS functions under the direction of the Front, which must approve every decision of the union.

National Workers' Union (Seychelles) (NWUS)

Address. P.O. Box 154, Mahé
Phone. 24030
Telex. SZ 2226
Leadership. Olivier Charles (national chairman); Michael Memee (national secretary)
Membership. 30,000.
History and character. Formed in 1978, the National Workers' Union states that it "represents all workers irrespective of colour, creed or political inclinations", and all workers who contribute to the state social security fund are automatically members. It is the sole negotiating body for workers, and is, with the Seychelles Women's Organization, the Youth League, and the People's Defence Forces, integrated into the structure of the ruling Seychelles People's Progressive Front.
Publication. The People.
International affiliation. OATUU. As at the end of 1987, the NWUS was listed as an affiliate by the ICFTU, but this affiliation was not acknowledged by the NWUS.

Sierra Leone

Capital: Freetown   **Population: 3,938,000**
                                                            (1988)

Political system. Sierra Leone is an independent republic within the Commonwealth. It is a one-party state with the head of the armed forces, Maj. Gen. Joseph Momoh, as President.

Economy. Sierra Leone's economy is based on agriculture (principally at subsistence level) and mining, notably of gold and diamonds. It has a chronic debt problem exacerbated by rigid market management and smuggling. In 1986 it failed to meet IMF conditions to halt the economic decline. In November 1987 a state of emergency was declared, the key points of which included a crack-down on smuggling, but the country entered the 1990s still deeply in debt. A large number of public servants failed to receive regular pay.

System of industrial relations. Sierra Leone ratified ILO Convention No. 87 (Freedom of Association and Protection of the Right to Organize, 1948) and No. 98 (Right to

399

Organize and Collective Bargaining, 1949) in 1961. It also ratified Convention Nos. 29 and 105 on forced labour in 1961, but the ILO has noted the continued imposition of compulsory cultivation and of forced labour as a punishment for political dissidence.

Trade unionism. Trade unions were recognized by the British colonial authorities just before World War II and were well established by independence.

Trade unionism is well developed and there is a dominant central confederation, the Sierra Leone Labour Congress, which is affiliated to the ICFTU and OATUU. This was reported as affiliating all the unions within the country, following the re-admission to membership in 1985 of the Sierra Leone Motor Drivers' Union. The country's main unions tend to be in industry, which accounts for less than 6 per cent of the workforce, whereas agriculture employs around 65 per cent.

Sierra Leone Labour Congress (SLLC)

Address. P.O. Box 1333, Freetown
Phone. 26869
Leadership. Momodu Sulimani Kemoh (national president); Kandeh Yila (general secretary)
Membership. 40,000 in 19 affiliated unions.
History and character. The SLLC was founded in 1966 succeeding the Sierra Leone Council of Labour which had been subject to a series of splits in the early 1960s. In 1981 the SLLC came into conflict with the government, rejecting the latter's emphasis on external factors as responsible for the country's economic difficulties; instead the SLLC put forward a programme of domestic reforms, including proposals for the administration of the state, steps to discourage smuggling, effective price controls (especially in respect of rice), and improvements to the economic infrastructure and to welfare services. Strikes organized by the SLLC in September 1981 led to looting, the detention of numerous trade union leaders, and a number of deaths. Ibrahim Langley, then the SLLC president, was appointed a nominated MP by President Stevens in October 1982, shortly after he had announced the dismissal as SLLC general secretary of James Kabia, the main organizer of the 1981 strikes. There was further labour unrest in 1984–85 over non-payment of salaries and bonuses. Discontent has since continued in protest at austerity measures imposed by President Momoh. Sweeping emergency regulations giving the government extensive powers were introduced in November 1987 following a series of strikes by public sector workers over salary non-payment. The emergency powers were extended for 12 months in March 1988.

Affiliated unions. The main affiliated are the Clerical, Mercantile and General Workers' Union; Railway Workers' Union; Dockworkers' Union; Motor Drivers' Union; Teachers' Union; Transport, Argicultural and General Workers' Union; United Mineworkers' Union; General Construction Workers' Union; Municipal and Local Government Employees' Union; Public Utility Workers' Union; National Seamen's Union;

International affiliations. ICFTU; OATUU.

Singapore

Capital: Singapore City   **Population: 2,639,000**
                                                        (1988)

Political system. Singapore is an independent republic within the Commonwealth. Although in form a multi-party democracy, in practice, it has been ruled since 1965 by the increasingly conservative and authoritarian People's Action Party (PAP) led by Mr Lee Kuan Yew until 1990 and then by Goh Chok Tong.

Economy. Singapore has a highly developed free market economy: it is a major regional manufacturing, trading and financial centre. It has experienced rapid economic growth since independence.

By 1988 growth was at the striking rate of 11 per cent. The same year unemployment dropped to 3.3 per cent and for the first time problems of labour shortage began to appear, prompting both unions and government to suggest that from 1992 the retirement age should be not 55 but 60. Of a labour force of 1,250,000; 410,000 were employed in industry in 1988, 760,000 in services and 19,800 in agriculture.

System of industrial relations. The basic framework for labour relations is provided by the Industrial Relations Act of 1960, as amended on several occasions. Singapore's Trade Union (Amendment) Act, which came into force in April 1983, caused a number of established unions to lose their recognition from the Registrar of Trade Unions. The Act requires unions to perform the function of regulating relations between employers and employees; thus trade unions of self-employed and contracted groups were efffectively de-registered and forced to switch to the status of societies. The National Wages Council (NWC), a tripartite body composed of representatives of the Government, employers and unions set up in 1972, fixes annual wage guidelines providing a framework for collective bargaining; however, the Singapore National Employers' Federation (SNEF) in 1985 recommended that these guidelines should be discontinued in favour of greater in-house bargaining and adaptability to market forces, and the NTUC indicated that it would be prepared to consider realistic proposals for ensuring that Singapore does not lose its competitive edge. During a period of economic recession in 1986–87, the NTUC accepted wage restraint and a cut in its membership's Central Provident Fund contributions. Economic recovery in 1988 led to a disagreement between the NTUC and SNEF over the question of wage increases. The NTUC in mid-1988 advised trade unionists to urge employers to raise salaries and give bigger annual increments if they wished to recruit and retain workers in an increasingly tight labour market. In response, the SNEF issued a series of guidelines on what employers should do in the face of what it described as a "visible building of pressure" by unions for big wage increases. There was no indication that the dispute would lead to any form of industrial action; the last major strike in Singapore had taken place at Metal Box in 1977.

Singapore ratified ILO Convention No. 98 (Right to Organize and Collective Bargaining, 1949) in 1965 but has not ratified Convention No. 87 (Freedom of Association and Protection of the Right to Organize, 1948).

Trade unionism. Trade unions developed after World War II and became associated with opposition to British colonial rule. A Singapore Trades Union Congress appeared in the 1950s in association with the People's Action Party (which took power when Singapore achieved internal self-government in 1959); this split in 1961 into the National Trades Union Congress (NTUC) and a leftist Singapore Association of Trade Unions, the latter collapsing in 1963. Today 98 per cent of the organized workers belong to unions affiliated to the NTUC, which professes to have a "symbiotic relationship" with the government. Development of unions outside the NTUC structure has been discouraged by the strong growth of the Singaporean economy and the provision of extensive welfare services. Of 83 registered unions in Singapore (with around 1,000 local branches) 70 are affiliated to the NTUC. Union density in 1988 was 16.5 per cent.

National Trades Union Congress (NTUC)

Address. Trade Union House, Shenton Way, Singapore City, 0106

Phone. 2226555
Telex. RS 24543
Cables. SOLIDCOM
Leadership. Oscar Oliveiro (president); Ong Teng Cheong (general secretary)
Membership. In mid-1988, 70 of Singapore's 83 registered unions were NTUC affiliated. NTUC membership had fallen from a peak of 31 per cent of the organizable workforce in 1979 to some 17 per cent in 1988.

History and character. Since its creation in 1961 the NTUC (which is also referred to as the Singapore National Trades Union Congress — SNTUC) has been closely linked to the ruling People's Action Party, and the current general secretary is also the Second Deputy Prime Minister. It describes its orientation as being to democratic socialism and anti-communism. The NTUC has favoured policies of industrial co-operation intended to promote growth and attract foreign investment, and in 1986 agreed to an indefinite wage freeze, following the 1985 economic downturn, in line with a recommendation of the National Wages Council. However, economic recovery in 1988 led to renewed demands by the NTUC for wage increases, a move criticized by the national employers group. The NTUC provides its members with a wide range of services, including shops, health services, insurance facilities and recreational and holiday facilities. In parliamentary elections held on Sept. 3, 1988, a small number of NTUC officials ran as opposition candidates. Three of the officials, Shariff Yahya, M. Ramasamy and George Situ, were subsequently dismissed from their union posts. Chaim Se Tong, leader of the opposition Singapore Democratic Party, proposed a three-month boycott of the NTUC-owned Fairprice shops in protest at the dismissals.

Publication. NTUC News.
International affiliations. ICFTU; ICFTU-APRO.

Solomon Islands

Capital: Honiara   **Population: 304,000**
                                                              (1988)

Political system. The Solomon Islands is an independent member of the Commonwealth. The British monarch, represented by a Governor-General, is head of state. The two main political parties, the Solomon Islands United Party (SIUP) and the People's Alliance Party (PAP), won 13 and 12 seats respectively in the October 1984 general election to the 38-seat National Parliament.

Solomon Mamaloni became Prime Minister in March 1989 following the election victory of his People's Alliance Party. He resigned as party leader in October 1990 but remained as Prime Minister, at the head of a coalition government of "national unity".

Economy. The economy is heavily dependent on agriculture, which accounts for about 60 per cent of GDP. Subsistence farming plays a greater role than commercial production. The manufacturing industry is largely restricted to the processing of local primary commodities. Only 10 per cent of the population was in organized employment in 1985.

System of industrial relations. The Solomon Islands joined the International Labour Organization in 1984 but has yet to ratify ILO Convention No. 87 (Freedom of Association and Protection of the Right to Organize, 1948) and No. 98 (Right to Organize and Collective Bargaining, 1949).

Trade unionism. The initial signs of formal organization among workers in the Solomon Island were first noted in the early 1960s. Organizations formed at this time were not always successful, but they were effective in making the employers and the government increasingly aware of the workers' organizational capacities. The emergence of the Solomon Islands General Workers' Union (subsequently known as the Solomon Islands National Union of Workers—SINUW) in the mid-1970s precipitated an increased level of unionization. Workers and their leaders saw the need to protect and further their interests through the process of collective bargaining and political participation. In 1986 a trade union centre was formed, the Solomon Islands Council of Trade Unions (SICTU), based in Honiara. At the end of June 1987 there were 21 registered trade unions with over 21,000 members, indicating that over 90 per cent of the country's workforce are unionized. The two main unions are SINUW and the Solomon Islands Public Employees' Union (SIPEU).

Solomon Islands National Union of Workers (SINUW)

Address. P.O. Box 271, Honiara
Leadership. Joses T. Tunhanuku
History and character. The SINUW was founded in the mid-1970s and is also known as the Solomon Islands General Workers' Union (SIGWU). The SINUW advocates a nuclear-free Pacific, favours the liberation struggle of the Kanak population of New Caledonia, and is critical of the operations of transnational corporations in the Solomon Islands.
International affiliation. WFTU.

Solomon Islands Public Employees' Union (SIPEU)

Address. P.O. Box 360, Honiara
Leadership. Roger Tauriki (general secretary)

Somalia

Capital:Mogadishu   **Population: 6,089,000**

Political system. Until 1991 the Socialist Democratic Republic of Somalia was a one-party state ruled by the left wing Somali Revolutionary Socialist Party. Major-General Mohammed Siad Barre, who seized power in a bloodless *coup* in 1969 was himself deposed in January 1991. He was replaced by Ali Mahdi Mohammed of the United Somali Congress, who promised free elections. However Somalia faces the threat of secession in that part of its territory which was British Somaliland where a Somaliland Republic was proclaimed by separatist forces in May 1991.

Economy. Somalia is heavily dependent on the rearing of livestock (the main source of export earnings) which supports up to three-quarters of the predominantly nomadic population. Food production falls far short of the country's requirements. There is a serious refugee problem and chronic external debt. Relations with the IMF and the World Bank were effectively severed in September and November 1987 respectively.

In 1985–87 the labour force of Somalia was divided between agriculture (75.6 per cent), industry (8.4 per cent) and services (16 per cent). Economic growth in 1990 was projected to reach 5 per cent and efforts would be made to keep inflation below 60 per cent. The 1990 budget made provision for a 103 per cent general salary increase and in a separate

403

measure designed to improve living standards customs duties on imported essential goods were reduced as from Jan. 1, 1990.

System of industrial relations. Somalia has been a member of the International Labour Organization since 1960 but has ratified neither ILO Convention No. 87 (Freedom of Association and Protection of the Right to Organize, 1948) nor No. 98 (Right to Organize and Collective Bargaining, 1949). However Somalia ratified Convention Nos. 29 and 105 on forced labour in 1960 and 1961.

Trade unionism. Only one national trade union centre has been identified, the General Federation of Trade Unions.

General Federation of Somali Trade Unions (GFSTU)

Address. P.O. Box 1179, Mogadishu
Phone. 80961, 80927
Cable. SHASOMA P O Box 1179
Leadership. Mahamud Shire Ismacil (president, elected April 1988)
Membership. 180,000.
History and character. The GFSTU was founded on May 1, 1977. Its third congress was held in April 1988.
Affiliated unions. Eight national unions are affiliated.
International affiliations. OATUU, ICATU.

South Africa

Capital: Pretoria   **Population: 36,000,000**

Political system. South Africa is ruled according to the system of apartheid with three racially separate houses elected from among the white, Asian and coloured (mixed race) population. Black South Africans (comprising about two-thirds of the country's total population) have no political representation within this system. South Africa has been ruled since 1948 by the National Party (NP) which has recently been threatened by the hard-line Conservative Party (CPSA) and from internal and external opposition to apartheid.

In June 1986 a State of Emergency was proclaimed in South Africa which led to at least 25,000 activists being detained. In February 1988 the United Democratic Front and 16 other organizations opposed to apartheid were banned while restrictions were placed on the political activities of trade unions. Under the Constitution Act of 1983 there was no provision for a parliamentary vote for blacks, and a Mass Democratic Movement was launched in the summer of 1989 to protest against the whites-only election held in September 1989.

President Botha had been succeeded by President De Klerk earlier in 1989 and he now moved rapidly. The liberation movements—notably the African National Congress (ANC) and the Pan-African Congress (PAC)—were un-banned on Feb. 2, 1990 and nine days later President De Klerk released Nelson Mandela, Deputy President of the ANC, from jail after 26 years' incarceration. Segregation in South African hospitals was abolished in law in May and in October the separate Amenities Act (enforcing apartheid in public places) was repealed. The State of Emergency was lifted on Oct. 18. On Feb. 1, 1991 President de Klerk announced that three main pillars of apartheid—the Population Registration Act, the Group Areas Act, and the Land Act—would be abolished. However controversy persisted around the 1,000 political prisoners still detained and the large number of those wishing but as yet unable to return to South Africa. The Internal Security Act remained on the Statute Book and the issue of one person, one vote was unresolved.

In 1991 the eradication of apartheid was dogged by two developments: the continuation of right-wing opposition to the measures taken by the De Klerk government, and the intense conflict between the ANC and the Inkatha movement led by Chief Gatsha Buthelezi. Thousands of deaths occurred in the period 1989–91 during clashes between the two in which, the ANC charged, the security forces had sided with Inkatha.

Economy. With exceptionally rich mineral wealth, notably in gold which provides up to half of export earnings, a diversified economic structure and a developed manufacturing sector, South Africa provides Western style living standard for white citizens, 90 per cent of whom live in urban areas. In 1988 the composition of the population was 26,970,000 blacks, 920,000 Asians, 3,120,000 coloureds and 4,950,000 whites.

Of total civilian employment of 8,370,000, 1,400,000 are employed in manufacturing and some 780,000 in services. The true size of the agricultural workforce is unknown. The workforce grew at 2.5 per cent annually in 1988, leading to dire projections of future unemployment in South Africa. One reason for the gloom was the great dependence of the economy on government for job creation. It has been estimated that between 1980 and 1988 the number of government employees rose from 850,000 to nearly 1,300,000; the private sector created just 30,000 jobs in the same period. Extensive job losses have resulted form municipal privatization. The white/black differential in wages has tended to narrow due to increasing success by the black unions in winning rises ahead of the inflation rate. However, reliable figures for price inflation are hard to come by. Sanctions hit the South African economy progressively hard in the 1980s but in 1991 the EC rescinded some of its economic measures in response to President De Klerk's reforms.

System of industrial relations—The Labour Relations Amendment Bill and the emergency regulations, 1988. In February 1988, amid widespread national and international condemnation, the government issued an order severly restricting and in some cases banning the activities of the COSATU, the UDF and 16 other organizations. A series of raids and detentions of unionists followed. The government also brought the Labour Relations Amendment Bill before parliament, with a view to curbing "politically-motivated" strikes. The ILO described the bill as "probably the most serious attack on the emerging unions since the early 1970s". It proposed to give the Minister of Manpower wide-ranging powers to intervene in labour disputes and to determine "unfair labour practices", thereby narrowing the definition of legal strike action. The bill provided for the imposition of a 15-month cooling off period before industrial action could be repeated over the same issues, such as a wage demand or pay agreement; it allowed employers to choose which union they would recognize and to claim damages for production lost through strikes; and it made it illegal for unions to call sympathy strikes or to organize boycotts. Sweeping reform of the industrial court was also proposed. Further legislation, the Foreign Funding Bill, was intended to give the government power to prevent unions and other organizations from receiving funds from abroad.

The introduction of the proposed new legislation prompted widespread protest among unions, with numerous work stoppages and demonstrations. Opposition to the restrictions and the Labour Bill encouraged co-operation among the rival union groupings, bringing them closer together. At a special congress in May the COSATU called for a three-day protest in June against the Labour Relations Amendment Bill and the bannings and restrictions imposed in February 1988. The NACTU followed suit. Between one and three million workers responded to the call between June 6–8, with the strongest response in the Johannesburg commercial-industrial complex and in Durban. The car industry was brought to a halt, diamond and coal mining was disrupted, and the commercial sector hit, but the gold mines were seriously affected. Fourteen people were killed in the course of the stayaway.

Union strategy was to renegotiate expanded recognition agreements with employers to by-pass the restrictions proposed in the law; this was pursued with some success by the COSATU-affiliated Metalworkers' and Mineworkers' unions and by NACTU. The three-day strike and employers' objections apparently made the government consider a redrafting of the bill, but shortly before representatives of the government, unions and employers were due to meet to discuss changes to the proposed legislation, the bill was promulgated in August, to come into effect at the beginning of September. The day before the bill was passed, the COSATU and NACTU had reached an agreement with the South African Employers' Consultative Committee on Labour Affairs (SACCOLA) which by implication specifically excluded several of the provisions of the new legislation. After the bill was made law the COSATU and NACTU called upon the employers' organization to honour its agreement and not to utilize the new Act's provisions, but employers nevertheless used the new law against the unions and numerous lockouts were reported. Talks with SACCOLA were broken off and the COSATU and NACTU called a summit at the end of 1988 to discuss further action against the new legislation.

In January 1989 it was announced that trade unions would enter the Labour Commission in surrogate fashion via the umbrella organization South African Trade Union Co-ordination Council (SATUCC) whose observer status would now be upgraded. There would be one seat for each organization, government, unions or employers. The SATUCC, founded in 1983, included the national labour centres from nine Southern African states. In practice, the concession did little to conciliate the domestic-based South African trade unions which continued to press for agricultural, public sector and domestic workers to be brought within the ambit of the Labour Relations Act.

On Sept. 6, 1989 South Africa held a whites-only election. In protest at the exclusion of the black population the unions helped launch the Mass Democratic Movement (MDM) which organized a two-day "stay-away" from work. It was distinguished from the township uprisings organized by the UDF and others by its greater discipline, and received widespread support.

The release of Mandela and the unbanning orders of February 1990 were greeted by a nationwide wave of celebratory strikes. Nevertheless, both COSATU and NACTU called for the maintenance of sanctions. They agreed however to meet the Manpower Minister in March 1990 to discuss changes to employment legislation, thus initiating the talks which were to lead to the passage of the 1991 Act (*see below*).

A growing concern of the unions was intimidation, especially at the hands of the Inkatha Movement. A number of members of the COSATU-affiliated NUMSA were killed or wounded in attacks in the early part of 1990. COSATU pressed for freedom of association in Natal which, in its view, would destroy the basis of the Buthelezi movement. It also charged that the police were tolerating Inkatha attacks and called for an independent inquiry.

In the public sector, conflict first burst into the open in 1980 with a strike by 12,000 Johannesburg City Council workers. In 1987 there were strikes on the railways and among port workers; in 1988 by the post office workers. In 1987 for the first time the government committed itself to remunerating equal work at equal value but, although blacks had enjoyed trade union rights since 1979, opportunities for advancement were few. The insistence of the main union centres on public sector rights reflected the much lower level of organization in this growing part of the economy and increased union interest in the extension of coverage of the law.

In February 1991, following three years of negotiations between COSATU, NACTU and the employers' federation SACCOLA, Parliament passed a new Labour Relations Amendment Act which repealed the restrictions placed on union activity by its 1988 predecessor. The Labour Relations Amendment Act 1988 curtailed the right to strike, defined unfair labour practice anew, removed protection against unfair dismissal, placed limits on negotiating rights in the case of redundancy, and encouraged racially based unions. The new Act re-installed the pre-1988 definition of an unfair labour practice and removed from the Labour Court the power to ban lawful strikes and lockouts. It also absolved unions from responsibility for illegal, unoffical strikes and made easier the conciliation process between unions and employers. Shortly after the passage of the new Act the South African government agreed to an ILO visit to investigate a COSATU complaint against aspects of the 1988 Act

NACTU greeted the Act as "a victory for the workers who sacrificed jobs and livelihoods in defence of the rights of the unions" but called for further legislation to ensure that farm and home workers, as well as those in the public sector, would be covered by it as well. COSATU hailed it as "the first time in the history of South Africa that measures that came as a result of consultations with representative organizations have become law", and called for similar extension of its coverage. The significance of farm work was underlined when the South African Agricultural Union (SAAU) which represents farmers and landowners requested the National Manpower Commission to allow them to employ child labour remunerated only with pocket money. The Commission passed on the request to the government; it was opposed by the South African Farmworkers' Co-ordinating Committee.

With the passage of the 1991 Act the way was cleared for the entry in April of the unions into the statutory advisory body the National Manpower Commission (NMC). COSATU has argued that its powers should be enhanced beyond the advisory, and that its remit should be broadened to cover other matters such as training. In effect the Minister would have to ratify decisions jointly reached by the unions and the employers. Along with NACTU it believes that places should be gained not by ministerial appointment but in proportion to size of organization represented, a change which would have the effect of reducing the influence of white right-wing unions. An early priority for the unions at the NMC was further revamping of the Act in respect of collective bargaining rights, extension of the right to strike and recognition of rights for unions at companies.

With the 1988 definition of an Unfair Labour Practice eliminated, an Unfair Labour Practice Code was envisaged by all parties to reflect the 1991 legislative position. The unions wish to see congenial standards applied in the Homelands, whose future is in doubt following the democratization measures which the government has introduced since 1989. In Bophuthatswana for example the only unions allowed to operate are those with a head office in the Homeland. They also seek changes in the Labour Appeal Court, a purely judicial and legalistic structure which they wish to see staffed by labour lawyers.

In 1991 the main union centres were less confident that they could continue to win wage settlements that were above the rate of inflation. This shift of attention was reflected in the broadening of their demands at bargaining meetings with employers, to embrace issues such as job security and training.

Disputes. After the turbulence of 1987, there were less strikes in 1988 when the number of days lost was around 1,600,000. In 1989 however strikes again soared and 3,000,000 days were lost as a result. Some 14,000 motor workers struck in August; there were metal industry strikes; and the longest strike in the history of the mining industry was mounted at a platinum refinery. Many chain stores were hit. However other industries, notably diamonds, settled their annual claims without a strike on the basis of an improved offer from employers. Large numbers of black unions were able to gain settlements ahead of the rate of inflation. An unwelcome feature of the industrial unrest was growing violence. A rail strike began in November 1989 which lasted two months and claimed 30 lives. There were also deaths at a strike at South African Breweries, but few of these disputes could be regarded from the union viewpoint as a success.

In 1990, there were strikes at the State-run Broadcasting Corporation, in the mines, in the paper industry and in the chain stores of the OK Bazaars group. The government responded to higher pay claims by announcing that salary increases in the public sector would not be higher than 10 per cent.

Trade unionism. Trade unions first developed among white workers in the 1880s, and a white Federation of Trade Unions was recognized in 1911. White workers are represented by the South African Confederation of Labour (SACL), which has favoured employment policies based on racial discrimination. The Trade Union Council of South Africa (TUCSA) included white, coloured and Asian members and some blacks in dependent organizations, but folded in 1986. The principal federations now representing black and other non-white workers are the Congress of South African Trade Unions (COSATU) and the National Council of Trade Unions (NACTU).

Early black trade unionism. The first trade union organizing blacks appeared as early as 1917, followed by the Industrial and Commercial Workers' Union of Africa in 1919. During the 1930s some black unions affiliated to the white-dominated South African Trades and Labour Council (SATLC), and after 1941 other black unions joined the Council of Non-European Trade Unions, which claimed 119 unions with 158,000 members in 1945. However, black trade union activity was suppressed after the National Party came to power in 1948; in addition the SATLC was disbanded in 1954 and replaced by TUCSA, which excluded independent black unions from affiliation. In response, 14 former SATLC members formed the South African Congress of Trade Unions (SACTU) in 1955, the Council of Non-European Trade Unions merging with the SACTU in the same year. The SACTU developed as the highly politicized trade union arm of the African National Congress, claiming 53,000 members by 1961. From 1962–65, the SACTU was crushed by the government and has since then operated underground. Black trade unionism had little organized expression by the end of the 1960s.

Unionization after the 1979–81 reforms. Following the Soweto riots of 1976–77 and in accordance with the recommendations of a commission of inquiry headed by Professor N. E. Wiehahn, the South African government in the 1979 Industrial Conciliation Act and the 1981 Labour Relations Amendment Act brought in major reforms affecting the status of black trade unionism. Under these reforms, which were the most substantial consequence of a phase of liberalization of government policy in the late 1970s, freedom of association and a right to strike were extended to all workers regardless of race, and legal black trade unions were recognized for the first time. However, farm workers, domestic servants and state employees were excluded from collective bargaining, and unions could not affiliate to political parties or support illegal strikes out of union funds. An Industrial Court was also established, with wide powers to settle disputes quickly, and most forms of job reservation for whites were also ended. Unions could be racially based or inter-racial, and could register with the government; registered unions enjoyed certain privileges, but unregistered unions were not illegal. Some black unions were refused to apply for registration to avoid any appearance of collaborating with the government. One advantage of registration was access to the government's arbitration and conciliation service, but registration also gave the government powers over the union's internal constitution.

SACTU. The external focus of black trade unionism was the South African Congress of Trade Unions (SACTU). The SACTU was formed in 1955 and from the first emphasized that the workers' movement in South Africa must fight for political freedom and against racial division in addition to trade union objectives. It was in exile from the mid-1960s and had an essentially political programme, emphasizing its character as a revolutionary organization working for the overthrow of the South African state. SACTU was a member of the Congress Alliance and worked in close co-operation with the African National Congress.

Rogers Mevi (Vernon Nkadimeng), an official of the ANC and SACTU and the son of the SACTU general secretary, was killed by a car bomb in Botswana on May 14, 1985, an act attributed by the SACTU to the Botha government.

SACTU urged the affiliation of all trade unions to the United Democratic Front, formed in August 1983, arguing that the class struggle within South Africa must take place within the context of a national struggle for political rights (i.e. directed against apartheid). It also called for the unification of the progressive trade union movement, opposing the "policy of collaboration" of the former TUCSA, and welcomed the formation of COSATU in November 1985 urging that it "must become a truly democratic centre of organized activity for all workers who are determined to liberate our country from its existing oppressive and exploitative social system". SACTU noted, however, that "as long as the oppressive apartheid régime exists, where the above-ground trade unionists face detention without trial, torture and murder at the hands of the police . . . there will always be a need for the SACTU", which would continue to maintain its "underground structures." Early in 1988 SACTU expressed its support for the COSATU, the UDF and the mass democratic movement, and in particular for the campaign against the Labour Relations Amendment Bill. Following the liberalization measures of February 1990 little purpose was seen in prolonging the life of SACTU. At a meeting with COSATU in Zambia on March 18–20 SACTU determined to dissolve. It advised its members to join COSATU's affiliates and the two organizations formed a joint committee to see the process through.

Trade unions and political unrest. In general black trade union activists from 1979 emphasized the goal of building effective industrial strength, with strike action built around issues specifically concerning trade unions, and the widespread unrest in South Africa from September 1984 was led predominantly by community and student groups. However, in November 1984 several hundred thousand black workers in the Transvaal followed a call by FOSATU, CUSA and student and community leaders for a two-day stoppage against police action in the townships, and 1,500,000 black workers took part in a "stay-away" from work on May 1, 1986, to demand an official May Day holiday (this being described as the largest strike in South African history). Under the renewed state of emergency imposed on June 12, 1986, statements calculated to encourage or promote "disinvestment or the application of sanctions or foreign action against the Republic" or "calculated to incite any person to take part in any unlawful strike" were defined as subversive, and in July 1986, 200 trade union officials were reported as being among 4,500 detained under the state of emergency, while others were in hiding. Among those detained for periods were the COSATU leaders Elijah Barayi and Jay Naidoo, and Phiroshaw Camay, the CUSA general secretary. According to the ICFTU there were 312 trade unionists detained as of January 1987.

The attitude towards affiliation to the United Democratic Front (UDF—the principal grouping of community groups opposing the South African government) caused a certain amount of division among the unions, opponents of affiliation arguing variously that the UDF is not solely working-class in composition, that the unions have members of differing political groupings, and that such affiliation is too overtly political.

Repression of the labour movement escalated. Seven strikers were shot dead in April 1987 during a strike of 20,000 railway workers. The COSATU headquarters in Johannesburg were raided and many officials arrested; the office was later bombed.

Another mass one-day stayaway was organized on June 1987 to mark the 11th anniversary of the Soweto riots; it was followed by further repression. Ten miners were killed in clashes with the police and vigilantes in August 1987. In October 1987 Moses Mayekiso, general secretary of the recently formed National Union of Metalworkers, was brought to trial for treason under the emergency regulations, together with four co-defendants, for involvement in a community organization in Alexandra township. He was not cleared until 1989 (*see below*).

The struggle between the labour movement and the government continued in other areas. The unions accused the authorities of using "dirty tricks" to discredit them, by sowing divisions between the COSATU and NACTU, and between the leadership and rank and file of individual unions. Alfred Makeleng, a COSATU and UDF official, died in police custody in suspicious circumstances after 26 months' detention under the emergency regulations. An anti-apartheid conference called by COSATU for September was hamstrung by the arrest and detention of 28 union leaders together with other anti-apartheid activists. Leaders of the Post and Telecommunications Workers' Association were detained, the unions's offices burgled and another official died in suspicious circumstances, against the background of negotiations to secure the reinstatement of postal workers dismissed during a strike in 1987. Twenty members of the COSATU affiliate, the Paper, Wood, Printing and Allied Workers Union (PPWAWU), were detained under the emergency regulations while involved in strikes in the Transvaal. Striking municipal workers in Soweto were in serious conflict with the police in August. 31,000 metalworkers went on strike for two weeks in the same month and won improved benefits from employers. The unions also gave tacit support to the boycott of October's municipal elections; they were banned under the emergency regulations from campaigning openly.

Despite the repression, unionization continued to gather momentum. The PPWAWU claimed a 40 per cent increase in membership in 1987–88 as a result of a well-organized recruiting drive. Efforts to form a single teachers' union affiliated to COSATU made some progress early in 1988. Unionization of the crucial agricultural sector also made headway. The National Union of Farmworkers, affiliated to the NACTU, was launched early in 1988 with a membership of 20,000 claimed. The National Union of Farm and Agricultural Workers of South Africa, affiliated to COSATU, was launched at the same time. Other unions already existing, including those affiliated to federations and those that are independent, set up wings recruiting farm workers.

International relations. Following the merger of the Council of Unions of South Africa (CUSA) into the CUSA-AZACTU federation, the ICFTU was left without an affiliate in South Africa; the WCL is likewise without an affiliate, and the WFTU's affiliate was the African National Congress-linked South African Congress of Trade Unions.

Independent black trade unionism in opposition to the accomodationist policies of the Trade Union Council of South Africa (TUCSA—*see below*), found expression in the formation of the Federation of South African Trade Unions (FOSATU), which was ideologically non-racial, in 1979 and the Council of Unions of South Africa (CUSA), which stressed black leadership, in 1980. Several important unions remained outside these federations. Largely regionally based, they were non-racial, like FOSATU, but they were opposed to registration. They included the Cape-based Food and Canning Workers' Union, the Western Province's General Workers' Union, and the South African Allied Workers' Union, organized mainly in East London and Durban. The issue of registration was a source of major division within the various groupings, but in the mid-1980s a further restructuring of black trade unionism occurred. In 1985 the FOSATU joined the new Congress of South African Trade Unions (COSATU, and in 1986 CUSA merged with the small Azanian Confederation of Trade Unions (AZACTU) to form the National Council of

Trade Unions (NACTU). Chief Ghatsa Buthelezi, the Zulu leader, formed the United Worker's Union of South Africa in 1986 to oppose disinvestment from South Africa by foreign companies and the other black unions. The most significant organization of blacks since the 1979–81 reforms occurred in the key mining sector, where the National Union of Mineworkers developed to become the largest black union. In contrast blacks working on farms, as domestic servants, and as state employees, are almost entirely unorganized. Mass dismissals occurred after industrial action, and many employers were active in attempting to frustrate trade union activities, in some cases hiring their own company security forces to break up meetings, etc. The threat of deportation to the homelands or the neighbouring states was a potent weapon to curb strikes. Numerous activists were also detained incommunicado without charge under the Internal Security Act, and a number of trade union officials died in police custody.

Among the new unions formed by amalgamation was the South African Domestic Worker's Union. Launched late in 1986, with an all-female executive and a membership of 50,000, it was aimed at the estimated one million mainly women domestic workers in the country; it is affiliated to COSATU. The National Union of Metalworkers of South Africa was launched in 1987, with a membership of 130,000, the result of a merger of seven black trade unions in the engineering, automobile and metal working industries; it is also affiliated to COSATU. The Amalgamated Clothing and Textile Workers' Union of South Africa, also affiliated to COSATU, was launched with 68,000 members later in 1987. Other unaffiliated unions covering textile and garment workers and other sectors have also recently been formed.

Dissolution of the TUCSA. The Trade Union Council of South Africa (TUCSA), formed in 1964, dissolved itself on Dec. 2, 1986, its membership having fallen to 120,000 from nearly 500,000 at its peak in 1983 (when it was the largest federation), with 25 member unions disaffiliating during that period. According to its president, Robbie Botha, the TUCSA had been the only truly non-racial federation in South Africa, and had lost membership because of the rise of politicized unions which saw industrial conflict as the key to broader political change. Botha argued that the dual system of unionism, which allowed unregistered unions to operate legally, had favoured unregistered unions which were willing to engage in political wildcat strikes, whereas registered unions—like those affiliated to the TUCSA—were obliged to observe the constraints of the Labour Relations Act. The TUCSA became fully open to all races in 1980, and was white-run. It foundered despite the use of closed shop agreements with employers designed to discourage the defection of blacks to other independent unions. The TUCSA was opposed to economic sanctions against South Africa and had a system of "parallel unions", under which black workers were recruited into separate subsidiary sections of white unions, these parallel black unions having some 32,00 members in 1984.

With most restrictions on trade union activity lifted, COSATU thrived, pushing its membership towards 1,000,000. In February 1990 it joined in a revolutionary alliance with the ANC and the South African Communist Party. SACTU was phased out in its favour in March 1990. NACTU's membership grew at a lower rate, partly because of its emphasis on black exclusivism and partly because of factional fighting between supporters and opponents of the PAC. COSATU favoured unity with NACTU but the latter suspected COSATU's political alliances. Each organization held a conference in 1990 and the two continued the series of inter-union summits begun in 1989.

Congress of South African Trade Unions (COSATU)

Address. P.O. Box 1019, Johannesburg 2001

Leadership. Elijah Barayi (president; also vice-president of the National Union of Mineworkers);

Chris Dlamini (first vice-president; Sweet, Food and Allied Workers' Union); Jay Naidoo (general secretary, Sweet, Food and Allied Workers' Union)

Membership. Around 1,000,000.

History and character. The COSATU was formed on Dec. 1, 1985, following four years of negotiations, by 33 mainly black unions with 558,000 members as a trade union federation which would emphasize opposition to apartheid on a non-racial basis. It absorbed the former Federation of South African Trade Unions (FOSATU), which had nine affiliates, and also incorported the National Union of Mineworkers (which left the Council of Unions of South Africa, CUSA). Membership is open to whites, although in practice is overwhelmingly black.

Federation of South African Trade Unions (FOSATU). The nine affiliates of the FOSATU (which was dissolved in 1985) were absorbed into the COSATU at its formation, and the FOSATU's president Chris Dlamini became COSATU's first vice-president. The largest FOSATU affiliates were: Chemical Workers' Industrial Union; Metal and Allied Workers' Union; National Automobile and Allied Workers' Union; National Union of Textile Workers; and Sweet, Food and Allied Workers' Union. Total FOSATU membership was over 100,000. The FOSATU was formed in April 1979, with an initial membership of 30,000 based in the motor, metal and textile industries. Its policies included: (i) industrial unionism, with one union in each major industry; (ii) non-racism; (iii) worker control; and (iv) collective bargaining at plant level. The membership was predominantly non-white, but with a number of white organizers; the FOSATU had no party political links and no international affiliations. The Federation suffered official repression and harassment from the outset. Andries Raditsela of the Chemical Workers' Industrial Union, a member of the FOSATU executive committee, died of head injuries in May 1985, two days after being taken into police custody.

The founding congress of COSATU made the following demands: (i) the repeal of the pass laws; (ii) the repeal of the state of emergency; (iii) withdrawal of troops and police from the townships; (iv) unconditional release of Nelson Mandela and all political prisoners, and the repeal of all banning orders; (v) the dismantling of the *bantustan* (homelands) system; and (vi) an end to the migrant labour system. The COSATU committed itself to worker control, representation based on paid-up membership, broad-based industrial unionism, and non-racial recruitment, the demand for a national minimum wage, an end to overtime, sexual equality, and support for disinvestment by foreign firms and economic sanctions against South Africa. These demands were reaffirmed at the confederation's first congress held in mid-1987. COSATU pursued a successful "living wage" campaign, resulting in substantial pay rises. It was also a "one union, one industry" campaign with the object of establishing 13 industry-based unions to strengthen bargaining power. While achieving some success in the food industry, with the expansion of the Food and Allied Workers' Union, efforts in other sectors have been less productive. COSATU also made overtures to white workers, in particular to those in the public sector, the subject of a government wage freeze.

COSATU was aligned ideologically with the United Democratic Front, an alliance of community, Church and trade union groups claiming a membership of 1,500,000 which was itself regarded by the government as the internal wing of the then exiled and illegal African National Congress (ANC). COSATU was widely seen as the effective successor to the ANC-backed South African Congress of Trade Unions, which had no significant industrial influence within South Africa, and representatives of the COSATU, SACTU and the ANC held discussions on strategy in Lusaka in March 1986.

COSATU suffered from serious harassment from 1987 onwards. Officials were detained, and offices were raided and sabotaged. With clamp-down on the UDF and other anti-apartheid groups under the State of Emergency, COSATU was impelled further into the political arena. It was prominent in the organization of the 1986 and 1987 May Day strikes and the June 16, 1987 stayaway. At its 1987 congress the confederation adopted the Freedom Charter and reaffirmed its support for international sanctions against South Africa. The great increase in strikes in 1987 was partly attributable to COSATU's heightened political profile. In response the government proscribed it from engaging in a wide range of specified political activities, as part of a package of still greater restrictions on anti-apartheid organizations introduced early in 1988. Despite the clamp-down, COSATU was in the forefront of the campaigns against the new restrictions and against the Labour Relations Amendment Bill, culminating in the three-day mass stayaway of June 1988 (*see above*).

Affiliates. COSATU was formed by 33 unions with 558,000 members. The intention at formation was to fuse the member unions, which included unions in the same industry, into 13 amalgamated industrial unions.

In 1989 COSATU claimed a paid-up membership of 925,000 and a signed-up membership of over 1,000,000. More quickly than NACTU it moved to rationalize its members into an industrial structure so that from 1989 there were 13, one per industry. An important merger during the year led to the formation of the South African Clothing and Textile Workers' Union (SACTWU), from the Amalgamated Clothing and Textile Workers' Union of South African and the independent Garment Workers' Union. SACTWU is now COSATU's third largest affiliate with 185,000 members. Another merger in November 1989 led to the formation of the South African Commercial, Catering and Allied Workers' Union (SACCAWU, General Secretary Vivian Mtwa) with 75,000 members, COSATU's fifth largest affiliate.

During 1989 a number of its affiliates achieved important negotiating successes. The mineworkers gained the agreement of the Chamber of Mines to establishing a new provident fund while the Steel and Engineering Industries Federation of South Africa agreed to a NUMSA demand to change the industry's pension fund into a flexible benefit fund. The Chemical Workers' Union made progress towards achieving a retirement fund. In the motor industry NUMSA staged a two-week strike to prevent the employers decentralizing bargaining arrangements. COSATU's four public sector unions created united local and regional structures to mount a campaign against privatization.

Leading affiliated unions:

National Union of Mineworkers (NUM). (General secretary, Cyril Ramaphosa; spokesman, Marcel Golding.) The NUM, formed only in 1982, is now the largest trade union in South Africa, claiming the membership of 360,000 of the 550,000 black miners, and was formerly the main affiliate of the CUSA. The NUM won recognition from the employers' organization, the Chamber of Mines, for bargaining purposes in 1983 and staged the first legal strike by black mineworkers in September 1984, when seven miners died in clashes between strikers and police and non-strikers. Cyril Ramaphosa is also president of the Southern African Miners' Federation, which includes miners in five countries and was formed in November 1985. A key issue for the NUM has been its campaign against "job reservation", whereby the best-paid jobs are reserved for whites, and most of these restrictions have now been ended; the Mines and Works Amendment Bill of June 1987 and a ruling of the Industrial Court in September 1988 removed the last of them in law. Thousands of miners were deported to homelands or to Lesotho, Swaziland or Mozambique in 1985 after taking part in illegal strikes, but were rehired after negotiations with the NUM. The NUM organized a major strike in 1987 over pay and conditions, but although it demonstrated the union's organizational capacity the strike was largely unsuccessful in achieving its objectives.

The NUM opened its 1990 wages campaign with a demand for an average increase of 35 per cent, its aim being to narrow the gap between the companies. At the same time it announced that it had founded a scheme to sponsor university studies in mining disciplines for 100 black miners.

National Union of Metalworkers of South Africa (NUMSA). (General secretary, Moses Mayekiso—re-elected May 1989). Membership in 1989 stood at 188,013. NUMSA is the second largest independent black union in South Africa: its membership grew by 45 per cent in the two years to 1989. At its May 1989 Congress it resolved to concentrate on organization and formed a National Campaign Committee to co-ordinate activity. Its General Secretary Moses Mayekiso, who was also a township community leader, was arrested in June 1986 and charged with treason. He spent 903 days in prison, during which he was the subject of an international campaign (he was arrested at the airport on his return from a union visit to Sweden). The charges were only dropped in April 1989. At its May 1989 Congress NUMSA was the first union to debate the possibility of negotiations with the government.

Political stance of COSATU. COSATU has been political from the outset, but it has been at the forefront of events at least since the emergence of the Mass Democratic Movement, of which it was perhaps the moving spirit. Before 1989 the "workerist" faction argued for a concentration on industrial activities but the leadership now seems to have support for its political dimension. COSATU attended the two workers summits of March and September 1989 in a much more unified state than

413

NACTU. Following the phasing out of the SACTU in February 1990, COSATU replaced it in a tripartite "revolutionary alliance" with the ANC and the South African Communist Party, while retaining its own independence under democratic control "as a matter of principle and practice". The launch of COSATU's Workers' Charter, which is intended to place the demands of labour at the heart of the democratic struggle, dates from July 1990. But COSATU's political stance also rendered it a target and a number of COSATU activists have fallen victim to violent attacks by Inkatha supporters.

In March 1990 COSATU announced that it was to publish a detailed economic programme. It was stimulated to do so by the ANC's reffirmation of its 1955 Freedom Charter nationalization objectives while a number of South African employers were espousing monetarism with increasing stridency. Alec Erwin, the COSATU Education Officer, announced that it would favour "coherent planning" which would accept the failures of Eastern Europe but also acknowledge that the free market was not the answer.

COSATU followed up its Workers' Charter initiative with discussions within all affiliated unions and the circulation of questionnaires. In October 1990 COSATU convened its "Workers' Charter" conference in Johannesburg. Its purpose was to define the constitutional position of the trade union movement. COSATU had always favoured independence from political parties but the discussion was directed towards further defining the concept of trade union independence. There was no agreement as to whether or not it was legitimate for union officers to hold political office, nor as to whether it would be permissible to have non-working class allies after apartheid was abolished. But there was agreement that trade unions must stay independent in a future democratic state. COSATU committed itself to the proposition that a constitution could be drafted only at a constituent assembly, and determined that it would participate to ensure that basic workers' rights (such as freedom of assembly) should be entrenched. The findings of this conference were scheduled to be debated at the 1991 Biennial Congress.

Publication. COSATU News.

National Council of Trade Unions (NACTU), formerly the Council of Unions of South Africa-Azanian Confederation of Trade Unions (CUSA-AZACTU)

Address. P.O. Box 10928, Johannesburg 2000

Leadership. James Mndaweni (president, formerly CUSA president); Cunningham NguKama (general secretary)

Membership. Claimed 244,000 at its September 1990 Congress.

History and character. This organization was formed, under the provisional name of the CUSA-AZACTU federation, on Oct. 11, 1986, by the merger of the former Council of Unions of South Africa (CUSA) and Azanian Confederation of Trade Unions (AZACTU). The CUSA, the principal element in the new federation, was founded in September 1980, with the majority of the membership coming from the NUM after its formation in 1982. The CUSA favoured economic sanctions against South Africa and an end to investment by foreign capital in the homelands; it did not call for total disinvestment of foreign capital from South Africa, however, but demanded that foreign-owned companies should oppose apartheid in the workplace and the military training of their white workers.

In contrast to the non-racial orientation of the rival COSATU, the new federation was identified with black consciousness, rejecting white support. The CUSA withdrew from the talks which led to the creation of COSATU because of the CUSA's principle that blacks should always hold the leadership positions in unions even if (as is the case with some CUSA unions) they have some non-black members (AZACTU unions admitted only blacks). The AZACTU was affiliated to the Azanian People's Organization and the CUSA was associated with the Pan Africanist Congress. The new federation was weakened by the disaffiliation from the CUSA of the National Union of Mineworkers (NUM) which became a founding member of the COSATU.

In a statement at the launching of the new federation, Mndaweni stated that the federation was based on the principles of worker control, black working-class leadership, and non-affiliation to political organizations (i.e., in particular, the UDF). However in 1987 NACTU representatives met in Tanzania with the PAC, with which the union organization closely associated; early in 1988 the NACTU and the PAC agreed a five-point programme for the defeat of apartheid. Later in 1988 the federation's president and general secretary also met ANC representatives in Harare, in a move

414

which reflected a *rapprochement* between the rival union groupings against the background of increasing government repression and in particular the introduction of the Labour Relations Amendment Bill. The NACTU participated alongside the COSATU in the three-day strike of June 1988 against the government restrictions and the labour bill. NACTU held its second congress in August 1988, at which 24 unions were represented; Mndaweni and Camay were re-elected to office.

By 1989 NACTU's paid-up membership had reached 150,000, and its signed-up membership 250,000. An important merger of four unions within its ranks led to the formation of the Metal and Electrical Workers' Union of South Africa (MEWUSA). At this point it was increasingly "Africanist" in orientation; several of its officials were members of the Pan Africanist movement which was founded in 1989. This trend however provoked opposition to the Black Consciousness movement within its ranks. There were as a result major internal clashes over workers' summits with COSATU in March and September 1989 and with the MDM at a Conference for a Democratic Future in December of that year. NACTU withdrew from the March summit just before it opened, arguing for a postponement to discuss the question of unity. When some 11 NACTU affiliates participated in the first of these meetings and eight in the second against the wishes of the federation, it led to the resignation of Piroshaw Camay, its General Secretary in December.

Camay charged his PAC critics with reneging on commitments to working class unity and being responsible for a decline in membership which was thought by mid-1990, to have fallen below 100,000. The third (September 1990) Biennial Congress reaffirmed the leadership which had replaced Camay and claimed that membership had risen to 244,000. It resolved to set a six-month limit for mergers to achieve one affiliate per sector, but it lost the affiliation of the Black Allied, Mining and Construction Workers' Union—an opponent of Pan-Africanism—which was expelled for non-payment of fees. It resolved to work for a new Workers' Summit with COSATU and other unions, and called for greater tolerance between groups and firm adherence to the principle of freedom of association.

South African Confederation of Labour (SACL, SACOL or SACLA)

Address. P.O. Box 19299, Pretoria West 0117
Leadership. G. Diederiks (president); L. N. Celliers (secretary)
Membership. 90,000 (all white)
History and character. The SACL, which was founded in 1957, has favoured apartheid and has had links with the right-wing Herstigte National Party (HNP). The decision of the South African government to endorse the main lines of the Wiehahn commission report, which led to the 1979 reforms permitting black trade unions, split the SACL, its executive approving the government's position by 13 to 11. As a consequence, the Mineworkers' Union left the SACL, condemning the government's action as the "biggest betrayal ever of the white South African worker", though it later rejoined.
International affiliation. None.

United Workers' Union of South Africa (UWUSA)

Membership. Claims 150,000.
History and character. This organization was launched on May 1, 1986, by Chief Gatsha Butehelezi, the Chief Minister of the KwaZulu tribal homeland and the leader of the Inkatha movement, at a rally attended by 70,000 Zulus. The policies of the new organization include: (i) opposition to economic sanctions against South Africa and to disinvestment by foreign firms (under the slogan "Jobs—not hunger"); (ii) hostility to the COSATU; (iii) opposition to socialism; and (iv) the resolution of political disputes "through negotiation rather than violence". The UWUSA appears to be almost exclusively Zulu-based, and has some strength in the mines in opposition to the NUM. It is currently a general union but intends to form separate unions for different industrial sectors. The UWUSA concluded a number of collective bargaining agreements with employers in the Transvaal and Natal.

The UWUSA claimed approximately 150,000 members in 1989. In April of that year it dismissed its President over charges that he had acted inconsistently with its constitution and the interests of the workers.

Spain

Capital: Madrid   **Population: 39,240,000**

Political system. Spain is a constitutional monarchy with a multi-party parliamentary democracy (installed after the death of Gen. Franco in 1975). There is a decentralized regional government structure with elected local parliaments. It is a member of the EC and NATO.

The Socialist Party of Felipe González (PSOE) came to power in 1982, won the next two general elections and must next go to the polls in 1993.

Economy. Of a total civilian employment of 12,250,000 in 1989, 4,020,000 worked in industry. 1,590,000 worked in agriculture, and 6,620,000 in services. Spain's economic expansion at the end of the 1980s was spectacular, bringing great employment growth and drawing unemployment below 2,500,000 for the first time since 1984.

System of industrial relations. Spain has been a member of the International Labour Organization since 1956, having earlier been a member form 1919 to 1941. It ratified ILO Conventions No. 87 (Freedom of Association and Protection of the Right to Organize, 1948) and No. 98 (Right to Organize and Collective Bargaining, 1949) in 1977.

The former system of works councils was abolished by decree in 1977, and staff delegates (forming works councils in large enterprises) are now the sole legal representatives of all the workers, regardless of their trade union affiliation, and the unions compete to secure representation on these bodies. Delegates are elected for four-year terms. The status of these bodies is regulated by the 1980 Workers' Statute, as amended in 1984.

An agreement reached between the UGT and the government in early 1986 provided for unions to have board-level representation in publicly owned concerns (APEP).

Law of Trade Union Liberty of 1985. This legislation, which was passed in July 1984 and promulgated in August 1985, superseded legislation on trade union association adopted in 1977. The Act guarantees full freedom to employees to join and to form unions, other than for members of the military and parliamentary forces and the judiciary and public prosecutors (with non-military security forces to be covered by separate legislation); self-employed workers, the unemployed and the retired may join existing unions but not set up unions of their own. The unions are free to draw up their own rules and may not be dissolved or suspended except through the courts in the event of a serious breach of the law. Unions are empowered to engage in collective bargaining, organize activities both on and off working premises, strike, and put forward candidates for election as workers' delegates. The Act also provides for a system of representational status (affecting a union's participation in collective bargaining, representation before government, etc.) whereby to be considered "most representative" at national level a union must obtain the votes of at least 10 per cent of staff delegates in the country as a whole (only the CCOO and the UGT currently qualify—*see below* for 1986 trade union election results); "most representative" status at regional level may be obtained by securing at least 15 per cent of staff delegates (but with a minimum of 1,500 delegates) provided that the union is not affiliated to a national federation or confederation. Workers' representatives at all levels are entitled to unpaid leave to carry out union functions and to paid leave to participate in collective bargaining, and in the civil service may not be dismissed in the event of staff cutbacks. All workers are required to pay a subscription (*canon económico*) to the recognized negotiating union unless they explicitly withdraw from doing so. The legislation was opposed by some regional unions as imposing on them excessive difficulties in securing representational status (1,500 delegates being half the total in some autonomous regions) while favouring unions which were nationally strong but weak in some areas; it was also opposed by the executive staff organization CEOPC for failing to create a separate electoral college for executive staff, and by the Worker's Commissions (CCOO) which rejects such framework legislation. Occasionally, ministers in the PSOE government have talked about changes to employment legislation but insisted that they would not alter the right to strike.

A two-year social and economic pact (AES) between the UGT, the employers organizations and the government in October 1984 led to the containment of most pay settlements in 1985 within AES guidelines (i.e. close to the level of price inflation), despite the opposition of the CCOO. Some 6,000,000 workers were covered by collective agreements in 1985, and 1,100,000 days were lost in strikes compared with 7,800,000 in 1984 (when no agreemnt was in force). A package of measures introduced by the government in May 1985 to combat unemployment was criticized by both the UGT and the CCOO (the former because of the unilateral modification of the AES), and both confederations, with the support of some small employers, staged a national strike on May 20 to protest against the removal of restrictions on the operating hours of enterprises.

Plans announced in April 1985 to reduce pension entitlements led to a one-day general strike (the first since the restoration of democracy) on June 20, led by the CCOO; the strike was not supported by the UGT, although this opposed the reduction and secured some modifications to the proposals (which were approved on July 23).

Trade union elections (to elect workers' delegates with a four-year mandate) held in September-December 1986 resulted in the UGT winning 71,327 delegate seats of the total of 177,484, compared with 60,816 won by the CCOO. However, the CCOO won a dominant position in the great majority of companies with more than 750 employees and in key public sector areas including the railways, Iberia airlines, telephones, gas and energy, and major banks, as well as in the two principal industrial cities of Madrid and Barcelona. The UGT and the CCOO together took 74.5 per cent of the delegate seats, compared with 70 per cent in the last elections in 1982. The Unión Sindical Obrera (USO) came third with 6,791 (3.83 per cent of the total), the ELA-STV fourth with 5,190 (but came first in its own Basque region) and fifth place was taken by a regional organization, the Intersindical Nacional de Trabajadores Gallegos—INTG—(in Galicia), which won 1,120 seats. The balance of seats was won by smaller unions and unaffiliated delegates. The elections were characterized by mutual allegations of fraud by the UGT and CCOO.

Since 1986 the UGT has increasingly distanced itself from the continuing austerity programme of the González government (see below) and consequently moved towards greater unity in action with the CCOO. Negotiations over a new social pact ended in deadlock in February 1987 with the UGT demanding a wage increase of 7 per cent and the employers holding firm to a ceiling fixed at the projected inflation rate of 5 per cent. The CCOO, which was not a party to the previous AES and did not participate in the negotiations over its renewal, entered the 1987 pay round demanding increases of 7–8 per cent.

The breakdown of the social pact, and divergence in bargainig positions between the unions and employers and the increased co-ordination of action between the UGT and the CCOO led to an upsurge in industrial conflict. The number of strikes rose from 272 in 1986 to just under 400 in 1987, and days lost due to industrial dipsutes increased from under 630,000 to nearly 3,000,000 over the same period. Wage settlements averaged an increase of close to 6.8 per cent in 1987, well above the projected rate of inflation.

The UGT and the CCOO also moved towards greater unity in opposing the economic and social programmes of the Socialist government. In October 1987 the two unions sponsored demonstrations of public employees in Madrid and Barcelona protesting the 4 per cent pay increase planned in the 1988 budget. Early in 1988 they likewise agreed on a platform of joint action, including demands for a minimum wage increase of 6 per cent (compared to the projected inflation rate of 3 per cent), abandonment of a proposed pay freeze, extension of unemployment benefit from the one-third of unemployed who receive it to 48 per cent, greater job security and more investment for job creation. Although the UGT re-entered discussions with the PSOE over employment and economic policy in 1988, by the end of the year the two nominal allies were openly feuding. The UGT joined the Workers' Commissions in support of a day of industrial action in the public sector and some private industries in November, followed by a one-day general strike on Dec. 14 and a mass rally in Madrid two days later. The general strike was the first since 1934 supported by the UGT. Some 7,800,000 workers (two-thirds of the working population) joined in the stoppage in what was viewed as a humiliating defeat for the government.

The general strike appeared to have widespread support among the population and the high rate of participation marked a major success for the unions. Its immediate impact was the withdrawal of the government's Youth Employment Plan (PEJ) and during the next six months the government met the unions on their other demands. However little concrete progress was made before the October general elections which saw the PSOE keep its absolute majority while losing some ground to the Left.

The UGT-CCOO response was to draw up a 20-point Trade Union Priority proposal (PSP) for presentation to the government and the employers, though they wished to meet them separately. The Prime Minister acceded to this request and during the rest of 1989 and early 1990 a number of issues were settled including inflation compensation for public sector salary and pension losses and greater union influence over contracts of employment. In the next stage of the talks the government's objective was to secure wage restraint in advance of Spain's integration into the Internal Market in 1992. However, with inflation twice expectations, the UGT approached the 1990 pay talks looking for increases in the order of 9 per cent. In 1991 the unions again sought 9 per cent in protest against what they considered were inadequate government guidelines, and mounted a mini-general strike at the end of May.

Trade unionism. The anarchist Confederación Nacional del Trabajo (CNT) and the socialist Unión General de Trabajadores (UGT) were the largest centres before the civil war of 1936–39, although the trade union movement was highly fragmented. Under Franco a corporate vertical trade union structure was imposed, with only one central organization. The National Trade Union Office (NTUO), which controlled the lower-level unions, and employers were incorporated in the membership of the trade unions. The unions predominantly provided social servies and strikes were illegal. The UGT, CNT and the Basque union, ELA-STV, maintained some underground activity, with headquarters in exile, and workers' commissions developed at shop-floor level in the 1960s, contributing to the weakening of the official trade union structure in the latter part of Franco's rule. In 1977, following the return to democratic government, the Francoist trade union structure was dissolved and free trade unionism has since developed. Today the most important confederations nationally are the Workers' Commissions (CCOO), close to the Communist Party of Spain (PCE), and the socialist UGT which traditionally was almost the *alter ego* of the ruling PSOE. However traditional union-political relationships have been disrupted as the UGT moved into increasingly fundamental opposition to the economic orientation of the González government. From 1986 the UGT actively sought a *rapprochement* with the CCOO and in February 1988 the two organizatins signed a pact to work together for a "social shift" in the government's policy. UGT relations with PSOE were not helped by declining financial support for the unions from the state: in 1988 for example subsidies for parties were uprated in line with inflation but subsidies for the unions were not. PSOE disenchantment may also be understood from the way the number of its members who were also in the UGT fell between 1980 and 1986 from 59 per cent to 54 per cent, at a time when its gross membership doubled. More than 10 per cent of UGT members are PSOE members, but the UGT has declined to organize a faction in PSOE.

In 1987 and 1988 the party-union split deepened. PSOE allies in the leadership of affiliated federations (for example Antonio Puerta's metalworkers) were prepared to settle below UGT guidelines for wage agreements in 1987 in line with government counter-inflationary goals. This led to a revolt and Puerta's overthrow, consolidating the Redondo leadership which became further entrenched as a result of the December 1988 general strike.

In effect the UGT has swapped partners, embracing the CCOO as an industrial ally in place of the political PSOE. The CCOO won the first two post-democratization workplace elections in 1978 and 1980 but the UGT polled much more strongly in 1982 as it was uplifted by its alliance with the ascendent PSOE while the CCOO were hampered by their political alliance with the factionalized PCE. In 1986 the CCOO again did well, and the UGT seems to have concluded that it had suffered from too close an alliance with the government. The two will always be rivals to a certain extent because they organize in the same areas of the economy: there is no natural division of labour and they are of comparable size, each having around 750,000 members.

The anarchist trade union tradition in Spain survives, courtesy of the CNT and its rival CNT-AIT, but anarchism has ceased to be a political force. The two CNTs and the politically independent USO are much smaller than the two main centres. There is also a Confederation of Independent Unions (CSI) which has a number of affiliates, including the Civil Servants' Union Confederation (CSIF). There are three regional federations, one each for the Basque Country, Catalonia and Galicia.

Confederación Nacional del Trabajo (CNT)
National Confederation of Labour

Address. Sagunto 15, 28010 Madrid
Phone. 447-5769
Leadership. Emilio Lindosa (secretary-general)
Membership. Claims 150,000.
History and character. Founded in 1910; anarchist. The CNT rivalled the UGT in importance before the Civil War. However, since the restoration of trade union freedom in 1977, it has failed to sustain a leading position and has also been badly affected by schisms. A major split in 1979 was followed by a unity congress held in 1982, at which it was accepted that the CNT would participate in elections and recognize the legitimacy of labour laws. In a further rift an attempt was made by a faction known as CNT-AIT to unseat José March (elected as secretary-general at the 1982 congress), but his position was upheld by a Madrid court in June 1986, which also found that the organization led by March was the legitimate successor to the CNT founded in 1910.
International affiliation. None.

Confederación Nacional de Trabajo (CNT-AIT)
National Confederation of Labour—International Labour Alliance

Address. Plaza de Tirso de Molina, 5–6, 28012 Madrid
Phone. 227-9608
Leadership. Vicente Villanova Gardo
History and character. CNT-AIT is a breakaway faction from the CNT. Until its Bilbao (April 1990) Congress its General Secretary was José Luis García Rúa. Congress resolved to seek better relations with the other union centres.

Confederación Sindical de Comisiones Obreras (CCOO)
Workers' Commissions

Address. Fernández de la Hoz 12, 28010 Madrid
Phone. 4191750

Telex. 455226
Leadership. Antonio Gutiérrez (secretary-general); Marcelino Camacho (president)
Membership. Around 700,000.

History and character. The CCOO is close to the Communist Party of Spain (PCE), which adheres to a Eurocommunist line, and is not a member of the WFTU. The workers' commissions developed in the 1960s to defend workers' interests at shop floor level, and participated in frequent (although illegal) strikes and industrial action, despite prosecutions of their leaders.

The CCOO opposed through a programme of industrial action government restructuring plans affecting the steel and shipbuilding sectors implemented from 1983, and has generally opposed austerity measures, moves to cut back the public sector and "liberalize" the economy under the Socialist government. It is dominant in the workers' councils in most large enterprises following the 1986 trade union elections.

Marcelino Camacho, a founder and long-serving secretary-general of the Workers' Commissions, announced his intention to make way for a younger leader early in 1987. At the fourth congress of the CCOO in November 1987 he was replaced by the 37 year-old Antonio Gutiérrez, a member of the executive committee since 1976 who was generally viewed as less flamboyant but a hard-headed negotiator. His election with a majority of nearly 75 per cent of the vote represented a substantial victory for the *gerardistas*, supporters of the moderate Communist Party leadership of Gerardo Iglesias, and a defeat for Julian Ariza, the candidate of the previously influential *carrillistas* who back the breakaway party of the former PCE leader, Santiago Carrillo.

International affiliation. None, but has applied to join the ETUC.

Confederación de Sindicatos Independientes (CSI)
Confederation of Independent Unions

Address. c/ Veneras 9, 28013 Madrid
Phone. 542 7355
Leadership. Oscar González Soto
Affiliated unions and structure. Among the affiliates is the Civil Service Union Confederation (CSIF).

Unión General de Trabajadores (UGT)
General Union of Workers

Address. Horteleza 88, 28004 Madrid
Phone. 308-3333
Leadership. Nicolás Redondo (secretary-general)
Membership. 700,000 paid-up members. There are 15 affiliated federations for the various occupational sectors.

History and character. Founded in 1888, the UGT claimed 2,000,000 members on the eve of the Spanish Civil War in 1936. Its leadership was in exile in France during the Franco period. In 1976 the UGT held its 30th congress in Spain, and in 1977 was legalized.

The UGT is linked to the Spanish Socialist Workers' Party (PSOE), which has formed the government since 1982, and maintained its support for the government until 1987 notwithstanding some tension caused by the government's adoption of austerity policies which has led Redondo to criticize its "neo-liberal tendencies". The UGT favours full integration into the European Communities and the adoption of a more expansionist economic policy to deal with unemployment. Redondo has opposed NATO, although there has been division within the UGT on the issue. (A national referendum on March 12, 1986, resulted in a majority in favour of continued membership of NATO, as had been urged by the government but not all sectors of the PSOE). The UGT took the largest number of delegate seats in the trade union elections held in 1982 and 1986, but its claim to be the leading trade union centre is weakened by the dominance of the CCOO in major enterprises.

The UGT held its 34th congress in April 1986 and emphasized the objective of adapting to meet changed social conditions, notably by seeking to organize in the growing services sector, among professional and executive staffs, and among pensioners, the unemployed and those employed only part-time. The congress endorsed the social and economic pact (AES) formed in October 1984 between the UGT and the government, which provided a framework for collective bargaining and "social dialogue".

Since the breakdown of negotiations over the renewal of the social pact in 1987 relations between the UGT and the governing Socialist Party have become increasingly acrimonious. Rival factions within the Catalonian metal workers' federation of the UGT attacked each other with bottles and iron bars in March 1988 during a meeting to choose delegates for the union's congress. Antonia Puerta, the leader of the metal workers and a government supporter, subsequently led a breakaway congress but attracted only a small minority of delegates. The official congress drew some 76 per cent of the delegates and voted to replace Puerta with Manuel Fernández, a Redondo loyalist. The agreement between the UGT and the CCOO in support of a one-day general strike in December hardened the rift as the PSOE attempted to mobilize its supporters within the UGT against the leadership of the union.

At its 35th Congress, held in Madrid in April 1990 the UGT symbolized its estrangement from PSOE by all inviting all groups represented in the Parliament to attend. After being unanimously re-elected as leader of the Union, Nicolás Redondo reported that the UGT had consolidated its understanding with the Workers' Commissions and the Basque Union ELA-STV, "leaving behind the confrontational relationship of previous years". The Congress also discussed new organizational initiatives to give branches greater autonomy to make agreements and to strengthen sectoral federations and territorial unions. It called for the creation of investment funds and appealed to the government for tax relief on union subscriptions.

Publications. Unión (official bulletin, 55,000 copies); *Técnicos y Cuadros* (monthly, 7,000 copies); *Claridad* (2,000 copies); *International Communication* (250 copies, English and French). Several affiliated federations also publish their own journals.

International affiliations. ICFTU; ETUC; TUAC.

Unión Sindical Obrera (USO)
Workers' Union

Address. Príncipe de Vergara 13-7°, 28001 Madrid
Phone. (5)77 41 13
Telex. 45694
Fax. (5)77 29 59
Leadership. Manuel Zaguirre Cano (secretary-general)
Membership. 60,000.
History and character. Founded in 1961, the USO is politically independent and pluralist and is organized into territorial structures and professional federations. It held its fourth congress in 1986 and set a goal of increasing its membership to 100,000 in four years. The USO supports an extension of industrial democracy, alternatives to unemployment, solidarity with the weakest social groups and disarmament.

Publications. El Proyecto (3,000 copies); *Unión Sindical* (70,000 copies).
International affiliations. WCL.

Regional trade union confederations

Confederación Sindical de Cataluña (CSC)
Catalonian Confederation of Labour

Address. Pelai 40, 2-2, 08001 Barcelona
Phone. 318-8639
Leadership. Miquel Porter i Moix

Euzko Langilleen Alkarasuna/Solidaridad de Trabajadores Vascos (ELA/STV)
Basque Workers' Solidarity

Address: Calle Barrainkunkua 15, 48009 Bilbao
Phone. 94 424 33 00

Fax. 94 424 17 30

Leadership. José Miguel Leunda Etxeberria (president); Jose Elorrieta Aurrekoetxea (general secretary)

Membership. 110,000.

History and character. The ELA/STV was founded in Bilbao in 1911, and operated underground under Primo de Rivera from 1923 to 1929 and then under Franco from 1939 to 1976. It is politically independent but Basque nationalist in orientation and close to the Basque Nationalist Party (PNV), which favours full regional autonomy but opposes the violence of the ETA movement. The ELA/STV and the Polish Solidarity are unique in Europe in that they hold dual ICFTU/WCL affiliation.

The ELA/STV has held only six congresses in its history, in 1929, 1933, 1976, 1979, 1982 and 1986. In the elections for workers' delegates held in enterprises in 1986 (see above), the ELA/STV took first place in the Basque region, with 34.9 per cent of the delegates, entitling it to"most representative" status at regional level.

Publication. Igual.

Affiliated unions and structure. There are seven affiliated unions in the following sectors: metals; construction; food, chemicals, textiles and paper; transport; public services; and other services.

In January 1990 ELA/STV held its Seventh Congress and resolved to give greater emphasis to autonomy and self-determination for the Basques. Among its guests was the UGT General Secretary Nicolás Redondo. The significant shift in leadership which had occurred in November 1988 was confirmed. In that year's enterprise elections secured 37.84 per cent of the delegates and the Congress heard that membership had risen by 8 per cent.

International affiliations. WCL; ICFTU.

Intersindical Nacional Gallego (INTG)
Galician National Confederation

Address. Emilia Pardo Bazán 27-3, 15005 La Coruña
Phone. 24-1662
Leadership. Juan Carballo (secretary-general)

Sri Lanka

Capital: Colombo   **Population: 16,881,130**
                                                                  (1989)

Political system. The Democratic Socialist Republic of Sri Lanka is an independent member of the Commonwealth with an executive President and a unicameral legislature. In the 1980s the country was brought to a state of crisis and near civil war as a result of communal tension between the majority Sinhalese and minority Tamil populations.

The arrival of Indian troops, first to assist the Tamils but later as a police force against the "Tamil Tigers" did not resolve civil disorder. In March 1991 the Minister of Defence was assasinated in an attack attributed to the Tamil Tigers.

Economy. Sri Lanka's economy is principally agricultural, with tea, rubber and coconuts as the main crops. There is also a large textile manufacturing sector. Labour migration constitutes a significant source of foreign exchange. Since 1977, the governments of the United National Party (UNP) have sought to reduce the role of the state in the economy. There is a considerable external debt and a growing dependency on foreign aid.

System of industrial relations. Collective bargaining is extensively practised in the private sector but does not exist in the public sector. Conciliation and arbitration services are available through the Department of Labour. Sri Lanka ratified ILO Convention No. 98 (Right to Organize and Collective Bargaining, 1949) in 1972 but has not ratified Convention No. 87 (Freedom of Association and Protection of the Right to Organize, 1948).

Legislation in 1979 provided for the establishment of employees' councils in state undertakings, and for worker representation on the boards of such undertakings.

An Act of 1979 empowered the government to prohibit strikes in essential services. Many employees (up to 100,000) were dismissed after a general strike in July 1980 supported by the opposition (most of these have now been reinstated), and emergency powers have been used on other occasions since then to curb strikes. The ICFTU has called on the government to abandon this practice, and opposition trade unions have organized protests against the use of such powers, the use of military operations rather than political negotiations in dealing with the Tamil question, and against aspects of government policy including privatization and wage controls.

In 1988, the government attempted to address some of the wider issues of unemployment and poverty which have long preoccupied Sri Lanka's trade unions. In a report entitled *Poverty Alleviation through People-based Development* commissioned by the government, the number of unemployed was established to be around 1,200,000 (18 per cent of the 6,000,000 potential workforce). Three million were considered to be "the poorest of the poor". The government promised to establish a Rural Works Programme with the intention of employing up to 6,000 workers. It envisaged a minimum wage of Rs. 600 and expected to employ at least one person from families where no member is currently employed. The government also hoped to extend its scheme of greater employment to the private sector where businesses will be requested to train up to 60,000 young people. Business incentive schemes would be encouraged and more job opportunities were foreseen following the repatriation of workers of Indian origin under the terms of the Indo-Sri Lanka Agreement.

In 1986–88 there were less than 100 strikes annually. Though there were no major work stoppages, production was continually interrupted in response to calls by Sinhalese and Tamil organizations.

Trade unionism. Trade unions were given legal recognition under colonial rule in 1935, by which time substantial development had occurred. Since independence, trade union freedoms have been substantial but subject to periodic modification or suspension according to political conditions. Only seven persons are needed to form a union and this factor in combination with ethnic, linguistic and ideological divisions has fragmented the labour movement. There is no clearly dominant trade union centre, although some moves in this direction were made in 1986 following the reorganization of the Sri Lanka Independent Trade Union Federation (SLITUF) as the Sri Lanka Nidahas Sewaka Sangamaya (SLNSS) which seeks to create a single, national trade union centre. The largest organization, the Ceylon Workers' Congress (CWC) organizes almost exclusively in the plantations.

Trade unions exist in both the public and private sectors; however, members of the police force, the judiciary and armed forces may not join unions, and unions in government services may not confederate. At the end of 1987, there were 903 unions with a membership of 1,677,208.

All Ceylon Federation of Free Trade Unions (ACFFTU)

Address. 94 1/6 York Building, York Street, Colombo 1

Phone. (1) 31847
Cable. ENDUBLEWCE
Fax. 447884
Leadership. Mrs M.C. Rajahmoney (president); Antony Lodwick (general secretary)
Membership. 70,000.
History and character. The ACFFTU was created in 1956 by the National Workers' Congress (which remains by far its largest constituent organization—see separate entry) to assist inter-union collaboration. It is politically non-aligned.

Affiliates. National Workers' Congress (which itself has a number of affiliates in different sectors); Mercantile Executives' Association; Ceylon National Union of Clerks and Estate Staff; National Union of Teachers (private schools); National Fisheries and Maritime Workers' Congress.

Publication. *National Worker* (bi-monthly); *Voice of Youth* (quarterly).
International affiliation. None.

Ceylon Federation of Trade Unions (CFTU)

Address. 71 Malay Street, Colombo 2
Phone. (1) 34516
Leadership. M. G. Mendis (president)
History and character. Founded in 1941 and linked with the pro-Soviet Communist Party of Sri Lanka. The CFTU wishes to "retain Sri Lanka as a unified country while ensuring regional autonomy for the Tamil nationality", and is opposed to the operations of transnational corporations and banks in the country. It has campaigned vigorously for the reinstatement of strikers dismissed in 1980.

International affiliation. WFTU.

Ceylon Workers' Congress (CWC)

Address. 72 Ananda Coomaraswamy, Mawatha, P.O. Box 1294, Colombo 7
Phone. 573059; 573980; 575708
Cables. CEYWORKER, COLOMBO
Leadership. Savumyamoorthy Thondaman (president); M. S. Sellasamy (general secretary)
Membership. 367,000 direct members (172,000 of them female) in the plantations. The CWC states that this represents 56 per cent of the workforce in the plantation sector, and that 200,000 plantation workers are organized in other unions. There are in addition two small affiliates from other sectors, the Ceylon Teachers' Congress and the Ceylon Estates Staff Congress.

History and character. Throughout its history the CWC has recruited overwhelmingly among plantation workers of Indian Tamil descent, who have for decades suffered institutionalized discrimination. It is regarded as the largest and most influential trade union organization in Sri Lanka.

The Ceylon Indian Congress Labour Union was founded in 1940 as the labour wing of the Ceylon Indian Congress (CIC), itself formed in 1939 by Shri Nehru as the envoy of Mahatma Gandhi. In the early years the principal objective of the CIC was to secure independence from British rule, and following the achievement of this in 1948, the Labour Union was renamed as the Ceylon Workers' Congress and became a trade union with a separate political wing, rather than vice versa, in 1950. In 1977 the CWC's political wing became a political party (also called the Ceylon Workers' Congress, and in effect indivisible from the union) and the union/party president, S. Thondaman, was returned to parliament, taking office in 1978 as Minister for Rural Development (a position which he still holds) in the United National Party (UNP) government of Junius Jayewardene. Using this position within the government coalition, the CWC was able to secure constitutional revisions which extended basic rights to so-called "stateless" persons, most of whom were of Indian descent. Thondaman is regarded as the leader of the Indian Tamil community in Sri Lanka, and has been influential in mobilizing electoral support among that population for the United National Party, a circumstance which has increased the influence of the CWC with the government. (The Indian Tamils have not supported the separatist demands of the indigenous Sri Lankan Jaffna Tamils of the northern and eastern parts of the country.) In January 1986, partly in response to CWC pressure, the governments of India and Sri Lanka reached an agreement providing for the extension of Indian or Sri Lankan citizenship to several hundred thousand stateless Indian Tamils in Sri Lanka.

The CWC opposes all disrimination based on race, creed, caste or religion, and declared 1986 a "Year of Peace, Amity, and National Reconciliation". In 1987 it focused its energies on the problem of homelessness among estate workers.

The CWC favours public ownership throughout the economy. It seeks to break down the "captive labour" system by converting plantations into villages; it is has established a vocational training complex and a construction consortium with the help of the ICFTU, and has launched credit schemes and a project to create a number of small dairy farm co-operatives on plantations.

The CWC is represented on the board of the Janatha Estates Development Board, which administers the state-owned tea and rubber plantations.

Publications. Congress (fortnightly, in Tamil; circulation 50,000); *Congress News* (fortnightly, in English; circulation 5,000).

International affiliations. ICFTU; IFPAAW; PSI.

Democratic Workers' Congress (DWC)

Address. 82-1/2 Sri Vajiragnana Mawatha, Dematagoda Road, P.O. 1009, Colombo 9

Phone. (1) 691279

Leadership. V. P. Ganesan (president); P. Sivasamy (general secretary)

Membership. Claims 231,600.

History and character. The DWC emerged in 1956 as a result of a split within the Ceylon Labour Congress. Since then, it states that it has sought "to secure speedy improvement in the conditions of work and life and the status of workers in industry and society, ... to foster the spirit of solidarity, service, brotherhood, co-operation and mutual help among the workers" and to "improve the present living conditions of the workers".

Affiliates. Mather Sangam (Women's Front); *Valiber Munneny* (Youth Front).

Publications. Jananayaga Thozhilali (monthly, in Tamil).

International affiliation. WFTU.

Lanka Jathika Estate Workers' Union (LJEWU)

Address. 546/4 Galle Road, Colombo 3

Phone. 573528; 573992

Leadership. Gamini Dissanayake (president); Rajah Seneviratne (general secretary)

Membership. 380,000.

History and character. The LJEWU stands for the "extension of the retirement age to 60 years for Estate staff"; "equal wages for plantation workers"; "assured six days work per week"; "enhanced reimbursements on funeral expenses", "compensation for workers who are retrenched"; "allocation of two acres of land for Estate schools"; "overseas leave for purposes of employment"; "contributions for the construction and development of temples"; "a new housing policy and loans to build houses", "compensation for premature retirement"; "maternity benefits for casual workers"; and "paid leave for seminar participants".

Affiliates. National Estates Services Union; Jathika Sevaka Sangamaya; Jathika Guru Sangamaya; National Public Services Union; National Nurses Union; National Agricultural Association; National Traders Association; National Railway Services Union; Up Country United Youth Front; Hill Country Sports Federation.

Publications. Muster (in English); *Jathika Jeevaya* (in Sinhala) and *Thesiyamurasoli* (in Tamil).

International affiliation. International Federation of Chemical, Energy and General Workers' Unions, (ICEF) and the International Federation of Plantation, Agricultural and Allied Workers (IFPAAW), both associates of the ICFTU.

National Workers' Congress (NWC)

This is a component part of the All-Ceylon Federation of Free Trade Unions (ACFFTU), whose address it shares (*see above*).

Leadership. S. Wattegama (acting president); Antony Lodwick (general secretary)

Membership. 65,000.

History and character. Founded in 1952; politically independent and non-sectarian. Emphasizes worker education.

Publication. National Worker (monthly).

International affiliation. WCL.

Public Service Workers' Trade Union Federation (PSWTUF)

Address. 35/5-19,20, Main Street, Colombo 11

Phone. (1) 31125

Leadership. Palitha Gamage (president); W. H. Piyadasa (general secretary)

Membership. 100,000.

International affiliation. Trade Unions International of Public and Allied Employees, an associate of the WFTU.

Sri Lanka Nidahas Sewaka Sangamaya (SLNSS), formerly
Sri Lanka Independent Trade Union Federation (SLITUF)

Address. 301 T.B. Jayah Mawatha, P.O. Box 1241, Colombo 10

Phone. 93405; 94074

Leadership. Sirima R. D. Bandaranaike (honorary president); Leslie Devendra (secretary-general)

Membership. 128,000.

History and character. The SLNSS was formerly known as the Sri Lanka Independent Trade Union Federation (SLITUF) which was established in 1960 and affiliated to the Sri Lanka Freedom Party. Following a reorganization in 1986, the SLITUF was superseded by the SLNSS which merged "all affiliated unions to form one single national union under the present name". It has five "sectoral sub-divisions" representing State corporations, plantations, transport, local government and co-operatives, and private sector employees.

Publications. Nidahas Mawatha (bi-monthly).

International affiliation. WFTU.

Sudan

Capital: Khartoum

Population: 23,200,000
(1987)

Political system. Sudan is politically divided between the Arab, Moslem north, including the capital, Khartoum, and the mainly Christian, African south where there has been a strong movement for autonomy, resulting in civil war. Since the overthrow of President Jaafars al Nemery's one-party régime in 1985, Sudan has been governed by a series of unstable coalitions.

In June 1988 the civilian government of Sadek-el-Mahdi was overthrown in a military *coup* led by General Oumar El Beshir who dissolved the Assembly and abolished the constitution.

Economy. Sudan's principally agricultural economy has been severely damaged by drought, famine, civil war, political instability and heavy foreign indebtedness, estimated at US$10,300 million in February 1988. Also in February 1988, the IMF announced Sudan's ineligibility for further funds because of its failure to repay debts.

The Civil War (which began in 1983) is estimated to cost around $1,000,000 a day while inflation in the later 1980s was estimated to have run at 50 per cent annually.

System of industrial relations. Sudan ratified ILO Convention No. 98 (Right to Organize and Collective Bargaining, 1949) in 1957, Convention No. 87 (Freedom of Association and Protection of the Right to Organize, 1948). The ILO observed that the state of emergency declared in July 1987 has seriously restricted trade union rights. Sudan ratified Convention Nos. 29 and 105 on forced labour in 1957 and 1970, but the ILO noted that some punishments may involve imposition of compulsory labour.

Trade unionism. Trade unions developed after World War II. In 1971 Nemery abolished all existing trade unions and the Sudan Workers' Trade Union Federation was established. This organization affiliated to the OATUU but broke the affiliation of the previous Sudanese Federation of Workers' Trade Unions with the WFTU. Following the overthrow of Nemery in April 1985 the trade unions were once again re-organized, and the new Sudanese Federation of Workers' Unions re-affiliated to the WFTU. According to a spokesman for the new trade union structures in late 1985, the trade union legislation under the "tyrant Nemery" had "managed to make the trade unions servile, by granting full powers to the Ministry of Labour".

Following the overthrow of Nemery there were two indentifiable unions, the Sudanese Workers' Trade Union Federation (SWTUF), and the Sudanese Federation of Employees and Professional Trade Unions (SFEPTU). Like all parties and newspapers, all trade unions were dissolved by General Beshir on his assumption of power. The SWFTU leaders kept their personal freedom following the 1988 *coup* but their activities were outlawed; most members of the SFEPTU were arrested however. In the summer of 1990, Dr Ali Fadul of the Sudan Doctors' Union died in prison as the result of torture.

Surinam

Capital: Paramaribo   **Population: 408,000**

Political system. Surinam has under the 1987 constitution, a National Assembly elected by universal adult suffrage: the coalition Front for Democracy and Development won a resounding victory in the 1987 elections bringing to an end seven years of military rule.

Though a new National Assembly was elected in May 1991, the political future of Surinam was dominated by the civil war waged by Col. Bouterse at the head of the country's armed forces with Amerindian insurgents led by Ronnie Brunswijk. Col. Bouterse continued to oppose the government of President Shankar from a semi-independent position.

Economy. Surinam's economy is dominated by the mining of bauxite and its processing into alumina and finished aluminium. There is self-sufficiency in most food crops with an exportable surplus of rice (the main staple). There is a small light manufacturing sector.

System of industrial relations. Surinam ratified ILO Convention No. 87 (Freedom of Association and Protection of the Right to Organize, 1948) in 1976, but has not ratified Convention No. 98 (Right to Organize and Collective Bargaining, 1949).

In December 1984 the then military government formed a tripartite Labour Advisory Council. In 1988 it was succeeded by a State Council to review employment legislation, but early in 1989, two federations, De Moederbond and C-47 informed the government that they would not participate unless its structure was changed to improve union representation. The years 1988–89 brought few industrial disputes but in May 1989 there was a general strike against the refusal of the government to acknowledge union concerns about a deteriorating economic situation.

Trade unionism. The president of the ICFTU-affiliated trade union AVVS, "De Moederbond", was among 15 opponents of the left-wing military régime executed in December 1982, following accusations of their participation in a "counter-revolutionary plot" being prepared in complicity with the USA, Netherlands and the former Surinam politicians. Following this, Lt.-Col. Desi Bouterse, the leader of the National Military Council, stated that the time had come "for us to form a truly revolutionary government in which the working class and the oppressed can recognize themselves", and in February 1983 he announced the formation of a new Cabinet under the premiership of Errol Alibux, a member of the leftist Progressive Workers' and Farm Labourers' Union (PALU) party.

From 1983, however, there was a shift away from leftist positions and to improved relations with the USA. Further strikes in the bauxite industry and other sectors calling for free elections and opposing price and tax increases were staged in the winter of 1983–84; following this Alibux was dismissed as Prime Minister. The nominated National Assembly formed in January 1985 to draft a new constitution preparatory to the proposed return to democratic rule, comprised 14 military officers, 11 trade union leaders and six representatives of the private sector and in September 1985 the Assembly announced the creation of a commission to draft a new constitution, the commission including a representative of De Moederbond. Trade union nominees participated in the government, and in December 1985 André Willem Koornaar, a leader of the Progressive Workers' Organization (PWO) was appointed Minister of Labour following an incident in which his predecessor had threatened a group of trade unionists with a gun at a meeting in his office. The ICFTU's *Trade Union Rights; Survey of Violations 1985–86* stated that the "atmosphere of uncertainty and fear reigning in the country" since the execution of Daal "has seriously limited the full exercise of trade union rights". However, an ICFTU mission to Surinam in 1988 found that, following the end of military rule, greater freedom had been restored to the trade unions.

By 1989 organized labour was thought to represent about 50 per cent of the workforce, assisted by a Dutch pro-union cultural bias. There are five union federations, four of which come together in the Foundation of Competing Labour Federations in Surinam (SSVS) which was founded in 1957 to receive international assistance. The SSVS today functions mainly as a supervisory board for the country's Union College. The largest federation is probably still De Moederbond which regained its ICFTU membership after suspension during the military years. The left-wing C-47 may be of comparable size, as indeed may the civil service federation CLO. The WCL-affiliated PWO is rather smaller as is the newer OSAV, which originated in C-47 but does not form part of the SSVS. All membership figures should be treated with caution.

Algemeen Verbond van Vakverenigingen in Surinam "De Moederbond" (AVVS) General Alliance of Labour Unions in Surinam

Address. Coppenstraat 134, Paramaribo

Leadership. Fred van Russel (chairman)

Membership. Some 12,000 in 46 unions, notably in banking, insurance, agriculture, government and commercial companies.

History and character. De Moederbond was founded in 1951. On Dec. 8, 1982, the National Military Council declared a state of martial law, destroyed the offices of De Moederbond, and summarily executed its president, Cyrill Daal, and other opponents of the régime. Following this other leaders of De Moederbond went into exile. These events followed a general strike called by De Moederbond in early November intended to hasten the transition to democratic civilian rule.

International affiliation. The affiliation of De Moederbond to the ICFTU was suspended by the ICFTU executive board in November 1986 when the board stated that De Moederbond was now participating in a government that denied human and trade union rights. In December 1988, however, the board lifted the suspension finding that De Moederbond had now been restored to democratic principles. It is also a member of the CCL.

Centrale Landsdienaren Organisaties (CLO)
Federation of Civil Service Organizations

Address. Kernkampweg 62, Paramaribo
Leadership. Hendrik Sylvester (chairman); Hugo Blanker (general secretary)
Membership. Claims 16,000 members in 60 unions, all state employees.
History and character. Founded in 1971
Affiliated unions and structure. The largest single block of CLO members is that of the teachers, whose history of organization dates back to 1895.
International affiliations. The CLO is not affiliated to any of the world centres but has contacts with civil service internationals.

Organisatie van Samenwerkende Autonome Vakbonden (OSAV)
Organization of Co-operating Autonomous Trade Unions

Address. Keizerstraat 18, Paramaribo
Leadership. Waldo Bijnoe (chairman); August Wong (secretary)
Membership. Claims 6,000.
Affiliated unions and structure. OSAV has 11 member unions, most of which joined after leaving other federations. This was most recently the case with Suralco, the biggest union on the bauxite sector which defected from C-47.
History and character. OSAV was founded in 1985 after a dispute over the leadership of De Moederbond, of which most of its officers were members. It is not a member of the SSVS and has poor relations with the other federations

Progressieve Vakcentrale 47 (C-47)
Progressive Labour Federation 47

Address. Wanicastraat 230, Paramaribo
Leadership. Fred Derby (chairman); Frans Menckeberg (general secretary)
Membership. C-47 claims to have 15,500 members in 66 member unions.
History and character. C-47 was founded in 1970 by members of the PNR and advocates a radical position in line with that party's view. Teachers and civil servants are prominent among its members. It maintains an office in the Netherlands via which it receives financial assistance.
International affiliations. C-47 was accepted into the ICFTU in March 1989 and has close links with the IMF.

Progressieve Werknemers Organisatie (PWO)
Progressive Workers' Organization

Address. Limesgracht 80. P.O. Box 406 Paramaribo
Phone. 75840
Membership. Around 4,000 members in 18 affiliated unions.
Leadership. Ramon Cruden (chairman); Marius Ment (general secretary).
History and character. The PWO was founded in 1948 by Father Josephus L. Weidmann, a Dutch Catholic priest, and a former associate of his is still the general secretary.
International affiliations. Although the PWO is still affiliated to the WCL, its CLAT affiliation ceased in 1989 following accusations of a too-close relationship to the former military régime.

Swaziland

Capital: Mbabane

Population: 737,000
(1988)

Political system. Swaziland is an independent kingdom within the Commonwealth. Political parties are banned.

Economy. Swaziland's economy is based on the production and processing of sugar cane and wood pulp. About 60 per cent of the population is supported by subsistence level farming. It has close economic ties with South Africa and relies on a sustained flow of foreign aid to offset current account deficits in the balance of payments.

System of industrial relations. Swaziland joined the International Labour Organization in 1975 and ratified ILO Convention No. 87 (Freedom of Association and Protection of the Right to Organize, 1948) and Convention No. 98 (Right to Organize and Collective Bargaining, 1949) in 1978.

Trade unionism. The development of trade unions has been weak and fitful in Swaziland and in 1977 the number of unions in the entire country was reported to be as low as three. The Swaziland Federation of Trade Unions is the only national centre, and has affiliates in electricity supply and the civil service. In the summer of 1990 a number of its members were tried and acquitted of seeking to form a political party.

Swaziland Federation of Trade Unions (SFTU)

Address. P.O. Box 1158, Manzini
Leadership. Obed Meanyana (general secretary)
Membership. 26,000 (according to the ICFTU).
History and structure. Founded in 1973, the SFTU became the central trade union organization in the mid-1980s, with members from both the public and private sectors, and including agricultural workers.

Four of the 11 defendants who in the summer of 1990 faced charges of trying to form a political party were members of the Federation, including Zodwa Mkhonta, Chair of the Federation Women's Committee. They were acquitted of all charges in October.

International affiliations. OATUU. The SFTU affiliated to the ICFTU in May 1987. It hosted the triannual conference of the ICFTU's African Regional Organization (AFRO) in Mbabane in May 1988.

Sweden

Capital: Stockholm

Population: 8,527,000

Political system. Sweden is a constitutional monarchy governed under a system of multi-party parliamentary democracy. As a result of elections held in September 1988, the Social Democratic Party of Mr. Ingevaar Carlsson was returned to power, but it was forced into coalition with the Communist Left Party and Centre Party in 1990.

Economy. Sweden has a highly developed economy with a relatively heavy dependence on international trade. Despite having trimmed over-capacity in some of its main heavy industries during the 1980s, Sweden has one of the lowest official unemployment rates in the industrialized world (under 2 per cent in 1987). There is an acute shortage of skilled labour. A very high level of welfare provision is sustained through heavy taxation.

During 1989, labour shortages drove up wage costs although growth continued for the seventh year in succession. Average wage increases for the year averaged 9.5 per cent. The rate of growth slowed however, falling to 1.8 per cent though unemployment fell to 1.4 per cent. It has not passed 3 per cent since 1974. Civilian employment was 4,470,000, of whom 1,320,000 worked in industry, 16,000 in agriculture, and 2,990,000 in services. Prices rose by 6.7 per cent during the year.

System of industrial relations. Sweden ratified ILO Convention No. 87 (Freedom of Association and Protection of the Right to Organize, 1948) in 1949 and Convention No. 98 (Right to Organize and Collective Bargaining, 1949) in 1950.

Collective bargaining. At national level, negotiations in the private sector are conducted between the Swedish Employers' Confederation (SAF) and the LO and PTK (the Federation of Salaried Employees in Industry and Services, representing 544,000 members of eight TCO unions and 48,000 members of 14 SACO/SR unions). In the state sector, negotiations are conducted by the Swedish National Agency for Government Employers (SAV) with the Section for State Employees of the TCO (TCO-S), the LO State Employees' Union, and SACO/SR. In the local government sector, negotiations are conducted by the Swedish Association of Local Authorities and the Federation of Swedish County Councils with KTK (the Federation of Salaried Local Government Employees representing eight TCO unions), the LO-affiliated Swedish Municipal Workers' Union, and SACO/SR. These central bargaining cartels negotiate framework recommendations within which the various unions conclude agreements. Centralized bargaining set fairly rigid patterns from the 1950s, but in the 1980s the SAF began to press strongly to negotiate as far as possible with the individual unions on a decentralized basis. In the public sector the government has since 1982 increasingly intervened indirectly to emphasize the priority of restraining inflation.

In general most issues between employers and workers are resolved through collective bargaining, but legislation provides a regulatory framework for matters such as job security, co-determination, status of shop stewards, etc. The Co-determination Act of 1977 requires employers to advise and consult employees before making any significant changes in company operation. Collective agreements are binding and industrial action may not be taken while in force, except in circumstances where an employer has refused to enter into a co-determination agreement on matters concerning company management and work supervision.

Closed shops do not exist, although union membership is typically 80 per cent or more in most sectors. In general, unions are active with significant membership participation, and have generally favoured technological adaptation and innovation.

Wage-earner funds. Swedish trade unions have successfully campaigned for economic democracy in the form of wage-earner funds. In 1975 LO called for the creation of employee funds and this led to a bitter disagreement between both sides of industry. A number of models for such funds were presented, and in 1983 Parliament decided to introduce a system of five regional funds as from January 1984.

Each fund has a nine-member board of directors including five trade union representatives. Roughly SEK 2,000 million a year is collected from companies in the form of 20 per cent of net profits exceeding a certain level (after adjustment for inflation) plus an employer fee totalling 0.2 per cent of payrolls. The funds are used to buy shares in Swedish companies for the benefit of all Swedish citizens covered by the National Pension Insurance Funds (ATP). The funds are not permitted to own more than 50 per cent of the voting rights in any one company. Wage-earner funds were introduced for an experimental period until 1990, when the system was to be reviewed. The SAF (the main Swedish employers' federation) is still bitterly opposed to the funds; employers advocate company-based profit-sharing as an alternative.

Before 1990 it was already apparent that the Swedish model was under increasing strain. The 1989 (two-year) agreement between the SAF and the LO provided for renegotiation in the event of price inflation passing 4 per cent. This occurred and the employers were reluctant to agree to compensate for this faster rate of increase. The Social Democratic government responded to increasing economic difficulties in early 1990 by proposing an austerity package including a wages and prices freeze coupled with a ban on strikes until the end of 1991. The package was at first accepted by the LO whose Vice President Rune Molin had been appointed Industry Minister the previous month. However union opposition swiftly gathered and the LO reversed its stance. When all opposition parties combined to defeat the Carlsson government, the Prime Minister formed a new administration with Communist Left Party and Centre Party support. A new economic stabilization package in April did not contain measures to constrain strikes and focused on cutting public expenditure instead.

The SAF proposed to its members associations in December 1989 that it should no longer negotiate central wage agreements with the LO, though it partially relented four months later by being prepared to discuss voluntary wage restraint. The LO struggled to retain the "Swedish Model" which many believed died as a result of the February 1990 government crisis.

Trade unionism. Numerous socialist-influenced trade unions appeared in the 1880s and in 1889 these were influential in the formation of the Social Democratic Labour Party (SDP), which functioned both as a political party and as a trade union centre. From this the blue-collar Swedish Trade Union Confederation (LO) was formed in 1898. In 1906 the Swedish Employers' Confederation (SAF) was formed and this recognized the LO and the right of workers to bargain collectively. In 1938 the two sides concluded their first "Basic Agreement". Most LO members are still manual workers. Organization among white-collar workers began in the 1930s, and this sector is also now highly organized (about 80 per cent), with its own trade union centre, the Swedish Confederation of Professional Employees (TCO), and also a Central Organization of Swedish Professional Workers (SACO/SR). The SDP was in office continuously from 1932 to 1976 (returning in 1982) and its welfare state policies and association with the LO have contributed to general industrial peace and a climate favourable to trade union activities. The SDP was returned to power again in September 1988 but was defeated over its austerity programme in 1990 and formed a coalition with the Communist Left and the Centre Parties.

For 1988 union density in Sweden was 86 per cent, though it is known that 1989 saw a slight decline in the number of members. The dominant LO entered a period of re-appraisal of its role, for so long almost synonomous with that of the Social Democratic Party. For more than 90 years the two organizations have shared support and leadership, a common factor underlined again when the LO Vice President joined the government as Industry Minister early in 1990, but by that date the "Swedish Model" of industrial co-operation was under unprecedented strain. Trends hostile to union dominance started to make themselves felt: the employers (equally organized and centralized in the SAF) rejected central pay bargaining; the SDP was forced into a coalition with two other parties; and signs accumulated of rejection of membership among younger workers. The slight falls in LO membership in 1988 and 1989 were the first it had recorded in decades, but the TCO (which had lost members in 1986 and 1987) resumed growth, expanding by 2 per cent; SACO increased its membership by 4 per cent.

In general the LO and the TCO have maintained a co-operative relationship, which has been enhanced by the trend to equalization of pay and conditions between the manual and white-collar sectors. The LO and the TCO have demarcation agreements to reduce intrusions on their various areas of recruitment, but there are few such agreements between the TCO and the SACO/SR.

The LO and the TCO co-operate with the Swedish International Development Authority (SIDA) and distribute SIDA funds to unions in developing countries through the LO/TCO Council of International Trade Union Co-operation. The 1986–87 budget was SEK 44,000,000. In 1978 the Swedish unions founded the International Centre of the Swedish Labour Movement (AIC) to co-ordinate their international work.

Landsorganisation i Sverige (LO)
Swedish Trade Union Confederation

Address. Barnhusgaten 18, 105 53 Stockholm
Phone. (8) 769 25 00
Telex. 19145 LO-PRESS
Fax. (8) 24 52 28
Cable. SVELOFACK STOCKHOLM
Leadership. Stig Malm (president); Rune Molin (vice-president and Industry Minister since February 1990).
Membership. 2,260, 204 (1989).
History and character. The LO was created in 1898 by the Social Democratic Labour Party (SDP), and has remained close to the party. The SDP first came to power in 1932, applying Keynesian policies to counter the depression; in 1938 the LO reached the first "Basic Agreement" with the employers' confederation—SAF—and thereafter pursued in conjuction with the SDP (which held power until 1976) "middle way" policies of social and industrial reform. A political levy is paid to the SDP, and some local unions have collective membership in the party. Relations with the SDP government which took office in 1982 have been strained at times by the adoption of policies of relative austerity, although the relationship has not been fundamentally weakened.

The LO favours the extension of worker participation and co-determination in the workplace. It is represented on numerous governmental bodies such as the National Labour Market Board, the National Board of Occupational Safety and Health, the National Social Insurance Board, etc. Each LO affiliate maintains its own unemployment fund, with members entitled to benefit equivalent to over 90 per cent of earnings for 300 days (450 for those over 55). These funds receive state grants.

Structure. Most LO affiliates work on the industrial union principle (i.e. organizing all workers in a workplace in the same union regardless of trade). This does not apply in the case of the building trades unions, which are craft-based. The majority of LO affiliates organize about 80–90 per cent of the workers in their fields, except in retailing and services. At workplace level there are union clubs; these form branch unions; and above these come the national unions. The national unions are run by an executive and a union council, with congresses (normally every four years) as their ruling bodies. The highest decision-making body of the LO is its delegate congress; between congresses the highest authority is the general council, which comprises about 130 members elected by the affiliates and the 15 members of the executive council, who are elected by the congress, and which meets at least twice each year. The executive council, which normally meets fortnightly, comprises the president (who functions as a general secretary), vice-president, secretary and negotiations secretary and 11 others, who are usually presidents of affiliated unions.

Publications. LO-tidningen (circulation 72,000). SDP and the LO also jointly publish 21 newspapers.

Affiliated unions. Membership figures relate to 1989.

Agricultural Workers' Union.
President: Leif Hékansson
Membership: 13,976.

Clothing and Textile Workers' Union
President: Arne Lökken
Membership:30,824.

Commercial Workers' Union.
President: Bengt Lloyd.
Membership: 160,872 (merged with the Hairdresser Workers' Union).

Construction Workers' Union.
President: Bertil Whinberg.
Membership: 156,164

Electricians' Union.
President: Hans Schoug.
Membership: 31,975.

Factory Workers' Union.
President: Uno Ekberg.
Membership: 99,200.

Foodstuffs Workers' Union.
President: Lage Andreasson.
Membership: 62,952.

Forest Workers' Union.
President: Arne Johansson.
Membership: 19,143.

Graphic Workers' Union.
President: Valter Carlsson.
Membership: 48,314.

Hairdresser Workers' Union.
President: Ake Rytteblad.
Membership: Merged with the Commercial Workers' Union.

Hotel & Restaurant Workers.
President: Seine Svensk.
Membership: 42,739.

Insurance Workers' Union.
President: Berje Johansson.
Membership: 24,176.

Maintenance Workers' Union.
President: Bert-Ove Pettersson.
Membership: 39,919.

Metalworkers' Union.
President: Leif Blomberg.
Membership: 465,935.

Mine Workers' Union.
President: Anders Stendalen.
Membership: 8,499.

Musicians' Union.
President: Gert-Ake Wallden.
Membership: 7,787.

Municipal Workers' Union.
President: Lillemor Arvidsson.
Membership: 633,999.

Painters' Union.
President: Arne Dahlberg.
Membership: 22,734.

Paper Industry Workers.
President: Ingvar Jansson.
Membership: 35,814.

Seamen's Union.
President: Anders Lindström.
Membership: 10,541.

Sheet Metal Workers' Union.
President: Sixten Johnsson.
Membership: 6,449.

State Employees' Union.
Members: Curt Persson.
Membership: 207,904.

Transport Workers' Union.
President: Johnny Grönberg.
Membership: 60,597.

Wood Industry Workers.
President: Ove Fredriksson.
Membership: 69,691.

International affiliations. ICFTU; ETUC; TUAC; NFS. All the LO affiliates also belong to at least one international trade secretariat of the ICFTU.

Tjänstemännens Centralorganisation (TCO)
Swedish Confederation of Professional Employees

Address. Linnégatan 14, P.O. Box 5252, 102 45 Stockholm
Phone. 7829100
Telex. 19104 TCO S
Cable. TECEOCENT
Fax. 08 6637520
Leadership. Björn Rosengren (president)
Membership. 1,276, 236 (1990). Women have constituted a majority of the membership since 1977.

History and character. Unions of salaried employees did not exist in Sweden before the 1920s. In 1931 a white-collar centre, DACO, was formed in the private sector, this won statutory rights to association and collective bargaining for private sector white-collar employees in 1936, and in 1937 the TCO was created to campaign for such rights in the public sector. The DACO merged with the TCO in 1944, and freedom of association for white-collar workers was won progressively in the public sector from the 1940s to 1966. The membership of the TCO includes members of the police and armed forces, who are not barred from union membership or industrial action. The TCO has generally co-operated with the LO, but never aligned itself politically, and opinion surveys indicate that its membership is broadly representative of the Swedish population as a whole in its political balance.

The TCO opposes statutory incomes policies and favours free collective bargaining and a shift to indirect taxation. It advocates public spending as a solution to unemployment problems. A portion of membership dues is allocated to the Unemployment Benefit Fund, which also receives state support.

Structure. Congress, meeting every four years, is the ruling body; the supreme body between congresses is the representative, which comprises 100 federation representatives; the executive committee, which is elected by the congress, has 15 members and normally meets fortnightly. The TCO has since 1977 also built a structure at district level.

Publication. TCO-Tidnigen (33 per year, circulation 90,000). All the affiliated federations also produce journals.

Affiliates. TCO affiliates are organized on both the industrial union and craft (occupational) basis. Membership figures relate to 1989.

Bank Employees' Union (SBmf)
President: Rolf Blom.
Membership: 54,531.

Civilian Defence Employees' Union.
President: Lennart Elvgren.
Membership: 13,220.

Commercial Employees' Union (HTF).
President: Lars Hellman.
Membership: 123,110.

Customs Employees' Union (STF).
President: Karl Gunnheden.
Membership: 5,742.

Folk High School Teachers' Union.
President: Kerstin Mustel.
Membership: 1,982.

Insurance Company Employees' Union
President: Ingvar Lundqvist.
Membership: 20,201.

Journalists' Union.
President: Claes Leo Lindwall.
Membership: 16,180.

Union of Local Officers (SKTF).
President: Sture Nordh
Membership: 185,859.

Pharmacy Employees' Union.
President: Kerstin Beckman-Danielsson.
Membership: 6,716.

National Union of Officers.
President: Ivan Bill.
Membership: 14,491.

Police Union.
President: Gunno Gunnmo.
Membership: 21,212.

Federation of Civil Servants (ST).
President: Olle Söderman.
Membership: 125,170.

Teachers' Union (SL).
President: Slveig Paulsson.
Membership: 73,771.

Theater Employees' Union.
President: Tomas Bolme.
Membership: 6,338.

Union of Employees in Health and Medical Care (SHSTF).
President: Inger Ohlsson.
Membership: 99,766.

Union of Forestry and Agricultural Employees.
President: Gert Magnusson.
Membership: 1,972.

Union of Technical & Clerical
Employees in Industry (SIF).
President: Inge Granqvist.
Membership: 301,745.

Vocational Teacher's Union (SFL)
President: Christer Romilson.
Membership: 104,510.

The Union of Foremen and Supervisors (SALF).
President: Björn Bergman.
Membership: 89,629.

Professional Musicians' Union.
President: Peter Höglund.
Membership: 1,739.

International affiliations. ICFTU; ETUC; TUAC; NFS. Affiliated unions are also members of the relevant ICFTU international trade secretariats.

Sveriges Akademikers Centralorganisation (SACO)
Swedish Confederation of Professional Associations

Address. P.O. Box 2206, 103 15 Stockholm
Phone. 8 613 48 00
Telex. 88105225
Fax. 8 24 77 01
Leadership. Jorgen Ullenhag (chairman)
Membership. Claimed 335,000 in 1990.
History and character. SACO, which was founded in 1975 by merger of the Swedish Confederation of Professional Associations (SACO) and the National Federation of Civil Servants (SR), is a confederation of 25 professional associations, graduate organizations, and organizations of government officials.
Affiliated unions. Membership figures relate to 1989.

Association of Graduates in Applied Agricultural Sciences, Industrial and Environmental Planning.
President: Olle Windfridsson.
Membership: 4,449.

Union of Acrhitects, Interior Designers, & Landscape Architects.
President: Olof Thedin.
Membership: 5,559.

Association of Graduates in Business Administration and Economics (CR).
President: Jan Eskil Jörby.
Membership: 11,139.

Association of Graduates in Documentation, Information and Culture (DIK).
President: Britt Marie Hüggström.
Membership: 11,220.

Association of Occupational Therapists.
President: Inga-Britt Lindström.
Membership: 5,634.

Society of College Engineers.
President: Lars Hjeltman.
Membership: 7,779.

Federation of Lawyers, Social Scientists & Economists.
President: Anders Forsberg.
Membership: 31,694.

National Association of Registered Physiotherapists (LSR).
President: Carina Svensson.
Membership: 8,463

National Union of Secondary School Teachers (LR).
President: Ove Engman.
Membership: 46,858.

Central Organization of Military Reserve Officers.
President: Sten-Ingvar Nilsson.
Membership: 6,657.

Association of Headmasters & Directors of Education.
President: Nils Arndt.
Membership: 5,074.

SACO/SR General Group.
President: Tore Sjöberg.
Membership: 7,093.

Association of Clergymen.
President: Bernt Waltmark.
Membership: 5,307.

Association of Military Officers (SOF).
President: Leif Törnquist.
Membership: 10,714.

Association of Graduate Engineers (CF).
President: Thomas Sidenbladh.
Membership: 50,118.

Pharmaceutical Association.
President: Barbro Hammarström.
Membership: 5,992.

Association of Masters in Forestry (SJFR).
President: Alvar Ohlen.
Membership: 1,656.

Railway Officers' Association.
President: Orjan Ersson.
Membership: 4,369.

Medical Association.
President: Anders Milton.
Membership: 30,509.

Association of Scientists (SN).
President: Göran Bengtsson.
Membership: 6,235.

Psychological Association.
President: Birgit Hansson.
Membership: 6,340.

Union of Social Workers, Personnel & Public Administration.
President: Agneta Bygdell.
Membership: 25,437.

Dental Association (STF).
President: Göran Koch.
Membership: 11,547.

Association of University Teachers.
President: Leif Lewin.
Membership: 9,896.

Veterinary Association (SV).
President: Herbert Lundström.
Membership: 1,887.

Independent unions

Swedish Worker's Centrla Organization (SAC), the Syndicalists

Leadership. Ingemar Nilsson (secretary)
Membership. 15,325.

The Swedish Dockworkers' Union,

Leadership. Gunnar Nordberg (chairman)
Membership. 1,762 (1988).

Swedish Airline Pilots' Association

Leadership. Kurt Ivarsson (chairman); Erik Levin (managing director)
Membership. 1,800.

Switzerland

Capital: Berne   **Population: 6,610,000**

Political system. The Swiss Confederation is a republic comprising 23 cantons. Executive power is exercised by the Federal Council whose seven members are elected from the popularly-elected bicameral legislature, the Federal Assembly. The constitution lays down procedures for the use of popular referenda to decide a range of major policy issues.

Economy. Given the country's lack of signficant natural resources, the Swiss economy is based on light industry and services, and is heavily dependent on exports. Switzerland's strong flow of invisible earnings from the banking and commercial sectors covers its visible trade deficit and produces an overall balance-of-payments surplus on the current account.

The country is increasingly dependent on services, which employ 58 per cent of the labour force. In 1988 only 4 per cent of the working population was employed full time in agriculture. Unlike a number of European countries, Switzerland experienced full employment in the late 1980s and skilled labour shortages caused increasing concern. The country partly met its skills deficit by importing foreign labour: it has more than 800,000 resident aliens and a further 75,000 come in for seasonal work.

System of industrial relations. Switzerland is noted for being an almost strike-free economy. Where social peace is concerned, the merit is generally attributed to the total non-dispute labour clause enshrined in the historic agreement signed in 1937 between the employers and unions in the metal trades, of which the Federation of Metalworkers and Watchmakers (FOMH) is by far the most important. That agreement established collectively agreed industrial relations between both sides of industry on the basis of mutual good faith, with each party undertaking, for the length of the contract, to forego any industrial action for whatever purpose. In exchange, disputes, including those concerned with the fixing of wages, are dealt with in the last resort by an arbitration tribunal agreed upon through collective bargaining. Strikes can take place, but rarely do, once the agreement reaches the end of its term and agreement is not reached upon its immediate renewal. It should be emphasized that arbitration provisions are exceptional—most of Switzerland's 1,300 collective agreements are reached by simple compromise.

A principle previously unknown to Swiss labour law was established in January 1987 by the Labour Tribunal when it ruled on an appeal made by the Italian-speaking section of the Federation of Metalworkers (FTMH), which two years previously had not been allowed to become a party to a 1981 collective labour agreement or to participate in discussions or renewal of that agreement. The tribunal ruled that in future signatories to a collective agreement must accept the adherence of other parties unless there are strong reasons against it. The decision only applies to participation in signing of an existing collective agreement and the Tribunal did not rule on the right of a minority organization to take part in collective bargaining.

Conditions of work are extensively regulated by the Federal Labour Act and the Swiss Code of Obligations, which lay down minimum standards, through not a minimum wage. In 1988 a new agency, the Federal Office for Equal Pay for Men and Women, was established. Under the code of obligations a collective agreement legally binds the parties who may not attempt to modify any of its terms through coercive action.

Switzerland ratified ILO Convention No. 87 (Freedom of Association and Protection of the Right to Organize, 1948) in 1975, but has not ratified Convention No. 98 (Right to Organize and Collective Bargaining, 1949).

Trade unionism. The trade union movement is fragmented, but the two major centres are the socialist Schweizerischer Gewerkschaftsbund (SGB/USS), which is affiliated to the ICFTU, and the Christian Christlichnationaler Gewerkschaftsbund der Schweiz (CNG/CSC), which is a WCL affiliate.

Unionization of the workforce in 1988 was 28 per cent, with density highest in the postal service and the railways. the textile and shoe industries, which employ large numbers of women and foreign workers, have low density. Unions do have in their armoury the right to push issues to a popular vote and occasionally the raising of an issue has led to legislation. However there is no sign that recourse to a referendum automatically leads to success. Under the circumstances, the willingness of employers to reach a compromise agreement probably reflects not trade union strength but the involvement of unions in running public affairs—through consultation machinery, through Socialist participation in government, and through direct democracy.

Christlichnationaler Gewerkschaftsbund der Schweiz (CNG)
Confédération des Syndicats Chrétiens de Suisse (CSC)
Swiss Confederation of Christian Trade Unions

Address. Case postale 2630, 3001 Berne
Phone. (31) 452447
Leadership. Guido Casetti (president)

Membership. 107, 453 (1987).

History and character. The CNG/CSC was founded in 1907 and developed as the Catholic trade union centre. It has now absorbed the former small Protestant centre, Schweizerischer Verband Evangelischer Arbeitnehmer/Association Suisse des Salariés (SVEA/ASSE). The orientation is Christian socialist. It has two deputies in the National Council and one in the Council of States.

Affiliates. There are 14 affiliated unions. Most of these are organized by industrial sector, but also included are the former Protestant centre SVEA/ASSE (which has 3,885 members) and federations for Hungarian and Czechoslovak workers in Switzerland (VUCA/TVCA, with 793 and 146 members respectively). The two largest affiliates are the construction workers' federation (FCTC), with 39,044 members, and the metalworkers' federation (FCOM), with 23,882 members (1987 figures).

Publications. Aktiv (45,000 copies); *Verkehrs- und Staatspersonal* (17,000 copies); *Service et Communauté* (17,000 copies); *Actif* (13,000 copies); *Action et Solidarité* (8,000 copies).

International affiliations. WCL; TUAC; ETUC.

Landesverband Freier Schweizer Arbeitnehmer
Union Suisse des Syndicats Autonomes
Swiss Union of Free Trade Unions

Address. Badenerstrasse 41, 8004 Zurich

Phone. (1) 2410757

Fax. (1) 241 14 09

Leadership. Jakob Züst (president); Alfred Meyer (secretary)

Membership. 22,500.

History and character. Founded in 1919.

Affiliated unions. Personalverband der Schweizerischen Fotobranche; Schweizerische Zahntechniker-Vereinigung; Forstpersonal-Verband der Schweiz; Berufsverband Floristinnen und Floristen der Schweiz; Schweizerische Gärtner-Verband; Schweizerische Organisation Lichtpaus- und Plandruck; Angestellter.

Schweizerischer Gewerkschaftsbund (SGB)
Union Syndicale Suisse (USS)

Address. Monbijoustrasse 61, 3007 Berne

Phone. (31) 455666

Telex. 33299 SYNUN CH

Cable. SINDICALUNION BERNE

Leadership. H.Walter Renschler (president)

Membership. 441, 400 (1989)

History and character. The SGB/USS was founded in 1880 and is the largest Swiss trade union centre, with a moderate socialist orientation.

International affiliations. ICFTU; TUAC; ETUC.

Affiliated unions. In 1989 SGB/USS affiliates were as follows (with changes shown over 1988):

	1988	*1989*	*Difference*	*%*
Gewerkschaft Bau und Holz (GBH)	118,981	122,304	+ 3,323	+ 2.8
Schweiz. Metall- und Uhren-arbeitnehmer-Verband (SMUV)	115,185	111,310	− 3,875	− 3.4
Schweiz. Eisenbahner-Verband (SEV)	57,910	57,430	− 480	− 0.8
Schweiz. Verband des Personals öffentlicher Dienste (VPOD)	40,564	40,796	+ 232	+ 0.6
Union Schweiz. Post-, Telefon- und Telegrafenbeamter (PTT-Union)	27,839	27,938	+ 99	+ 0.4

	1988	1989	Difference	%
Gewerkschaft Verkauf Handel Transport Lebensmittel (VHTL)	26,393	26,002	− 391	− 1.5
Gewerkschaft Druck und Papier (GDP)	15,661	16,290	+ 629	+ 4.0
Gewerkschaft Textil Chemie Papier (GTCP)	12,195	11,984	− 211	− 1.7
Schweiz. Lithographenbund (SLB)	6,992	7,089	+ 97	+ 1.4
Verband Schweiz. Postbeamter (VSPB)	6,555	6,619	+ 64	+ 1.0
Verband Schweiz. Telefon- und Telegrafenbeamter (VSTTB)	3,923	3,909	− 14	− 0.3
Verband Schweiz. Zollpersonal (VSZP)	3,830	3,789	− 41	− 1.1
Verband der Bekleidungs-, Leder- und Ausrüstungsarbeitnehmer der Schweiz (VBLA)	3,145	3,001	− 144	− 4.6
Schweiz. Syndikat Medienschaffender (SSM)	2,124	2,232	+ 108	+ 5.1
Schweiz. Verband der Seidenbeuteltuchweberei (SVSW)	385	396	+ 11	+ 2.9
Vereinigung des Schweizerischen Flugsicherungspersonals (VSFP)	338	360	+ 22	+ 6.5
Total	442,020	441,449	− 571	− 0.1

Syria

Capital: Damascus   **Population: 12,028,000**

Political system. The Syrian Arab republic is a "socialist popular democracy". The popularly-elected legislature (*Majlis al-Sha'ab*) has only limited powers; the Prime Minister and Cabinet are appointed by the President. The government is dominant by the Baath ("Renaissance") Arab Socialist Party.

Gulf War participation assisted Syria to end its isolation of many years, facilitated a *rapprochement* with Egypt, and gave her a free hand to crush the Maronite rising of General Aoun in the Lebanon.

Economy. The state-controlled areas of Syria's economy account for about 70 per cent of GDP and include much of the country's manufacturing industry. Syria exports low-grade crude oil and imports higher grade oil.

Syria benefited greatly from its participation in the anti-Iraq coalition during the Gulf War, receiving large subventions from the Gulf states. In 1989, helped by buoyant oil revenues, it recorded its first current account surplus for 30 years, though this success may prove difficult to sustain in view of its dependence on a large volume of exports to the USSR.

System of industrial relations. Syria ratified ILO Convention No. 87 (Freedom of Association and Protection of the Right to Organize, 1948) in 1960 and Convention No. 98 (Right to Organize and Collective Bargaining, 1949) in 1957. The ILO has criticized apparent contraventions of Convention No. 87: the single union system does not allow workers to form unions outside the established structure; there are restrictions on the rights of foreign, non-Arab workers; and trade union administration is not free from interference by the public authorities. The government in Damascus has consistently failed to answer these points.

Trade unionism. Under a decree of 1968 a single-trade-union system is in force, organized by the General Federation of Trade Unions, which has powers to dissolve the executive committee of any union. A decree of 1969 gives the Ministry of Labour powers of supervision over the financial affairs of the unions. Trade union membership was widened in the civil service by legislation adopted in 1986. Peasants are organized separately in the General Federation of Peasants.

Ittihad Naqusbat al-'Ummal al-'Am fi Suriya
General Federation of Trade Unions

Address. P.O. Box 2351, Damascus
Phone. 39900
Telex. 411974
Cable. ALARINE DAMASCUS
Leadership. Izzedine Nasser (chairman)
Membership. 485,891 (1986).
History and character. Founded in 1948.
International affiliation. WFTU; ICATU.

Taiwan

Capital: Taipei   **Population: 20,130,000**

Political system. Taiwan, the Republic of China, has been ruled since 1949 by the Nationalist Party (KMT) which is fundamentally anti-communist in orientation. With the lifting of martial law in July 1987, there has been a significant political liberalization with several independent political parties being formed and a greater political role being accorded to the indigenous Taiwanese population as opposed to the Nationalist élite.

Economy. Taiwan's free market economy, based on manufacturing, has achieved one of Asia's highest growth rates in the past 38 years. It is heavily reliant upon export trade, principally in the late 1980s, in electronic goods, textiles and metal and plastic products.

Taiwan's growth rate was above 7 per cent in 1988 and 1989, helping to reduce unemployment to 1.57 per cent in 1989. In fact a number of Taiwanese manufacturing firms shed labour in 1989, but most of those who lost their jobs were absorbed by the country's burgeoning service sector. Civil employment in 1989 was 8,260,000 of which 3,490,000 were employed in industry, 1,170,000 in agriculture and 3,700,000 in services. With the labour market tight, wages rose by more than 50 per cent between 1985 and 1989.

System of industrial relations. In August 1984, a Labour Standards Law (LSL) was passed which gave more than 3,000,000 workers improved pension and severance benefits as well as restrictions on night-time and overtime work for women. Despite the unions' legal right to participate in drafting such legislation, the CFL had not been involved in any discussion of the bill.

One of the first government decisions in the aftermath of the lifting of Martial Law in mid-1987 was the establishment, on Aug. 1 of a Cabinet-level Council of Labour Affairs (CLA), which was authorized to recommend changes to the country's 1929 Trade Union Law (last amended in 1975). The establishment of the CLA had been partly motivated by a recent increase in labour unrest and also by a perceived challenge to General System of Preference privileges on the basis of alleged violations of union rights. In November 1987 a Labour Party was formed, which looked to the country's workers as its principal support base. During 1988 the Labour Party worked within individual unions, attempting to weaken traditional KMT control. In some unions, members rejected KMT candidates for leadership posts, voting instead for non-partisan or opposition figures.

Vital support for the new party came from unions in the Kaohsiung area and in Hsinchu. The party's vice-chairman, Lou Mei-wen, was a veteran union activist who gained a high profile in mid-December 1987 when he successfully led a campaign to reinstate a textile worker in Tsungli who had been dismissed because of his union activities. In March 1988 Kang Yi-yi, a Labour Party member, was elected Chairman of the China Petroleum Corporation Union, the first non-KMT member to head a major union. Also during 1988, a number of unions organized into "voluntary associations", in order to challenge the CFL's role as the sole legal labour centre. The two main such associations were (i) the Brotherhood of Unions and (ii) the Labour Union Alliance.

During 1987 there were over 1,600 labour dispute cases in Taiwan, most of which were technically illegal; however, for the most part the authorities tended to choose not to

444

enforce the letter of the law. During February 1988 workers in several factories took industrial action in support of their demands for greater profit-sharing and larger (lunar) new year bonuses. On May 1 the first island-wide work stoppage took place, when 95 per cent of the country's train drivers claimed their right (as enshrined under the 1984 LSL) to take leave on a national holiday. A demonstration by farmers in Taipei on May 20 in support of their demands for medical insurance developed into the country's worst rioting since 1947. In the following months large numbers of workers in public utilities and nationalized industries took industrial action of some sort; many of the actions appeared to be aimed at obtaining a more thorough enforcement of the LSL.

The Arbitration Dispute Law was revised on June 17, 1988, allowing workers to legally resort to strike action after one round of mediation, but requiring that they return to work if a second arbitration phase was called. Bus drivers in Miaoli tested the new law on Aug. 8 when they staged Taiwan's first technically legal strike, albeit for only three hours after which the CLA compelled the drivers to go to arbitration. During the same period the country's first Labour Courts were established, under the aegis of the Judicial Yuan, to deal with labour-management disputes.

The number of disputes rose by nearly 50 per cent between 1988 and 1989 though few ended successfully for the unions.

The Council began the work of revision of the Labour Standards Law in 1989 with a view to extending its coverage. The Council also has under consideration revision of the Trade Union Law of 1975. In both cases the Presidential and Assembly elections delayed progress. However progress was more rapid with the Law Governing Labour Disputes, the first major legislative revision since the lifting of martial law, where the establishment of a neutral mediation and arbitration agency is under control. It is expected that the CLA will eventually be upgraded to a fully-fledged Ministry of Labour.

Trade unionism. The process of political liberalization in Taiwan, which started in October 1986 and culminated in the lifting of Martial Law after 38 years in mid-1987, heralded a period of unprecedented change in the country's labour relations. Under Martial Law provisions, strikes had been forbidden, as were demonstrations, marches or picket lines. The only approved union centre, the Chinese Federation of Labour (CFL), was widely perceived by workers as being a tool of management. Unions generally limited their activities to organizing leisure activities and the provision of credit facilities, and officers (who were often managerial-level company employees) rarely involved themselves in collective bargaining or promoting improvements in working conditions. In 1988, only 12 per cent of the 2,400 large private enterprises had written collective contracts, as did a third of public enterprises. High wage levels and low unemployment rates only increased the lack of interest workers showed in their unions. By the mid-1980s only some 1,300,000 workers were unionized, despite constitutional and legislative guarantees, principally a 1929 Labour Union Law, providing the right to union membership to approximately 4,000,000 workers in manufacturing, mining, transport and other sectors. Civil servants, teachers, defence industry workers and administrators acting on behalf of employers are prohibited from organizing. Nevertheless, the union membership ratio rose during the 1980s, from 16.6 per cent in 1980 to 22.9 per cent in 1987. Over the same period the number of unions rose from 1,679 to 2,471.

At the end of 1989, Taiwan had 3,562 unions with 2,530,000 members, an increase over 1988 of nearly 16 per cent. In the same year union density was 30.5 per cent, a sharp rise from the 1988 figure of 26.4 per cent. Much of the growth in unions was achieved by independent organizations outside the Chinese Federation of Labour (CFL) whose origins lie in the history of the Kuomintang. The independent unions declined in 1990 in concert with the regression in the fortunes of the Labour and Workers' Parties, both of which did poorly in the December 1989 elections for the Legislature.

Chinese Federation of Labour (CFL)

Address. 11th Floor, 201-218 Tung Hwa North Road, Taipei
Phone. (2) 7135111
Cable. CHINFOL TAIPEI
Leadership. Hsieh Shen-San (president); Chiu Ching-hwei (secretary-general)
Membership. In 1987 there were 1,874,669 members in 2,471 unions, a membership proportion of 22.9 per cent.

History and character. The CFL traces its origins back to a Kuomintang labour organization founded in mainland China in 1928 and, remains to this day closely controlled by the ruling Kuomintang (KMT). It is the only legal confederation of unions and is organized vertically with seven industrial federations below it. Of the CFL's 2,471 affiliated unions, 1,276 are craft based and the remainder are industrial unions. Following the lifting of Martial Law in July 1987, other union centres, organized as "voluntary associations", formed to challenge the CFL's monopoly. The CFL responded to the challenge by electing a new leadership in April 1988. Hsieh Shen-shan, the new president, was elected to the KMT's central committee and central standing committee at the party's 13th congress held in July 1988.

Publication. Chinese Trade Unions.
International affiliation. ICFTU/APRO.

Tanzania

Capital: Dar es Salaam   **Population: 23,174,336**
                                                          (1988)

Political system. The United Republic of Tanzania is an independent member of the Commonwealth. It is a one-party state ruled by the left-wing Chama Cha Mapinduzi (CCM).

Economy. Tanzania's economy is primarily agricultural; about 70 per cent of its output is produced on a subsistence basis. It has a chronic foreign debt problem.

System of industrial relations. Collective agreements must be submitted for the approval of the Permanent Labour Tribunal, which is required to take account of the needs of the national economy. Labour legislation also provides for compulsory arbitration in industrial disputes, making it possible to declare strikes illegal and punishable by imprisonment.

Tanganyika and Zanzibar ratified ILO Convention No. 98 (Right to Organize and Collective Bargaining, 1949) in 1962 and 1964 respectively, and this ratification now applies in respect of Tanzania. Convention No. 87 (Freedom of Association and Protection of the Right to Organize, 1948) has not been ratified. Tanzania ratified Convention Nos. 29 and 105 on forced labour in 1962; Zanzibar followed suit in 1964. However the ILO has noted that compulsory cultivation may still be imposed, that the Human Resources Deployment Act of 1983 obliges citizens to work, and that other legislation permits the exaction of compulsory labour for public purposes and development schemes. Compulsory labour may also be imposed on offenders.

Trade unionism. Trade unionism in Tanzania has followed the pattern of many other African states. In 1964 the Tanganyika Federation of Labour was dissolved and replaced as the sole union central organization by the National Union of Tanganyika Workers (NUTA), which was linked by law to the ruling party. After a series of changes the central organization was designated the JUWATA (the Union of Tanzanian Workers) in 1978.

Private employers are required to apply the check-off system and collect contributions on behalf of JUWATA; the power to appoint its president and secretary-general are vested in the Tanzanian President. However, whereas NUTA was formally affiliated to TANU, JUWATA is constitutionally an outgrowth of the CCM, one of its "mass organizations" and is oriented towards the promotion of production.

Union of Tanzania Workers (JUWATA)

Address. P.O. Box 15359, Dar es Salaam
Phone. 26111/3
Telex. 41205
Leadership. H. Kolimba (chairman); Joseph Rwegasira (secretary-general)
Membership. 443,570.
History and character. The NUTA, formed in 1964, was expanded in 1978 to incorporate trade unions in Zanzibar and was renamed as JUWATA, which is a designated mass organization of the ruling CCM. The union is represented in parliament and in late 1987 Joseph Rewegasira was appointed Minister for Industry and Commerce.
Affiliates. JUWATA comprises seven sections: Commercial, Construction and Haulage; Government Civil Servants and Medical; Teachers; Industry and Mines; Agriculture; Domestic, Hotels, General Workers and Municipal; and Transport, Communications and Railways.
Publication. Mfanyakazi newspaper.
International affiliations. OATUU; CTUC.

Thailand

Capital: Bangkok   **Population: 54,960,000**

Political system. Thailand is a constitutional monarchy. Although it is formally a multi-party democracy, the dominant political force continues to be the military. Prime Minister Chatichai Choonhaven came to power in August 1988 after the eight-year premiership of Prem Tinsulanonda, but his government—the first democratic experience for the Thais in many years—was overthrown in a military *coup* on Feb. 23, 1991. Though a civilian Cabinet was appointed under Anand Panyarachun, power continues to rest with the military junta's National Peacekeeping Council (NPKC). A total of 148 of the 292 members of the Legislative Assembly appointed in March 1991 are officers.

Economy. Thailand has a broad-based, diversified economy. It is one of the world's largest net exporters of food, with rice as the principal export crop by value. In the mid-1980s textiles formed the largest single manufactured export. The government pursues a cautious fiscal policy and has taken account of the structural reform proposals put forward by the World Bank, Thailand's largest creditor.

By the late 1980s Thailand had the fastest growing economy in Asia: growth was 12 per cent in 1988 and 10.8 per cent in 1989, led by tourism, construction, light manufacturing for export, mining and energy. The country's principal economic problems were shortages of skilled workers and managers, including graduates; in 1989 the first shortages of unskilled labour occurred in the Bangkok area. More than 250,000 Thais work abroad,

150,000 of them in Saudi Arabia. Wages are also starting to rise. Civil service pay rose in 1989 for the first time in six years, and went up again in 1990. Inflation nevertheless was only 3.8 per cent in 1988; unemployment 4.6 per cent the following year, through this may inadequately reflect the position in rural areas which have tended to be left behind by Thailand's development. Of a civilian workforce of 28,440,000 in 1988, 7,270,000 were employed in industry, 17,880,000 in agriculture, and 3,290,000 in services.

An area of great economic conflict at the end of the 1980s was the government's programme of privatization. Its Finance Minister Pramual Saphawasu identified the country's 61 public enterprises as a means of raising funds without crashing through the foreign borrowing ceiling. In 1989 a number of key state holdings were given at least partial listings despite vociferous union opposition. These protests culminated early in 1990 in a strike by dockworkers against plans to privatize a new deep sea container port at Laem Chabang. Ominously, the strikers—technically acting outside the law which forbids public sector strikes—called on Thailand's highly politicized military for support, and the strike was only ended in February 1990 by talks in which the Acting Chief of the Armed Forces General Chavalit, was seen to have taken the initiative. Finally in March the Prime Minister—faced with threats of strikes by other groups of workers—announced a postponement of all privatizations pending the creation of a tripartite State Enterprise Labour Relations Promotion Committee (SELRPC).

System of industrial relations. Thailand has been a member of the International Labour Organization since 1919 but has ratified neither ILO Convention No. 87 (Freedom of Association and Protection of Right to Organize, 1948) nor No. 98 (Right to Organize and Collective Bargaining, 1949). All trade unions were dissolved in 1958 and workers were not permitted to associate again until 1972. The Labour Relations Act, providing for the registration of trade unions, was enacted in 1975; under this Act, a minimum of 10 employees are required in order to form a union. Strikes in the public sector are banned, but unions do sometimes strike under the guise of "extended extraordinary meetings".

Thailand until the 1991 *coup* had a panoply of industrial relations bodies including a tripartite National Labour Development Advisory Board (NLDAB) with the task of developing consensual policy options. There is also a Labour Relations Committee and a system of Labour Courts, both tripartite and with mediating responsibilities. Four union leaders are appointed members of the Upper House (the Senate). Prime Minister Chatichai acknowledged the importance of organized labour and had a programme for developing industrial relations institutions. Union pressure led the NLDAB to notify the Ministry of the Interior to restrict the use of temporary employment in October 1989 and this it did the following month. During 1990 the goverment introduced a bill to establish a Ministry of Labour, thus meeting another long-term objective of the unions.

The vehemence of the unions' stand against privatization originates in the disparity of employment conditions in the private sector where pay can be very low and mass dismissals are frequent. Thailand is also the location of widespread child labour: its factories employ perhaps 100,000 12–15 year olds according to an AFL-CIO estimate. Apart from politicized disputes (*see above*) strikes over economic issues were few in 1989.

Trade unionism. Union density in Thailand is little more than 3 per cent of the industrial workforce, though in 1989 the number of registered union members grew to 309,000 while the number of registered unions grew from 503 to 562. The strongest unions, and half the membership, are to be found in the public sector. Though a State Enterprise Labour Relations Group has been established to co-ordinate public sector unions, their effectiveness and that of those in the private sector, is dispersed because of the existence of four competing centres. In 1987, the ICFTU affiliates LCT and TTUC set themselves the goal of merging and in April 1989 they set up a Joint Council but by 1990 they were no nearer achieving their goal. However the LCT, TTUC and NCTL are able to come together in common causes quite often, a feature they do not share with the NFLL. An exception to this rule occurred in October 1989 when all four came together to organize opposition to temporary employment contracts. The attempt by Senator Preechap Simisap of the metalworkers' union, to form a fifth centre early in 1989 seems to have come to nothing.

Thailand's labour movement has traditionally enjoyed the support of the ICFTU and other Western agencies such as the US-based Asian-American Free Labour Institute and the private West German foundation, the Friedrich Ebert Stiftung. However, in October 1987 a WFTU meeting, sponsored by the federation's leather industry branch, was convened in Bangkok. Observers saw the meeting as a significant development, underscoring Soviet inroads into non-communist Asia.

On Feb. 25, 1991 leaders of the new military junta called in union leaders for talks, offering them the chance to keep their four seats in the senate and an increase in the minimum wage. Subsequently it appeared that the military aimed to rescind the coverage of the public sector by the Labour Relations Act, a move which would have the effect of disbanding state unions and preventing the formation of new ones. The LCT and TTUC jointly identified the plans of the military as "a return to the dark days of the 1960s".

Labour Congress of Thailand (LCT)

Address. Neramit Court Building, 3rd Floor, 1193 Paholyothin Road, Sarmsen-Nai Phayathai, Bangkok 10400

Leadership. Thanong Po-arn (president)

Membership. Less than 70,000 in 40 unions (1986).

History and character. The LCT was created in 1978. According to its founder, Paisal Thawatchainant, who left the LCT to found the TTUC, the LCT was taken over in 1982 by a faction led by two executives of the State Railways of Thailand (SRT), Ahmad Khamthesthong and Sawas Lukdod, with the assistance of the army-controlled Internal Security Operation Command. Ahmad (who became LCT president) and Sawas were appointed to the Senate in 1983; in 1985, however, Ahmad was dismissed from the SRT for leading illegal strikes, and both he and Sawas were subsequently arrested in September 1985 on charges of involvement in an attempted *coup*. Plans to merge with the TTUC were announced in early 1988, but have not come to fruition. However the LCT was able to co-operate with the TTUC on a number of significant issues and put out a joint statement in response to the proposals of the military following the February 1991 *coup*.

International affiliation. ICFTU.

National Congress of Thai Labour (NCTL)

Address. 30/1 Soi 61, Sukumvit Road, Bangkok

Leadership. Att Sri-Art (president)

Membership. Some 80 unions and 25,000 members.

History and character. Founded with the assistance of the WCL in 1978. The NCTL holds the majority of trade union seats on the Labour Court, voting for which is based on the number of affiliated unions rather than size of membership.

International affiliation. WCL.

National Free Labour Union Congress (NFLUC)

Membership. Some 80 unions and 25,000 members.

State Enterprise Labour Relations Group (SELRG)

Leadership. Ekkachai Ekharnkamol (secretary-general)

History and character. SELRG was founded in 1987 to co-ordinate union opposition to privatization. Its general secretary is the leader of the metropolitan water workers' union.

Thai Trade Union Congress (TTUC)

Leadership. Wattana Ieumbumroong (president)
Membership. The TTUC is the largest of the four national trade union centres with some 100,000 members.
History and character. The TTUC was founded in 1982 by Paisal Thawatchainant, who had earlier founded the Labour Congress of Thailand (LCT). In early 1988 plans were announced to merge the TTUC and the LCT within three years, but these have not come to fruition. However the TTUC was able to co-operate with the LCT on a number of significant issues and put out a joint statement in response to the proposals of the military following the February 1991 *coup*.
International affiliation. ICFTU (affiliated 1987).

Togo

Capital: Lomé

Population: 3,023,000
(1988)

Political system. The Republic of Togo is a one-party state, ruled since the military *coup* of 1967 by the Rassemblement du Peuple Togolais (RPT).
Economy. Togo's economy is primarily agricultural; following the adoption of the "Green Revolution" policies in 1977, Togo achieved agricultural self-sufficiency in the mid-1980s. Since its severe debt crisis in the early 1980s, it has adhered closely to the IMF recommendations for structural adjustment, thereby obtaining not only the fund's financial support, but also debt repayment concessions.
System of industrial relations. Togo ratified ILO Convention No. 87 (Freedom of Association and Protection of the Right to Organize, 1948) in 1960 and Convention No. 98 (Right to Organize and Collective Bargaining, 1949) in 1983. Apprenticeship contracts and conditions are regulated under a law of December 1988.
Trade unionism. All previously existing trade unions were dissolved in 1972 and the Confédération Nationale des Travailleurs du Togo (CNTT) was established by the ruling RPT in the following year. There is no formal establishment of a single-trade-union system; however, trade union dues are deducted automatically from all wages and salaries, and no unions exist outside the structure of the CNTT.

Confédération Nationale des Travailleurs du Togo (CNTT)
National Confederation of Togolese Workers

Address. Bourse du Travail, 160 Boulevard-circulaire, B.P. 163, Lomé
Phone. 215739
Leadership. Mr Houyengah
Membership. 105,000 in 43 affiliated unions.
History and character. The CNTT was created in January 1973, absorbing the previous Union Nationale des Travailleurs du Togo (UNTT), founded in 1962, and the Confédération Syndicale des Travailleurs du Togo (CSTT), which was founded in 1946 and was affiliated to the WCL. The CNTT

devotes itself to the defence of the workers' interests within the context of "responsible participation" in the overall development of the country. It is represented on the RPT central committee and in the National Assembly.

In 1977 the CNTT founded a co-operative movement Coopsynto with a view to providing cheap food. Disappointing financial results led to the inauguration of training for union leaders of Coopsynto from 1986, with the assistance of the ICFTU and the French *Force Ouvrière*.

Publication. ETRATO: l'Eveil du Travailleur Togolais.

International affiliation. OATUU.

Tonga

Capital: Nuku'alofa

Population: 101,000
(1988)

Political system. Tonga is an independent member of the Commonwealth with its own hereditary monarchy. There are no political parties.

Economy. Tonga's economy is primarily agricultural. Food production is mostly on a subsistence basis and there is a heavy dependence on food imports. There is a limited, growing light manufacturing sector.

Trade unionism. Although there exists a legal base for the formation of trade unions in Tonga, the authorities refused to allow them to organize until 1990. In that year it was reported that FITA/TNA, the Tonga Teachers' and Hospital Workers' Association had been formed.

Trinidad and Tobago

Capital: Port of Spain

Population: 1,241,000
(1988)

Political system. Trinidad and Tobago is an independent republic within the Commonwealth. The National Alliance for Reconstruction, formed in February 1986 through the merger of four opposition parties won a landslide victory in the December 1986 general election, leaving the People's National Movement (which had held power continuously since independence in 1962) with only three seats in the House of Representatives.

Economy. Trinidad and Tobago's significant (but declining) oil reserves form the basis of the economy which has consequently been affected by the drop in the world oil prices.

System of industrial relations. Trinidad and Tobago ratified ILO Conventions No. 87 (Freedom of Association and Protection of the Right to Organize, 1948) and No. 98 (Right to Organize and Collective Bargaining, 1949) in 1963. On Convention 87, the *Report of the Committee of Experts on the Application of Conventions and Recommendations (1988)* notes that it has been asking the government "for several years" to amend laws of 1966 which effectively prevent civil servants, firemen and prison officers choosing, by majority vote, their own representative associations; and to further amend the Industrial Relations Act of 1972 (as amended in 1978) to enable a simple majority of workers in a bargaining unit to call a strike and to restrict the Ministry of Labour's criteria for intervention to "essential services" (that which would endanger life, personal safety or health of the whole or part of the population) or in the event of an acute national crisis. It also notes "with regret" that "minority unions" (i.e. lacking less than 50 per cent of workers in a unit) cannot negotiate collectively, in contravention of Convention No. 98; and that Convention No. 105 (Abolition of Forced Labour, 1957, ratified 1963) is still being contravened because penalties involving compulsory labour can be imposed for breaches of discipline or for participation in strikes which do not endanger individual or national life. The government maintained it has established a Joint Consultative Council to review and monitor the operation of the industrial relations system.

Industrial relations in Trinidad and Tobago are conducted within the framework of legislation from the 1970s and 1980s. Where bargaining is deadlocked the issue in dispute is referred to the Ministry of Labour and may progress to a strike or a lock-out only when the Minister himself declares it unresolved. The country's Labour Court was by 1989 overburdened with a lengthening queue of cases to judge.

Trade unionism. Trade union activities date back to the formation of the Working Man's Association in 1919, and the 1972 Industrial Relations Act made provision for collective bargaining. The principal trade union centre is the Trinidad and Tobago Labour Congress (TTLC), which is affiliated to the ICFTU. In 1975 trade unionists (not including the TTLC) led by Basdeo Panday (of the All Trinidad Sugar and General Workers' Trade Union—*see below*) formed the United Labour Front (ULF) in opposition to the ruling People's National Movement, and in the 1976 elections the ULF took 10 of the 36 seats in the House of Representatives, campaigning on a programme which included worker participation, nationalization of key enterprises, and land reform. The ULF is now part of the moderate socialist National Alliance for Reconstruction. The Council of Progressive Trade Unions (CPTU) and the TTLC accused the government of "economic madness" in 1988 condemning proposals for free trade zones, privatization of state enterprises and sale and lease agreements which they believe would be harmful to the country and working people. They called for a meeting between the unions and the ministries involved, while threatening to withdraw from all tripartite bodies as a protest against the government's plans.

The TTLC is the larger of the two confederations by a ratio of about 2:1 against the WFTU-affiliated CPTU. Outside their ranks stand the All Trinidad Sugar and General Workers' Trade Union (ATSGWTU), and the Trindad and Tobago Unified Teachers' Association (TTUTA) which claims 10,000 members in elementary and secondary teaching. Union density is assessed at 22 per cent.

All Trinidad Sugar and General Workers' Trade Union

Address. Rienzi Complex, Exchange Village, Southern Main Road, Couva
Phone. 809-636-2354
Leadership. Basdeo Panday (president); San Maharaj (general secretary)
Membership. 10,000.
Publication. Battlefront. (monthly).
History and character. Established in 1937 as a Sugar Workers' Union. Constitution changed in 1978 to represent workers in industries outside sugar: at present, represents workers in 40 companies involved in rum production, contracting, construction, entertainment, air line, transport, food

processing, garment manufacturing, animal food production. The union is involved in activities such as culture, education, politics and business. Membership in 1981 was 18,000, reduced to 10,000 at present through retrenchment, plant closures and contracting national economy.

Basdeo Panday, the ATSGWTU President, was leader of the defunct ULF and now leads the new United National Congress Party, whose work is closely integrated with that of the Union.

International affiliations. CLAT; WCL.

Council of Progressive Trade Unions (CPTU)

Address. 143 Charlotte Street, Port of Spain
Phone. 623 6094; 623 3115
Fax. 652 7170
Leadership. Albert Aberdeen (acting president); Cecil Paul (general secretary)
Membership. 28,000.
History and character. The CPTU was founded in 1972. It describes its activities as promotion of legislation in the workers' interest, publishing statements of interest to workers, conducting educational activities and training, and representation on various agencies, boards and institutions. The most influential union within it is the Oilfield Workers' Trade Union (OWTU) which claims 10,500 members in the oil industry and the country's Electricity Commission. Its President-General Errol McLeod has denounced the collective bargaining process as "a rotting corpse" and called for the intervention of the working class in Trinidadian politics. A number of CPTU leaders, including Mcleod are supporters of the radical Committee on Labour Solidarity which is intended to pave the way for a new political party.

Affiliated Unions and Structure. The following are recorded at the time of writing:

1. **Communication Workers Union (CWU)**

2. **Sugar Boilers' Associations (SBA)**

3. **Transport and Industrial Workers' Union (TIWU)**

4. **General Poultry Farmers' Association (GPFA)**

5. **Union of Commercial and Industrial Workers (UCIW)**

6. **National Farmers' and Workers' Union (NFWU)**

7. **National Foodcrop Farmers' Association (NFFA)**

8. **Oilfields Workers' Trade Union (OWTU)**

9. **Steel Workers' Union of Trinidad and Tobago (SWUTT)**

10. **Trinidad Islandwide Rice Growers' Association (TIRGA)**

11. **Aviation Communication Allied Workers' Union (ACAWU)**

12. **Customs and Excise Extra Guards' Association (C&EEGA)**

International affiliations. WFTU; CTUC.

Trinidad and Tobago Labour Congress (TTLC)

Address. Workers' Bank Building, Independence Square, Port of Spain
Leadership. Vernon Glenn (president); Carl A. Tull (general secretary)
Membership. Claims 100,000 members but records only 58,811 as paid.
International affiliations. ICFTU; CCL.
Affiliated unions and structure. Four of the six largest unions are TTLC affiliates including the National Union of Government and Federated Workers (NUFGW, 26,500 members); the Public Services' Association (15,651 members); and the Seamen and Waterfront Workers' Trade Union (5,242 members).

History and character. The TTLC was founded in 1966. It is a largely pragmatic body, mainly concerned with promoting collective bargaining and quite willing to extend the process to employees of multinational companies active in Trinidad and Tobago. It is the country's largest union confederation.

Tunisia

Capital: Tunis   **Population: 7,900,000**

Political system. The republic of Tunisia has an executive President and a Council of Ministers, headed by a Prime Minister. It achieved independence from France in 1956. From 1963–1981 the Destour Socialist Party (PSD) was effectively the sole legal party. Since then other parties have been legalized but they all boycotted the 1986 elections. In 1987 President Bourguiba was deposed and a new government, headed by President Ben Ali embarked on a programme of liberalization.

Economy. Tunisia has a relatively well-developed economic base and a high per capita income by African standards. Petroleum exports and tourism are the main sources of foreign exchange. Agriculture is impeded by a lack of irrigation. Remittances sent by migrant labourers abroad make a significant contribution to the balance of payments. Debt servicing accounts for a significant proportion of GDP.

Official statistics assess 33 per cent of the Tunisian workforce as being employed in agriculture, 36 per cent in industry and mining, 6 per cent in tourism and 25 per cent in public administration and other services. Some 400,000 Tunisians work abroad. The workforce is growing more rapidly than the population.

Unemployment in 1989 was thought to be in excess of 15 per cent, prompting the government to set itself the target of creating 48,000 new posts during 1990. Government-ordained price rises of 17 per cent for staple items prompted fierce complaints about the impact on living standards, but substantial wage rises were ordered in the 1990 budget.

System of industrial relations. The Tunisian wide-ranging Labour Code was enacted in 1966 but between 1985 and 1987 there were fierce confrontations between unions and the government as the latter moved to restrict union activity. A change of emphasis occurred with the arrival of a new government in 1987 which marked the passing of the worst period of trade union repression. President Ben Ali inaugurated a period of liberalization. Nevertheless the number of strikes more than doubled in the years 1987–1989 as some UGTT affiliates tested out their renewed independence. President Ben Ali announced important wage rises for government employees in 1990 and urged the private sector to emulate them.

In April 1990 the UGTT and the employers' organization UTICA reached an agreement to establish a tripartite commission to oversee wage negotiations, and embarked on bargaining for a three-year agreement which was meant to usher in a period of social peace. In the same month President Ben Ali announced that he intended to revoke the 1985 decree restricting union activity at the workplace.

Tunisia ratified ILO Conventions No. 87 (Freedom of Association and Protection of the Right to Organize, 1948) and No. 98 (Right to Organize and Collective Bargaining, 1949) in 1957.

Trade unionism. Trade unions developed under French rule and were associated with nationalist politics. The Union Générale Tunisienne du Travail (UGTT), which is affiliated to the ICFTU, has been the sole or only significant trade union centre since independence. Since 1978 UGTT relations with the government and the ruling party have fluctuated sharply.

Though the oldest and best established union centre in Africa, the UGTT was severely weakened in the middle of the 1980s as it combatted the repression of the Bourguiba régime and then became engulfed in internal strife (*see below*). However the 1989 (Sousse) conference ended factional fighting and led to the emergence of a new leadership able to meet the formidable Tunisian employers' organization UTICA on equal terms in 1990. Union density in Tunisia is assessed at 11 per cent.

Union Générale Tunisienne du Travail (UGTT)
Tunisian General Federation of Labour

Address. 29 Place M'Hamed Ali, Tunis
Leadership. Ismail Sahbani (secretary-general)
Membership. Assessed at around 300,000.
History and character. The UGTT was founded under French rule in 1946 by Fahrat Hached (assassinated by French agents in 1952) and was involved in the struggle for independence in association with the Neo-Destour Party (renamed the Destour Socialist Party—PSD—in 1964) of Habib Bourguiba. An early leader, Ahmed Tlili, opposed Bourguiba's decision to establish a one-party state. In January 1978 the UGTT (the only organized grouping in Tunisia outside the PSD and the armed forces, and hitherto allied with the PSD government) called a general strike during which several dozen people were killed in clashes between strikers, police and troops. Following this, Habib Achour, the UGTT secretary-general and a vice-president of the ICFTU, who had already resigned from the political bureau and central committee of the PSD, was removed from his post at the UGTT, being replaced by Tijani Abid. In October 1978 the State Security Court sentenced Achour and other former UGTT leaders to imprisonment with forced labour following conviction on charges of plotting to overthrow the government and incitement to violence, looting and murder. In November 1979 Achour, who had been released into house arrest, was re-elected a vice-president of the ICFTU at the ICFTU's 12th congress, causing the new leadership of the UGTT to suspend relations with the ICFTU. All other detained members of the former UGTT leadership were released during 1980, and following the failure of the new UGTT leadership to achieve international recognition or support within the Tunisian labour movement, a unity congress of the UGTT was held in April–May 1981, this resulting in the formation of a new 13-member executive bureau which included 11 members of the executive arrested in January 1978, one of whom, Taieb Baccouche, was appointed secretary-general. Achour remained the only former UGTT leader still barred from office.

Tunisia's first multi-party elections since independence in 1956 were held on Nov. 1, 1981, and were won by an alliance of the PSD and the UGTT which took all 136 seats in the National Assembly, 27 of the seats going to candidates of the UGTT. Following this President Bourguiba on Nov. 30, 1981, granted a full pardon to Achour, who was immediately appointed as chairman of the UGTT and a member of the executive bureau. In November 1983 the UGTT administrative commission dismissed seven of the 14 members of the executive bureau after they had charged Achour with anti-democratic methods, poor financial management and use of UGTT funds for bribery and secret deals. These seven members in February 1984 formed the Union Nationale des Travailleurs Tunisiens (UNTT), with Abdelaziz Bouraoui as secretary-general. In December 1984 the 16th regular congress of the UGTT elected a new executive committee with Achour returning as secretary-general in succession to Baccouche.

During 1985 relations between the government and the UGTT again deteriorated as a consequence of the UGTT's campaign of strikes to demand increases in public sector salaries, which had been frozen for two years, set against a background of acute economic difficulties which had caused widespread unrest and "bread riots". Trade union meetings were banned, strikers dismissed, the UGT newspaper *Ech Chaab* suspended, and the check-off system for union dues ended. By mid-November 1985, 100 UGTT activists were in detention, including Achour, and regional offices of the UGTT had been occupied by so-called "provisional committees" assisted by the police. An agreement between the executive bureau of the UGTT on Dec. 4 to end the crisis proved ineffective, and on Dec. 31, 1985, Achour was sentenced to one year's imprisonment (later reduced to eight months) on charges of breaking and entering the premises of a fishing co-operative in a case originally dating from 1982. On Jan. 21, 1986, control of the national headquarters of the UGTT in Tunis was handed over by the police to a "provisional committee", and on Jan. 29 the UGTT administrative commission, meeting under the supervision of a "National Co-ordination Bureau" at the Tunis headquarters, announced that it had ceased to recognize the executive bureau and endorsed the work of the National Co-ordination Bureau towards the reconstruction of the trade union movement. On April 5, 1986, Achour was sentenced to a further two years' imprisonment for mismanagement of a union-funded insurance company and on April 30 the "provisional committees" held an extraordinary congress in the name of the UGTT at which they elected a new executive bureau with Ismail Lajeri as secretary-general. In September 1986 the UGTT also absorbed the UNTT, the merged organization being called the UGTT. The remodelled UGTT failed to secure significant grass-roots support within the Tunisian trade union movement, however, and in December 1986 a new executive bureau was formed with Ismail Lajeri replaced as secretary-general by Abdelaziz Bouraoui. In January 1987 the UGTT held an extraordinary congress at which it addressed a "message of faithfulness" to President Bourguiba and pledged itself to responsible participation in the tasks of national recovery. The congress, which was boycotted by most of the bodies elected under Achour but attended by President Bourguiba, elected a new executive bureau comprising five representatives of the former "provisional committees", four representatives of the former UNTT, and four representatives of the old UGTT leadership who had broken recently with Achour. Bouraoui was confirmed as secretary-general, on the recommendation of President Bourguiba. Since the bloodless *coup* on Nov. 7, 1987, when President Bourguiba was deposed by his Prime Minister, Zine el Abidine Ben Ali, there has been some lessening of the split within the union movement. Habib Achour, still recognized by the ICFTU and the WFTU as the legitimate Secretary-General of the UGTT, was freed from house arrest. In May, 1988, ICFTU General Secretary, John Vanderveken, visited Tunisia for talks with government officials and unionists and reported that the normalization of the trade union situation was making good progress. A National Trade Union Commission had been set up to organize a new Congress of the UGTT and the government gave assurances that all public sector workers sacked for involvement in the strikes of 1984 and 1985 were being reinstated. In addition, dismissed private sector workers were to be the subject of talks between the government and employers' federation.

Regional elections were held in early 1989 at which those leaders deposed by President Bourguiba (*legitimistes*) were mostly returned to office. The UGTT then held a Special Congress at Sousse in April 1989 at which a unified list of delegates was put forward for election, and Ismael Sabhani, the metalworkers' union leader was elected General Secretary. The Congress also resolved to establish a commission to examine internal structures, to bring back the automatic check-off, and to grant autonomy to regions and federations. Following the Congress, the 50 UGTT Federations held elections which, like those of the regions, led to the return of those officers deposed earlier in the decade.

Publication. Ach-Chaab (resumed publication in 1989 after being suspended for 18 months).

International affiliations. ICFTU; OATUU; ICATU.

Turkey

Capital: Ankara   **Population: 54,115,000**

Political system. A new Constitution approved by referendum in November 1982 began a gradual return to a democratic system of government in the Republic of Turkey after a period of rule by a National Security Council (NSC) set up following a military *coup* in

1980 (the third in 20 years). The formation of political parties was reauthorized in April 1983 (although extreme left-and right-wing parties remained banned), and elections to a new unicameral Grand National Assembly in November 1983 were won by the centre-right Motherland Party led by Turgut Özal. Mr Özal's government was returned to power in elections in November 1987, and he was subsequently made President under Turkey's indirect election system. By the end of 1988 10 enterprises had been privatized under his programme of economic liberalization

Economy. Civilian employment in Turkey was over 16,500,000 in 1987, of whom, 2,300,000 were employed in industry, 4,900,000 in services and 9,400,000 in agriculture. The unemployment rate in 1988 was 14.4 per cent, driven partly by a fast-growing workforce, but also by a slowing growth rate. In 1988 inflation was running at 75 per cent, easily outstripping the annual rate of wage increases. All these statistics fail to cover a large unregulated and unregistered economy which may employ more than 2,500,000 workers. There are, moreover, perhaps 1,250,000 Turkish workers abroad. Nevertheless the early impact of the Özal government's privatization drive seems to have been positive for employment as more than 330,000 jobs were created in 1988, the first complete year of the programme.

System of industrial relations. Turkey ratified ILO Convention No. 98 (Right to Organize and Collective Bargaining, 1949) in 1952 (it has not ratified Convention No. 87. Freedom of Association and Protection of the Right to Organize, 1948), and the 1961 Constitution guaranteed the right to form trade unions and to engage in collective bargaining. The 1961 Constitution, partially suspended after the 1980 *coup*, was super-seded by a new Constitution approved in November 1982. Under the various provisions of the 1982 Constitution and labour legislation adopted in 1983, the right of association is guaranteed except where associations are closed down by a court order or (in the case of emergencies) by the Minister of the Interior, collective bargaining is authorized, and strikes are permitted. However, trade unions may not pursue political ends or co-operate with political parties (though the law in this respect was relaxed in 1988); unions may not be authorized to negotiate if they have as members less than 10 per cent of the workforce in a given industry or 50 per cent in a given workplace; cooling-off periods and compul-sory arbitration may be imposed by the government; general strikes, political strikes, and sympathy strikes are prohibited; the internal affairs of unions are closely regulated; civil servants and workers in public services (including banks, schools, electricity, water and petroleum) may not organize; and trade unions require official approval to form interna-tional affiliations although this approval is officially described as merely procedural.

Collective bargaining resumed in 1984, and the first legal strike since 1980 occurred over a pay claim in the docks in October 1984, while at the end of that month it was announced that trade unions would not henceforth be required to seek official permission to begin a strike.

Recent changes in the labour laws in response to strong criticism from the ILO and other international and national union bodies (see below) have resulted in what many see as only cosmetic improvements. As of 1988 unions were allowed to make political statements but were still barred from having any links with political parties or other organizations. Union finances must now be inspected by government officials only before their general confer-ences instead of annually. However, no significant changes have been made to the stringent restrictions on the rights to organize trade unions or engage in strikes.

Despite the legal constraints trade union activity has revived in recent years. The number of strikes increased from seven in 1986 to 389 in 1987, and the number of days lost due to industrial disputes in the latter year was the highest ever recorded. However, organizations such as Amnesty International, Helsinki Watch and the US Commission on Security and Co-operation in Europe have continued to document human rights' abuses of trade union activists. An attempt to hold a commemorative meeting on May 1, 1988 for 36 people assassinated on Labour Day 1977 was blocked by police and resulted in 80 arrests. Aziz Çelik, an organizer of the meeting and educational director of Kristal-İş (the glass-workers union), was later arrested and allegedly tortured. Mustaia Dilmen, president of Kristal-İş, was also arrested a few weeks later and claimed to have been tortured during his week-long detention. 1988 brought sharp battles between employers and employees. The number of workdays lost to strikes (nearly 1,900,000) was the highest since the 1960s, and there were no less than 112 lock-outs. The enhanced militancy of TISK encouraged action as the Confederation argued that real wages had fallen far behind Turkey's rampant inflation rate. Private sector employees generally succeeded in obtaining higher increases than those gained in the public sector, but the latter enjoyed superior non-wage benefits. The unions have strong interest in maintaining the size of the public sector which accounts for nearly half of all organized workers.

Early 1989 was marked by widespread industrial action which was only partly resolved when Türk-İş negotiated a two-year agreement with the government on behalf of public sector workers. Given the ban on strikes, Turkish public sector trade unionists resorted to such subterfuges as mass visits by doctors' to workers complaining of physical and psychological distress due to malnutrition! Some industrial action continued after the agreement was made, notably at the Karabuk and Isdemir steel plant which was stopped for more than four months until the employers obtained a court order for a return to work in September 1989.

For a brief period it seemed that the unions and the government might draw closer together. A Tripartite Board (with Türk-İş participation) had the official job of policing the minimum wage, and a High Arbitration Board (to which Türk-İş was again a party) was meant to arbitrate in cases where there was no legal right to strike. Mr Ozal himself was a former employers' association official and his Minister of Labour had worked for employers and Türk-İş. These hopes foundered when no agreement could be reached on the definition of the minimum wage and the Confederation found itself out-voted on the Arbitration Board by the combined employer–government bloc, and relations again deteriorated.

The unions gained some ground when they mounted a successful legal challenge to an attempt by the Ozal government to buy them out of state enterprises by offering employees non-union contracts at higher wages. However, January 1991 brought the Gulf Crisis which led to an intensification of industrial relations severity. A Council of Ministers decree banned all strikes (thus reaching beyond the constitutional provision which gives powers to forbid only those affecting national security or public health) and ordered those currently striking to return to work immediately. By the same decree all collective bargaining was postponed, leading the main union centre Türk-İş to make an immediate reference to the ILO.

Trade unionism. Trade union activities have been severely restricted since the 1980 *coup*. The Confederation of Turkish Trade Unions Türk-İş is affiliated to the ICFTU. In December 1986 a military court ordered the dissolution of the leftist Confederation of Progressive Trade Unions, DISK, formerly the second largest confederation after Türk-İş, whose activities had been suspended since 1980. Outside Türk-İş, which has slowly moved to a more oppositionist position, there are several large independent unions, and two smaller federations with political alignments. Türk-İş has found its international connections useful as it battles constantly against restrictions on its industrial activity.

The pressure from international and national labour organizations has intensified, especially given Turkey's application to become a full member of the European Community. Turkey was sharply critized at the June 1987 meeting of the ILO for failing to fulfil an undertaking to change its restrictive labour laws to meet ILO standards and presently stands under threat of expulsion from the organization. The AFL-CIO recommended in 1987 that the United States deny Turkey "most favoured-nation status" and the benefits of the Generalized System of Preferences unless trade union rights improved. The ETUC has similarly resolved to oppose any attempt to admit Turkey to the EC until the legal restrictions are lifted. On Dec. 10, 1988 (Human Rights Day) Nafiz Bostani, a prominent trade unionist in exile, returned to Turkey in the face of probable arrest in order to maintain the pressure to restore full trade union and human rights.

Confederation of National Unions (MISK)

History and character. MISK was aligned with an extreme nationalist faction of Alparslan Turkes, but has virtually disappeared.

DISK
Confederation of Progressive Trade Unions/Confederation of Revolutionary Workers' Unions

Leadership. Abdullah Baştürk (president); Fehmi Işiklar (secretary-general)

Membership. Claimed about 700,000 in 1980 (independent estimates about 400,000).

History and character. DISK was formed by leftist unions in 1967 as a breakaway from Türk-Iş, and associated itself with the Turkish Workers Party (TIP). It assumed the character of a militant socialist labour organization with a Marxist wing, and operated primarily in the private sector, where it organized many strikes. Before 1980 it was the second largest Turkish trade union confederation, behind Türk-Iş. DISK was often a target for right-wing terrorist attacks during the escalating political violence of the 1970s. Its president and founder, Kemal Türkler, was assassinated in July 1980, shortly before the military seized power. DISK and its affiliates were suspended and many of their leaders detained following the 1980 army *coup*, and a mass trial of DISK members was initiated before a military court in 1981, continuing until December 1986. Initially indictment charges were brought against 52 (later 78) DISK leaders under Article 146 of the Turkish Penal Code (concerning "attempts to overthrow the constitutional order"), which allows for the death penalty, while others were charged under Article 141, providing for terms of imprisonment of up to 15 years for offences such as intending the overthrow of "the social and economic order of the country" or "organizing to establish the supremacy of one class over another" (Article 141 requiring only evidence of intent and not of actions). At its peak the trial involved close to 3,700 defendants, although the number dropped to 1,477 by the time of the verdict. In addition, an estimated 2,000 other union members fled the country during this period to avoid prosecution. All charges under Article 146 were withdrawn in January 1986, but on Dec. 23, 1986, the court sentenced 264 leaders and members of DISK for terms of up to 15 years' imprisonment under Article 141. Some 1,169 of the defendants were acquitted and the cases against 44 others had been abandoned. The heaviest sentences were imposed on a group of key leaders, including Abdullah Baştürk (the DISK president) and Fehmi Işiklar (the DISK secretary-general) who each received 10 years, and Ceytin Uygur, a member of the DISK executive council and leader of Yeralti Maden-Iş (the underground metal-workers union), who received 15 years and 8 months. Many of those condemned were eligible for immediate or early release having spent extended periods in custody during the trial, although all those convicted would remain for a period equivalent to one-third of their sentences under supervision in places decreed by the court. The court also stripped those convicted of their basic civil and political rights for life, including the right to take part in trade union activities, and ordered the dissolution of DISK and 28 of its 30 affiliated unions, whose assets would be confiscated by the state. The court's decisions were apppealed to the military High Court of Appeals and the case remains in limbo.

DISK had been actively supported by the WFTU, WCL and the ICFTU throughout the trial, these international organizations emphasizing that no evidence had been produced to demonstrate that DISK had advocated or resorted to violence in pursuit of its ends or had participated in any plot to overthrow the state. The ICFTU and WCL, in conjunction with ETUC and national trade union centres, have also opposed the increasing normalization of relations between Turkey and western Europe while trade union rights continued to be infringed. DISK leaders maintained throughout the trial that they adhered to Turkey's 1961 Constitution and the principles of free, democratic trade unionism, and rejected violence as a means. There were numerous allegations that defendants had been tortured during the early phase of detention. However, defendants were subsequently allowed out of prison and Baştürk was permitted to travel abroad, returning to Turkey after the announcement of the verdicts. Subsequently, Baştürk won a seat in parliament in the elections of November 1987, and was joined there by the DISK Secretary-General and a president of a DISK affiliate, all as members of the Social Democratic Populist Party.

International affiliation. ETUC.

HAK-Is

Membership. Around 35,000 members in six unions.

History and character. Hak-Is was formerly affiliated to Erbaken's fundamentalist party and now shares the outlook of the Prosperity Party.

Türkiye Işçi Sendikalari Konfederasyonu (Türk-Iş)
Confederation of Turkish Trade Unions/Turkish Confederation of Labour

Address. Bayindir Sokak 10, Yenischir, Ankara

Phone. (41) 333125

Leadership. Şevket Yilmaz (president); Orban Balta (general secretary)

Membership. Claimed around 1,800,000 (independent estimates about 1,000,000).

History and character. Türk-Iş was formed in 1952 during a phase of liberalization in Turkey's social and political conditions, and developed as the general confederation of the labour movement. Some of its membership formed the more left-wing DISK in 1967, but Türk-İş remained the larger centre. It adopted a politically centrist character and was influenced by the model of the US AFL-CIO.

Following the suspension of DISK in 1980, Türk-Iş was permitted to function by the military régime, and its general secretary Sadik Şide took office as Minister of Social Security, leading to the suspension of Türk-İş by the ICFTU (it is now re-admitted to full membership).

The premier position of Türk-Iş is acknowledged by the government through its membership of the Tripartite Board which determines the minimum wage, and in its supply of members to the High Arbitration Board. However it withdrew from the Tripartite Board when the government refused to accept its view that the minimum wage should be set for the maintenance of the worker and three other persons, and from the High Arbitration Board in protest against the way its views were always overruled by the combined government–employer vote. From 1985 Türk-Iş (which has been attacked for being too conciliatory to the government) took an increasingly oppositional stance.

In February 1986, Türk-Iş organized its first demonstration since the 1980 *coup*, calling for economic reforms and a restoration of trade union freedoms, and its congress held in December 1986 adopted a declaration calling for an active struggle to secure pro-worker policies based on free democracy.

Şevket Yilmaz, the Türk-Iş president, stated that the outcome of the DISK trial filled him with "sadness and concern". However, the posture of Türk-Iş during the trial had been criticized by trade unionists both inside and outside Turkey as being one of relative indifference to the fate of DISK.

Relations between the confederation and the government have come under increasing strain. Türk-İş has taken a lead in the revival of trade union activity in recent years, initiating demonstrations, symbolic protests (such as boycotts of works' canteens) and adopting a platform in February 1987 which did not exclude possible recourse to a general strike. In March 1987 police surrounded the central offices of the organization to prevent its representatives from marching to parliament to hand in a petition. The ETUC accepted Türk-Iş into membership of its executive council in April 1988.

There was a brief thaw between government and Türk-Iş in 1987 and 1988 when a former union and employers' official was appointed to the Ministry of Labour, but privatization and high wage demands pushed the two sides apart again. At the December 1989 conference of Türk-Iş, Sevket Yilmaz was elected for his third successive term as President in opposition to Social Democratic and nationalist candidates. He called for the restoration of pluralist democracy in Turkey and the reintroduction of a genuine collective bargaining system. The Union's head office was wrecked by a bomb in February 1990 but the motive for the attack was not established. In January 1991 about 90 per cent of the Türk-İş membership stopped work to demand a democratic system and the respect of civil and trade union rights, but the response of the government was to open legal proceedings against union leaders, a number of whom were detained in custody. Their action merged with that of the miners, striking since November for better pay and conditions.

International affiliations. ICFTU; TUAC; ETUC.

Unaffiliated unions

Celik-Is
Iron and Steel Workers

Membership. 50,000.

Orman-Is
Public Sector Forestry Workers

Membership. 64,000.

Otomobil-Is
Car and Metalworkers

Membership. 58,000.

Ozdemir-Is
Iron and Steel Workers

Membership. 70,000.

Tuvalu

Capital: Funafuti   **Population: 8,500**

Political system. Tuvalu, an independent member of the Commonwealth has the British monarch (represented by a Governor-General) as its head of state. There are no organized political parties, but rather groupings around dominant political personalities.

Economy. Tuvalu is exceptionally dependent upon foreign aid. Earnings from copra (the main cash crop) fall far short of expenditure on food imports to supplement local subsistence production.

System of industrial relations. Tuvalu is not a member of the International Labour Organization.

Trade unionism. There is only one registered trade union, the Tuvalu Overseas Seamen's Union (TOSU).

Uganda

Capital: Kampala

Population: 16,195,000
(1988)

Political system. Uganda is an independent republic within the Commonwealth. Since the National Resistance Army (NRA) assumed power in 1986, political parties have been banned.

Economy. The Ugandan economy is based on agriculture which provides two-thirds of government revenue, and virtually all export earnings. It is heavily dependent upon foreign funding for the reversal of the economic deline engendered under the Amin régime (1971–9) when manufacturing and tourism were severely damaged.

System of industrial relations. Uganda ratified ILO Convention No. 98 (Right to Organize and Collective Bargaining, 1949) in 1963, but has not ratified Convention No. 87 (Freedom of Association and Protection of the Right to Organize, 1948). Under the Trades Dispute (Arbitration and Settlement) Act of 1964, workers in "essential services" may be prevented from terminating their contracts of service and strikes may be prohibited. ILO Convention Nos. 29 and 105 on forced labour were ratified in 1963, but the ILO has noted that compulsory labour may be imposed on offenders.

Uganda has a tripartite framework, which brings together the national union centre NOTU with the Federation of Ugandan Employers and the Minister of Labour. Bargaining is highly centralized.

Trade unionism. Trade unions developed after 1940 under British colonial rule and were given legal recognition in 1952. There is now one trade union centre, the National Organizaiton of Trade Unions (NOTU), to which all unions are by law affiliated.

National Organization of Trade Unions (NOTU)

Address. P.O. Box 2150, Kampala
Phone. 233020
History and character. The Uganda Trade Union Congress (UTUC), the first national trade union centre, was formed in 1955 with the assistance of the ICFTU. In 1964, however, a Federation of Uganda Trade Unions (FUTU), with affiliation to the WFTU, was formed as a splinter from the UTUC. In 1966 the trade unions reunited in the Uganda Labour Congress (ULC), and this was succeeded in 1974 by the NOTU. The NOTU states that it is non-political and seeks to build a strong labour movement in Uganda without interference in the internal affairs of other organizations. It is represented on a number of government bodies such as the Industrial Court, Social Security Fund and the Industrial Training Council. All Ugandan unions are affiliated to the NOTU.
Publications. Produces study materials.

Union of Soviet Socialist Republics

Capital: Moscow   **Population: 280,000,000**

Political system. The Union of Soviet Socialist Republics is, according to its 1977 constitution, "a socialist state of the whole people" in which the Communist Party (CPSU—the only legal party) is "the leading and guiding force of the Soviet society and the nucleus of its political system, of all state and public organizations". The country is a federation of 15 Union Republics (Armenia, Azerbaijan, Byelorussia, Estonia, Georgia, Kazakhstan, Kirghizia, Latvia, Lithuania, Moldavia, Russian Federation, Tadjikistan, Turkmenia, Ukraine and Uzbekistan), each of which has its own constitution and government, while at national level the country is administered by the bicameral Supreme Soviet (parliament), which elects the Presidium, whose Chairman is the country's head of state, and the Council of Ministers.

In March 1991, a Union-wide referendum returned a 76 per cent "yes" vote to the continuation of the "Union of Soviet Socialist Republics as a renewed federation of equal sovereign republics in which human rights and freedoms for all nationalities will be fully guaranteed". However the status of this vote was disputed: some republics (Georgia, Armenia, Moldavia, Estonia, Latvia and Lithuania) did not participate; Russia (easily the largest) added a question asking for approval of direct elections for the Republic Presidency and the Ukraine one on independence. Georgia held a referendum on independence and Armenia planned one for September.

The USSR furthered its experience of contested direct elections in 1991 when the President of Georgia, Zviad Gamasakhurdia, and the Russian President Boris Yeltsin were re-elected to their positions. Elections for the Union Presidency, currently held by Mikhail Gorbachev, are likely to be held in 1992.

Economy. Until the 1980s, the Soviet economy was based on state or collective ownership, centrally planned, with production targets dictated by five-year development plans.

Since the election of Mikhail Gorbachev as CPSU general secretary in March 1985, a policy of economic "restructuring" (*perestroika*) has been adopted which aims to reverse the stagnation of the 1970s. This means trimming bureaucracy, paying greater attention to improving efficiency and product quality and modernizing production processes, while recent legislation has given autonomy of decision-making to managers in individual enterprises, allowed limited private enterprise, and permitted joint ventures with foreign companies.

In 1989 a plan was prepared by Soviet Deputy Prime Minister Leonid Shatalin to shift the economy to a market in 500 days. This plan was progressively diluted and finally defeated during the course of 1990. But in 1991 economic reform was returned to by the Soviet authorities. On April 2 a three-tier pricing system was introduced: basic goods rose by between 20 and 200 per cent, luxury goods prices (about 30 per cent of the whole) were decontrolled, and price ceilings were introduced on those goods in between. To compensate wages and pensions were also raised, but since many Soviet goods were sold below the official price there was still a loss of purchasing power. These measures were not enough to stop output sliding in the first quarter and the growing crisis forced a meeting of President Gorbachev and some republic presidents to agree a joint approach in April. In May the republics (only Estonia and Georgia demurred) agreed a new economic reform plan. Like the Shatalin Plan it incorporated privatization and increased foreign investment attracted by investment guarantees. Two thirds of small and medium-sized enterprises were to be sold by the end of 1992 but the sale was more likely to occur than the Shatalin proposals because it was put in the hands of the republics. The republics also gained the right to issue export licences and a number of steps were taken towards convertibility of the rouble, including a commitment to complete price liberalization in September 1992.

In 1989 the Soviet workforce numbered around 160,000,000. Of these, 28.7 per cent were employed in industry, 24.7 per cent in services, 18.2 per cent in agriculture, 10.4 per cent in construction, 8 per cent in transport and communications, 7.8 per cent in trade and catering and 0.5 per cent in financial services. Unemployment is estimated to be in the range 3–6,000,000 but as many as 28,000,000 may be under-employed.

System of industrial relations. The USSR has been a member of the International Labour Organization since 1954, having earlier been a member from 1934 to 1940. It ratified ILO Conventions No. 87 (Freedom of Association and Protection of the Right to Organize, 1948) and No. 98 (Right to Organize and Collective Bargaining, 1949) in 1956 (when ratification also took place in the name of the Byelorussian SSR and the Ukrainian SSR).

The ICFTU has frequently complained that applicants for permission to emigrate have been dismissed or suffered work discrimination, in violation of ILO Convention No. 111 (Discrimination-Employment and Occupation-Convention, 1958), ratified by the USSR in 1961.

Until 1989 strikes were neither banned nor approved in Soviet law. However on Oct. 9, 1989 the Supreme Soviet introduced a new right to strike. There is now a clearly defined arbitration procedure, which must be adhered to, comprising a search for a compromise by a joint conciliation committee (which has five days to find a solution), followed by the intervention of an outside arbitrator. The strike cannot be officially declared until 12 days after the grievances have been announced. Certain sectors, whose work was deemed "essential or vital" namely communications, energy, defence, government administration, and factories on continuous shifts, were excluded from coverage by the Statute. Strikes remained formally banned if their aim was "to overthrow by force the structure of government and society" or if they sought to destroy the equality of rights between nationalities or ethnic groups. The text of the new law also ended the exclusive right of the official unions to handle industrial disputes. Any organization could now be involved, provided it was so authorized by the work collective. In October 1989, during the stormy debate on the law in the Soviet Parliament, Mr Gorbachev suddenly brought forward a proposal to ban strikes entirely for a 15-month period, but this was later withdrawn after meeting fierce opposition.

From 1987 there has been a series of disputes in the USSR, some of them of major significance. 1989 brought a wave of strikes, including miners' strikes, which mixed industrial with political demands such as for the cancellation of the results of recent elections for the Supreme Soviet. A total of 7,300,000 days were lost in strikes from all causes in 1989 as a whole.

New disputes occurred in 1990 both industrial and political, with national minorities and republics prepared to use the strike weapon in order to reinforce their demands. In early March 1991 a miners' strike began which spread to virtually the whole country. Beginning as a call for better pensions, more investment and the ploughing back of profits, the strike became explicitly political, centering on demands for the resignation of President Gorbachev and his government, dissolution of Parliament and the removal of the CPSU from all state institutions. Such was the industrial impact of the strike that 1,200,000 working days were lost in March alone. Considerable support was lent to the miners by the Russian president Boris Yeltsin, but even he was repudiated by the strikers when he put his name to a settlement proposal.

Trade unionism before 1989. Trade unions developed in the early years of the twentieth century, reflecting the impact of rapid industrialization and the abortive revolution of

1905–6, which weakened somewhat the repressive apparatus of the Tsarist state. However, they were still of little importance compared with their counterparts in other major European countries on the eve of the 1917 Bolshevik revolution. Elements opposed to the Bolsheviks and emphasizing the autonomy of the trade unions from any party had considerable influence at the time of the 1917 revolution, but these were eliminated in the subsequent communist consolidation of power, and the unions were subordinated to the new ruling party, being used primarily to mobilize and discipline the workers behind the objectives of the revolution and to secure greater productivity. Subsequently, all trade unions were organized within the All-Union Central Council of Trade Unions (AUCCTU). Throughout the 1930s and 1940s the unions were of little significance, collective agreements were abolished, and there was no AUCCTU congress between 1932 and 1949. Expanded rights and obligations were accorded from the late 1950s onwards and these were consolidated, extended and codified in legislation adopted from 1970 to 1974, and were also given recognition in the national Constitution of 1977.

Trade unions were organized on the industrial union principle (i.e. so that all employees in a workplace were in the same union, regardless of occupation), and 98 per cent of workers were union members. Managers were included in the same unions. There were no trade unions outside the AUCCTU, although there are non-affiliated professional associations such as the Architects' Union and the Journalists' Union. Members of farm collectives are also involved in trade unions.

Trade union monopoly. The single-trade-union system in operation in the USSR since the Bolshevik revolution served as a model for the construction of similar systems in eastern Europe since World War II and in numerous Third World countries from the 1960s. According to the Soviet government the labour legislation of the Soviet Union and its federated republics did not prohibit the establishment of trade unions outside the structure of the AUCCTU, but rather the unification of the workers had been brought about at the wish of the workers themselves. The ILO Committeee of Experts on the Application of Conventions and Recommendations observed, in contrast, that were such independent unions ever formed they would be unable to exercise the functions of defending the interests of their members, these functions being by legislation reserved to the trade unions within the existing structure, and that a trade union monopoly had consequently been created indirectly by law. Article 6 of the national Constitution defined the Communist Party as the leading and guiding force and nucleus of all "public organizations" (into which category fall the trade unions), and although the Soviet authorities denied that the trade unions are under the direction of the party the rules of the AUCCTU stated that "the trade unions conduct all their work under the guidance of the Communist Party of the Soviet Union". In theory this guidance was of an "ideological-political" character and excluded direct administrative control. The AUCCTU historically followed the shifting positions taken by the party, and there was a close interlocking of party membership and trade union office-holding at all levels. Symptomatically, a purge of government and party officials begun after the appointment of Uri Andropov as General Secretary of the CPSU in November 1982 and stepped up after the election of Mikhail Gorbachev to that post in March 1985 was paralleled by the removal of many hundreds of trade union officials in an attempt to "strengthen discipline" in the trade unions.

Social functions of trade unions. The officials unions are widely involved in the fields of education, health, leisure and social life, and it is in these areas that they possess the greatest significance for the average worker. They administer much of the extensive social insurance system (using funds provided by the state), including disability and maternity benefits and some pensions, and have wide responsibilities in the construction, allocation and maintenance of housing, the provision of accommodation in sanatoriums, holiday camps and homes, and Young Pioneer Camps, and in supervising shops, services and public transport. They also provide a legal advice service, library facilities, sports stadiums, educational courses (through "people's universities"), organize social and cultural activities, and run local "palaces of culture".

Workplace organization. A new state enterprise law took effect on Jan. 1, 1988. Under its provisions workers "self-management" gives new substance to structures for workers' power and participation which had existed previously but had often been purely formal. The law gives workers' meetings, which customarily discuss all matters relating to the operation of an enterprise or collective, the right to elect managers at all levels, and if necessary to call them to account. Workers' meetings elect an executive trade union committee to represent them in negotiations with management, and they are also represented in standing production conferences (these being elective bodies working under the trade union committtes and involving workers, managers, the party and other public organizations). Annual collective agreements reached between management and trade union committees cover an extensive range of topics, including production assignment, investment, introduction of new technology, provision of facilities, worker education, medical services, housing and leisure, laying down the mutual obligations of workers and management. The drafts of such agreements must be discussed by the workers' meeting, where amendments may be suggested (which must be considered by the management and the trade union committee). Where management and the trade union committee are unable to agree, the draft of the agreement is referred to higher trade union and economic management bodies. Collective agreements are legally binding on management but not on the trade union committee, which is accountable only to the collective which elects it, and the trade union may appeal to the administrative authorities to intervene if the management disregards the agreement. Furthermore, workers cannot be dismissed without the approval of the trade union committee.

Financial autonomy of enterprises on a profit-and-loss accounting basis is another feature of the new law, and has meant that enterprises now take greater responsibility for wage fixing. This was previously centrally controlled within the system of national economic planning, but is now to be closely related to the performance of enterprises. Financial autonomy also means that unprofitable enterprises are to be allowed to go bankrupt, although full employment is still officially guaranteed to all workers, and severance pay and retraining are offered in cases of redundancy. There are a number of forecasts which predict massive unemployment in the USSR by the year 2000.

Protection of workers. Before 1990, a principal function of the official trade unions was to mobilize workers behind productivity targets and to secure economic growth, an objective which was seen as entirely compatible with the defence of workers' interests in the context of socially owned production where the workers enjoy the fruits of their own labour. However, the AUCCTU also recognized an ambiguity in this function, stating that the unions must also serve to "protect the masses against excessive departmental zeal, against bureaucracy by officials who distort the policy of the party and the state, against officials who, incapable of correctly organizing production, strive to ensure plan fulfilment at any cost, not infrequently by violating labour laws . . . ". The unions, not the state, were responsible for the enforcement of labour legislation, and technical and legal union inspectors (operating under the direction of the central committees of the sectoral unions) could close down unsafe working areas, issue orders binding managers, and make cases for the disciplining of managers. Managers were not infrequently dismissed for violations of safety or other standards following complaints of trade union inspectors, and it was officially acknowledged that the drive for increased productivity has led to increasing difficulties in this area, while it had also been noted by the AUCCTU that the financial rigours of the new state enterprise law had made some enterprise managers cut expenditure on workers' social benefits in order to meet profit targets.

Non-official trade unions. The "Free Interprofessional Association of Soviet Workers" (*Svobodnoye Mezhduprofessionalnoye Obshchestvo Trudyashchikh*—SMOT) was formed in 1978 (when it unsuccessfully sought registration with the Soviet authorities), but it faced systematic persecution and there was no indication that it has existed in any form other than that of a tiny dissident group with no organized mass base. A number of SMOT activists were imprisoned for "anti-Soviet agitation and propaganda", and one of the SMOT founders, Mark Morozov, died in prison in August 1986. The ICFTU has one small affiliate—with only 166 members in 1985—with the status of a union-in-exile from part of the Soviet Union. This is the Eesti Meremeeste Union (EMU—Estonian Seamen's Union, P.O. Box 5365, S-102 46 Stockholm, Sweden; Nikolaus Metslov, general secretary). Its antecedent union was founded in (then independent) Estonia in 1920, and was liquidated under Soviet rule, before being reformed in exile in 1943.

Trade unionism from 1990. As late as the autumn of 1989, there were few signs of change in the official AUCCTU. By 1990 however massive threats to its Union-wide coverage had forced internal reform. Early in 1990 the official unions announced far-reaching reforms of their role and reorganized themselves leading up to a Congress in October at which they were relaunched as the General Confederation of Unions of the USSR (GCTU). While changing the old statutes, delegates voted to retain unitary control of the assets of the AUCCTU in the GCTU. The new President Vladimir Scherbakov defined the immediate objective of the Federation as defending workers' interests during the transition to a market economy.

The GCTU proclaims itself to be a voluntary alliance, to be independent of all political parties and of state bodies. It recognizes the right of primary organizations independently to determine their structure, activity and affiliation, and it explicitly repudiates democratic centralism. The GCTU continues to claim a large number of affiliates, comparable to those of the AUCCTU which it has replaced and whose assets it has inherited. Its claimed membership is also identical to the figure claimed by the AUCCTU. It seems likely however that there is an overlap with membership of non-affiliated organizations.

An example of the difficulties encountered by the reforming official unions is the evolution of the miner's organizations. The AUCCTU mining affiliate convened its 15th Congress in March 1990 and invited representatives of the miners' strike committees to attend. They concluded from observing the proceedings that no change was going to take place and immediately resolved to establish a new and independent union (*see below*). But membership of the GCTU no longer implies subservience to the régime. Early in 1990, even before its formation, members of the offical oil and gas workers' union threatened to strike if equipment prices were not frozen and more investment not made. This became a generalized threat from the AUCCTU in opposition to rises in industrial prices and the organization went so far as to establish a Commission on Price Rises which was starting to prepare an all-USSR strike. The Commission was only disbanded when the government assured the AUCCTU that while the increases would go ahead all the enterprises hurt by higher input costs would be compensated. A year later in April 1991, the (claimed) 60,000 strong Federation of Independent Trade Unions of the RSFSR (Deputy Chairman Yevgeny Arapov), organized a one-hour strike against high prices.

Unofficial trade unions. The threats to the AUCCTU's position were of three kinds. It faces a small yet potent all-Union challenge in the form of the Confederation of Labour (which co-ordinates most of the Workers' Committees and many unions which have seceded from the official unions). Second, in the Republics, separatist views are held to a greater or lesser degree. Where the drive for autonomy is strong, as in Georgia or the Ukraine, the trade unions tend to reflect it and seek to organize outside the AUCCTU (*see above*). But in all parts of the USSR there appear to be movements towards independent organization. This may reflect political objectives which are distinct from those of the

CPSU—such is the case with Sotsprof (*below*)—or it may reflect a desire after decades of political integration to concentrate on more purely industrial objectives.

The summer 1989 strike wave in the USSR led directly to the establishment of Workers' Committees. Of the challenges which the official AUCCTU faces these are probably the most formidable since they have built the embryo of a Union-wide organization. The Workers' Committees are to be found in the north (Vorkuta region), in the Ukraine (Donbass in the Don Valley), and East of the Urals (Kuzbass). However, they, like some of the new organizations which have emerged in Eastern Europe, face definitional difficulties for despite their title they are commonly regarded by union members with their own organizations in the Confederation of Labour (*see below*) as embryonic parties rather than unions.

Most Workers' Committees are in contact with the Confederation of Labour (Konfederatsya Truda) whose President is Vyatsheslav Golikov. The Confederation was founded in May 1990 by a joint congress of strike committees and support groups. It is reported to have organized regular subscriptions and to be planning a strike fund. It has established extensive contacts with western unions and an all-Union newspaper is planned. Its declared aim is to unite all progressive forces, so that not only unions and strike committees, but also support organizations and political parties are found within it. The new organizations being founded increasingly have a Republic base. The Confederation of Independent Trade Unions of Georgia (CITUG) was founded in 1990, when the Georgian unions seceded from the AUCCTU. It claims that some budgets of Georgian unions have been turned over to Moscow-run centres in the AUCCTU and opposes the All-Union body's decision to set up from the centre branches in the armed forces, a number of which are located in Georgia. CITUG has also called for a law to be passed in Georgia which would ban the activities within its territory of non-Georgian Republic bodies. This would effectively bar the AUCCTU from activity in Georgia.

One of the main independent unions in the USSR is the Federation of Socialist Trade Unions (Sotsprof), whose President is Serguei Khramov. It claims a membership of 20,000 and it successfully promoted candidatures in elections to the Supreme Soviet of the Russia Federation. Sotsprof aims to be a confederation with contacts across the USSR and explicitly intends to rival the official unions. It is very decentralized but has a twin structure which would permit expansion: horizontal for territories, and vertical for sectors. At an early stage, Sotsprof leaders were approached by some in the AUCCTU to participate in it and help rejuvenate it. The Sotsprof leaders declined but there is no exclusivity about membership, and many Sotsprof members are also affiliated to the AUCCTU. Sotsprof views the new industrial relations law as undemocratic, an attempt to limit the right to strike *de jure* when it had already been won *de facto* by the industrial actions of the miners and others. Its ideology is firmly socialist and it affiliates to the Socialist Committee; in this it is sharply demarcated from many of the other independent unions that have sprung up.

In 1990, *Free Labour World* reported that in Leningrad there was the Union of Workers' Committees grouping over 20,000 people in 30 workplaces; another group, Workers' Initiative, gave practical support and had had some success in helping the foundation of an independent farmers' union. In the Ukraine, Solidarity of the Ukraine Workers (Yedinist) covered seven towns and had about 6,000 members. In Lithuania, where independent unionism began in 1988, the first independent organization was the Lithuanian Workers' Trade Union (President Kazimierz Uoka). In Moscow the Independent Union of Soviet Journalists (President, Serguei Grigoriants) was also founded at a congress in 1988 and publishes a review *Glasnost* in Paris and New York. An independent union "Shield" was reported to have been formed with the support of 40,000 middle ranking army officers in 1989 in defence of their economic and legal rights.

The increasingly strong and independent miners' union grew like so many new organizations out of the 1989 strikes. The strikes themselves were organized outside the official structures and concluded with the signing of a comprehensive agreement with the government covering wages, conditions, supplies and industrial organization. A tripartite commission of the committees, the official unions and the government was established to monitor implementation. After the strikes ended the strike committees remained in place.

The 2,500,000 strong AUCCTU-affiliated Miners Union renewed its leadership by electing a number of strike leaders at its March 1990 Congress. A number of other strike leaders walked out of the Congress in protest at the continued inclusion in the union of managers and engineers: they wished to confine membership to underground workers. This dissident group attempted to found its own union at a congress in Donetz three months later but the proposal was rejected. Certain decisions were taken including one to open any new organization to all in the mining industry regardless of the material they worked. It was the Recall Congress of October 1990 which finally decided to establish a new union. A General Agreement (statement of aims) was approved and an Executive Bureau was also elected. This Congress was attended by 880 delegates, 648 of whom approved of the ambition to establish a new union. The attitude of the Soviet government to the new union is unclear: its Congress was addressed by the responsible minister, and its headquarters are located in the coal ministry offices. In the Spring of 1991 there was still a considerable overlap between the new miners' union and the official one, making reliable membership figures hard to obtain. The confusion was heightened by the eruption of a further miners' strike (*see above*) which had its origins in frustration at the non-implementation of aspects of the agreement which concluded the 1989 dispute but rapidly broadened its demands to include others of a political nature.

General Confederation of Trade Unions of the USSR (GCTU)

Address. Leninsky prospekt 42, Moscow 117119
Phone. 9387215
Telex. 411010 VKP SU
Fax. 9382155
Leadership. Vladimir Shcherbakov (president); Gennady Bashtanyuk, Vladimir Kuzmenok and Albert Yakovlev (vice-presidents).
Membership. 140,000,000.
History and character. Formed in October 1990 at the 19th Congress of Trade Unions of the USSR as a lawful successor of the All-Union Central Council of Trade Unions (AUCCTU).

Following the October revolution of 1917 the Bolsheviks held the first All-Russian Congress of Trade Unions in January 1918. This congress formed a Provisional All-Russian Central Council of Trade Unions which became the All-Union Central Council of Trade Unions in November 1924.

The function of the AUCCTU and the lower-level trade union organizations was to organize the workers behind the development of Soviet society, giving recognition to the guiding role of the Communist Party, and to safeguard the interests of individual working people. Under the trade union rules the AUCCTU "promoted socialist emulation and the movement for a communist attitude to work". The AUCCTU had powers to initiate legislation in the social and economic field and participated in its formulation and implementation, and participates in setting rates of pay. Under Article 7 of the Constitution of the USSR trade unions "participate in accordance with the aims laid down in their rules, in managing state and public affairs, and in deciding political, economic and social and cultural matters", and under Article 100 nominate candidates to state bodies.

The AUCCTU was constructed on the principle of democratic centralism, whereby all trade union bodies were elected and the decisions of higher bodies were always binding on lower bodies.

The 18th AUCCTU congress held in February 1987 was dominated by self-criticism, following the lead given by CPSU General Secretary Gorbachev who told the congress that the trade unions had failed to defend adequately the interests of the workers. As a result the congress unanimously adopted a modification of its statutes extending the rights and duties of trade unionists in accordance with a resolution which insisted on the "independence" of trade union action to "defend the legitimate rights and interests of the workers" and its importance "in the process of democratization of Soviet society." The new provisions of the AUCCTU constitution establish that "the trade unions are one of the important links in the political system of Soviet society, and of people's socialist self-management" and stipulate the possibility of multiple candidates for election to trade union bodies. Shalayev stated that the trade unions "give their unreserved support to the policy of acceleration, restructuring and democratization led by the CPSU", and delegates stressed the need for openness, democracy and flexibility, and the need to counter bureaucratic formalism.

According to its Constitution the GCTU is "a voluntary alliance of trade unions of the USSR ... which have been united with a view of co-ordinating and strengthening their actions to defend the employment, social, economic and cultural rights and interests of employees, students and pensioners, rendering mutual support in achieving common aims at a nationwide level and consolidating the trade union movement of the country".

While functioning within the framework of the Constitution of the USSR the GCTU is independent of any political parties and movements, State and economic bodies. It is founded on the principles of rallying working people on a voluntary basis in trade union organizations formed at their members' workplaces or educational institutions; the right of primary organizations to determine independently their structure, activity orientation and affiliation to a particular trade union; to establish a higher-level trade union body and to vest it with appropriate authority; the electivity of trade union bodies, collectivity and openness in work, regular report-making and plurality of views.

This means the renunciation of the principle of democratic centralism formerly applied in the Soviet trade union system.

The principles referred to above are declared by the Law on Trade Unions, Rights and Guarantees of Their Activities which became effective Jan. 1, 1991. The Law provides for the right of trade unions to initiate legislation, their participation in formulating the State policy of employment and in exercising control over the observance of relevant laws, the preference right of collective bargaining and concluding collective agreements, their involvement in outlining measures for the social protection of working people, the right to organize and go on strike—the latter being for the first time throughout the history of the USSR. The Law stipulates guarantees for these rights as well as for the status of trade unions and their officers at workplaces, trade unions property and funds.

Soviet trade unions are represented in the parliaments of the USSR and component Union Republics and in local government bodies.

Structure. The GCTU Congress is convened at least every five years. The governing body between congresses is the Confederation Council where every GCTU affiliate is represented—currently by seven members from each sectoral federation (union) and 14 members from each republican federation. At present there are 33 sectoral unions *(see below)* and 11 Republican federations affiliated to the GCTU, in all the Union Republics of the USSR excluding Georgia, Estonia, Latvia and Lithuania. The Confederation Council also includes the President and Vice-Presidents of the GCTU. The Council forms a Presidium which consists of the GCTU President and Vice-Presidents and representatives of all the GCTU affiliated organizations (one person from each of them). There are standing commissions formed from among the Council members, which deal with the main aspects of trade union activities. The Council plenary meetings elect its Secretaries.

The funds of the GCTU are made up by the contributions paid by its affiliates, which are mutually agreed upon and endorsed by the Confederation Council, as well as by receipts from business, commercial, external economic and other activities of the Council. The Council sets up a Solidarity Fund, co-ordinates the administering of the Social Insurance Fund of the USSR, guides the activities of the organizations subordinate to the GCTU which are responsible for sanatorium and health-resort facilities and recreation centres provided for working people and their families, tourist and excursion, cultural and sports activities etc. Soviet trade unions have established a Trade Union Bank, a Building Concern and other cost-accounting undertakings.

Publications. Trud, daily newspaper, circulation over 18,000,000, and a number of other newspapers and magazines, as well as "Profizdat", the GCTU publishing house.

Affiliates. Aircraft Industry Workers' Union; National Federation of Civil Aviation Workers' Unions, Associations and Societies; National Federation of Automobile Transport and Highway Workers' Unions; Automobile and Farm Machinery Industries Workers' Union; Federation of Agro-

Industrial Complex Workers' Unions; Nuclear Power Engineering and Industry Workers' Union; Federative Independent Union of Water Transport Workers; Federation of Armed Forces Workers' and Employees' Unions; National Federation of Geology, Geodesy and Cartography Workers' Unions; Federation of Mining and Metallurgical Industries Workers' Unions of the USSR; Federation of State Institutions Workers' Unions of the USSR; Railway and Transport Construction Workers' Independent Union; National Federation of Health Service Employees' Unions; National Federation of Cultural Workers' Unions; National Federation of Wood Industries Workers' Unions; Engineering and Instrument Making Industries Workers' Unions; Federation of Local Industries and Public Services Workers' Unions; National Federation of Public Education and Scientific Workers' Unions; Scientific-Technical and Scientific-Industrial Co-operatives, Enterprises and Organizations Employees' Union; Oil and Gas Industries and Construction Workers' Union; Defence Industry Workers' Union; General Engineering Workers' Union; Radio and Electronic Industry Workers' Federative Union; Fish Industry Workers' Union; Federation of Communication Workers' Unions of the USSR; Construction and Building Materials Industry Workers' Union; Shipbuilding Workers' Union of the USSR; Textile and Light Industry Workers' Union; National Federation of Trade, Public Catering and Consumers Co-operatives Workers' Unions; Heavy Engineering Workers' Union; Coalminers' Union; National Federation of Chemical Industries Workers' Unions; "Electroprofsoyuz" National Federation of Trade Unions; Federation of Independent Trade Unions of the RSFSR; Ukraine Federation of Independent Trade Unions; Federation of Byelorussian Trade Unions; Federation of Trade Unions of the Uzbek SSR; Federation of Trade Unions of the Kazakh SSR; Azerbaijan Republican Trade Union Council; Moldova Federation of Independent Trade Unions; Kyrghyzstan Federation of Trade Unions; Tadzhik Republican Trade Union Council; Armenian Republican Trade Union Council; Federation of Trade Unions of the Turkmen SSR. As the reorganization of trade unions affiliated to the GCTU has not been accomplished yet, it is still impossible to give the addresses of their governing bodies.

In addition to the above unions, in the USSR there are a few autonomous trade union organizations with most of which the GCTU of the USSR maintains relations based on agreement.

International affiliation. WFTU. Bilateral relations are maintained with almost all countries of the world. Representatives of the GCTU and its affiliates participate in the work of the ILO and the activities of the United Nations, UNESCO and other international organizations as well as in the NGO system.

United Arab Emirates

Capital: Abu Dhabi Town   **Population: 1,544,000**

Political system. The UAE is a federation comprising the Emirates of Abu Dhabi, Dubai, Sharjah, Ras al Khimah, Fujairah, Ajjman and Umm al Quwain, which each have hereditary rulers with absolute power over non-federal matters. There are no political parties.

Economy. The UAE's economy is based on petroleum exports and is therefore directly affected by fluctuations in the global oil price. There is a large population of migrant labourers from abroad, mostly South Asia.

Only 4.5 per cent of UAE labour was employed in agriculture in 1985–87, 38 per cent in industry and 57.3 per cent in services.

System of industrial relations. UAE has been a member of the International Labour Organization since 1972, but has ratified neither Convention No. 87 (Freedom of Association and Protection of the Right to Organize, 1948) nor Convention No. 98 (Right to Organize and Collective Bargaining, 1949).

471

Trade unionism. Trade unions are illegal and there is no evidence of any form of activity.

UNITED KINGDOM

Capital: London

Population: 57,019,000
(1988)

Political System. The United Kingdom of Great Britain and Northern Ireland is a constitutional monarchy. It has a cabinet government with a powerful prime minister. There are two main political parties, Conservative and Labour, although a number of other parties representing the middle ground or nationalist movements in Scotland, Wales and Northern Ireland regularly gain over 20 per cent of the vote between them. At the 1987 general election the Conservatives won 376 seats in the House of Commons, Labour 229 and the others 55. There is an unelected upper chamber, the House of Lords, which can amend draft legislation before final referral to the Commons.

Economy. The UK has a mixed economy, although the public sector is declining and now accounts for under 4,000,000 (almost all in national or local administration, education and health) of an employed labour force of 22,000,000. Since the 1970s there has been a major decline in manufacturing and substantial growth in services, primarily banking and finance. In 1989 the UK recorded its first ever manufacturing deficit and the largest-ever balance of payments deficit in its history; these deficits continued throughout 1990. In 1979 North Sea oil began contributing to the balance pf payments, peaking in 1989.

After the severe recession of the early 'eighties the UK economy grew strongly through the mid- to late eighties. However, in 1989 inflation was rising and the government raised interest rates, precipitating a sharp recession in 1990. Unemployment began to rise in late 1989 and reached 2,000,000 (9 per cent) in early 1991. Inflation peaked at 10.9 per cent in late 1990 and began to fall sharply in early 1991. The UK joined the exchange rate mechanism (ERM) of the European Community in October 1990, thus making more difficult any further downward drift or devaluation of sterling. Average earnings continued to rise at the same rate as, or slightly above, inflation throughout 1990. Some real pay cuts began to emerge, mainly in manufacturing, early in 1991 although on a very limited scale. Much 1980s' investment has been from foreign-owned multinationals which now dominate the UK manufacturing economy and are increasing their share of the finance sector owning, for example, 60 per cent of the insurance industry.

Trade unionism. The UK trade union movement is the oldest in the world and emerged in three distinct phases. First was the mid-19th century emergence of skilled craft unions in, for example, engineering or printing; second was the 1890 explosion of activity which formed the major general unions of unskilled or semi-skilled workers; third was the early-20th century emergence and consolidation of white collar and professional organisations, often in public administration, education and health.

Within UK unions patterns of organisation vary considerably, largely reflecting bargaining systems among the membership. The craft unions have typically had a well developed local shop steward (workplace representative) system; their organization tends to give considerable authority to elected lay officials: there are often strong branches or regions. The general unions, where membership turnover is often higher, tend to have larger, but less autonomous, branches. Shop stewards may rely more on the help of professional full-time union officials who have relatively greater authority. White collar unions are usually organized along semi-craft lines, although there is often less emphasis on pay bargaining and the unions have traditionally offered a wider range of membership benefits such as travel, legal advice and insurance, as well as actively developing members' professional interests. However, all this is rapidly changing with changes in collective bargaining, methods of communication, and declining resources (*see below*). The Trades Union Congress (TUC) was founded in 1868, since when it has been virtually the sole national trade union centre. Unlike the unions of many other industrial nations, Britain's unions founded the Labour Party (in 1900), rather than a Labour or Social Democratic party helping to set up trade unions. The TUC is itself a wholly independent body, but the majority of members of its constituent unions have always been affiliated to the Party and have a majority vote at the Labour Party conference. At the 1990 TUC congress 77 unions, with 8,404,827 members were represented. Thirty one unions, with 5,000,000 members, were affiliated to the Labour Party, including the Electricians' Union (EETPU), currently outside the TUC.

The authority of the TUC is relatively small; it has no direct role in bargaining and its powers over affiliated unions are limited to recommendations or disputes over membership. However, its history and unity gives its considerable force as the voice of the UK union movement. Since 1918 it has rarely represented less than three-quarters of union members. Until 1979 governments consulted the TUC over a wide range of issues and it had representatives on a number of economic planning, industrial, training, educational, community, and health bodies. Since 1979 consultation has been reduced or ceased altogether, and many tripartite (government/industry/union) bodies have been abolished. Those that remain, such as the Health and Safety Commission, the Advisory, Conciliation and Arbitration Service (ACAS) and the National Economic Development Office have seen one of the (usually three) TUC representatives replaced by representatives of non-TUC unions. Historically the main non-TUC unions have been in education, the civil service, or health. although the electrical workers' EETPU was expelled in 1988 for refusing to abide by the TUC's "Bridlington" agreement on non-poaching of members.

System of industrial relations (history). Until the mid-nineteenth century employers were hostile to trade unionism, which could be rendered unlawful as a "conspiracy". In 1871 the Trades Union Act finally permitted collective bargaining and laid the foundation for the UK's system of "immunities", in which unions had no positive legal right to act but enjoyed legal immunity from, for example, employer claims for damages, provided their acts fell within the definition of trades disputes, representation, etc. Successive (increasingly imaginative and restrictive) definitions of permissible union action led Parliament to introduce successive Acts to restore or widen legitimate union activity and collective bargaining: notably in 1906 when the *Trades Dispute Act* gave protection against civil conspiracy; the 1913 Act which permitted some political action; the 1927 Act which prevented action to pressurize governments (even when employers); the 1946 Act which repealed the 1927 Act; the *Equal Pay Act* 1970 and the 1978 *Employment Protection (Consolidation) Act* which gave a range of individual rights, for instance against unfair dismissal and set up ACAS. Within this legal framework, throughout most of the century until the late 1970s, most collective bargaining was typically conducted nationally at industry level: for example, in engineering, chemicals or the health service. Major companies or organizations often bargained independently. On top of these rates local establishments commonly negotiated top-up rates, bonuses, etc. Such two-tier bargaining was the norm in manufacturing and the private sector; single-tier national agreements were the public sector norm. Such collective bargaining covered over three-quarters of all employees: usually not covered were the service sectors and professional occupations.

As regards the changing importance of industrial relations institutions, the chief industrial relations institution is the Advisory, Conciliation and Arbitration Service, set up in 1974 with a duty to promote good industrial relations. Funded entirely by government it is run by a council appointed by the Secretary of State for Employment but comprising trade union, employer and independent (usually academic) members. Prominent throughout the 'seventies and early 'eighties, it has changed emphasis from crisis management to more advisory work.

The Certification Office (CO) was set up in 1976 and took over the duties of the old Registrar of Friendly Societies originally established in 1871. The CO has a duty to keep lists of unions and employers' associations, as well as to administer funds for ballots, and oversee mergers, political funds and union accounts. The CO will only register independent unions: in 1990 he refused a certificate to the staff association set up at the Government Communications Centre at Cheltenham after the government had banned union membership—causing great controversy and union anger—deeming it to be under the control of the Director. The addition of responsibility for political funds and ballots has given the CO more prominence. As at December 1990 there were 323 unions registered with the CO: the latest membership figures relate to December 1989, when there were 10,043,606 members in 342 unions.

The 1988 Act also set up the Commission for Trade Union Rights, an agency designed to give advice and funds to members with a complaint against their union. It has dealt with only a handful of cases and has had very little impact.

Recent developments, and particularly with reference to the 1980s have included industry agreements declining in favour of company agreements; collective bargaining weakened and was reduced in scope as employment patterns have sharply moved towards service and professional occupations; and reasserted managerial authority reduced the scope for local bargaining. Britain's highly developed system had been based on a relatively tolerant legal framework, which encouraged voluntary collective bargaining. In many sectors closed shop agreements were established, requiring employees to be union members. However, a series of Acts in the 1980s removed the encouragement to collective bargaining; virtually outlawed the closed shop; withdrew legal rights, for example, to recognition or to taking industrial action in many circumstances. The impact of these Acts (summarized in more detail below) has undoubtedly been to weaken trade unions, and thus the scope for collective bargaining. Nevertheless, the vast majority of changes to the industrial relations pattern have been wrought by economic and employment changes; very few employers have de-recognized unions, although this may now be changing (*see below*). Overall, old patterns and procedures have shown remarkable resilience.

One feature of 1990 was an upsurge of interest in pay policy. Following entry to the ERM at a fixed exchange rate, and with high unemployment (it topped 2,000,000 or 7.5 per cent in early 1991 and was forecast to reach 3,000,000 by the year end) critics argued that intervention was needed to reduce UK unit labour costs and curb unemployment. The 1990 TUC Congress carried a resolution based on a GMB/UCW proposal seeking discussion on pay co-ordination and widening the bargaining agenda to include productivity and training, although also opposing traditional across-the-board pay policy. Several influential commentators argued the case for some form of pay restraint or advisory pay board. The government, under the new premiership of John Major, showed some tentative interest as frequent calls for pay restraint were plainly having little effect. However, the moves toward fragmentation of bargaining structures and weakening of union and employer organizations' influence, posed a major difficulty. The Labour Party proposed an annual national economic assessment, fixed after tripartite discussion, which would aim at influencing pay negotiators. Settlements would, in turn, influence the level at which a government could establish both Labour's proposed statutory minimum wage, as well as the social wage. There was no support from any quarter for a return to pay norms. Meanwhile, wage and price inflation continued to run higher than forecast, and well above the EC average.

Trade unions began the decade of the 'eighties with their highest-ever membership (13,300,000 in 1980) but after a series of largely public sector disputes over pay policy. The 1978/79 "winter of discontent" (involving refuse, hospital, transport and cemetery workers) had heavily contributed to the May 1979 defeat of the Labour government and the election of a Conservative Party pledged to curb the power of the unions. Previously the unions had achieved great influence within the Labour government in the "social contract", which conceded pay policy for a major extension of collective and individual rights contained, for example, in the 1975 Act. The "winter of discontent", when the government's 5 per cent pay policy was comprehensively breached, was thus widely seen as the graveyard of the social contract approach and of Labour's claim to be able to work with the unions. Under the onslaught of rapidly rising unemployment and a hostile climate, TUC membership fell rapidly from its all-time peak of 12,173,000 in 1981. The number of unions also shrank, reflecting mergers in the face of wholesale membership loss: from 109 in 1981 to 77 in 1989. Almost all of this fall reflects drastic employment falls in "smokestack" industries which were all well organized: coal, steel, shipbuilding, the docks. There is little evidence that the propensity to join unions has changed over the decade; union density has remained stable in the public sector and in what is left of the traditional private manufacturing sector. However, unions have not been recruiting in the newer industries like banking, finance or retailing, at the same rate as employment expansion. Overall, despite a 2.5 per cent employment rise in 1989, TUC membership continued to fall, by 247,000, or 2.9 per cent.

A series of Acts passed by the Conservative government (re-elected in 1983 and again in 1987) has hampered union activity. The 1980 *Employment Act*: (i) gave public funds for secret ballots to elect union officers, amend union rules, or end industrial action; (ii) made it unfair to dismiss an employee with a deeply held religious belief or reason of conscience against joining a closed shop; (iii) said any new closed shops should have 80 per cent membership support in a secret ballot; (iv) protected workers against unreasonable non-acceptance into a union or expulsion from a union where an existing closed shop was in force; (v) limited immunity to picketing at an employees's own place of work (i.e. "secondary" picketing at a different place of work would render the pickets or union officials liable to a civil claim for inducing a breach of contract); (vi) removed immunity from organizers of secondary action unless the action directly affected the employer in the primary dispute; (vii) reduced unfair dismissal conpensation and (viii) gave the Secretary of State the power to issue non-binding codes of practice aimed at improving industrial relations after consultation with ACAS, but which would be used as evidence in courts and tribunals. One such code ruled that pickets should rarely exceed six in number and extended police discretion to further reduce the number of pickets where they feared possible disorder.

The 1982 *Employment Act*: (i) gave the Secretary of State power to compensate individuals dismissed for non-membership of a union before the 1980 Act came into force; (ii) further reduced the possibility of being fairly dismissed for non-membership of a union; (iii) increased compensation for dismissal for non-membership of a union or for non-participation in union activities (although employers could fairly dismiss either selectively or collectively for participating in, for instance, strike action); (iv) ended clauses in contracts stipulating union-only labour; (v) brought legal immunities for unions (and employers' associations) into line with those for individuals so that individuals could be held liable for action outside a trade dispute (i.e. not covered by immunity); (vi) set out a scale of damages which could be awarded (i.e. as fines against unions, and (vii) further narrowed the definition of a trade dispute as being a conflict over terms and conditions of employment, thus rendering unlawful all political strikes or protests against government policy, and drastically reducing the possibility of sympathy action.

The *Trade Union Act* 1984 provided that: (i) all voting members of union executives (their governing body) should be directly elected by secret postal ballot at least every five years; (ii) only industrial action supported by a clear majority in a secret ballot would have immunity and (iii) all members of unions with political funds should be balloted on the continuation of those funds and, if approved, such funds should be subject to re-approval in further secret ballots every 10 years. Ever since 1913 unions had been allowed to undertake political objects provided members gave initial consent. A separate political levy was set up to fund such activity and individuals could opt out of the levy if they wished. Most unions with political levies used most of their political fund to support the Labour Party, so this provision was seen by some as an attack on the major opposition party's finances. In the event, all 36 unions with political funds retained them with large majorities and 18 new funds were set up. The Act also required unions to set up an accurate register of members' names and addresses (workplace addresses were permitted); this became essential to run the elections and ballot now legally required. A great many unions had always balloted or voted at meetings on, for example, elections and strikes. However, the Act required very much tighter procedures which caused considerable difficulty in multi-employer disputes or among scattered membership.

The 1988 *Employment Act* provided: (i) members with rights against being "unjustifiably disciplined" by their unions (for example by being fined for strike breaking); (ii) extended the balloting requirement to key non-voting executive members (for example general secretaries, presidents, and other chief policy makers); (iii) removed the last vestige of support for the closed shop (i.e. the immunity from unfair dismissal even if a closed shop had been supported by 80 per cent in a secret ballot) and (vi) established a Commissioner for Trade Union Rights to help members to bring cases against their unions. The Act also prevented postal ballots at the workplace: only fully postal ballots, where members posted their votes from outside work, would confer immunity unless demonstrably impractical.

Lastly, the 1990 *Employment Act*, which took effect from November 1990 provided: (i) that unions would be liable for any form of industrial action (including unofficial action not sanctioned by union ballots and procedures) which had been organized or supported by officers or members *unless* the union explicitly repudiated the action in writing to every member who either had taken part, or might take part, in such action; (ii) employers would have the right to *selectively* dismiss anyone taking part in unofficial action (previously employers had normally been able to dismiss all those taking part in action, or none) and (iii) if a union then took action, official or unofficial, in support of such dismissed workers that action would be unlawful and not covered by any immunity. However, most industrial action in the UK takes the form of short unofficial disputes involving few employees although the majority of days lost derive from official disputes. Unofficial disputes are often ratified by a subsequent ballot after they have begun. Thus the 1990 Act could have a major impact. Critics, including the Institute of Personnel Management, have argued that management may use it to enable them to selectively sack "troublemakers" after provoking a dispute, and that effective repudiation will be difficult and costly for unions. The Act is widely seen as a move back to the infamous 1906 *Taff Vale Judgement* (reversed by the 1906 *Trade Disputes Act*) which held that a union can be held liable for acts done by any of its members, authorized or not.

Recent disputes. Throughout the early and mid-1980s there was a series of major disputes against the run-down of traditional industries; the decline in public sector pay relative to private sector earnings; and the introduction of new technology. Strikes in the steel industry, the civil service, among teachers, miners and printers followed each other in successive years. The most important of these was the extremely bitter 12-month 1984/85 miners' strike, which resulted in fines of over £500,000 being levied against the union (the NUM), and ended in defeat for the miners. With over 200,000 members before the dispute, its 1989 membership had fallen to only 60,000—entirely due to pit closures. In 1988 print-workers in SOGAT and the NGA took action against wholesale redundancies and the closure of national newspaper plant as it moved to new premises, new technology and a new workforce: partially organized in a rival union (the EETPU) which was subsequently expelled from the TUC for this and other breaches of TUC rules over membership rights. Like the NUM, both SOGAT and the NGA suffered very substantial fines for what was held to be sympathy action.

Since those disputes union tactics have changed to ensure compliance with the law, win public support, and minimize the cost both to the union and its members. In the summer of 1989 NALGO undertook its first-ever national strike over pay and bargaining structure, involving local authority staff on a carefully selected rolling basis, partly financed by a membership levy. This rapidly succeeded in raising the employers' offer and secured a 9.5 per cent agreement. Similar tactics were successfully employed at the BBC. Also in the summer of 1989 underground rail workers took unofficial action, but won widespread public sympathy, at the same time as railway workers took official action, also with some public sympathy. Both disputes were eventually resolved with the help of ACAS and the unions (NUR and ASLEF) claiming victory. Critics said impractical balloting require-ments had forced the underground workers to take unofficial action, although it is widely believed that the 1990 Act was a response to such tactics. This "summer of discontent", as it was dubbed, also saw the start of other disputes which ran over into 1990. The first involved ambulance workers and officially began in November. Almost uniquely in UK union history, union members did not strike, but continued to work voluntarily on an emergency basis—often after having been locked out of vehicle depots by management. Such tactics, combined with extremly professional presentation by the main union involved (NUPE) won overwhelming public support, with millions of pounds being donated. The final settlement, in the spring of 1990, involved a settlement of 17.6 per cent over two years, with both sides claiming victory.

The second dispute involved North Sea oil rig workers operating through an unofficial Offshore Industry Liaison Committee. Beginning in April 1990, and continuing throughout the summer, an overtime ban and series of one-day stoppages were held to protest against health and safety policy (the Piper Alpha disaster in 1989 killed 167) in a demand for union recognition and for improvements in pay and conditions. The employers (a wide range of operators, contractors and maintenance subcontractors) refused to co-operate in balloting arrangements, thus rendering it virtually impossible to remain within the law and causing the main union involved (MSF)—like the NUR and ASLEF—to have little incentive to make the dispute official. The offshore employers reacted strongly, dismissing over 1,000 employees and refusing recognition. The dispute ended in stalemate in August 1990, although subsequently the employers conceded some pay improvements and informal negotiations.

A third dispute has attracted less attention, but arguably been more important. In November 1989 engineering talks, aimed at reducing the working week from 39 to 35 hours, broke down and the unions (principally the AEU, but also the GMB, MSF and TGWU, collectively organized through the CSEU) embarked on a lengthy series of short selective strikes in target companies, supported by a levy of all members, and after meticu-lous balloting arrangements to remain within the law. By August 1990 the Engineering

Employers Federation claimed that only one quarter of their members had made concessions, while the unions claimed over one third of companies, involving almost half the employees in the industry (including some in non-EEF firms), had agreed reductions to 37 hours, usually financed by changed working practices.

Overall, therefore, 1990 saw a renewed confidence among many union members, coupled with stronger public support and more sophisticated tactics. However, union issues often still attract great controversy. For example, an issue attracting great attention in 1990 was the report by Gavin Lightman QC, into Daily Mirror allegations of improper use by NUM senior officers of funds collected in the UK and the Soviet Union during the miners' strike. The Lightman report criticized both the NUM and the International Mineworkers' Organization, which had received much of the money, although it exonerated officials from accusations of personal gain. The government has not ruled out further union legislation.

Employment policy developments. The break-up of collective bargaining arrangements has continued, although at a slower pace than many would have predicted. By the summer of 1990 almost all national newspaper journalists and several provincial groups had moved over to individual pay contracts. In 1988 and 1989 managers at British Telecom, British Rail and the Ports had been removed from bargaining and placed on individual contracts. There were few other moves on this scale in 1990. Despite fears of "union-busting" only Cable & Wireless decided to derecognize all their unions; although other employers derecognized some minority unions, preferring to deal with a single organization. British Coal insisted that it would negotiate with the minority UDM (which had broken away from the NUM during the 1984/5 strike); the NUM refused to negotiate alongside the UDM and was thus effectively barred from pay talks.

A continuing feature was also the introduction of flexibility within national agreements. The 1990 settlements in local authorities, the entire education sector, the health and civil services, incorporated further elements of local discretion and flexibility, allowing managers to vary pay rates in response to local labour market pressures or individual performance—often measured by newly introduced staff appraisal schemes. However, early in 1991, the government dropped its plans to restore teachers' bargaining rights (removed in 1987) preferring to set up an advisory pay review body and thus retaining a national agreement. Moreover, there is little sign that employers (public or private) are willing to devolve more than a small amount of control over pay. Private companies in water, chemicals and telecommunications, which moved away from national agreements in 1989 and 1990, did not move to geographical (local labour market) but to functional (company sector or profit centre) agreements. Under the impact of the 1990 recession many restored pay control to the centre.

Demographic pressures, reducing the supply of women and younger workers at a time of increasing demand (which had been strong in 1989) continued, but much more weakly, in 1990. Graduate starting salaries rose only slightly faster than general non-manual earnings. Some groups of women, on the other other hand, benefited from a number of legal decisions under equal pay and sex discrimination law (strengthened in 1986 at EC insistence) which coincided with supply shortages to produce some large pay rises. In November 1989 an equal pay for work of equal value claim awarded a Sainsbury's supermarket checkout operator equal pay with warehousemen, and in March 1990 both Sainsbury's and Marks & Spencer awarded rises of up to 22 per cent to checkout staff. However, women as a whole continued to lag far behind men: manual women earned 72 per cent of the male wage and non-manual women only 61 per cent; part time women (comprising the majority of women employees) fared worst of all, earning 64 per cent of the male manual and only 49 per cent of the male non-manual wage. A significant judgement in the European Court (Barber v GRE Assurance) established that men and women should have the same retiring age and benefit opportunities, with potentially enormous pension scheme cost implications.

Developments in trade unions. The 12 months of 1990 saw a continuation of the mergers and planned mergers among UK unions. The NUR and NUS merged to form the NURMTW; BETA and ACTT formed the BCTU; the Health Visitors Association merged with MSF; hosiery and footwear workers formed the NUKFAT; the National Union of Tailors and Garment Workers merged with the GMB; NGA and SOGAT moved closer towards merger; as did the UCW and NCU; while the largest merger of all, involving COHSE, NUPE and NALGO, moved a stage further after joint adoption of a merger blueprint in March 1991. This new union would become the UK's largest and the biggest public service union in western Europe. It would also facilitate merger of manual and staff pay scales in many areas. Several of these mergers were prompted by financial pressures, which also affected the large unions. The TGWU froze all recruitment of staff and sought to cut spending by 15 per cent. Less drastic cuts were also implemented in the GMB, NUPE, NALGO, MSF, and a number of other unions.

Divisions between unions over acceptance of the 'eighties' legislation largely ended in 1990. The autumn 1990 TUC and Labour Party conferences reached agreement on a package of labour law policies. These would leave in place most of 1980s' legislation, but allow: (i) some sympathy action where a direct working link could be shown between groups of workers; (ii) introduce a statutory minimum wage fixed initially at half male median earnings (£130 in 1990) but moving towards a two-thirds target; and (iii) introduce an employee's charter giving individual rights to, for instance, minimum health and safety standards, holidays and sick pay, irrespective of union membership. A 1991 TUC proposal to allow statutory recognition rights for unions (in steps depending on level of union membership) could also be endorsed in some form. Many of these issues, for example, pay policy, minimum wage and rights' legislation and collective union rights, were thought likely to figure in the coming general election campaign.

Summing up this complex picture, general themes emerge. The economic background worsened sharply in 1990 and unemployment rose, prompting a sharp cut in pay and earnings, although inflation also fell quickly; demand for managerial, professional and lower paid service workers (often part-time women) grew, while prospects for male manual workers worsened; flexibility and discretion grew, although not at the expense of national agreements; disputes continued, although in different forms and at a lower level; the corporatism and tripartism of the 'seventies largely disappeared as both unions and the Labour Party finally accepted the legislation of the 'eighties.

The key question at the end of 1990 is whether the "new industrial relations" (NIR) of the 1980s has had a lasting impact on employers and employees, or whether it has been a temporary phenomenon due to restrictive legislation and high unemployment. Many observers said the faltering of the "productivity miracle" of the early 1980s and upturn in strike activity show that fundamental attitudes were largely unchanged. A wide-ranging academic study concluded tentatively that: "there is reasonably good evidence of specific attitude changes of an *instrumental* or *interpersonal* nature. However there is little or no evidence to suggest that a variety of NIR practices has altered workers' largely negative view of management in general and of union – management relations ... ten years of 'new industrial relations' has so far made little impact on 'them and us' attitudes in industry". ("Them and us: Social psychology and the 'New Industrial Relations'", *British Journal of Industrial Relations* – John Kelly and Caroline Kelly, March 1991).

Trades Union Congress (TUC)

Address. Congress House, 23-28 Great Russell Street, London WC1B 3LS

Phone. 071-636 4030
Fax. 071-636 0632
Cable. TRADUNIC LONDON
Leadership. Norman Willis (general secretary; elected September 1984. Willis had been deputy general secretary since 1973 under Len Murray)
Membership. Membership was 8,404,827 (2,861,143 women) in 77 unions in 1990, a drop of 3,000,000 over seven years.
History and character. The TUC was founded in 1868, since when it has been the sole national trade union centre. There is also a Scottish Trades Union Congress (STUC), and unions may affiliate to both the STUC and TUC. Trade unions in Northern Ireland are represented by the Irish Congress of Trade Unions (Northern Ireland Committee), although most organized workers in Northern Ireland are members of British-based unions which are affiliated to the TUC. There is also a Wales Trade Union Council within the TUC. Regional committees within England help organize education, research and campaigning.

The TUC works to co-ordinate the activities of its affiliates and represents the trade union movement to government and internationally. Its member unions are autonomous, however, and the TUC does not instruct them or negotiate on their behalf. The TUC has no political affiliation, although the majority of its major affiliates support the Labour Party both morally and financially, and the trade unions also control a large majority of the votes at Labour Party conferences. Historically, the trade unions have constituted the core of the centre and centre-right of the Labour Party, and the party's own constituency members the left-wing. Trade unions sponsor over 100 Labour MPs, but full-time serving trade union officials do not sit as Members of Parliament (and consequently do not serve in government).

TUC leaders were prominent in the 1960s and 1970s as participants in the tripartite formulation of economy policy, and the TUC assumed great power and status. Since the election of a Conservative government in 1979, however, the TUC has been excluded from access to government policy-making. The main employer organization, the CBI, has also suffered a parallel, if lesser, diminution in influence.

Following the election of the Conservative government in 1979, the TUC refused to co-operate with its industrial relations plans. It responded to the 1980, and especially the 1982, *Employment Acts* with campaigns of mass opposition which did not, however, deter the government. When the *Trade Union Bill* 1984 appeared after the Conservatives were returned to power in the 1983 general election, the TUC's campaigning stance was based on the voluntarist tradition whereby British unions ordered their own affairs. Once the Bill became an Act of Parliament, TUC and union policy shifted to accommodation with the law. The TUC did not, for example, support the NUM's opposition to a ballot during the 1984/85 strike.

While most unions have, in practice, accepted the law's new provisions (ballots for instance are now commonplace) there is still an occasional defiance in the TUC stance. Its rejection of the *Employment Act* 1988 illustrates how it remains as opposed *in principle* to the government's approach as before. Yet Congress delegates voted in 1988 to withdraw from co-operation with its youth training proposals against recommendations from their own General Council and the Labour leader Mr Neil Kinnock. The Secretary of State, Mr Norman Fowler, swiftly retaliated by abolishing the Training Commission on which TUC representatives sat, one of the few surviving examples of tripartitism. Such defiance was not evident at the 1989 or 1990 Congresses.

Like the American unions, the TUC has resolved to examine its practices in order to improve efficiency and promote a positive image. A Special Review Body (SRB) was established at the 1987 Congress and through 1988 it examined recognition and inter-union relations (including single union and no-strike deals); the promotion of trade unionism; the extension of union organization; the expansion and development of services; and the role of the TUC.

The report of the SRB to the 1990 Congress emphasized its work in developing local recruitment projects in two pilot areas: Trafford Park in Manchester, and Docklands in London. Both had mixed success: some 900 new members were reported by autumn 1990 in Trafford Park; the Docklands campaign took place somewhat later and recruited fewer members. Nonetheless the concerted advertising and union co-operation during the campaigns worked well—the first time the TUC has directly been involved in such direct union recruitment activity. The SRB also reported on the launch in 1990 of a TUC credit card (sponsored by a famous footballer), which was being used by 6,250,000 members in 27 unions (70 per cent of TUC membership) at the time of the autumn Congress. A UNIONLAW scheme has also been launched, giving members some free legal advice, and further financial services are planned.

TUC structure changed at the 1989 Congress. Previously the 48 General Council seats had been filled very largely by male delegates from the large unions. The new system guaranteed between one and six seats in steps for unions with between 100,000 and 1,200,000 members; for unions with over 200,000 members, of whom at least 100,000 were women, at least one of their General Council delegates should be a woman. Unions with fewer than 100,000 members had eight seats between them, and a further four seats were reserved for women to be elected from all unions with up to 200,000 members. The 1990 General Council comprised 15 women (seven more than on the old 48-member body) and 39 men.

TUC finances have been hit hard by falling membership and the 1988 expulsion of the EETPU. A report to the 1990 Congress was followed in October by agreement to abolish nine committees and reorganize local TUCs (trades councils). The final package of cuts and affiliation fee increases aimed to reduce staff numbers through natural wastage by up to 15 per cent, and should remove the projected £2,000,000 deficit (which would otherwise have occurred in 1991) by 1992.

Affiliated organizations

Only affiliates with over 10,000 members are listed. Italic figures denote female members, where known within total membership.

1. **Amalgamated Engineering Union**, 110 Peckham Road, London SE15 5EL.
   Phone: (071) 703 4231. Fax: (071) 701 7862.
   General secretary: Gavin Laird.
   Membership: 741,647 (*105,022*).
   History and character: Affiliated to IMF, EMF and the Labour Party; publishes *AEU Journal* monthly; founded 1851. Long-established craft union which has recently broadened membership to unskilled and, with less success, white collar workers. Has separate sections for engineering, foundry, construction and staff. Successfully took selective strike action in 1990 to reduce the working week.

2. **Associated Society of Locomotive Engineers and Firemen**, 9 Arkwright Road, Hampstead, London NW3 6AB.
   Phone: (071) 431 0275. Fax: (071) 794 6406.
   General secretary: Derrick Fullick.
   Membership: 18,685 (*66*).
   History and character: Affiliated to Labour Party; founded in 1880. Represents train and underground drivers and others.

3. **Association of First Division Civil Servants**, 2 Caxton Street, London SWIH OQH.
   Phone: (071) 222 6242. Fax: (071) 727 6547.
   General secretary: Elizabeth Symons.
   Membership: 10,411 (*2,144*).
   History and character: Highly independent; founded in 1919; publishes *FDA News* monthly. Represents top civil servants.

4. **Association of University Teachers**, United House, 1 Pembridge Road, London W11 3HJ.
   Phone: (071) 221 4370. Fax: (071) 727 6547.
   General secretary: Diana Warwick.
   Membership: 31,807 (*4,771*)
   History and character: Affiliated to ETUCE; publishes *AUT Bulletin* monthly and *AUT WOMAN* thrice yearly; founded in 1917. Represents academic and related staff in university and equivalent institutions; has close links with NATFHE.

5. **Bakers, Food and Allied Workers' Union**, Stanborough House, Great North Road, Stanborough, Welwyn Garden City, Hertforshire AL8 7TA.
   Phone: (0707) 260150/9. Fax: (0707) 261570.

General secretary: Joe Marino.

Membership: 34,379 (*17,189*)

History and character: Affiliated to IUF, ECF and Labour Party; publishes *The Foodworker*; founded in 1861. Represents mainly manual and technician bakery workers; relatively decentralized and with a high ethnic minority and female membership.

6. **Banking, Insurance and Finance Union**, Sheffield House, 1b Amity Grove, Raynes Park, London SW20 OLG.

Phone: (081) 946 9151. Fax: (081) 879 3728.

General secretary: Leif Mills.

Membership: 170,481 (*94,392*)

History and character: Independent; publishes *BIFU Report* monthly; founded in 1946 on merger of English and Scottish early twentieth century unions. Has grown steadily in '70s and '80s and diversified membership into expanding financial services sector. Sector-, occupational- and company-based structure has enable BIFU to recruit a wide range of staff, over half women.

7. **British Actors' Equity Association**, 8 Harley Street, London WIN 2AB.

Phone: (071) 637 9311. Fax: (071) 580 0970.

General secretary: Peter Plouviez.

Membership: 44,269 (*21,842*)

History and character: Affiliated to IFA, CEU and PA; publishes *Equity Journal* monthly. Early twentieth century union which maintains strong closed shop; membership gives professional status.

8. **Broadcasting and Cinematograph Technicians Union**, 181–185 Wardour Street, London WIV 4B.

Phone: (071) 439 7585. Fax: (071) 434 3974.

General secretaries: Tony Hearn; Alan Sapper.

Membership: 61,695 (*20,839*).

History and character: Affiliated to WFTU, ICFTU and Labour Party; publishes *Film & Television Technician* and *BETA News*. Formed in 1991 on merger of two early mid- twentieth century unions representing private sector and BBC film technical and production staff; mainly London-based and facing derecognition, introduction of individual contracts and casualization.

9. **Ceramic and Allied Trades Union**, Hillcrest House, Garth Street, Hanley, Stoke-on-Trent ST1 2AB.

Phone: (0782) 272755.

General secretary: Alf Clowes.

Membership: 29,872 (*13,704*).

History and character: Affiliated to Labour Party; founded in 1827. Represents pottery workers, almost all in Staffordshire.

10. **Civil and Public Services Association**, 160 Falcon Road, London SW11 2LN.

Phone: (071) 924 2727.

General secretary: John Ellis.

Membership: 127,976 (*90,802*).

History and character: Publishes *Red Tape* monthly. Formed in 1969 from merger with smaller, early twentieth century Civil Service Clerks Unions. Centralized, but now devolving, union representing middle and lower level civil service staff and clerical officers.

11. **Communication Managers' Association**, Hughes House, Ruscombe Road, Twyford, Reading, Berkshire.

Phone: (0734) 342300. Fax: (0734) 342087.

General secretary: Terry Doogan.

Membership: 19,229 (*3,462*).

History and character: Affiliated to PTTI; publishes *New Management* monthly. Represents post office managers.

12. **Confederation of Health Service Employees**, Glen House, High Street, Banstead, Surrey SM7 2LH.
    Phone: (0737) 353322. Fax: (0737) 370079.
    General secretary: Hector MacKenzie.
    Membership: 209,461 (*166,417*).
    History and character: Affiliated to Labour Party; publishes *Health Services* monthly; founded early twentieth century. Represents nursing and paramedical staff, mainly in mental institutions; has completed first stage of merger with NALGO and NUPE.

13. **Educational Institute of Scotland**, 46 Moray Place, Edinburgh EH3 6BH.
    Phone: (031) 225 6244. Fax: (031) 220 3151.
    General secretary: Jim Martin.
    Membership: 45,571.
    History and character: Affiliated to ETUCE and WCOTP; publishes The *Scottish Educational Journal*; founded in 1847, unusually with a prestigious royal charter. Represents all teachers, except in universities in Scotland; well organized and influential.

14. **Engineers' and Managers' Association**, Station House, Fox Lane North, Chertsey, Surrey KT16 9HW.
    Phone: (0932) 564131. Fax: 0932(567707.)
    General secretary: Tony Cooper.
    Membership: 41,079 (*415*).
    History and character: Affiliated to FIET; publishes *Electrical and Power Engineer*. Formed in 1976 as federation of engineering and managers' unions, although dominated by the Electrical and Power Engineers Association.

15. **Fire Brigades Union**, Bradley House, 68 Coombe Road, Kingston-upon-Thames, Surrey KT2 7AE.
    Phone: (081) 541 1765. Fax: (081) 546 5187.
    General secretary: Ken Cameron.
    Membership: 49,121 (*1,002*).
    History and character: Affiliated to PSI and Labour Party; publishes *Firefighter* monthly; founded 1918. Represents almost all firefighters and clerical staff and many managers; radical and well organized.

16. **Furniture, Timber and Allied Trades Union**, 'Fairfields', Roe Green, Kingsbury, London NW9 0PT.
    Phone: (081) 204 0273. Fax: (081) 204 3476.
    General secretary: Colin Christopher.
    Membership: 42,900. (5,109).
    History and character: Affiliated to Labour Party; publishes *FTAT Record* monthly; founded mid-nineteenth century. Represents both manual and craft workers, declining and likely to merge.

17. **GMB**, 22/24 Worple Road, Wimbledon, London SW19 4DD.
    Phone: (081) 947 3131. Fax: (081) 944 6552.
    General secretary: John Edmonds.
    Membership: 823,176 (267,984).
    History and character: Affiliated to FIET, ICFTU and Labour Party; publishes *GMB Journal* and *ACCESS* monthly and wide range of pamphlets, etc. Founded 1924 upon merger of three late ninteenth century general unions. Has a high profile centrist position and strongly advocates modernizing unions and bargaining; it is now developing a stronger industrial or trade group structure to absorb recent major craft and staff union mergers; the latter forming the "APEX Partnership" section.

18. **Inland Revenue Staff Federation**, Douglas Houghton House, 231 Vauxhall Bridge Road, London SW1V 1EH.
    Phone: (071) 834 8254. Fax: (071) 630 6258.
    General secretary: Clive Brooke.
    Membership: 51,171 (31,726).

History and character: Affiliated to PSI; publishes *Assessment* quarterly. Formed 1936 from merger of three (formerly 20 small) tax clerks' unions.

19. **Institution of Professionals, Managers and Specialists**, 75–79 York Road, London SE1 7AQ.
Phone: (071) 928 9951. Fax: (071) 928 5996.
General secretary: Bill Brett.
Membership: 89,730 (10,026).
History and character: Founded in 1919 as union for middle ranking professional and scientific civil servants; changed name to IPMS 1989 as privatization had moved many members to private sector.

20. **Iron and Steel Trades Confederation**, Swinton House, 324 Gray's Inn Road, London WCIX 8DD.
Phone: (071) 837 6691. Fax: (071) 278 8378.
General secretary: Roy Evans.
Membership: 65,000 (2,623).
History and character: Affiliated to EMF, IMF, ICFTU and Labour Party; publishes *Phoenix* quarterly, founded mid-nineteenth century. Represents craft, technician and manual metal-workers. Merged with the Wire Workers in 1991.

21. **Manufacturing Science Finance**, Park House, 64–66 Wandsworth Common-North side, London SW18 2JH.
Phone: (081) 871 2100. Fax: (081) 877 1160.
Membership: 668,901 (*141,763*).
General secretary: Roger Lyons.
History and character: Affiliated to ICFTU and Labour Party; publishes *MSF Journal* monthly. Formed 1988 from merger of two major late-nineteenth century unions; TASS, representing engineering technicians and management, and ASTMS, representing wide range of finance and manufacturing white collar staff. Has radical, modern and European perspective; has absorbed many small staff unions and associations, successfully recruiting despite some derecognition.

22. **Musician's Union**, 60–62 Clapham Road, London SW9 OJJ.
Phone: (071) 582 5566. Fax: (071) 582 9805.
General secretary: Dennis Scard.
Membership: 40,762 (*7,981*).
History and character: Affiliated to FIM and Labour Party; publishes *Musician* quarterly; founded 1921. Now the second largest musicians' union in the world, representing all professional musicians; as with Equity, membership is proof of professional competence.

23. **National and Local Government Officers' Association**, 1 Mabledon Place, London WCIH 9AJ.
Phone: (071) 388 2366. Fax: (071) 387 6692.
General secretary: Alan Jinkinson.
Membership: 750,502 (*398,660*).
History and character: Affiliated to PSI and EULAS; publishes *Public Service* monthly, *NALGO News* and wide range of booklets, etc; founded 1905. Now represents majority of local authority and public utility clerical, specialist and managerial staff. Faced with privatization and loss of status the union has become more radical, although also provides many professional services; a highly centralized organization, it is changing structure as it merges with NUPE and COHSE to become the largest public service union in western Europe.

24. **National Association of School Masters/Union of Women Teachers**, 22 Upper Brook Street, London W1Y 1PD.
Phone: (071) 629 3916/7. Fax: (071) 409 1193.
General secretary: Nigel de Gruchy.
Membership: 118,230 (*56,068*).
History and character: Affiliated to ETUCE and ICFTU; publishes *Schoolmaster and Career Teacher*. Formed 1975 on merger of early-twentieth century men and mid-20th century women teachers' unions; similar to NUT.

25. **National Association of Teachers in Further and Higher Education**, 27 Britannia Street, London WC1X 9JP.
Phone: (071) 837 3636. Fax: (071) 837 4403.
General secretary: Geoff Woolf.
Membership: 80,981 (*27,670*).
History and character: Affiliated to WCTOP; publishes *NATFHE Journal* monthly and a professional triennial journal; formed 1976 from two smaller mid-twentieth century teacher unions. Organized in two sections, representing lecturers in higher and further education.

26. **National Communications Union**, Greystoke House, 150 Brunswick Road, London W5 1AW.
Phone: (081) 998 2981. Fax: (081) 991 1410.
General secretary: Tony Young.
Membership: 157,060 (31,579).
History and character: Affiliated to Labour Party; publishes *NCU Journal* monthly; formed 1985 from merger of clerical and engineering telephone workers. Membership declining following privatization and competition in telecommunications industry.

27. **National Graphical Association (1982)**, Graphic House, 63–67 Bromham Road, Bedford, Bedfordshire MK40 2AG.
Phone: (0234) 351521. Fax: (0234) 270580.
General secretary: Tony Dubbins.
Membership: 125,003 (*7,970*).
History and character: Affiliated to Labour Party; publishes *Print* monthly; founded 1849. Long standing craft printworkers' union which has recently broadened membership to include clerical and semi-skilled workers; merger with SOGAT (82) planned for 1992.

28. **National Union of Civil and Public Servants**, 124–130 Southwark Street, London SE1 OTU.
Phone: (071) 928 9671. Fax: (071) 928 0751.
General secretary: Leslie Christie.
Membership: 115,606 (*41,723*).
History and character: Affiliated to PSI and PTTI; formed in 1988 from merger of two early-twentieth century civil service unions. Represents specialist, middle and clerical ranks.

29. **National Union of Knitwear, Footwear and Apparel Trades,** The Grange, Earls Barton, Northampton NN6 OJH.
Phone: (0604) 810326. Fax: (0604) 812496.
General secretary: George Browett.
Membership: 68,049 (*42,834*).
History and character: Affiliated to ICFTU, TGLWF and Labour Party; publishes monthly journal; formed from a merger in 1991 between two late-nineteenth century footwear and clothing unions. Branch-based with little regional structure; represents manual and craft workers, largely women, but declining as industry contracts.

30. **National Union of Journalists**, Acorn House, 314–320 Gray's Inn Road, London WC1X 8DP.
Phone: (071) 278 7916. Fax: (071) 837 8143.
General secretary: Steve Turner.
Membership: 30,055 (*9,856*).
History and character: Publishes *The Journalist* monthly; founded 1907. Represents print, television and radio journalists, although membership is declining after derecognition and introduction of individual contracts in some areas.

31. **National Union of Marine, Aviation and Shipping Transport Officers**, Oceanair House, 750–760 High Road, Leytonstone, London E11 3BB.
Phone: (081) 989 6677. Fax: (081) 530 1015.
General secretary: John Newman.
Membership: 18,459 (231).
History and character: Affiliated to the ITF; publishes *The Telegraph* monthly. Represents engineers and officers though membership is declining with shrinkage of UK merchant fleet.

32. **National Union of Mineworkers**, Holly Street, Sheffield S1 2GT.
Phone: (0742) 766900. Fax: (0742) 766400.
President: Arthur Scargill.
Membership: 58,861.
History and character: Affiliated to IMO and Labour Party; publishes *The Miner* monthly; emerged in 1945, on nationalization, out of a federation of regional bodies dating from the mid-nineteenth century. Still highly regionalized, although dominated by Yorkshire; membership has halved as widespread pit closures followed defeat in traumatic 1984–85 strike.

33. **National Union of Public Employees**, Civic House, 20 Grand Depot Road, Woolwich, London SE18 6SF.
Phone: (081) 854 2244. Fax: (081) 316 7770.
General secretary: Rodney Bickerstaffe.
Membership: 604,912 (*453,684*).
History and character: Affiliated to the Labour Party; publishes *NUPE Journal* monthly and a wide range of highly professional leaflets, packs, booklets, etc. Founded 1888, reorganized 1928; grew rapidly in the 'sixties and 'seventies partly at the expense of the GMB with which there is longstanding rivalry. A radical union comprising low-paid, predominantly female, manual workers in health, utilities, education and local government. Has campaigned hard and successfully for adoption of statutory minimum wage policy; has completed first stage of merger with COHSE and NALGO.

34. **National Union of Rail, Maritime and Transport Workers**, Unity House, Euston Road, London NW1 2BL.
Phone: (071) 387 4771. Fax: (071) 387 4123.
General secretary: Jimmy Knapp.
Membership: 123,308 (*6,198*).
History and character: Affiliated to ITF and Labour Party; publishes *The Seamen* and *Transport Review*; formed in 1990 on merger of seamen's and rail unions, each dating from late-nineteenth century. Highly centralized, but reorganizing with regionalization and privatization of parts of British Rail; seamen's section declining.

35. **National Union of Tailors and Garment Workers**, 16 Charles Square, London N1 6HP.
Phone: (071) 251 9406.
General secretary: Alec Smith
Membership: 73,122 (*66,541*).
History and character: Affiliated to Labour Party; publishes *The Garment Worker* monthly; founded 1939 on merger of several mid-nineteenth century bodies. Over 90 per cent female membership, low-paid and declining; based in East Midlands.

36. **National Union of Teachers**, Hamilton House, Mabledon Place, London WC1H 9BD.
Phone: (071) 388 6191. Fax: (071) 387 8458.
General secretary: Doug McAvoy.
Membership: 171,990 (*123,287*).
History and character: Affiliated to ETUCE, ICFTU and WCTOP; publishes *The Teacher* weekly and several books, professional guides, etc; founded 1870, affiliated to TUC in 1970. Represents all teachers; traditionnally the least moderate of teaching unions but has lost members heavily to rivals AMMA and NAS/UWT.

37. **Prison Officers' Association**, Cronin House, 245 Church Street, Edmonton, London N9 9HW.
Phone: (081) 803 0255. Fax: (081) 803 1761.
General secretary: David Evans.
Membership: 24,251 (*1,831*).
History and character: Founded 1919 although not recognized until 1939; publishes *Gatelodge* bi-monthly; represents almost all prison officers.

38. **Society of Graphical and Allied Trades '82**, Sogat House, 274–288 London Road, Hadleigh, Benfleet, Essex SS7 2DE.
Phone: (0702) 554 111. Fax: (0702) 559737.

General secretary: Brenda Dean.

Membership: 176,144 (*49,849*).

History and character: Affiliated to ICEF, FIET and Labour Party; publishes *SOGAT Journal* monthly; founded 1982 through merger of two large print unions each deriving from late-nineteenth century. Strong craft tradition, although new technology creating rapid change; shortly to merge with NGA ('82).

39. **Society of Telecom Executives**, 1 Park Road, Teddington, Middlesex TW11 OAR.

Phone: (081) 943 5181. Fax: (081) 943 2532.

General secretary: Simon Petch.

Membership: 29,961 (*3,486*).

History and character: Founded 1912; represents middle and senior management in British Telecom.

40. **Transport and General Workers' Union**, Transport House, Smith Square, Westminster, London SW1P 3JB.

Phone: (071) 828 7788. Fax: (071) 630 5861.

General secretary: Ron Todd.

Membership: 1,270,776 (*207,229*).

History and character: Immensely influential and important union. Affiliated to Labour Party, ICFTU, PSI; publishes *The Record* monthly, *The Landworker* monthly, *Highway* quarterly (for drivers), *ACTS Magazine* bi-monthly (for members in ACTS staff section). Founded 1922 on merger of three large late-nineteenth century dock, transport and general unions; represents employees in almost every sector and at every level, although predominantly unskilled and semi-skilled in manufacturing and public services. Traditionally militant and with a strong emphasis on local shop steward organization; facing severe cuts as membership declines in early 'eighties was not reversed in late 'eighties, despite major recruitment drive among low-paid, part-time and women workers.

41. **Transport Salaried Staffs' Association**, Walkden House, 10 Melton Street, London NW1 2EJ.

Phone: (071) 387 2101.

General secretary: Richard Rosser.

Membership: 36,052 (*8,761*).

History and character: Affiliated to Labour Party; publishes *TSSA Journal* monthly; founded 1892. Represents middle and some senior British Rail staff.

42. **Union of Communication Workers**, UCW House, Crescent Lane, Clapham, London SW4 9RN.

Phone: (071) 622 9977. Fax: (071) 720 6853.

General secretary: Alan Tuffin.

Membership: 202,500 (*30,104*).

History and character: Affiliated to PTTI and Labour Party; publishes *The Post*; founded 1921 from mergers of smaller late-nineteenth/early-twentieth century organizations. Highly central-ized but seeking mergers and re-organization as sections of the Post Office move into the private sector.

43. **Union of Construction, Allied Trades and Technicians**, UCATT House, 177 Abbeville Road, London SW4 9RL.

Phone: (071) 622 2442. Fax: (071) 720 4081.

General secretary: Albert Williams.

Membership: 258,342 (2,578).

History and character: Affiliated to Labour Party; publishes *Viewpoint* monthly; founded 1971 on merger of several craft building unions each dating from early-nineteenth century. Represents all building workers but mainly semi-skilled and skilled.

44. **Union of Shop, Distributive and Allied Workers**, Oakley, 188 Wilmslow Road, Fallowfield, Manchester M14 6LJ.

Phone: (061) 224 2804. Fax: (061) 257 2566.

General secretary: Garfield Davies.

Membership: 375,891 (228,543).

History and character: Affiliated to Labour Party; publishes *Dawn* monthly; founded 1974 on merger of two early-twentieth century unions. Represents shopworkers and some dairy and food workers; high proportion of low-paid, women, part-time and ethnic minority members; campaigned successfully against Sunday trading; has strong women's and race relations committees.

45. **United Road Transport Union**, 76 High Lane, Chorlton-cum-Hardy, Manchester M21 1FD.
Phone: (061) 881 6245. Fax: (061) 862 9127.
General secretary: Frank Griffin.
Membership: 20,372 (*1,410*).
History and character: Affiliated to ITF, IUFW; publishes *Wheels*, grew out of late-nineteenth century carters' union. Now represents road haulage drivers.

Other organizations

1. **General Federation of Trade Unions**, Central House, Upper Woburn Place, London WC1H 0HY.
Phone: (071) 388 0852. Fax: (071) 383 0820.
General secretary: Peter Potts.
History and character: Founded 1899; has 31 unions affiliated. None of these unions has more than 100,000 members and many are locally based organizations with far fewer; to them the GFTU provides a central service of information, research, education (through its Educational Trust) and dispute benefit. The GFTU is not a rival to the TUC and many of its members are also TUC affiliates; it has one regular publication; *Federation News*, seasonally.

2. **Scottish Trades Union Congress (STUC)**, Middleton House, 16 Woodlands Terrace, Glasgow G3 6DF.
Phone: (041) 332 4946. Fax: (041) 332 4649.
General secretary: Campbell Christie.
History and character: STUC is separate from, but has reciprocal arrangements with the TUC. Occupies position to left of the labour movement and the TUC; nevertheless affiliates tend to correspond between the two bodies except (as in the case of NUT and EIS) where there is a clear national organizing boundary.

The Wales TUC functions in the same way as an English region of the TUC.

Significant organizations not affiliated to the TUC

1. **Assistant Masters and Mistresses Association**, 7 Northumberland Street, London WC2 5DA.
Phone: (071) 930 6441. Fax: (071) 930 1359.
General secretaries: Peter Smith; Joyce Baird.
Membership: 135,000.
History and character: Founded 1978 through merger of separate men's and women's teachers' unions; publishes *Report* monthly. Originating in non-state schools; cautious on strike action and took many members from main teacher unions during mid-'eighties period of strikes.

2. **Barclays Group Staff Union**, Oathall Road, Haywards Heath, West Sussex RH16 3DG.
Phone: (0444) 458811. Fax: (0444) 416248.
Contact: W.E. Gale.
History and character: Together with Lloyds Bank Group Staff Union and Nat West Staff Association (*see below*), one of the three major bank staff associations which have over 150,000 members between them. They came together to form the clearing Bank Union (*see below*) when the banks agreed to negotiate collectively. However in 1986 negotiations reverted to the individual banks.

3. **Clearing Bank Union**, Tuition House, 27–37 St Georges Road, Wimbledon, London SW19 4EU.
Phone: (081) 879 3766.

Contact: Margaret Platt.

History and character: Formed when the banks agreed to negotiate collectively, but since 1986 when individual banks again dealt with their own pay deals, the CBU has lost its major role.

4. **Lloyds Bank Group Staff Union**, Jansel House, 648 Hitchin Road, Luton, Belfordshire LU2 7XH.
Phone: (0582) 25433
Contact: I.K. Patridge.
Membership: *See* Barclays Group Staff Union *above*.

5. **Nat West Staff Association**, 8–10 Dean Park Crescent, Bournemouth BH1 1HH.
Phone: (0202) 293616. Fax: (0202) 555673.
Contact: C. Carthy.
Membership: *See* Barclays Group Staff Union *above*.

6. **Electrical, Electronic, Telecommunications and Plumbing Union (EETPU)**, Hayes Court, West Common Road, Bromley, Kent BR2 7AU.
Phone: (081) 462 7755. Fax: (081) 462 4959.
General secretary: Eric Hammond.
Membership: 329,914.
History and character: Expelled from TUC in 1961 following ballot-rigging scandal involving communists; expelled again in September 1988 for signing single-union recognition agreements in defiance of TUC instructions. Electrical and Plumbing Industries Union formed in 1988 by dissident EETPU members has, however, had little success in winning over EETPU members. EETPU, which prides itself on its training facilities, has set up a small federation of some 16 small non-TUC unions and staff associations but this has not emerged as a serious rival to the TUC.

7. **National Association of Head Teachers**, 1 Heath Square, Boltro Road, Haywards Heath, RH 16 1BL.
Phone: (0444) 458133. Fax: (0444) 416326.
General secretary: David Hart.
Membership: 34,000.
History and character: Affiliated to ESMA, IFTA, WCTOP; founded 1897; publishes *Head Teachers Review* quarterly. Represents heads and deputies; emphasizes professionalism and has set up training/consultancy company.

8. **Professional Association of Teachers**, St. James's Court, Friar Gate, Derby DE1 1EZ.
Phone: (0332) 372337. Fax: (0332) 290310/292431.
General secretary: Peter Dawson.
Membership: 39,000.
History and character: Publishes *Professional Teacher*; founded 1970 as no-strike alternative to mainstream teacher unions; highly centralized; stresses professionalism.

9. **Royal College of Nursing of the United Kingdom (RCN)**, 20 Cavendish Square, London W1.
Phone: (071) 409 3333. Fax: (071) 355 1379.
General secretary: Christine Hancock.
Membership: 290,000.
History and character: Publishes *The Nursing Standard* weekly. World's largest professional union for nurses; in 1988 a members' ballot reaffirmed the College's traditional no-strike stance. Highly independent; after spectacular growth in the 'eighties membership is levelling off and RCN is consolidating some professional services.

10. **Union of Democratic Mineworkers**, the Sycamores, Moor Road, Bestwood, Nottingham NG6 8UE.
Phone: (0602) 763468.
Contact: J.P. Liptrott.
History and character: Set up in 1985 as a moderate breakaway from NUM; membership not published but probably 10,000 (approx); largely based in Nottingham.

BERMUDA

Capital: Hamilton

Population: 56,000
(1988)

Political system. Bermuda is a British dependency with a system of internal self-government introduced in 1968 and a bicameral parliament. The government has since 1968 been formed by the multiracial United Bermuda Party while the opposition has been formed by the predominantly black Progressive Labour Party.

Economy. Economically Bermuda is almost wholly dependent on receipts from tourism, which account for about a quarter of the country's labour force, and from the growing (offshore) financial services sector. However, tourism is heavily dependent upon economic conditions in the United States and Canada, and the banking sector also has faced strong competition from the increasingly important US offshore market. There is little agriculture and only a small manufacturing sector.

System of Industrial Relations. As a dependency Bermuda is not separately represented at the ILO.

Trade unionism. The first trade union in Bermuda, the Bermuda Workers' Union (later Association) was founded among workers on US bases in 1943 during World War II. About one-third of the 35,244 workforce is organized in the seven registered unions. The union with the largest membership on the island is the Bermuda Industrial Union (BIU) with 6,000 paid up members. Other unions are the Bermuda Public Service Association (BPSA), the Amalgamated Bermuda Union of Teachers (ABUT), the Firemen's Association, the Musician's Union and the Prison Officers' Association. Each of these unions have collective agreements signed with various employers throughout the island and in some 30 enterprises.

Bermuda Industrial Union (BIU)

Address. 49 Union Square, Hamilton HM 12
Phone. 809-292-0044
Telex. BERINDUN
Leadership. Ottiwell Simmons (president); Helena "Molly" Burgess (general secretary)
Membership. 6,000.
History and character. The BIU was founded in 1946. Its founding president was the late Dr. E.F. Gordon. The union draws its membership from some 25 industries and enterprises. There are some 75 employers, including the Government who have signed collective bargaining agreements with the union. There are many foreign workers among the union's membership. The BIU prides itself with a policy of "out of many workers—one membership". The Union operates a credit union, a taxi co-op, a fuel station, a movie theatre and it initiated the Bermuda Workers Co-operative Society, a successful supermarket. The BIU, while politically autonomous, generally supports the Bermuda Progressive Labour Party and relies on the PLP to support the union on all social legislation and other political issues. The centrist National Liberal Party (formed August 1985) has made overtures to the BIU for its support.
Publication. The Worker's Voice (fortnightly).
International affiliations. ICFTU, CCL, ITF, IFBWW.

Bermuda Public Services Association (BPSA)

Address. P.O. Box 763, Hamilton HMCX
Phone. 809-2926985/2926484.
Telex. BEPSA.
Fax. 809-2921149
Leadership. Stephen W. Emery (president); Eugene Blakeney (general secretary)

Membership. 2,240.

History and character. The Bermuda Civil Service Association was formed in 1952, becoming a registered trade union under the 1946 Trade Union Act in 1966. The present name was adopted in 1971. The membership comprises civil servants, hospital employees, telephone company clerical employees, cable and wireless employees, city hall workers, private sector pharmacists and staff employed by the Bermuda College.

Publication. Feedback (monthly).

International affiliations. Public Services International (PSI); Postal, Telegraph and Telephone International (PTTI); Caribbean Public Services Association (CPSA).

FALKLAND ISLANDS

Capital: Port Stanley   **Population: 1,900**

Political system. The Falkland Islands were heavily occupied by British troops following the Argentine invasion and war of 1982. The islands have no political parties, but have Legislative and Executive Councils.

Economy. Sheep are the mainstay of the economy, but the British government has sought since 1982 to encourage diversification.

Trade unionism. There is one general union, the Falkland Islands General Employees' Union, founded in 1943.

Falkland Islands General Employees' Union (FIGEU)

Address. Ross Road, Port Stanley

Phone. 21151

Leadership. Gavin Short (chairman); Raymond Robson (vice-chairman); Mary Jennings (secretary-treasurer)

Membership. 150.

History and character. Formed on Oct. 28, 1943. The recent decrease in membership has been due entirely to the large sheep farms being sub-divided and consequently employees' buying their own farms and subsequent reduction of labour.

International affiliation. ICFTU.

HONG KONG

Capital: Victoria   **Population: 5,674,000**
                                                                                    (1988)

Political system. Under the agreement of September 1984 (ratified in May 1985), Hong Kong is due to revert to China in 1997; meanwhile the administration of the colony lies with the Governor (appointed by the United Kingdom government) and with the appointed executive council and a partially elective legislative council. There are no political parties as such.

Economy. In 1989 the Hong Kong workforce had 2,800,000 people, of whom 23.7 per cent were in manufacturing, 32.5 per cent were in wholesale and retail trades, restaurants and hotels, 18.6 per cent were in social and personal services, 9 per cent in transport, storage and communications, 8 per cent in finance and 7.9 per cent in construction. The economy is operating at full capacity and unemployment is little more than 1 per cent. With labour shortages in prospect the unions may be able to overcome their traditional weakness.

System of industrial relations. Hong Kong is not a member of the ILO in its own right and so the UK makes declarations on its behalf concerning the various conventions. By 1989 Hong Kong had applied 29 of these in full and 18 others with modifications and according to the China–UK agreement these will continue to apply after the territory reverts to Chinese sovereignty from which time it will participate in the ILO as an associate member. The Basic Law will include current employment rights and the right to strike. A 1990 Employment Ordinance extended the rather limited protection of the employment laws to non-manual workers.

However, in a memorandum submitted to the Basic Laws Drafting Committee the ICFTU argued that without a representative government existing in Hong Kong before the transfer of sovereignty to China there was a risk to the Dependency's trade unions. The Legislative Council, argued the Memorandum, was mostly drawn from business circles with little union representation and thus unions would have little opportunity to influence the course of events. The ICFTU expressed particular concern over those ILO Conventions not ratified by China and which therefore could not be the subject of complaint for non-fulfilment; it called for the Basic Law to spell out union rights to join international bodies without prior approval of the authorities. At an August 1990 conference held in Hong Kong, the ICFTU denounced "the alliance between the Chinese communist authorities and the business community which, for different reasons, are in league against the independent trade union movement".

Hong Kong has a Labour Advisory Board whose membership, like that of the Legislative Council, is determined on a " one union one vote" rule, a device which encourages fragmentation while spreading representation.

Trade unionism first appeared early in the twentieth century, although it had to wait until 1948 to achieve legal status. Union density in Hong Kong was 15.6 per cent in 1989, when there were 472 registered trade unions covering 437,302 workers. For many years Hong Kong trades unionism was clearly divided between the Hong Kong and Kowloon Trade Union Council (HKTUC) and the Hong Kong Federation of Trade Unions (HKFTU), each founded in the aftermath of legalization. The HKTUC is allied to the (Taiwanese) Chinese Federation of Labour and has a Taiwanese orientation. Its membership is small. The larger HKFTU has a China orientation and much of its activity is geared towards providing services. Apart from these two centres there is a large number of independent unions. A growing number of these are affiliated to a new centre, the CTU, whose influence has grown rapidly since 1989.

Independent unions are mostly found in the civil service and service industries and they have grown at the expense of the other two centres. The total number of independent unions was last estimated at 278 and their membership at 190,000.

Altogether Hong Kong's unions had pushed up density to nearly 16 per cent by the end of 1989, but there are signs that the CTU is gaining ground. Both CTU and HKTUC delegates attended an APRO/ICFTU conference in Hong Kong in August 1990.

492

Hong Kong Federation of Trade Unions (HKFTU)

Address. 3rd Floor, 142 Lockhart Road

Membership. 175,200 workers organized in 81 unions with principal support in the shipyards, textile mills, public transport and public utilities.

History and character. The HKFTU was founded in 1948 and supports China. It resembles the Chinese model of trade unionism in its orientation towards service provision. In 1990 the HKFTU began to develop these services, building a new trade union school and offering goods from its own shop at reduced prices to members. The rival HKTUC charges that it is in receipt of increased aid from China and that Hong Kong employers are under pressure to grant it sole negotiating rights.

Hong Kong and Kowloon Trades Union Council (HKTUC)

Address. Labour Building, 11 Chang Sha Street, Mongkok, Kowloon

Phone. (3) 845150; 850743

Telex. 36866 PPIHK HX

Fax. 770 5396

Cable. TRACOUNCIL HONGKONG

Leadership. Tong Woon Fai (president); Liew Nan Kiem (general secretary).

Membership. 17,100 in 1989, organized in 71 unions with chief strength in the catering and building trades.

International affiliation. ICFTU.

Independent unions

Confederation of Trade Unions of Hong Kong (CTU)

Leadership. Lee Cheuk-Yan

Membership. Claims over 90,000 members.

History and character. Established in response to the Tianamen Square events and the approach of transfer of sovereignty to China. The CTU prioritizes the defence of workers' rights and trade union recognition. In 1990 the CTU set itself the target of increasing membership by 80,000 in order to overtake that of the HKFTU and establish a strong base before transfer to China. It boycotted the 1990 Asian Games in China.

Affiliated unions and structure. Unions in textiles, buses and public services (President Michael Siu Yin-ying); teachers (President Szeto Wa).

International affiliations. Is supported by the ICFTU.

TURKS AND CAICOS ISLANDS

Capital: Cockburn Town   Population: 7,900

Political system. The Turks and Caicos Islands have a Governor representing the British Monarch and an Executive Council and a partially elective Legislative Council. The centre-left People's Democratic Movement is currently in power.

Economy. Hitherto one of the least developed economies in the Commonwealth Caribbean territories, the Turks and Caicos Island's economy has diversified in the 1980s to include tourism and offshore financial services.

System of industrial relations. As a dependent territory the Turks and Caicos Islands are not members of the ILO.

Trade unionism. One organization has been reported, the St George's Industrial Trade Union (address, Cockburn Harbour, South Caicos; president, James Sylvester Williams), founded in 1942 and with about 250 members.

United States of America

Capital: Washington **Population: 248,231,030**
(1989)

Political system. The United States of America is a federal republic of 50 states with an executive President and a bicameral legislature (Congress). Since 1980, the Presidential elections have been won by the Republicans while Congress generally had a Democrat majority.

Economy. As the world's leading economic power, the USA plays a key role in influencing the international trading and monetary environment and the formation of economic policy in other non-communist states. It is self-sufficient in most raw materials except petroleum (of which it is nevertheless one of the world's largest producers). In recent years there has been a shift in emphasis from heavy industry to "high technology" with a corresponding decline in the proportion of manufacturing employment to total employment. The USA has the lowest proportional tax receipts and lowest public expenditure of any major OECD country except Japan.

Despite structural balance of payments problems and a chronic budget deficit, the United States experienced seven continuous years of growth to the end of the 1980s. Yet at the end of 1989 there were 6,700,000 workers unemployed in the United States, many of them casualties of the continued relative decline of manufacturing. Nevertheless, unemployment had been over 6 per cent in 1987, and the average figure for 1990 was a bare 5 per cent. Of those in work, the "contingent" (i.e. flexible) section is computed to have expanded by between 17 and 23 per cent: its size in 1987 is estimated at between 29 and 35,000,000.

System of industrial relations. The United States has ratified neither ILO Convention No. 87 (Freedom of Association and Protection of the Right to Organize, 1948) nor Convention No. 98 (Right to Organize and Collective Bargaining, 1949).

The United States withdrew from the ILO in 1977, with the support of the AFL-CIO, stating that the ILO had "in recent years increasingly disregarded its basic principles and procedures. There are four particularly alarming trends. They are the selective application of human rights; the denial of due process; the introduction of political considerations outside the ILO's mandate; and the erosion of the principle of tripartite representation". According to the US Chamber of Commerce, a "coalition of communist and Third World countries" within the ILO "repeatedly allowed violations of these conventions in their own countries while strongly condemning such violations in non-communist countries". The United States returned to membership in 1980, President Carter citing the greater attention given by the ILO since US withdrawal to human rights questions, reinforcement of due process, a reduction in "politicization", and a strengthening of tripartism.

After a gap of 35 years, the United States again ratified an ILO Convention in February 1988 when the Senate approved Tripartite Consultations to promote the Implementation of International Labour Standards, 1976 (No. 144) and the Merchant Shipping (Minimum Standards) Convention, 1976 (No. 147). These ratifications bring the number endorsed by the USA to nine and there is a consensus that more will now follow.

The General Accounting Office of the Labour Department recorded a 250 per cent increase in offences against the Child Labour laws between 1983 and 1989, with 24,000 violations in the latter year alone. The ILO has urged the United States to ratify its *Convention on Child Labour*.

Unions win the right to bargain collectively (and to represent all the workers) in a workplace by securing a majority of votes in an election acceptable to the National Labour Relations Board (NLRB). A majority of contracts in the private sector provides for a union shop or agency shop requiring all workers to pay union dues (although this is illegal in some states). Under the *Taft-Hartley* Act, persons defined as "supervisors" may join unions, but do not enjoy the right to collective bargaining. Other professional workers are permitted to engage in collective bargaining, but a collective bargaining unit may not include both professional and non-professional staff unless a majority of the professional staff votes for inclusion. Federal employees were extended the right to join unions in 1962, and about 25–30 per cent are now dues-paying union members (and 60 per cent are represented by unions). All federal employement is open shop; unions cannot negotiate pay, which is determined by a special mechanism, and federal employees may not strike. Their principal weapon is direct lobbying of Congress. Farm workers are excluded from the provisions of the *National Labour Relations Act* and consequently from the right to collective bargaining (although this right is extended in some states, notably California, by state legislation). Secondary boycotts (i.e. in which an aggrieved party boycotts a third party in a dispute) are illegal under the *Taft-Hartley Act*, and on this basis the US Supreme Court held in April 1982 that the International Longshoremen's Association had acted unlawfully in refusing to handle goods being sent to or from the Soviet Union following that country's military intervention in Afghanistan in December 1979. Litigation is commonplace in disputes.

Management assertiveness. Whereas the 1970s was a time of management retreat, employers adopted a more aggressive stance in the 1980s. And, while this stance initially reflected the impact of the severe recession of the early 1980s, it continued throughout the economic upturn. Unemployment, has also remained high by historical standards, with a concentration in unionized industries. In some cases employers broke free from "pattern bargaining" (setting uniform rates across industries) to force concessions in their own plants, with a knock-on impact on other employers, and several national bargaining groups broke up. Employers in some sectors (such as the airlines and auto industry) in return for reducing job losses successfully demanded "give-backs" of earlier concessions, including wage cuts, the ending of automatic indexing of wages to the retail price index (cost-of-living adjustment, COLAs), reduced holidays and pension rights, "no-strike" agreements, and two-tier wages scales (where new employees are permanently or for an extended period paid at substantially lower rates than existing workers). Such concessions by unions, although not universal, were made on a scale not seen since the 1930s. US employers also sought to use non-union strikebreakers to defeat unions in disputes, reviving a tactic which was once common but had sharply declined in the post-World War II period. Employers were able to do this because of the relatively high levels of unemployment, and in July 1986 the NLRB ruled that employers could lawfully keep operating by hiring temporary replacement workers in economic disputes where there was no specific proof of anti-unionism (workers legally have the right to strike without being dismissed). Some disputes were settled with only a proportion of the strikers being taken back, to work alongside replacements who broke the strike. Furthermore the US Supreme Court in June 1985 upheld an NLRB ruling that unions could not discipline members who resigned during a strike (the NLRB having in earlier years broadly permitted unions to determine their own internal rules). In the context of US industrial relations, where loyalty to the union and unwillingness to cross picket lines have been key union advantages, these trends assumed particular significance. Disputes involving such strike-breaking efforts not infrequently generate high levels of violence on all sides, and dispute-related intimidation, bombing and murder have historically been more prevalent in the United States than in most other industrial countries (it is not a federal crime to commit violence on a picket line and according to "right-to-work" advocates, local police forces in strong union areas are reluctant to take action against strikers).

Pay. The US Bureau of Labour Statistics reported a rise in labour costs of 5 per cent in 1988 and 5 per cent in 1989. AFL-CIO figures compute the difference between union and non-union wages at $5.26 an hour. In November 1989 President Bush assented to a compromise figure for the Minimum Wage which raised it from $3.35 an hour to $4.25 in April 1991. This was the first increase since 1981. A sub-minimum wage of 45 cents below the Minimum was inaugurated for trainees in April 1990. It can be paid for 90 days with a 90-day extension if the Department of Labour agrees, but only for a quarter of the workforce. However, pay disparities between the public and private sectors were sufficiently great for the President's Advisory Committee on Federal Pay to recommend increases of 10 per cent in 1990 and 1991. It found that the differential ranged from 20 per cent at the bottom of the pay-scale to 36.6 per cent at the top.

In 1990 annual average wage increases were kept below 4 per cent and management's objective for 1991 was to settle at between 2 and 4 per cent. The demand for wage freezes which was evident in the 1980s has declined and the search for "give-backs" has virtually disappeared. Key settlements during the year 1990 included that of the UAW with GM which covered 300,000 workers for three years from October: it embodies a 3 per cent rise in each year, a significant apprentice intake, strengthened profit-sharing arrangements and better job security; in return the unions are committed to flexibility over work reorganization.

Union recovery at the end of the 1980s. This agreement seems to have been the model for several more at Chrysler and Ford. The period 1989 and 1990 saw some significant victories for unions involved in industrial disputes. There was a greater willingness to strike and days lost to strikes hit 17,000,000—the numbers involved quadrupled between 1988 and 1989—and the strikes themselves achieved more. Around 1,990 striking miners at the Pittston (West Virginia) company were out for over 10 months and finally succeeded in making the company pay into a pension fund for the mining workforce; 58,000 machinists at Boeing struck for six weeks for higher wages and bonuses; and the Communications Workers of America (CWA) struck several times to stop the company imposing contributions to health insurance. A dispute at Eastern Airlines did not end in victory for the American Association of Machinists though the company was also unsuccessful when it filed for protection under the Bankruptcy Code.

The Pittston strike brought the UMWA to the brink of financial ruin. During the course of the dispute fines to the value of $50,000,000 were imposed on it, not least because 40,000 other miners struck in solidarity for nearly one month during the course of the dispute. It ended in February 1990 after 10 months and the union claimed a clear victory for the miners with four out of five jobs at the coalfield reserved for miners dismissed during the strike. Wages rose by $1.20 an hour and each miner received a bonus of $1,000. A Health Insurance scheme agreed in 1988 (the revocation of which by the company was a key factor in starting the strike) was extended to cover all workers and their families, including the retired.

Most symbolic for the unions was the Boeing dispute for it came in the industry which had seen the crushing of the air traffic controllers by President Reagan (1981) and the busting in 1983 of three unions (including the International Association of Machinists, IAM) by Continental Airlines' President Frank Lorenzo. In 1985 a walk-out by Pan Am pilots and flight attendants won them an increase but failed to restore an earlier pay cut, and Boeing itself had in 1983 and 1985 achieved the principle of lower rates for new entrants. However the final 1989 Boeing package (constructed by the Federal Mediator) gave a 10 per cent wage increase over the three years, yearly lump sum payments and a pre-paid cost-of-living increase in the first year, together with higher overtime pay and an easing of mandatory overtime provisions.

The circumstances which had allowed President Reagan to replace the air traffic controllers of 1981 were also changed by a Supreme Court ruling of April 1990. The Court found that companies replacing strikers cannot assume that new workers are opposed to the union and must therefore continue to recognize the unions and negotiate with them. This ruling took its origin from a change in policy by the National Labour Relations Board which in 1987 for the first time undermined the assumption of anti-union preferences and began to evaluate each strike on an individual basis. The effect of the Court's ruling is to put the onus on the employer to prove that the new employees do not wish to be represented by the union. Under Board regulations this will prove difficult unless it can be shown that the union is supported by less than half of employees.

Disputes over health costs were a growing factor in causing strikes in 1989. In 1986 only 45 per cent of workers were fully covered by health insurance compared to 72 per cent six years earlier. They became an issue around the same time: from causing only 18 per cent of stoppages in 1986 they accounted for 78 per cent three years later. In a country where health cares for those of working age in entirely private, the cost falls on employers or on employees, but health care costs spiralled in the late 1980s, sparking disputes such as the Pittston strike of the UMW. The AFL-CIO has called for a universal health care scheme particularly addressed to the needs of those 37,000,000 Americans who lack coverage.

While 1990 lacked high-profile strikes of the kind 1989 had witnessed, there were disputes at Greyhound Bus (where the Amalgamated Transport Union faced a $30,000,000 dispute and a picket was killed when run over by a working driver) and by a number of local groups. There is some evidence that the more powerful groups among wage earners pulled ahead. The (unorganized) and low-paid sector had to make do with increases below the rate of inflation. Three million contracts were due for renewal in 1990 and in most cases the outturn seems to have been above the 1989 level.

Trade unionism. Trade unions which organized on a national scale developed in the middle decades of the nineteenth century, and the American Federation of Labor-Congress of Industrial Organizations (AFL-CIO), today the sole trade union centre, has a continuous history dating back (through the AFL) to the early 1880s. The strength of trade unionism was consolidated under the New Deal of the 1930s, especially through the *National Labor Relations Act* of 1935, which guaranteed the right to collective bargaining and established a National Labor Relations Board (NLRB) to supervise and protect trade union acitivities. Organized labour suffered some reverses in the Cold War period, notably in the *Taft-Hartley Act* of 1947, but has retained substantial legal immunities. Despite this, however, the trade unions have never achieved the central status in US society and politics enjoyed by their counterparts in most other western industrial nations, and have been affected by a culture which stresses private enterprise and individual liberty as against collective or class rights. The mainstream of the labour movement has throughout the twentieth century espoused "business unionism" (i.e. emphasizing "bread-and-butter" issues of wages and conditions rather than broader political or social objectives) and has not sustained a socialist party. Since the 1930s the trade unions have been such closer to the Democratic Party than to the Republicans, but the AFL-CIO is officially non-partisan and candidates for office tend to be supported on an individual basis.

Declining popularity. Trade unions have suffered declining popularity at shop-floor level. They are commonly regarded by women workers as male-dominated and have suffered from an image of being old-fashioned, dominated by powerful union bosses, and unresponsive to changes in working conditions, these problems being reflected in the lack of organizational success in the white-collar clerical and professional fields. In no year before 1974 did unions lose more than half of the several thousand elections held each year to decide if they should secure workplace bargaining rights, but since 1974 they have never won more than half. Furthermore, decertification elections, held to expel a union from the workplace, which were rare before the 1970s, have occurred with increasing frequency in recent years. There has also been a greater tendency for union members to break ranks in strikes by crossing picket lines. Against this background employers have proved more resistant to union demands. If a labour board certifies an election, the employer is legally obliged to negotiate with the successful union, but according to the AFL-CIO, a third of the elections won by unions do not result in signed contracts with the employer within five years. (This problem has been compounded by serious delays in the consideration of cases by the NLRB.) Furthermore the NLRB ruled in May 1984, reversing its previous policy, that unions must show majority support among workers to gain bargaining rights regardless of unlawful conduct by employers to deter union activity, and there has been a growth in the number of consultants retained by employers to provide advice on techniques to influence workers against trade unions.

The tale is not one of uniform decline. The Service Employees' International Union (SEIU) and others have increased the organized percentage of health care workers from 14 to 20 per cent. The SEIU, the fifth largest AFL-CIO affiliate increased its membership by nearly 50,000 in 1986. The National Air Traffic Controllers' Association (NATCA) which replaced the decertified PATCO after the failure of the 1981 strike has now won bargaining rights on behalf of 12,800 controllers in an election supervised by the Federal Labour Relations Authority. But while there are signs of workforce problems affecting the level of safety in air traffic control, the employers still opposed the rehiring of the strikers.

Political climate. The early years of the Reagan administration (i.e. from 1981) were particularly unfavourable to organized labour, President Reagan making "anti-union" appointments to the NLRB, and adopting policies of cutting social programmes to the advantage of the wealthy. In 1981 President Reagan dismissed all 11,345 members of the (federal employees') Professional Air Traffic Controllers' Organization (PATCO) for illegally striking and ordered the complete dissolution of the union. By 1986 only a few hundred of those dismissed had won individual reinstatement (a new National Air Traffic Controllers' Association was formed in September 1986 with AFL-CIO support, and it pledged to avoid confrontation). In 1982 a rail strike was ended when Congress passed special legislation requiring the Brotherhood of Locomotive Engineers to accept a new contract recommended by a special presidential arbitration commission, which included a suspension of the union's right-to-strike until the end of the contract period in mid-1984. However, "right-to-work" advocates have not persuaded the administration to prohibit the union shop by federal law, and in his second term (since 1985) President Reagan made some attempt to improve his relations with organized labour.

The political climate remained difficult for trade unions though there were some encouraging signs. In March 1988 the Supreme Court upheld a federal Law denying food stamps (coupons for use in retail stores) to striking workers and their families unless they were poor enough to qualify before going on strike. In June the Court ruled that a union cannot require non-members who pay "agency fees" rather than dues to finance political lobbying for policies with which they do not agree: this ruling is likely to force expensive changes in union accounting procedures.

However, in July of that year Congress approved a bill requiring companies with 100 or more employees to give 60 days' advance warning of closures or large-scale lay-offs affecting one-third or 500 of their workers. This provision had previously been vetoed by President Reagan when it lay within a wider trade bill. Now, confronted by strong bipartisan support for it in an election year, he allowed it to pass into law. And the Supreme Court also decided that job selection criteria which have a disproportionate impact on minority group members are illegal.

But polling evidence suggests that after its trough in the mid-1980s union popularity is now recovering in the United States. Figures from the Bureau of Labor Statistics indicate that the United States had 17,000,000 union members in 1990, a number unchanged since 1985. However workforce growth meant that union density declined over the same period from 18 per cent to 16.4 per cent. In 1953, the figure was 32.5 per cent. Density varies greatly from the public to the private sectors. There were 10,500,000 union members working for private companies in 1990, a density of 12 per cent; in the government sector 6,400,000 union members resulted in density of 37 per cent. Faced with a trend which was still adverse, unions continued to seek new ways of attracting members, offering credit cards and setting up "employee partnership funds" to be used to buy company shares.

An important focus of union agitation in 1991 was the Bush administration's proposed free trade treaty with Mexico intended by the President as a step towards a North American trading bloc. Opponents, including the unions, feared that the Mexican Treaty would undercut American jobs, already at risk from the burgeoning *maquiladora* sector. This sector, consisting of some 1,800 factories employing perhaps 500,000 workers directly or indirectly became the cheapest assembly centre in the hemisphere as a result of measures to provide employment for Mexicans denied entry into the United States. Even before the *Free Trade Treaty* was mooted, the existence of the sector had drawn sharp condemnation from unions such as the UAW. But a major lobbying effort by the AFL-CIO and the Teamsters failed to prevent the Senate voting to extend "fast-track" authority for the Mexican negotiations at the end of May.

American Federation of Labor and Congress of Industrial Organizations (AFL-CIO)

Address. 815 16th Street NW, Washington, DC 20006
Phone. (202) 637 5000
Telex. 710 822 9276 AFL-CIO WSH A
Fax. (202) 637 5058
Leadership. Lane Kirkland (president); Thomas R. Donahue (secretary-treasurer)
Membership. 14,400,000 in 90 unions.
History and character. The origins of the AFL-CIO lie in the formation of the Federation of Organized Trades and Labor Unions of the United States and Canada in 1881: five years later the American Federation of Labour was born. It grew by emphasizing craft-based organization and trade unionism directed towards immediate bargaining over wages and conditions rather than broader political and social objectives. In the mid-1930s, however, under the impact of the economic depression and the favourable political climate of the New Deal, some AFL unions sought to organize in the mass-production industries on the industrial union principle, forming the Committee for Industrial Organization within the AFL and becoming involved in many strikes. This led to the creation of the Congress of Industrial Organizations (CIO) in 1938. The two streams of the trade union movement were united in 1955, and there is no other trade union centre.

The AFL-CIO seeks to co-ordinate the activities of its affiliates, and to represent the union movement in government. It also settles jurisdictional disputes between its affiliates. It has no political affiliation but is at the national level closer to the Democratic Party, and this relationship has tightened under the (Republican) presidency of Ronald Reagan. In 1984 the AFL-CIO leadership strongly supported the Democratic candidate, Walter Mondale, for the presidency. He was heavily defeated, winning only 55 per cent of the vote in union households. Since then the Democratic Party nationally has sought to emphasize that it is not a captive of the "special interest" of organized labour. The AFL-CIO gives financial support to individual Congressional candidates of both parties (reflecting the status of the parties as diverse coalitions), but mostly favours Democrats.

In the 1988 presidential election, the AFL-CIO was less closely identified with the Democratic candidate Michael Dukakis than it had been with Walter Mondale four years earlier, having failed to endorse anyone during the nominating process. A union like the Auto Workers (UAW) had substantial numbers of its members backing at least four of those who hoped to gain the Democratic nomination and this uncertainty was evident among other affiliates. Nevertheless there was no question of neutrality after Dukakis was finally nominated in the summer of 1988, especially since the voice of the Republican-inclined Teamsters was muted during their battle with the Federal Government.

The sharp falls in union membership, high unemployment, renewed assertiveness by managements, and anti-union posture of the Reagan administration encouraged the AFL-CIO in the 1980s to seek new approaches. A report from its Committee on the Evolution of Work, which was approved by the executive council in February 1985, included proposals to: (i) broaden categories of union membership to include workers not covered by contracts and workers who leave their jobs; (ii) emphasize mediation or arbitration rather than strikes as a technique in collective bargaining disputes; (iii) expand social services, job training, and other benefits to members; (iv) seek to employ consumer, church and financial pressures (such as pressurizing companies with interlocking directorates with financial corporations by shifting major pension reserves) as methods in disputes; (v) encourage further mergers of AFL-CIO unions (50 of the 96 affiliates having fewer than 50,000 members each); (vi) place new emphasis on organizing smaller non-union plants; and (vii) emphasize "pay equity" and comparable worth—i.e. the upgrading of pay for jobs disproportionately held by women, as compared with higher-paid jobs of comparable skill disproportionately held by men. The report also noted the need to reverse the "near invisibility" of American trade unions and their members in television and radio programming. Other concepts discussed within the AFL-CIO have included a drive for increased worker participation in management (although this has never been a significant factor in industrial relations, and stands in opposition to the conflict-orientated traditions of US unions).

The 1987 Biennial convention of the AFL-CIO defined the overhaul of the "harsh, anti-worker, labor laws we confront" as its highest priority, citing the exclusion of many public employees from collective bargaining rights and the non-observation of those rights in important areas of the private sector. A Committee on the Evolution of Work was established earlier in the 1980s to monitor unions' effectiveness in the face of the management and Federal offensive. However, the 1987 convention recorded its view that "labor's message is not reaching most Americans. We have permitted a negative image of labor to grow up around us without an effective response...". It resolved to mount a positive campaign to raise the level of public understanding of unions and increase the disposition of younger American workers to join them.

In May 1988 the AFL-CIO launched "Union-YES", a campaign designed to promote the positive side of the movement by a number of means including networked TV commercials.

Particular emphasis is placed by the AFL-CIO on the need for trade legislation to put US industry on equal terms with imports from Japan and elsewhere. It opposed cuts in social spending in the federal budget and has called for a large-scale job creation programme of public works.

The relationship between the AFL-CIO and the mainstream of western trade unionism has been an uneasy one. The AFL and the CIO both participated in the formation of the ICFTU in 1949, but never fully accepted the heavily socialist and social democratic orientation of the ICFTU, and withdrew in 1969. (The AFL-CIO remained a member of, and the dominant factor in, the ICFTU's regional organization for the Americas, ORIT, which was often hostile to Christian unions, and individual affiliates remained within ICFTU international trade secretariats.)

The AFL-CIO has a Department of International Affairs, which oversees the work of four institutes: the Asian-American Free Labor Institute (AAFLI), founded in 1968; the African-American Labor Centre (AALC), founded in 1964; the American Institute for Free Labor Development (AIFLD), founded in 1962, which covers Latin America; and the Free Trade Union Institute (FTUI). Launched in 1977, the FTUI is the most recently formed of the institutes and originates in a desire to assist the Iberian countries' unions away from state control. It has supported Solidarnosc in Poland and sponsors "research on human and labor rights". Unlike the other three institutes, FTUI is not tied by regional terms of reference.

The 1987 budget for the institutes exceeded US$28,000,000, of which the AFL-CIO directly provided only 2.5 per cent. Nearly US$5,000,000 comes from the National Endowment for Democracy, a Congress-funded private entity formed in 1983 by the AFL-CIO and the US Chamber of Commerce and backed by both major political parties. But the bulk of the funding, some 80 per cent, was provided by the Federal Agency for International Development. The use of government funds contrasted with the traditional reluctance of labour movements such as those of Britain to use them, but the AFL-CIO argued that the setting of its own priorities had the support of both parties in Congress and pointed to its clashes with the Reagan administration in the implementation of overseas programmes.

Under George Meany (to 1979), the AFL-CIO supported the war in Vietnam, opposed detente under President Nixon, and was vehemently anti-communist and highly suspicious of social democrats. Its position shifted somewhat after Lane Kirkland assumed the presidency in 1979, and it rejoined the ICFTU. In 1986, Kirkland assumed the Presidency of TUAC.

At its 1987 Biennial Convention, the AFL-CIO endorsed the "Arias Plan" to resolve Central America's problems peacefully and condemned the provision of covert aid to the Contras by the Administration. It did not however support the Sandinista government of Nicaragua and backed the call for that country's Confederation of Trade Union Unity for the withdrawal of US and Soviet/Cuban military assistance to the two sides.

The President's Commission of Organized Crime in March 1986 identified three AFL-CIO unions (the International Longshoremen's Association, the Hotel and Restaurant Employees' and Bartenders' International Union, and the Labourers' International Union of North America), all of whose presidents sat on the AFL-CIO executive council, as having "histories of control or influence by organized crime". The Commission criticized the AFL-CIO leadership for a failure to take action to deal with this issue.

Substantial efforts have been made to reintegrate unions beneath the AFL-CIO umbrella. At the 1987 Biennial Convention the decision was taken (despite some evidence of misgivings) to readmit the controversial Teamsters' Union to membership. But the possibility that the Mineworkers' Union would amalgamate with the affiliated Oil, Chemical and Atomic Workers' Union receded in February 1988 when talks collapsed on the verge of an announcement. Among recent mergers have been those of the 175,000 strong International Union of Electrical, Radio and Machine Workers (IUE) with the 21,000 members of the United Furniture Workers of America, and the decisions of the International Typographical Union and the United Telegraph Workers to join the Communications Workers of America, thus bringing their membership to 600,000.

Structure. The AFL-CIO is a loose federation with no power to instruct its affiliates, and within many of its affiliates there are conflicts as to whether authority lies with the local union or at national level. Policy is made by the Biennial Convention, which last met in October 1987. The affiliates each set their own collective bargaining policies, but the 35-member AFL-CIO executive council, made up principally of the leaders of affiliated unions and which leads the federations activities, has recently sought to become more involved at an earlier stage. In February 1986 the executive council approved a new arbitration pact intended to reduce mutual competition for members by referring disputes to umpires selected by the AFL-CIO.

The AFL-CIO Convention met in Washington in November 1989 and was attended by 800 delegates. It was strongly influenced by the wave of strikes that was then at its peak and condemned employers who were resorting to "the brutal anti-labour tactics of a previous era to crush unions". President Lane Kirkland asserted that the current disputes disproved the argument that unions were no longer necessary "in this age of warm and cuddly management". The Convention was addressed by a succession of foreign union leaders including Lech Walesa, Manuel Bustos (Chile), and Phiroshaw Camay (then the General Secretary of NACTU, South Africa). In 1984 the AFL-CIO had secured an amendment to the aid programme to the effect that benefits would be suspended for countries that did not honour internationally recognized employment standards; however it was not always successful in its submission of countries to be covered by the amendment. The Convention reiterated its position and called on the United States government to link its trade or aid policy to the human rights' record of recipient countries. Duties were reimposed on Burma and the Central

African Republic under the Generalized System of Preference in 1989. The AFL-CIO also called for the 1990 GATT round to be extended to include a social clause.

Affiliates. The following are the major AFL-CIO affiliates (membership figures are the latest available).

1. **Actors and Artistes of America, Associated**, 165 West 46th Street, New York, NY 10036.
   Phone: (212) 869 0358.
   Leadership: Frederick O'Neal (international president).
   Membership: This organization associates nine member unions and individual members join.

2. **Aluminium, Brick and Glass Workers International Union**, 3362 Hollenberg Drive, Bridgeton, Mo 63044.
   Phone: (314) 739 6142.   Fax: (314) 739 1216.

3. **Automobile, Aerospace and Agricultural Implement Workers of America International Union, United**, 8000 East Jefferson Avenue, Detroit, Mi 48214.
   Phone: (313) 926 5000.   Telex: 810 221 1523. Fax: (313) 823 6016.
   Leadership: Owen Bieber (president).
   Membership: 1,029,000.

4. **Bakery, Confectionery and Tobacco Workers' International Union**, 10401 Connecticut Avenue, Kensington, Md 20895.
   Phone: (301) 933 8600. Fax: (301) 946 8452.
   Leadership: John DeConcini (president).

5. **Boilermakers, Iron Ship Builders, Blacksmiths, Forgers and Helpers, International Brotherhood of**, 570 New Brotherhood Building, 8th Street at State Avenue, Kansas City, Ks 66101.
   Phone: (913) 371 2640. Telex: 42279. Fax: (913) 371 5335.
   Leadership: C. Jones (international president).
   Membership. 100,000.
   Publication: *Boilermaker Reporter*.

6. **Bricklayers and Allied Craftsmen, International Union of**, 815 15th Street NW, Washington, DC 20005.
   Phone: (202) 783 3788. Telex: 892400 IUBAC WSH. Fax: (202) 393 0219.
   Leadership: John T. Joyce (president).

7. **Carpenters and Joiners of America, United Brotherhood of**, 101 Constitution Avenue NW, Washington, DC 20001.
   Phone: (202) 546 6206. Telex: 89561 CARPENTERS WSH. Fax: (202) 543 5724.
   Leadership: S. Lucassen (president).
   Membership: 620,000.

8. **Chemical Workers' Union, International**, 1655 West Market Street, Akron, Oh 44313.
   Phone: (216) 867 2444.
   Leadership: Frank D. Martino (president).

9. **Clothing and Textile Workers Union, Amalgamated**, 15 Union Square, New York, NY 10003.
   Phone: (212) 242 0700. Fax: (212) 255 7230.
   Leadrrship: J. Sheinkman (president).
   Membership. 284,000.

10. **Communications Workers of America**, 1925 K Street NW, Washington, DC 20006.
    Phone: (202) 728 2300. Telex: 892785 CWA WSH. Fax: (202) 728 2559.

11. **Electrical Workers, International Brotherhood of**, 1125 15th Street NW, Washington, DC 20005.
    Phone: (202) 833 7000. Telex: 8-9405 IBEWIO A WSH. Fax: (202) 467 6316.
    Leadership: J.J. Barry (international president).
    Membership: 950,000.

12. **Farm Workers of America, United**, P.O. Box 62, Keene, Ca 93531.
Phone: (805) 822 5571.
Leadership: Cesar Chavez (president).

13. **Fire Fighters, International Association of**, 1750 New York Avenue NW, Washington, DC 20006.
Phone: (202) 737 8484.
Fax: (202) 737 8418.
Leadership: Alfred K. Whitehead (president).
Membership: 185,000.
Publication: *International Fire Fighter*.

14. **Flight Attendants, Association of**, 1625 Massachusetts Avenue NW, 3rd Floor, Washington DC 20036.
Phone: (202) 328 5400. Fax: (202) 328 5424.

15. **Food and Commercial Workers' International Union**, 1775 K Street NW, Washington, DC 20006.
Phone: (202) 223 3111. Telex: 892791 UFCW WSH.
Fax: (202) 466 1562.
Leadership: William H. Wyun (international president); Jerry Menapace (international secretary-treasurer).
Membership: 1,300,000.

16. **Furniture Workers of America, United**, 1910 Airlane Drive, P.O. Box 100037, Nashville, Tn 37210.
Phone: (615) 889 8860.

17. **Glass, Molders, Pottery, Plastics and Allied Workers' International Union**, 608 East Baltimore Pike, P.O. Box 607, Media, Pa 19063.
Phone: (215) 265 5051. Fax: (215) 565 0983.
Leadership: J. Hatfield (international president).
Membership: 100,000.

18. **Government Employees, American Federation of**, 80 F Street NW, Washington, DC 20001.
Phone: (202) 737 8700.
Leadership: J. Sturdivant (national president).
Membership: 200,000.

19. **Graphic Communications International Union**, 1900 L Street NW, Washington, DC 20036.
Phone: (202) 462 1400.

20. **Hospital and Health Care Employees, National Union of**, 330 W. 42nd Street, Suite 1905, New York, NY 10036.
Phone: 947 1944. Fax: (212) 695 0538.

21. **Hotel Employees and Restaurant Employees International Union**, 1219 28th Street NW, washington, DC 20007.
Phone: (202) 393 4373. Fax: (202) 333 0468.

22. **Industrial Workers of America, International Union, Allied**, 3520 West Oklahoma Avenue, Milwaukee, Wi 53215.
Phone: (414) 645 9500.

23. **Iron Workers, International Association of Bridge, Structural and Ornamental**, 1750 New York Avenue NW, Suite 400, Washington, DC 20006.
Phone: (202) 383 4810. Telex: 892429 IRONWRKER WSH. Fax: (202) 638 4856.

24. **Laborer's International Union of North America**, 905 16th Street NW, Washington, DC 20006.
Phone: (202) 737 8320. Fax: (202) 737 2754.

25. **Ladies' Garment Workers' Union, International**, 1710 Broadway, New York, NY 10019.
Phone: (212) 265 700. Fax: (212) 265 3415.
Leadership: J. Mazur (president).
Membership: 200,000.

26. **Letter Carriers, National Association of**, 100 Indiana Avenue NW, Washington, DC 20001.
Phone: (202) 393 4695.
Leadership: V. Sombrotto (president).
Membership: 314,000.

27. **Longshoremen's Association, International**, 17 Battery Place, Room 1530, New York, NY 10004.
Phone: (212) 425 1200. Telex: 128254 INTILLONGSH NYK. Fax: (212) 809 6826.
Leadership: J. Bowers (president).

28. **Machinists and Aerospace Workers, International Association of**, 1300 Connecticut Avenue NW, Washington, DC 20036.
Phone: (202) 857 5200. Telex: 892472 IAM WSH. Fax: (202) 296 1638.
Leadership: William Winpisinger (president).

29. **Maintenance of Way Employees, Brotherhood of**, 12050 Woodward Avenue, Detroit, Mi 48203-3596.
Phone: (313) 868 0490. Fax: (313) 863 5122.
Leadership: M. A. Fleming (president).
Membership: 75,000.

30. **Musicians of the United States and Canada, American Federation of**, 1501 Broadway, New York, NY 10036.
Phone: (212) 869 1330. Telex: 125662 AFM NYK. Fax: (212) 764 6134.

31. **Office and Professional Employees International Union**, 265 West 14th Street, Suite 610, New York, NY 10011.
Phone: (212) 675 3210.

32. **Oil, Chemical and Atomic Workers International Union**, P.O. Box 2812, Denver, Co 80201.
Phone: (303) 987 2229. Fax: (303) 987 1967.
Leadership: Joseph M. Misbsenet (president); Anthony Mazzocchi (secretary-treasurer).
Membership: 110,000.

33. **Operating Engineers, International Union of**, 1125 17th Street NW, Washington, DC 20036.
Phone: (202) 429 9100. Telex: TWX 710 822 9316 IUOE WASH. Fax: (202) 223 3741; (202) 429 9100.
Leadership: Frank Hanley (president); N. Budd Coutts (general secretary-treasurer).
Membership: 370,000.
Publication: *International Operating Engineer*.

34. **Painters and Allied Trades of the United States and Canada, International Brotherhood of**, 1750 New York Avenue, NW, Washington, DC 2006.
Phone: (202) 637 0720.   Fax: (202) 637 0711.

35. **Paperworks International Union, United**, 3340 Perimeter Hill Drive, Nashville, Tennessee 37211, P.O. Box 1475, Nashville. Tennessee 37202.
Phone: (615) 834 8590.
Fax: (615) 834 7741.
Leadership: Wayne E. Glenn (international president); James H. Dunn (secretary-treasurer).
Membership: 240,000.
Publication: *Paperworker*.

36. **Plasterers' and Cement Masons' International Association of the United States and Canada**, 1125 17th Street NW, Washington, DC 20036.
Phone: (202) 393 6569.

37. **Plumbing and Pipe Fitting Industry of the United States and Canada, United Association of Journeymen and Apprentices of**, 901 Massachussetts Avenue NW, Washington, DC 20001.
Phone: (202) 628 5823. Telex: 89564. Fax: (202) 628 5024.
Leadership: M. Boede (general president).
Membership: 325,000.

38. **Postal Workers Union, American**, 1300 L Street NW Washington, DC 20005.
Phone: (202) 842 4200. Fax: (202) 842 4297.

39. **Professional and Technical Engineers, International Federation of**, 8701 Georgia Avenue, Suite 701, Silver Spring, Md 20910.
Phone: (301) 565 9016. Fax: (301) 565 0018.
Leadership: James E. Sommerhauser (industrial president); John H. Dunne (secretary-treasurer).
Membership: 26,000.
Publication: *The Outlook*.

40. **Retail, Wholesale and Department Store Union**, 30 East 29th Street, New York, NY 10016.
Phone: (212) 684 5300.
Leadership: L. Miller (president); Guy Dickinson (secretary-treasurer).
Membership: 130,000.
Publication: *The Record*.

41. **Rubber, Cork, Linoleum and Plastic Workers of America, United**, URWA Building, South Street, Akron, Oh 44308-1893.
Phone: (216) 376 6181. Telex: 810 431 2078.
Leadership: M. Stone (international president).
Membership: 110,000.

42. **Seafarers' International Union of North America**, 5201 Auth Way, Camp Springs, Md 20746.
Phone: (301) 899 0675. Fax: (301) 899 7355.
Leadership: Michael Sacco (president).
Membership: 85,000.
Publication: *Seafarer's Log*.

43. **Service Employees' International Union AFL-CIO**, 1313 L St. NW, Washington, DC 20005
Phone: (202) 898 3200. Fax: (202) 898 3438.

44. **Sheet Metal Workers' International Association**, 1750 New York Avenue NW, Washington, DC 20006.
Phone: (202) 783 5880. Telex: 701 822 1175. Fax: (202) 737 2424.
Leadership: E. Carlough (general president).
Membership: 150,000.

45. **State, County and Municipal Employees, American Federation of**, 1625 L Street NW, Washington DC 20036.
Phone: (202) 429 1000. Telex: 892376 AFSCME. Fax: (202) 429 1272.

46. **Steelworkers of America, United**, Five Gateway Center, Pittsburgh, Pa 15222.
Phone: (412) 562 2400. Fax: (412) 562 2317.
Leadership: Lynn Williams (president); Edgar L. Ball (international secretary-treasurer).
Membership: 750,000.
Publication: *Steelbar*.

47. **Teachers, American Federation of**, 555 New Jersey Avenue NW, Washington, DC 20001
Phone: (202) 879 4400. Fax: (202) 879 4545.

48. **Teamsters Union**—see separate main entry below.

49. **Transit Union, Amalgamated**, 5025 Wisconsin Avenue NW, Washington, DC 20016.
Phone: (202) 537 1645. Fax: (202) 244 7824.

50. **Transport Workers Union of America**, 1980 Broadway, New York, NY 10023.
   Phone: (212) 873 6000.

51. **Transportation Communications International Union**, 3 Research Place, Rockville, Md 20850.
   Phone: (301) 948 4910. Telex: BRAC ROVE 710 828 9780. Fax: (301) 948 1369.
   Leadership: Richard I. Kilroy (international president).
   Membership: 200,000.

52. **Utility Workers of America**, 815 16th Street NW, Room 605, Washington, DC 20006.
   Phone: (202) 347 8105.
   Leadership: J. Joy (national president); Marshall M. Hicks (national secretary-treasurer).
   Membership: 60,000.
   Publication: *Light* (monthly).

53. **Woodworkers of America, International**, 25 Cornell Avenue, Gladston, Or 97027.
   Phone: (503) 656 1475.

Publications. Free Trade Union News;, AFL-CIO News.
International affiliations. ICFTU/ORIT; TUAC.

Teamsters, Chauffeurs, Warehousemen and Helpers of America, International Brotherhood of, (IBT)

Address. 25 Lousiana Avenue NW, Washington, DC 20001
Phone. (202) 624 6800. Fax: (202) 624 6918.
Leadership. William J. McCarthy (president); Weldon Mathis (secretary-treasurer)
Membership. 1,700,000.
History and character. The IBT (or Teamsters) is the largest and most powerful single union in the United States.

The position of the IBT was weakened by the deregulation of the trucking industry in the early 1980s, which led to the creation of many small non-union companies, and by 1986 only about 200,000 truckers worked under the master agreement of the IBT, compared with 400,000 a decade earlier. However, the IBT has sustained its membership by organizing in other sectors, including clerical, service and high technology workers, and has in this respect benefited from not being subject to AFL-CIO demarcation restrictions. Its greatest asset has been its reputation for winning high wage settlements as a result of its bargaining strength as the largest union.

According to the President's Commission on Organized Crime, reporting in March 1986, the leaders of the IBT "have been firmly under the influence of organized crime since the 1950s". These criminal associations, which include the use of the union's multi-billion dollar Central States Pension Fund to finance activity controlled by the Mafia, led to the expulsion of the IBT from the AFL-CIO in 1957. In 1967 James R. Hoffa, the IBT president, was imprisoned for involvement in misuse of pension funds; he was released in 1971 (in exchange for an agreement that he would stand down as president) but disappeared in 1975 and is generally presumed to have been murdered. The union was led by Frank E. Fitzsimmons from 1971 to 1981. His successor Roy L. Williams was convicted in December 1982 of conspiracy to bribe a US senator in return for favourable trucking legislation, and stood down in favour of Jackie Presser, who was in turn indicted by a Cleveland grand jury on embezzlement and racketeering charges in May 1986 (but was re-elected as IBT president at the national convention five days later). Many local and regional IBT officials have also served prison terms. A dissident faction within the IBT opposed to criminal links is known as "Teamsters for a Democratic Union" but this has failed to become a major force and is opposed by the "Brotherhood of Loyal Americans and Strong Teamsters" (BLAST).

DRIVE (Democratic, Republican Independent Voter Education) was launched by the IBT in 1963; it is the largest labour political action fund, raising some US$10,000,000 in 1987, and has supported both Democratic and Republican candidates (more particularly the former). The IBT was the only union which supported President Reagan in the 1980 and 1984 election campaigns, and Presser served in 1980–81 on the President's White House transitional team.

The Teamsters finally reaffiliated to the AFL-CIO in October 1987. Their return came at a critical moment. For some 15 years there had been talks about the possibility of readmission, but now the Federal Justice Department was preparing a civil lawsuit against them aimed at removing the entire executive and placing the union under a trustee appointed by the Court. This was the culmination of decades of efforts by Washington to remove what it alleged were links between the Teamsters and organized crime. Nor did their increased respectability as an AFL-CIO affiliate divert legal proceedings: the suit was filed in June 1988 under Federal racketeering laws with the Department charging that Cosa Nostra figures had played a part in the election of Presser and his predecessor.

The AFL-CIO and some Congressmen responded that the government was interfering with the right of union members to choose their own leaders. Some labour experts questioned whether state control was really the most effective way to deal with crime in the union and proposed stiff regulation instead. Union reformers also took the view that enforcement of elections was the surest way to purge felons from its ranks: their strength was becoming more apparent as opposition mounted to some recently signed contracts including the Master Freight Agreement which covered 200,000 drivers. A new organization, Americans Against Government Control of Unions was launched with support from diverse figures such as Jesse Jackson and Alexander Haig. A few days later the situation was further complicated when Presser, whose own trial had been delayed due to his serious ill-health, died in hospital.

Teamsters for a Democratic Union (TDU) had campaigned through the 1980s for constitutional reform, notably "one person, one vote" elections of the union leadership. Pressure from the TDU and others did lead to important changes at the end of the decade. Thus is October 1988 the IBT Executive ruled that all future contracts (agreements) would require majority ratification. This followed some two years when the membership in a number of locals had refused to ratify contracts in protest against the then rule whereby only a one-third vote was required. In March 1989 the racketeering case was settled but in a manner which opened the door to constitutional reform. A Court order required all delegates to the 1991 Convention to be elected by the membership, thus meeting a key demand of the TDU which had long opposed the way local union officers dominated representation at these quinquennial events. At this Convention the delegates will nominate for all officers of the Union, with a 5 per cent minimum threshold. Six months from its conclusion, officers will be elected by the membership.

Sixty-nine year-old William McCarthy was elected president in July 1988 following the death of Jackie Presser. He dismissed a number of key union figures associated with the previous régime. However this approach was coupled with political conservatism, given Mr McCarthy's preference for the Republicans; his rival in the presidential selection, Weldon Mathis, being a close associate of Michael Dukakis, the Democrats' nominee.

Publication. International Teamster Magazine (circulation 1,886,000).

International affiliation. International Federation of Chemical, Energy and General Workers' Unions.

Other unions

Major unions not affiliated to the AFL-CIO include the National Education Association of the United States (1202 16th Street NW,Washington, DC 20036; phone: (202) 833 4000); the United Electrical, Radio and Machine Workers of America (535 Smithfield Street, Pittsburgh, Pa 15222; phone: (412) 471 8919); the International Longshoremen's and Warehousemen's Union (1188 Franklin Street, San Francisco, Ca 94109; phone: (415) 77550533; the United Mine Workers of America, International Union (900 15th Street NW, Washington, DC 20005; phone: (202) 842 7200); the American Nurses' Association (2420 Pershing Road, Kansas City, Mo 64108; phone: (816) 474 5720); the National Alliance of Postal and Federal Employees (1628 11th Street NW, Washington, DC 20001; phone: (202) 939 6325); and the United Transportation Union (14600 Detroit Avenue, Cleveland, Oh 44107; phone: (216) 228 9400).

507

PUERTO RICO

Capital: San Juan   **Population: 3,400,000**

Political system. Described in its 1952 constitution as a "free state associated with the USA", Puerto Rico is also a member of the Commonwealth.

Economy. The Puerto Rican economy, which is based on industries such as textiles, petrochemicals and pharmaceuticals is largely dependent upon the USA, its main trading partner, from which is receives 30.7 per cent of its GDP in federal aid.

System of industrial relations. The divestment of the Puerto Rican Telephone Company in 1990 provoked major union opposition. There was a one-day general strike in March against the absence of guarantees that there would be no redundancies.

Trade unionism. The labour movement is fragmented, with the Puerto Rican Federation of Labor (AFL-CIO) as the major organization.

Central Puertorriqueña de Trabajadores (CPT)
Puerto Rican Workers' Centre

Address. P.O. Box 4084, San Juan 00936
Phone. 7659700
Telex. CPT 9148
Leadership. Federico Torres
History and character. The CPT was founded in November 1982, and a year later claimed 20,000 members in 15 affiliates. The CPT is the successor to the Frente Unido de Trabajadores formed in 1964, and is politically non-aligned with a Third World orientation.
International affiliations. WCL/CLAT.

Federación del Trabajo de Puerto Rico (AFL-CIO) (FTPR)
Puerto Rican Federation of Labor

Address. P.O. Box S-1648, San Juan 00903
Leadership. Hipólito Marcano (president)
Membership. 60,000 (1983).
History and character. Founded in 1957 by merger of federations linked to the (previously rival) US AFL and CIO (which merged in 1955).
International affiliations. ICFTU/ORIT.

Unión General de Trabajadores (UGT)
General Workers' Union

Address. P.O. Box 29247, Estacíon 65 Infantería Rio Pío Piedras, PR 00929
Phone. 751-5350
Leadership. Osvaldo Romero Pizarro (secretary-treasurer)
Membership. 5,300
International affiliation. WFTU.

Uruguay

Capital: Montevideo

Population: 3,004,000
(1988)

Political system. In 1984, after 11 years of military rule, Uruguay returned to constitutional government, with the liberal Colorado Party (CP) holding a dominant position but not an outright majority.

The Colorado government of President Sanguinetti was replaced in March 1990 by a new coalition government under President Lacalle, the victor in the November 1989 elections.

Economy. Services account for the biggest proportion of Uruguay's employed workforce followed by agriculture and industry, but agricultural employment—dominated by livestock farming—may be understated by being outside the formal economy. The Uruguayan economy, heavily burdened by external debt, stagnated in 1989 while inflation—already high at 62 per cent in 1988—rose to more than 89 per cent by the end of the year. The Lacalle administration entered office pledged to bring down the fiscal deficit from 6.7 per cent of GDP to 2.5 per cent. Among its early measures were a rise in indirect taxes and in tariffs, higher social security contributions and selected price rises. Trade unions calculated that real wages in the public sector (covering one fifth of the country's workforce) were by March 1990 6.5 per cent below their level of a year before. Unemployment for the first quarter of 1990 was 9.3 per cent.

System of industrial relations. Uruguay ratified ILO Conventions No. 87 (Freedom of Association and Protection of the Right to Organize, 1948) and No. 98 (Right to Organize and Collective Bargaining, 1949) in 1954. Following a wave of public sector strikes, President Sanguinetti stated in June 1986 that strikes in "essential services". including the social security administration, the ports and the hospitals, would be met with sanctions. The new government had to that point failed to take drastic action against strikers, partly to avoid any appearance of a return of the methods of the dictatorship, and partly because of Sanguinetti's view that the unrest was an inevitable result of tensions built up under military rule, and of the inexperience of the union leaders.

Up until 1989 the orientation of government was towards consensus building, and the Ministry of Labour continued to act as a mediator where disputes arose. In November for the first time two Uruguayan businesses were closed down for discriminating against trade union employees. Nevertheless there were sizeable disputes during the year in the port of Montevideo and by the municipal workers of the city. Primary school teachers staged a month-long strike in September and October. In some cases the government invoked its powers under the essential services regulations to deal with the effects of the disputes. The PIT-CNT mounted three general strikes in 1989 against eroded living standards.

President Lacalle had been elected on a programme whose centrepiece was employment law reform. Proposals he brought before the Uruguayan parliament in the summer of 1990 stipulated steps to be taken (including secret ballots) before strike action can be initiated within the law. Under this legislation employers may dismiss all workers participating in an illegal strike.

The unions responded swiftly to the Lacalle economic programme. Two general strikes were called in March 1990 by the PIT – CNT which protested that real wages would fall by 10 per cent in the year and that workers were paying the cost of the adjustment package. As the year wore on there were protest stoppages in transport, health and banking.

Trade unionism. Trade unionism began in Uruguay as early as the 1880s and the first national confederations appeared early in the twentieth century. Trade union activities continued under generally constitutional rule and in notably favourable conditions by Latin American standards until the armed forces assumed power in 1971. The Convención Nacional de Trabajadores (CNT) was dissolved in 1973 when it staged a general strike, following which independent treade unionism was crushed. The Confederación General de Trabajadores del Uruguay (CGTU)—founded in 1951 as the Confederación Sindical del Uruguay—which was an ICFTU affiliate, came firmly under government control and was suspended by the ICFTU in May 1978 and subsequently disaffiliated. The new civilian government which took office in March 1985 immediately adopted legislation repealing various forms of restrictive labour regulations imposed under military law, restoring the situation applying in 1973, when there were few regulations governing labour relations or restricting or specifically according the right to form unions or to strike. After the restoration of democracy, the PIT – CNT emerged as a unified centre supported by all sections of the labour movement. During 1987–88 it organized a series of strikes, in both the public and private sectors, to oppose President Sanguinetti's austerity policies which were geared to ensuring that the foreign debt repayments were met and which, according to the unions, meant (for meeting the interest payments alone) the equivalent of a wage cut of US$41 per month. The unions also strongly opposed his government's programme of "re-structuring" the economy, especially the development of "Free Trade Zones" which, they claimed, gave foreign multi-national capital a free hand while plundering the country's natural and human resources.

By 1989 the PIT-CNT's position as the peak union association was unchallenged though several unions announced their decision to leave. The Communist Party maintained its control of the Confederation. The PIT-CNT mounted three general strikes in opposition to the fall in the value of real wages in the last months of the Sanguinetti administration and fiercely opposed the economic orientation of his successor President Lacalle. The WCL-affiliated ASU does not rival the PIT-CNT.

Plenario Intersindical de Trabajadores-Convención Nacional de Trabajadores (PIT–CNT)
Inter-Trade Union Assembly-Workers' National Convention

Address. Buenos Aires 344, Montevideo

Phone. 952383

Membership. PIT-CNT unions have about 230,000 members and bargain on behalf of perhaps 400,000 workers.

Affiliated unions. The PIT–CNT has 200 unions and 40 federations affiliated. In 1990 a number of autonomous unions left the confederation, including the Merchant Seamen, the Technical School Employees' Union, and the Bus Drivers' Union

History and character. The CNT formed in 1964, bringing together all the major unions, but was dissolved by President Bordaberry in 1973, following which 18 members of the CNT central council "disappeared". Trade union acitivities re-emerged in 1983 under the name of the PIT, which was banned in January 1984 when it led a general strike. The fused PIT–CNT was restored to legal status on March 1, 1985 and held a congress in November 1985 under the slogan "Consolidating Democracy". The congress was attended by representatives of the ICFTU, WCL and the WFTU. Since its legalization, the PIT–CNT has led numerous strikes. At its Congress of June 1987, 1,200 delegates endorsed not only a continuing campaign against the Sanguinetti government's austerity measures but maintained the call for the prosecution of those guilty of crimes under the years of dictatorship. It also reinforced its committtment to workers in struggle in Latin America.

Vanuatu

Capital: Port Vila

Population: 151,000
(1988)

Political system. Vanuatu became an independent republic within the Commonwealth in 1980. The left-wing Vanuaaku Party (VP) is currently in power, having last been elected in 1987. A former General Secretary of the Vanuatu Trade Union Congress Kenneth Satungia founded an opposition Labour Party.

Economy. While there have been attempts to diversify the economy since independence, copra exports and agriculture have remained the mainstays. Tourism and the processing of primary products, offshore banking and a "flag of convenience" shipping register help to offset the country's visible trade deficit.

Vanuatu remains one of the least developed countries of the Pacific.

System of industrial relations. Vanuatu is not a member of the International Labour Organization.

Trade unionism. The country's first trade unions were formed in 1984 and soon organized into the Vanuatu Trade Union Congress (VTUC). In April and May 1988, municipal workers and dockers in Port Vila and other cities, went on strike in support of demands for better pay and conditions. A number of workers were subsequently sacked and some reports claimed that the government was considering revoking or amending legislation protecting trade unions.

National Union Blong of Leba (Vanuatu)

Address. P.O. Box 911, Port Vila
International affiliation. Affiliated to WFTU in 1988.

Vanuatu Trade Union Congress (VTUC)

Address. VTUC, P.O. Box 608, Port Vila
Leadership. Ephraim Kalsakau (general secretary)
Membership. 1500 in 13 unions.
History and character. The VTUC held its first national congress in December 1985. Affiliated unions include the Vanuatu Waterside, Maritime Allied Workers' Union, and the Oil and Gas Workers' Union. It has been assisted by ICFTU-APRO in organizing rural workers in the outer islands.
International affiliations. ICFTU; ICFTU/APRO.

511

Vatican City

Political system. The state of the Vatican City (the Holy See) which came into being in 1929, is the seat of the central government of the Roman Catholic Church.

Economy. In the 1980s, the Vatican City has suffered both debt and financial scandal. Employees are engaged in administration and communications.

System of industrial relations. In 1989 the Vatican agreed to the creation of a Labour Council to deal with social questions and to settle disputes between the Holy See and its employees. Employees elect four of the 11 Council members. The establishment of the Labour Council marked a clear departure from the paternalistic pattern of industrial relations at the Vatican and represented a victory for the Association of Vatican Lay Workers, which had campaigned for such a structure since 1979.

Trade unionism. The Vatican City has about 2,500 employees, the majority of whom are now members of the Association of Vatican Lay Workers (ADLV). The Vatican City is not a member of the International Labour Organization.

Associazione Dipendenti Laici Vaticani (ADLV)
Association of Vatican Lay Workers

Address. Arco del Belvedere, 00120 Citta del Vaticano
Phone. (6) 6985343
Leadership. Mariano Cerullo (president); Alessandro Cartoni (secretary)
Membership. 1,250.
History and character. The ADLV originated in the early 1980s. According to its president, workers' requests had hitherto been "met with silence" by the Vatican authorities, wages had been seriously eroded by inflation, and there were no internal Vatican labour regulations. The ADLV seeks to secure labour regulations based on international standards which should also "reflect the social doctrine of the Church and serve as an example to the world". It was reported in 1986 that the Vatican had established a three-member commission, including a representative of the ADLV, to draw up such regulations.

The ADLV organized the first ever strike in the Vatican on Feb. 29, 1988. Called in protest at a unilateral decision by the pontifical administration to pay differential wages, 1,400 of the 1,800 lay workers supported the strike in a response which exceeded union expectations. The Vatican authorities were equally surprised, as the president of the committee of staff affairs declared it a "totally unacceptable" form of protest.

International affiliation. ICFTU.

Venezuela

Capital: Caracas   **Population: 18,759,000**
                                               (1988)

Political system. Venezuela is a federal republic of 20 states and two federal territories. It is a multi-party democracy, ruled by the left of centre Democratic Action (AD) which was victorious in the elections of December 1988, paving the way for the return to power of President Carlos Andrés Pérez who succeeded President Lusinchi.

Economy. The petroleum industry is the dominant factor in the formal economy, and revenues from this source have been adversely affected by depressed world oil prices since the mid-1980s. The government has sought to meet the problems caused by weak economic performance and heavy external indebtedness through a tripartite "social pact" to implement austerity measures.

In 1988 the economy grew by 4.2 per cent and the unemployment rate dropped appreciably while inflation fell slightly. Employment is dominated by services, which account for more than half of it, with industry responsible for less than one quarter. Public sector employment continued to expand to the end of the 1980s. In September 1989 President Pérez announced the creation of an Employment and Social Investment Plan to stimulate labour-intensive activities in the construction industry.

System of industrial relations. Industrial relations in Venezuela have been generally good, and notably so by Latin American standards, since 1958, although the AD government's implementation of austerity measures in the mid-1980s has led to tensions between it and the CTV. There is no right to strike in the public sector, where a form of compulsory arbitration controlled by the government is in use, and the right to strike in other areas is also weakened by compulsory arbitration procedures. Although there is a strong legislative tradition governing employment conditions, largely designed to protect the worker, it applies only to large enterprises, whereas small and medium sized workplaces operate outside legal constraints in what is a large "informal sector" (whose share of the national workforce has been steadily growing until, in 1985, out of every 100 employed persons, 46 were in the informal sector, 33 in the modern private sector and 21 in the public sector). The trade unions have yet to come to grips with this trend, although plans by the CTV to reorganize on a sectoral instead of an enterprise basis could succeed in spreading protective legislation to small businesses. Indeed, since 1980, the CTV has taken a more "global" approach to national social and economic issues, especially with rising inflation eroding wages. However, even though it was instrumental in the formation of such tripartite bodies as the National Price Cost and Wage Commission in 1984 (CONACOPRESA), such critical measures as the fixing of the minimum wage has remained the preserve of presidential decree, a situation which appears to breach ILO Convention No. 26 on the need for tripartite consultation in the setting of such wage levels (which Venezuela ratified in 1974). During 1987, due to an inflation rate of 30 per cent, the CTV broke with the government, being particularly opposed to President Lusinchi's determination to repay the foreign debt regardless of the impact on the national economy.

Venezuela was a founding member of the International Labour Organization, but withdrew briefly in 1957–58. It ratified ILO Convention No. 98 (Right to Organize and Collective Bargaining, 1949) in 1968 and Convention No. 87 (Freedom of Association and Protection of the Right to Organize, 1948) in 1982.

For most of 1988 few collective agreements were signed due to reluctance to be committed ahead of the elections due in December. With the return of President Pérez there was a speedy announcement of stringent economic adjustments to meet Venezuelan inflationary and other problems while continuing to comply with its external debt servicing requirements; in the short term these entailed sharp rises in the price of basic goods which provoked great popular unrest outside the normal institutional channels. The unrest was put down at the cost of hundreds of deaths but its longer term implications were for the CTV which had been by-passed and whose leaders began to speak openly about the need to distance themselves from the government.

Trade unionism. The development of trade unions before 1945 was restricted by predominantly military rule. From 1945 to 1948, however, the founder of Democratic Action, Rómulo Betancourt, headed a revolutionary *junta* with wide labour support which became organized in the Confederación de Trabajadores de Venezuela (CTV). The AD government was overthrown and replaced by a military dictatorship under Pérez Jiménez in 1948, and trade unions were dissolved. Pérez Jiménez fell from power in 1958, and AD candidates served as elected presidents form 1959 to 1969. During this period the re-founded CTV consolidated its position as the dominant trade union centre, maintaining a close relationship to the AD, which provided it with financial assistance. Though it remains close to the AD, the CTV has representatives of other parties on its board.

By 1989 union density in Venezuela was estimated to be 30-35 per cent. Up to 90 of the country's union members are in the ICFTU-affiliated CTV which has a semi-official character. There are also two WCL and one WFTU affiliates, as well as a small number of independent unions.

Central Unitaria de Trabajadores de Venezuela (CUTV)
Venezuelan Workers' United Centre

Address. Av. Lecuna, Esq. Miseria, Edificio San Luis, Oficinas 16, Caracas
Phone. 5456572
Leadership. Not available
Membership. 40,000.
History and character. The CUTV was formed in the early 1960s by communist-influenced unions expelled from the Confederación de Trabajadores de Venezuela (CTV) over the issue of attitudes to the Cuban revolution. Its president, Hemmy Croes, a member of the Venezuelan Communist Party (PCV), was assassinated in Caracas in March 1985.
International affiliation. WFTU.

Confederación General de Trabajadores de Venezuela (CGT)

Address. Toro a Cardones, Edificio Fristol, Local 3, Parroquia Altagracia, Caracas
Leadership. Pedro Leon Trujillo (president)
History and character. The CGT held its fourth national congress in November 1986 and is described as politically independent.
International affiliations. WCL/CLAT.

Confederación de Trabajadores de Venezuela (CTV)
Confederation of Workers of Venezuela

Address. Edificio Las Mercedes, Esq. de Tienda Honda, Caracas
Leadership. Juan José Delpino (president); José León (secretary-general)
Membership. 1,100,000. Major affiliates include the peasants' union—FCV—with 700,000 members, the construction workers' union FETRACONS (100,000 members) and FETRASALUD (health workers).
History and character. The CTV was originally formed in 1947 in close association with the ruling AD party; it was dissolved under the dictatorship of Pérez Jiménez, but reformed in 1959, since when it has been the principal Venezuelan trade union centre. Its relationship with the social democratic AD has always been close, but the CTV criticized austerity measures and the working of the tripartite social pact under the AD government of Jaime Lusinchi from February 1984, arguing that a disproportionate share of the burden of the debt crisis was being borne by labour. The CTV also expressed dissatisfaction with the workings of the tripartite (but government-dominated) National Commission of Costs, Prices and Salaries (created in July 1984).

Its closeness to government received a severe jolt with the unforeseen popular unrest of February 1989 against the retrenchment programme of President Pérez. An extraordinary conference of April 1989 put forward special trade union proposals for resolving the crisis.
International affiliations. ICFTU/ORIT.

Movimiento Nacional de Trabajadores Para La Liberación (MONTRAL)

Address. P.O. Box 51236 Av. Las Palmas, Edificio FTC, Entre Av. Los Apamates y Rio de Janeiro, Caracas Z.P. 1050

Phone. (781)-39-55; (781)-37-66

History and character. Founded in 1974 and is a co-ordinating body for Christian-influenced unions.

International affiliations. WCL/CLAT.

At the May 1990 Congress José d'Elia stood down from the post of Secretary General.

Other organization

Acción Sindical Uruguaya (ASU)
Uruguayan Trade Union Action

Address. Avenida José E. Rodó 1836, Montevideo

Leadership. Mitil Ferreira (president)

Membership. 30,000 activists and sympathizers.

History and character. Supports the PIT-CNT and does not consider itself as a trade union centre or a trade union but as an organization to promote trade union autonomy and peace.

Publication. Avanzada.

International affiliations. WCL/CLAT.

Vietnam

Capital: Hanoi   **Population: 66,820,544**
                                                                                    (1989)

Political system. The Socialist Republic of Vietnam is a one-party state in which the Communist Party of Vietnam holds power.

Economy. Since 1987 there have been moves away from rigid orthodoxy towards a more "reformist" line incorporating decentralization, a shift towards light industry, a recognition of private enterprise as legitimate, and attempts to attract foreign investment. Vietnam's economy is primarily agricultural, but there is also a significant and diverse mining industry and manufacturing sector. Most foreign trade is with the Soviet Union and Eastern Europe.

System of industrial relations. Vietnam became the 140th member of the International Labour Organization in 1980 (South Vietnam having earlier been a member from 1950 to its collapse, ratifying ILO Convention No. 98 — Right to Organize and Collective Bargaining, 1949 — in 1964). On June 1, 1983, however, Vietnam suspended its participation in the ILO because of "unfounded allegations" by ILO member countries relating to the employment of Vietnamese guest workers in the Soviet Union (these focusing on the alleged deduction of a proportion of the earnings of such workers to pay Vietnamese obligations to the Soviet Union), and withdrew from the ILO effective May 31, 1985.

Trade Unionism. In the Democratic Republic of Vietnam (North Vietnam) established in 1945 trade unions were organized on the pattern of other communist countries in the Vietnam Confederation of Trade Unions (VCTU, renamed in 1988 the Vietnam General

Federation of Labour), whereas in South Vietnam trade unions were affiliated to the anti-communist Confédération Vietnammiene du Travail (CVT), founded in 1949, which in its latter years was affiliated to the WCL. Following the fall of the South to Northern forces in 1975, however, the VCTU was established throughout Vietnam. The former secretary-general of the CVT, Nguyen Van Phong, spent 10 years in a "re-education camp" following the fall of South Vietnam, and died in 1986. According to the ICFTU in June 1986, 20 former CVT officials were still detained in re-education camps.

No signs of discontent with the single union system have been reported to parallel developments in Eastern Europe. The emphasis on greater autonomy for the Confederation's primary unions which its leading bodies stressed in the later 1980s did not signify that their role was to be differently conceived.

Vietnam General Federation of Labour

Address. 82 Tsan Hung Dao, Hanoi.

Cable. TOCODO HANOI.

Leadership. Nguyen Van Tu (chairman); Cu Thi Hau (vice-chairman); Duong Xuan An (vice-chairman)

Membership. 89.5 per cent of the more than 4,000,000 workers and public employees in the state sector are reported to be members.

History and character. The Vietnam Confederation of Trade Unions (VCTU) held its sixth national congress from Oct. 17–20, 1988. Attending the congress were 839 delegates representing trade union organizations in all provinces and cities, branches and central offices. Delegates agreed to re-name the VCTU the Vietnam General Federation of Labour "in keeping with the requirements of expanding objectives". Delegates also approved a political report which criticized "negative manifestations" among some workers and the "red tape and rightist-leaning attitude" of some trade unions. In an interview given after the congress, the newly elected chairman, Nguyen Van Tu, said that workers' incomes were too low, and that trade unions and production management agencies had a responsibility to resolve the problem "practically and not in a perfunctory manner".

In 1989 the Executive Committee of the Confederation reviewed progress in implementing the decisions of the Sixth Congress. It also resolved to give greater autonomy to its primary trade unions in the provision of leisure, rest and convalescence service provision. This commitment to decentralization however did not alter the nature of the unions, which were still enjoined to "overcome difficulties, raise production-business, and work efficiency".

The primary unions were encouraged to achieve greater participation of their members in organization. The Executive set itself the task for 1989 of establishing labour associations in small industry and among handicraft workers, to build unions in non-government establishments, and to organize unions among the expatriate Vietnamese workforce.

International affiliation. WFTU.

Western Samoa

Capital: Apia

Population: 168,000
(1988)

Political system. Western Samoa is an independent member of the Commonwealth with its own head of state. There is a Cabinet government under a Prime Minister commanding majority support in the unicameral legislature (*Fono*). Organized parties began to play a role in the country's politics during the first half of the 1980s, although party allegiances remain highly volatile.

Economy. The Western Samoan economy is predominantly agricultural with some manufacturing. Important flows of foreign exchange earnings are remitted by migrant workers abroad.

System of industrial relations. Western Samoa is not a member of the International Labour Organization.

Trade unionism. The Public Service Association, which is the principal local trade union, has affiliated to the ICFTU.

Western Samoa Public Service Association (WSPSA)

Address. P.O. Box 1515, Apia
Phone. 24-134
Leadership. Peseta Sinave Isara (president); Tautulu Roebeck (vice-president and general secretary); Anae Tony Pereira (vice-president and treasurer)
Membership. 2,500, out of a working population estimated at 40,000 in 1988.
History and character. The WSPSA took strike action for 90 days in 1981 in pursuit of a pay claim, reducing many essential services to emergency manning levels, in what was considered the most nationally divisive issue for 50 years. Particular controversy resulted from the government's attempt to persuade the *matai* to exert their traditional authority to influence strikers to return to work, and the dispute caused tensions within the traditional structure of Western Samoan society. Since 1985 the WSPSA has been actively involved in the campaign against nuclear contamination of the environment. Negotiations with the government aimed at obtaining a 10 per cent general wage increase for public servants began in 1986; as of September 1988 the government had granted a five per cent wage increase and negotiations were continuing. In February 1988 the Prime Minister recognized the WSPSA as a non-government organization under his jurisdiction.

In 1989 the WSPSA made representations to the government against draft legislation which would make all civil service posts subject to political nomination.

Publications. PSA bulletin, distributed every three months to the general membership.
International affiliations. ICFTU/APRO.

Yemen

Capital: San'aa (political).
    Aden (economic and commercial)

Population: 11,207,000

Political system. The Republic of Yemen was formed in May 1990—six months ahead of plan—by the unification of the Yemen Arab Republic (North Yemen) and the People's Democratic Republic of Yemen (South Yemen). Lieutenant-General Ali Abdullah Saleh, outgoing President of North Yemen, became President of the united state, while Ali Salim al-bid, Secretary-General of the Yemen Socialist Party in former South Yemen, became Vice President. In 1990 a Provisional House of Representatives, an Advisory Council and a Yemen Council of Ministers were created. As many as 60 political parties were founded during the year, following the decision to legalize opposition groupings North and South and permit them representation in the Provisional House of Representatives.

Economy. In 1985–87, the North Yemen workforce was divided between agriculture (68.8 per cent), industry (9.2 per cent), and services (22.1 per cent); the South Yemen workforce was divided between agriculture (41 per cent), industry (17.5 per cent), and services (41.2 per cent). In the North important industries include cement and textile production; in the South, industrial activity is centred on the oil refinery at Aden.

Yemen suffered severe consequences from its decision to abstain in the Arab League and on the UN Security Council on sanctions and military intervention against Iraq. The united country already had debt equivalent to 110 per cent of GNP, and by November 1990 had to act as home to some 800,000 expatriates who had left Saudi Arabia following abolition of their privileges. In February 1991 US Aid to Yemen was also cut.

System of industrial relations. North Yemen joined the International Labour Organization in 1965, ratifying ILO Conventions No. 87 (Freedom of Association and Protection of the Right to Organize, 1948) and No. 98 (Right to Organize and Collective Bargaining, 1949) in 1976.

South Yemen became a member of the International Labour Organization 1969, when it ratified ILO Convention No. 98 (Right to Organize and Collective Bargaining, 1949). It did not ratify Convention No. 87 (Freedom of Association and Protection of the Right to Organize, 1948).

Trade unionism. Trade unions first appeared in the 1960s in North Yemen but workers' organization was strictly regulated by the labour code and there was little indication of significant trade union activity.

South Yemen had a single trade union system in place. The Aden Trades Union Congress, which was affiliated to the ICFTU and the ICATU, participated in the struggle for independence from Britain, which was achieved in 1967. The trade unions were subsequently reorganized in the General Confederation of Workers' Trade Unions, which joined the WFTU trade union bloc.

General Confederation of Workers' Trade Unions

Address. P.O. Box 1162, Ma'alla, Aden
Leadership. A. Karim Nasir Ahmed (secretary-general)
Membership. 77,708 (October 1986), reported as 73 per cent of the workers in South Yemen, organized in 886 trade union committees.

History and character. The Confederation was the single trade union system of South Yemen. The fifth congress was held in October 1986 under the slogan "for the strengthening of the role of the working class of Yemen and of the trade unions of Yemen, for the defence of the Yemeni revolution, for the realization of the five-year plan and for achieving Yemeni unity".

International affiliations. WFTU; ICATU.

Yugoslavia

Capital: Belgrade   **Population: 23,688,000**
                                                                           (1989)

Political system. The Socialist Federal Republic of Yugoslavia is a federation of six republics (Bosnia-Herzegovina, Croatia, Macedonia, Montenegro, Serbia and Slovenia) and two autonomous provinces (Kosovo and Vojvodina—both part of Serbia), in which effective political power is exercised by the League of Communists of Yugoslavia (LCY), the only political party. Under the 1974 Constitution there is, at federal level, a bicameral Federal Assembly (parliament), which elects the President and members of the Federal Executive Council (i.e. the Prime Minister and the Cabinet); each of the constituent republics and provinces also has its own government and parliament. In 1971 a system of collective leadership involving the regular rotation of posts was introduced in an attempt to unify the various nationalities, and since the death in 1980 of Marshal Tito the functions of head of state have been rotated on an annual basis among the members of a collective state presidency. Since the early 1980s the weakness of the Federal administration compared with those of the republics and provinces, resurgent nationalism, and the significant variation in regional prosperity hava all threatened the stability of the federal system.

This process of disintegration accelerated in the later 1980s as the communist régimes in Yugoslavia's neighbouring countries collapsed. Its expression was the political and economic diversity of the republics. Thus by 1991, Slovenia (with a relatively prosperous economy, a multi-party system and involved in a privatization process) was considering a declaration of independence; Montenegro showed little sign of active political life; Serbia was under strong and centralized control with a charismatic leader in Slobodan Milosevic who had rebuilt a socialist identity for his communist party. Croatia was swept at the polls in May 1990 by the right-wing Croation Democratic Union of Franjo Tudjman.

In all the republics except Slovenia (which is overwhelmingly Slovene and Catholic) there were ethnic tensions: Catholic and Croat Croatia has a large Serb and Orthodox minority increasingly oppressed by the Tudjman government; Bosnia has a large group of Muslim Slavs but substantial Serb and Croat populations; Montenegro and Macedonia each have Albanian minorities; the largest republic, Orthodox Serbia, while fiercely independent of the federal state, has abolished the autonomy of its provinces like Kosovo (largely Albanian Catholics or Muslims) and Vojvodina (with a large minority of Hungarians who are mainly Catholics).

The ability of the Federal Government to control the republics and defuse tensions is limited by its lack of a democratic base. From 1989 the Communist Prime Minister Ante Markovic tried to liberalize Federal institutions and abolish the CPY monopoly; in practice his writ did not run in all the republics. There were clashes between Federal and Croation troops in 1991. President Tudjman obtained a mandate for independence by referendum and threatened secession, while President Milosevic affirmed Serbia's commitment to Federal Yugoslavia (in which the Serbs are the biggest nation). Slovenia, like Croatia, had a timetable for independence if deadlocked negotiations on constitutional change were not resolved to its satisfaction. The early summer of 1991 brought a major constitutional crisis when the Serbs refused to accept the handover of the Presidency to the Croation Stipe Mesic and several republics withdrew from the collective presidency. This objection to what had historically been a routine transfer to maintain equal access to a Federal post posed a grave threat to the compromise on which Yugoslavia's existence was predicated.

Economy. As a consequence of over-ambitious foreign borrowings and a persistent trade deficit, Yugoslavia experienced serious economic difficulties from the end of the 1970s, and despite successive austerity programmes adopted by the government in 1980, 1983 and 1988, assistance by the International Monetary Fund, and agreements with foreign creditors to reschedule several of the country's medium- and long-term debts, its overall economic position deteriorated.

Of 9,500,000 civilian employees in 1989, 2,700,000 were employed in industry, 2,800,000 in agriculture and 3,700,000 in services. Unemployment was 15 per cent the same year. By 1989 inflation—already in excess of 200 per cent in 1988—was no less than 2,600 per cent. The response of the Markovic government was first a series of liberal economic reforms, and second a shock anti-inflation programme centred on pegging the currency to the German Deutschemark, squeezing the money supply and freezing wages. At the end of 1989 the impact of these policies began to be felt sharply.

System of industrial relations. Yugoslavia has been a member of the International Labour Organization since 1919, but withdrew from 1949–1951. It ratified ILO Conventions No. 87 (Freedom of Association and Protection of the Right to Organize, 1948) and No. 98 (Right to Organize and Collective Bargaining, 1949) in 1958.

In November 1988 the right to strike was constitutionally guaranteed though the Federal government failed to carry through a draft strike bill into law. In this vacuum the local union councils in the republics adopted their own strike codes. The state intervened in strikes on two occasions during the year. Official CTUY figures showed that roughly 470,000 workers participated in 1,900 strikes in 1989, a modest increase over 1988. However the trend of strikes was upward at the end of the year when the wage freeze was introduced. It was also noticeable that more than half of them were locally led.

In September 1989 the Federal Assembly passed a new law on Employment Relations, which for the first time introduced the concept of collective agreements. The Law, effective from 1990, regulated the making of agreements at Federal or republic level rather than at the level of the enterprise. For the rest most of the old self-management structure remained in place: though further new legislation placed private business on a par with socially owned business, the latter dominates the economy.

Trade unionism. Trade unions of conflicting orientations existed in the inter-war period, and in 1935 the monarchy also attempted to establish its own official Yugoslav Workers' Federation (JUGORAS). The United Federation of Workers' Unions of Yugoslavia (URSSJ), founded in 1922 by social democrats but by the late 1930s heavily influenced by the communists, claimed 100,000 members in 1940, when it was banned. The trade unions of the 1980s owed little to these early developments, however, and were essentially the product of the establishment of communist rule after World War II and the subsequent re-modelling of the economy and political and social relations through the principle of self-management. The Confederation of Trade Unions of Yugoslavia (Savez Sindikata Jugoslavije—CTUY) originated in January 1945 and took its present name in 1948.

Neither the national Constitution of 1974 nor the law prohibit the formation of unions outside the structure of the SSJ, although as a named organization it is accorded various rights and responsibilities under legislation, and the national Constitution also provides that unions shall pursue the objective of building and defending a self-managing socialist society. No unions outside the SSJ appeared before 1988. Prior to this Yugoslav trade union officials had stated to an ILO mission in 1983 that any such development would be inconceivable within the context of the system of self-mangement. All workers, including self-employed persons who do not employ others and co-operate with the social sector, members of farmers' co-operatives, policemen and civilian employees of the army (but not members of the armed forces), and the temporarily unemployed, have the right to join unions. Membership is voluntary but up to 99 per cent of workers are union members in the social sector (much less in the private sector), the position of those who are not organized being explained as arising form job mobility or personal dissatisfaction. In practice all applicants for union membership are accepted.

Role of trade unions under self-management. Under the 1974 Constitution and the Associated Labour Act of 1976 workers "associate" in self-managed enterprises in "basic organizations of associated labour" (BOALs), which may combine in multi-departmental "organizations of associated labour" (OALs) in larger enterprises. The basic trade union units are also formed at BOAL level, on the industrial union principle (i.e. whereby all workers of whatever occupation in the same enterprise belong to the same union), and federate within OALs. Unions also include the managers. An elected workers' council, constituted as the executive of the basic workers' assembly, serves as the decision-making body of each self-managing organization, with powers (which are exercised) to appoint and dismiss managers, who are in any case subject to periodic re-election. (In small BOALs of less than 30 persons the workers' assembly itself functions as the workers' council.) The role of trade unions within this system is principally to ensure the participation of the workers in the exercise of self-management, to prepare for and monitor elections to the workers' councils, to ensure that workers understand the issues and broader social responsibilities involved in decision-making, and to ensure that managers and technical experts do not achieve dominance within the enterprise at the expense of the workers, either individually or collectively. In this they are guided by the policies established by the higher levels of the CTUY. The trade unions play a large role in encouraging steps to raise productivity, and in leading the discussion of draft proposals from management before their adoption by the organs of self-management. Although in theory governed by the collective decisions of their members, in some cases trade union basic organizations have limited practical worker participation and are close to the management of the enterprise, with which they may work in concert. The actual status of the trade union within the enterprise under self-management is unusually dependent on the character and ability of the individuals involved in its operation. This dependency is emphasized by the range of competing centres of influence present within the enterprise (managers, the party, workers' council, etc.), all with claims to influence its basic strategic operations.

Proposals drawn up by a federal government commission in 1988 to deregulate the economy and introduce "a free commodity, money and labour market" raised the possibility that the BOAL system might be abandoned and enterprises reorganized along traditional company lines, with the role and powers of workers' self-management being scaled down and the concept of social ownership preserved by issuing shares to the workers. Constitutional amendments embracing such changes received final approval by the Federal Assembly on Nov. 25, 1988.

Self-management agreements. The basic trade union organizations participate in the discussion of (and must approve) self-management agreements which regulate working conditions, income, and prices. The Associated Labour Act stipulates various binding conditions in respect of working conditions, and also that workers must receive a guaranteed minimum income regardless of the profitability of the enterprise, and further guidelines are provided by social compacts reached at higher levels (from the commune level upwards) on a multipartite basis involving the trade unions. All enterprises must also follow the criteria laid down in national plans. As the self-managing organization must provide for investment as well as personal income, in effect the trade union is often in the position of explaining to workers why they should forfeit a greater immediate share of the proceeds from their labour, and the problems associated with this position have been exacerbated in recent years by the economic crisis. The same problem exists in respect of securing assent for differentials intended to foster productivity. Direct state intervention, to prevent enterprises from inflating prices and to control wages, has grown in importance, and this has led to difficulties with the trade unions which have emphasized the self-management rights of the enterprises.

Trade unions also participate in the distribution of social benefits, using funds from enterprises or the self-managed social services, and have a major role in providing welfare, sports, and cultural facilities. The unions have been criticized within Yugoslavia as being too deeply involved in such activities at the expense of defending workers' interests.

Representatives of the self-managed enterprises and other employers form the economic chambers, which at national level form the Federal Economic Chamber, with parallel chambers in the republics. These chambers assist in concluding self-managing agreements, and provide a component of a form of tripartism, with some resemblance to employers' organizations.

Trade unions also have members employed in the small private sector, and negotiate collective agreements on their behalf at the commune level. Union membership rates are much lower in this sector. Private employers may form associations, and have done so in some cases, and these associations are represented in the economic chambers. Associations of farmers owning their land but pooling labour and equipment may form self-managing organizations with close relations to the economic chambers.

Somewhat different factors apply in the social and public services, where "self-managing communities of interests" have as their supreme organs bicameral assemblies, comprising co-equal chambers representing the staff of such services (e.g. teachers, hospital workers) and the users of the services. These are intended to regulate the supply of services and the provision of resources to pay for them, although in practice direct state funding is still involved. Trade unions play a role in influencing and leading the discussions of such assemblies.

Relationship to party (LCY). In the 1950s the trade unions functioned as a "transmission belt" between the LCY and the working masses. This relationship is no longer acknowledged in theory in Yugoslavia, where the practical relationship has also become more ambiguous. Before 1990 the CTUY took "its guidance from the programme and the ideological and political orientation of the League". However, it enjoyed autonomy within this context, and leading officials did not simultaneously hold leading posts in the LCY.

Relationship to government. The CTUY is consulted by the government on a range of issues, and is required to participate in the area of planning, but retains autonomy from the state and has on occasions taken public positions contrary to those of the government. Owing to the degree of decentralization involved both in self-management and the Yugoslav government itself, the government normally sought consent from the CTUY before attempting new departures in policy. The CTUY is not subsidized by the state but depends on membership dues, which are shared between the various levels. The ILO Committee of Experts on Conventions and Recommendations has never expressed any views on the relationship between the government and trade unions in Yugoslavia.

Disputes. Individual grievances may be taken up through the trade union (although the union will also consider the viewpoint of the other party); and the union, if unable to achieve a satisfactory solution through discussion with management, may have recourse to the workers' council (i.e. the supreme body of the enterprise), or, in cases of general principles, to the courts of associated labour. In the case of collective disputes the trade union will seek to find a solution by assisting discussion; if this fails and the dispute may lead to a stoppage, the workers must appoint delegates who with representatives of the trade union, political organizations (such as the LCY) and the workers' assembly form a joint committee for settlement of the dispute, the trade union functioning in effect as a mediator rather than as a party to the dispute. Where this procedure breaks down stoppages occur, normally at the single-plant level, and the existence of strikes is acknowledged by the Yugoslav authorities, according to which strikes indicate a breakdown of the proper functioning of the system of self-management and also of the trade union. The CTUY has itself never organized strikes, which arise spontaneously, but in November 1987 the then CTUY president, Zvonimir Hrabas, stated that if the working class had no other available means to resolve problems, the trade unions must support workers who resorted to strike action, although he reaffirmed that legalization of strikes was not envisaged. Hrabas also said that the demands and daily problems of workers could be dealt with more effectively if more worker delegates participated in government, rather than those who "passed themselves off as workers". Strikes did in fact occur throughout the 40 years of Yugoslavia's communist history.

The evolution of the CTUY was less abrupt than that of the official unions in most other European countries. Already in 1988 different levels had played a part in organizing protests, marches and even strikes. The 97,000-strong Croatian Union for Educators and Cultural Workers threatened a strike in December 1988 against a cut in public spending; the Belgrade city unions late in 1988 threatened a boycott of electricity payments if a price increase were not rescinded; the Croatian council threatened legal proceedings to obtain a "no-confidence" vote against Federal economic policy. At Federal and republic level there was discussion about the union role throughout 1989; statutes were reviewed in preparation for the June 1990 (11th) CTUY Congress. Preliminary agreement was reached that the officials should be independent, that membership be voluntary in fact as well as in theory, and that craft or industrial unions—not political councils—should be the core of the structure.

When it met, the Congress arranged its business in a new way. It acknowledged that the demand for an independent organization was nearly unanimous, and promulgated for the first time ever an action programme. It withdrew from the Socialist Alliance of Working Peoples of Yugoslavia, the co-ordinating body for all communist institutions in the country, and accepted that it would have to function in a pluralistic environment.

But in parallel to the threat to the Federal centre of the state, there were diverse tendencies in the CTUY. In Slovenia freedom of association was incorporated in the constitution during 1989 and the union council was the first to adopt an independent programme. In Croatia, the union council also adopted freedom of association and began to draw up statutes for a multi-party system. There was a discussion about changing its name to the "League of Independent Unions of Croatia". Local union leaders who formed an independent rail union were given the council's blessing, and backing was given to a group of workers seeking to organize an independent private sector union.

During 1989 three noteworthy independent unions were formed. After a major strike in December 1988 railway engineers formed a new union in Slovenia and North-West Croatia, 1,500 strong; railway engineers in Zagreb (also in Croatia) took the same step after their strike of September 1989. With republic-wide support this group was able to mount a successful strike in January 1990. Finally, airline pilots formed their own independent union in December 1989.

Yet the structural changes of 1990 did not immediately lead to behavioural changes. In Serbia where the rule of the Serbian Socialist (formerly communist) Party of President

Slobodan Milosevic was legitimized by a 70 per cent vote in December 1990, the unions continued to support the republic government.

Savez Sindikata Jugoslavije—Véce SSJ
Confederation of Trade Unions of Yugoslavia—CTUY Council

Address. Trg Marksa i Engelsa 5, 11000 Belgrade
Phone. (11) 330481/9. Also (11) 330922 for international trade union co-operation
Telex. YU-CEVESI 11121
Leadership. Rotating presidency
Membership. Over 6,000,000.

History and character. The CTUY was established (as the United Trade Union of Workers and Employees) in 1945, and took its present name at the first congress in 1948.

Ideologically, the CTUY exists to organize the workers to enable them to realize their interests, influence and constitutional position as the ruling force in society. It is constituted as a socio-political organization within the Socialist Alliance of the Working People of Yugoslavia. Decisions of the higher-level bodies of the CTUY are binding on lower-level bodies, although the exercise of this authority is limited by the difficulty of maintaining discipline within the self-management system. At federal level the CTUY signs social compacts, regulating incomes and other basic social and economic factors, and these compacts are used as the framework for compacts agreed at lower levels and for agreements within enterprises. The CTUY currently emphasizes the role of the trade unions in implementing the government's Long-Term Economic Stabilization Programme, which it participated in drafting. This includes a drive to restructure the economy, increase production and exports, the closer linking of incomes to productivity, and efforts to curb inflation. Elements emphasized by the CTUY include the protection of the lower-paid (including protection by subsidies to offset inflation), and retraining and flexibility with greater geographical and occupational mobility of labour. The unions have their delegates in the assemblies of socio-political communities at all levels, and a significant part of CTUY activity is in the area of political action, although this activity is often regarded with indifference at lower levels where narrowly trade union issues predominate.

The June 1990 (11th) Congress introduced major changes into the structure of the CTUY and into its statutes. The extent to which these changes have been implemented is in doubt and the description which follows reflects the pre-Congress position.

Structure. Basic trade union organizations are formed at the BOAL self-managing department level. There are about 50,000 basic trade union organizations, with an average membership of 120, but ranging up to 2,000 or more members. These units may federate at enterprise level in large concerns. The CTUY is structured both territorially (commune, inter-commune, republican or provincial levels) and sectorally. The ruling body of the CTUY is the congress, which meets normally every four years and is composed of delegates elected in commune, republican and provincial organizations. Between congresses the 117-member CTUY council is supreme, this comprising 15 representatives from each of the six republic organizations, 12 from each of the two provincial organizations, two from the Federation of Pensioners and one from the Federation of Disabled Persons. The council elects a 22-member presidency (presidium) from among its membership (again with balanced territorial representation), and this forms the executive body, under the president of the CTUY council. The presidency appoints the secretariat. The principle of rotation of office-holders is in force at all levels of the CTUY, whose statutes provide that a member cannot be elected more than twice to the same body (single terms of office being two years in basic-level organizations, and four years at higher levels).

Affiliated unions. There are 15 sectoral federal trade union committees; these are all located at Trg Marksa i Engelsa 5, 11000 Belgrade, except where shown, and have the common telex number YU-CEVESI 11121.

1. **Federal Committee of the Administration, Jurisdiction and Finance Workers' Union**
   Phone: (11) 330943.

2. **Federal Committee of the Agricultural, Food and Tobacco Workers' Union**
   Phone: (11) 332481.

3. **Federal Committee of the Building Workers' Union**
   Phone: (11) 331510.

4. **Federal Committee of the Catering and Tourism Workers' Union**
   Phone: (11) 340343.

5. **Federal Committee of the Chemical and Non-Metallic Minerals Workers' Union**
   Phone: (11) 335893.

6. **Federal Committee of the Commerce Workers' Union**
   Phone: (11) 340344.

7. **Federal Committee of the Communal Economy and Handicrafts Workers' Union**
   Phone: (11) 337159.

8. **Federal Committee of the Education, Schooling, Science and Culture Workers' Union**
   Phone: (11) 335196.

9. **Federal Committee of the Energy and Petrochemical Workers' Union**
   Phone: (11) 330220.

10. **Federal Committee of the Forestry and Woodworking Workers' Union**
    Phone: (11) 333603.

11. **Federal Committee of the Health and Social Security Workers' Union**
    Phone: (11) 335196.

12. **Federal Committee of the Metal Production and Manufacturing Workers' Union**
    Phone: (11) 332337.

13. **Federal Committee of the Printing, Newspaper, Editing and Information Workers Union**
    Phone: (11) 332953.

14. **Federal Committee of the Textile, Leather and Footwear Workers' Union**
    Phone: (11) 331582.

15. **Federal Committee of the Transport and Communications Workers' Union**, Miloša Pocerca 10, 11000 Belgrade.
    Phone: (11) 646321.

The Federation of Pensioners of Yugoslavia and the Federation of Disabled Persons of Yugoslavia have collective membership of the SSJ.

Republic and provincial councils of the CTUY. There are six republic councils (for Bosnia-Herzegovina, Croatia, Macedonia, Montenegro, Serbia and Slovenia) and two provincial councils (for Kosovo and Vojvodina).

Publications. Rad (weekly, 70,000 copies); *Jugoslovenski Sindikati* (*Yugoslav Trade Unions*; every two months, also published in English, French, Spanish and Russian). Newspapers and journals are also published by constituent organizations.

International affiliation. None (the SSJ withdrew from the WFTU in 1950). Unusually for a communist centre, the CTUY is a long-standing participant in TUAC. In November 1989 it applied for affiliation to the ETUC.

Zaïre

Capital: Kinshasa **Population: 34,442,000**

Political system. Zaïre is a one-party state ruled since the military *coup* of 1965 by President Marshal Mobutu Sese Seko, leader of the Mouvement Populaire de la Révolution (MPR).

Political reforms which would lead to a multi-party system in 1991 were announced in May 1990. As part of the transition President Mobutu announced his resignation as head of the MPR; by the end of 1990 more than 60 opposition parties had been formed. In early 1991 the transition was bedevilled by a dispute over the influence of the President over a national constitutional conference to bring in the reforms.

Economy. Zaïre's economy is plagued by chronic debt. Since 1983, the government has co-operated closely with the IMF and external aid donors in implementing reforms designed to re-establish foreign confidence in the economy. The first five-year plan, adopted in 1985, emphasized the need for sustained private investment and decentralization.

Some 38 per cent of Zaire's population lives in urban areas. The labour force is divided between agriculture (71.5 per cent), industry (12.9 per cent) and services (15.6 per cent).

System of industrial relations. Zaïre ratified ILO Convention No. 98 (Right to Organize and Collective Bargaining, 1949) in 1969, but has not ratified Convention No. 87 (Freedom of Association and Protection of the Right to Organize, 1948). The National Labour Council is a tripartite body with advisory powers in respect of minimum wage rates, and under a National Inter-occupational Collective Agreement between UNTZa and the employers' organization, ANEZA, wages and prices have been fixed jointly on an annual basis, with government supervision. Zaïre ratified Convention No. 29 on Force Labour in 1960, but the ILO has noted that though compulsory civic service has been abolished in law, citizens may be obliged to carry out development work, and compulsory labour may be exacted from tax defaulters and other offenders. The government is reported to be revising the Labour Code so as to bring legislation in line with ILO conventions.

Trade unionism. The trade unions were consolidated into the Union Nationale des Travailleurs du Zaïre (UNTZa) in 1967, and this remains the sole trade union centre.

Union Nationale des Travailleurs du Zaïre (UNTZa)
National Union of Workers of Zaïre

Address. B.P. 8814, Kinshasa

Leadership. Kombo Ntonga Booke (president); Bwensa Dia Malosa (general secretary).

History and character. Founded 1967. The UNTZa launched a contributory national health insurance scheme (UPM) in August 1986 in co-operation with the WCL and the ICFTU. It has also established a number of education, health, rural co-operative, agricultural, banking and other projects. The UNTZa protested in the late 1980s against the steady decline in the purchasing power of Zaïrean workers, which it attributes to currency depreciation and abuse perpetrated under the guise of economic "liberalism".

Publication. The UNTZa publishes *Mosali*, a periodical, and occasional trade union studies.

International affiliation. OATUU. Has relations with the ICFTU, WCL and WFTU.

Zambia

Capital: Lusaka

Population: 7, 875,448
(July 1989)

Political system. Zambia is a one-party state ruled by the socialist United National Independence Party (UNIP) under the President, Dr Kenneth Kaunda.

Economy. Zambia derives around 90 per cent of its export earnings from copper (and most of the balance from other minerals) and was severely affected by the fall in world copper prices which occurred in the late 1970s and the 1980s. In May 1987, Zambia dropped the IMF programme for repayment of its huge foreign debt.

Zambia has been a member of the International Labour Organization since 1964 but has not ratified Conventions No. 87 (Freedom of Association and Protection of the Right to Organize, 1948) or No. 98 (Right to Organize and Collective Bargaining, 1949). However it has ratified Conventions covering forced labour (1964, 1965), pay and organization among agricultural workers (1964, 1972, 1978), equal remuneration (1972), and discrimination (1979).

In general, the government has sought to involve the unions in the restructuring of the economy on the basis of tripartite consultations. All wage settlements must be approved by the Prices and Incomes Commission, which must take account of the government's prices and incomes policy, and there is compulsory arbitration by the Industrial Relations Court where agreement cannot be reached through conciliation and mediation.

Trade unionism. Trade unions first developed in the copper belt in the 1930s. There is one trade union centre, the Zambia Congress of Trade Unions (ZCTU). Trade unions are required to register under the *Industrial Relations Act* whereupon they are deemed to be affiliated to the ZCTU. By African standards, the labour movement is large, independent and influential, and the principle of collective bargaining is well established.

The ZCTU has always resisted official status, and in 1990 went further than ever before in making its distance from the Kaunda régime. Its Chairman-General Frederick Chiluba advocated muti-party democracy and sponsored a pro-democracy movement; the government responded by threatening to suppress the check-off system. At the end of the year ZCTU severed all ties with the ruling United National Independence Party.

Zambia Congress of Trade Unions (ZCTU)

Address. P.O. Box 20652, Kitwe
Phone. 211999
Leadership. Frederick J. Chiluba (chairman-general); Newstead Zimba (secretary-general)
Membership. 400,000.
History and character. The ZCTU was formed in 1965 in succession to the former United Trades Union Congress (UTUC). Its leadership has been one of the main sources of criticism of the government. The ZCTU has consistently tried to distance itself from the government and ruling party so as to avoid the fate of other organizations which have been incorporated into the régime. It has opposed government moves requiring all "mass organizations" to affiliate to the ruling UNIP.

Frederick Chiluba, Newstead Zimba and 15 other prominent trade unionists were expelled from the UNIP in January 1981 following a wave of strikes which the government related to a thwarted plot to stage a *coup*. The expulsions were followed by protest strikes in the copperbelt and other sectors, and in April 1981 the expelled trade unionists were re-admitted to the party. Chiluba and Zimba and others were detained in July 1981 following further industrial unrest, Dr Kaunda stating that the detained trade unionists were instigating illegal strikes with the aim of toppling the UNIP leadership. However, all the detained trade union leaders were released on the order of the courts by November 1981. The labour movement has come under increasing pressure in recent years. Early in

1985, in response to a wave of wildcat strikes triggered by the imposition of austerity measures required by the IMF, the government banned strikes in various sectors of the economy and ordered employers to end the statutory "check-off" of union dues for illegal strikers. These measures were revoked in 1986, but the labour movement still complained that it was hamstrung by legal restrictions, censorship and pressure to succumb to the demands of the ruling party. The passports of Chiluba and Zimba were withdrawn in 1987. At the end of that year Chiluba was expelled from his own union, the 27,000-member National Union of Building, Engineering and General Workers, amid charges of constitutional irregularities. However the ZCTU alleged that this internal discord was engineered by the government as part of its campaign to disable the labour movement. Chiluba retained his position as ZCTU chairman and the courts later ruled that the ZCTU could over-rule his expulsion from the NUBWEGW. Tensions between the government and the labour movement were increased in the run-up to presidential and parliamentary elections held at the end of 1988. Meanwhile the standard of living for Zambian workers has continued to fall steeply following riots against austerity measures at the end of 1986 and the country's break with the IMF in mid-1987.

At the end of October 1990 Chiluba was re-elected as Chairman-General of ZCTU at its Congress which went on to reject participation in government-sponsored committees. In July he had become Deputy Chairman of the Zambian pro-democracy campaign, and shortly after was briefly detained by the police for taking part in an unauthorized meeting. At the end of the year it was reported that ZCTU had severed all ties with the Party.

Affiliates. There are 19 affiliated unions, including (with memberships as of the end of 1987 for the largest): Airways and Allied Workers' Union; Civil Servants Union of Zambia (27,000); Guards Union of Zambia; Hotel Catering Workers' Union of Zambia; Mineworkers' Union of Zambia (48,000); National Union of Building, Engineering and General Workers (27,000); National Union of Commercial and Industrial Workers (28,000); National Union of Plantation and Agricultural Workers; National Union of Postal and Telecommunications Workers; National Union of Public Services' Workers (67,155); National Union of Transport and Allied Workers; Railway Workers' Union of Zambia; Zambia Electricity Workers' Union; Zambia National Union of Teachers; Zambia Typographical Workers' Union; Zambia Union of Financial Institutions; Zambia United Local Authorities Workers' Union; University of Zambia Allied Workers' Union.

International affiliations. OATUU; CTUC.

Zimbabwe

Capital: Harare   **Population: 9,400,000**

Political system. Since independence in 1980, Zimbabwe has been an independent republic within the Commonwealth. In 1987, it moved from parliamentary government to a presidential-style government and *de facto* one-party rule under the Zimbabwe African National Union (Patriotic Front) ZANU(PF), led by Dr Robert Mugabe.

Economy. Zimbabwe has a relatively well-diversified economy with a strong infrastructural base to facilitate further development.

In 1989 inflation was running at 20 per cent (though government specified only minimum 10 per cent increase, and the employers' organization EMCOZ claims wages have fallen by 13 per cent since 1980). The unemployment rate of 25 per cent does not fully reflect the position in the unregulated economy, but this sector is probably the best hope of absorbing a large proportion of the 300,000 school leavers joining the workforce annually in the 1990s.

System of industrial relations. Zimbabwe has been a member of the International Labour Organization since 1980 but has yet to ratify either ILO Convention No. 87 (Freedom of Association and Protection of the Right to Organize, 1948) or No. 98 (Right to Organize and Collective Bargaining, 1949).

ZCTU has pressed the government to define in law which are the "essential industries" where strikes may not be held under emergency powers, but without success. The government is closely involved in industrial relations, and its powers under the normally renewed State of Emergency are formidable. It also has powers under the *Labour Relations Act* 1985 and the *Parastatals Commission Act* 1987. The *Labour Relations Act* excludes from its coverage those provided for by the Constitution, and so covers perhaps a quarter of Zimbabwe's workers; the Parastatal Commission on the other hand is responsible for more than half of them. Civil servants fall under a separate Commission. Domestic and agricultural workers, the worst paid of all, are excluded from these arrangements. The system has come under criticism from employers and unions.

Collective bargaining takes place in June and July within guidelines established by the government. Its locus is the Employment Board, of which there are 42, each corresponding to an industry. There are 19 National Employment Councils for non-union industries where a government-ordained minimum wage is set. Zimbabwe's Labour Relations Tribunal has fallen into disuse, but the lower level Labour Relations Board is still operational.

Trade unionism. Since independence in 1980, previously competing trade union centres representing European and African workers have been reconstituted into the Zimbabwe Congress of Trade Unions (ZCTU), now the sole trade union centre. The ZCTU has attempted to remain independent and to maintain a working relationship with the government without compromising its effectiveness. Nevertheless from time to time the government has used controversial legislation inherited from the previous régime of Ian Smith to suppress labour unrest. Emergency powers outlawing the disruption of essential services and providing for prison sentences of up to five years for strikers were used to break a five-day strike by railway workers in 1982, and suspended prison sentences were imposed on 215 workers. In March 1985 a number of trade unionists were arrested and held in detention, again under emergency powers dating from the Smith era, in what was described as a "concerted attack" on trade unionists. The government also intervenes in pay bargaining and determines wage levels through the revised Labour Relations Act of 1985.

Union density in 1988 was assessed at 17 per cent, but comparisons with other countries are difficult because Zimbabwe's unions are national bodies of which the ubiquitous worker committees tend to act independently. In the late 1980s the ZCTU became more outspoken, culminating in the arrest in October 1989 of Morgan Tsvangirai, its secretary-general, after his condemnation of the closure of the University of Zimbabwe, once again under powers inherited from the Smith régime. He was held for two months in defiance of High Court orders to free him and refused to join other ZCTU officials in endorsing the re-election of President Mugabe in March 1990.

In April 1990 the President responded to these criticisms by appointing the ZCTU Vice-President Florence Chitauro (a ZANU member) to Parliament but he blocked a ZCTU demand for a say in the planning and budgetary process.

One fissure appeared in the ZCTU's monopoly representation position in September 1989 when non-graduate teachers formed the Zimbabwe Teachers' Union (ZIT) in opposition to the Zimbabwe Teachers' Association (ZIMTA) with the objective of gaining better representation for lower paid teachers. When in March 1990 a salary increase was awarded to graduate teachers alone, non-graduate teachers staged the longest strike in Zimbabwe's history during the 18 days to June 11 when they returned to work without achieving a settlement.

Zimbabwe Congress of Trade Unions (ZCTU)

Address. P.O. Box 3549, Harare
Phone. 793092
Leadership. J. Mutandare (president); M. Tsvangirai (secretary-general)
Membership. 162,835.

History, structure and policies. The Zimbabwe Congress of Trade Unions was founded in February 1981. Policy is decided by a congress which meets every four years. A smaller conference is held bi-annually to review progress. The ZCTU is run by a general council comprising representatives of affiliated unions and elected officials, a 19-member national executive and a secretariat. At its 1985 congress the ZCTU resolved to participate fully in the tripartite organizations of government, employers and unions, to assist in the formulation of development plans, and to promote workers' education and co-operatives. A policy of pan-africanism and non-alignment was adopted. The ZCTU is strongly opposed to apartheid in South Africa and is in favour of sanctions. In 1986 it organized a seminar on the impact of sanctions in Zimbabwean workers and launched a Sanctions Unemployment Fund to help mitigate the undoubted adverse effects sanctions would have on the country's workers.

Following research carried out in conjunction with the ICFTU, the ZCTU pressed in 1987 for an increase in the minimum wage together with a six-monthly pay review. A *Minimum Wages Act* was passed in 1980, but the wage set then and subsequent adjustments have long been overtaken by inflation. The ZCTU advocated a monthly minimum of Z$277 (as against the current minimum scale of Z$85–Z$158), and further argued that the minimum wages system constrained collective bargaining, since unions could rarely press for more than the minimum. However the government imposed a wage freeze in July 1987, and minimum wages remained the same until March 1988 when they were increased by a maximum of 15 per cent under Emergency Powers regulations. The ZCTU has repeatedly protested that government intervention into collective bargaining and the curtailment of the right to strike have rendered meaningful negotiations with employers almost impossible.

Since 1989 ZCTU relations with the government have deteriorated steeply. The climax came when Morgan Tsvangirai used the closure of the University of Zimbabwe to launch a general attack on the Mugabe government: "its attempts to suppress the growing disenchantment of the masses over the cost of living, transport problems, unemployment, destitution and many other negative socio-economic developments . . . have brought about the naked use of brute force and the suppression of individual rights". He spent October and November 1989 in custody for these remarks, and was unreconciled to the President the following spring.

Affiliated unions. There are 30 national sectoral unions, including (with memberships for the largest); the Associated Mine Workers' Union (26,000); Construction Workers' Union (15,000); Commercial Workers' Union (7,000); Plastics, Chemicals and Allied Workers' Union; Ziscosteel Workers' Union; Catering and Hotel Workers' Union (9,500); Textile Workers' Union (6,345); Tobacco Industrial Workers' Union; Union of Journalists; Posts and Telecommunications Workers' Union (5,628); United Food and Allied Workers' Union (6,000); Leather, Shoe and Allied Workers' Union; Federation of Municipal Workers' Union (9,282); Zimbabwe Radio, Television Manufacturers Workers' Union; Air Transport Workers' Association; Air Transport Union; General Agricultural and Plantation Workers' Union (10,000); Graphical Union; National Engineering Workers' Union (8,500); Amalgamated Railwayman's Union (13,599); Motor Industry Workers' Union (6,410); Transport and General Workers' Union; Education, Scientific, Social and Cultural Workers' Union (9,000); Furniture and Cabinet Workers' Union; National Union of Zimbabwe Electricity Supply Authority; Union of Musicians; and the Zimbabwe Society of Bank Officials.

Publication. The Worker.

International affiliation. OATUU. The ZCTU also chairs the Southern African Trade Union Co-ordinating Council (SATUCC).

INTERNATIONAL ORGANIZATIONS

There are three world organizations of national trade union centres, all of which are recognized by the UN and its agencies as representative of labour at the world level. The International Confederation of Free Trade Unions (ICFTU) comprises trade unions of the western world, including the American Federation of Labor-Congress of Industrial Organizations (AFL-CIO) in the United States, the West German DGB, and the British TUC. Most of its affiliates function in systems where trade union diversity is permitted, but in a minority of cases ICFTU affiliates are the sole authorized centres (as in Singapore and Taiwan) with close links to the ruling party. The World Federation of Trade Unions (WFTU) is dominated by the trade union centres of the Soviet bloc countries, but also includes numerous affiliates from Third World one-party states (where there is typically only one legal trade union centre) and a number of left-wing centres functioning within pluralist capitalist societies, notably the French CGT. Most of the significant affiliates of the (much smaller) World Confederation of Labour (WCL) are in Latin America, where there are connections with the Roman Catholic Church, or are Christian unions within western Europe. Each of the three world centres maintains its own regional organizations: of these arguably the most important are the ICFTU's ORIT and the WCL's CLAT, both of which are in Latin America, where trade unionism tends to be pluralistic, vigorous and highly politicized.

The Organization of African Trade Union Unity (OATUU) was founded in part in an attempt to rid the African continent of the ideological divisions created by extra-continental affiliations, and the world centres are weakest in Africa. However, the OATUU itself has been riven by internal conflict and its status is also diminished by the absence or minimal development of organized trade unionism (on either the ICFTU or the WFTU model) in much of Africa.

International and regional organizations of national trade union centres

All Africa Teachers' Organization (AATO)

Address. P.O. Box 7431, Accra, Ghana
Phone. 221515
Telex. 2269 AFCINE
Leadership. T.A. Bediako (secretary-general)
Membership. Claims over 3,000,000.
International Affiliations. WCOTP; OATUU; friendly relations with the three world centres.
Publications. AATO Newsletter.
Affiliated unions and structure. SYNEMB (BENIN); BTU (BOTSWANA); SNEA (BURKINA FASO); FETRASSEIC (CONGO); SNEPPCI, SYNESCI (COTE D'IVOIRE); GTU (GAMBIA); GNAT (GHANA); FSPE (GUINEA); KNUT (KENYA); LAT (LESOTHO); NTAL (LIBERIA); TAM (MALAWI); SNEC (MALI); GTU (MAURITIUS); SNE (MOROCCO); SNEN (NIGER); NUT (NIGERIA); SADTU (SOUTH AFRICA); EER (RWANDA); SNEEL (SENEGAL); SLTU (SIERRA LEONE); SNAT (SWAZILAND); CHAKIWATA (TANZANIA); SELT (TOGO); SGEP (TUNISIA); UTA (UGANDA); FENEZA (ZAIRE); ZNUT (ZAMBIA); ZIMTA (ZIMBABWE); NANTU (NAMIBIA); ONP (MOZAMBIQUE); ETA (ETHIOPIA); SYNEDD-TO (TOGO); JUWATA (TANZANIA); FENESCU (ZAIRE).

History and character. Founded in 1974 and keeps in touch with affiliates through conferences, workshops, meetings and seminars. Aims to promote closer contact between national teacher organizations, to defend teachers' rights, to promote cultural advance through education, to promote international understanding, to foster the improvement of the curriculum and teaching methods. AATO has intervened in a number of countries to defend teachers' organizations and has supported teachers in the front line states in the struggle against apartheid.

Asian-Pacific Trade Union Co-ordination Committee (APTUCC)

History and character. APTUCC was formed at a conference of Asian and Pacific unions held in Manila (Philippines) on Aug. 13–15, 1987. It is not-aligned but its executive accepts as permanent "guests" the three main world centres. The conference elected Bonifacio Tupaz (Philippines) as chariman and K. R. Srivastava of India as secretary. APTUCC's head office is in New Delhi.

Caribbean Congress of Labour (CCL)

Address. Room 407, Norman Centre, Broad Street, Bridgetown, Barbados.
Phone. 429-5517
Cable. CARCONLA
Leadership. Lascelles Beckford (president); Kertist Augustus (secretary-treasurer)
Membership. 122,605.
History and character. Founded in 1960, the CCL now has 26 affiliates in 17 countries. It represents the views of organized labout in regional fora such as CARICOM, the Caribbean Common Market.

The CCL in 1988 continued its efforts to promote regional unification with high level seminars and symposia. It also made presentations to the Heads of State meetings in Antigua (July 1988) and Grenada (July 1989) outlining concerns over issues affecting workers' rights in view of the parlous economic position of a number of Caribbean countries. The Barbados-based Secretariat carried out education and training programmes in 1988 and 1989 as well as research; it also hosted a Caribbean regional seminar on education and research in conjunction with the ICFTU. In mid-1988 the CCL recruited a Women's Trade Union Programme Co-ordinator. In November 1989 the CCL held its Tenth Triennial Conference of Delegates in Curaçao.

Commonwealth Trade Union Council (CTUC)

Address. Congress House, Great Russell Street, London WC1B 3LS
Phone. 071 631 0728
Telex. 266006 CTUC G
Fax. 071 436 0301
Leadership. Shirley Carr (president); Patrick Quinn (director)
History and character. The CTUC is a Council established in 1979 grouping national trade union organizations in the 50 Commonwealth countries.

It embraces 30,000,000 organized workers. The CTUC aims to promote the interests of workers in the Commonwealth.

Practical assistance is given to trade unions in developing countries—especially in trade union education—through the CTUC Charitable Trust.

In addition the CTUC also promotes Development Education with Trade Unionists in industrialized countries, aimed at raising awareness of international issues.

The CTUC also represents the interests of Commonwealth trade unionists to Commonwealth governments and institutions. A General Session is held once a year where representatives of member organizations can decide CTUC policy.

Trade union leaders from Africa, the Americas, Asia, the Pacific and Europe make up the CTUC's Steering Committee and meet at least three times a year. The CTUC is financed by contributions from member organizations and official aid-giving bodies.

Publication. The CTUC publishes a quarterly newsletter *Update*. It also has available reports of its main educational activities in the different parts of the Commonwealth.

Congreso Permanente de Unidad Sindical de Los Trabajadores de América Latina (CPUSTAL)
Permanent Congress of Trade Union Unity of Latin American Workers

Address. Ribera de San Cosme No 22, Office 105, Mexico 4 DF, Col. San Rafael C.P. 06470, Mexico
Phone. 566 0530
Membership. Claims 20,000,000.
History and character. Founded in 1964 by representatives from 18 countries, CPUSTAL now has affiliates in 25 Latin American or Caribbean countries. It is autonomous but has close links to the WFTU. It claims to have experienced difficulties in co-ordinating actions with ORIT and CLAT, both of which are larger in this continent. CPUSTAL was seriously weakened by the suppression of the Chilean CUT after 1973. It has lately devoted much of its time to agitation against the foreign debt burden of many Latin American countries.

Council of Nordic Trade Unions (NFS)
Nordens Fackliga Samorganisation

Address. Barnhusgatan 16, S–105 53 Stockholm, Sweden
Phone. 796 25 00
Telex. 13712 LABMOV
Fax. 789 88 68
Leadership. Sune Ahlen (general secretary)
Membership. 7,200,000.
International affiliations. None directly, but all members are affiliated to ICFTU and ETUC.
History and structure. NFS was founded in 1972 though organizations grouping the Nordic labour movement can be traced back to 1886. The national trade union centres in Sweden, Denmark, Finland, Norway and Iceland are all affiliated to NFS. NFS also co-operates with some 30 Nordic trade secretariats. Among these secretariats are (total membership in brackets): the Nordic Union of Hotel, Cafe and Restaurant Workers, c/o HRHL r.y. PL327, 00531 Helsinki, Finland, phone 90-77561, fax 90-7756-223, chairman Jorma Kallio (131,000); the Nordic Federation of Factory Workers' Unions, Box 1114, S–111 81 Stockholm, Sweden, phone 786-85-00, general secretary Nils Kristoffersson (400,000); the Nordic Transport Workers' Federation, c/o NFS, Barnhusgatan 16, S–105 53 Stockholm, Sweden, phone (08) 796 5510, chairman Anders Lindstrom (272,000); the Nordic Federation of Building and Wood Workers, Hagagatan 2–3 tr, Box 190 13, S–104 32, Stockholm, Sweden, phone (08) 728 48 00, fax (08) 34 50 51, general secretary Anita Wetterberg-Normark (565,402); and the Nordic Union of Textile and Garment Workers, Box 1129, S–111 81 Stockholm, Sweden, phone 247150, fax 242354 (111,000). The Nordic unions report the highest proportion of women members in Europe, with over 50 per cent of all organized workers in Denmark, Sweden and Finland being female.

European Civil Service Federation (ECSF)
Fédération de la Fonction Publique Européene (FFPE)

Address. 48 rue Franklin, B-1040 Brussels, Belgium
Phone. 733-22-59
Telex. 21877 COMEU B
Fax. 236-23-94
Leadership. Loek Rijnoudt (secretary-general)
History and character. The ECSF was founded in 1962 to unite officials within the administration of European communities irrespective of their political, religious or philosophical beliefs. It describes itself as a "pluralist professional organization, with the same status as a trade union" and as "resolutely against the old model of outdated trade-unionism which is traditionally based on relations that are by definition a conflict between employers and employees".
Publication. Eurechos.

European Federation of Building and Woodworkers (EFBWW)

Address. Wolvengracht 38, bus 5, B–1000 Brussels, Belgium
Phone. (2) 218 12 18
Leadership. Albert Williams (president); Jan Cremers (secretary)
Membership. 33 organizations in 12 EC member states.

European Federation of Chemical and General Workers' Unions (EFCGU)

Address. 109 avenue Emile de Béco, B–1050 Brussels, Belgium
Phone. 32-2-648 24 97
Telex. 20847 ICEFBX B
Fax. (32-2) 648 43 16
Leadership. Hermann Rappe (president); Franco Bisegna (secretary-general)
Membership. 2,000,000 in 44 affiliated unions in Western Europe.
International affiliation. ETUC.

European Trade Union Confederation (ETUC)
Confédération Européene des Syndicats (CES)

Address. 37–41 Rue Montagne aux Herbes Potagères, 1000 Brussels, Belgium
Leadership. Normal Willis (president); Emilio Gabaglio (general secretary).
Membership. Represents about 47,000,000 workers in 21 countries. Affiliates most of the national trade union centres of the European Communities (EC) and European Free Trade Area (EFTA) countries, as well as centres from Malta, Cyprus, Turkey (Confederation of Progressive Trade Unions-DISK).

Following the admission of the communist-led Italian CGIL, the Spanish Workers' Commissions (CCOO) were admitted at the 1991 Congress, but the General Confederation of Portuguese Workers (CGT-Intersindical) and the French CGT have not been allowed entry. Eastern European unions were not accepted into membership up to the time of the 1991 Congress, but the ETUC has established the European Trade Union Forum as a half-way house.

History and character. The ETUC was formed in 1973 by the merger of the previous European Confederation of Trade Unions in the EC with the European Free Trade Area Trade Union Committee. In 1974, the members unions of the WCL's European organization also joined. The ETUC shares the same address as the ICFTU and works with it and the WCL on the basis of a mutually agreed division of tasks. Its research and educational arm is the European Trade Union Institute (ETUI) which was founded in 1978 and publishes research reports and a newsletter. (ETUI, 66 bd. de l'Impératrice, Box 4, 1000 Brussels, Belgium. Phone (02) 512-30-70. Fax (02) 514 17 31. Director Günter Köpke.

Until the end of the 1980s it functioned mainly as a lobbying body within Community institutions on such issues as the need fot a shorter working week.

At the Sixth Congress of the ETUC, held in Stockholm during May 1988, the agenda was dominated by unemployment and the prospect of the Single European Market, although not all ETUC affiliates are in Member Countries of the Community. In October 1989 the ETUC convened a conference of nearly 1,000 shop stewards and representatives from the 12 Member Countries to discuss the European Social Charter. In 1990, the ETUC Executive established three objectives for the December Intergovernmental Conferences on Community Treaty Reform, namely the building of a social dimension, extended majority voting, and democratization of Community institutions.

The 1991 Congress, held in Luxembourg in May 1991 heard the President of the European Commission M. Jacques Delors, denounce the lack of progress in the Community over the Social Charter. The Congress voted to support his call for an extension of majority voting in order to expedite the progress of the Social Charter.

It also resolved to overhaul its own organization in order to upgrade itself from a lobbying body and to double its £5,000,000 budget over the next five years. The restructuring will have the effect of giving more power to the ETUC's industrial committees which are expected by some observers to be the cutting edge of European-wide collective bargaining. In 1990 the ETUC Executive Committee resolved that European Committees of Representatives in multinationals should meet twice yearly with the cost being funded by the company concerned. The European Metalworkers' Federation (EMF) has made considerable progress in this respect, taking over the role of international shop stewards committees, and supervising embryonic multinational agreements with a number of companies including Airbus, Bull, Thomson and Volkswagen. A European structure for Ford is also under discussion, but in this and other multinationals the absence of major communist-led unions such as the CGT may prove a handicap to adequate organization.

European Union of Local Authority Staffs (EULAS)
Union Syndicale Européene de la Fonction Publique Locale et Régionale (UEFPC)

Address. BP 438, 2014 Luxembourg
Phone. 4796-3047
Leadership. Carlo Becker (general secretary)
Membership. 800,000. There are nine member organizations in Western Europe.

Fédération Africaine des Syndicats des Mineurs et des Enérgeticiens (FASME)

Address. 17 rue de la Liberté, Algiers
Phone. 213 2 634266/213 2 750154
Telex. 66489
Fax. 213 2 634266
Leadership. Zitolini Lemtai (secretary-general)
Membership. 51 affiliated organizations of which 10 are in electricity.
History and character. FASME (formerly FASM) held its first consultative conference in Nairobi in 1979, its second in Algiers in 1981, its third in Cairo in 1986 and is scheduled to hold its fourth during 1991. It has recently added to its mining interests a campaign to co-ordinate those of unions in the electricity industry.
Affiliates:

Fédération Pan-Africaine des Travailleurs des Industries Alimentaires (Food Industry Workers), Maison du Peuple, Place du 1er Mai, Algiers, Algeria.

Fédération des Travailleurs Africains en France (FETAF — African Workers in France), Esplanade Benoit Frachon, 93100 Montreuil, France.

Regional organizations associated with OATUU.

Southern African Trade Union Co-ordination Council (SATUCC), P.O. Box 727, Maseru, Lesotho.

Organisation des Travailleurs de l'Afrique Centrale (OTAC), Avenue Mutombo Katsh/Zone de la Gombe, BP 5230, Kinshasa 10, Zaïre.

Organization of Trade Unions of West Africa (OTUWA)

Organisation des Travailleurs de l'Afrique de l'Ouest (OTAO), BP 11240, Niamey, Niger. Phone. Niamey 723656. Telex INEO 5438 NI.

Publication. Le Mineur Africain.
International affiliations. OATUU.

Union of Workers of Arab Maghreb (UWAM)

Address. c/o UGTT, 29, Place M'Hamed Ali, Tunis
History and Character. UWAM was formed in 1990 with the primary aim of protecting the interests of Maghreb workers employed in Europe.

Federation of International Civil Servants' Associations (FICSA)

Address. palais des Nations, Room PS 125, CH-1211, Geneva 10, Switzerland
Phone. (41) 022 798 58 50
Fax. (41) 22 733 0096
Leadership. Edward J. Freeman (president); Bradford P. Cross.
Membership. Around 30,000 staff members of the UN or its agencies.
History and Character. FICSA was established in 1952 and promotes the interests of the staff of the United Nations and its specialized agencies. FICSA assesses the conditions of service of international civil servants and makes recommendations on the management of human resources to interagency bodies and administrations. It seeks fair treatment for all staff on matters of remuneration and benefits, and conditions of security at all duty stations. It develops authoritative research papers on international human resource management to support its efforts to improve conditions of service within the UN system. Its activities are financed primarily by the contributions of members.
Affiliated unions and structure. There are 28 member associations or unions:

1. **Economic Commission for Latin America and the Caribbean (ECLAC)** (Santiago, Chile).

2. **Food and Agriculture Organization of the United Nations (FAO) — Association of Professional Staff** (Rome).

3. **FAO—Field Staff Association** (Rome).

4. **General Agreement on Tariffs and Trade (GATT)** (Geneva).

5. **International Atomic Energy Agency (IAEA)** (Vienna).

6. **International Agency for Research on Cancer (IARC)** (Lyon).

7. **International Civil Aviation Organisation (ICAO)** (Montreal).

8. **International Labour Organization (ILO)** (Geneva).

9. **International Fund for Agricultural Development (IFAD)** (Rome).

10. **International Centre for Advanced Technical and Vocational Training (CATVT)** (Lyon).

11. **International Maritime Organization (IMO)** (London).

12. **International Telecommunication Union (ITU)** (Geneva).

13. **United Nations Office at Vienna (UNOV)** (Vienna).

14. **United Nations Development Programme/United Nations Fund for Population Activities (UNDP/UNFPA)** (New York).

15. **United Nations Educational, Scientific and Cultural Organization (UNESCO)** (Paris).

16. **United Nations Industrial Development Organization (UNIDO)** (Vienna).

17. **United Nations Relief and Works Agency for Palestine Refugees in the Near East (UNRWA)** – Area Staff Union (Vienna).

18. **Universal Postal Union (UPU)** (Berne).

19. **World Health Organization (WHO)** (Geneva).

20. **WHO/AFRO – Regional Office for Africa** (Brazzaville).

21. **WHO/EMRO – Regional Office for Eastern Mediterranean** (Alexandria).

22. **WHO/EURO – Regional Office for Europe** (Copenhagen).

23. **WHO/PAHO – Pan American Health Organization** (Washington).

24. **WHO/SEARO – Regional Office for South-East Asia** (New Delhi).

25. **WHO/WPRO – Regional Office for Western Pacific** (Manila).

26. **World Intellectual Property Organization (WIPO)** (Geneva).

27. **World Meteorological Organization (WMO)** (Geneva).

28. **World Tourism Organization (WTO)** (Madrid).

Publications. FICSA Newsletter; Annual Council Report.

International Confederation of Arab Trade Unions (ICATU)

Address. P.O. Box 3225, Damascus, Syria
Phone. 459544
Cable. Ommarels-Damascus
Telex. 411913-Syria
Leadership. Ahmed Jalloud (general secretary)
History and character. The ICATU was founded in 1956, and was based in Egypt until it moved in 1978 because of its opposition to the international policies of the late President Sadat. It has member unions in 16 countries and accepts observers from several others. In most Arab countries, trade unions are either prohibited or entirely controlled by the régime. The ICATU leadership works closely with the WFTU: in April 1988 the two organizations issued a joint statement on international affairs.

International Confederation of Free Trade Unions (ICFTU)
Confédération Internationale des Syndicats Libres (CISL)
Confederación Internacional de Organizaciones Syndicales Libres (CIOSL)
International Bund Freier Gewerkschaften (IBFG)

Address. 37–41 Rue Montagne aux Herbes Potagères, 1000 Brussels, Belgium. The ICFTU also maintains branch offices at 46 Avenue Blanc, 1202, Geneva, and at the United Nations, Room 104, 104 East 40th Street, New York, NY 10016
Phone. (02) 217 80 85
Telex. 26785 ICFTU BRU
Fax. (02) 218 8415
Leadership P. P. Narayanan (president, Malaysia); John Vanderveken (general secretary)
Membership. In January 1991, the ICFTU had 144 organizations with 99,918,875 members in 101 countries. A geographically representative sample taken at the end of 1990 disclosed that 34 per cent of the ICFTU affiliated membership were women. The corresponding figures for 1978 and 1984 were 27 per cent and 30 per cent respectively.
History and character. The ICFTU was formed in 1949 by unions in Western countries which broke away from the WFTU, founded four years earlier. However some of its associated international trade secretariats are of earlier origin. At the time of its formation the principal organizations involved were the AFL and the CIO, the British TUC and the Dutch NVV, which is a manifesto stated that the WFTU was "completely dominated by communist organizations, which are themselves controlled by the Kremlin and the Cominform". The AFL-CIO left the ICFTU in 1969, being unable to come to terms with the views held on several matters by some social-democratic trade union centres, but it has since rejoined.

With the collapse of the régimes in Eastern Europe in 1989, the opportunity was granted the ICFTU to transcend the divisions of the Cold War. It gained the adherence of unions in Poland and Czechoslovakia which offset the implications of declining memberships in longer established affiliates. As a result the membership rose from 87,000,000 in January 1988 to nearly 100,000,000 three years later.

Affiliated unions and structure. The ICFTU is predominantly a confederation of national trade union centres, though it does permit some individual union affiliations. Affiliates must be free of the control of any other body, although a few of them operate in countries where social organizations are effectively controlled by a single party.

Supreme authority at the ICFTU is vested in a Quadriennial Congress, composed of delegates from the member federations in proportion to the size of their membership. Congress elects an Executive Board, which directs activities between Congresses. Day to day authority is exercised by the Brussels-based Secretariat, under the direction of the General Secretary. The ICFTU is financed solely by its member organizations. At the 1988 Congress it was resolved that a Quadriennial Women's World Conference be established to meet between Congresses.

There are 16 associated International Trade Secretariats (ITSs) as follows:

1. **International Federation of Building and Woodworkers (IFBWW)**, International Centre Cointrin (ICC), Immeuble 'A', 20 route de Pré-Bois, 1216 Cointrin-Geneva, Switzerland. Phone: (22) 788.08.88 Telex: 415327 FITB CH. Cable: INTERBUILD GENEVA. Fax: 022/788.07.16 General secretary: Ulf Asp. Membership: 3,500,000 in 118 affiliates in 58 countries.

2. **International Federation of Chemical, Energy and General Workers' Unions (ICEF)**, 109 avenue Emile de Béco, B-1050 Brussels, Belgium. Phone: (2) 647 0235. Telex: 20847 ICEFBX B. Fax: (2) 648 4316. Secretary general: Michael Boggs. Membership: 6,300,000 members in 189 unions in 59 countries.

3. **International Federation of Commercial, Clerical, Professional and Technical Employees (FIET)**, 15 avenue de Balexert, 1219 Châtelaine-Geneva, Switzerland. Phone: (22) 796 27 33. Telex: 418736. Fax: 796 53 21. Acting general secretary: Philip J. Jennings. Membership: 10,000,000 in 304 unions in 96 countries.

4. **International Federation of Free Teachers' Unions (IFFTU)**, Nieuwe Zijds Voorburgwal 120–126, 1012 5H Amsterdam (C), Netherlands. Phone: (31) 206 249072. Telex: 17118 IFFTU NL. Fax: 020-6381089 General secretary: Fred Van Leeuwen. Membership: 8,500,000 members in 58 countries.

5. **International Federation of Journalists (IFJ)**, IPC building, boulevard Charlemagne 1, Bte 5, 1041 Brussels, Belgium. Phone: (2) 238.09.51. Telex: 61275. Cable: INTERFEDJOUR BRUSSELS. Fax: (2) 230 36 33. General secretary: Aidan White. Membership: 175,000 members in 37 unions in 32 countries.

6. **International Federation of Plantation, Agricultural and Allied Workers (IFPAAW)**, 17 rue Necker, 1201 Geneva, Switzerland. Phone: (22) 7313105. Telex: 412494 Cable: AGRIPLANT GENEVA. Fax: 738 01 14. General secretary: Börje Svensson. Membership: 2,000,000 members in 100 affiliates in 65 countries.

7. **International Graphical Federation (IGF)**, 17 rue des Fripiers, Galerie du Centre (Block 2), 1000 Brussels, Belgium. Phone: 031-45 99 20. Telex: 913 274. General secretary: Robert W. Tomlins. Membership: 835,386 members in 37 countries.

8. **International Metalworkers' Federation (IMF)**, route des Acacias 54 bis, Case Postale 563, 1227 Geneva, Switzerland. Phone: (22) 743 61 50. Telex: 423298 METL CH. Cable: INTERMETAL GENEVA. Fax: 743 15 10. General secretary: Marcello Malentacchi. Membership: 12,616,391 members in 170 unions in 70 countries.

9. **International Secretariat for Arts, Mass Media and Entertainment Trade Unions (ISETU/FIET)**, c/o FIET, 15 avenue de Balexert, 1219 Châtelaine-Geneva, Switzerland. Phone: (22) 7962733. Telex: 418736 FIET CH. Fax: 796 53 21. ISETU/FIET secretary: Irène Robadey. FIET acting general secretary: Philip J. Jennings. Membership: 100,000 members. This organization was integrated into FIET as an autonomous section in 1984.

10. **International Textile, Garment and Leather Workers' Federation (ITGLWF)**, 8 rue
Joseph Stevens, 1000 Brussels, Belgium.
Phone: (2) 5122833. Fax: 511 09 04.
General secretary: Neil Kearney.
Membership: 5,500,000 in 145 unions.

11. **International Transport Workers' Federation (ITF)**, 133-135 Great Suffolk Street, London
SE1 1PD, United Kingdom.
Phone: (071) 403 2733. Telex: 8811397. Cable: INTRANSFE. Fax: 071-357 7871.
General secretary: Harold Lewis.
Membership: 4,110,577 members in 398 unions in 88 countries.

12. **International Union of Food and Allied Workers' Associations (IUF)**, 8 rampe du
Pont-Rouge, 1213 Petit-Lancy, Switzerland.
Phone: (22) 7932233. Telex: 429292 UITA CH. Cable: FOODUNION GENEVA. Fax: 793 22
38.
General secretary: Dan Gallin.
Membership: 2,178,828 members in 212 unions in 64 countries.

13. **Miners' International Federation**, 109 avenue Emile de Beco, 1050 Brussels, Belgium.
Phone: (2) 6462120
General secretary: Peter Michalzik.
Membership: 1,600,000 members in 36 countries.

14. **Postal, Telegraph and Telephone International (PTTI)**, 36 avenue du Lignon, 1219
Le Lignon-Geneva, Switzerland.
Phone: (22) 7968311. Cable: INTERTELEPOST GENEVA.
General secretary: Philip Bouryer.
Membership: 4,200,000

15. **Public Services International (PSI)**, 45 avenue Voltaire, 01210 Ferney-Voltaire, France.
Phone: (50) 406464. Telex: 380559. Fax: (50) 40 73 20.
General secretary: Hans Engelberts.
Membership: 8,995,968 members in 73 countries.

16. **Universal Alliance of Diamond Workers**, Lange Kievitstraat 57, Bus 1, 2018 Antwerp,
Belgium
Phone: (3) 2329151.
General secretary: Constant Denisse.
Membership: 10,100 in six countries.

The 143 affiliates of the ICFTU, their membership figures and reference date are as follows:

Antigua—Antigua Workers' Union (AWU), 5,000 (March 1989).

Argentina—Confederación General del Trabajo de la República Argentina (CGT), 6,000,000
(May 1989).

Australia—Australian Council of Trade Unions (ACTU), 1,800,000 (Dec. 31, 1989).

Austria—Österreichischer Gewerkschaftsbund (ÖGB), 1,644,408 (Dec. 12, 1989).

Bahamas—Commonwealth of the Bahamas Trade Union Congress (CBTUC), 10,300 (Dec. 12,
1988).

Bangladesh—Bangladesh Jatio Shramik League (BJSL), 550,000 (March 1988); **Jatiya Sramik
Party (JSP)**, 295,781 (Feb. 2, 1987); **Bangladesh Free Trade Union Congress (BFTUC)**, 105,000
(Dec. 31, 1989); **Bangladesh Jatyatabadi Sramik Dal (BJSD)**, 122,000 (Feb. 15, 1990);

Barbados—Barbados Workers' Union (BWU), 15,000 (Dec. 31, 1989).

Basque Country—Solidaridad de Trabajadores Vascos (STV-ELA), 110,000 (Dec. 31, 1989)

Belgium—Fédération générale du Travail de Belgique (FGTB), 1,029,074 (1987)

Bermuda—Bermuda Industrial Union (BIU), 4,941 (February 1990)

Botswana—Botswana Federation of Trade Unions (BFTU), 18,000 (1986)

Brazil — Confederaçâo Nacional dos Trabalhadores em Comunicaçôes e Publicidade (CONTCOP), 117,000 (Jan. 1, 1988)

Burkina Faso—Organisation nationale des syndicats libres (ONSL), 6,000 (March 1988)

Canada—Canadian Labour Congress (CLC), 1,300,000 (Dec. 31, 1987)

Central African Republic—Union Syndicale des Travailleurs du Centrafrique (USTC), 15,000 (March 1988)

Chad—Union Nationale des Syndicats du Tchad (UNST), 7,610 (July 1990)

Chile — Central Democrática de Trabajadores (CDT), 160,000 (Jan. 1, 1987); Comité de Coordinación y Enlace entre la CIOSL y el Movimiento Sindical Chileno, 111,544 (Jan. 1, 1987)

China—Chinese Federation of Labour (CFL), 1,000,000 (June 1989)

Colombia—Confederación de Trabajadores de Colombia (CTC), 50,000 (March 1988); Frente Unitario de Trabajadores Demócraticos (FUTD-CUT), 411,582 (October 1988)

Costa Rica—Confederación Costarricense de Trabajadores Democráticos (CCTD), 12,000 (March 1988); Confederación Nacional de Trabajadores (CNT), 18,403 (March 1988); Confederación Auténtica de Trabajadores Democrática (CATD), 26,312 (Oct. 31, 1988)

Curaçao—Sentral di Sindikatonan di Korsou (SSK), 6,000 (March 1988)

Cyprus — Cyprus Workers' Confederation (SEK), 51,581 (Dec. 31, 1988); Cyprus Turkish Trade Unions Federation (TÜRK-SEN), 9,536 (Dec. 31, 1986)

Czechoslovakia — Czech and Slovak Confederation of Trade Unions (CS KOS), 6,098,738 (April 30, 1990)

Denmark—Landsorganisationen i Danmark (LO), 1,412,767 (Jan. 1, 1989); Funktionaerernes og Tjenestemaendenes Faellesrad (FTF), 321,671 (Dec. 31, 1989)

Dominica — Dominica Trade Union (DTU), 1,000 (Dec. 31, 1986); Waterfront and Allied Workers' Union (WAWU), 3,000 (March 1988)

Dominican Republic — Confederación Nacional de Trabajadores Dominicanos (CNTD), 110,000 (November 1988)

Ecuador—Confederación Ecuatoriana de Organizaciones Sindicales libres (CEOSL), 150,000 (Dec. 31, 1989)

El Salvador—Central de Trabajadores Democráticos de El Salvador (CTD), 84,539 (March 1988)

Estonia—Eesti Meremeeste Union (EMU), 163 (Dec. 31, 1989)

Falkand Islands—Falkland Islands General Employees' Union (FIGEU), 74 (April 1988)

Fiji—Fiji Trades Union Congress (FTUC), 40,000 (August 1990)

Finland — Suomen Ammattiliittojen Keskusjärjestö (SAK) r.y., 1,074,174 (Dec. 31, 1989); Toimihenkilö-ja Virkamesjärjestöjen Keskusliitto (TVK) r.y., 325,000 (November 1989)

France—Confédération générale du Travail—Force Ouvrière (CGT – FO), 930,000 (1989); Confédération Française Démocratique du Travail (CFDT), 900,000 (October 1988)

French Polynesia—A Tia I Mua, 5,000 (May 1990)

Gambia—Gambia Workers' Union (GWU), 3,000 (March 1988)

Germany—Deutscher Gewerkschaftsbund (DGB), 7,100,000 (Dec. 31, 1989)

Great Britain—Trades Union Congress (TUC), 8,652,318 (Dec. 31, 1989)

Greece—Greek General Confederation of Labour (GSEE), 300,000 (March 1988)

Grenada—Grenada Trade Union Council (GTUC), 7,532 (Sept. 30, 1989)

Guatemala—Confederación de Unidad Sindical de Guatemala (CUSG), 191,893 (May 1989)

Guyana—Guyana Trades Union Congress (GTUC), 15,000 (Sept. 1, 1989)

Honduras—Confederación de Trabajadores de Honduras (CTH), 35,000 (March 1988)

Hong Kong—Hong Kong and Kowloon Trades Union Council (HKTUC), 83,769 (Dec. 31, 1988)

Iceland—Althydusamband Islands (ASI), 56,000 (Sept. 1, 1990); **Bandalag starfsmanna rikis og beaja (BSRB)**, 17,055 (Dec. 31, 1989)

India—Hind Mazdoor Sabha (HMS), 2,800,000 (Dec. 31, 1989); **Indian National Trade Union Congress (INTUC)**, 5,123,655 (Dec. 31, 1989)

Indonesia—Kongres Buruh Islam Merdeka (KBIM), 130,000 (March 1988); **Gabungan Serikat 2 Buruh Islam Indonesia (GASBIINDO)**, 150,000 (March 1988); **Gerakan Organisasi Buruh Sjarikat Islam Indonesia (GOBSI)**, 50,103 (May 1, 1985); **Sarikat Buruh Muslimin Indonesia (SARBUMUSI)**, 100,000 (Dec. 31, 1985)

Israel—General Federation of Labour in Eretz-Israel (HISTADRUT), 800,000 (Dec. 31, 1986)

Italy—Confederazione Italiana Sindacati Lavoratori (CISL), 3,288,369 (Dec. 31, 1986); **Unione Italiana del Lavoro (UIL)**, 1,000,000 (Jan. 1, 1989)

Jamaica—National Workers' Union of Jamaica (NWU), 60,000 (March 31, 1990); **Bustamante Industrial Trade Union (BITU)**, 115,212 (March 1988); **Trades Union Congress of Jamaica (TUCJ)**, 4,000 (Jan. 1, 1988); **Jamaica Association of Local Government Officers (JALGO)**

Japan—Japanese Trade Union Confederation (JTUC-Rengo), 8,000,000 (Jan. 1, 1990)

Kiribati—Kiribati Trades Union Congress (KTUC), 2,600 (February 1990)

Korea—Federation of Korean Trade Unions (FKTU), 1,666,255 (1989)

Lebanon—Ligue des Syndicats des Employés et des Ouvriers dans la République libanaise (LIGUE), 13,000 (March 1988); **Fédération des Syndicats-Unis des Employés et Ouvriers au Liban (SYNDICATS-UNIS)**, 10,000 (March 1988); **Fédération ouvrière des Offices autonomes et des Enterprises publiques et privées au Liban (OFFICES AUTONOMES)**, 13,000 (March 1988); **Federation of Petroleum Trade Unions in Lebanon (PETROLEUM)**, 1,700 (March 1988); **Fédération des Syndicats des Employés de Banques au Liban (BANQUES)**, 5,000 (March 1988); **Federation of Insurance Sector Employees in Lebanon (INSURANCE)**, 1,000 (March 1988); **Fédération des Syndicats des Employés du Commerce au Liban (COMMERCE)**, 1,000 (March 1988); **Federation of Sindicates of Health and Education Sector in Lebanon (HEALTH & EDUCATION)**, 2,500 (March 1988); **Workers' Syndicates Federation of Sea Transport in Lebanon (SEA TRANSPORT)**, 8,000 (March 1988); **Federation of Airline Companies Employees and Labourers of Lebanon (AIRLINE COMPANIES)**, 4,000 (March 1988); **Fédération syndicale des Employés et Ouvriers des Offices autonomes et services publics au Liban (OFFICES AUTONOMES & SERVICES PUBLICS)**, 9,000 (March 1988); **Fédération des Syndicats d'Ouvriers des Imprimeries et de l'Information au Liban (IMPRIMERIES)**, 5,000 (Dec. 31, 1986); **Fédération des Employés des Hôtels, Restaurants et Lieux de Loisirs au Liban (HOTELS)**, 2,800 (March 1988)

Lesotho—Lesotho Labour Congress

Liberia—Liberia Federation of Labour Unions (LFLU), 10,000 (March 1988)

Luxembourg—Confédération générale du Travail du Luxembourg (CGTL), 44,000 (Dec. 31, 1985)

Madagascar—Fivondronamben'ny Mpiasa Malagasy (FMM), 30,000 (March 1988)

Malawi—Trades Union Congress of Malawi (TUCM), 26,000 (April 1, 1985)

Malaysia—Malaysian Trades Union Congress (MTUC), 300,000 (Dec. 31, 1989)

Malta—General Workers' Union (GWU), 36,316 (Jan. 1, 1989)

Mauritius—Mauritius Labour Congress (MLC), 33,471 (Dec. 31, 1989)

Mexico—Confederación de Trabajadores de Mexico (CTM), 1,300,000 (March 1988)

Montserrat—Montserrat Allied Workers' Union (MAWU), 1,000 (Dec. 31, 1984)

Morocco—Union Marocaine du Travail (UMT), 438,000 (April 1990)

Netherlands—Federatie Nederlandse Vakbeweging (FNV), 967,312 (January 1990)

New Caledonia—Union des Syndicats des Ouvriers et Employés de Nouvelle Calédonie (USOENC), 3,584 (Dec. 1, 1989)

New Zealand—New Zealand Council of Trade Unions (NZCTU), 511,000 (March 30, 1989)

Nicaragua—Confederación de Unificación Sindical (CUS), 21,000 (March 31, 1988)

Norway—Landsorganisasjonen i Norge (LO), 782,376 (September 1989)

Pakistan—Pakistan National Federation of Trade Unions (PNFTU), 150,000 (Dec. 31, 1985); **All-Pakistan Federation of Labour (APFOL)**, 265,000 (March 1988); **All-Pakistan Federation of Trade Unions (APFTU)**, 591,021 (Dec. 31, 1989)

Panama—Confederación de Trabajadores de la República de Panama (CTRP), 50,000 (March 1988)

Papua New Guinea—Papua New Guinea Trade Union Congress (PNGTUC), 70,000 (Dec. 31, 1988)

Peru—Confederación de Trabajadores del Perú (CTP), 350,000 (Jan. 1, 1984); **Confederación Nacional de Trabajadores (CNT)***, 120,000 (Nov. 30, 1986)

Philippines—Trade Union Congress of the Philippines (TUCP), 475,000 (Jan. 1, 1988)

Poland—NSZZ "Solidarnosc", 5,000,000 (Jan. 1, 1987)

Portugal—União Geral dos Trabalhadores (UGT-P), 1,048,000 (February 1988)

Puerto Rico—Federación del Trabajo de Puerto Rico (AFL-CIO) (FTPR), 30,000 (Dec. 12, 1985)

St. Helena—St. Helena General Workers' Union (GWU), 685 (March 1988)

St. Kitts–Nevis—St. Kitts–Nevis Trades and Labour Union (TLU), 873 (Dec. 31, 1986)

St. Lucia—St. Lucia Seamen, Waterfront and General Workers' Trade Union (SWGWTU), 1,200 (Dec. 31, 1989); **St. Lucia Workers' Union (WU)**, 1,000 (March 1988)

St. Vincent—Commercial, Technical and Allied Workers' Union (CTAWU), 2,000 (March 1988)

San Marino—Confederazione Democratica Lavoratori Sammarinesi (CDLS), 1,809 (July 31, 1990)

Seychelles—National Workers' Union (Seychelles) (NWUS), 25,000 (March 1988)

Sierra Leone—Sierra Leone Labour Congress (SLLC), 45,000 (Dec. 31, 1986)

Singapore—Singapore National Trades Union Congress (SNTUC), 150,000 (Dec. 31, 1989)

Spain—Unión General de Trabajadores (UGT), 600,000 (September 1990)

Sri Lanka—Ceylon Workers' Congress (CWC), 177,000 (March 1989)

Surinam—Algemeen Verbond van Vakverenigingen in Suriname "DE MOEDERBOND", 7,000 (March 1988); **Progressive Federation of Trade Unions (C-47)**, 12,000 (September 1988); **Centrale van Landsdienaren Organisaties (CLO)**, 17,500 (Dec. 1, 1989)

Swaziland—Swaziland Federation of Trade Unions (SFTU), 26,00 (Dec. 31, 1986)

Sweden—Landsorganisationen i Sverige (LO), 1,997,058 (Dec. 31, 1989); **Tjänstemännens Centralorganisation (TCO)**, 1,144,007 (Dec. 31, 1989)

Switzerland—Schweizerischer Gewerkschaftsbund (SGB), 442,020 (Dec. 31, 1988)

Thailand—Labour Congress of Thailand (LCT), 90,000 (Dec. 31, 1988); **Thai Trade Union Congress (TTUC)**, 123,150 (July 1990)

Tonga—Friendly Islands Teachers' Association/Tonga Nurses' Association (FITA/TNA), 450 (March 31, 1990)

Trinidad and Tobago—Trinidad and Tobago Labour Congress (TTLC), 50,000 (March 1988)

Tunisia—Union générale tunisienne du Travail (UGTT), 200,000 (March 1988)

Turkey—Türkiye Isçi Sendikalari Konfederasyonu (TÜRK-IS), 800,000 (Dec. 31, 1989)

Uganda—National Organization of Trade Unions (NOTU), 130,000 (June 1983)

United States—American Federation of Labor and Congress of Industrial Organizations (AFL-CIO), 14,090,000 (Dec. 31, 1989); **United Mine Workers of America (UMWA)**, 100,000 (March 1989)

Vatican—Associazione Dipendenti Laici Vaticani (ADLV), 1,400 (Dec. 31, 1989)

Venezuela—Confederación de Trabajadores de Venezuela (CTV), 700,000 (March 1988)

Western Samoa—Public Service Association (PSA), 2,184 (March 1988)

* The 98th Executive Board meeting (Tokyo, Dec. 5–7, 1990) decided to keep in abeyance the rights and privileges of the Confederación Nacional de Trabajadores (CNT), Peru, as an affiliate of the ICFTU.

Regional Organizations of the ICFTU. For Asia and the Pacific: **ICFTU-APRO** (Trade Union House, 3rd Floor, Shenton Way, Singapore 0106. Phone: 222 62 94. Telex: ICFTU RS 24480. President: Gopeshwar; general secretary: Takashi Izumi). APRO has now established a co-ordinating body for trade unions in the South Pacific and Oceania, under the title South Pacific and Oceanic Council of Trade Unions (SPOCTU).

Representation in the Americas in through the **Organización Regional Interamericana de Trabajadores (ORIT)** (Inter-American Regional Organization of Workers), Vallarta No 8, 3er Piso, CP 06030 Mexiso DF, Mexico. Phone: 535 13 36. Telex: 1771699 ORITME. Fax: 592 73 29. President: Alfonso Sánchez Madariaga; secretary general: Luis A. Anderson. ORIT was founded in 1951. Throughout its history it has been strongly influenced by the AFL-CIO and its American Institute for Free Labor Development (AIFLD), which received funds from the US government and corporate sources, and its relations with the ICFTU have sometimes been strained. Particular criticism was directed in the past towards ORIT's alleged accommodation with military régimes. ORIT maintains that its orientation is social-democratic, and seeks to advance free trade unionism, oppose dictatorship and consolidate democracy with the strong support of affiliates outside the region.

International Federation of Petroleum and Chemical Workers

Address. 435 So Newport Way, Denver, Co 80224, USA
Phone. 303-388-9237
Leadership. Curtis J. Hogan (secretary-general)
Membership. Affiliated and co-operating unions with over 2,000,000 members in 74 countries.

International Miners' Organization (IMO)
Organisation Internationale des Mineurs

Address. 119 Rue Pierre Semard, 93000 Bobigny, France
Phone. 48 95 96 87
Telex. 233419
Fax. 48 95 96 88
Leadership. A. Scargill (president); A. Simon (general secretary)
Membership. Claims the affiliation of 46 unions covering 6,000,000 members.

History and character. The IMO was formed in September 1985 as a new independent organization aspiring to cross Cold War boundaries. It gained the adherence of the British National Union of Mineworkers, and the WFTU-affiliated Trade Union International of Miners and Energy Workers agreed to its mining affiliates leaving to join the IMO.

In 1990 a major controversy erupted in Britain over the role of the IMO in channelling international miners' donations. It was precipitated by the report of Mr Gavin Lightman QC into the financial affairs of the NUM during and after the strike by members of the British NUM in 1984–85. In his report Mr Lightman focussed on the dual role of Mr Scargill as President both of the NUM and the IMO, and complained that without the co-operation of M. Simon (a former executive member of the French CGT), the finances of the IMO were "impenetrable". He endorsed the view expressed in some quarters of the British press that as much as £2,000,000 of Soviet money intended for the NUM had been diverted by Mr Scargill and other NUM officers to the IMO. The NUM and the IMO later reached an understanding over the payment of a substantial amount to the British organization. However further revelations in May 1991 indicated that it was the Soviet government which had diverted the donations via an international solidarity fund of the WFTU-affiliated Miners' Trade Union International, later to be controlled by the IMO, which was not founded until after the conclusion of the British miners' strike. The establishment of an international solidarity fund rather than direct donations to the NUM was done to avoid embarrassment to President Gorbachev at a delicate point in his *rapprochement* with the West.

North Atlantic Labour Movement

Membership. Comprises the ASÍ in Iceland, SIK in Greenland, and the major trades unions in the Faeroes Islands (where there is no federation).

Organization of African Trade Union Unity (OATUU)
Organisation de l'Unité Syndicale Africaine (OUSA)

Address. P.O. Box M 386, Aviation Road, Accra, Ghana
Phone. 774531/772574/772621
Telex. 2673 OATUU GH
Fax. (233) 21 772261
Leadership. Salem Jalloud (president); Alhaji Hassan Sunmonu (secretary-general)

History and character. The first African international trade union federation was the All-African Trade Union Federation (AATUF), founded in Casablanca in May 1961. In an attempt to exclude the influence of the ICFTU and the Christian unions, which were seen as damping militancy and "revolutionary zeal", AATUF insisted on the principle of disaffiliation of all its member national centres from any non-African union organizations. National centres which maintained affiliation to the ICFTU or the Christian federation, IFCTU, (the forerunner of the WCL) or which were unwilling to accept this policy formed the African Trade Union Confederation (ATUC) in January 1962. The ATUC itself, however, did not affiliate to an extra-continental body. In 1973 these two rival federations, and a third smaller grouping known as the Pan-African Workers' Congress, were merged into the Organization of African Trade Union Unity (OATUU), under the auspices of the Organization of African Unity (OAU). The OATUU held its first congress at Tripoli, Libya, in April 1976, when Ali El-Nafeshy (Libya) was elected president and James Dennis Akumu (Kenya) secretary-general. The OATUU has continued to oppose in principle the affiliation of African centres to the world trade union organizations. In some cases, OATUU affiliates are active members of these organizations, however, either directly or through their sectoral (trade) organizations, or maintain strong informal links. The ICFTU and more particularly the WCL claim as affiliates a number of African centres which appear not to regard themselves as possessing such an affiliation. The OATUU signed a co-operation agreement with the WCL in March 1988.

In February 1986 the OATUU split into two rival camps, principally over the issue of the management of its financial affairs under secretary-general Dennis Akumu. Those countries involved in the formation of a breakaway group, which was ideologically disparate, were Algeria, Angola, Benin, Cameroon, Cape Verde, Central African Republic, Chad, Congo, Gabon, The Gambia, Guinea-Bissau, Lesotho, Liberia, Madagascar, Malawi, Mali, Mauritius, Niger, Nigeria, Rwanda, Senegal, Sierra Leone, Swaziland, Togo, Tunisia, Zaïre, Zambia, and Zimbabwe. According to the rump organization, in which the key posts of president and secretary-general remained in the hands of Ali El-Nafeshy and Akumu, respectively, the breakaway was motivated by "imperialists" (such as those associated with the African-American Labour Centre) who were seeking to disrupt African unity. In a reconciliation meeting in October 1986, Alhaji Hassan Sunmonu, a former president of the Nigerian Labour Congress, was elected secretary-general, after Akumu withdrew, while Ali El-Nafeshy was re-elected as president. El-Nafeshy died in office in February 1987.

The second Executive Committee meeting held in Abidjan (Côte d'Ivoire) on Feb 10–11, 1987 appointed Adiko Niamkey, Secretary-General of UTGCI as Acting President after the death of President Nafeshy; the Tenth Session of the OATUU General Council met in Cairo on May 12–15 and appointed Joseph Rwegasira, Secretary-General of JUWATA (Tanzania) as President. When Mr Rwegisira was made Minister of Commerce in Tanzania, Salem Jalloud of Libya was elected President in his place. This election occurred at the Eleventh session of the General Council on May 8–11, 1988.

OATUU remains independent of any international trade union organization, but keeps fraternal relations with trade union organizations throughout the world. It strongly maintains Article 8 of its Charter which insists on the principle of non-affiliation.

Publication. Voice of African workers.

Specialized agency of OATUU. African Trade Union Co-ordinating Committee against Apartheid and Colonialism, BP 380, Kinshasa 1, Republic of Zaïre.

Pacific Trade Union Community (PTUC)

Address. c/o Australian Council of Trade Unions, 393–397 Swanston Street, Melbourne, Victoria 3000, Australia.

Leadership. I. Ross (convenor). There is an executive co-ordinating committee

Membership. Trade union centres in 14 countries.

History and character. The PTUC was established in 1980 as the Pacific Trade Union Forum, and has held conferences in Vanuatu (1981), New Caledonia (1982), Fiji (1984) and New Zealand (1986), adopting its present name at the 1986 conference. Its objectives are to campaign for a "nuclear-free Pacific" and to foster co-operation between trade unions in the region.

Pan-African Federation of Agricultural Trade Unions (PAFATU)

Address. 20 Zamzam Street, Dokki, Giza, Egypt

Phone. 360 2801

Leadership. Moukhtar Abdel Hamid (president); Kwaku Haligah (secretary-general).

Membership. Claims 1,500,000.

Affiliated unions and structure. Twenty-six unions as follows:

1. **Algeria—Union Nationale de Paysans Algériens (UNPA).**

2. **Burkina Faso—Confédération Nationale des Travailleurs du Burkina Faso (CNTB).**

3. **Congo—Fédération Syndicale des Travailleurs de l'Agriculture et des Forêts du Congo (FESYTRAF).**

4. **Côte D'Ivoire—Union Générale des Travailleurs de la Côte D'Ivoire.**

5. **Djibouti—Union Générale des Travailleurs de Djibouti.**

6. **Egypt—General Trade Union of Workers in Agriculture and Irrigation (GTUWAIE).**

7. **Ethiopia—Agriculture, Forestry, Hunting & Fisheries Union.**

8. **Ghana—General Agricultural Workers Union of TUC.**

9. **Liberia—National Union of Plantation, Agricultural, Forestry and Allied Workers (NUPAFAW).**

10. **Malawi—Plantation and Agricultural Workers' Union (PAWU).**

11. **Mali—Syndicat National de la Production (SYNAPRO).**

12. **Mauritius—Plantation Workers' Union.**

13. **Morocco—Fédération Marocaine de l'Agriculture.**

14. **Nigeria—Agricultural & Allied Workers' Union of Nigeria (AAWUN).**

15. **Rwanda—Centrale Syndicale des Travailleurs du Rwanda (CESTRAR).**

16. **Senegal—Confédération Nationale des Travailleurs du Sénégal.**

17. **Somalia—GTU of Workers in Agriculture.**

18. **Sudan—GTU of Agriculture; GTU of GUIZERA Project Workers; GTU of Workers in Agriculture & Irrigation.**

19. **Swaziland—Swaziland Agricultural & Plantation Workers' Union (SAPWU).**

20. **Tanzania—Union of Tanzanian Workers.**

21. **Togo—Syndicat National de l'Agriculture et des Services Connexes du Togo (Synascot).**

22. **Tunisia—Union Générale de Travailleurs Tunisiens.**

23. **Uganda—National Union of Plantation & Agricultural Workers (NUPAW).**

24. **Zaire—Syndicat de l'Agriculture et Elévages; Union Nationale des Travailleurs du Zaïre/ Fédération Nationale des Travailleurs de PEBC–ZAIRE.**

25. **Zambia—National Union of Plantation & Agricultural Workers (NUPAW).**

26. **Zimbabwe—General Agriculture Union.**

Pan-African Federation of Petroleum and Allied Workers, P.O. Box 1031, Tripoli, Libya.

Pan-African Federation of Banks, Insurance and Financial Affairs, P.O. Box 14807, Tripoli, Libya.

PANACOM, BP 1673, Brazzaville, Congo.

International affiliation. OATUU.

South Asian Regional Trade Union Council (SARTUC)

History and character: Union organizations from India, Pakistan, Sri Lanka, Bhutan, Bangladesh, Nepal and the Maldives formed SARTUC at a convention held in Colombo on Jan. 28, 1988. SARTUC's second board meeting was held in New Delhi in July 1989.

Southern African Trade Union Co-ordination Council (SATUCC)

Address. c/o Botswana Federation of Trade Unions, P.O. Box 440, Gaborone, Botswana

Leadership. B. C. Ntune (chairman); Chakufa Chihana (secretary-general). The chairman of the host country's trade union federation (i.e. currently the Botswana Federation of Trade Unions) is automatically also the chairman of the SATUCC.

Membership. The SATUCC claims to represent more than 10,000,000 workers in the Southern African region and has nine member trade union organizations in Southern African countries.

History and character. The SATUCC was founded in December 1984 as a regional body for the member states of the Southern African Development Co-ordination Conference (SADCC). It is, however, independent of the SADCC.

Trade Union Advisory Committee to the OECD (TUAC)
Commission Syndicale Consultative Aupres de l'OCDE

Address. 26 avenue de la Grande-Armée, 75017 Paris, France

Phone. 47-63-42-63

Telex. OCDE 620 160

Fax. 47 54 98 28

Leadership. Lane Kirkland (president); John Evans (general secretary)

Membership. There were 39 affiliates in 1987 with a total membership of over 66,000,000 in 23 of the 24 OECD countries (New Zealand being the exception).

History and character. The Trade Union Advisory Committee to the OECD (TUAC) was founded in 1948. It began as an advisory committee to the European Recovery Plan which brought together most of the non-communist union national centres in western Europe. Today the TUAC is a non-governmental organization enjoying consultative status with the OECD and regularly meets OECD specialist committees. Its membership is composed of national trade union centres in OECD countries, and international organizations (ICFTU, WCL, ETUC, Nordic Trade Union Council); international trade secretariats also participate in its work. Particular concerns of the TUAC are multinational corporations, structural changes in the labour market and employment prospects generally.

Structure. Plenary sessions, involving representatives of all the affiliates and the international organizations, are held twice-yearly and make policy decisions and approve the budget. An administrative committee oversees administration and draws up the budget; it comprises representatives of the DGB (Germany), TUC (United Kindgom), AFL-CIO (United States of America), FO and CFDT (France), CISL (Italy), Rengo (Japan), ÖGB (Austria), TCO (Sweden), and CSC (Belgium) representing the WCL, and the general secretary. There are also various working groups. Decision-making is generally by consensus. The TUAC office comprises the general secretary and four staff.

Affiliated unions. Australia, ACTU; Austria, ÖGB; Belgium, CGSLB, CSC, FGTB; Canada, CLC, CSN; Denmark, FTF, LO; France, CFDT, CGC, CGT-FO, FEN; Finland, SAK, TVK; Germany, DGB; Greece, GSEE; Iceland, ASÍ, BSRB; Ireland, ICTU; Italy, CISL, UIL; Japan, Rengo, Sohyo; Luxembourg, CGT-LG, LCGB; Netherlands, CNV, FNV; Norway, LO; Portugal, UGT-P; Spain, STV, UGT; Sweden, Lo, TCO; Switzerland, CNG, USS; Turkey, Türk-Is; United Kingdom, TUC; United States of America, AFL-CIO.

World Confederation of Labour (WCL)
Confederación Mundial del Trabajo (CMT)
Confédération Mondiale du Travail (CMT)

Address. 33 rue de Trèves, 1040 Brussels, Belgium

Phone. (2) 230 6295
Telex. 26 966 CMTWCL B
Cable. MUNDOLABOR
Fax. (2) 230 87 22
Leadership. Willy Peirens (ACV-CSC, Belgium); Carlos Luis Custer (ATE, Argentina).
Membership. The WCL claims that its affiliates represent 15,000,000 members, but Bendiner puts the figure at less than 6,000,000 (Bendiner, B., *International Labour Affairs*, Oxford, 1987).

History and character. The WCL was founded, as the International Federation of Christian Trade Unions (IFCTU), at the Hague in 1920. At its 1968 congress the organization changed its name to the World Confederation of Labour, ending the explicit association with the Christian Church. Its core membership, however, is still Christian in character in Europe and Latin America, whereas in Africa and Asia significant affiliates are not Christian in character. The changing geographical composition of its membership is reflected in the fact that delegates from only three non-European countries took part in the 1952 congress, whereas 82 countries, predominantly in the Third World, were represented at the 1977 congress. With the disaffiliation in 1986 of the Canadian Confédération des Syndicats Nationaux (CSN), the WCL lost its significant foothold in North America (where it now claims only the US National Alliance of Postal and Federal Employees—NAPFE—as an affiliate), and it is weak generally throughout the industrialized world. However, in October 1987, the WCL accepted the affiliation of the independent Polish union Solidarnosc.

The 22nd congress of the WCL, held in Caracas from Nov. 20–25, 1989, decided that during the coming years it would give priority to: (i) making concrete human rights and trade union freedoms across the world and in particular the Third World, Central and Eastern Europe and South Africa; (ii) defending rural workers, domestic workers in the Third World towns, and the most vulnerable in the industrialized countries; (iii) meeting the new needs of workers for information, education and organization; (iv) furthering the active participation of women in union and social life, combating all forms of domination and exploitation, achieving equality of access to education and re-training, and equal pay, conditions and rights at work, and providing information on family affairs; (v) promoting effective environmental policies, and (vi) alleviating the social consequences of external debt.

The WCL adopts a non-aligned position in global power politics, and emphasizes the right to national self-determination for the countries of the Third World. In the economic sphere it works for the liberation of the workers through self-management and democratic socialism in opposition to the multinational corporations. The WCL believes that man's fulfilment must have a spiritual as well as a material dimension, and that workers possess individual human rights in addition to their collective rights, and opposes Marxism in the same measure as capitalism.

WCL's work with other international trade union bodies is co-ordinated by the International Solidarity Foundation. The Foundation provides resources, funds campaigns and backs projects intended to promote independent trade unionism. It enjoys consultative status with the ILO, the Economic and Social Council of the United Nations, UNESCO, the FAO, IAAE, UNCTAD, UNIDO, UNICEF, IMCO, ICEM and the OECD. Permanent representation at the ILO is guaranteed by maintenance of a bureau at Geneva.

Structure. Congress, which meets every four years (most recently in 1989), is the ruling body; it is made up of delegates from national centres, regional organizations and trade internationals, sets overall policy and elects the confederal board. The confederal board, consisting of 34 members (representing the continents and the trade sections) elected for four-year terms, meets annually and is the ruling body between congresses. The 10-member executive committee, composed of the president, the vice-presidents, the secretary-general, the deputy secretary-general and the treasurer is responsible for the concrete implementation of policies laid down by the congress and the confederal board and meets at least twice a year. The secretariat in Brussels (led by the general secretary) is responsible for day-to-day affairs.

The internal organization of the WCL differs from that of the other two major world federations in that it accepts direct affiliations on individual unions rather than basing itself primarily on national centres. A mixture of both may be found in the affiliated organizations below.

Regional organizations. The most important of the regional organizations of the WCL is CLAT, which was founded in Santiago in 1954. It campaigns for trade union organization, for the defence of human and civil rights, against dictatorship, for the integration of the countries of the continent, for democracy, for research into the political solution of conflicts, and for mobilization in the interests of peace and social justice.

In Latin America CLAT tends to occupy a mid-point between the business unionism of the United States backed ORIT (the regional ICFTU organization) and WFTU-backed organizations such as CPUSTAL. Much of its success lay in the establishment of new independent unions on the continent, often in collaboration with the worker-priest movement. As a result of this the centre of gravity of the WCL today lies in Latin America, rather than in Europe, its original base.

CLAT's administration of its region is through four sub-regional bodies covering Mexico and Central America, the Andean Zone, the Southern Cone and Brazil, and the Caribbean, and it also maintains the University of Latin American workers (UTAL), based in Caracas, which is supported by 19 national trade union centres on the continent. CLAT claims the adherence of 42 national organizations in 39 Latin American countries, as well as 13 professional federations and two action organizations.

The Asian organization of the WCL is BATU which was created in 1963 and is based in Manila. BATU has affiliates or professional organizations in 11 countries and has established a sub-regional network. In Africa, FOPADESC was founded in 1970, but changed its statutes in 1973 to dissolve its sub-regional body UPTC in order to minimize its rivalry with the Organization of African Trade Union Unity—OATUU. It has member unions in 14 countries and four sub-regional organizations. Representation of the WCL in North America is minimal, confined to one United States union (NAPFE) and a Canadian associate.

In 1973 the WCL regional organization for Europe (OE-CMT) was dissolved in favour of pressing affiliates' interests through the European Trade Union Confederation—ETUC, though they continue to meet twice a year. Eleven countries in Europe are claimed to have WCL affiliates and there are also two extraordinary members. However the international affiliation status of at least one of these —Solidarnosc of Poland—remains unclear. The relative decline of the WCL in Europe stems from the gradual secularization of some of its affiliates, either by a change of objective (as with CISL of Italy and CFDT of France, which switched their affiliations to the ICFTU on losing their confessional character), or through a process of merger (such as that which in the Netherlands brought together the Catholic Industriebond NKV with the Socialist Industriebond NVV). Nevertheless the WCL retains affiliates in Europe, and notably in the Low Countries, which are growing in membership and thus strengthen the international centre.

The four regional centres of the WCL, their addresses and other details are as follows. For Africa: **Fondation Panafricaine pour le Développement Economique, Social et Culturel—FOPADESC** (Route Internationale d'Atakpame, B.P. 4401 Lomé-Agoenyive, Togo. Phone: 21 07 10. Fax: 21 61 13. Secretary-general: Eugène Akpemado). For Latin America: **Central Latinoamericana de Trabajadores — CLAT** (Apartado 6681, 1010-A Caracas, Venezuela. Phone: 58 32 720794/720878/721549. Telex: 29873 LAWTU VC. Fax: 58 32 720643. Cable: CLAT-Caracas. Secretary-general: Emilio Maspero). For Asia: **Brotherhood of Asian Trade Unionists—BATU** (Dr Antonio Vasquez Street, 1839 Malate, P.O. Box 163, Manila, Philippines. Phone: 50 07 09. Telex: 65018 BATU PN. FAX: 63 25 21 835. Cable: BATUM-MANILA. President: Juan C. Tan). For North America: **National Alliance of Postal and Federal Employees—NAPFE** (1628, 11th Street, N.W., 20001 DC Washington, USA. Phone: (202) 939 6325. Fax: (202) 939 6389. President: James McGee).

Publications. Labor (monthly, five languages); *Flash* (fortnightly, five languages—trade union news); press releases; *Events* (twice per year, five languages).

Affiliates: The WCL reported the following affiliates by region as of early 1991:

Africa

Pan-African Regional Organizations: Comité Africain de Coordination et d'Action Syndicale contre l'Apartheid et le Colonialisme; Organisation des Travailleurs de l'Afrique Centrale (OTAC); Organisation des Travailleurs de l'Afrique Occidentale (OTAO); Organisation de l'Unité Syndicale Africaine (OUSA)

Benin

Fédération des Travailleurs de la Terre et des Animateurs Ruraux du Bénin (FETRABENIN); Syndicat National des Postes et Télécommunications (SYNPOSTEL)

Burkina Faso
Confédération Nationale des Travailleurs du Burkina (CNTB)

Central African Republic
Confédération Nationale des Travailleurs Centrafricains (CNTC); Syndicat de Base des Agents de la Presse

Chad
Groupement Carré Nangoto; Union Nationale des Syndicats du Tchad (UNST)

Gambia
Gambian Trade Union Congress (GTUC)

Ghana
Railway Enginemen's Union of TUC

Liberia
Bong Mines Workers' Union; Co-ordinating Committee FOPADESC — WCL; Federation of Transport Union Inc.; National Agriculture and Allied Workers Unions of Liberia (NAAWUL); National Seamen, Port and General Workers Union (NSPPGWU); National Teachers' Association of Liberia; National Transport and General Workers Union of Liberia (NTHWU)

Madagascar
Sendika Krisitianina Malgasy (SE.KRI.MA); Union des Syndicats Autonomes de Madagascar (USAM)

Mauritius
Cartel; Confédération Mauricienne des Travailleurs; Fédération Syndicale des Corps Constitués (FSCC); Fédération des Syndicats du Service Civil (FSSC); Organisation Unitaire des Artisans (OUA)

Namibia
Namibian Christian Social Trade Unions (NCSTU)

Niger
Syndicat National de l'Industrie; Syndicat National des Postes et Telecommunications du Niger (SYNPOSTEL); Syndicat National des Travailleurs de l'Energie; Syndicat Unique des Agents des Travaux Publics et l'Habitat et des Transports (SUATP/H/T); Syndicat Unique des Travailleurs des Eaux et Forêts (SUTEF)

Senegal
Syndicat National des Postes et Télécommunications (SYNAPOSTEL)

Sierra Leone
Medical, Dental and Health Services Workers' Union; Plantation, Forestry and Agricultural Workers Union (PFAWU); Sierra Leone Union of Securities Watchmen and General Workers (including agricultural industry); Transport, Agriculture and General Workers' Union (TAGWU); Union of Mass Media, Financial Institutions, Chemical Industries and General Workers (UMSDIFIC)

Togo
Fédération Nationale des Syndicats des Services Publics et Assimilés du Togo (FENASYSPATO); Syndicat des Couturières et Tailleurs du Togo (SYNCTATO); Syndicat des Enseignants Catholiques du Togo (SECT); Syndicat des Enseignants Protestants du Togo (SEPT); Syndicat du Personnel de la Santé Publique du Togo (SYNPERSANTO); Syndicat National des Coiffeurs et Coiffeuses du Togo (SYNACOIFTO); Syndicat National des Conseillers d'Orientation Scolaire et Professionnelle (SYNCOSPTO); Syndicat National des Dockers (SYNADOCKTO); Syndicat National des Inspecteurs de l'Education Nationale du Togo (SIENT); Syndicat National des Mineurs du Togo (SYNAMITO)

ASIA

Asian Regional Organization: Batu Social Institute (BSI)

Bangladesh
Bangladesh Sanjukta Sramic Federation (BSSF)

Hong Kong
Joint Organization of Unions-Hong Kong (JOU-HK)

India
Batu India

Indonesia
Batu Indonesia
(joint secretariat BATU affiliated organizations)

Iran
Democratic Union of Iranian Workers (DUIW, extraordinary member)

Japan
BATU WCL liaison office

Korea
BATU Korea

Malaysia
BATU Malaysia

Pakistan
All Pakistan Trade Union Congress (APTUC)

Philippines
Federation of Free Workers (FFW)

Singapore
BATU Singapore

Sri Lanka
National Workers' Congress (NWC)

Taiwan
BATU Taiwan

Thailand
National Congress of Thai Labour (NCTL)

Vietnam
Brotherhood of Vietnamese Workers (BVW)

EUROPE

Austria
Fraktion Christlicher Gewerkschafler im ÖGB (FCG/ÖGB)

Belgium
Confédération des Syndicats Chrétiens (Algemeen Christelijk Vakverbond—CSC-ACV)

Cyprus
Democratic Labour Federation of Cyprus (DEOK); Pancyprian Federation of Independent Trade Unions (POAS)

France
Confédération Française des Travailleurs Chrétiens (CFTC)

Italy
Associazioni Cristiane Lavoratori Italiani (ACLI—extraordinary member)

Liechtenstein
Liechtensteiner Arbeitnehmerverband (LAV)

Luxembourg
Luxemburger Christlicher Gewerkschaftsbund (Confédération des Syndicats Chrétiens Luxembourg —LCGB)

Malta
Confederation of Malta Trade Unions (CMTU)

Netherlands
Christelijk Nationaal Vakverbond (CNV)

Poland
NSZZ Solidarnosc (Offices for National Executive Commission and Foreign Co-ordination Bureau)

Portugal
BASE-FUT (extraordinary member)

Spain
Confederacio Sindical de Catalunya (CSC); Solidaridad de Trabajadores Vascos (ELA/STV); Unión Sindical Obrera (USO)

Switzerland
Christlich-Nationaler Gewerkschaftsbund der Schweiz (CNG)

LATIN AMERICA

Latin American Regional Organizations: Confederación Centroamericana de Trabajadores (CCT); Consejo Sindical de Trabajadores Andinos (CSTA); Consejo de Trabajadores del Caribe (CTC); Consejo de Trabajadores del Cono Sur (CTCS/CLAT); Universidad de los Trabajadores de América Latina (UTAL)

Antigua
Antigua Trades and Labour Union (ATLU)

Argentina
Consejo Co-ordinador Argentino Sindical (CCAS)

Aruba
Federación de Trabajadores Arubanos (FTA)

Belize
Christian Workers' Union (CWU)

Bolivia
Comité de Relaciones Intersindicales y Solidaridad Laboral (CRISOL)

Bonaire
Federación Boneriana di Trabao (FEDEBON)

Brazil
Confederação Brasileira Trabalhadores Cristãos (CBTC—extraordinary member); Co-ordenação Autónoma de Trabalhadores (CAT)

Chile
Consejo Co-ordinador de Trabajadores (CCT)

Colombia
Confederación General del Trabajo (CGT)

Costa Rica
Central de Trabajadores Costarricenses (CTC)

Cuba
Solidaridad de Trabajadores Cubanos (STC)

Curaçao
Central General di Trahadornan di Corsow (CGTC)

Dominica
Dominica Amalgamated Workers' Union (DAWU)

Dominican Republic
Confederación Autónoma de Sindicatos Clasistas (CASC)

Ecuador
Central Ecuatoriana de Organizaciones Clasistas (CEDOC)

El Salvador
Central de Trabajadores Salvadoreños (CTS); Confederación General del Trabajo (CGT)

French Guiana
Centrale Démocratique des Travailleurs de la Guyane (CDTG)

Guadeloupe
Central Sindical de Trabajadores de Guadelupe (CSTG)

Guatemala
Central General de Trabajadores de Guatemala (CGTC)

Guyana
National Workers' Union (NWU)

Haïti
Confédération des Travailleurs Haïtiens (CTH—Haïti)

Honduras
Central General de Trabajadores (CGT)

Martinique
Centrale Démocratique Martiniquaise des Travailleurs (CDMT)

Mexico
Frente Auténtico del Trabajo (FAT)

Nicaragua
Central de Trabajadores Nicaragüenses (CTN)

Panama
Central Istmeña de Trabajadores (CIT)

Paraguay
Central Nacional de Trabajadores (CNT)

Peru
Co-ordinadora Nacional de Organizaciones de Base (CNOB—extraordinary member)

Puerto Rico
Central Puertorriqueña de Trabajadores (CPT)

St. Kitts
National Allied Workers' Union (NAWU)

St. Lucia
National Workers' Union (NWU)

St. Maarten
Windward Islands Federation of Labour

St. Vincent
National Workers' Movement (NWM)

Suriname
Co-ordinadora Surinameña de Organizaciones Autónomas de Trabajadores (OSAVE—extraordinary member)

Trinidad

All Trinidad Sugar and General Workers Trade Unions (ATS/GWTU)

Uruguay

Acción Sindical Uruguaya (ASU)

Venezuela

Confederación General de Trabajadores de Venezuela (CGT); Movimiento Nacional de Trabajadores Para la Liberación (MONTRAL)

NORTH AMERICA

Canada

Christian Labour Association of Canada (CLAC-extraordinary member)

USA

National Alliance of Postal and Federal Employees (NAPFE)

International trade federations. The WCL's network of nine trade federations is less comprehensive in its coverage than that of the two larger world centres. All are based in Belgium.

1. **International Association of Professional Cyclists (AICPRO)**

2. **International Federation of Employees in Public Services (INFEDOP)**

3. **International Federation Textile-Clothing (WCL)**

4. **International Federation of Trade Unions of Transport Workers (FIOST)**

5. **World Federation of Agricultural and Food Workers (FEMTAA)**

6. **World Federation of Building and Woodworkers Unions**

7. **World Federation of Clerical Workers (WFCW)**

8. **World Federation of Industry Workers (WFIW)**

9. **World Confederation of Teachers (WCT)**

World Confederation of Organizations of the Teaching Profession (WCOTP)

Address. 5 avenue du Moulin, 1110 Morges, Switzerland
Phone. (021) 801-74-67
Telex. 458 219 WCTP CH
Fax. (021) 801 74 69
Leadership. Mary Hatwood Futrell (president); Robert Harris (secretary-general)
Membership. Around 13,000,000 in 191 organizations in 120 countries.
History and character. WCOTP, which was founded in 1952, is an independent and non-political confederation of teaching unions. Its two constituent federations are the International Federation of Teachers' Associations (IFTA) and the International Federation of Secondary Teachers (FIPESO).
Publications. Echo (quarterly, in English, French, Spanish and Japanese).
International affiliation. None.

World Federation of Trade Unions (WFTU)
Fédération Syndicale Mondiale (FSM)

Address. Na Dobesce 35, Branik, 14000 Prague 4, Czechoslovakia
Phone. 462684; 463244
Telex. 121525 wftu c

Fax. 235 43 93

Cable. FESYMOND PRAGUE (Czechoslovakia)

Leadership. (Leadership elected November 1990) president: Ibrahim Zakaria (Sudan); vice presidents: Ernest Boatswain (Australia), J.M. Bokamba-Yangouma (Congo), Pedro Ross Leal (Cuba), Avraam Antoniou (Cyprus), Ms. Nélsida Marmolejos (Dominican Republic), Tadesse Tamerat (Ethiopia), Henri Krasucki (France), Indrajit Gupta (India), Elias El-Habre (Lebanon), Valentin Pacho Quispe (Peru), Alfred Miodowicz (Poland), Izzedine Nasser (Syria), Vladimir P. Shcherbakov (Soviet Union), Nguyen Van Tu (Vietnam); general secretary: Alexander Zharikov (Soviet Union); deputy general secretary: Alain Stern (France)

Membership: 188,000,000.

History and character. The WFTU was formed in 1945, in succession to the International Federation of Trade Unions (IFTU), itself formed in 1901. Pro-western unions broke away in 1949 to form the ICFTU. Until 1990 it was dominated by the trade unions of the Soviet bloc (by far the largest affiliate being the AUCCTU of the USSR), but also included as members the trade union centres of Third World Marxist states and left-wing organizations operating in capitalist economies. In the 1980s the WFTU emphasized the objective of building closer relations with the ICFTU and the WCL and their affiliates, by developing themes of common concern such as "peace and disarmament" and action to oppose multinational companies. Its major western affiliate is the French CGT, which criticized the dependence of Soviet bloc trade unions on the state and called on them to play a role which was "original, responsible, and active".

The political changes that have occurred in Eastern Europe and other parts of the world since 1989 have had a major impact on the composition of the WFTU. It lost the collapsing single trade union centres of Bulgaria (the Central Council of Trade Unions), Czechoslovakia (the URO), the German Democratic Republic (the Federation of Free German Trade Unions, FDGB), Hungary (SZOT), and Romania (UGSR). In Poland the re-formed centre OPZZ decided in 1991 not to renew its affiliation (though some of its individual unions continue to affiliate to the WFTU's Trade Union Internationals (TUIs, see below). However, the General Confederation of Trade Unions of the USSR—the re-formed AUCCTU—has stayed an affiliate and remains easily the largest. The WFTU remains attractive to a large number of unions in the Third World, and in France, the sometimes critical CGT continues to affiliate.

Affiliates. The new affiliates ratified at the November 1990 (Moscow) Congress were as follows:

1. **The Confederation of Workers of Costa Rica (CTCR)**
   (Confederación de Trabajadores de Costa Rica)

2. **Majority Centre of the Workers of the Dominican Republic**
   (Central de trabajadores mayoritaria Santo Domingo)

3. **Confederation of Haitian Workers (KOTA)**

4. **Democratic Workers' Movement of Bangladesh**
   (Bangladesh Ganotantrik Sramik Andolon)

5. **National Workers' Federation of Bangladesh**
   (Jatio Sramik Federation, Bangladesh)

6. **National Workers' League of Bangladesh**
   (Jatio Sramik League, Bangladesh)

7. **United Trade Union Centre (Lenin Sarani), India**

8. **All Pakistan Trade Union Federation**

9. **Sri Lanka Mahajana Trade Union Federation**

10. **Bolivian Workers' Centre**
    (Central Obrera Boliviana)

11. **Federation of Sudanese Professionals' and Technicians' Trade Unions**

12. **All Pakistan Trade Union Organization**

13. **All Pakistan Federation of Labour—Durrani Group**

14. **General Confederation of Labour of Zaïre (CGTZ)**

The Twelfth World Trade Union Congress took place in Moscow on Nov. 13–20. The representation was Africa: 97 delegates and observers from 39 organizations; America: 201 delegates and observers from 129 organizations; Asia and the Pacific: 227 delegates and observers from 119 organizations; Europe: 332 delegates and observers representing 130 organizations; Middle East: 71 delegates and observers representing 29 organizations. It was noteworthy for the presence of a large number of organizations (more than half) which were not WFTU members, although the ICFTU instructed its affiliates not to attend and this did lead to the absence of observers from some important national centres.

The Congress introduced changes into its structure which reflected the changes made by trade unions in the Eastern European countries and the USSR. It was resolved to draw up a new constitution which stressed the independence of trade unions from governments, to establish a number of new regional offices (Africa, Asia, Latin America and the Middle East) and cut back heavily on the number of head office staff. The Trade Union Internationals were asked to work towards financial independence. It renewed its plea for world trade union unity and heard a number of pleas from non-members for the international centres to come together. Ibrahim Zakaria of the Sudan became President and was replaced as General Secretary by Alexander Zharikov, the former head of the AUCCTU International Department.

Structure: The ruling body is the Congress, which last met in Moscow from Nov. 13–20, 1990, and elects the General Council; the latter is made up of representatives of the affiliated national centres and trade union internationals, meets three times between Congresses and plans agendas and elects the president, general secretary and secretariat officers; the presidential council, with 20 members, elected by the General Council meets twice a year and conducts most of the executive work of WFTU; the secretariat, appointed by the general council, comprises the secretary-general and five secretaries, and is responsible for the general running and co-ordination of WFTU activities.

The WFTU has the following regional offices: *Asia*: Debkumar Ganguli (regional secretary); address: c/o AITUC, 24 Canning Lane, New Delhi, India; Phone: 387320; 386427; fax: 386427. *Africa*: Messeambia Koulimaya (regional secretary); address: B.P. 2161, Brazzaville, Congo; Phone: 831923; telex: 5304 cosygo; fax: (242) 835954. *America*: José Ortiz (regional secretary); address: Oficina regional de la FSM, Calle 32, No. 1, entre la y Mar, Miramar, Municipio Playa, Havana, Cuba; Phone 294531; telex 511263 ra fsm cu; fax 290385.

The WFTU has the following associated trade union internationals:

1. **Trade Unions International of Agricultural, Forestry and Plantation Workers**, Bolshaia Serpoukhovskaia 44, 113093 Moscow M93, USSR.
   Phone: 230 2070. Telex: 411040 UIS AG SU.
   General secretary: André Hemmerlé.

2. **Trade Unions International of Chemical, Oil and Allied Workers (ICPS)**, Foldvary ut. 4.1. EM 26, H 1097 Budapest, Hungary.
   Phone: 361 113 211. Telex: 22 4408 att.icps-h.
   Cable: INTERCHIMIE.
   General secretary: Alain Covet.

3. **Trade Unions International of Energy Workers**, Kopernika 36/40, 00-924 Warsaw, Poland.
   Phone: 264316. Telex: 816 913 UISTE pl. Fax: 635 86 88.
   General secretary: Eugeniusz Mielnicki.

4. **Trade Unions International of Food, Tobacco, Hotel and Allied Industries Workers**, Stamboliysky 3, Sofia, Bulgaria.
   Phone: 885 759. Telex: 24237 UIS BG. Cable: UIS MOP Sofia.
   General secretary: Ricardo Martínez Masdeu.

5. **Trade Unions International of Metal Workers**, P.O. Box 158, Ul. Pouchkinskaia 5/6, Moscow K-9, USSR.

Phone: 200 02 23. Telex: 411 370 activ su. Fax: 200 02 23.
General secretary: Gilbert Lebescond

6. **Trade Unions International of Public and Allied Employees**, Wilhem-Wolff Strasse 21, Berlin 1110, Germany.
Phone: 48 27 914 Telex: 115 037 fise dd. Cable: UNSYFO.
Acting general secretary: S. Galkin.

7. **Trade Unions International of Workers in Textile, Clothing, Leather, Shoe and Allied Industries**, Opletalova 57, 110 00 Prague 1, Czechoslovakia.
Phone: 222 882.
Secretary: E.A. Sidorov.

8. **Trade Unions International of Transport Workers**, Vaci ut. 73, 1139 Budapest, Hungary.
Telephone: 120 9601. Cable: INTERTRANSPORT.
General secretary: Jozsef Toth.

9. **Trade Unions International of Workers of the Building, Wood and Building Materials Industries (UITBB)**, Box 281, 00101 Helsinki, Finland.
Phone: 693 1050. Cable: INTERBATIMENT.
Fax: (3580) 693 1020.
General secretary: Mauri Perä.

10. **Trade Unions International of Workers in Commerce**, Opletalova 57, 110 00 Prague 1, Czechoslovakia.
Phone: 220 680.
General secretary: Alvaro Villamarin.

11. **World Federation of Teachers' Unions (FISE)**, 14 rue de Strasbourg, 93200 Saint Denis, France.
Phone: (331) 48 20 72 51. Telex: 97660 fise f.
Fax: (331) 48 20 72 50.
General secretary: Gérard Montant.

Affiliates. The WFTU reported the following affiliates as of June 1991.

Afghanistan
Central Council of Afghan Trade Unions (CCATU)

Albania
Këshilli Qëndror i Bashkimeve Profesionale të Shqiperisë

Angola
União Nacional dos Trabalhadores Angolanos (UNTA)

Argentina
Coordinadora Nacional de Agrupaciones (CONAT)

Austria
Fraktion des Gewerkschaftlichen Linksblocks im ÖGB

Bahrain
Bahrain Workers' Union

Bangladesh
Bangladesh Trade Union Kendra (BTUK); Jatio Sramik Jote; Jatio Sramik League; Ganotantrik Sramik Federation; Jatio Sramik Federation; Jatio Sramik League of Bangladesh

Benin
Union Nationale des Syndicats de Travailleurs du Bénin (UNSTB)

Bolivia
Central Obrera Boliviana

Burkina Faso
Union Syndicale des Travailleurs Burkinabês (USTB)

China
All-China Federation of Trade Unions (ACFTU)

Congo
Confédération Syndicale Congolaise (CSC)

Costa Rica
Confederación Unitaria de Trabajadores (CUT); Confederación de Trabajadores de Costa Rica

Cuba
Central de Trabajadores de Cuba (CTC)

Cyprus
Pankypria Ergatiki Omospondia (PEO); Devrimci İşçi Sendikalari Federasyonu (Dev-Iş)

Dominican Republic
Central Unitaria de Trabajadores (CUT); Central de Trabajadores Mayoritaria

Ecuador
Confederación de Trabajadores del Ecuador (CTE)

El Salvador
Federación Unitaria Sindical Salvadoreña (FUSS)

Ethiopia
Ethiopian Trade Union (ETU)

France
Conféderation Générale du Travail (CGT)
    French Guiana: Union des Travailleuers Guyanais (UTG)
    Guadeloupe: Confédération Générale du Travail de la Guadeloupe (CGTG)
    Martinique: Confédération Générale du Travail de la Martinique (CGTM)
    New Caledonia: Confédération Syndicale de Nouvelle Caledonie (CSNC); Union des Syndicats
    des Travailleurs Kanaks et Exploités (USTKE)
    Réunion: Confédération Générale du Travail de la Réunion (CGTR)
    St Pierre et Miquelon: Union Intersyndicale CGT (associate status)

Gambia
Gambia Labour Congress (GLC)

Guatemala
Federación Autónoma Sindical Guatemalteca (FASGUA)

Guinea-Bissau
União Nacional dos Trabalhadores da Guiné (UNTG)

Guyana
Guyana Agricultural and General Workers' Union (GAWU)

Haiti
Confédéracion Ouvrière des Travailleurs Haïtiens

Honduras
Federación Unitaria de Trabajadores de Honduras (FUTH)

India
All-India Trade Union Congress (AITUC); United Trade Union Centre (Lenin Sarani)

Indonesia
Sentral Organisasi Buruh Seluruh Indonesia (SOBSI)

Iran
Commission de Liaison des Syndicats Iraniens

Iraq
General Federation of Trade Unions of Iraq

Jamaica
Independent Trade Unions Action Council (ITAC); University and Allied Workers' Union (UAWU)

Jordan
General Federation of Jordanian Trade Unions (GFJTU)

Kampuchea
Kampuchea Federation of Trade Unions

North Korea
General Federation of Trade Unions of Korea

Kuwait
Kuwait Trade Union Federation

Laos
Fédération des Syndicats du Laos

Lebanon
Fédération Nationale des Syndicats des Ouvriers et des Employés du Liban (FENASOL)

Madagascar
Fédération des Syndicats des Travailleurs de Madagascar (FISEMA); Fédération des Travailleurs Malagasy Révolutionnaires (FISEMARE)

Mauritius
General Workers' Federation (GWF)

Mongolia
Central Council of Mongolian Trade Unions

Namibia
National Union of Namibian Workers (NUNW)

Nicaragua
Confederación General de Trabajo Independiente (CGT)

Oman
National Committee of Omani Workers

Pakistan
All-Pakistan Federation of Labour (Durrani Group); All-Pakistan Trade Union Organization; Pakistan Trade Union Federation (PTUF); All Pakistan Trade Union Federation (APTUF)

Palestine
Palestine Trade Union Federation

Panama
Central Nacional de Trabajadores de Panama (CNTP)

Peru
Confederación General de Trabajadores del Perú (CGTP)

Philippines
National Association of Trade Unions (NATU); Trade Unions of Philippines and Allied Services (TUPAS); National Congress of Workers (KATIPUNAN)

Puerto Rico
Union General de Trabajadores (UGT)

St Vincent and the Grenadines
Progressive Trade Union Centre

Saudi Arabia
Workers' Union of Saudi Arabia (associate status)

Senegal
Union des Travailleurs Libres du Sénégal (UTLS)

Solomon Islands
Solomon Islands National Union of Workers (SINUW)

South Africa
South African Congress of Trade Unions (SACTU)

Sri Lanka
Democratic Workers' Congress; Ceylon Federation of Trade Unions; Sri Lanka Mahajana Trade Union Federation; Sri Lanka Nidakas Sewaka Sangamaya

Sudan
Federation of Sudanese Professionals and Technical Trade Unions; Trade Union Front of Sudan

Syria
General Federation of Trade Unions

Trinidad and Tobago
Council of Progressive Trade Unions

Union of Soviet Socialist Republics
General Confederation of Trade Unions of the USSR

Venezuela
Central Unitaria de Trabajadores de Venezuela (CUTV)

Vietnam
General Confederation of Labour

Yemen
General Federation of Yemen Trade Unions

Zaïre
Confédération Générale du Travail du Zaïre

Publication. World Trade Union Movement (quaterly, in English, French, Spanish); *Flashes from the Trade Unions* (fortnightly, in English, French, Spanish).

Select List of Acronyms

The following is a select list of acronyms of international trade union organizations

AATO	All Africa Teachers' Organization
APTUCC	Asian–Pacific Trade Union Co-ordination Committee
CCL	Caribbean Congress of Labour
CPUSTAL	Permanent Congress of Trade Union Unity of Latin American Workers
CTUC	Commonwealth Trade Union Council
ECSF	European Civil Service Federation
EFBWW	European Federation of Building and Woodworkers
EFCGU	European Federation of Chemical and General Workers' Unions
ETUC	European Trade Union Confederation
EULAS	European Union of Local Authority Staffs
FASME	Fédération Africaine des Syndicats des Mineurs et des Energeticiens
FICSA	Federation of International Civil Servants' Associations
ICAATU	International Confederation of Arab Trade Unions
ICFTU	International Confederation of Free Trade Unions
IMO	International Miners' Organization
NFS	Council of Nordic Trade Unions
OATUU	Organization of African Trade Union Unity
PAFATU	Pan-African Federation of Agricultural Trade Unions
PTUC	Pacific Trade Union Community
SARTUC	South Asian Regional Trade Union Council
SATUCC	Southern African Trade Union Co-ordination Council
TUAC	Trade Union Advisory Council to the OECD (TUAC)
UWAM	Union of Workers of Arab Maghreb
WCL	World Confederation of Labour
WCOTP	World Confederation of Organizations of the Teaching Profession
WFTU	World Federation of Trade Unions

Index of English Trade Union Centre Names and Vernacular Acronyms

575